The Descendants of Thomas & Rose Ann Mould
of
Peterborough, England

by

Joan Bolton
and
Richard Klapper

Order this book online at www.trafford.com
or email orders@trafford.com

Most Trafford titles are also available at major online book retailers.

Printed in the United States of America.

ISBN: 9781426943386 (sc)
ISBN: 9781426943393 (e)

Our mission is to efficiently provide the world's finest, most comprehensive book publishing service, enabling every author to experience success. To find out how to publish your book, your way, and have it available worldwide, visit us online at www.trafford.com

Trafford rev. 09/11/2010

 www.trafford.com

North America & international
toll-free: 1 888 232 4444 (USA & Canada)
phone: 250 383 6864 ♦ fax: 812 355 4082

Table of Contents

Introduction

In 1963 Joan Mould of Peterborough, England made a trip to the United States as a twenty year old and visited her relatives around the country. One of the relatives she met was a cousin, Richard Klapper, who was a teenager at the time. They did not have any contact again until nearly 40 years later when Richard became interested in tracking down the descendants of his great great grandparents, Thomas & Rose Ann Mould of Gunthorpe, England. Knowing that this would require a major effort on both sides of the Atlantic, he contacted Joan (now Joan Bolton) who was living in Dorset, England to see if she would like to join in this endeavor. Joan was very interested and immediately agreed. They shared the information they each had and the project which resulted in this book was begun.

Authors Joan Bolton and Richard Klapper transcribing John Mould's headstone in Helpston churchyard

During the past several years we have pored over GRO indexes, censuses, parish registers, coroners reports, newspaper articles and talked to dozens of family members to ferret out details on the descendants of Thomas and Rose Ann. In the course of this research, Richard made a trip to England and he and Joan visited the cemeteries and churchyards in Peterborough and the surrounding villages where Thomas, Rose Ann, their ancestors and their descendants lived. We found, transcribed and photographed grave headstones as well as talked to other cousins found along the way. Little by little the information on each line of descendants was uncovered and recorded.

In addition to collecting data and family stories, we have attempted to collect photos, documents and newspaper articles relating to the family. Our major concern was that some of these photos and documents could be lost forever in another generation or two. After some discussion it was agreed that the best way to ensure their preservation would be to document them in a book. We had two main objectives in undertaking this project, (in addition, of course, to prolonging the fun of collaborating!) One was to provide useful information for descendants wanting to know more about our family history and the other, hopefully, to help and encourage any future family historians/enthusiasts to build on our research.

Since Thomas' ancestors and family lived for many years in the area around Peterborough we have found a significant amount of information on his grandparents, parents, aunts, uncles and siblings. Although Rose Ann's parents and siblings have been identified, we have not yet been able to find her grandparents. To aid future researchers, we have included this information in the book as well.

Before embarking on this book, a decision had to be made on how Peterborough and its environs would be referred to, in terms of the county in which they reside. For most of the time frames covered here, Peterborough and its nearby villages were included in the county of Northamptonshire (Northants). But between 1865 and 1972, the Peterborough area was merged with Huntingdonshire (Hunts). In 1972 it was incorporated into Cambridgeshire, which was the case up until 1998, when Peterborough became a United Authority. To simplify matters and, hopefully, to avoid confusion, we have chosen to consistently describe these areas as being in Northants.

We have devoted one chapter of this book to Thomas and Rose Ann and one chapter to each of their nine children who lived past infancy. In each of the children's chapters we have included Thomas and Rose Ann's grandchildren in some level of detail. All later generations are contained in the genealogy report found in Chapter 11. The same criteria is followed in the appendicees that contain descendant pictures in which only three generations are shown in pictures. One of our goals was to keep the cost of the book down. Interesting stories or documentation of interest to future researchers are also to be found in the appendices.

Both Richard and Joan have contributed chapters to this book, (Joan the second and tenth chapters; Richard all of the remainder) and therefore the reader will find a different spelling of various words depending on whether it was written by the American or English cousin. Such words as center (centre), theater (theatre), favor (favour), labor (labour), etc. will appear in the book. We have not tried to reconcile the different spellings between British and American English.

This introduction would not be complete without noting that the collection of the information for a book like this would be impossible without the help of many other family members who shared with us their data, stories, documents, newspaper articles and photos. Although they are far too numerous to mention here individually, we want to thank them all.

We would like to express our deep appreciation to Peter Kershaw of Bridport, Dorset for his help in sending scans of pages across the Atlantic. His efforts helped us immensely and served to speed the review process along. Special thanks also to Alan Marks who generously gave permission to use his detailed maps of Paston Churchyard. Grateful acknowledgements are also due to the following people: Family Historian, Jane Ferentzi-Sheppard, whose courses were the starting point for Joan's research; Richard Hillier, in charge of the Family History Section at Peterborough Library, for his help in tracing relevent events in the local newspaper archives and also to Councillor Charles Swift, for the generous loan of two most useful books on Peterborough: one entitled The GNR Schools and the other: The History of New England. In the course of our research, we have naturally had recourse to many County Record Offices. In Huntingdon, the then Deputy Archivist went out of her way to provide a tiny - but vital - piece of the jigsaw. Similarly, the archivists at Dulwich College offered us invaluable help. Many other contributors may find that they have become 'part of the story': we hope they will not object! Equally, if anyone should feel overlooked we are sorry.

But we surely owe very special thanks to our two spouses, Linda and Reg. With his extensive knowledge of British history, Reg was able to make a valuable contribution by setting some of the events in their historical context. While they did not perform research or interviews, they put up with our spending hundreds of hours in Family History Centers and Record Offices as well as countless hours of phone calls between Texas and Dorset. Linda even spent almost a week in Peterborough area village churchyards and cemeteries helping us read and record 150 year old grave headstones. Squinting at these barely legible inscriptions for four days is certainly going beyond the call of duty! For all of these things we are in their debt.

Thomas and Rose Ann Mould

Chapter 1

Thomas & Rose Ann Mould

Etton Parish Church

Thomas and Rose Ann Mould were both born in the English county of Northamptonshire. Thomas was born the seventh of ten children of William and Mary Edith (Pick) Molds on September 8, 1827 in Woodcroft, a small place with few inhabitants, known mainly for its castle. He was six weeks old when, on October 21st, his parents took him to the parish church in nearby Etton to be baptised. A year and a half later, on March 20, 1829, Rose Ann Mackness was born in Brigstock and was baptised there on August 30th. (The village of Brigstock is situated close to the town of Corby, to the southwest of Peterborough and about fourteen miles from Woodcroft.) Rose was the fifth of nine children of Mary (nee Wade) and Jabez Mackness. Both Thomas and Rose Ann were from working class families with their fathers being designated 'agricultural labourers'. Thomas's relatives and ancestors are described in Appendix I and Rose Ann's in Appendix II. It should be noted that throughout the records the spelling of 'Mould' changes depending on the whim of the person writing the name. We have found it spelled Mould, Moulds, Mold, Mole, Molds, Mowles and Moules.

In the 1841 census, Rose Ann is shown as a twelve-year-old girl living with her parents at Syke Row in Brigstock, whilst Thomas who was not yet fourteen, had already left home. He was working in Gunthorpe as a 'servant' for a twenty year old farmer named Thomas Brown. Mr. Brown had three male servants, probably all farm hands who worked in his fields.

By the time of the 1851 census, Rose Ann was twenty-two years old, and working as a servant for the Bell family in Deeping Gate near Maxey. This was in Lincolnshire, just over the Northamptonshire border.

The cottage in Gunthorpe where Thomas and Rose Ann lived

Unfortunately, we have not (as yet) been able to find Thomas in this census, though he was certainly not living under his father's roof. (His mother, Mary, had died four years previously, aged fifty-five.) However, at the time of his marriage one year later, Thomas gave Etton as his place of residence. Significantly, perhaps, the villages of Etton and Deeping Gate (or Maxey) are only a mile or so apart.

Thomas Mould with his cows.

So, did the young couple meet while she was in service, or had they already become engaged to marry? If it was the latter, might not Thomas have helped Rose to find employment close to where he himself was then working in the Maxey area? All of this is supposition! But what we do know is that the couple were married in Etton Parish Church on April 5, 1852, and that their first child, Jane, was born on 1st May the following year. On the birth certificate, Rose put 'Greatford' as their place of residence at the time. But the little family must have moved to Gunthorpe not long afterwards since their second child, Betsy, was born there in the February of 1855 and subsequently, the rest of their children also. (Gunthorpe, of course, was the place where Thomas had been living at the time of the 1841 census.) Sadly, the cottage where they lived no longer exists, having been demolished in the early 1970's to make way for the new development of Greater Peterborough. It is generally thought that the original site is now occupied by the Brookside Methodist Church, which was completed in 1976.

Thomas Mould (in hat) with his men working in field. The men may be his sons.

Up until 1871, Thomas described himself as an 'Agricultural Laborer', but from the 1881 census onwards, he appeared as a 'Dairyman' or 'Cottager'. When his youngest son, George, moved into Peterborough in 1911 to set up Rock House Dairy, his business card claimed that the family milk business had been operating since 1876. Joan Bolton, however, feels it would be misleading to suggest that, in those early years, Thomas had done much more than sell milk from his few cows to the local inhabitance.

Thomas and Rose Ann had eleven children over a twenty year period, nine of whom lived to adulthood. Two sons died in infancy. They were Jabez A. (b: October 4, 1860, d: January 14, 1862, aged fifteen months) and

7

William Jabez (b: December 6, 1862, d: January 1, 1863, just under four weeks old). Both of these infant sons were buried in Paston Churchyard. The children of Thomas and Rose Ann in order of birth were Jane, Betsy, Mary, Rose, Jabez A., William Jabez, Joseph, Jabez, Rebecca, Charles and George. Of the nine children who lived to become adults, three emigrated to the US and six stayed in England.

Two of the daughters, Becky and Rebecca, married cousins on the Mackness side. There are currently descendants of Thomas and Rose Ann in England, the U.S. and even a few in New Zealand.

In those days, large families were the norm and, when there were too many mouths to feed, it was quite usual for daughters to be sent 'into service', working for a wealthy family as live-in servants. This was the case with the Mould family since it would

Brookside Methodist Church in Gunthorpe sits on the site of Thomas and Rose Ann's cottage.

appear that all four daughters were in service before they married. As for the sons, the family smallholding could only support two of them, in addition to Thomas and Rose. The two who stayed to help their father were Joseph, the eldest, and George, the youngest but the two middle sons were forced to make their living elsewhere.

At some point prior to 1881, Jabez was put on the train to Irthlingborough in order to look for work. From there he had to walk into Rushden where he managed to find employment as an apprentice in one of the shoe factories. Soon after Charles turned thirteen, he was sent to join his older brother in Rushden where he too found work in the shoe trade. The two brothers lived under the same roof even when Jabez first married. (Both men had met their wives in Rushden.) But, whereas Charles remained in England all his life, Jabez and his wife emigrated to America in 1919, joining their three children who were already there.

After marrying Fannie Mills in the autumn of 1898, George brought his wife back to Gunthorpe where they lived with his parents and older brother, Joseph. Six of their children would be born there before George moved the family into Peterborough in 1911 to start up his own dairy. By that time, however, the cottage had become a sad place, for not only had Thomas and Rose 'passed on', but also, Joseph had pre-deceased them, having taken his own life. This tragic event took place in 1900, on the last day of March. Almost thirty-six years of age, Joseph was unmarried and still living at home. (The Coroner's Report can be found in Appendix IV.)

With the help of his son, George, as well as Betsy and Jim Mackness, (his daughter and son-in-law - both now living at the cottage,) Thomas managed to struggle on with the smallholding until his death on January 26, 1906: he was seventy-eight. A family story has it that the old man ate his lunch one day without first washing his hands and got food poisoning, which resulted in his death. This may be at least partially correct since, on Thomas's death certificate, the cause is given as: 'Diarrhea 4 days. Sudden heart failure.' He was buried in Paston Churchyard, within a few yards of his son's grave.

Rose Ann survived her husband by two and a half years and died in Rushden on July 25, 1908, aged seventy-nine. The death certificate indicates that she died of 'Hemiplegia (paralysis on one side of the body) and Cardiac Failure'. The informant was her daughter Mary 'Polly' Avery. It appears that after Thomas died, Rose went to live with Polly and husband, Jim, in Rushden. Her funeral, however, took place in Paston where she was was buried in the same grave as Thomas at Paston Church. (Further information on the burial location appears in Appendix XVIII.)

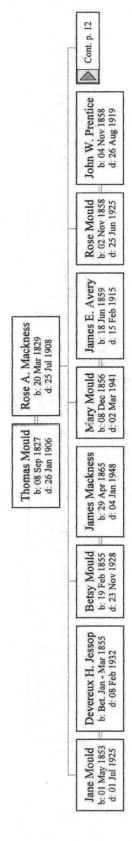

Cont. p. 12

Thomas Mould
b: 08 Sep 1827
d: 26 Jan 1906

Rose A. Mackness
b: 20 Mar 1829
d: 25 Jul 1908

Jane Mould
b: 01 May 1853
d: 01 Jul 1925

Devereux H. Jessop
b: Bet. Jan - Mar 1855
d: 08 Feb 1932

Betsy Mould
b: 19 Feb 1855
d: 23 Nov 1928

James Mackness
b: 29 Apr 1865
d: 04 Jan 1948

Mary Mould
b: 08 Dec 1856
d: 02 Mar 1941

James E. Avery
b: 18 Jun 1859
d: 15 Feb 1915

Rose Mould
b: 02 Nov 1858
d: 25 Jun 1925

John W. Prentice
b: 04 Nov 1858
d: 26 Aug 1919

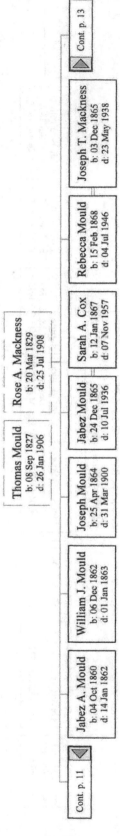

Thomas Mould
b: 08 Sep 1827
d: 26 Jan 1906

Rose A. Mackness
b: 20 Mar 1829
d: 25 Jul 1908

Jabez A. Mould
b: 04 Oct 1860
d: 14 Jan 1862

William J. Mould
b: 06 Dec 1862
d: 01 Jan 1863

Joseph Mould
b: 25 Apr 1864
d: 31 Mar 1900

Jabez Mould
b: 24 Dec 1865
d: 10 Jul 1936

Sarah A. Cox
b: 12 Jan 1867
d: 07 Nov 1957

Rebecca Mould
b: 15 Feb 1868
d: 04 Jul 1946

Joseph T. Mackness
b: 03 Dec 1865
d: 23 May 1938

Cont. p. 11

Cont. p. 13

Thomas Mould
b: 08 Sep 1827
d: 26 Jan 1906

Rose A. Mackness
b: 20 Mar 1829
d: 25 Jul 1908

Charles Mould
b: 15 Nov 1871
d: 03 Mar 1945

Emily J. Whitbread
b: 18 Aug 1872
d: 21 Apr 1942

Fanny Mills
b: 19 Nov 1870
d: 15 Feb 1947

George Mould
b: 05 Nov 1873
d: 10 Apr 1953

Dorothy Ayres
b: 20 Jul 1900
d: 07 Feb 1985

Cont. p. 12

Jane Jessop with daughters Naomi Jane and Rose Anna.
Picture probably taken in September 1886 while
attending wedding of Jane's sister Rose.

Chapter 2

Devereux and Jane Jessop

$\mathbf{T}$homas and Rose Ann's first child was a daughter named Jane.

She was born May 1, 1853 in Greatford, Lincolnshire quite a few miles from Gunthorpe, Peterborough, where the rest of Rose Ann's children were born. Although it was not unusual for a woman to go back to her own mother for the birth of the first baby, in Rose Ann's case the Macknesses were still in Brigstock, (to the south east of Corby and a good twenty miles from Greatford). A clue to the Lincolnshire connection could lie in the census for 1851 where Rose Ann was found "in service" with a family in Deeping Gate, situated only three or four miles from Greatford. Could it be that she continued to work there after marrying? Interestingly when she marries Thomas in 1852, it is at Etton Parish Church, in his parish, instead of in Brigstock.

By the time of the 1861 census, Jane was almost eight years old and living with her parents in Gunthorpe with four younger siblings, but has not been found so far in the census for 1871. She was not living at home with her parents and, since she would have been nearly eighteen years old, it is assumed she had been sent off to work, probably as a servant. This would be consistent with her sisters who were all sent into service as soon as they were old enough.

Janes next mention in the records was when she married on October 23, 1878 in the parish church at Paston. The bridegroom was Devereux Henry Jessop from Clapham, Surrey (now known as Greater London) who gave his occupation as a painter. But how had Jane met her husband? The most likely scenario is that their paths crossed whilst 'Jinny' (as she was known within the family) was in service with a family in the Clapham area and 'Harry', as he was generally known, came to the house to do some decorating. (This is where the 1871 census entry for Jane would have proved invaluable!) That the bride's place of 'residence at the time of marriage' should be 'Gunthorpe' could simply mean that she had returned home a few weeks in advance in order to prepare for the wedding - a logical move. The ages of both bride and groom are given as 'full': Jane was, in fact, twenty five (and a half) whilst her husband was almost two years younger, having been born at Little Stonham in Suffolk, with the birth registered during the March Quarter of 1855.

Another intriguing question is how someone from an ordinary working family, (the son of one Henry Jessop, a plumber,) had come to be named Devereux. (Robert Devereux, the second Earl of Essex, had been a favorite courtier of Queen Elizabeth I, three centuries before!) Probably having experienced some teasing at school, the lad had decided to call himself 'Harry', a variation on his second name. Significantly, Harry's son, Devereux Henry Jessop, was obviously known as Henry, as proved by the newspaper report on his death. The Christian name, DEVEREUX, still survives in the Jessop family, with Jane and Devereux's great-grandson christened Michael Devereux Jessop in 1968.

It is more than likely that the newly-weds first set up home at 5 Pickett Street, off Temperley Road, Clapham since this was the address given when the birth of their first child, a daughter, was registered in the summer of 1879. By December of 1880, however, when Jane gave birth to a son, the family had moved the short distance to 55 Balham Grove, which probably offered more room for their growing family. Fifteen months later, in fact, the 1881 census recorded six people living there. In addition to Devereux and Jane were their two small children, eighteen-month-old Naomi Jane, born August 19, 1879, and a three-month old son, Devereux Henry, born December 16, 1880. The 'birthplace' for both children was Balham, Surrey.   The fifth person living there was the Jessops' lodger, one Edward Olive, aged twenty-four. But the sixth occupant at 'Number 55' was a thirteen-year-old girl, mistakenly listed as "Rebecca <u>Jessop</u>.... Sister" who turned out to be Rebecca <u>Mould</u>, (or 'Becky'), Jane's youngest sister. Undoubtedly, Becky would have been delighted to escape from Gunthorpe in order to give Jane some help with her babies, and at the same time experience the excitement and bustle of London. (There could scarcely have been a greater contrast!) As for her parents, Rose Ann and Thomas, the prospect of "one less mouth to feed" would surely have been welcomed. Subsequently, two more children were born at Balham Grove: another son, Frederick Thomas on April 6, 1882, and a second daughter, Rose Anna, on September 24, 1885. Searching for the Jessops at the Balham Grove address on the 1891 census proved fruitless; they had moved, and more than likely to Balham High Road.

Fifteen years later, the 1901 census provides an informative 'snapshot' of the Jessops, (leaving aside the misspelling of Naomi as 'Naino' and the fact that she has been relegated to the second-born, after brother Devereux!) All of the four children were still living at home but the family had moved again. This time it was to 86 Balham High Road, though still in the same area. Naomi, now 21 years old, is a 'cashier' (presumably in a shop), Devereux, 20, is described as a 'groom', Fred, 18, is working as a 'commercial clerk', but there is no occupation given for fifteen-year-old Rose. Head of the family and father, Devereux/ 'Harry' Jessop, still describes himself as a House Decorator - but will have 'promoted' himself to the status of 'Master Builder' by the time of his elder daughter's wedding just three years later!

On May 23, 1904, Naomi Jane Jessop married Herbert Alphonsus Baldwin at the Victoria Baptist Chapel, situated on the Wandsworth Road. Aged 25, and just a few months older than his bride, Herbert was living in Honeybrook Road, Clapham and was also a master butcher. (All of this information is revealed on the marriage certificate.) If we add in the facts that both fathers were in the building trade, (Phillip Baldwin a joiner and Harry Jessop a builder/decorator/plumber), that Naomi worked as a cashier and that, as a master butcher, Herbert would have owned at least one shop, then the temptation to speculate is irresistible. Both fathers worked in the same area and on the same projects from time to time. Harry's daughter was looking for a job and Phillip Baldwin's son needed an assistant. The two young people worked together and fell in love - the rest is history!

Herbert and Naomi Baldwin. Based on the car's identification by Reg Bolton, the little boy is most likely their son John Rupert.

But in fact, Naomi's granddaughter, Virginia Manning (nee Parsley), confirmed that this could indeed have been how her grandparents met. Naomi was a good-looking girl with her lovely fair hair and would certainly have made an instant impression on her employer. Furthermore, she was highly intelligent and very good with figures (or 'numbers') - so much so that Eric Parsley, her schoolmaster son-in-law, described Naomi's mental arithmetic skills as 'incredible'. Obviously, Omi was not "just a pretty-face" but also an excellent cashier - and a real asset to Bert as they built up the business together.

Herbert and Naomi had three children: Muriel Naomi, born March 26, 1905, Douglas Herbert, born November 23, 1908 and then John Rupert, born almost eight years afterwards on August 25, 1916. It was the birth of this third child that posed something of a conundrum.

During WW1, Herbert and two of his brothers were sent to Dartmoor prison for being conscientious objectors. (According to the 1901 census, Herbert was the second eldest of six children, having four brothers and a sister and, coincidentally, all living with their parents in St. Alphonsus Road!) Since Herbert was a butcher by trade, he was given the opportunity to supply meat to the British army, but declined. Naomi, however, was a very determined woman and had no difficulty in visiting her husband in Dartmoor, especially since money would change hands. Besides, her husband seemed to be on good terms with the warders. (In fact, one came from the Epsom area and Bert found him a job in one of his shops after the war.) But still, the puzzling question was this: how had Naomi managed to have a child during the summer of 1916, mid-way through the war and with her husband still in prison? An explanation eventually came from an unexpected source: apparently, the couple were able to enjoy the privacy of their own room in the prison for conjugal visits! Bert was released after the war and his life gradually returned to some sort of normality. But sadly, John Rupert's life would be very short as he died from T.B. just before his eighth birthday.

During the 1920's and 1930's, the Baldwins owned nine butcher shops, all in the Sutton area of London. The first shop - named 'Henry' was in Sutton High Street. Then there was one in Ewell West, one in Ewell East, two in Epsom High Street, (The Top Shop and the Bottom Shop), one in Leatherhead, one in Ashtead, one in Carshalton, known as Woodmans' and another in Motspur Park. Jane Fletcher expressed her immense admiration for Herbert, her grandfather, whom she considered a prime example of a 'self made man'. Starting out as a butcher's delivery boy on leaving school, he had managed to work his way up until he eventually owned a whole chain of butcher's shops in the capital; quite an achievement! His hard work and shrewd business acumen also made Herbert a wealthy man and he left a quarter of a million pounds when he died, aged only fifty-nine. Having become a successful businessman, Herbert was able to capitalise on this prominence in order to run for parliament. He stood for election as the Labour Party candidate for Acton in 1923 and 1924, but was unfortunately defeated on both occasions. (For additional details of these campaigns, see Appendix XXII.) The second defeat - on October 29, 1924 - must have been especially hard for Herbert, coming as it did just three months after the death of John, their youngest child.

GENERAL ELECTION, 1923.

POLLING DAY, Thursday, December 6th, 1923.
7 A.M. to 9 P.M.

PUBLIC MEETINGS

THE LABOUR CANDIDATE.
TO-NIGHT, Friday, at Acton Baths.

Mr. J. F. SHILLAKER,

SATURDAY, Dec. 1st, Acton Market Place.
MONDAY, Dec. 3rd, Southfield Road Schools.
TUESDAY, Dec. 4th, All Saints' Parish Hall.
WEDNESDAY, Dec. 5th, EVE OF POLL RALLY.
At CENTRAL HALL, PRIORY SCHOOLS.

ELECTORS! TRY REAL PROTECTION and
VOTE for BALDWIN

Article in the Acton Gazette and Express concerning Herbert Baldwin's candidacy for the Labor Party candidate for Parliament.

But Bert did have other interests too. The chief of these was horse riding, which he did not take up until the late 1920's, on reaching fifty. He soon became a member of the East Surrey Hunt and went out drag hunting most Saturdays. According to Mona, her father-in-law liked nothing better than to do the round of his shops straight after his Saturday hunting sessions. Fired up after being in the saddle he would bellow at his staff over any perceived shortcomings, leaving them quaking in their shoes! On a more positive note, Jane Fletcher told of many cups her grandfather had won with his hunting and how she felt that her own passion for horses undoubtedly came

Herbert Alphonsus Baldwin on a horse.

down through him. His interest in trade unions indicated a genuine interest in his employees.

After these disappointments came sadness when Jane Jessop died on July 1st 1925, just two weeks after her 72nd birthday. She died at 62 Lenham Road, Sutton, the home of her daughter, Rose Brushett. Devereux survived her by six-and-a-half years, dying on February 8th 1932, aged 76. According to the death certificate, he died at '26, Wolverton Avenue, Kingston Urban District, Surrey'. Since Kingston Hospital backed onto Wolverton Avenue then (as now), 'Number 26' might possibly have been a nursing home. Devereux was buried beside his wife in the Sutton Cemetery on February 11.

Naomi and Herbert's daughter, Muriel, would have been eleven-and-a-half years old in September of 1916 when she was sent to the North London Collegiate School. But it seems that she was a rather rebellious student (as well as something of a tomboy,) and was eventually expelled. Muriel was then sent to 'lodge' in Hendon where she was taught privately by the head of the household, Mr. Leonard Parsley, a former merchant at the London Corn Exchange. Their son, Eric, was a pupil at Christ's Hospital in

Horsham and five years older than Muriel. The two first met when he came home for the holidays and, although thirteen at the time, the young 'lodger' was immediately drawn to this kind, thoughtful young man. Being a very able scholar himself and excelling at languages, Eric was possibly drafted in to assist his father with Muriel's instruction, whenever he came home.

It was at about this time that the Parsleys learned their son had won a Classical Scholarship to Keble College, Oxford. However, his studies were interrupted when he left Christ's Hospital to serve with the Royal Horse Artillery towards the end of the First War, afterwards returning as a pupil for two more terms. When Eric finally went up to Oxford in 1919, his friendship with Muriel continued, and, by the time he graduated in 1923 with a First in Modern Languages, the pair were courting in earnest. He had already been appointed Master in charge of French at Dulwich College, starting in the September. Two years later, they were married. The wedding took place on Saturday, 25th July, 1925, in the centre of London, followed by a reception at Harrod's.

Eric Parsley's career at Dulwich was a most distinguished one and extended over thirty- seven years. He quickly established his reputation as a dedicated and inspiring teacher, later becoming an excellent housemaster as well. He was a natural musician, able to play the piano for any occasion and also had a fine baritone voice. Eric was most adept at producing school plays and sketches, as well as possessing good debating skills. Always immaculately dressed and with a great sense of style, he could be very amusing and genuinely good company. In his book, 'Dulwich College - A history 1616-2008', J.R.Piggott documents Eric Parsley's considerable contribution to the Scouts, and also, as an officer, to the Junior Training Corps. He writes: 'During the Second World War Eric Parsley, a famous master at the College, raised money from Alleynians to carry out a highly successful and ambitious scheme to encourage Old Alleynian prisoners of war, dispatching Red Cross parcels of books, gramophone records and tins of cigarettes to their camps, each with 'cheering' individual letters; it was reported that most of the parcels got through.'

After a long illness, courageously fought, Eric Parsley died near Cambridge, (where he had chosen to retire,) in July 1972. Just a few weeks before, he had been awarded a second French decoration, 'Chevalier des Arts et Lettres'. He was seventy-two. Writing Eric's obituary in The Alleynian, George Way summed up his former colleague thus: "Few, if any, Dulwich masters of this century will be remembered with greater respect and affection for all that he did by those who had the privilege of working with him or of studying under him. He had a wonderful sense of humour, combined with a great dignity, and a never-failing kindness for the many who brought their problems to him."

But what part did Muriel Parsley play in all of this? For an answer, we again turn to George Way who maintained that 'the sustaining influence throughout most of Eric's life had been his happy family relationship, and especially his wife, Muriel.' He goes on to say: 'With similar predilections, they were supremely happy in their own company and delighted in furnishing their successive homes with exquisite taste.' Muriel survived her husband by more than twenty years, dying in the spring of 1993, aged 88 years. (The fascinating story of how Eric came to possess a rare first edition manuscript of Racine's play "Athalie", resulting in his being honoured by the French Government, is to be found in Appendix XIV.)

The Parsleys had two children: a son, David, born in 1927 and a daughter, Virginia (known as 'Bar'), who was born in November 1928. (In correspondence with Joan Bolton, she explained how her 'little brother' had always called her 'Bar'- and this name had stuck.) Tragically, David was killed in a plane crash over Egypt in 1949 when he was returning to Britain prior to his sister's wedding that summer: a cruel blow for the family. Virginia and John Manning had four children, a son and three daughters, two of them twins.

It was Virginia who told Joan that the last she'd heard of her mother's brother, Douglas Baldwin, he and his family had been living in Ringwood, Hampshire. (It was apparent that there had been little contact between brother and sister over the years, but neither had there been any falling out, to Virginia's knowledge.) She knew that her uncle and his wife had a son and a daughter and that the boy was called Christopher. There was only one 'C.Baldwin' in the phone book Joan found for that area, but it was the number she needed! The two cousins had a cordial chat for several minutes before Chris came out with a surprising revelation: his mother, Mona, was still alive, living independently in her own flat and 'hale and hearty' for her 94 years! Better still, (as Joan discovered two weeks later when she went over to Ringwood to meet her), Mona had retained an excellent memory too! The information Mona Baldwin provided for this book has proved invaluable and her personal insights fascinating. (Clearing up the "mystery" surrounding John Rupert was just one of her contributions.)

From the outset, it was clear to Mona that Douglas would always have difficulty in pursuing his own path in life. For a start, Herbert, his successful father, was a hard act to follow, whilst Naomi was 'very controlling', (to use Mona's words.) Their son had really wanted to go into engineering but received no encouragement in this direction. It was most probably on turning fourteen at the end of 1922 that Douglas left school (St. George's, Harpenden). His first job was as an errand boy at one of his father's shops, whilst living with his parents in Reigate. He then found himself an apprenticeship with a bus company where he was very happy, but unfortunately his mother was not. Naomi did not like the dirt and grease so Douglas was soon 'persuaded' back into another of his father's shops. He was next sent off to Kenya on a business mission his father had organized and later landed up in South Africa, driving organized parties of wealthy people around on safari trips. Since he always liked driving, this was a happy interlude for Douglas, with the added advantage of being free from his parents' influence. When he found that his money was running short, however, his only option was to return home.

Douglas's next move was to the Argentine where his father had found him work on the ranches owned by Armours, the country's number one beef canning company. There was no better place than on the 'haciendas' for him to learn the butchery trade from beginning to end. Being a good horseman, (one interest at least that he and his father shared,) Douglas was in his element rounding up the cattle. Here in Argentina, he was able to indulge his love of yachting too. This proved to be another happy period in his life, and even more so when he became engaged to a young lady he had met out there; Douglas could imagine himself staying on forever!

But he had not bargained for his parents, or, more especially, for his controlling mother. Douglas' 'good news' certainly did not meet with her approval. He was summoned back to England forthwith and the engagement was broken off.

Naomi seemed to have difficulty showing any maternal affection towards her son, according to Mona. In any case, she had made little attempt to disguise the fact that the younger son, - her "darling John"- had always been her favourite and his premature death had only reinforced this preference. When Douglas returned from South America early in 1934, Naomi and Herbert had travelled to Bristol in order to meet Douglas from the boat. But when his mother saw how much luggage he had brought back, she turned to her husband and said: 'Bert, we cannot possibly have him home with all that stuff! You will have to find him a flat.' So Douglas had to move into a flat above his father's latest shop in Motspur Park, near Wimbledon, where he didn't know a soul. Fortunately, he did not have long to wait before meeting the young woman who would change his life.

In the 1930's, both the Skeltons and the Baldwins were living in the Epsom area where Mona's father, Fred, ran his well-established family building business, Skelton and Sons. Fred and his wife, Hannah (nee Sale), had five children - one son and four daughters. Hannah Skelton was one of Herbert Baldwin's best customers, buying her meat from the 'top shop' in Epsom High Street, where she was often served by Herbert himself. Aware that Mrs Skelton was a regular churchgoer, Bert would sometimes ask her to 'say a little prayer' for him if, for example, he was in pain after one of his hunting accidents. At the same time he would give her a generous donation for the church.

One day when Mona's mother went for her meat, the conversation turned to family matters. Bert told her that his son was back from the Argentine and wondered if Hannah's daughters, Mona and Olive, might be interested in joining them to follow the hunt. The answer was in the affirmative. When Douglas arrived with the car to collect the sisters, Mona sat in front, next to him - and that was how the romance began!

Just as Douglas had broken off his engagement, so Mona had to disentangle herself from a lengthy involvement with her fiancé, Cecil, whom she had met through joining a church youth group in Epsom. (She was working in London as a telephonist/telephone operator at the time.) Cecil aspired to become a parson and was studying for the Anglican ministry, but the ending of the relationship came as a huge relief to the Skelton household. Cecil had scarcely endeared himself to Mona's parents on his visits by taking along his classical textbooks and insisting on silence while he studied! Worse still in Fred Skelton's eyes, Cecil was a High Church "pot slinger". (In other words, his task was to swing the censer during the service.) Apparently, the pungent smell of incense on the young man's clothes put them off their Sunday lunch and they were glad to see the back of him!

After a short courtship, Douglas and Mona were married on November 8th 1934; both were twenty-five years old, though the groom was, in fact, older by nine months. Herbert gave his son the job of managing one of his butcher's shops in Epsom High Street - the 'top shop', (the one that Hannah Skelton patronised,) and the newly-weds lived in the flat above. In the December of 1935, the young couple's first child was born: a daughter they named Jane.

The following year, Herbert asked Douglas to take over the running of the Carshalton shop, called 'Woodmans', a 'high class' establishment specialising in expensive cuts of meat. This time, instead of having a flat above the shop, the family made their home in nearby Cheam. (It was from Woodman's that they witnessed the huge fire that destroyed Crystal Palace on Sydenham Hill in 1936.) It was probably during this same year that Herbert had a bad fall from his horse and, as a consequence, had to endure a long spell in London's Maudesley Hospital, (which specialized in head injuries,). But on the weekends that he was free to go home, Bert preferred to escape to be with his son and daughter-in-law, rather than return to Naomi in Hove. Even though the older couple were living under the same roof, to all intents and purposes, their marriage had broken down. Both Naomi and Bert were strong characters who had grown apart over the years. Bert was notoriously prone to bouts of severe depression and could give vent to a violent temper. Naomi, of course, could be very difficult too but the realization that her husband was seeking other female company could hardly have improved matters.

Herbert obviously enjoyed his weekends spent with Douglas and Mona (with the added attraction of seeing little Jane, his first grandchild, of course.) For their part, the young couple were more than happy to welcome him. But it may have been a very different story had Naomi wished to visit too. Unfortunately, the relationship between Mona and her mothe-in-law had been difficult from the beginning. Both women were strong-willed, fiercely independent - and neither was afraid to speak her mind!

One illuminating episode took place soon after Douglas and Mona married and were living above the shop in Epsom. Naomi called at the flat one day, catching her new daughter-in-law alone. She was concerned that her son seemed so tired these days. Being a butcher, he had to rise very early in order to get to the Smithfield Market every morning, of course, but she had reason to suspect that the newly-weds were burning the candle at both ends. (In fact Omi had taken to driving slowly past their flat at night to see if the lights were still on. And often they were!) Over a cup of tea, the older woman soon dispensed with the 'small talk' and broached the topic that was uppermost on her mind. Douglas seemed very tired these days, she thought. Could it possibly be that Mona was denying him his sleep at night? Without missing a beat, Mona was ready with her reply. "oh yes," she said, "and we're making the most of the dinner hour too."

But what especially rankled with Mona was Naomi's implication that Douglas 'had married beneath him'. Her retort was two-fold: <u>one</u>, her own family, the Skeltons, were 'proper builders', (clearly suggesting that Naomi's father, Harry Jessop, was not!) And, <u>two</u>, Fred Skelton was a pillar of respectability who did not frequent public houses - unlike Harry Jessop. (Mona knew well that Naomi's younger brother, Bill, regularly waited up to restrain their father when he came in late, "the worse for wear".)

There was, however, one thing at least that Naomi and Mona did have in common - both celebrated their birthdays on the nineteen of August, (though thirty years apart.) Perhaps this is why the two women seemed so incompatible: they were too alike!

In due course, Bert was well enough physically to be discharged from the Maudesley, but it became obvious that he was suffering from a severe mental breakdown and had to be admitted to a residential home. At the same time, Naomi acquired 'power of attorney' over Bert's financial affairs. A wealthy woman in her own right, she had nevertheless lost a great deal of money on her stocks and shares in the 1930's, especially those invested in Cunard and in gold. Soon afterwards and very much against her husband's wishes - Naomi decided to sell the chain of shops.

The spring of 1937 heralded two significant events for Douglas and his wife: on 1st March, Mona gave birth to a son they named Christopher. It was also at this time they learned that Woodmans had finally been sold and that Douglas's parents were to set him up in a new venture. It was another butchery business in the small town of Witheridge in Devon, but this time it would involve buying the animals, slaughtering them and selling the meat on to the butchers. This was not a prospect that Douglas relished at all but, once again, he had to 'fall in line'! (To be fair here, it was the young couple themselves who were set on fulfilling their ambition to live in the country'.)

The move down to Devon took place towards the end of March, with the furniture van going ahead the night before. Douglas drove the family down, with the snow falling so heavily all the way that the windscreen wipers stopped working. It was a nightmare, especially as the children were so young, with Jane fifteen months and Christopher only three weeks old. They spent the night at a hotel in Tiverton before setting off again the next day, still in wintry conditions.

The young couple had never seen the house before but soon noticed that it was on a steep slope. The removal men, who had been impatiently waiting for the new occupants to arrive, were intent on off-loading all the furniture as quickly as possible before any more snow fell. Instead of following the room plan as intended, they simply pushed everything through the door and rushed off, leaving a scene of utter chaos. It was not a propitious start! Indeed, Douglas's misgivings proved to be justified. Not only did he have little experience of buying the livestock, but he also hated slaughtering the animals. Mona did all she could to help her husband; for

24

example, it was her job every week to make a large quantity of both lard and fat and fill a tin bath with each. It was fortunate that she was able to employ some help with the care of the children, but by the end of the year they had had enough, sold up and moved to Hampshire.

Probably realising from the outset that the business venture in Devon was unlikely to succeed, Douglas had sensibly contacted one of his Baldwin cousins who managed a taxi business in Portsmouth. Driving was an occupation that Douglas enjoyed, so that when the cousin advised him that they had a vacancy, he and Mona went down for the weekend, found a house to rent and agreed a date for Douglas to start. After all the stress of the business in Devon, it was sheer bliss for Douglas, driving a taxi around the town and doing a job he liked. But, unfortunately, the initial gratitude for his cousin's help was short lived. One day Douglas went into work to learn that his relative was in deep disgrace: he had broken into the safe and stolen a large sum of money. The outcome was a short spell in prison for the offender and a great deal of trouble and inconvenience for Douglas and Mona as they tried to help him. During this period, however, there was a far more dramatic event, which caused real upheaval in their lives. It occurred over the Easter weekend in mid-April, 1938, when Douglas and family were newly settled in Portsmouth.

That weekend, Mona had two of her sisters, Brenda and Olive, staying there. On the Bank Holiday Monday, 18th April, they had all finished lunch and Mona was reading the newspaper while her sisters washed the dishes. It was just a small item inside which arrested her attention: Mr Herbert Baldwin had disappeared overboard from a Channel ferry (the 'PARIS') that had sailed from Newhaven on the Friday night!

Mona's first thought was to find Douglas without delay in order to break the dreadful news herself. With the two small children strapped into the double pram, the three sisters set out to walk into Portsmouth. Mona knew that her husband regularly stopped at three garages in order to find his next 'fare' but couldn't find him at any of them. She therefore decided to catch the bus home, leaving Olive and Brenda to push the children back in the pram. Mona arrived back just in time to see Douglas pushing his bike up the drive. As he propped it against the side of the house, she could tell from his face that he had already heard the news.

Herbert was fifty-nine years old. His body was never found so that no death certificate could be issued, (as was the case in such circumstances.) This terrible act had clearly been planned over a period of time and was not carried out on a sudden impulse. There was, however, one serious oversight that almost thwarted his plans at the outset. Being a conscientious objector, (hence his imprisonment during WWI,) Herbert had no passport, but had learned that this requirement was waived over Easter. Through some misunderstanding, or possibly because of his state of inner turmoil, he had set off to catch the Newhaven-to-Dieppe ferry a week too early! He then had no choice but to return home to Naomi in Hove and try again the next weekend, which he did. This time he thought it might be advisable to carry a suitcase onto the ship in order to avert suspicion. It so happened that Naomi had recently dismissed a girl who had been working for them (because she thought that her husband was becoming too friendly with her!) and this gave Herbert the perfect excuse: he said he would take this girl the belongings she'd left behind - in the suitcase.

Herbert had maintained a close friendship with a married woman who lived at Tadworth on the Epsom Downs, so he first drove there to say good-bye before visiting the young helper with her things. He then set off for Newhaven a second time and succeeded in boarding the night boat for what would be his last journey.

So, what was it that drove Herbert to take his own life? Suggestions have come from several quarters. Mona Baldwin thought that the serious head injury her father-in-law sustained from his hunting accident could have triggered the bouts of depression, while Herbert's granddaughter, Virginia, enlarged on this theory in a letter (to Joan) written in 2003: "As you will know, Herbert was a prisoner in Dartmoor during the 1914-18 war. Later, he became acutely depressed as he thought (quite rightly, as it turned out) that there was going to be another war and couldn't face being imprisoned again. Hence his suicide." If we add to this his understandable disappointment after two thwarted attempts to enter Parliament, as well as the continuing difficulties in his marriage, then the tragic picture becomes clearer. (Quite obviously, the marital problems were a significant factor in all this. Mona recalled her father-in-law's dreadful temper, something that Omi had no doubt experienced at first hand on many occasions. But then, both Omi and Bert had always been very forceful characters.)

Devastated as the family were by this dreadful event, there were practical matters to deal with. Their first priority was Naomi. For all the difficulties that she and Herbert had experienced, Naomi was now in a state of complete shock and grief. As soon as Muriel and Eric, heard of the tragedy, they went down to the south coast to take her back to Dulwich. It was there the following day, Easter Sunday, 1938, that Naomi was interviewed by a reporter from a national paper, the Daily Mirror, and the story appeared the next day, Bank Holiday Monday. (This was, most probably, the same account that Mona read.) Naomi was quoted as saying: "He has been kissing me good-bye for weeks past and we could not understand the pathetic farewells. I thought he might be thinking he would die within a short time."

Since Herbert's remains were never found, there could be no conventional funeral to bring the family any sense of 'closure'. Instead, they had to gather up the threads of their lives again, as best they could. Naomi herself lived for twenty more years, dying at the age of seventy-nine in Hove at the beginning of 1959.

So, what was Naomi really like? And who better to tell us than her granddaughter, Jane Baldwin Fletcher? As we have already seen, Naomi was not very motherly, as Jane confirms: "Naomi was certainly not a 'hands-on' mother; in fact, she was not very good with children at all, preferring to keep them at a distance! She was, however, a very good cake-maker, and also made sweets - such as crystallised fruits - to a professional standard. When children visited, Naomi had all the cakes set out on a table in another room and would say: 'Now you can go in there for your tea - and just be quiet!' Omi was 'a bit of a fusspot', lived on her nerves and was prone to headaches."

Both Jane and her mother, Mona, saw Naomi as a very manipulative woman. Apparently, she and Herbert tried to compete for the children's affection, as well as to see which one could have more influence over them. For instance, if Bert denied them something, then Naomi would probably give it.

Jane also revealed a 'snobbish' side to her grandmother with this little story: Occasionally Naomi would invite Douglas and Mona to make up the numbers at a bridge party. But, before setting off, she would remind them not to 'let on' (i.e. reveal) that they were 'in trade'. Always mindful of her perceived station in life, to be thus employed seemed 'common' to Naomi! Jane also offered her opinion on the thorny issue of her grandparents' marriage: she felt that Herbert and Naomi had simply grown apart over the years. It was the familiar story of a successful businessman 'leaving his wife behind', but a divorce in those days would have been out of the question.

In her final years, however, Naomi became a rather pathetic figure, according to Mona. Back in Hove again on the south coast, she was often to be found wandering aimlessly along the seafront and speaking to complete strangers. No longer bothering about her appearance either, Naomi was now only a shadow of the proud and confident womanshe had been. She died at a nursing home there on 12th February 1959, after suffering a brain haemorrhage.

By the time war broke out in 1939, Douglas and Mona were running a ten-acre smallholding in Ringwood, with chickens and pigs, as well as a few goats. But Douglas felt a compulsion to 'sign up', possibly not wanting to be labelled a 'conchie', (a conscientious objector) like his father. He joined the RAC - the Royal Armoured Corps - initially as a driver and subsequently, with his regiment, became part of the Eighth Army, fighting across North Africa, from Egypt to Tunisia. By that point, Douglas had become batman (personal attendant) to an officer. In the summer of 1944 he took part in the Normandy landings, driving one of the amphibious landing craft, known as 'ducks'. Although Douglas had never enjoyed robust health, it could have been during the war that he contracted TB and was forced to spend time in hospital.

But while her husband was away, it was a real struggle for Mona to keep the smallholding going, as well as caring for the children and all they had to survive on was Douglas' pay as a soldier! The long winter of 1939-40 was one of the coldest and snowiest of the century and the Spartan conditions with which Mona had to contend made it especially difficult. There was no mains sewerage, no electricity or gas - just paraffin for heating, cooking and light. Mona eventually went down with influenza and was so ill that she had to go into a nursing home for three weeks. Jane and Christopher went to stay with their mother's family and all the livestock had to be sold at market.

Asked whether Naomi had given the couple any financial help at this critical time, Jane was not aware of any. Furthermore, she added, her father never felt that he had been adequately rewarded in the early days for managing the family shops. However, in a letter to Joan in 2004, Mona wrote, (with undoubtedly some bitterness): "...but I'm sure you will be pleased to hear that, on Douglas's return to England after the war, his mother repaid our mortgage on the smallholding, which I had struggled to pay.' This gesture was something that Jane also remembered, though neither woman would have described her as generous.

Although not lavish with others, Naomi was certainly given to extravagance in her own life, ensuring that she herself lived very comfortably. During the Second World War, for instance, she went to live in a hotel in Gloucester in order to get away from the bombing. In fact, she moved about a great deal, renting a series of flats and houses in various places.

Douglas was thirty-five when the war ended and he was able to return to England. Once back, he had to undergo more treatment for TB, but his inability to completely give up smoking was clearly an obstacle to his recovery. He found employment with an engineering firm called Wellworthys where he worked as an instructor on the lathes. Sadly, Douglas did not live to enjoy retirement since he died after a heart attack in the autumn of 1971 at the age of sixty-two.

As we have seen, the Baldwins' youngest child, John Rupert, was born in August 1916, eight years after Douglas, whilst Muriel, his sister, was thirteen and a half years older. Inevitably, as the baby of the family, John was somewhat spoilt by all the attention, but when he was diagnosed with tuberculosis at an early age, everyone doted on him even more. Since the exposure to fresh air was considered an important part of the treatment, his parents had made him a little house in the garden that could be swivelled round to face the sun.

When he reached school age, John was sent to a private sanatorium somewhere on the East Coast' where he was also able to receive tuition from Montessori teachers. Mona recounted a sad story in connection with this. Apparently, John's mother, accompanied by her own mother, Jane Jessop, used to take the small boy to the railway station. There they would hand him over to an escort who then accompanied him to his destination. "But", said Mona, "the poor child was so distraught at being parted from Naomi that his screams could be heard long after the train pulled out of the station."

Sadly, John finally succumbed to the tuberculosis, dying in the July of 1924, a few weeks short of his eighth birthday. Naturally, all of the family were heartbroken, but no-one more so than Naomi; forever after she would refer to him as "my darling John". But, although Herbert may not have shown his own emotions so readily, it is inconceivable that he would not have been deeply affected. Coming so soon after the couple's twentieth wedding anniversary, the tragic loss might even have contributed to their marriage problems.

Naomi lived another twenty-one years and died in Hove on February 12, 1959.

Devereux and Jane's second child was a son, born on 16th December 1880 and named Devereux Henry, after his father. The 1901 census reveals that he was working as "a groom", (a servant.) Almost a decade later, on September 13th 1910, he married Jessie Anscombe at the Baptist Church in Sutton High Street. Henry (as he was now known) was almost thirty years old whilst Jessie was eight years younger. (The marriage certificate gives her age as twenty but, with her birth having been registered during the last quarter of 1888, Jessie was nearer to twenty-two.) The groom is described as a "master butcher" and it is virtually certain that he is managing one of Herbert Baldwin's two shops situated in Epsom High Street. Not unusually, no 'profession' is given for the bride and, up to this point, the only other document providing information about herself and the Anscombes is the census for 1901. From this we learn the following: (1) Her parents were Joseph and Eliza, then aged 45 and 43 years respectively. (2) Jessie was the third of five children, four girls and a boy. (3) The two older sisters had been born in Penge, Surrey, whilst Jessie and her two younger siblings were born in the London Borough of Southwark. But in 1901, they were all living at 23 Dagmar Road, New Windsor in Berkshire. (4) Jessie's age was recorded as '12', (which, incidentally, closely matched the registration date in the GRO records, referred to above.)

Once again, we ask ourselves how the young couple came to meet and, just as in Naomi and Herbert's case, the marriage certificate could well hold the clue. This time both fathers give their occupation as 'House Decorator' and so could easily have met through the building trade. (Two years previously, on his daughter Rose's wedding certificate, Devereux had described himself as a 'Builder'.) For his 'profession', the bridegroom writes "Butcher (master)" and gives his residence at the time of marriage as "High Street, Epsom". It was more than likely that the couple set up home together in the flat above the butcher's shop in Epsom, where Henry Jessop was already living - and working.

They did not have long to wait to start a family. Their first child was born on 25th June the following year and was christened Devereux Frederick Jessop; the parents could not know that he would also be their last. Tragedy was to strike on the evening of the 12th June 1914 when the young couple decided to call on Herbert and Naomi in order to discuss some business matters. The Baldwins lived in Holland Avenue, just a ten-minute drive away by motorbike; Henry was at the controls with Jessie travelling in the sidecar. Their small son was safely tucked up in bed, possibly being minded by Jessie's parents who were not too far away, in Benhill Wood

Road, Sutton.

Once the discussions were over, it could have been Bert who suggested going for a spin on the motorbike. It was a nice evening and they headed for Epsom Downs with Bert riding pillion behind his brother-in-law and Jessie again in the sidecar. That Naomi was not included in the outing would have been a great relief to her! If she was to travel, she liked to do so in style, preferably in a smart car. And in any case, the two children, nine year old Muriel and five year old Douglas, had to be put to bed.

EPSOM.
(See also Page 6).

MOTOR CYCLE FATALITY.

On Wednesday evening Mr. Jessop, manager of Messrs. Baldwin Bros., butchers, High-street, Epsom, was motor cycling along the Banstead road with his wife, who was in a side-car, when the machine by some means got out of control and ran into a tree. Both Mr. Jessop and his wife were thrown out, the former being killed instantly, whilst his wife was seriously hurt. Mr. Jessop was a brother-in-law of Mr. Baldwin, one of the members of the firm of Baldwin Bros.

The inquest was opened at the Banstead Institute yesterday (Friday). Evidence of identification having been taken, the inquiry was adjourned. Mrs. Jessop, who was taken to Holland-avenue, Sutton, is stated to be progressing favourably.

Newspaper account of the motorcycle death of Devereux Henry Jessop.

The three of them went along Banstead Road and then onto Drift Way Road (or "Firtree Road", as it appeared on maps at the time.) As Henry attempted to take the left hand bend, he lost control of the bike and crashed into a tree. The impact killed him instantly and threw Herbert and Jessie to the ground. Although Herbert got off lightly, his sister-in-law suffered serious injuries. From a report in The Surrey Advertiser three days afterwards, we learn that Jessie had been "taken to Holland Avenue, Sutton" where she was "progressing favourably". Presumably, this referred to the Baldwins' comfortable home, where Omi possibly employed someone to nurse poor Jessie. Fortunately, the young woman eventually made a full recovery. (Further details on the death of Devereux Henry are in Appendix XXI.) Young Devereux was buried in the same grave in which his parents were later buried in Sutton.

So, after just four years of marriage and aged only twenty-five, Jessie Jessop was left a widow, with a young son two weeks short of his third birthday. It should be said that it was entirely due to the memories that Mona Baldwin shared with Joan Bolton during one of their meetings that this tragic incident came to light - and, of course, saved the authors the effort of searching for more children, as well as ending speculation as to whether Devereux Henry had been killed during WWI, (although nothing had been found in the war records.) Being only four years old at the time of the accident, Mona heard about it later from her parents (the Skeltons) who, when out driving, would regularly point out the large beech tree where the crash had occurred.

And there were many other reminiscences from Mona's childhood in the Epsom/Sutton area. Not only did Fred and Hannah Skelton know the Jessops, but they also knew the Anscombes. In fact, as a small girl, Mona had attended the same infants' school as Devereux Jessop, though two classes ahead of him, being older. (Little did she know then that one day she would be married to his cousin!) Hannah Skelton would probably have exchanged greetings with Jessie at the school gate. However, she was somewhat disapproving of the young widow, describing Jessie as "a flighty piece"! All the same, being good at dressmaking herself, Mona's mother certainly admired the way Jessie dressed.

Jessie had been a widow for just over five years when she remarried, becoming the wife of a Mr. William B.S. Parker. The wedding took place in Epsom, and was registered in the final quarter of 1919. And so, the eight-year-old Devereux acquired a stepfather. No more children were born, so he remained 'an only one'.

Up until the late summer of 2006, the only other information we had on this son (whom we dubbed "Devereux III") was that, on 23 July 1939, aged twenty-eight, he had married a Miss Kathleen Mary Weeks at St. Paul's Church, Clapham, (London) in the county of Surrey. The bride had been born in the London district of Wandsworth during the latter part of 1915, was therefore twenty-three and working as a secretary at the time of the wedding. Her mother's maiden name was Bennett. Her father, William Henry Weeks, a linotype operator, had already died, as had the bridegroom's father. (One of the two witnesses to the marriage signed himself 'Sidney Arthur Weeks'. This *could* have been Kathleen's uncle - her late father's brother - who quite possibly gave her away too.) As for the bridegroom himself, he gave his occupation as 'Shop Proprietor' and his 'place of residence at the time of marriage' as '88 Edgeley Road', (the same address as his bride!)

Disappointingly however, a careful search through the GRO records for the ten years after this wedding failed to reveal any children born to the couple. Since they had married shortly before the outbreak of WW2, could it have been that Devereux was killed? But, just as in his father's case, no evidence of this was discovered in the war records. During the run-up to the war, of course, many young men made hasty marriages before they were called up, and if they themselves were fortunate enough to survive, not all of these marriages did. Had this been the case with Devereux and his wife?

This mystery was finally solved by an amazing stroke of 'happenchance' on Friday 25th August, 2006, and involved the services of Margaret Milree, a Dorset archivist working from the Coach House Museum in Bridport. "Googling" Devereux's full name into her computer, Margaret brought up the ANNIVERSARIES web page for a Roman Catholic church in Wimbledon and this lead Joan directly to his second wife, Nuria Jessop. Their first real contact was over the telephone, followed by a proper meeting soon afterwards in Basingstoke.

Born in May 1928 in the small town of Igualada (near to the famous Monastery of Monserrat) to the north west of Barcelona, Nuria Ribera Marimon had first met her husband whilst nursing in London in the 1950's. They had married in June 1963, set up home in the capital and had two sons named Michael (Devereux), born 29 February 1968 and Mark (Frederick), born 12 January 1973. Seeming delighted to be in contact with her husband's English family at long last, Nuria was able to impart a great deal more information too.

But there was one big disappointment: sadly, Joan had missed meeting her second cousin by just two years! The reason that Devereux's name had appeared on the 'Anniversaries' website of The Sacred Hearts Church on that particular day was precisely because it marked the second anniversary of his funeral. He had died in Wimbledon on 17th August 2004 and his funeral had taken place eight days later on Wednesday 25th, in the Chapel at the Merton and Sutton Cemetery, where he was then laid to rest. Devereux was ninety-three years old. (The supreme irony was that Joan had been in London the very day he died, carrying out some more 'Mould Family' research at the Newspapers Museum in Colindale.)

Nuria had first come over to England in the summer of 1953 as a twenty-five year old nurse. She had travelled with another Spanish girl and both headed for Bristol where they were offered work at the Barrow Gurney Psychiatric Hospital - mainly as ward orderlies, since their Spanish qualifications were not accepted for general nursing duties. With the long unsocial hours, the young women soon felt isolated. Also, they hadn't realised that English winters could be so cold! Learning that a hospital in London was eager to recruit Spanish nurses, they decided to apply and were soon heading for the bright lights of the capital. At St. Olave's in Bermondsey, Nuria and her friend found they were in good company with no fewer than two dozen other Spanish recruits - all but one from Barcelona. In 1955, after working there for a year, Nuria decided that she would embark on a two-year course to specialise in midwifery at the East End Maternity Hospital, and it was at about this time that she met Devereux.

Moving from Bristol to London had certainly proved to be a good move socially. Although the 'Swinging Sixties' were still only on the horizon, the coffee bar culture was all the rage by the late 1950's, and Nuria wanted to be a part of it. One evening, she and a Finnish nurse decided to try 'El Cubano' in Knightsbridge. Seated next to them at the bar, a gentleman asked Nuria if she would pass the sugar. He was Devereux Jessop and this was how the couple met.

Though somewhat guarded about his age, Dev was clearly quite a bit older than Nuria and her assumption that he had been married proved correct. He told her he had married a girl called Kate just before the outbreak of WW2, but that, while he was in Canada training to be a pilot with the R.A.F., she had been unfaithful. (Apparently, when Dev turned twenty-one, he had bought two newsagents shops with the legacy his father had left him and put in managers to run them while he was away. It was with one of these men that his wife had had 'a fling'.) On his return to England, it was clear that their marriage had broken down and Kate had eventually "gone off with an American," he said, "and moved up north."

But for quite a while, Nuria had sensed there was some evasiveness on

Devereux's part concerning his divorce, and she was becoming wary. Until this matter was settled, there could be no formal engagement - however fond they were of one another. (In fact, coming from a traditional Spanish family as she did, Nuria was very aware that her parents were not at all in favour of her marrying a divorcee.) Her emotions were in such turmoil that she decided she had to get away from London - and from Devereux - to 'sort herself out'. In 1960 she applied for a nursing job in Switzerland - which seemed the ideal escape. If Nuria had also wanted to put her boyfriend to the test, the ploy was successful. Absence certainly made *his* heart grow fonder. He visited her in Geneva on several occasions during the two years she was there, finally persuading her to return to London, where they eventually married.

The ceremony took place at Caxton Hall, Westminster, in early June 1963. The bridegroom had chosen no ordinary Registry Office; this was the most prestigious one in central London, where all the celebrity weddings took place! Nuria's family were represented by her brother and his wife, who had travelled over from Spain. (Her mother had already died and her father was unable to attend.) Afterwards, the couple flew to North Africa for the honeymoon. To an outside observer, it all appeared idyllic - but, according to Nuria, that was certainly not the case. In fact, the discovery she made on the eve of their wedding made her so angry that she was no longer sure she wanted to go ahead. Dev had been going through some papers in readiness for the big event and amongst these was his birth certificate, which Nuria asked to see. Since he had been thirty-nine when they first met in 1955, now - eight years on - he would be a couple of weeks short of his forty-seventh birthday, (or so she thought.) But a shock was in store when she read the date of birth: "twenty fifth of June 1911"! As if an age gap of twelve years was not enough, Nuria now discovered that Devereux was soon to turn fifty-two. What infuriated her most was that he had deceived her over such a long time. As she explained to Joan: "If it were not for the fact that my brother and sister-in-law had travelled over especially for the wedding, I would have called the whole thing off!" It was not an auspicious start to the marriage.

Although the newly weds had surely resolved their differences by the end of the honeymoon, there was another challenge for Nuria to face on their return to London. For several years prior to this marriage, Devereux had been living in Thames Ditton with his mother, Jessie Parker, now a widow again. This arrangement was to continue - with Nuria moving in as the new Mrs. Jessop. Even though it was a fairly sizeable three-bedroom flat, Nuria felt this start to married life was far from ideal, especially as her mother-in-law was in the first stages of Parkinson's disease. Also, the fact that Jessie was obviously not used to 'foreigners' did nothing to make Nuria feel at ease in her new home. But she was determined to be a good daughter-in-law and, with her nursing skills, could offer the ailing Jessie some valuable help. She died on 1st May 1970, aged eighty-one. Poor Jessie! As well as the good times, she had experienced more than her share of hardship and sadness. The tragic loss of her first husband had made the mother-and-son bond especially close and, even if Dev tried to conceal his grief when his mother died, he would have missed her very much. But, at least, Jessie lived long enough to see her first grandson, Michael. However, there was one little puzzle that Jessie left behind for those who came after to solve. Having learned from Nuria when it was that Jessie had died, Joan looked for the death in the GRO index, hoping to discover her exact date of birth, and this is the entry she found: "About 1895". Thus, for much of her later life, it seems that no-one knew her precise age and that she was in fact seven years older than she claimed.(Jessie was actually born during the December quarter of 1888) One person must have realised, of course, and that was her son. But Dev might have had reason to 'keep mum'!

If Devereux claimed that he was not too worried about having a family, Nuria most certainly was! As a midwife, she had helped many mothers with their babies and, quite naturally, now wanted children of her own. They had been married for almost five years by the time their first son, Michael Devereux, was born in 1968, and when Mark arrived five years later, Nuria was well into her forties while Dev had turned sixty.

But in spite of the age-gap, Devereux had made it clear to his wife from the outset that he did not want her to continue working after they married. This came as a disappointment to Nuria, since she really enjoyed her nursing and had hoped to make a career in midwifery. However, by her own admission, Dev was a very hard worker and a good provider - and had no intention of giving up work at the customary retirement age of sixty-five.

But now, thanks to the information provided by his widow, we can go back to 1914 to fill in some of the gaps in the 'Devereux III' story. It is hard to imagine the effect that his father's tragic accident had on both himself and Jessie, (although, of course, as WW1 got underway, many families would suffer similar bereavement.) While his mother was being nursed back to health at the home of his Aunt Naomi, the three-year-old would have been without both parents. In addition, since they had all lived in the flat above Uncle Bert's shop, he and Jessie would have had to vacate that too. Nuria recalled Dev telling her that the flat where he had grown up was in Chutters Grove, Epsom. (She could never forget the unusual name!) Were any of their family - on either side - able give them help, whether practical or financial? We do not know. But certainly one serious consequence of her husband's death was that Jessie found herself in dire financial straits, since he had been 'the breadwinner' and so, in order to make ends meet, she was reduced to taking in lodgers, as well as turning to dressmaking again. (Devereux Henry's money had all been left in trust for their son to inherit when he was twenty-one.) Fortunately, since Epsom was considered a 'very good area', Jessie could be confident of attracting a 'better class' of lodger.

One who came to lodge there was a Mr. Sidney Parker who worked in London for Thomas Cook, the renowned travel company, managing their banking department. (His full name was William Brewster Sidney Parker, known as Sid.) He was immediately captivated by the lively young widow and it was not long before he was proposing marriage. Although Sid Parker was a good bit older than she was, Jessie was impressed by this well-educated gentleman with his good position in the City. Marrying him would enhance her own status, she felt, as well as giving her some financial security. The wedding took place at the Epsom Register Office on 3rd October 1919. According to the marriage certificate, the groom's age was forty-four, whilst the bride's - as on a previous occasion - was reduced by two years to 'twenty-nine'. In the column headed 'Residence at the time of Marriage', both wrote "Buena Vista, Chase Road, Epsom". This, presumably, was the house where all three had been living.

Nuria never knew Mr Parker. In fact, she was fairly certain he had been dead for quite a while when she and Dev started courting. Jessie did tell her, however, that he had been the manager at Thomas Cook's Piccadilly Branch, (which more or less corresponded with his occupation on the marriage certificate, ie "Bankers' Manager".) In the column headed "Condition", Jessie is down as a 'Widow', (as we would expect) and Parker as a 'Bachelor' - which would appear to cast some doubt on the story that "he had been married before and had a daughter".

Very unfortunately for both Jessie and her son, this second marriage did not work out as she had hoped. It became increasingly clear that her husband 'liked his drink' and that, when he was 'the worse for wear', he quickly became violent. Dev witnessed his mother being ill treated on many occasions and grew to hate his stepfather, speaking of him only very rarely in later life. But, to be fair to Sidney Parker, it is possible that the bad memories obscured the good ones in young Devereux's mind. Was it he, for example, who instilled in his stepson the ambition to get a good education and a desire to see more of the world? Dev was an intelligent lad, gaining a place at Sutton Grammar School for Boys when he was eleven. He proved to be a good athlete too and ran competitively, winning a cup for the fastest mile in 1928.

The summer of 1932 marked a special milestone for Devereux when he turned twenty-one and inherited the money left by his father. After giving the matter considerable thought, he decided to buy two newsagents shops, both in the Morden area, to the south of Epsom. (This venture proved successful, with both shops making a good profit for the first few years.) It was at about this time that Jessie had a 'good win' at the races - so good, in fact, that she was able to purchase a new Austin car, which she let Dev drive to take them out and about. Owning a car was also a great advantage for getting to his shops each day, as well as for collecting the newspapers at crack of dawn. Although Devereux employed regular staff, of course, the ultimate responsibility always rested with him - seven days a week.

Being a typical young man, Dev probably liked to impress his various girlfriends by having a car - a great luxury that few could afford in the 1930's. Then, as we know, Dev married Kate Weeks in the summer of 1939, just before the outbreak of war. Although not enlisting straight away, he eventually decided to join the R.A.F. and found himself in Canada, training to be a pilot. His chief role was to move planes from place to place; he wasn't a bomber pilot. When the war finished, Dev apparently joined BOAC as a pilot, flying within the British Isles for a couple of years. When

Dev got back home to London, it was to find not only his marriage in ruins but his business also. The managers he had put into the two shops proved dishonest and unreliable, turning profit into loss. It must have been doubly galling for Devereux when he learned that Kate had been having an affair with one of them. It seems that his wife eventually went off with an American, though when exactly the divorce came through, and if and when she re-married, are still unresolved.

Having sold the newsagents business, Dev was at a loss to know what to do next. But, fortunately, he was able to call on his 'old school network'! He had always remained in touch with Raymond Bloye, a good friend from their days at Sutton Grammar School. Having first worked as an accountant for the Milk Marketing Board, Raymond had subsequently built up a chain of butcher shops, called 'Matthews the Butchers' during WW2. He achieved this by purchasing shops which became vacant when young men were called up to fight. (For Dev, this would have brought back recollections of his uncle, Bert Baldwin's similar enterprise, twenty years before.) Ray was only too pleased to help his friend, offering him the job of Poultry Buyer for the Matthews chain. Starting there in the late 1940's, Dev stayed with the company for some twenty years until about 1979, when he was three years over the usual retirement age of sixty-five. But still not ready for his pipe and slippers, Raymond then helped him find another job - this time as a part-time driver for the Milk Marketing Board. Dev kept this up for a further three years or so, before finally retiring in the early 1980's.

By this time, the Jessop family were living on a housing estate in Epsom, where they had moved in the late 1960's. But in 1991 - the year in which Dev turned eighty - Nuria decided they would be better off living closer to London and so they moved to Wimbledon.

Devereux was fortunate to be blessed with such good health and had the energy of someone ten years younger. He enjoyed working in his garden where, to his wife' amusement, he always wore a tie! He had various interests, including reading and had even tried his hand at writing a novel. It was a romantic novel, which he never got around to publishing, but Nuria still has the manuscript. When he died in the August of 2004, he was ninety-three years old and had enjoyed two decades of retirement. Throughout their marriage, Devereux had often accompanied his wife when she attended Mass at the Roman Catholic Church and he was given a Catholic funeral. The service was conducted by Father Simonson in the Chapel at the Merton and Sutton Cemetery, followed by interment.

Devereux and Jane's third child - and second son - was Frederick Thomas Jessop, born at 55 Balham Grove on April 6, 1882. For some reason that no one has been able to explain, he became known as Bill. At the time of the 1901 Census, a few days short of his nineteenth birthday, Bill was employed as a commercial clerk and went on to become an accountant. By all reports, he was a likeable, generous man and, looking at the photograph of him on his motorbike, obviously handsome too. But

Frederick Thomas "Bill" Jessop.

although there was the suggestion of at least one romantic involvement, Bill remained a bachelor. With no conventional family to keep his story alive, it would be easy to assume that he had lead a rather dull life, (or certainly a less exciting one than the Baldwins.) But, as a young man, he did serve in the military in India for several years and one of his nieces, Virginia Manning, remembered him bringing her parents some exotic souvenirs on his return to England. Sadly, we have no details of this period abroad.

Perhaps it was because he was single that he had the time and inclination to maintain links with the wider family. He must have seen Naomi and Bert fairly regularly, since he acted as their accountant. He apparently considered his sister to be far too extravagant and suggested ways in which her household expenditure could be reduced. (For one thing, he said, she was buying too many varieties of bottled sauce when one or two should have sufficed!) But not all of Bill's visits were taken up with business. One charming photo, taken at Omi and Bert's home when their children were small, shows Muriel and Douglas perched happily on their Uncle Bill's knee.

Jane Fletcher, one of the Baldwin grand children, pointed out that Bill also helped her parents, Douglas and Mona, with their tax returns when they ran a smallholding in Ringwood. In a letter written to Joan Bolton, she described an unexpected encounter with Bill in the late 1940's:

"Late one afternoon when I was about thirteen or fourteen years old, as I stepped off the bus from school, an elderly gentleman also alighted. He then asked me if I knew where Mr and Mrs Baldwin lived, so I said I would show him, as they were my parents. We had about a mile and a half to walk so had plenty of time to talk (though I seemed to do most of the chatting!) He told me that he was my Grandmother's brother, my Great Uncle Bill. I reminded him that he was also my God Father. You can imagine the astonishment at home when we walked in! My Father had not seen him since before the war and this was about 1949.There was a shock for Bill, too, on discovering that his elder sister, Omi, (my Granny) was also there at the house.

He visited us several times as he was an Accountant and, since my parents were self-employed running a smallholding, he was able to help them with their tax affairs. One Christmas, he and Granny came to stay, I remember. But it wasn't a success as far as my brother (Christopher) and I were concerned because it was far too quiet. For much of his working life, Bill lived in Sunbury on Thames, in lodgings. He remained there until the last few years of his life, moving to the south coast in about 1950.

My remaining memory is rather materialistic because, when he died, he left all his great nieces and nephews £200 each - quite a lot of money in those days. We were not able to touch it until we were 21 but at that time it was very helpful." (Bill's will can be found in Appendix XXIII.)

Bill, of course, had lost his only brother, Devereux, years before. It must have come as a terrible shock in the summer of 1914 to learn the grim news of his death in a motorbike accident on Epsom Downs. Only thirty-three years old, he had left a young widow and a little son. We do not know whether Bill offered any help to Jessie, or if he played any part in little Devereux's upbringing but, knowing what we do about him, it would be surprising if he had not offered some support.

There is one revealing little story about Bill and this nephew, related by Devereux's widow, Nuria Jessop. It goes back to the 1930's, when Devereux was running his newsagent's business in London. One day a middle-aged gentleman appeared in one of the shops and asked if he could speak to Mr Jessop, explaining that he was his Uncle Bill. The employee went into the back of the shop to tell him about his visitor but, instead of returning with Devereux, all he had was a message: "He's too busy to see you now. You'll have to come back." Needless to say, after this discourteous reception, Bill never bothered again.

Undoubtedly he would have maintained contact with his younger sister, Rose, and her husband, Fred Brushett. Their only child, Joan, remained single and seemed to make the most of her independence, travelling here and there to visit friends and relatives. In this case, there was a close bond between Uncle and Niece and the pair had regular get-togethers whilst Bill was based in Sunbury on Thames. Joan continued to visit her uncle in Seaford (near Eastbourne) when he moved down to the South Coast from London after being diagnosed with cancer. Bill died there, at the Berrow Nursing Home in Carew Road, on August 12, 1953. He was seventy-one years old. Unlike the great nephews and nieces, Joan Brushett did not receive a legacy as such. Instead, Bill left her 'the residue' of his estate, after all the bequests and expenses had been settled, probably leaving his niece considerably better off.

The Last Will and Testament left by Frederick Thomas Jessop, (known as "Bill",) was drawn up on November 15th 1951, nearly two years before his death on 12th August 1953, aged 71. He died (of cancer) at the Berrow Nursing Home in Eastbourne but, at the time of writing this document, his address was given as 74 Vicarage Road, Sunbury-on-Thames, Middlesex, where, according to his great niece, Jane Baldwin, he was 'in lodgings'. (He begins: "I, Frederick Thomas Jessop, of 74 Vicarage Road....")

In the Legacies section, the following Beneficiaries are listed:-

(a)   To my Great Niece - Mrs Virginia Manning of Dulwich College, London, the sum of £200.

(b)   To my Great Niece - Jane Baldwin of St Leonards, Ringwood, Hampshire, the sum of £200

(c)   To my Great Nephew - Christopher Baldwin (of the same address) the sum of £200

(d)   To my God Daughter - Ruth Young of 'Dikoya', Croft Drive, Caldy, Cheshire, the sum of £200

(e)   To my friend - Mrs Esme Green of 86 Surbiton Road, Kingston on Thames, the sum of £100 as a memento of her long friendship

(f) To my friend - William Brown of the Old Coach House, Cailfail, Lewes, Sussex, the sum of £100 as a memento of his long friendship.

After this, he continues: "All the residue of my estate... (etc.) I give and bequeath unto my Niece, Helena Joan Brushett of 'Avonside', 68 Lenham Road, Sutton, Surrey." (This was his sister Rose Brushett's only child, known as Joan, who never married. She died in November 1996 aged eighty-six.)

The two witnesses are:-(1) Alex Wilfred Ganley of 42, Zealand Avenue, Harmondsworth, West Drayton, Middlesex, described as a Chartered Mechanical Engineer, and

(2) L M Stovold of 74, Vicarage Road, Sunbury-on-Thames, a Housewife.

Joan Bolton feels that the will raises some interesting questions. First and foremost, since the address of the second signatory, Mrs Stovold, was clearly where Bill Jessop was also living at the time the document was drawn up, was she his 'landlady', or was the relationship perhaps a closer one? One of the Jessop family claimed to have heard a rumour that not only was there a romantic attachment between lodger and landlady, but also a daughter. The informant added that both Mother and Daughter were Beneficiaries of the Will. (The case remains open!)

And there is another puzzling matter: On the first page of the Declaration issued from the Probate Registry, issued in October 1953, it gives Bill's address at the time of death as being "5 Milldown Road, Seaford, Sussex", adding "formerly of 74 Vicarage Road, Sunbury on Thames." So, had he and Mrs. Stovold bought the Seaford property together after his illness was diagnosed? If this were the case, why was this lady not listed to receive a legacy? (Unless, of course, Bill had 'helped' her to purchase the Milldown Road property in her name?)

Whatever the answers to these questions, his life was far from humdrum. In fact, in the end, our Bill proved to be something of a dark horse!

Devereux and Jane's fourth and last child was a daughter named Rose Anna, born on September 24, 1885. Naomi's wish for "a little sister" was finally granted, but she had already turned six when Rose arrived. Even without the age gap, however, the two sisters could scarcely have been more different.

In the photograph which fronts this Chapter, the eleven-month-old Rose sits on her mother's knee, understandably apprehensive of the camera, whilst her seven-year-old sister looks confidently ahead. Rose has dark hair whilst 'Omi' is fair. Even at this young age, her older sister has all the appearance of someone who would make her mark in life and be noticed. In Rose's case, it must be said, her life rarely seemed to transcend the ordinary. {The date for this photograph was almost certainly the occasion of Rose Mould's wedding to John William Prentice, which took place in early

September 1886 at Paston Church, Peterborough, almost eight years after Jane's own wedding to Devereux. (The main evidence to support this theory is that Devereux's signature appears as a witness on the Prentices' marriage certificate.) As well as wanting to attend her sister's wedding, Jane would see this as an ideal opportunity to visit her family in Gunthorpe. The journey from London to Peterborough in those days would be made most easily by train, on the Great Northern line from King's Cross up to Scotland via Peterborough. This would have been a great adventure for all the family and especially for the Jessop boys, Devereux being nearly six and Bill four-and-a-half. Even though there are no photographs of the young brothers positively linking them to this occasion, it is most unlikely they had been left behind. However, because of the expense involved, this might have been one of very few excursions the Jessops undertook to visit the family in Northamptonshire.

Like Devereux, (or 'Harry') Jessop, Rose's new husband was also 'in trade'. John Prentice was working as a baker in the village of Peakirk at the time of his marriage and he too had aspirations. A few years later, he had become a 'Master Baker and Grocer,' with his own shop. The general consensus was that Rose had "done rather well for herself."}

Rose first appeared on a census in 1891, aged five, and then again, of course, on that of 1901, by which time she was fifteen years old (or fifteen-and-a-half, to be precise.) That no occupation was given for her is somewhat surprising, as observed earlier. Almost certainly, her mother would have been working by that age and most likely 'in service'. By the time of the 1911 Census, not only was Rose married but she also had a baby daughter.

The marriage took place on September 21 1908 at St. Peter's Presbyterian Church, Wandsworth, just three days before Rose's twenty-third birthday. The bridegroom was Frederick Thomas Brushett, aged twenty-eight and a Cheesemonger's Assistant. (Since his father, Frederick William Brushett, gave 'Cheesemonger's Manager' as his occupation on the marriage certificate, we might assume that father and son were working together at the same shop.) The Brushetts set up home at number 254 Upper Tooting Road, apparently in the same street as the Jessops' home, where Rose had been living until the time of her marriage. Just over two years later, on October 11th 1910, their daughter, Helena Joan, was born. Joan (as she liked to be known) would be the couple's only child.

One can only surmise how Fred and Rose had met. If Naomi had come to know her husband, Bert Baldwin, through working in one of his shops, then Rose might have bought cheese from Fred Brushett. But how had Fred come to manage a high-class butcher shop, having started out as a cheesemonger? Once again, (thanks to the miracle of the internet!) Richard Klapper received some most helpful information on the Brushetts, going back to the 1930's. Philip Adkins from Hampshire e-mailed, explaining how his Mother had come to know Fred Brushett when he was the manager of an established butcher shop, called 'Henry', situated in Sutton High <u>Street.</u> Richard immediately recognised this as being one of the Baldwin chain. When a vacancy came up for the position of Manager there, Bert probably saw his brother-in-law as the ideal person for the job. (We know that by the mid 1920's the Brushetts had moved to Lenham Road, Sutton, just a few minutes' walk from the High Street.) Unfortunately, however, cutting up meat required rather more skill than slicing through cheese, as Fred discovered to his cost after losing part of a finger!

Speaking of Fred's working life, Mona Baldwin described him rather dismissively as "doing a bit of this and that." He certainly changed jobs at least once more, ending up as an Insurance Agent for the London and Manchester Insurance Company prior to his retirement. (He would have reached sixty-five in 1945.)

But what do we know about Rose herself? Sadly, the answer has to be 'very little'. Mona again: "Rose was less buxom than Naomi and shorter; very old-fashioned, too, in the way she dressed, and so was her daughter." Apparently, both mother and daughter chose to wear dresses made of Macclesfield silk, usually striped. They always wore hats when going out and, occasionally, when indoors too. And another thing Mona revealed: all three of the Brushetts belonged to a strict religious sect.

It was left to Philip Adkins to identify this organisation as The Glanton Brethren, a small, exclusive sect, very similar to the better-known Plymouth Brethren. Members were reserved, 'keeping themselves to themselves', and aspired to remain untainted by such worldly distractions as the cinema or television, and so on. (Joan did, in fact, have a television eventually, once she had greater independence in her own flat / apartment.)

In one of the emails, Eileen Adkins, Philip's wife, made two interesting observations. The first concerned the family's financial situation. It was always thought, she said, that Mrs Brushett 'had money' because they were able to send Joan to Sutton High School and, she added: "For a butcher's employee to afford private school fees was quite unusual at that time." So, if Rose was indeed 'well off', where had the money come from? Joan Brushett would probably have moved to her new school in the autumn of 1921, aged almost eleven. Seeing how well their eldest grandchild, Muriel Baldwin, was doing at her private school in Dulwich (*before* her expulsion, that is), the Jessop grandparents might well have decided to offer some help with Joan's schooling. (Being older, Muriel was six years ahead of her cousin, of course.) Or, could there have been a kind benefactor? Naomi and Bert might have decided to fund their niece's education, now that their shops were doing well, or even generous Uncle Bill - by that time nearly forty, but with no family of his own.

By whatever means her education was funded, Joan certainly seemed to have benefited from it, ending up as a Dispenser at the Sutton and Cheam Hospital. In those days, more than twenty years before the inception of the National Health Service, it was quite usual for employees to 'train on the job', without having to go to college. This would seem to be the more likely option for a young woman like Joan Brushett, with such a restrictive upbringing.

The Adkins' second revelation was more intriguing. Eileen continued: "The other story about Mrs. Brushett's family was that she had some Spanish blood. She and Joan were slightly swarthy in colour, as the Spanish are." It should, perhaps, be explained here that the Adkins' main purpose in contacting the authors was to scan and send (to Richard) some photos of the Brushetts which had come into their possession; an offer which was accepted with alacrity, of course! The photo which caused most excitement was the one mentioned above - of Joan and a colleague, taken in the hospital dispensary - because this was the only one of her as a young woman. Also, going back to Eileen's comment, the photo would seem to back up her theory: Joan certainly does look Spanish, even down to the severe hairstyle (which does her no favours!) It is a pity that she is overshadowed here by her pretty colleague but, with a smile on her lips, Joan comes over as a pleasant, friendly lady.

Joan Brushett on left in the hospital dispensary where she worked.

This question of possible Spanish (or foreign) ancestry remains unresolved. Any such exotic links on the Mould side seem highly unlikely! But the Jessop family has scarcely been researched, (although the unusual choice of Devereux's Christian name was considered earlier,) and therein might lie the key to the mystery.

At the time of the 1871 census, the Jessops were living in the village of Little Stonham in Suffolk. There were five in the household: the parents, Henry and Caroline Jessop, with their three children, sixteen-year-old Devereux, Frederic (sic), aged ten, and Louisa, three. Louisa, (or 'Louie', as she became known) never married. After retiring, she moved to Hove on the south coast, where she died in 1944 at the age of seventy-seven. Apparently, her nephews and nieces (Naomi, Bill and Rose) were regular visitors at Aunt Louie's home. Indeed, Omi liked the resort so much that she and Bert decided to make their home there in the 1920's, residing at 27, Bigwood Avenue. Joan Brushett, Louie's great-niece, was also a regular visitor there in the 1930's.

Another family she liked to visit were the Prentices, who first farmed in a little place called Cold Ashby in Northamptonshire before moving to the Cotswolds. The Prentices had two children: a son, John Trevor, and a daughter called Sheila, both ten years younger than Rose. But it was their mother, Lillian, who always made Joan welcome and, as Sheila herself said, "Joan was always very fond of my mother." Apparently, after Joan's parents had passed on, she used to visit Sheila and Dick Rose once or twice a year in Oxfordshire. She would take advantage of a coach trip from London to Blenheim Palace (not far from where the Roses lived), be collected and driven back to her cousins' home for the day. Then back to Blenheim Palace again in the evening to meet up with the coach! "She was very pleasant company", Sheila recalled, "and had a nice sense of humour, in her quiet way."

As we know, Joan remained single all her life. Whether marriage was ever contemplated is not known. Or did she perhaps allow herself to be dissuaded from marrying? She certainly appeared to be a most dutiful daughter, living with her parents and looking after them as they grew older. The residential care home the couple chose was situated in Worcester

Road, (not far from Lenham Road). It was called 'Eothen', (a Greek word meaning 'towards the dawn'), possibly inspired by a book with that title by Alexander Kinglake, which came out in 1844. Unsurprisingly, the Brushetts' care home had religious connections. What was unusual, however, was that Joan was allowed to have a room there too!

Both her parents died in 1968, within four months of each other: Rose on April 18th and her husband on August 24th, aged eighty-two and eighty-eight respectively. Rose and Fred had always been a devoted couple and their daughter was devoted to *them*. Understandably, Joan was devastated by their deaths. At the age of fifty-eight, she would have to learn to live independently. The blow was softened, however, when the owners of 'Eothen', (presumably members of the Brethren,) offered her the chance to buy a small bungalow in the grounds. Sheila Rose remembered Joan showing her some photos of this bungalow during one of her visits and observed: "Small it certainly was! It consisted of a bed-sitting room, a small kitchen and a bathroom." But one big advantage for Joan was that she had some kind (if elderly) folk nearby, able to offer help and sympathy at a difficult time.

Sheila did not think her cousin had ever had many friends, apart from her church community. But when she eventually moved from 'Eothen' and found herself a flat in the Sutton area, she met a lady called Dorothy Adkins - the sister of Philip. Dorothy, too, was single, (but quite a bit younger than Joan) and was willing to help her in practical ways, such as decorating the new flat. Indeed, when Joan subsequently moved home once more, her friend was there to assist. According to Philip Adkins, his mother, too, was very kind to Joan after her parents died and was happy to be adopted "as a sort of surrogate mother".

Joan outlived her parents by twenty-eight years, dying on Monday, 4th November, 1996 at the age of eighty-six. Sheila Rose attended her funeral and gave this account of the occasion: 'My elder son, Richard, drove me to London for the funeral, which took place at the Cheam Hall Chapel. It was a rather strange service as there was no minister in charge, just contributions from the Brethren. Afterwards we all went to the cemetery for the burial. But I was pleased that my son and I had made the effort, because we were the only ones there from our side of the family."

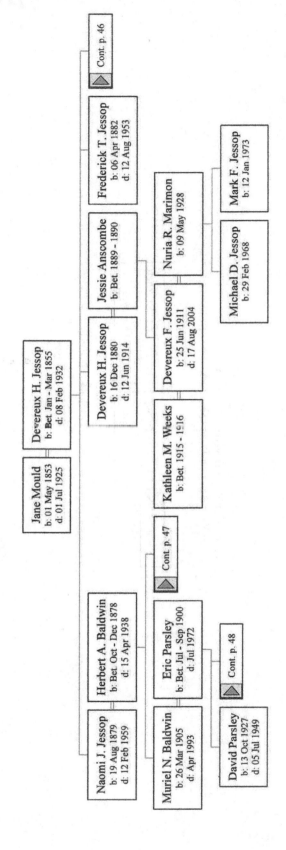

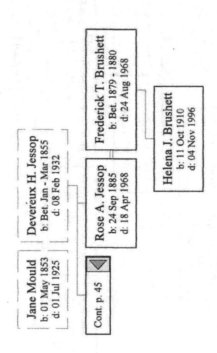

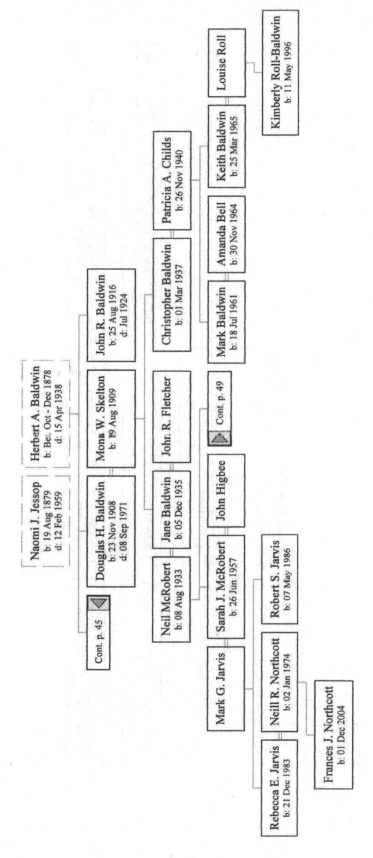

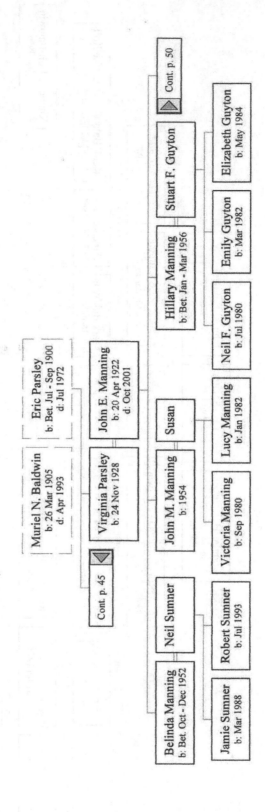

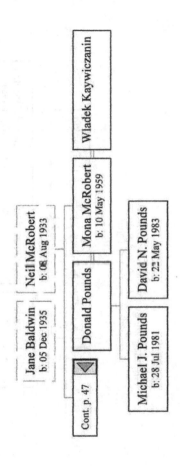

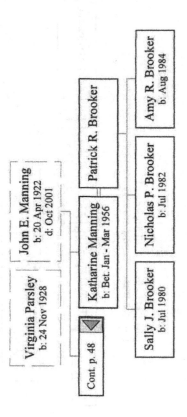

Virginia Parsley
b: 24 Nov 1928

John E. Manning
b: 20 Apr 1922
d: Oct 2001

Patrick R. Brooker

Katharine Manning
b: Bet. Jan - Mar 1956

Cont. p. 48

Sally J. Brooker
b: Jul 1980

Nicholas P. Brooker
b: Jul 1982

Amy R. Brooker
b: Aug 1984

(Printed by authority of the Registrar General)

CERTIFIED COPY of an ENTRY OF MARRIAGE
Pursuant to the Marriage Act 1949

TG 504236

M. Cert.
S.R./R.B.D.& M.

| Registration District | | | PETERBOROUGH | | | | | |

1894. Marriage solemnized at the Parish Church _____ in the
District of Parish of Paston _____ in the _____ County of Northampton.

No.	When married	Name and surname	Age	Condition	Rank or profession	Residence at the time of marriage	Father's name and surname	Rank or profession of father
384	August 15	James MACKNESS	29	Bachelor	Shoe Finisher	Rushden	Jabez MACKNESS	Shoe Finisher	----
	1894	Betsy MOULD	39	Spinster	------	Gunthorpe	Thomas MOULD	Cottager

Married in the Parish Church according to the Rites and Ceremonies of the Church of England _____ by _____ by me,

This marriage was solemnized between us,
James Mackness
Betsy Mould

in the presence of us,
Thomas Mould
Fannie Mills

F W Robinson
Rector

Certified to be a true copy of an entry in a register in my custody.

Registrar
Superintendent Registrar }

Date _____ 28/8/2001

CAUTION—It is an offence to falsify a certificate or to make or knowingly use a false certificate or a copy of a false certificate intending it to be accepted as genuine to the prejudice of any person or to possess a certificate knowing it to be false without lawful authority.
WARNING: THIS CERTIFICATE IS NOT EVIDENCE OF THE IDENTITY OF THE PERSON PRESENTING IT

Marriage record for James Mackness and Betsy Mould.

Chapter 3

James and Betsy Mackness

Thomas and Rose Ann's second child, Betsy, was born February 19, 1855 in Gunthorpe and was baptized at the Parish Church in Paston five weeks later on March 25, 1855. Although the registers for Paston and the surrounding parishes have been reviewed, Betsy is the only child of Thomas and Rose Ann whose baptism record has been found.

In 1871, at the age of sixteen, Betsy was working as a servant for two sisters in the village of Glinton; they were Mary and Jane Burgess. On the 1881 census, Betsy was still working for these sisters as a general servant. Mary was then eighty-one years old and Jane seventy-nine. By the time of the 1891 census, it appears that the two sisters had died, whilst Betsy is found as a visitor at the home of her younger sister Mary (Polly) and her husband James (Jim) Avery. They were all living in Harborough Park Road in Rushden. Aged thirty-six Betsy is listed as having 'no occupation'.

But, three and a half years later, everything had changed. On August 16, 1894, Betsy married her first cousin James Mackness, in the Parish Church at Paston. He was the son of Rose Ann's brother, Jabez Mackness. Born on April 29, 1865, at Port Mulgrave, Hinderwell in Yorkshire, James was twenty-nine years old - and ten years younger than his bride. The signatories to the marriage were Betsy's father, Thomas Mould and Fannie Mills who would later become the wife of George Mould, Betsy's youngest brother.

In the 1891 census James was living on Park Road, Rushden with his uncle's wife, Rebecca, and her sister Elizabeth and was working in the shoe industry as a 'finisher'. Prior to his marriage, James was still working there, while Betsy had moved back to Gunthorpe. This was for two reasons: <u>one</u>, to establish residency in her home parish of Paston in order to marry there, and <u>two</u>, to get everything ready for the wedding. The 1901 census, however, indicates that, by then, the couple had moved to Gunthorpe to live with Betsy's parents. This time James's occupation is listed as 'dairyman' and it is most likely that they returned to help Thomas with his milk business after the sudden death or his eldest son, Joseph in 1900.

Sometime between 1901 and 1928 James and Betsy moved north to Loftus in Yorkshire. Although we have no documentary evidence in support of any one specific year, it was most likely to be after Thomas Mould's death in 1906. We know that Betsy's brother, George, moved out of the Gunthorpe home and into the middle of Peterborough with his wife in 1911, probably selling the cottage and the land at about the same time. Still only thirty-six years old, James would need to seek new employment. One obvious solution was to return to Yorkshire! There he found work in the iron mines and set up home again with Betsy at 4 Liverton Road. James, of course, was 'going back to his roots', for he had been born at Hinderwell, a mere five or six miles along the coast to the east of Loftus. James had a brother called Nathaniel, who lwas living at Marske near Guisboro. Loftus, too, was close to Guisborough and, although his brother had already died (in 1897) before their move, the presence of other relatives must surely have played a part in this decision. James was a banksman (working below ground) at the ironstone mine near Loftus. We know from Betsy's death certificate that he had retired before she died on November 23, 1928, aged seventy-three. Since James was then sixty-three, he had probably stopped working a few years before.

Betsy died at home in Liverton Road with James by her side. She died of "heart failure, periferal neurites and senility" and was buried in Loftus cemetery on November 26 in unconsecrated ground. (Plot A: F/26.)

At some point after this bereavement, James moved to Huddersfield, which was about eighty miles south of Loftus - though still in Yorkshire. It would appear that this move was again prompted by the wish to be near his family, since his nephew, Lawrence Mackness, was living there, as indeed was his father, William Mackness, James' brother.

James survived his wife by almost twenty years, dying at St. Luke's Hospital on January 4, 1948. The cause of death given on the certificate was "senility" and the informant was Lawrence Mackness. He had been living at 17 Poplar Street, Moldgreen, Huddersfield and was buried in Edgerton Cemetery, Section 27, plot 128. James and Betsy had no children.

Mary "Polly" Avery

Chapter 4

James and Mary Avery

Thomas and Rose Ann's third child was born December 8, 1856 and was a daughter they named Mary. Mary was known as "Polly" for most of her life and in her latter years she was known as "Aunt Polly" to those who knew her, including those outside the family.

Like most of the children of Thomas and Rose Ann, Mary was sent to work at an early age. Although Mary has not been found in the 1871 census, she was not living at home with her parents at Gunthorpe. At this time she would have been fourteen years old and already working.

Ten years on, in 1881 Mary was twenty-four and working as a domestic cook for the Webster family who lived in Town Street, Glinton. George Webster owned 220 acres and employed six men and three boys in addition to Mary as cook and a 15 year old girl named Martha Dale who was the housemaid. The fact that Mary was working in the same household as Martha Dale is significant, because a relative of Martha's (probably her brother), James Dale was also living on Town Street. Cupid did not disappoint! Three years later, on June 2, 1884, Mary married James Dale in Glinton. The bride was twenty-seven and her groom some three years younger. In fact, he had added the last name, 'Avery', thus becoming James Dale Avery. And, as he always referred to his wife as 'Polly', let us do the same from now on!

By 1891, James and Polly had moved to Rushden where he was working as a shoe finisher in Rushden's thriving shoe factories and living on Harborough Park Road. Polly's sister Rebecca and her husband Joseph Thomas Mackness were also living on the same street as were Joseph's older brother John and his wife Eliza.

James and Polly lived in Rushden for quite a number of years. The 1901 census shows them at 76 Harborough Road with James still working in the shoe factories as a boot trade foreman. When Polly's mother, Rose Ann, died July 25, 1908 she was living with them in Rushden. Polly was present at her mother's death.

St. Pegas Churchyard in Peakirk. James Avery's grave is just beyond the door.

At some time prior to 1915, James and Polly left Rushden and moved to the village of Peakirk near Peterborough. The move seemed to come about after Rebecca and Joseph Mackness emigrated to America in 1906. Seeing how much his wife missed having her sister nearby, James probably realized that Polly would never be happy until they moved to Peakirk in order to be near to her sister Rose (Prentice). This meant, of course, that James had to give up his job as a factory foreman and be content to take a job as a general labourer.

On February 15, 1915, James died in Peakirk aged only fifty-five; he was found to be suffering from heart disease. After the funeral at St. Pega's Church, he was buried in the churchyard, not far from the main entrance porch. Polly continued to live in Peakirk until September 1921 when she, too, emigrated to America to join her sister, Rebecca and her husband who had gone over there fifteen years before.

Polly arrived in New York's Ellis Island on September 18, 1921 on the ship Berengaria. She had $175 with her and listed her final destination as Ellingson, South Dakota where she planned to join her sister Rebecca and noted that her intentions were to stay in the US permanently. In fact, she

ended up in Aberdeen, South Dakota living with her brother Jabez and his wife instead. Helen Klapper and her brother Alfred Bull remember "Aunt Polly" living with their grandparents, Jabez and Sarah Ann Mould in Aberdeen. She lived quietly with them doing what she could to help out by darning socks and other useful tasks but also spent much time reading her Bible.

Site of the house Mary Avery lived in with her sister Rebecca in Ellingson, South Dakota. The pile of rocks to the left of the bush is all that is left of the house. The water pump in the foreground is the one they used. Picture taken in 2003.

Following the death of Joseph Mackness in May 1938, Polly moved to Ellingson, South Dakota to live with her sister, Rebecca. The two women lived in this remote, desolate area of South Dakota for the rest of their lives. (For a description of the living conditions in Ellingson see Chapter 8.)

The two sisters lived together until Polly's death on March 2, 1941. She died of a "Cerebral Hemorrhage". Polly was buried in Ellingson Zion Cemetery near Joseph Thomas Mackness and close to the plot where Rebecca would later be buried.

James and Polly had no children.

John and Rose Prentice family. L-R: George Harold, Rose,
Lillian, John William, Ellen and John Frederick (in front o
Ellen). Picture taken about 1897.

Chapter 5

John and Rose Prentice

The fourth child of Thomas and Rose Ann was another daughter and they named her Rose. She was born November 2, 1858 in Gunthorpe. In 1871 when Rose was twelve years old she was living at home with her parents. But ten years later in 1881, the twenty-two year old was working in London as a servant for David and Mary Blelloch at 4 South Hill Park Gardens in Hampstead. David Blelloch was a retired Presbyterian minister. It is interesting to note that David had another servant in addition to Rose. She was Elizabeth Mackness, unmarried and fifty-four years old. Being the elder sister of Rose's mother, she was therefore Rose's aunt.

On September 7, 1886, Rose married a baker from Peakirk, John William Prentice. The ceremony took place at Paston Church, Peterborough.

The young couple set up house in Peakirk at 3 Rectory Lane, remaining in the village all of their lives. The building was a grocery and post office combined. (The mail slot in the front wall could still be seen in 2003.) At the time of the 1891 census the family were still living on Rectory Lane where John was listed as a baker and grocer and Rose as a grocer. Also residing there were their three children - Ellen, Lilian and George Harold - as well as two servants. The male servant was a baker's

3 Rectory Lane - building in Peakirk, England where John and Rose Prentice had a bakery and grocery store. Picture taken in March 2003.

assistant to John and the female was a general servant.

The 1901 census shows the Prentices were still living in Rectory Lane but there have been a few changes. For one thing, they have moved to a larger house (that was the former vicarage) and for another, there were two more children to fill it: John Frederick and Dora. The seventeen year old boy listed as a 'servant and baker' was obviously John's assistant in the bakery.

John and Rose were pretty well off financially as seen in the valuation of his property after his death. The valuation was done in September 1920 by the Peterborough firm of Fox & Vergette. John Prentice's estate was valued at approximately 4,000 pounds. John had six horses, four bullocks, one calf and approximately seventy five sheep. The valuation of John William's estate can be found in Appendix XVII.

John William's obituary indicated that he was the postmaster in Peakirk. It is interesting that in 1891 the Peakirk postmaster, per that year's census, was Rose's uncle, John Day (the husband of Thomas Mould's sister, Elizabeth). It is possible John William took over from his uncle who died shortly after the census was taken in 1891.

John William was taken ill while on his postal rounds. Rheumatic fever was followed by pneumonia and other complications. He died a week later on August 26, 1919 and was buried in Peakirk Churchyard. Rose lived nearly six more years before she died on June 25, 1925, aged sixty-six years. According to her obituary, Rose had been suffering from a long illness before she died. She was buried beside her husband in a coffin of polished oak with the inscription: "Rose Prentice, died June 25, 1925, aged 66 years.". Their grave is located immediately in front of the main door of Peakirk's Parish Church.

Of her siblings, only her brothers, Charles and George Mould, were able to attend the funeral. Her eldest sister, Jane Jessop, was herself on her death bed and died a week later.

John and Rose had five children. Ellen was born March 18, 1888 and baptized on April 15; Lilian was born March 9, 1889 and baptized on April 7;

1 Rectory Lane, Peakirk, England - House where the Prentice sisters lived (Ellen, Lillian and Dora). Picture taken in March 2003

George Harold was born June 13, 1890 and baptized on July 13; John Frederick was born June 30, 1893 and baptized on August 6; Dora Evelyn was born on January 2, 1899 and baptized on January 29. All of these baptisms took place at the Peakirk Parish Church. Although both sons married and had families, all of the daughters remained single. Since there was no school in Peakirk, the five children had to walk to the school in Glinton.

Ellen (who was always called Nellie) went to Germany prior to World War I and taught English in a German school. At the start of World War I she was repatriated in exchange for Germans who were in England. Upon returning to England she moved to Nottingham and taught German to

Harold and Nellie Prentice riding in a charabac in Berlin prior to 1914. Nellie is near right and Harold is next to her on the left. Both are marked with x's.

English children. She continued teaching in Nottingham until she had a stroke sometime between 1935 and the early 1940's. Following her stroke she was a semi-invalid and could not continue working. She went to Bledington to live with her brother Harold and his wife Lily. Occasionally she would go to Peakirk to stay for a month or two with her sister Dora. It

61

was during one of these visits that Nellie died on August 11, 1946; she was just fifty-eight years old. Nellie was buried in the Churchyard at Peakirk.

Lilian trained as a teacher and found a post in London, working in Special Education and teaching children with learning difficulties. She taught in the capital until her retirement and then moved back to the family home in Rectory Lane, Peakirk. There she lived with her younger sister, Dora, whom she outlived by a couple of years. Lilian died in Peakirk on November 16, 1967 aged seventy-eight. According to her death certificate, she was suffering from "bronchopneumonia, right hemiplagia, cerebral aeterio-schlerosis".

George Harold Prentice was always called Harold Prior to World War I he helped his father farm near Peakirk. During the war, he was in the army in the Royal Horse Artillery and served in France. After the war he returned home and married Lily Lake on July ⁻. 1919. His father died a month later in August

Harold Prentice during World War I

1919. Harold took over the farm after his father's death. In 1923 or 1924 he left Peakirk and moved to Cold Ashby, Northants to have more land to farm. England went through the depression and it became very difficult to continue farming. Finally, in 1935 or 1936, Harold gave up farming and moved his family to Oxfordshire. They lived in a cottage at Foxholeswhich that was situated a mile from the tiny village of Foscot, down a narrow lane.They later moved again, this time to the neighboring village of Bledington which is on the border of Oxfordshire and Gloucestershire. He became an Air Ministry Warden which was a policeman job. Harold and Lily stayed there until they retired and were getting up in years.

Lovells Lodge in Cold Ashby, Northants where George and Lily Prentice lived with their children

In about 1970, Harold and Lily moved to be with their daughter and son-in-law, Sheila and Dick Rose, who farmed at Churchill Heath, staying in a cottage on their farm. Harold died there in 1975.

It was a few years later, in about 1983, that Dick and Sheila gave up farming and moved to Wales to be near a cousin of Sheila's taking Lily with them. Sadly, Lily died there, on March 1, 1984; she was ninety. Harold and Lily had two children, a son, John Trevor and a daughter Sheila Margaret.

John Frederick Prentice, who was always called Frederick, completed his schooling and went to London to the Chelsea St. Marks Training College for teachers. He graduated and became a certified teacher in August 1913 and a certificate which has survived notes that he completed one year of service on January 14, 1915. Frederick then served in the British army during the war. He was a Lieutenant in the Royal Artist Rifles. He served in France and for a time in India. After the war he returned to England and landed a job in North London. He taught senior classes in the Bowes Road School. On

Frederick Prentice during World War I

April 11, 1925, Fred married Jessie Smellie in Bounds Green, London. Jessie had been working as a clerk to the Government. Jessie and Fred had two sons, John Robert, born in 1926 and Michael in 1928.

In 1926/1927 the family moved to nearby Palmers Green. Frederick still taught in Bowes Road School but the family now lived in a nicer neighborhood. They were still close enough to the school for Frederick to ride his bicycle to work every day. Jessie was very musical and had a beautiful contralto voice. She gave singing lessons and also sang in the 'BBC Chorus'. It is not surprising, therefore, that Jessie was invited to sing at the wedding of Muriel Baldwin and Eric Parsley, which took place in central London on July 25, 1925. It might well have been at ner ow wedding ro Frederick Prentice three months earlier that Jessie met the Jessop family. Frederick's mother, Rose Prentice and Muriel's grandmother, Jane Jessop, were sisters and had always remained close. (The Jane Jessop family is discussed in Chapter 2.)

The Prentices lived in Palmers Green until 1939 at which time Frederick received a headship at a school just outside Hayes in West London. Frederick taught there until he retired. He was a keen gardener and Jessie once said that she had never bought vegetables since she married. He also was an avid reader and was active in the local church where at one time he was church treasurer.

Shortly after becoming headmaster at Hayes and with the war imminent, Frederick and Jessie made arrangements with Frederick's brother Harold to allow their sons John and Michael to live with Harold and Lily in Foxholes. To get to the school in Chipping Norton where they were enrolled, John and Michael had to ride John's bike to Foscote to catch the bus at 8:15am each morning. The Prentice boys' escape from London certainly changed the direction of John's life, for it was on the school bus that he met Vivienne Rose (Dick Rose's sister) who would later become his wife!

After Frederick retired (presumably in the summer of 1958, on turning sixty-five), Jessie wanted to move to Angmering-on-Sea, the small coastal town in Sussex where her sister lived with her husband. So they packed up and moved to join them. They lived happily there together until Fred died on June 23, 1969 a week before his seventy-sixth birthday. (On his death certificate, the causes given were "haemorrhage, burst aorta (thoric), generalized arteriosclerosis"). Following her husband's death and that of her sister's husband, Jessie and her sister moved in together and lived in Angmering until Jessie died on October 18, 1983.

Door inside St. Pegas Church in Peakirk, England dedicated to Dora Prentice. Picture taken in March 2003.

Out of the five Prentice children, Dora was the only one who stayed in Peakirk for her entire adult life. As a young lady, she went to London to train at the Pitman College for Secretaries. She returned to Peakirk and was the secretary for a solicitor in Peterborough for a number of years. When the solicitor died she became the secretary to the Dean of Peterborough Cathedral. She was also the Treasurer of the Friends of Peterborough Cathedral an organization which supported the cathedral. She was very organized and efficient and knew how to get things done. Freda Neaverson of Peakirk remembers that during the war when food was strictly rationed, Dora could have cakes delivered from Blanchard's bakery in Nottingham for sale at the church bazaars. For many years Dora was a correspondent for the Peterborough Citizen and Advertiser. She was also very active in the Peakirk Church. She was a church warden, school manager and played the organ for many years. As it turned out, the day before her unexpected death, Dora had played the organ for the service of Nine Lessons and Carols. The side door of the Peakirk Church had a curtain rather than a real door which really bothered Dora. When she died of "cerebral haemorrhage, cerebrovascular disease" December 20, 1965, she left money to the church with the stipulation that the money be used to purchase a real door for the church. A door was purchased and a plaque affixed which said " In memory of Dora Evelyn Prentice 1899 - 1965". For some unknown reason, her sister Lillian, was unable to attend Dora's funeral according to Dora's obituary.

Close-up of inscription on door of St. Pegas Church in Peakirk, England dedicated to Dora Prentice. Picture taken in March 2003.

The story of Lilian and Dora's burials is rather interesting and has been confirmed with several people present at the time. It seems that after Ellen was buried in the Peakirk churchyard both Lilian and Dora wanted to be buried in the grave with Ellen. Unfortunately for Dora, she died first and Lilian promptly had her cremated and her ashes interred in the grave, thus leaving room for Lilian to be buried according to her wishes when she died two years later.

Another story of interest is that John William had a brother named Will who went to Germany prior to World War I and became a naturalized German citizen. Will married and had a son named Victor. Following World War II, Ellen and Lilian went to Germany and took tea and sugar to Victor.

He wrote them a letter thanking them for coming over and bringing him these staples.

. FOOTNOTE

Returning home to Dorset from a Yorkshire holiday in October 2001, Joan and Reg Bolton made a detour to the Cotswolds in order to visit Sheila (nee Prentice) and Dick Rose. This was the first time that the second cousins had met and proved a most enjoyable occasion. After a delicious lunch, the foursome were joined by John (Robert) Prentice, Sheila's cousin who lived close by. During the course of the conversation, Joan learned two amazing things. The first was that Sheila's godchild, Pauline Evans (nee Edginton), lived quite near to the Boltons in West Bay, Bridport! (Sheila and Pauline's mother, Drucilla, had been friends for years.) But it was only later, when Joan spoke to Pauline, that she became aware of another coincidence, namely that John Prentice's daughter, Mary, had married Pauline's brother, Patrick Edginton! The third surprise came late in 2004, when the Boltons' new next-door-neighbours proved to be Pauline's daughter and family!

As if these coincidences were not enough, there was to be another when Joan visited a lady from her church. In the course of the conversation, they talked about the family research and the Prentices of Peakirk came up. Joan but could scarcely believe her ears when Sheila Flindt (yes, another Sheila!) revealed that she had known both Lilian and Dora Prentice in about the 1940's /1950's, when she herself was living and working in Peakirk. (Sheila had been a member of the Community at St. Pega's Hermitage.)

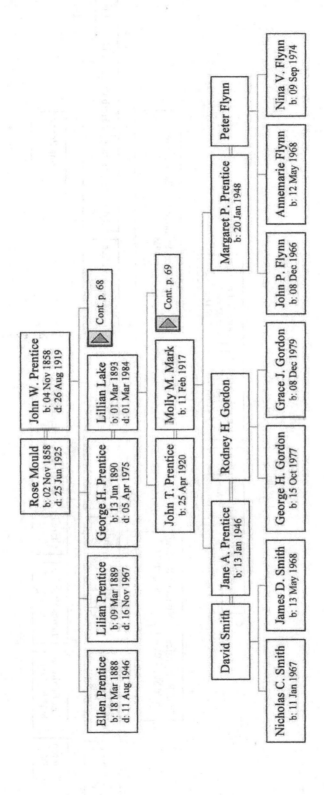

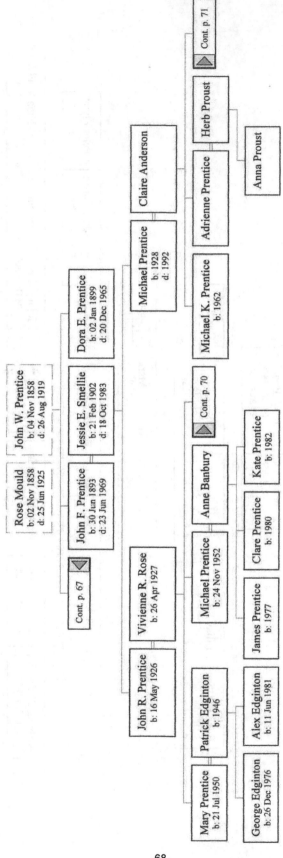

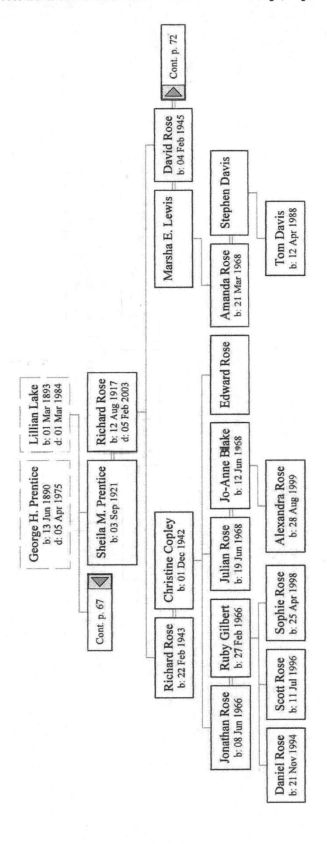

Cont. p. 72

Cont. p. 67

George H. Prentice
b: 13 Jun 1890
d: 05 Apr 1975

Lillian Lake
b: 01 Mar 1893
d: 01 Mar 1984

Richard Rose
b: 12 Aug 1917
d: 05 Feb 2003

Sheila M. Prentice
b: 03 Sep 1921

David Rose
b: 04 Feb 1945

Marsha E. Lewis

Stephen Davis

Amanda Rose
b: 21 Mar 1968

Tom Davis
b: 12 Apr 1988

Christine Copley
b: 01 Dec 1942

Richard Rose
b: 22 Feb 1943

Edward Rose

Jo-Anne Blake
b: 12 Jun 1968

Julian Rose
b: 19 Jun 1968

Alexandra Rose
b: 28 Aug 1999

Ruby Gilbert
b: 27 Feb 1966

Jonathan Rose
b: 08 Jun 1966

Sophie Rose
b: 25 Apr 1998

Scott Rose
b: 11 Jul 1996

Daniel Rose
b: 21 Nov 1994

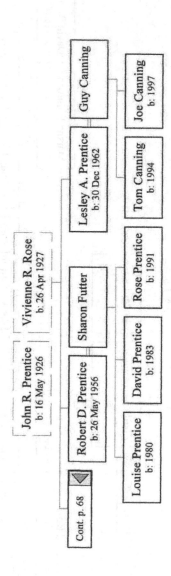

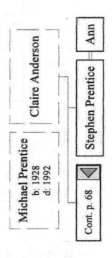

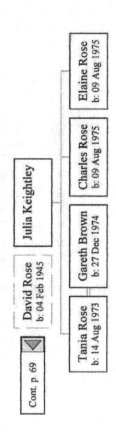

FC 005653

CERTIFIED COPY of an ENTRY
Pursuant to the Births and Deaths Registration Act 1953

Registration District				Peterborough				
1900. Death in the Sub-district of Peterborough					in the Counties of Hunts & Peterborough			
Columns:- 1	2	3	4	5	6	7	8	9
No.	When and where died	Name and surname	Sex	Age	Occupation	Cause of death	Signature, description and residence of informant	When registered	Signature of registrar
236	Thirtyfirst March 1900 Gunthorpe R.D.	Joseph MOULD	Male	35 years	Builder's Labourer	Suicide whilst temporarily insane by cutting his throat.	Certificate recieved from J H Buckle, Coroner for the Hundred of Nassaburgh. Inquest held 31st March 1900.	Thirtyfirst March 1900	J Buckle Registrar

Certified to be a true copy of an entry in a register in my custody.

_____ Superintendent Registrar

11·5·61 Date.

Death certificate of Joseph Mould

Chapter 6

Joseph Mould

Thomas and Rose Ann's seventh child was a son, Joseph, who was born April 25, 1864 in Gunthorpe. The two sons born just before Joseph both died in infancy, so Joseph was the first son to live to adulthood. Joseph appears to have spent his whole life in Gunthorpe. He never married.

Aged sixteen in 1881, Joseph was living with his parents and listed in the census as an 'agricultural labourer', almost certainly working for his father.

At the time of the 1891 census, he was still living at home and his occupation still given as a labourer. The fact that Joseph lived at home with his parents all his life and never married, causes one to suspect that he was not entirely normal. When he was a teenager in about 1880, he was examined as to his state of mind by a Dr. Paley while Joseph spent a week at the Union Infirmatory. In addition, Thomas Mould indicated that his son ".......had been queer in his mind at times."

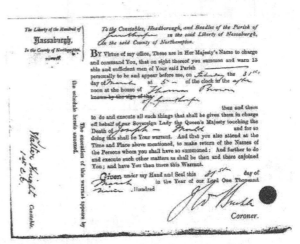

Coroner's jury summons in the death of Joseph Mould

By 1900, Joseph was working for William Rowe the butcher. On March 31, 1900, Joseph who was then thirty-five years old, committed suicide by cutting his own throat. He was living at home with his parents and had been ill with the influenza for two weeks during which he became despondent. He was found by his father in the morning lying in a pool of blood on the floor next to his bed. This must have been a terrible experience for his parents. A coroner's inquest was held at which Thomas Mould testified, as did a local Constable, Walter Knight. The Coroner ruled the death a suicide and Joseph was buried on April 3 in the Paston

.... findings of suicide in the death of Joseph Mould

Parish churchyard.

By 2003, Joseph's grave headstone had been broken by vandals. The pieces are still lying on the ground and others sadly missing. (Joseph's headstone inscription has been included in Appendix XXVI. The testimony of Thomas Mould and that of Constable Walter Knight at the Inquest into Joseph's death are included in Appendix IV.)

Jabez Mould family. L-R: George, Rose, Sarah Ann, Jabez, Annie Beatrice.

Chapter 7

Jabez and Sarah Ann Mould

The eighth child of Thomas and Rose Ann Mould was a son named Jabez born December 24, 1865. They seemed determined to have a son named Jabez since this Jabez was the third son with that name. The first two died in infancy but this Jabez lived to adulthood. As mentioned earlier, Thomas' small dairy operation was not big enough to support all of his children so when Jabez, or "Jabe" as he was called as a boy, was old enough, he was sent on the train to Irthlingborough to find work. He walked from Irthlingborough to Rushden and found employment as a shoemaker apprentice in this major shoemaking center in England. It is not known how old Jabez was when he left home but when he was barely fifteen in the spring of 1881 he was already in Rushden working in the shoe factories.

Sarah Ann Mould seated on far right in the middle row when she was a medical worker in England.

Four years later, on June 4, 1885 Jabez married Sarah Ann Cox. She was only eighteen years old and Jabez' father, Thomas, thought she was too young for Jabez to marry but when he gave in, he told Jabe that if he ever mistreated her he could and would still whip him. Sarah was the illegitimate daughter of a woman who gave birth to her in the Union Work House in Kettering. Her natural mother either couldn't take care of her (or didn't want to) so Sarah was raised by her Aunt and Uncle, Rowland and Mary Cox. Her aunt evidently resented having to raise her niece. Sarah recalled her saying "I didn't have children of my own so why should I end up with someone else's?" Mary Cox made her stand on a box and wash dishes when she was four years old. Her Uncle Rowland appears to have been kinder to her than her Aunt Mary as when she was cross with Sarah he would give her a coin and say "Go get yourself something and your aunt will be in a better mood when you get back." As a small child Sarah loved the music of the Salvation Army Band. She would sneak out to hear them and her Aunt would spank her but she continued to go because she liked the music so much. When she was a little older, Sarah was a medical worker (similar to a nurse).

4 Station Road in Rushden, England where Jabez and Sarah Mould lived in 1901.

Jabez and Sarah had five children, two of whom died as infants.

Jabez and his family moved around Rushden and Higham Ferrers for the next thirty-five years or so. During his years in Rushden/Higham Ferrers Jabez and his family lived on Higham Hill, Lancaster Street, at 4 Station Road and 13 Westfield Street.

Jabez worked in the shoe manufacturing industry as a shoe finisher the entire time. At some point Jabez was elected as a city councilman of Rushden. He was presented with a bamboo walking cane with an engraved plate recognizing him for his service. Jabez and Sarah, (called "Annie"), had five children: Rose Marion (born: January 1, 1885), George Ewart (born:

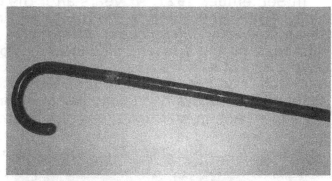

Bamboo cane with silver engraved band given to Jabez Mould when he was a city councilman in Rushden, England.

October 15, 1887), Bessie Lilian (born: 1Q 1890), Annie Beatrice (born: October 6, 1891) and Thomas Rowland (born:December 1899). Bessie and Thomas both died in infancy.

In 1906 Jabez' son George went to the U.S. and then returned to England. On May 1, 1911 George left England for good and took his sister Rose with him. A year later George sent the money to have his other sister Annie come out to the US. George finally convinced his parents to emigrate to the US and sent them money for the trip. Jabez and Sarah Ann arrived at Ellis Island on December 24, 1919 on the ship Orduna. George and his wife Kate went to New York to meet them when they arrived. When George saw his father's handlebar mustache he told him

Jabez and Sarah Mould's house and small grocery store at 111 8th Ave. S. W. in Aberdeen, South Dakota.

"We're going to have to get you de-horned since those aren't too popular over here."

Jabez and Sarah bought a house at 111 8th Ave. S.W. in Aberdeen. They opened a small grocery store in the front of it. George helped them set it up and supplied the cream and milk for them to sell. The store was called the Eighth Avenue Grocery and they ran it for about seventeen years. They may have been in America but they never lost their English roots. At tea time every afternoon they would go into their kitchen to drink tea and would not allow

Jabez and Sarah Mould in their grocery store in Aberdeen, South Dakota.

anything to interrupt them. If a customer came in during tea time, Sarah would call out from the kitchen to see who it was. She would then tell them to take what they needed and write it down. Sarah wouldn't leave her tea for business!

In September 1921, six years after the death of her husband, Mary "Polly" Avery emigrated to the U.S. from England and lived with Jabez and Sarah until after Jabez' death. After Polly's and Jabez' sister Rebecca Mackness' husband Joseph died in 1938, Polly moved to Ellingson, South Dakota to live with her sister.

Jabez enjoyed spending time with his grandchildren. Helen (Bull) Klapper remembers him taking her and her young friends down to the railroad station in Aberdeen to watch the trains come in from all over the country. Aberdeen was the hub of several different train lines so people came from all over. Helen remembers enjoying hearing all the different accents such as southern U.S., etc.

Charabac trip during Jabez Mould family trip back to England in 1928. Two standing on far right are Annie Bull and father Jabez Mould. Boy standing fifth from left is Annie's son Alfred.

In May 1928 Jabez, Sarah, their daughter Annie and Annie's son Alfred took a trip back to England to visit their relatives. Annie kept a daily diary of the trip and this diary is included here (as Appendix XV). We have shown this since it mentions a number of the descendants of Thomas and Rose Ann who were still living in 1928. In the diary Annie discusses visiting the cottage where Thomas and Rose Ann spent their last years and then walking across the fields to the Paston church to visit the graves of Thomas, Rose Ann and Uncle Joe (Joseph Mould). They visited Uncle Charlie (Jabez's younger brother) and various members of his family as well as Jabez' brother George.

Although Annie and Alfred came back to the U.S. in October 1928, Jabez and Sarah stayed on in England for a couple of years before returning. On June 4, 1935, Jabez and Sarah Ann celebrated their fiftieth wedding anniversary in Aberdeen. Their two daughters who lived in Aberdeen were there and their son, George (who by this time had moved to San Diego, California) came back for the celebration.

A year later on July 10, 1936 Jabez died at home in an upstairs bedroom. There was a heat wave in Aberdeen and several relatives who were there mentioned how incredibly hot it was in that bedroom. The death certificate indicates that Jabez died of heat stroke. It is interesting to note that Jabez' death certificate contains two mistakes. It indicates that he was widowed but Sarah Ann was still very much alive at the time. The death certificate also mistakenly indicates Jabez' birthplace was London, England although he was born in Gunthorpe. Jabez was buried in Aberdeen in Riverside Cemetery.

Following Jabez' death, Sarah Ann continued to run the grocery but she reduced the range of goods quite a bit. She sold bread, eggs, prepackaged cold cuts, milk, canned goods as well as some cereals and staples. She no longer carried tobacco, fresh meats or produce. Sarah and her son George both had severe allergies while living in Aberdeen. Sarah's nose always ran and she used a silk handkerchief to keep it from getting raw from wiping. George took a vacation to California and found his allergies didn't bother him there.

George had done very well in the creamery business so sometime prior to 1935 he sold out, retired at a young age and moved to San Diego, California. In 1946 Sarah's daughter Rose and her husband, George Lovell, who were living in Aberdeen retired and moved to San Diego as well. Sarah continued to run the little grocery store until 1949 or 1950 when she went into the hospital. Rose came back to Aberdeen and sold the goods in the store, sold Sarah's house and took her back to San Diego with her. Sarah lived in San Diego for about seven years until her death on November 7, 1957. She died in her daughter Rose's house in San Ysidro, California and was buried in Bonita, California (Near San Diego) in the Glen Abby Memorial Park.

Jabez and Sarah's oldest daughter, Rose was born on January 1, 1885 in Rushden. In England as a young woman, she was quite a popular singer. In 1911 she joined her brother George in emigrating to the U.S. arriving at Ellis Island on the ship Baltic on May 1. She and her brother travelled to Aberdeen, South Dakota and settled there. On May 8, she married George Lovell in Aberdeen. Her husband was born and raised in Higham Ferrers and had emigrated to the US in 1906, gone back to England and returned to the US again in 1908. George had gotten a job in 1907 at the pumping station and by 1912 he was the Chief Engineer. In August 1912 he and Rose lived at 918 South Lloyd Street.

On August 15, 1912 George was the subject of an article in the local newspaper. The article marveled at the fact that George had lived in

Aberdeen for over six years but had not been downtown in over five years. He worked midnight to noon at the pumping station and always went home to bed. One night, in spite of his difficult work hours and need for sleep, he decided to go downtown to learn what the Socialist party stood for and he and Rose heard the Milwaukee Socialist Mayor Emil Seidel speak. George had read about the new buildings downtown but had never seen them. On this night he marveled at the new buildings and vowed he would keep in closer touch with his town - even if it meant losing sleep!

Cottage Grocery in Aberdeen, South Dakota owned by George and Rose Lovell.

Rose started a grocery store in one room in her house on 7th Ave.

S.E. She named it the Cottage Grocery. It was located next to an apartment building so she did very well; - so well, in fact, that she was able to enlarge the store by building an extra room connected to the house by an interior hall. At first George wasn't too happy about Rose opening a grocery store but it did so well and made so much money that he finally quit his job at the pumping station to help her run it.

George and Rose Lovell in front of their Cottage Grocery in Aberdeen, South Dakota.

In 1926/1927 George was operated on for an accidental neck injury. During the operation the doctor cut a nerve to his thyroid causing George to bloat up to the point that he couldn't hear or see very well. The local doctors couldn't determine what was wrong with him so he finally went to the Mayo Clinic in Rochester, Minnesota. They diagnosed his condition and gave him thyroid pills. This solved the problem and he lost a lot of weight. When he returned to Aberdeen he was so thin everyone was shocked to see him.

In 1934 George took his nephew, Alfred Bull, to the Chicago World's Fair.

In 1946 George and Rose sold their grocery store and retired. They then moved to San Ysidro, near San Diego in California where Rose's brother had retired to earlier, remaining there until her husband George died on February 9, 1959. Rose continued to live there until her death on January 26, 1973. Both of them were buried in Glen Abby Memorial Park in Bonita, California. George and Rose Lovell had two children. They were Hazel Constance and James Arthur.

Jabez and Sarah's son George Mould was born on October 15, 1887 in Rushden. George's middle name was Ewart after a famous attorney in England. In the 1901 census George listed his occupation as a boot builder. On June 13, 1906 George arrived at Ellis Island on the ship Oceanic. He returned to England and came back to the US arriving at Ellis Island on the ship Baltic on May 1, 1911. At this time he was listed as a US citizen. George worked in a saw mill when he first came to Aberdeen and while working there he cut off one of his fingers.

On February 14, 1914 George married Kate Freeman in Aberdeen. Kate was a Rushden girl who had come to the U.S. It doesn't appear that she came through Ellis Island since no record of her arrival there has been found. George went to work for a man who owned a creamery in Aberdeen. In a few years George saved enough to buy out the owner. Under his management the business grew. He bought milk from local dairymen, processed it and also made cheese, butter, cottage cheese, etc. He owned trucks and hired drivers who delivered the products to various Aberdeen neighborhoods. The business was called Mould's Creamery.

George and Kate lived on 9th Ave. about a block from his parents. The creamery continued to be successful and George was able to retire at an early age. He had bad allergies in Aberdeen and for two or three years he took his family on vacation to the west coast where his allergies didn't bother him. They would go for three months each summer when school was out traveling from Washington down through Oregon to the San Diego area. In 1932 or 1933 George retired and sold his creamery. He and Kate moved to San Diego, California where they rented a house. Later the family moved to nearby National City where they rented a house on Third Street. George had enough money from selling his creamery that he didn't have to work for a long time. In the early 1940s George opened a deli which he ran for three or four years.

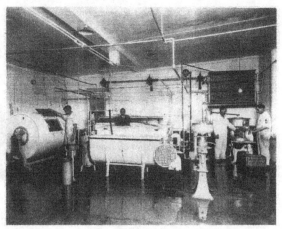

Mould Creamery owned by George Mould in Aberdeen, South Dakota in the 1930's.

The property was owned by Bank of America and they wanted to expand so they forced George out. He then went to work as a checker at a grocery store until he retired in about 1946/1947.

Kate had three sisters who all lived in the San Diego area. Every Friday they would ride the bus to downtown San Diego where they would spend the day window shopping.

On March 6, 1947 Kate died and was buried in Glen Abby Memorial Park in Bonita, California. George bought a house in Chula Vista and his mother, Sarah Ann and his daughter Marguerite lived with him. He lived another eighteen years and died on October 7, 1965. He was buried in Glen Abby Memorial Park next to his wife, his sister Rose, George Lovell and his mother Sarah.

George and Kate had four children. They were Constance Doreen, a stillborn infant, Irene Marguerite and Donald Thomas.

Jabez and Sarah's third child was a daughter they named Bessie Lilian. She was born in the first quarter of 1890. She lived only four years and died in February 1894. She was buried in Rushden on February 19, 1894. According to Annie (Mould) Bull, her sister became sick and was very hot. She got out of bed, opened a window to cool off from her fever which caused the illness to move into her chest and ultimately caused her death.

Jabez and Sarah's fourth child was born on October 6, 1891 in Rushden and was named Annie Beatrice. Annie only went to school through the third or fourth grade. She had to quit school because she kept fainting. The doctor said she needed to be outside not inside a school building. Her brother, George, had gone to the USA in 1906 and sent money to pay for Annie to emigrate to the U.S. She arrived at Ellis Island on board the ship Baltic on July 27, 1912. On her arrival papers she indicated she was a milliner in England. She traveled to Aberdeen where she worked in one of the stores there and also cooked and cleaned houses. On July 11, 1915 she married Fred Bull who had also been born in Rushden and had come to America.

Fred worked in the Bull Brothers Dairy which he and his three brothers had established in 1910. The dairy was located on what is now called "Old Road" about three and one-third miles west of Aberdeen. By 1913 they had

Bull Brothers' Dairy barn

done well enough to build a huge dairy barn. It was the largest structure of its kind in South Dakota. It was L-shaped and was 245 feet long and 36 feet wide. If it had been laid out in a straight line it would have been a city block long. It was very modern for the time with 125 stalls and a concrete floor. It could hold 150 cows. Fred and Annie lived upstairs in a small apartment along with Fred's brother, Arthur, and his family who lived in a second apartment. The dairy grew to be one of the largest in the northwest part of the state and the Aberdeen newspaper carried an article on the barn on July 13, 1913.

Trouble erupted between the Bull brothers and state health inspectors in 1917. The state began a program to inspect dairy cattle for tuberculosis and the Bull brothers refused to have their cattle tested. On June 25, 1917 the local newspaper carried a lengthy letter from the Bull brothers explaining their position on why they would not have their cattle tested. They maintained that a false positive test would cause a very expensive cow to be killed needlessly. They noted that some of their cows cost as much as $1,200 which in 1917 was a huge amount of money. The American newspaper columnist, Ripley, who became famous writing a column/cartoon called "Ripleys Believe It or Not", describing facts that were hard to believe, wrote about the Bull Brothers Dairyas follows: "A large percentage of Aberdeen, S.D. residents drink Bulls' milk".

In 1918 Fred and Annie left the Bull Brothers Dairy to start their own milk business called Willow Home Dairy which was located on the southeast side of Aberdeen near Riverside Cemetery. To buy cows for his new dairy, Fred rode the train to Ohio. The trip took about a week each way. He rode all the way back in a box car with the cows. He had to milk the cows twice a day and dump out the milk.

One day Fred was inside a fence with a large bull he kept on the farm and the bull knocked him down and began crushing him into the ground. He tried to get away under the fence but there was hog wire around the bottom of the fence so he was trapped. Fortunately a neighbor heard what was happening and ran over with a shotgun that he fired into the air and the bull was scared away. Although at the time it was not believed Fred suffered lasting damage, a doctor fifty years later found that one of his kidneys had been destroyed.

Milk wagon of Bull Brothers' Dairy.

Fred ran his dairy until it became almost impossible to hire men to help him operate it during World War II. He had no choice but to sell up. Besides milking the cows twice a day and processing the milk, Fred delivered milk to homes in Aberdeen in a horse drawn milk wagon. Later he bought a milk truck to use in his milk deliveries but he actually preferred the horse drawn

wagon. This was because the horse, over time, learned the route and when Fred would get off the wagon at the beginning of the block and ended up at the other after delivering to the houses, the horse and wagon would be there to meet him. With the truck, he had to walk back to the beginning of the block to get the truck after completing deliveries there.

Bull Brothers' Dairy barn after it burned in 1924.

In 1924 tragedy struck the Bull Brothers Dairy. The barn and silos burned to the ground. The fire started from a kerosene stove used to warm up food in the barn. After the fire, the brothers sold their herd and confined their activities to pasteurization of milk and making butter.

Annie became a naturalized U.S. citizen on February 24, 1925, and Fred had become one also five months earlier, on October 4, 1924.

As discussed above, in 1928, Annie and her son Alfred took a six month trip back to England to visit relatives. They raised chickens and sold the eggs to save money for the trip.

Annie's daughter, Helen, related an interesting story which probably happened in the mid-1930's. President Franklin Roosevelt visited Aberdeen and the entire town turned out to see him. He had had polio and was wheelchair bound. He arrived on a train and then rode in a car down the main street of Aberdeen. Annie had taken Helen to see the President and they were both shocked to see him having to be helped from the train to the car. Since everyone only heard him on the radio (there was no TV then) no one knew he was handicapped!

Fred and Annie sold their dairy at the beginning of WWII due to the shortage of help and moved to San Diego, California where Annie's sister, Rose, and brother, George had moved from Aberdeen. In San Diego Fred worked in a defense plant that manufactured warplanes. He worked there for several years until 1944 when his daughter, Helen, was transferred to Denver,

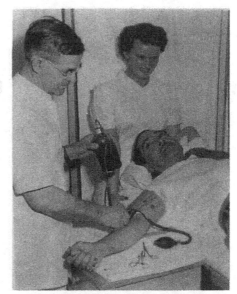

Fred Bull taking blood from the actor J. Carroll Naish at Fitzsimmons Hospital in Denver, Colorado.

Colorado. Fred and Annie then moved to Denver where he became a blood technician at Fitzsimmons Army Hospital until he retired in the early 1960's and moved back to Aberdeen. During the war various celebrities donated blood in order to encourage others to do the same. Fred took blood from a number of famous people such as the actor J. Carroll Naish and Mamie

Eisenhower when her husband was hospitalized at Fitzsimmons after a heart attack.

Annie and Fred lived in Aberdeen from 1960 until their deaths. Annie died on March 16, 1974 and was buried in Riverside Cemetery. Fred lived another eight years and died on November 24, 1982 and was buried next to Annie.

Fred and Annie had two children. They were Alfred Mould Bull and Helen Wrighton Bull.

More information on the Bull family can be found in the book, The Descendants of James and Eliza Bull of Rushden, England, by Richard J. Klapper, Trafford Publishing, 2004.

The Descendants of Thomas & Rose Ann Mould of Peterborough, England

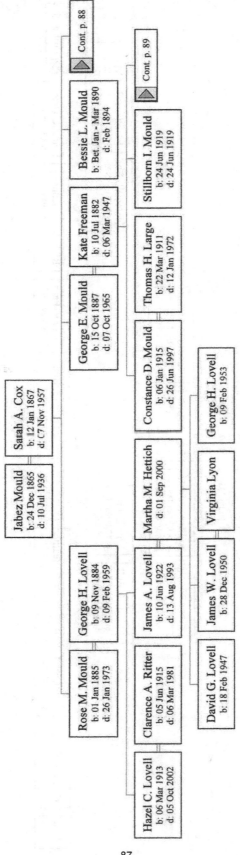

Cont. p. 88

Cont. p. 89

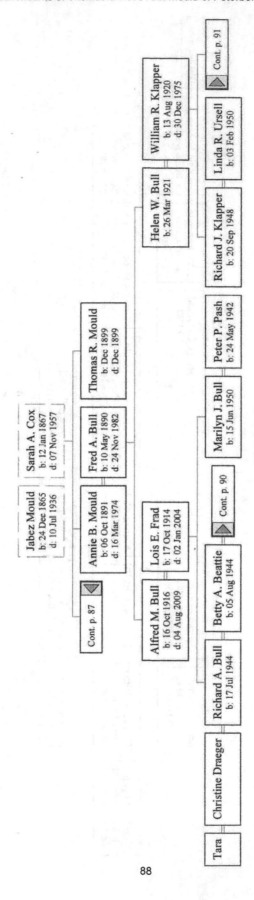

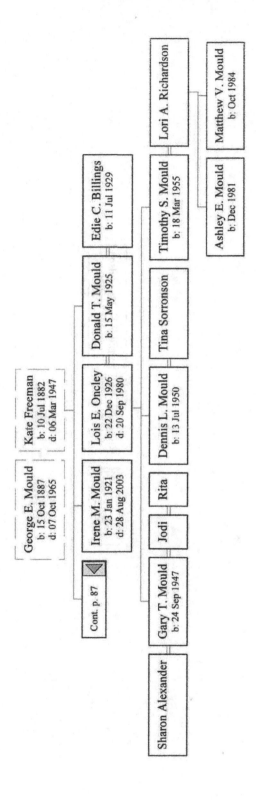

| Cont. p. 88 | Richard A. Bull b: 17 Jul 1944 | Linda K. Mendelson b: 05 Feb 1957 |

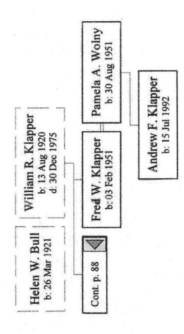

Joseph Thomas Mackness family. Seated: Joseph and Rebecca
Mackness. Standing: Frank Mackness.

Chapter 8

Joseph and Rebecca Mackness

Thomas and Rose Ann's ninth child was a daughter named Rebecca born in Gunthorpe on February 15, 1868. As expected, she appeared on the 1871 census as a child of three living in the family home. But on the following census ten years later, Rebecca was found to be living at 55 Balham Grove, London, with her married sister, Jane Jessop.Though married for barely three years, Jane and her husband, Devereux, already had two small children and the prospect of some help from her youngest sister must have seemed appealing.

Unfortunately for anyone pursuing the 1881 census sheets, Rebecca Mould was not easy to identify, and the reason was simply that her name had been incorrectly recorded as 'Rebecca Jessop'! But her age (13), place of birth (Gunthorpe) and relationship to the family (Sister), all pointed to this young girl being Jane's sister. (See Chapter 2 for more details.) It would be very interesting to know for how long Rebecca stayed with the Jessops: they went on to have two more children so that there would have been plenty to keep her busy. Or perhaps she moved on to work with some other family after gaining experience in London? As it is, the next record we have of her is from her wedding at Paston Church on May 28, 1890 when she gives her place of residence as Gunthorpe, her parents' home. But it was the custom of all 'spinsters' (single women) to spend a certain period of time in the parish where they intended to marry and to have 'the banns' read out in the parish church. These requirements meant that a bride-to-be would return home from wherever she had been living ('in service' for many young women, including the Mould sisters). She would also have to make preparations for her wedding.

Rebecca was twenty-two when she married. The bridegroom was her first cousin, Joseph Thomas Mackness, the son of Rose Ann's brother, William Mackness. Born in Brigstock on December 3, 1865, Joseph was two years older than Rebecca and living in Rushden where he was working as a shoe finisher. (Since both the 1881 and 1891 censuses list this as his occupation, he must have been working in the boot and shoe trade for at least ten years.) According to the 1891 census taken almost a year after they married, the couple were living in Harborough Park Road in Rushden; clearly a sound decision to set up home where Joseph's work was. Also, Joseph's older brother, John, and his wife, Eliza, were not only living in Rushden but in the same road. By the time of the 1901 census, Joseph and Rebecca had moved to York Road.

Two children were born to the young couple while in Rushden. A son, Frank, was born July 9, 1891 and a daughter, Nellie, in January 1894. Unfortunately, Nellie lived only sixteen months, dying in May 1895. She was buried on May 21 in Newton Road Cemetery in Rushden.

Joseph was very musical and was a member of the Rushden Temperance Band.

Sometime between 1904 and 1906, Joseph emigrated to the US and

Rushden Temperance Band. Joseph Mackness is on the front row far right.
Picture dated January 23, 1904.

settled in Aberdeen, South Dakota. We can narrow the date of his emigration to the US to between 1904 and 1906 since he is pictured in the Rushden Temperance Band on January 23, 1904 and he was listed as living in Aberdeen, South Dakota on Rebecca's arrival papers into Ellis Island in October 1906. Aberdeen was a popular place in the US for immigrants from England - particularly from Rushden. A large number of former inhabitants named Mackness, Mould and Bull seemed to end up in South Dakota! On October 16, 1906 Rebecca and her son Frank arrived at Ellis Island. The arrival manifest indicated that their final destination was to be Aberdeen where they would join Joseph.

According to Frank's daughter, Marge Redford, after living in Aberdeen for some period of time, they decided to move to Oregon but, most unfortunately, their house burned down! In 1914, Joseph and Rebecca took Frank and moved to the small "town" of Ellingson in Perkins County, South Dakota. Elingson consisted of a combination grocery store/post office, a Lutheran Church and a small school. It was named after the Ellingsons who ran the store and post office. The church sat next to the cemetery, and the store and school were close by. A number of small homesteads were nearby and Joseph and Rebecca homesteaded 160 acres about one and one-half to two miles southeast of the town. Joseph was given the 160 acres of land by the US government on October 15, 1914.

Joseph and Becky had a small two room house with a front door which faced east. It had a kitchen/living room which measured about 16' X 20' with a lean-to bedroom on the back (west) which measured about 16' X 8'. The main room also had an entry made of stone walls on the north side. The house had a basement and an outhouse.

Joseph and Becky had sod barns with cows and chickens. They would milk the cows and carry the cream to Ellingson. They

Homestead house very similar to the house owned by Joseph and Rebecca Mackness.

Seeder used by Joseph and Rebecca on their homestead in Ellingson, South Dakota. The seeder was still there when this picture was taken in September 2003. Wooden spoke wheels and wooden tongue have rotted away.

rode everywhere in a horse and buggy or horse and wagon since they didn't have a car. They raised vegetables in their garden and canned their produce. Their meat and produce was stored in the basement under their house. Joseph only plowed enough land to raise the produce the family needed. He left most of the land in prairie grass. There were frequent dry spells and if the land had been plowed the soil would blow away. Since Joseph did not plow all of his land, the prairie grass held the soil so he didn't lose it. Joseph lost an eye in an accident with a shotgun. He continued farming, however.

Joseph and Becky enjoyed music and had a windup phonograph on which Joseph played a collection of classical records. One Christmas their neighbors gave them a radio that ran on a big battery. They listened to the radio in the evening and Becky listened to the radio soaps during the day. According to Ruth Bertapelle, batteries were recharged from a windmill. Joseph had a good bass voice and sang in a quartet with the father of Robert Lewis who now lives in Hettinger, North Dakota. Joe wrote hymns - both words and music.

Joseph's grandson, Robert, traveled to Ellingson each summer to help his grandparents work the farm. After Joseph died he continued to go out each summer to help his grandmother. Ruth Bertapelle, who lived three miles from the Macknesses, remembers going to Joe and Rebecca's house at Christmas in a horse drawn sleigh and the wonderful cookies Aunt Beck made.

Joseph died of "carcinoma gastrica" on May 23, 1938 in Ellingson and was buried on May 26 in the Ellingson Cemetery. Rebecca transferred title to the homestead to her son Frank on September 22, 1938.

Rebecca's sister, Mary Avery, had immigrated to the US on September 18, 1921. Mary or "Polly" as she was known, first lived with her brother Jabez and his wife, Sarah, in Aberdeen, but after her sister Rebecca was widowed, Polly moved to live with her in Ellingson. Robert Lewis remembers Aunt Polly as jolly and happy while Aunt Beck was more quiet. They survived by taking care of their cows and chickens and raising vegetables in their garden. They didn't do any real farming since they were getting pretty old by that time. They probably leased out their land.

On March 2, 1941 Polly died and was buried in Ellingson Cemetery on March 6. Becky continued to live by herself until her death of "arterial schlerosis" on July 4, 1946. She was buried in Ellingson Cemetery next to Joseph and Polly. The town of Ellingson has disappeared. Directions to the Ellingson Cemetery are in Appendix III.

Following Rebecca's death, her son Frank sold the homestead property to Kurt E. Erdmann who sold the property to the current owner, Robert Lewis on February 19, 1991.

During the early years of his working life, Frank Mackness was a store manager within the Woolworth chain. In fact, this was how he came to meet his wife, Esther Mary Preston, who was one of the staff at a store he was managing. They fell in love and were married on December 10, 1918; Frank was twenty-seven and his bride was eighteen. Frank was frequently moved from one store to another, which could be unsettling for them both. When their first child, Robert, was born in December 1922, they were living in Omaha, Nebraska and by the time their daughter, Marjorie, was born in May 1926, they had been transferred to Huron, South Dakota.

In 1930 Woolworth wanted Frank to move again but he and Esther liked Huron so Frank quit and went into business for himself selling insurance. Unfortunately, the depression hit and he went bankrupt. The family moved to Lead, South Dakota where the two children grew up. In Lead, Frank worked for the Homestake Mine lawyer.

In 1943, the Homestake Mine was closed by Presidential order and the family moved to Ellensburg, Washington for a year. In September 1944, Frank and Esther moved to Portland, Oregon, following their daughter Marge who was working there. By that time their son, Bob, was in the military. He fought from Normandy through Germany. After the war he stayed in Berlin in the military government until 1949 as Secretary to the American Sector in Berlin.

In Portland, Frank found part time work, going door to door demonstrating Electrolux vacuum cleaners . It was while he was engaged in this work that he decided to reorganize their window and floor displays to better show off the merchandise. The company were so impressed that they hired him full time and Frank worked there until he retired in his mid-seventies. His wife was not in good health and he needed to stay home to take care of her.

Frank was a very kind and gentle man. Both he and Esther were members of the Knights of Pythias and Pythian Sisters.

Frank died in 1971 and was buried in a mausoleum in Portland, Oregon. Esther went to live with her daughter Marge Redford, in Torrence, California where she died in August 1975. She was buried beside her husband in Portland.

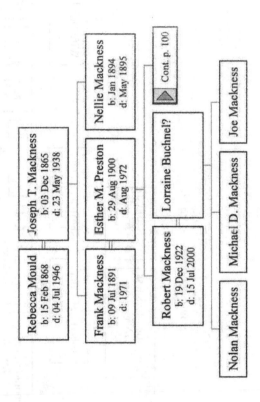

Cont. p. 100

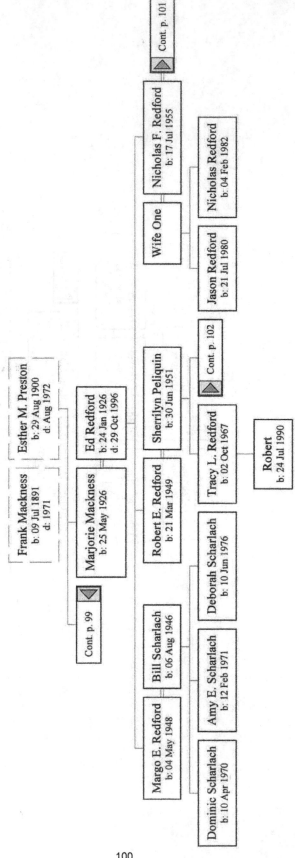

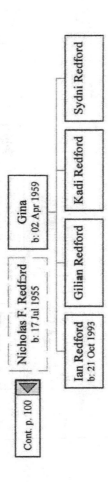

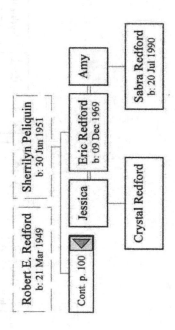

Picture taken at wedding of Bob Roberts/Violet Mould in 1920. Standing L-R: Bernard Mould, Bob Roberts, Charles Mould, Jessie Mould. Seated L-R: Lily Mould, Elsie Mould, Violet Mould, Emily Mould, Daisy Mould. Children in front: Ivy Mould and Percy Mould.

Chapter 9

Charles and Emily Mould

Thomas and Rose Ann's tenth child was a son named Charles. As detailed in previous chapters, the dairy business of Thomas was not of sufficient size to support all of the children so the two 'middle' sons, Jabez and Charles, had to earn their living elsewhere. After turning thirteen, Charles was sent to join his elder brother, 'Jabe' in Rushden, with a good prospect of finding employment in the flourishing boot and shoe industry there. The plan worked out and Charles, too, became a shoe maker. It was most probably in the spring of 1885 when Charles arrived in Rushden and was able to share his brother's lodgings at 13 Westfield Street in nearby Higham Ferrers. A decade later, in the 1891 census, Charles, is still living with his older brother, but Jabez is now married with three small children and there are six of them living at their new abode in Lancaster Street, Rushden. Charles is nineteen and his brother twenty-five; both men are working as 'shoe finishers'.

In July of 1891 Charles married Emily Whitbread, a local Rushden girl. Emily was a shoe machinist in Rushden. Ten years later in the 1901 census Charles and Emily were living in Westfields, Higham Ferrers with four children, Elsie, Jessie, Violet and Daisy. Later they moved to a flat in Rushden over a butcher shop on Queen St. just around the corner from High Street.

Sometime before late 1919 they again moved to Higham Ferrers to 2 Grove Street. This is known from the arrival records at Ellis Island, New York. On December 24, 1919 Chales' brother Jabez arrived at Ellis Island and listed as his nearest relative his brother, Charles, who was living at 2 Grove Street. Charles and Emily lived at the same address for the rest of their lives. Charles spent all of his working life in the shoe trade, working as a finisher for Messrs. B. Ladds of Rushden. Sadly, he was able to enjoy only three years of retirement before he died.

After her marriage Emily never worked outside the home, being fully occupied raising their eight children. She joined the Salvation Army, wore the distinctive bonnet

Higham Ferrers Methodist Church where Charles Mould was an elder and Sunday School supervisor.

and enjoyed attending their weekly band concerts. Prior to her death she had been associated with the Higham Ferrers Baptist Mission. Charles, however, was an elder in the Higham Ferrers Methodist Church. He was the Sunday School supervisor. In his latter years he attended the Milton Hall Chapel. He also spent a lot of time raising vegetables in his allotment.

Emily died of "Cerebral Thrombosis" on April 21, 1942 at the age of sixty-nine. She had been in failing health for about a year and seriously ill for about seventeen weeks prior to her death. It is interesting to note that she had two sisters who both lived to be over a hundred years old. Following

Emily's death, their daughter Ivy and her daughter Doreen left London to avoid the bombing and came to live with Charles, staying with him until he died of bronchial pneumonia on March 3, 1945. After being confined in Northampton General Hospital for fourteen weeks. Charles had returned home two weeks prior to his death. He was seventy-three.

Charles and Emily had nine children but the oldest, Emily May, died at one month of age. She was buried May 24, 1892 and the eight children who lived to adulthood were Elsie May, Jessie, Violet, Daisy, Lily, Bernard William, Ivy Doreen and Percy T. Whitbread.

Manor House where Elsie Mould cooked for Dr. Crew.

Elsie May was born May 23, 1893. She left school and became the cook for Dr. Crewe at the Manor House in Higham Ferrers. In the third quarter 1931 she married Charles Headland who was a widower. His first wife had died and been buried in Orlingbury. After their marriage Elsie and Charles lived in Queen Street in Rushden but later bought a nice house in Orlingbury and moved there. They actually owned two houses next door to each other in Queen Street. This was common among the working class in England in those days since the second house would be used to rent out for income after retirement. Charles and a partner, Mr. Austin, owned a small tanning factory on Commercial Street in Higham Ferrers. Charles commuted each day from Orlingbury in his car which he loved to drive. The

Queen Street house in Rushden where Charles and Elsie Headland lived.

factory was small with about a dozen employees. It specialized in delicate skins for gloves, handbags and so on. Charles Headland was an excellent dyer of leather and was the mainstay of the business. However, he was not as good at the administrative side so the factory was not as profitable as it might have been. Elsie was good at bookkeeping and kept the books for the factory. She was a forceful woman and often gave the orders to the workers in lieu of the partners.

When Elsie and Charles owned the two houses in Queen Street in Rushden and moved to Orlingbury, they rented one of them to Elsie's sister, Daisy and her husband, Jim Sharp. When the Headlands retired they moved back to Queen Street to the house they had been renting to Daisy and Jim. The Sharps then moved next door into the second house.

Charles was musical and was the organist at the Independent Wesleyan Chapel in Rushden for a period of time. He played the organ for the funeral of his brother-in-law, Jim Sharp on November 18, 1948. Charles died in the fourth quarter 1953 in Rushden.

Elsie continued to live in Rushden in her house on Queen Street until she died at the age of 90 in January 1984. Elsie had a housekeeper to help her. Elsie would often fall asleep in her chair downstairs rather than going upstairs to bed. But one morning her housekeeper came in to find Elsie dead in the chair. Elsie was cremated. The Headlands had no children.

Charles and Emily's third child was a daughter named Jessie who was born October 22, 1895. After leaving school, Jesse was sent to live with an elderly relative in Northampton to help and keep house. It was quite common in those days when someone had a large family for the girls to be farmed out this way. Jesse got a job in Northampton with Freeman, Hardy and Willis which was a national chain of boot and shoe stores. She became the manageress of the Northampton branch of the company. Jessie had some very good friends in Northampton and everyone assumed she would marry their son but, sadly, the young man died. She was forty-one years old when she married John William J. Barrett in the second quarter of 1937. John Barrett was fifty-four when they married, and possibly already retired. He was a widower with investments.

John and Jessie lived at 118 James Park Road in Northampton and both were staunch members of the Methodist Church. John collected records and had some of Lord Haw-Haw whose name was actually William Joyce, an Englishman who broadcast propaganda for the Germans every Sunday night during WWII. After the war, he was tried for treason and executed.

After a short illness, John died in Northampton General Hospital on May 9, 1957. The death certificate gave the following as causes:"Cerebro-vascular Episode with (L)hemiplegia, Parkinson's Disease."Jessie continued to live in Northampton. Later in her life she went into St. John's nursing home in Weston Favell (a part of Northampton). Jessie died July 2, 1977. She was cremated and her ashes buried in her parents' grave in Higham Ferrers. John and Jessie had no children.

Charles and Emily's fourth child was a daughter named Violet born November 23, 1897. In the fourth quarter of 1920, Violet married Robert Edward Roberts in the Methodist Church. Robert had volunteered for the army at sixteen by claiming to be eighteen. Bob had served in France in WWI and talked about how miserable it was in the trenches. Bob was in the Welsh Fusiliers and he met Violet when he was billeted in Higham Ferrers during WWI. After the war he returned home to England to marry her. He had no money but was very independent and self sufficient. He began working in a small leather factory.

He rented some land from the Duchy of Lancaster on the outskirts of Higham Ferrers. He managed to save enough money to buy some of the land and build a house on it. Bob and Violet were very frugal and later were able to sell their house and land and buy Crossweir Farm in Souldrop. They also bought a pair of houses across the road from the farm. For a time, Violet's sister Lily and her husband Hubert Eaton lived in one of the two houses. Joan Bolton remembers her father, Guilf Mould, purchasing pullets (young chickens) from the Roberts on more than one occasion.

Violet was Methodist but Bob was a member of the Church of England. This is reflected in the fact that the children were baptized in the Church of England but were raised Methodist. Bob and Violet lived on Crossweir Farm until they retired. They then moved to Wellingborough Road, Rushden while their son John continued to work the farm.

Bob died on February 12, 1971 and was buried in Higham Ferrers. Violet lived another eleven years and died of "Congestive cardiac failure, Myocardial Ischaemia, Coronary atherosclerosis" on January 8, 1982 at The Poplars, Thrapston Road in Finedon. Bob's grave is marked with a headstone. Violet is buried a few steps away from Bob in an unmarked grave.

![Wentworth Road house in Higham Ferrers where Jim and Daisy Sharp lived.](image)

Wentworth Road house in Higham Ferrers where Jim and Daisy Sharp lived.

Bob and Violet had three children, Jeffrey, Pauline and John.

Charles and Emily's fifth child was a daughter named Daisy who was born in the second quarter of 1900. Daisy worked in the closing room of a shoe factory. In the second quarter of 1927 Daisy married a WWI veteran Alfred James Sharp. Alfred, who went by the name of Jim, was in the army in France during WWI. He sufferred a gas attack and his brain was slightly damaged. After that he was always a little slow. This WWI brain damage would eventually lead to his death twenty years later.

Following their marriage they lived in Queen Street in Rushden in a house owned by Charles and Elsie. When the Headlands moved back from Orlingbury, Daisy and Jim moved next door to another house owned by Charles and Elsie. About five or six years later, they bought a house at 19 Wentworth Road in Rushden. Although they both worked in shoe factories, Jim and Daisy never had much money.

In November 1948 Jim went to a dentist to have some work done. The dentist gave him gas as an anesthesia. He couldn't be revived so they took him to Northampton but he never regained consciousness and died there on November 14, 1948. It is thought that the gassing he endured in WWI may have contributed to his death from the anesthetic. They were living at 19 Wentworth Road when Jim died. At Jim's funeral, his coffin was draped with the Union Jack. Daisy continued to work after her husband's death but spent every Sunday with Bob and Violet at Crossweir Farm in Souldrop. Daisy lived in Wentworth Road for many years until she moved into Fairlawns Nursing Home in Higham Road, Rushden where she died on January 29, 1995. Jim and Daisy are both buried in Higham Ferrers cemetery. They had no children.

Charles and Emily's sixth child was a daughter named Lily who was born March 9, 1902. Lily married Hubert

Shop in Commercial Street in Higham Ferrers owned by Hubert and Lily Eaton.

Eaton in the fourth quarter of 1929 and they lived in a cottage on the main street in Souldrop, Bedfordshire. They later moved to a house owned by Violet and Bob Roberts opposite Crossweir Farm. Lily never worked after their marriage but Hubert worked in a shoe factory in Higham Ferrers as a clicker. He rode his bicycle to work every day when he was young but rode the bus when he was older. Hubert served in the army in WWII.

Just prior to his retirement, Hubert and Lily moved to Higham Ferrers and lived on Westfield Terrace in back of High Street. They later moved to 20 Commercial Street at the corner of Northampton Road and Commercial Street in Higham Ferrers. Hubert lost his job at the shoe factory and he and Lily opened a general store on Commercial Street which they ran for some time.

Hubert died in the fourth quarter of 1981. Lily died on March 9, 1988 of bronchopneumonia. At the time of her death Lily was at the Poplars, a residential home in Marshall Road, Raunds.

Hubert and Lily had a son Peter. He married in England and had several children but later divorced and moved to Australia.

Charles and Emily's seventh child was a son, Bernard who was born August 20, 1905. Bernard left school at twelve years of age and worked on a farm. At that time you were allowed to leave school at twelve if you worked on a farm. Otherwise you had to go to school until fourteen. He

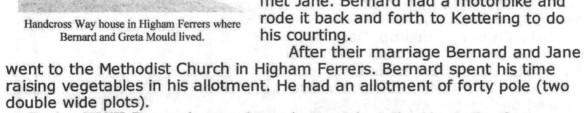

worked on a farm until he was fourteen and then went to work at the Victoria Leather Factory in Midland Road in Higham Ferrers.

On October 9, 1926 Bernard married Jane Margaretta Maycock (known as Greta) in the Silver Street Methodist Church in Kettering and set up home in Handcross Way. Jane's father was an officer in the Kettering Methodist Boys Brigade. Bernard was in the Higham Ferrers Boys Brigade. Every year the Nene Valley Battalion had a camp. One year they camped at Rhyl in Wales. Jane's mother always went to the camps and took her daughters, all staying in a B&B. It was in Rhyl that Bernard first met Jane. Bernard had a motorbike and rode it back and forth to Kettering to do his courting.

Handcross Way house in Higham Ferrers where Bernard and Greta Mould lived.

After their marriage Bernard and Jane went to the Methodist Church in Higham Ferrers. Bernard spent his time raising vegetables in his allotment. He had an allotment of forty pole (two double wide plots).

During WWII Bernard moved to a better job at the Harris Brothers Tannery in Northampton Road. He was also in the Home Guard. He later retired from Harris Brothers where he had been a forman.

Bernard died of "Myocardial Infarction, Left Hemiplegia" in the hospital in Wellingborough on February 19, 1982. He was cremated in Kettering. Jane died of "Broncho pneumonia, Progressive Cerebral Vascular disease" on

January 8, 1986 in the Rushden Hospital and was cremated in Kettering. Bernard and Jane had eight children who were in order of age; Joan Margaretta, Norman William, Phillip, Mary Gillian, Trevor Gilbert, Joyce Irene, Margaret Ann and Janet Elizabeth.

Charles and Emily's eighth child was a daughter named Ivy. In the third quarter of 1931, Ivy married Archibald Thomas Lovell who was known as Bob. Bob worked in a barber shop in London but during World War II he was called up to serve in the Army. Bob apparently served his time in England and never went to the continent during the war.

Bob Lovell's barber shop in Rushden, England

Because London was the major target of the Blitz, Bob sent his wife, Ivy, and his daughter, Doreen, to live with her father, Charles, in Higham Ferrers. This proved wise as the barbershop where Bob had worked and their house nearby were both destroyed during the bombing. Bob was an avid stamp collector and when he came home on leave he would trade stamps with other family members.

After he was demobbed, Bob returned to Higham Ferrers where his brother-in-law, Bob Roberts, convinced him to open his own barber shop rather than work for someone else. Bob opened a shop in Rushden at 40 High Street South. He and Ivy lived over the shop. His daughter worked with him until she married in 1952.

Bob worked in the shop until he retired. He died at home in 1965. After his death, Ivy had to sell the business and in doing so lost her home. She then moved to a new bungalow in Glassbrook Road in Rushden. She later moved to sheltered accommodation which was a group of houses with a warden who would come around twice a day to check the residents.

Ivy lived to be ninety-one and died in 1999. The Lovells had just one daughter, Doreen.

Charles and Emily's ninth and last child, named Percy, born in the second quarter 1910. He qualified as a motor mechanic and worked in the garage at the John Whites shoe factory in Rushden, carrying out the maintenance on their trucks. In 1933, Percy married Elizabeth Firkins and the couple set up home in Oakley Road, Rushden, later moving to Lime Street. In 1935 they had a son named Anthony but, tragically, he contracted meningitis and died at the age of three. Elizabeth was a restless person so she and Percy moved quite often. They moved from Lime Street to a house in Souldrop, and later, to one they had bought on Rose

Garage at John White's Bootware in Higham Ferrers where Percy Mould was forman.

Avenue, Rushden. Once again, they sold that house and bought a cottage in Souldrop. Their last move came when Percy was promoted to forman at John Whites. This promotion came with a house provided by the company and they moved to Paddock Lodge - later renamed 'The Paddocks' - in Higham Ferrers. (See photo.) As forman, Percy was in charge of John Whites entire fleet of vehicles.

Demolition of the John White's Bootware garage ir June 1992 where Percy Mould had been forman.

Percy and Elizabeth remained at Paddock Lodge even after his retirement. Elizabeth died on May 23, 1982; Percy lived for another eighteen months, dying on October 31, 1983, aged seventy-three. The couple had no more children after the loss of their small son.

The Paddocks in Hayway in Higham Ferrers where Percy and Betty Mould lived.

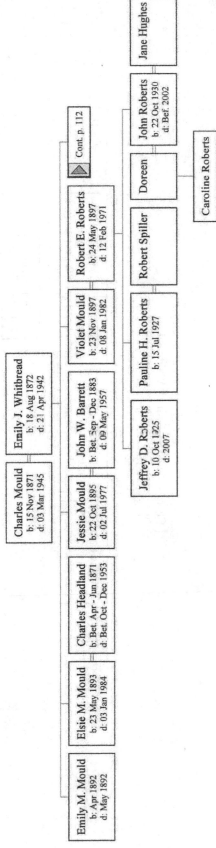

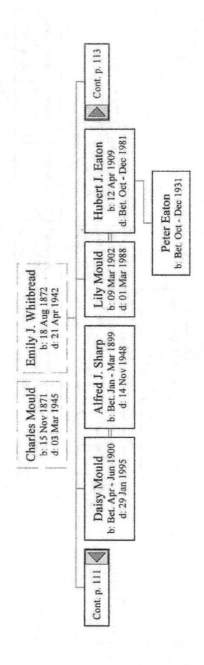

Charles Mould
b: 15 Nov 1871
d: 03 Mar 1945

Emily J. Whitbread
b: 18 Aug 1872
d: 21 Apr 1942

Daisy Mould
b: Bet. Apr - Jun 1900
d: 29 Jan 1995

Alfred J. Sharp
b: Bet. Jan - Mar 1899
d: 14 Nov 1948

Lily Mould
b: 09 Mar 1902
d: 01 Mar 1988

Hubert J. Eaton
b: 12 Apr 1909
d: Bet. Oct - Dec 1981

Peter Eaton
b: Bet. Oct - Dec 1931

Cont. p. 111

Cont. p. 113

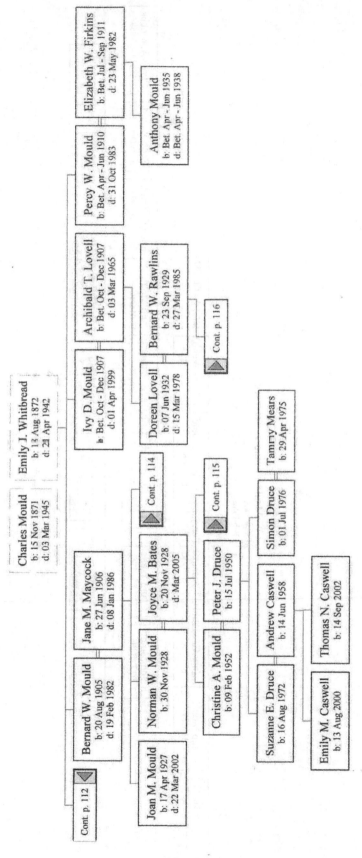

Charles Mould
b: 15 Nov 1871
d: 03 Mar 1945

Emily J. Whitbread
b: 13 Aug 1872
d: 21 Apr 1942

Bernard W. Mould
b: 20 Aug 1905
d: 19 Feb 1982

Jane M. Maycock
b: 27 Jun 1906
d: 08 Jan 1986

Ivy D. Mould
b: Bet. Oct - Dec 1907
d: 01 Apr 1999

Archibald T. Lovell
b: Bet. Oct - Dec 1907
d: 03 Mar 1965

Percy W. Mould
b: Bet. Apr - Jun 1910
d: 31 Oct 1983

Elizabeth W. Firkins
b: Bet. Jul - Sep 1911
d: 23 May 1982

Anthony Mould
b: Bet. Apr - Jun 1935
d: Bet. Apr - Jun 1938

Joan M. Mould
b: 17 Apr 1927
d: 22 Mar 2002

Norman W. Mould
b: 30 Nov 1928

Joyce M. Bates
b: 20 Nov 1928
d: Mar 2005

Christine A. Mould
b: 09 Feb 1952

Peter J. Druce
b: 15 Jul 1950

Doreen Lovell
b: 07 Jun 1932
d: 15 Mar 1978

Bernard W. Rawlins
b: 23 Sep 1929
d: 27 Mar 1985

Suzanne E. Druce
b: 16 Aug 1972

Andrew Caswell
b: 14 Jun 1958

Simon Druce
b: 01 Jul 1976

Tamrry Mears
b: 29 Apr 1975

Emily M. Caswell
b: 13 Aug 2000

Thomas N. Caswell
b: 14 Sep 2002

Cont. p. 112

Cont. p. 114

Cont. p. 115

Cont. p. 116

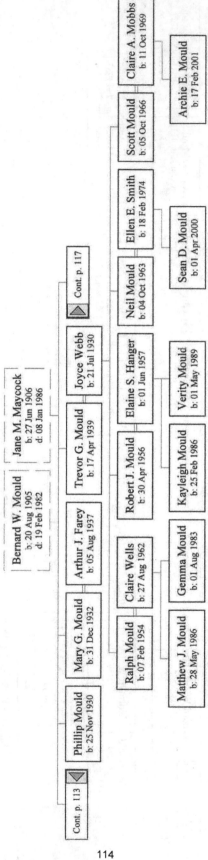

Bernard W. Mould
b: 20 Aug 1905
d: 19 Feb 1982

Jane M. Maycock
b: 27 Jun 1906
d: 08 Jan 1986

Phillip Mould
b: 25 Nov 1930

Mary G. Mould
b: 31 Dec 1932

Arthur J. Farey
b: 05 Aug 1937

Trevor G. Mould
b: 17 Apr 1939

Joyce Webb
b: 21 Jul 1930

Cont. p. 117

Ralph Mould
b: 07 Feb 1954

Claire Wells
b: 27 Aug 1962

Robert J. Mould
b: 30 Apr 1956

Elaine S. Hanger
b: 01 Jun 1957

Neil Mould
b: 04 Oct 1963

Ellen E. Smith
b: 18 Feb 1974

Scott Mould
b: 05 Oct 1966

Claire A. Mobbs
b: 11 Oct 1969

Matthew J. Mould
b: 28 May 1986

Gemma Mould
b: 01 Aug 1983

Kayleigh Mould
b: 25 Feb 1986

Verity Mould
b: 01 May 1989

Sean D. Mould
b: 01 Apr 2000

Archie E. Mould
b: 17 Feb 2001

Cont. p. 113

114

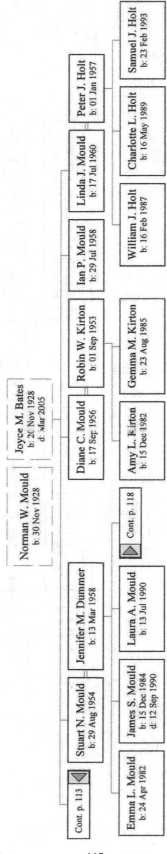

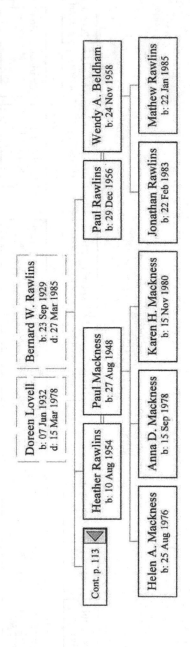

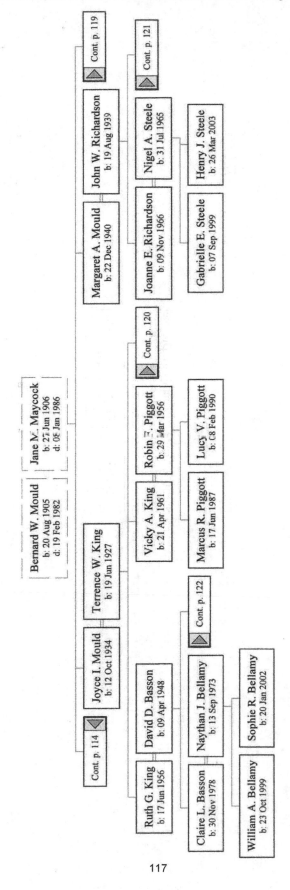

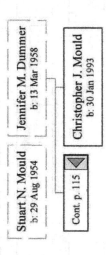

Stuart N. Mould
b: 29 Aug 1954

Jennifer M. Dummer
b: 13 Mar 1958

Christopher J. Mould
b: 30 Jan 1993

Cont. p. 115

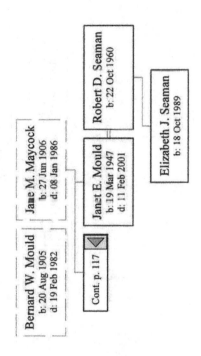

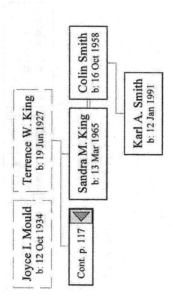

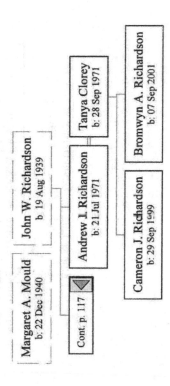

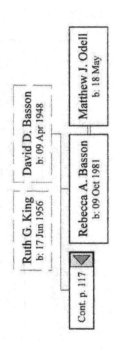

George and Fanny Mould

Chapter 10

George and Fanny Mould

Thomas and Rose Ann's youngest child was a son, George, born on November 5, 1873, in Gunthorpe, Peterborough. At this time, Gunthorpe was no more than a small hamlet, about a mile and a half from Peterborough's northern edge, with fields separating the two.

Twenty years had elapsed since the birth of Thomas and Rose's oldest child, Jane, and Rose was well into her forty fifth year.

From census information, it is clear that George's sisters went "into service" as soon as they were old enough, working as servants in private homes, normally with a family. From the 1881 census, it appears that Rebecca ("Becky") was living in London with her eldest sister Jane Jessop, and family: she was thirteen years old. At the Gunthorpe cottage not only would space be at a premium as the number of children increased but funds would be limited also.

George's brothers, Jabez and Charles, were sent by train to Irthlingborough, about 25 miles to the southwest of Peterborough, to find work, and ended up living and working in Rushden. Joseph and George, though, remained at home, working with their father who had set up a small "milk business". The latter may simply have involved selling and delivering milk from Thomas' cows. We know that George was involved with this from the age of eight and still at school (where he probably stayed until the age of twelve).

In later years, George was obviously a good letter writer. He expressed his ideas well and his handwriting was impressive, albeit painstakingly done, according to Olive, his eldest grandchild. He also found great pleasure in books. All of this suggests that he had received a sound educational grounding as a child.

But to go back for a moment to the middle years of the nineteenth century when Thomas and Rose were beginning married life and starting their family. At that time, Peterborough was a medium-sized market town, with a beautiful cathedral. However, the construction of the Great Northern Railway, linking London with the industrial Northeast of England, converted Peterborough into a bustling railway center and an industrial manufacturing town in its own right. The advent of a fast and reliable transport system attracted various manufacturers of agricultural and marine machinery.

These industries, in turn, attracted to the town former agricultural workers from the surrounding areas and beyond. To accommodate these people, various local "entrepreneurs" constructed streets and various areas of small up-to-date (for the age) terrace houses. The Great Northern Railway built its own houses - the GNR cottages - in the area of Peterborough now known as New England, all conveniently close to the marshalling yards, the coal hoists, the "loco" sheds, etc. to the north of the main station. (Many of these houses are still lived in, found on the west side of Lincoln Road.)

These new inhabitants, in the 1860's and onward, needed services such as shops, suppliers of services and so on. It was doubtless as a result of this that George Mould in 1911 seized the opportunity to set up home in Gilpin Street, New England, with the space for a dairy, from where his milk business could be run.

But another gentleman had been attracted to Peterborough before George Mould was even born and he too was called George. George Mills had been born in Kent in 1841 and came to the city as a young married man to work as a guard on the railway. At that time a guard was the man who sat at the rear of the train in the caboose and performed many of the duties of today's conductors and signalmen. At the time of the 1881 census, George Mills and his wife Mary (nee Ives) were living at number 176 New England (the

School teachers at Great Northern Railways School in late 1880's. Fanny Mills is at right end of front row.

GNR cottages mentioned above) with their five children, three daughters and two sons aged between twelve and two years old. Their second daughter, Fanny, was ten years old. By the time of the 1901 census twenty years later, she would be George Mould's wife and about to give birth to their first child.

Fanny was an intelligent young woman who wanted to be a teacher. As the child of a railway employee, she attended the Great Northern Railway Schools (the GNR Schools) in New England. Instead of leaving school at fourteen, she was encouraged to stay on as a pupil teacher, working with the children in the Infants' Department under the supervision of a senior, qualified teacher. These teachers were usually college trained and known as certified assistants.

An excellent little book entitled "The History of the Old Railway Church Schools" (or "The GNR Schools") was produced in 1957 to mark the schools' centenary that year. In it, Joan Bolton was able to pick out her grandmother in two of the staff photographs. In the one of all the teachers, (nineteen appear in the group), Fanny is sitting to the right on the front row. She looks to be about twenty years old, thus dating the photo as taken in about 1890.

In the other photo, Fanny appears in a smaller group of seven teachers, (all women), and the caption beneath reads: "Miss Thorne and her staff." Since Miss H. Thorne was the Infants' School head mistress, this confirms that Fanny Mills taught in that department. On this occasion, she looks rather ill at ease and, also, several years younger, (c. 1886 perhaps?). As a Pupil Teacher, the book

Late 1880's teachers at the Great Northern Railways school in Peterborough. Fanny (Mills) Mould is seated on the far left.

suggests that her starting salary would have been about two shillings a week, paid quarterly, (i.e. every thirteen weeks).

There was a close connection between the School and the Church of England. The Anglican Church of St. Paul's was built in New England and consecrated in 1869, with the first vicar, Canon C. R. Ball, appointed to the governing board of the school in that year.

We do not know how Fanny and George met but certainly George would have had customers for his milk in the New England area by the 1890's. He might have delivered to the GNR cottages and the Mills' home - or, even, to the school where Fanny was working. (Born in 1870, she was three years older than George. Interestingly, both had birthdays in November.)

At any rate, on August 10th, 1898 they were married at St. Paul's church. Fanny had to give up her teaching post since in those days women teachers were not normally allowed to continue after marriage. They went back to Gunthorpe to begin their married lives and Fanny had six of their nine children there. Doris was born in April 1901, Cyril in June 1902, Bernard in July 1903, Eric in January 1905, Guilford in August 1906 and Marjorie in September 1909.

As well as being the year they married, 1898 was the year George took over the milk business from Thomas. His parents were probably "feeling their age" by then, having worked very hard throughout their lives. The 1901 census showed George and Fanny liveing with Thomas and Rose in Gunthorpe along with Geroge's sister, Betsy and her husband, James Mackness. Fannie and George were then anticipating the birth of their first child, but the whole household were also recalling the tragic event that had taken place a year before. One night at the end of March, Thomas and Rose Ann's eldest son, Joseph, committed suicide by cutting his own throat. He was a month short of his thirty-sixth birthday and still living at home. His elderly parents probably never recovered fully from the shock. Thomas himself died six years later in January of 1906 and Rose moved to Rushden soon afterwards to live with her daughter "Polly" (Mary) Avery. It was there that she died in July 1908.

In 1911 the family made the move from Gunthorpe to 59 Gilpin Street in the New England area of Peterborough. This was about two miles north of Peterborough's center and the Cathedral. Number 59 was already built and named Rock House. It had enough space behind it for the dairy - basically a covered area where the milk churns were kept. No pasteurizing or bottling occurred. The milk was taken out by bicycle at first, in special cans hanging from the handlebars and poured into a jug

59 Gilpin Street known as Rock House. Picture taken in 2003

or similar receptacle which customers left in their front porches.

The move from Gunthorpe would not have been an easy time for the family and especially stressful for Fanny with six children to look after as they settled into their new surroundings. Doris, the eldest, was ten but little Marjorie just a toddler. But, on top of all this, even as they planned their move, Fanny discovered that she was expecting another baby.

A little boy they named George was born that autumn, with his birth and death both registered during the last quarter of 1911. So his life was a short one.

Was this infant - the couple's fifth son - named after his father because he was born close to George's birthday (November 5th)? One thing is certain; when George turned thirty-eight that month and Fanny was forty-one two weeks later, any celebrations would have been muted. It is more than likely that this baby arrived too early to survive as a consequence of all the upheaval and exertions his mother had experienced with the move.

Two more children were born at Gilpin Street; Iris in July 1913 and then, in February 1917, a bouncing baby boy they named Hubert. Since Fanny was 46 years old (at this time) it is not surprising that this child was their last!

Once settled into their new surroundings, their lives at Gilpin Street would have been very busy. The four oldest children had to adjust to a different school, most likely the school where their mother had been teaching thirteen years before. You can just picture Fanny, encouraging her "brood" to read, giving them the help a teacher could. But, in reality, she probably had her hands full with her housewife routine and with the additional responsibility of the milk business. The dairy was in their back yard and it was Fanny's job to wash the milk churns every day, as well as dealing with customers who came to buy milk at the back door.

With the dairy on the premises at Rock House, it was very much a matter of "living over the shop". With little separation between family life and the milk business, the Mould children all had to help when they were old enough and even when they were still at school, they would be asked to run around to Mrs. "So-and-so's" with a pint of milk.

The milk came from a farm in Gunthorpe, owned by George Speechley. Cyril Mould remembered going out there to collect it with his father by horse and cart, a trip of about three miles to the northeast of New England. Joan Bolton says, "I also remember going to this farm with my father when I was five or six years old. (This would be around 1948 and we went in the Morris Eight.) I have a clear recollection of one of George Speechley's naughty grandsons making faces behind the old man's back to make me laugh. Even my father had difficulty trying to keep a straight face."

Amongst various newspaper cuttings and photographs found in the writing bureau of Guilford Mould following his death was one of George Mould's business cards. There was some debate over the meaning of the phrase on the card "Deliveries twice daily". Did it mean they delivered milk to customers twice a day or that milk was delivered fresh to the dairy twice a day? It was Ursula Mould who settled the debate. Living at Rock House for over three years from August 1947, she was well placed to see what happened. She confirmed that Rupert Speechley, George Speechley's son, who was then in his thirties, did indeed bring the milk twice a day, and that certainly some customers, if not all, might have half a pint in the morning and then some more in the afternoon. So both assumptions

Business card of George Mould's dairy

were correct. Very few homes indeed would have a refrigerator before 1950 and, even though pantries were situated in the coolest part of the house with a concrete or stone floor, or a stone slab shelf for perishables , milk would quickly turn sour, especially in the summer months. The necessity for two deliveries probably explains why Guilford ate his mid-day meal so quickly when he came home for the main hot meal of the day, known as "dinner" in most working households. This always annoyed Mary, his wife, who had doubtless spent a considerable amount of time preparing the meal. But Guilford would be aware that his second milk round had to be done before he could sit down again, probably for a cup of tea at Gilpin Street.

The "sons" referred to after George Mould's name on his business card were Eric and Guilford. Both helped their father full-time upon leaving school, aged thirteen or fourteen. (In the early 1900's, youngsters were entitled to education up to the age of fourteen but no fuss was made if their parents wanted to remove them from twelve in order to work.) Quite why it was that these two boys were drawn into the milk business we don't know. Probably they had no say in the matter! Both liked being outdoors and were attracted by the prospect of greater freedom than they would have had in an office or in a factory. (Guilf himself would verify this in the 1960's.) Their father needed help in the family business as the number of customers increased and Eric and Guilf were prepared to join him. Also, the two boys got on well, being very close in age. Both would work in the business for thirty years until it was sold in 1950.

Eric's daughter, Ann, remembers her father going on his bike to deliver the milk, with a can hanging from each handlebar. The customers used to leave their jugs out in the front porch and Eric, Guilf or George, would ladle out the milk into them. Doris and Iris Mould would also deliver milk to customers living within walking distance of the dairy.

When they married in 1932, Eric and his young wife, Pollie, lived in Exeter Road, conveniently near to his milk round. When Guilf and Mary set up home in 1935, they were a bit further away, in Fulbridge Road, on the southern side of the railway line that crossed it. At about that time, Guilf bought a little Austin Seven, thus making his milk round easier. Later he bought a second-hand Morris Eight. It was maroon and black and Joan Bolton can still (no kidding) remember the registration number was BOH 780. Guilf removed the front passenger seat to make room for the milk churn. When he braked rather suddenly on one occasion, the churn lurched forward, spilling the milk. The smell lingered for weeks.

It needs to be made clear that the Gilpin Street dairy was far from being the 'high tech' enterprise that we would find today. As mentioned earlier, there was no pasteurizing or bottling plant; all pretty basic in fact. But by the 1940's the dairy industry was changing. Customers came to expect bottled milk, something that other dairies in Peterborough were already providing.

However, for George Mould, who was in his late sixties by 1940, the upheaval and huge investment required in order to convert to bottling were daunting, even if there had been the space at Rock House. With the tragic death of his wife during the bitterly cold February of 1947, George's mind was made up: he would sell the business. In 1950 it was bought by the Peterborough dairy, Brown and Sons, based in the Walton area.

By the time Eric and Guilf began working full-time at Gilpin Street, Cyril and Bernard were already out at work, though still living at home. By the late 1920's all four older brothers were courting and all married between 1928 and 1935. Cyril married Beatrice 'Beattie' Ward from near Boston, Lincolnshire, in the autumn of 1928, closely followed by Bernard and Annie, n'ee Green, from Crowland in February 1929. Eric married Pollie Giddings in 1932. Pollie was born in Blackheath, London and was working in Peterborough when they met. Guilf and Mary (n'ee Murden) married in May 1935. All four weddings took place in Peterborough. But when Doris married Ernest Maile in June 1932, the ceremony took place in St. Leonards-on-Sea in Sussex. Her two sisters, Marjorie and Iris, remained single.

Back row L-R: Hubert Mould, Kate (Freeman) Mould, Doris Mould, Bernard Mould, Marjorie Mould, Cyril Mould and Doreen Mould. Front: L-R: Fanny Mould, Marguerite Irene Mould, Iris Mould and George Mould. George Ewart Mould family trip to England in 1927.

Just as the eldest child chose to marry away from Peterborough, so did the youngest - Hubert. But in his case, it was much farther from home. Whilst serving with the British Army in Germany in 1945, he met his wife, Ursula, in Berlin and that is where they married in June 1947.

Although we have few first hand accounts to build up a picture of life at the dairy for the first twenty years after the move from Gunthorpe, it is

129

thanks to some American cousins that we can fill in a few of the gaps.

In the summer of 1927, Jabez's son, George Ewart Mould, visited Peterborough during his tour of England. With him were his wife, Kate, and their two daughters, Doreen and Marguerite. Their small son, Don, was only two years old , so he stayed behind. The photographs George Ewart took, both in Peterborough and in Higham Ferrers (where Charlie Mould's family lived) are literally snapshots of life with the Moulds. One, shown here, captures George and Fanny and their family in the garden of Gilpin Street. A ten year old Hubert (far left) looks distinctly reluctant to be photographed. Joan Bolton wondered why Guilf, then twenty one years old and Eric, a year older, were missing; she then realized that they would, of course, be working on their milk rounds seven days a week.

Another photo shows George Ewart sitting on his Uncle George Mould's special bike with the Rock House Dairy plate (sadly the only photo we have of this bike). This 'working' bike was actually a tricycle (for better balance). Ursula says that a milk churn could be carried in front of the handle bars. Although her memories are from the 1940's, others have confirmed that George did use a tricycle. It is unfortunate that the picture is double exposed but underneath we can make out the two older brothers, Cyril, twenty five years old, and Bernard, twenty four. Both are wearing uniforms - but what uniforms are they? Cyril's daughter Olive says that her father and Bernard began working as bus drivers in 1927, so these were most likely the uniforms they were wearing. (If sister Doris was working at the bus depot by then, she would probably have alerted her brothers to these vacancies.) The bus depot was on Lincoln Road, between Stone Lane and Oxford Road. It would have been a short walk or bicycle ride from Gilpin Street.

Although this American family's visit produced valuable snapshots, the following year some other American relatives came to England and produced a story-in-a-diary. In 1928 George's Mould's older brother Jabez (see Chapter 7) brought his wife, Sarah, his daughter, Annie Bull and her son, Alfred, to England to visit family for six months. They began their trip on May 19 and returned home to Aberdeen, South Dakota on October 12. The aim was to give them a chance to see their family again and to let Alfred meet his relatives in the old country. They visited both their Mould and Bull families. (Annie's husband was Fred Bull of Rushden.)

During this six month trip, Annie kept a fairly detailed diary of what they did and who they met each day: a most illuminating chronicle and an invaluable contribution to this family history. After visiting George Mould's brother Charles in Higham Ferrers, near Rushden, Annie and Alfred moved on to Peterborough, arriving by train on Monday 13th August, and stayed until the following Saturday, the 18th. Although George didn't own a car, we read that "Uncle George met us with a car - then home. Met Aunt Fanny and all the family...." Presumably he had hired a car or borrowed one for the occasion. No car is mentioned again. (In order to drive a car in England then, you did not need a driving license; someone showed you how and you just picked it up. See the Eric story).

Their Uncle George cycled about a great deal for pleasure, as well as when delivering milk, and accompanied Annie and Alfred when they cycled out to Peakirk, a small village about four miles north of Peterborough where cousins Dora and Lily Prentice lived. Aunt Rose (George's sister) and her husband John Prentice were dead by then, their eldest daughter, Ellen, was working in London, whilst Harold and Frederick, the two sons, had married and moved away.

It seems clear that Fanny did not go with them on such visits. (She is not mentioned as being at the get together with Charlie and family in Higham Ferrers either). She knew that someone had to stay home to see to the housework and to have a meal ready for the visitors when they returned. And not just the visitors; all eight of her children were at home, from Doris, aged 26 years down to ten year old Hubert. Quite a houseful!

By the summer of 1928, Bernard was probably engaged to Annie Green from Crowland. For Annie Bull's diary entry for Wednesday 15 August, she writes: "We had dinner at Bernard's girl's home in Crowland and had a very nice time - returning home in time for tea." (Note: Again "dinner" was the main meal and tea would have been taken at about 5:30pm with bread and butter, jam or savory spreads, cakes or pastries, etc., along with cups of tea of course!). At Rock House, trifles and jellies appeared regularly, too.

The last part of the diary entry for the 15th reads, "Spent a quiet evening at home with Aunt Fanny." Joan is certain that such quiet evenings were common at Gilpin Street, (and especially for Fanny). She is also certain that the family made every effort to welcome their American cousins, organizing visits to the cathedral and various places of interest, ensuring too, that they met up with Aunt Rose's daughters, Dora and Lily Prentice in nearby Peakirk. The visitors apparently had "a very enjoyable time" in Peakirk and were pressed to return for another visit before they left Peterborough.

There was an outing, too, on their first evening at Gilpin Street when they went to the New England Cinema in Occupation Road, only a five minute walk away. Annie writes: "In the evening went to a picture show - saw Jack Mulhall in the 'The Poor Nut'. The Mould family were great patrons of this cinema, often going twice a week when the films changed. [Annie's diary can be found in its entirety in Appendix XV.]

What a wonderful treat these outings must have been: an escape to look forward to during the hectic, repetitive routine at Rock House. The "pictures" would transport them into a different world, enlivened with drama, glamour, often laughter and fun. These last three were in short supply at Gilpin Street, especially for Fanny, but there would be dramatic events later........

Joan Bolton admits that she has only a vague recollection of her grandmother, since she was only four years old when her grandmother died in February 1947. Fortunately, Olive Coleman, Ann Antill and Enid Withers, have contributed their recollections to build up a clearer picture of their grandmother and Rock House. Ursula Mould's memories from the three and a half years she (and Hubert) spent at Gilpin Street (August 1947 - January 1951), have, of course, been invaluable, but it has to be remembered that her mother-in-law had died six months before Ursula arrived.

Joan had never expected to find anyone from outside the family who would remember Fanny Mould more than fifty years after her death. But just before the start of the new millenneum, she had cause to telephone a writer living in Peterborough - Margaret Winham, n'ee Blackwell. During their conversation, Joan was amazed to learn that Margaret's parents had lived on St. Paul's Road, New England, during the 1930's and '40's and had been her grandfather's milk customers. Better still, Margaret remembered being sent to Rock House to fetch some milk as a little girl of seven or eight, in the late 1930's. She remembered her first visit clearly. She made the mistake of knocking at the front door, but no one came. When she knocked a second time, and more loudly, she heard a woman's voice shout "Go to the back door, not the front!" Awaiting her at the "back" door was an old lady wearing a huge white apron with a bib to it. (Fanny would have been about seventy by then.) Under this garment she wore a black skirt which reached her ankles and a white blouse. On her feet she wore black boots. Fanny poured the milk into the white enamel can Margaret had brought with her.

The reprimand the little girl received for daring to knock at the front door, highlights the custom at that time: only special friends and visitors were admitted at the front, or someone of a high social standing, such as the family doctor, or the vicar, paying a call. The back door was "the tradesmen's entrance", except that in this case, no-one could remember the front door of Rock House ever opening.

Margaret Winham remembered something else on her visits: "Mrs. Mould cupped her hand to one ear and asked me to speak up, so I got the impression that she was a bit deaf." None of Fanny's grandchildren could confirm this, but, if true, suggests she would have enjoyed the cinema visits less once the silent (films) movies gave way to the "talkies" in the late 1920's.

When young Margaret walked round to the dairy from her home on St. Paul's Road, she headed in the direction of Lincoln Road. Turning left onto Gilpin Street, number 59 was the first house she would come to on her left. Rock House was a detached residence, facing (roughly) westwards towards the Lincoln Road and the railway beyond. The wide path to the side door was to the left of the house.

And now for a guided tour of the family home, with some of the memories it evokes, starting of course at the back door. This opened into a small lobby: to the left was the scullery and to the right a rather dark kitchen, with light coming in from just one sash window.

In the scullery there was a large sink below the window overlooking the yard at the back. From here, Fanny would attach a hose pipe to the cold tap (there was no hot tap) and pass it through the window to wash out the milk churns below. Like so many other chores, this one would fall to Marjorie on her mother's death. There was a large copper for boiling water and a mangle to squeeze out most of the moisture from the washing before it was hung up to dry. Here, too, lived the gas cooker, with gas rings on top and an oven underneath. The lavatory led off from the scullery.

Outbuildings behind Rock House. Picture taken in 2003.

Stepping into the kitchen, you had the window immediately to your right and then the black kitchen range, with its coal fire burning in the grate (except in summer) and its integral oven. The gas stove was used for most of the cooking, but Ursula remembered the vegetable saucepans being placed on the range - and forgotten - so the contents were often reduced to a pulp.

Beyond the range were some shelves and on the top one the family kept a box of loose change. All of them seemed to dip into this communal "purse", presumably intended for household necessities. Or was it primarily in order to have change for customers at the door? If the latter was the case, then some of the milk money kept it topped up. At any rate, this happy-go-lucky arrangement typified the milk business at Rock House.

On the other side of the kitchen was a large table standing by the wall, with a chair at each end. Ursula confirmed that, although the main meals (dinner and high tea) were taken in the dining room next door, George would have his breakfast at the kitchen table before setting out on his round. Eric too would often have some breakfast in the kitchen after completing his first round. Ursula's most useful memories of life at Rock House were, of course, from the three years she lived there with Hubert from August of 1947. After Fanny's death six months before, the family's routine would have changed considerably. But in any case, for most of her married life, Fanny had been acustomed to rising early, before everyone else and eating breakfast by herself.

But certainly in the Mould household where business and family merged, the hub of all the activity was the kitchen. The three "milkmen", George, Eric and Guilf, would be coming back to the dairy for more milk, often popping their heads round the kitchen door with a piece of news or a message. Before Cyril, the eldest brother, left to get married in 1928, there were ten people living at Gilpin Street.

With Fanny's day so taken up with work for the dairy and, doubtless, many other chores, she would have been pleased to see that from quite a young age, Marjorie was proving so capable in the kitchen. In fact, on leaving school, she was able to take over most of the cooking whilst sister Iris - though always rather "slow" - was content to make the custard and the gravy.

The meals served up every day were good and satisfying, according to Ursula, and she had no complaints, apart from the vegetables being overcooked, as mentioned earlier. Ursula also noticed the family's predilection for milk puddings, jellies and trifles. The main factor here, she soon realized, was not so much that they all had a "sweet tooth" but rather that Fanny and Doris (at least) had no teeth at all and seemed reluctant to wear their dentures!

A door at the far end of the kitchen led into the hallway, with another door into the dining room immediately to the left. Here the main feature was the dining table with a concealed "leaf" (or extension) at each end. One or both could be pulled out in order to accommodate more people at mealtimes, then slid back to leave more room space afterwards. Either side of the hearth was an armchair: in the evenings, Fanny used to sit to the right of the fire to do her bookkeeping for the dairy. After a long, tiring day and on her feet for much of the time, she must have relished this opportunity to sit by the fireside, even with the adding up to do. Not only were her feet tired, but her legs were badly ulcerated, something Fanny had to put up with for years. Olive had a clear recollection of her grandmother, sitting very close to the open fire. After removing the bandages, she positioned her sore legs directly in front of the flames. Olive remembered the smell. Was Fanny attempting to burn the ulcers or did the intense heat bring her some sort of relief? Did she ever seek treatment? Olive was eighteen when her grandmother died and it was only subsequently that she wondered if the ulcers had been cancerous. She believed there had been talk of Fanny going into hospital at some point. But even if she had, it is hard to imagine her following medical advice, especially if it involved resting or "taking it easy". She would have felt her presence at home was indispensable and that she had to "soldier on".

Whether George ever sat with his wife in the evenings is uncertain: Olive thought not. The couple's relationship had become strained with the passing years and Fanny must have suspected that someone else had supplanted her in George's affections - even in their "twilight years". She had always risen early to start her work before anyone else was around: it was not unusual for her to embark on the washing at 4am, after lighting the fires. This meant that, by eight o'clock at night, she was ready to collapse into bed, exhausted. George had to work hard, too, of course, possibly much harder than he had imagined when starting up the dairy. Getting up early everyday to deliver the milk, whatever the weather and no matter how you felt, required great self-discipline. Guilf Mould summed it up well: "You couldn't afford the luxury of being ill. If you felt off-colour, you had to drag yourself out of bed and do your round". Joan didn't think that Eric and Pollie, Guilf and Mary (her parents) or especially her grandparents, ever

134

managed so much as a weekend away together while they were involved with the dairy.

George and Fanny were very different in temperament: she,seemed serious, intense, "up-tight", whereas he was far more relaxed and easy going. He enjoyed a good read, liked writing letters (one to his brother Jabez' widow, Sarah Annie Mould, in the USA has survived), and apparently he also wrote poetry, though, sadly, none of this has come to light. In the summer he would go for long cycle rides in the surrounding countryside. The one he recorded in the letter took place in 1951 when George was in his seventy eighth year - so his milk rounds obviously kept him fit! He not only had other interests outside of his work but ensured that he made time for them. The question, then, is this: did he also ensure that his wife had time for herself and the opportunity to relax from the drudgery? There were surely many occasions when she must have felt resentful and "taken for granted".

As Fanniy pored over the accounts beside the dining room fire each evening, she grew increasingly annoyed by her husband's easy-going approach to the financial side of the business. It was quite obvious that some of the customers on his round were taking advantage of their kind milkman, allowing their debts to build up and then pleading poverty to avoid paying. Incredibly, George often let them off, even suggesting he would "wipe the slate clean" to give the errant customer a fresh start. Small wonder the Mould family had money problems! (Apparently the business came close to bankruptcy on at least one occasion.)

Hubert Mould told Ursula how, as a young man, he was given the unwelcome task of going round to the customers' doors to collect the money. When they came out with their "hard luck" stories, Hubert told them in no uncertain terms that if they didn't pay up, they would receive no more milk. "They soon found the money then!" Ursula observed.

It was Olive who told Joan that the dining room had French windows which looked onto the rear yard. She remembered this detail because as a girl (in the mid-to-late 1930's), she and her two younger brothers would go to Gilpin Street with their parents on Bonfire Night (5th November) to watch the fireworks. Their Uncle Hubert had the job of letting them off in the yard while the rest of the family enjoyed the spectacle from behind the french windows, in the comfort of the dining room. For Hubert, being master of the family fireworks was, doubtless far preferable to giving errant customers "a rocket" over their milk debts.

Now to leave the dining room behind, with all the associated memories, and peep into the remaining room downstairs - the front room. As in many homes of this period, the sitting room (or parlour) was only really used on special occasions - when visitors called, for instance, and at Christmas. This room at Gilpin Street was the only one with a bay window, looking on to the street. Mainly for reasons of privacy, most of the windows at Rock House had net curtains, as well as heavier ones which were drawn to at night. In

135

place of the heavy curtains, Margaret Winham remembered seeing wooden venetian blinds at some of the windows.

When Doris and Ernest came back to Gilpin Street to live in 1941, the front room became their bed-sitting-room, effectively depriving the family of its use. At Christmas, however, Fanny saw to it that the bed was pushed to the side, so that the room could be used when the family was invited round.

Upstairs there were three bedrooms and a small storage room which Marjorie used for storing hard fruits such as apples, later to be used in her pies and puddings. (Some fruits were preserved by bottling in glass Kilner jars.) There was no upstairs bathroom or toilet. The only occasion Joan Bolton went upstairs was to look at the glass cases containing stuffed birds on the landing.

So far there has been little mention of the outbuildings at Rock House, apart from the area where the milk churns stood, immediately behind the scullery's rear facing window under an awning. In warm weather, Ursula recalled, the churns would stand in a bath of cold water.

A second bath tub was kept in one of the brick outbuildings against the rear boundary of the yard: this was brought into the warmth of the kitchen so that all the family could have their weekly bath. In the adjoining store place the coal was kept. Also in one of the outbuildings, possibly where the bath was stored, was an old fashioned copper for boiling the washing, similar to the one in the scullery.

Also outside at the back was a covered area where a local coal merchant kept his cart. (In fact we know that George had purchased the property from a coal merchant so it could have been the same man.) Above the cart-house, young Hubert had made a small dark room for his photography, most likely in the mid-1930's when he was into his teens. He installed electric lighting in his loft, an event which helped persuade his mother to have electricity in the main house.

In another section of these outbuildings was "the barn", where a lovely big doll's-house was kept. Olive remembered being transfixed by this when she was a small girl.

To the south side of the house was a garden enclosed by wire fencing with a gate where the two pet tortoises roamed. (One was called Toby, the other was Joey.) There was a wooden summer house within this enclosed area. Marjorie used to tend this garden and grew flowers in it but after she died of cancer in 1953 it became neglected.

Not surprisingly, perhaps, Joan's happiest memories of Gilpin Street are of Christmas gatherings. There would be a special tea at the table (including a Christmas trifle, no doubt!). One memory that stands out is of her grandfather pouring some of his tea into the saucer to drink because it was too hot. Joan's mother concealed her disapproval, but Joan well knew her views on drinking - (or "slurping"!) tea in this way. Since George also had a rather droopy moustache, it was fascinating to see how the tea would reach his lips.

The meal over, they would adjourn to the front room to enjoy the open fire and conversation. Marjorie would put a record on the turntable of the gramophone and wind it up. (The records in that era, the late 1940's-early 50's, were "78's", which readily broke if handled roughly.)

Most ordinary homes were still lit by gaslight during the first part of the twentieth century. Fanny, who was rather resistant to change, had eventually agreed to have electricity installed but had retained a gaslight in the front room. This was something Ursula found enchanting the first winter after she arrived in 1947. As a child, Joan found all the rooms at Rock House very sombre and somewhat forbidding. There were arrangements of dried flowers - some in cases. Other cases contained stuffed birds - (even a small deer in one!), whilst the display cabinets were full of china (crockery) and ornaments.

Aunt Doris, a most fervent convert to the Roman Catholic church, would rattle off an account of the mass she had attended, with added details about the recent Saints' days, along with what she had said to the priest. Poor Ernest, her husband, who had contracted sleepy-sickness before they married, was by now a sad figure, slumped in his chair, his tongue lolling.

All of the family spoke quickly. Such gabbling must have proved a huge problem for Ursula, of course, when she arrived from Germany. The radio, which was on in the evenings, proved easier for her to follow but no one had time to listen to the radio during the day - they were far too busy.

It is not difficult to imagine the delight Fanny and George felt when their first child, Doris, was born at Gunthorpe on April 15th 1901. The couple had been married for two and a half years and Fanny was thirty years old.

In what was probably the earliest photograph of their little daughter, taken at the age of about fifteen months, we see a pretty, chubby-faced blonde child, astride a rocking horse. This might well have been taken in a photographer's studio - typically the prerogative of a family's first-born. (There is no evidence that any of Doris' seven siblings were similarly favoured!)

In a later photo, taken in about 1907, Doris is in the garden at Gunthorpe with her two younger brothers, Cyril and Bernard. Cyril is sitting in a deck chair while Doris is leaning against her father, one arm draped over the back of the chair. She is holding a book, smiling coyly at the camera and obviously posing for the unknown photographer. Even at the age of six, Doris looks intelligent. With her now dark hair curling down on to her shoulders, she is even prettier than before - and she knows it! She also has the air of a child who is used to getting her own way. As an experienced teacher, Fanny would have realized from early on that her eldest child might well prove to be a challenge.

Even before Doris was five and a half, she had been joined by four young brothers to compete for her parents' attention. In many families an older daughter can turn out to be a great help with younger brothers and sisters but this was not the case with Doris: she was never interested in such down-to-earth matters as household chores. In fact she seemed to live on an altogether different plane - and certainly in the world of her own imagination.

Doris' niece, Olive Coleman, treasures an essay her aunt submitted for a competition held by the Peterborough Citizen in 1913. In it, Doris extols the wild violet as a symbol of of spring and expresses herself in language far more sophisticated than that of the average twelve year old. Unsurprisingly, Doris' efforts won her the first prize.

Everyone in the family credited Doris with having a "marvelous brain",

Doris Mould - daughter of George and Fannie. Photo taken about 1903.

but did this make her something of a "loner"? Certainly no-one can remember her having many friends. Did Doris resent the fact that her mother was too busy tending to the younger children to give her all the attention she craved for herself? Did she then seek attention and approval through her academic achievements? At school she would surely have won the approbation of her teachers, even if ostracized by her classmates as a "teacher's pet".

It is perhaps surprising that Doris showed no inclination to follow in her mother's footsteps and become a teacher. Joan Bolton believes she went on to do shorthand and typing after leaving Lincoln Road School - possibly to Felix Bean's College in the Cathedral Precincts. This would have enabled her to take up a job in the Bus Depot offices at Millfield, in around 1917 or 1918, when she would have been sixteen or seventeen years old. Indeed , her marriage certificate is further evidence of this when she gives her job as being "Omnibus Company's Shorthand Typist" - no matter that this employment did not last long.

Of all the brothers, Eric and Guilf frequented Rock House the most at that time, since they were working on the family milk rounds. They saw first hand what was going on. Ann Antill remembers her father, Eric, relating how "Doris wouldn't get up in the morning" - a trait unlikely to endear her to any employer - and she was eventually given the sack from the depot. Joan recalls her father, Guilf, also being most critical of his sister, regretting that "she hadn't put her talents to better use", and that Doris was "a law unto herself".

As a young woman, Doris became very involved in religion. Her parents were Anglicans by upbringing but the family appeared not to be regular church attendees. Their local church, St. Paul's was at The Triangle, where Walpole Street (now Bourges Boulevard) joined Lincoln Road, with Occupation Road forming the base of the triangle. This would have been no more than a three-minute walk from Rock House. But, for some reason, it was to the Roman Catholic tradition that Doris was drawn, eventually becoming a convert. This involvement soon reached the point of obsession and she would walk up to All Saint's Church in Geneva Street virtually every day to attend mass, or to arrange the flowers there.

When Jabez Mould's son, George Ewart Mould, came over to England from the USA in the summer of 1927, he and his family visited Gilpin Street and took a photo of their English relations in the garden - Doris amongst them. Then twenty-six years old, she should have been "in her prime". But although quite pretty, she lacked the comely charms possessed by most young women her age: not so much 'slim' as 'thin as a rake', and it must be said, completely flat-chested. From the age of puberty, Doris came to hate the idea of womanhood. She would eat very little - her staple diet at one time seemed to be digestive biscuits with tea - and took purgatives and other medicine to suppress menstruation.

In view of all this, therefore, it must have come as something of a surprise to those who knew her when Doris began courting in the mid-1920's. The young man in question was Ernest Maile. Born in Peterborough in August 1932, he was the youngest of five children. His father, John, worked as a railway plate-layer.

Ernest was a pleasant, presentable young man, sixteen months Doris' junior and with an intellect to match hers. When they first met, he was probably still working at Baker Perkins factory. All of this was "the good news". But "the bad news" was that Ernest was already in the early stages of an illness known as sleepy-sickness (or encephalitis lethargica), which he and several other employees had contracted, possibly, from handling imported wood in the factory's oven shop. It was inevitable, therefore, that Ernest would eventually have to leave his job at the factory and review his future.

Although present-day members of the Mould family (mainly Doris' nieces) knew that she and Ernest had taken on a newsagent's shop near Hastings on the Sussex coast, no-one could say with certainty whether this was before or after the marriage. In either case, Joan assumed that the wedding itself would have taken place in Peterborough - the bride's town - as was customary. Her assumption was wrong: the couple did not marry in Peterborough at all but in Hastings (per the marriage certificate). The ceremony took place in the Roman Catholic church in Magdalen Road (St. Thomas' and the English Martyrs) on June 20th 1932 - a Monday. Doris was thirty one years old whilst Ernest was two months short of his thirtieth birthday.

The certificate makes it clear that the couple had already embarked on their business venture, since Ernest gives his "profession" as being a 'Master Newsagent'. (The word "master" in this context indicating that he employed people in the business, cf. George Mould - Master Dairyman).

More interestingly, in the column headed, 'Residence at the time of Marriage', both bride and groom gave the same address: "15 Mercatoria, St. Leonards-on-Sea". This could have been where the newsagents and tobacconists shop was situated, with living quarters possibly above. But any reader inclined to jump to a conclusion should read on.............

What can be stated with certainty is that this marriage was quite an event. Not for Doris the rather low-key wedding for which the four older Mould brothers settled; she was going to enjoy her "big day", with no expense spared - as the photographs prove.

The main group photograph certainly captures a happy occasion. The bride is wearing a long, elegant ivory dress with a train. The close-fitting Juliet cap is reminiscent of the headwear worn by Elizabeth Bowes-Lyon when she married the future King, George VI in 1923. She has three attendants - her two younger sisters, Marjorie and Iris, and a seven or eight year old bridesmaid, Beryl Maile.

This little girl is identified in the wedding report from the Hastings and St. Leonards Observer, as "Miss Beryl Maile, niece". She must, therefore, be the daughter of Ernest's only brother, Charles Maile, who was about twelve years his senior. The lady who is smiling at the very back of the group on the left, could well be Charles Maile's wife and the mother of the small bridesmaid: the girl certainly bears a striking resemblance to this lady. All three attendants are beautifully attired and are carrying such large "posies" that one imagines they would have had a problem if called on to hold the bride's train. Doris' bouquet of lilies is even bigger. The groom is smart too, of course, and smiling broadly.

Marriage of Doris Mould to Ernest Maile. L-R: Bridesmaid Iris Mould Best Man, Bill Toyne, Groom Ernest Maile, Mrs. Charles Maile, Bride Doris Mould, Florence Toyne, Emily and Charles Mould, Bridesmaid Marjorie Mould, George Mould. In front: Beryl Maile.

The wedding report also reveals that the priest conducting the ceremony was the Revd. Father O'Donoghue and the reception was held "at the home of the bridegroom", (presumably, at the Mercatoria address.)

The best man to the left of the group behind Iris is Bill Toyne, Ernest's brother-in-law. He was also the verger at St. Paul's Church in Peterborough, hence one source of the confusion over the place of marriage! The thin-faced rather stern looking lady at the back is Ernest's older sister, Florrie Toyne, wife of the best man. (Florrie was then forty years old and was identified in the photo by her niece, Mrs. Sylvia Watson, nee Toyne, from Peterborough.) The bride's father, George, stands to the far right, with his brother Charlie, from Higham Ferrers near him and behind Marjorie, his niece. The short lady, smiling from under her tall hat, has to be Charles' wife Emily.

The big question, surely, is this: Where is the mother of the bride? Fanny is nowhere to be seen! Had there been a falling out? Was she disappointed that the marriage didn't take place in St. Paul's in Peterborough? Or was it simply that she was "holding the fort" at home? As someone who was never comfortable at social gatherings, might Fanny not have found this a convenient excuse?

The demands of their business would have made it difficult for Doris and Ernest to get away for a long honeymoon but they certainly managed to have a few days in Hertfordshire. A newsagents shop then - as now - had to open seven days a week, closing only for public holidays. In order to have even a day off, the couple would have had to engage someone to cover for them. Not that Doris had any reservations about employing staff: far from it. Never having familiarized herself with the art of housework or cooking, she was content to pay someone to do this for them.

In spite of his encroaching disability, Ernest ran the shop, ordering all the stock - newspapers, magazines, tobacco, cigarettes and other items sold there, such as sweets. Although it was most unlikely that Ernest would get up at crack of dawn to collect the newspapers from the railway depot as they came off the London train, (presumably someone else did that for him), he, or somebody else, would have needed to sort the papers to be ready for the first customers calling in on their way to work, possibly as early as 5:30am. If the shop offered a home delivery service, then each paper boy's allocation of papers and periodicals had to be sorted. But, of one thing we may be sure: Doris would not have been the one overseeing these operations at such an early hour.

What no one seems to know is why Doris and Ernest chose to live in Hastings. If Ernest had had to give up his job at Baker Perkins in Peterborough, the prospect of taking on a shop in entirely different and attractive surroundings would have had its appeal, especially on the south coast where the combination of sunshine and sea air would be beneficial. There was no suggestion that the couple bought the business; far more likely that they saw a shop manager's position advertised in St. Leonards-on-Sea, applied for it and were taken on. With living accommodation provided too, this arrangement would have seemed doubly acceptable - work and "four walls" at a stroke, even if the remuneration would hardly be princely, with the rental deducted first.

When, by the late 1930's, it was learned that the Mailes were struggling to keep the business afloat, no one was surprised - least of all the Moulds.

When it finally foundered in 1941, they all marveled that it had lasted for nine years. Doris' sisters-in-law had wondered from the outset how she and Ernest would "make a go of it". Mary Mould, Guilf's wife, knew better than most how hard it was to run a business and a home and was scathing in her assessment, saying "Doris hadn't the faintest idea how to run a business", and that "it was ridiculous to be paying someone to cook and clean. No wonder they couldn't make ends meet." Guilf agreed, only too aware of his sister's shortcomings, especially having observed her on a daily basis while working for the Gilpin Street dairy. It is more than likely that George and Fanny were called on "to help Doris out" financially.

In the light of how things worked out (or didn't) in St. Leonards, it was possibly better for everyone that Doris and Ernest left Peterborough to start their new life and new venture. To have done so in the full gaze of their families - especially the Moulds - would have been a very bad idea.

But by 1941 there was only one option left for them - to return to Peterborough and the family home in Gilpin Street. This they did - and what a strain this must have put on everyone, especially Fanny. She had just turned seventy but looked a good ten years older. Hubert was twenty-four, working in Peterborough and still at home. Marjorie (thirty-two) and her younger sister Iris (twenty-eight) were living at Gilpin Street and seemed unlikely to marry.

The dairy work still had to be done, though Marjorie was able to take over some of this. Fanny had ulcers on both of her legs, which were now permanently bandaged; all this slowed her down. Undoubtedly she would not have relished the prospect of having two extra people under her roof, one a semi-invalid, the other her eccentric strong-willed daughter who, she knew, would offer little practical help.

But if the welcome for the returning "prodigal" did not quite match up to the Biblical benchmark, her parents doubtless did the best they could. Any deficiencies on Fanny's part were more than compensated for by George's solicitude for the couple's well being and the front parlor downstairs became their bed-sitting room. In all fairness, it must be said that for Doris, too, it would have been very difficult being back again with her parents after enjoying nine years of independence - and by now a married woman of forty. Many women in her situation would have seen it also as a loss of face and felt that they had failed. But there is no evidence that Doris viewed it in this way at all.

For Ernest, though, it must have been more difficult. He was now living under his in-laws' roof and no longer in control of his own destiny. One would like to think that, in difficult times, Doris and Ernest at least had each other to turn to for comfort and consolation. But, very sadly, the reality was otherwise. Theirs was no normal marriage and it is doubtful if any intimacy ever took place between them - much as Ernest might have welcomed it. The story goes that, on returning from their "honeymoon", Doris wrote to her parents, proudly announcing that she was still "virgo intacta"!

Once back in Peterborough, Doris and Ernest had to pick up the threads of their lives again. Always a good correspondent, Doris had maintained contact with her brothers' families, remembering all the birthdays with at least a card and, for the nephews and nieces, gifts of money.

Needless to say, she wasted no time in renewing contact with her former church 'family', returning to All Souls, often with Ernest on her arm. Close, personal friends, though, were few and far between.

As Ernest's health continued to deteriorate, Doris had to spend more time seeing to his needs. This would be her reason - or excuse - for not seeking another job.

What reaction did Doris meet with from her sisters, Marjorie and Iris on her return? By 1941, Marjorie had virtually taken over the cooking and general running of Rock House, with Iris helping with the simple tasks, such as making the gravy and the custard. Both might have accepted the extra work more readily if their sister had shown any inclination to "pitch in" and help. Unfortunately, Doris hadn't changed and was as impossible as ever. Iris had never gotten on with her eldest sister, becoming ever more grumpy when Doris appeared. Though slow in many ways, she was quick to retort when riled by Doris and it was left to Marjorie to arbitrate and restore sisterly harmony.

Rock House was still a hive of activity in 1941, with George in his late sixties still running the dairy with his two sons. The 'zoning system' introduced during the war made their work more complicated - their zone was now only to the eastern side of Lincoln Road, so they had to reorganize their milk routes. Then there were the milk coupons to cope with, due to the rationing.

Ann Antill recalled one Gilpin Street ritual that took place regularly. One evening a week, after their rounds were finished, her grandfather, George, her father, Eric, and uncle, Guilf, sat down at the dining table "to do the crossword". Although the family had long enjoyed this pastime - (probably a welcome opportunity to sit down after a hard day's work), by the 1940's it had become a seriously competitive activity, with good prizes at stake.

Their favored crossword appeared in a Sunday paper, the News of the World, noted for its rather lurid and sensationalist contents. Certain clue words were known as "bankers", (i.e. not to be changed or substituted on the entry coupons). There was much lively and, often, heated discussion about these. For other clues, two or three words could fit. The little syndicate would submit several entries to increase their chances of winning. Indeed, Eric and Guilf won some worthwhile cash prizes, and Ann would be surprised if George didn't also.

After returning to Gilpin Street to live in 1941, Doris would join in these sessions. With her extensive vocabulary, she had always excelled at crosswords and, for once, her contributions were welcomed. It is quite possible that her mother occasionally had a say too.

Cyril Mould's oldest son, Arthur, (Olive's brother), said that one of his abiding memories of Rock House was the bickering that went on. Often this was between the Mould sisters but it was certainly a regular occurence when they were hammering out the crossword, especially if Doris was present. There were, however, times when the three sisters worked together, setting aside their disagreements. It was noticeable that their father was taking longer to complete his milkround and returning home later than before. With all the contacts the Moulds had, it could not be very long before Fanny was enlightened. Sure enough, her husband's distinctive tricycle had been seen regularly, parked in a street at the town end of Lincoln Road - Manor House Street, in fact.

As already mentioned, Doris had wasted no time in renewing contact with the Roman Catholic church nearest to town - St. Peter and All Souls. Now forty years old, her devotion to her church was matched by her energy, and Doris became a familiar figure as she strode along Lincoln Road to attend mass, wearing her trademark mackintosh and wellington boots, whatever the weather. How convenient that All Souls, situated on the Park Road end of Geneva Street, was a mere stone's throw away from Manor House Street! It would have taken Doris just a minute or two longer to route herself along the latter, even allowing time to look out for the tell-tale bike.

Marjorie went along on some of these spying missions and although Iris stayed at home, she was well aware of what was afoot.

There were unlikely to be many milk customers in Manor House Street since it was at the furthest extremity of the dairy's zone. Once Doris had identified the right house, she could easily find the customer's name in her father's milkround book. Then a few "innocent" inquiries after mass whilst speaking to local worshippers, would be enough to establish that the householders were out at work during the week but employed a housekeeper. She was a single lady in her forties and her name was Dorothy Ayres.

Confirmation that something was indeed going on came from another quarter. Olive related how, as a twelve or thirteen year old schoolgirl, her grandfather asked her to do him a favor. Knowing how good she was at artwork, he wondered if she would paint "a nice card for a special friend". Olive agreed, but had express instructions not to take it round to Rock House: he would collect it himself. She made several cards like this one but, though curious, only found out later who the recipient was.

Olive's curiosity was further aroused when she took part in a concert, whilst still at secondary school in Beech Avenue. She had made friends with a girl in her class called Celia Anton whose father had formed a concert party - the Antonian Players. Another of Olive's talents was tap dancing, and she was invited to join the group. Since her grandfather had expressed a wish to see one of their shows, Olive decided to send him a ticket through the post. George went along to the Elwes Hall, (which was not far from Olive's school) and thoroughly enjoyed himself. However, speaking to his

144

granddaughter afterwards, he confided that the letter had been opened by his daughters. Their excuse was that the handwriting resembled their brother Guilf's. (All this happened round about 1942/43 during the Second World War when he was serving in the army, though based in England.)

It was only later that the truth dawned on Olive: her aunts were looking out for letters from this lady friend, doubtless hoping to discover what their father was getting up to. Was it the intention to tell their mother? Surely, at some point she must have guessed that something was going on?

The story has it that Fanny decided to write a letter to the lady concerned. Though the actual contents may never be known, it is easy to imagine the message conveyed, and very likely along these lines: "If my husband has told you that his wife doesn't understand him, please permit me to enlighten you. After being married to him for forty-five years and having borne him eight children, this wife understands him only too well. You should be aware that your association with him is causing myself and the family great distress. We would therefore request that you give him no further encouragement ....."

It was Doris who was entrusted with the task of delivering the letter in person, but (again, according to the "grapevine"), did not do so. Presumably, Fanny needed to be sure the letter was delivered or otherwise she would simply have posted it. But Doris could be devious: it seems as though she agreed to take it but then failed to deliver it, letting her mother believe that she had. More intriguingly, what was Doris' motivation in all of this? But then, she had always been "a law unto herself" and was well known within the wider family for making trouble.

Few families are without their problems, of course, and it should be remembered that the "back-drop" to everyone's life in Britain in the early 1940's was the war. The Moulds were fortunate; of their five sons, only one - Hubert, the youngest - was sent to fight abroad. Guilford, the next youngest, was thirty-three when war broke out. He served in England with the R.A.O.C. (Royal Army Ordinance Corps) but saw no action.

For many families though it was a very different story; their loved ones never returned, or they came back suffering from their injuries -- physical and mental. Amazingly, considering the importance of its industry and railway, Peterborough got off very lightly in so far as the bombing was concerned.

On Tuesday, May 8th, 1945, Germany surrendered to the Allies and the war in Europe was finally over. There was general rejoicing throughout Britain and, to celebrate this momentous victory in Europe V.E. Day parties were organized in every town and village, mainly for the local children. Because of the acute food shortages suffered during (and long after) the war, it took these communities a few days to pool their rations so that the "mums" could bake and lay on a celebration tea.

In another of her reminiscences, Margaret Winham well remembers the party she herself attended in Gilpin Street. Apparently, trestle tables were set up on the road itself in side streets (which were closed to traffic), but not on main thoroughfares such as St. Paul's Road, where her family lived. Unfortunately, the Gilpin Street organizers decided to have an open fire in the road, which damaged the tarmac surface. So, when V.J. Day (Victory over Japan) was celebrated in August, they were forced to enclose their fire in an old dustbin.

By the end of the war, the four older Mould brothers were married and had families of their own. George and Fanny now had seven grandchildren. Joan, the youngest of the seven, was two-and-a -half on V.E. Day and had good reason to remember the occasion. Less than a mile from Gilpin Street, the Fulbridge Road street party she attended was held opposite her house (number 97). She was sitting at a trestle table with a dozen other children (some were teenagers) after enjoying their special tea. The table had been set up on a large patch of grass next to the pavement and was parallel with Fulbridge Road. Suddenly Joan caught sight of her mother who had come to the garden gate at the opposite side of the road and, without any warning, dashed across straight into the path of an approaching car. Luckily, cars at that time travelled more slowly than today and had chassis that were higher off the ground. Even more fortunately for Joan, although knocked down, she lay safely between the car wheels as it passed over her and suffered only a few bruises. All the same, she was taken to hospital and kept there under observation for a day or two - possibly this was the small temporary hospital at the army camp in nearby Tennyson Road. One of the older children at this party was Michael Savage (later ordained into the Anglican church). Twelve years old at the time, he remembered the episode clearly sixty years later and was able to tell Joan that the driver of the car was a Mr. Jepson who had a garage at Dogsthorpe.

This little drama doubtless served to fix the event in the memories of the other children too .....and brought the party to an abrupt halt!

It was around the middle of January of 1947 that the Mould family received some very worrying news: Fanny had unexpectedly been admitted to hospital, but not to the Peterborough Memorial Hospital. She had been taken to Bracebridge Heath near Lincoln, forty minutes from Peterborough. There she died about four weeks later on Saturday 15th February, aged seventy six.

On her death certificate, the causes of death given were "1) Broncho Pneumonia" and "2) Arterio Sclerosis Senility". What was not mentioned was the fact that Fanny had made an attempt on her own life by cutting her wrists whilst at home. This explained why she was admitted to Bracebridge Hospital, since the Lincolnshire hospital had a "mental wing". Although the exact date of Fanny's admission to hospital is not known, we do know that it all coincided with one of the worst British winters on record - and the snowiest. The extreme weather conditions would have deterred the family from making the eighty mile round trip to see Fanny, even if they had transport. (The only member of the family to own a car was Guilf, for the purpose of the business.) Poor Fanny must have felt she had been abandoned. Or was she perhaps so ill that she was past caring?

Back at Rock House, it was a terrible struggle to keep things going, both in the home itself and on the business front where the supply of milk was a problem. The food rationing which had begun during the war (and which would continue until the early 1950's) became more severe during that winter (1946/47) and was exacerbated by an acute shortage of coal, because it had become frozen in the ground. This inevitably led to power-cuts being imposed throughout the country, causing factories to close. There was little respite at home either: with domestic coal in short supply, households had to eke out what little they had. Since nearly all homes were dependant on open fires for both heating and cooking, the misery experienced is hard to imagine. Even water was a problem: with so many main pipes cracked and leaking, as well as domestic pipes frozen solid, standpipes had to be installed in the streets. Notwithstanding the "successful" outcome of the war, it would be many years before daily life became easier for British families. The continuing privations and tribulations were enough to test even the most optimistic folk. Fanny had never belonged in this category and all of the circumstances probably combined to break her spirit.

It is difficult for people today to fully appreciate the stigma attached to suicide sixty years ago, but there is no denying its existence. The circumstances preceeding Fanny's admission to hospital remained a closely guarded secret within the family and were seldom mentioned. But this did not stop the speculation, of course.

So what could have driven Fanny to make her suicide attempt? There were several factors. Her health was not good, as has been seen, much of the problem being over-work. Yet she could get no respite from the workload of both home and dairy. In particular, her leg ulcers must have been debilitating.

Was Fanny embittered by the "hand" life had dealt her? Did she come to resent the fact that she had been obliged to give up her teaching career (and the status it carried) in exchange for domestic drudgery? Wives in those days had larger families than their counterparts today: Fanny might have found motherhood demanding and certainly all three of her daughters gave her cause for concern at times. Even within a few years of marrying, those who knew her felt she had "aged" beyond her years.

And then, within the marriage itself, (as already suggested), she had good cause to feel unappreciated and resentful, especially in later years, when she realized she had been supplanted in her husband's affections by someone else.

Much has been said already about the war but, quite apart from all the hardship, it had other repercussions. For one thing, Hubert, her youngest son, had gone to fight "the enemy" in Germany itself. Born ten years after Guilf when Fanny was forty six, Hubert doubtless became "the apple of her eye". She could not wait to see him safely back in Peterborough and perhaps married to a local girl. He was originally due to be "demobbed" in February 1947, but as the time approached, her hopes were dashed. She learned that he would not be returning then, after all. Instead he would return six months later, after marrying his German sweetheart in Berlin. This extension seemed like an eternity.

But there was a further concern: Hubert had asked if he and Ursula could live with them at Gilpin Street after their marriage that summer.

While George was writing his letter to the Oberlanders, (Ursula's parents) to assure them that their only child "would be made very welcome", Fannie was most probably worrying about how the already crowded house could be re-arranged to accommodate the newly-weds. That summer there would be nine adults at Rock House, now that Doris and Ernest were in residence.

Poor Fanny! She was not to know how well her new daughter-in-law would fit in, how hard she was prepared to work, nor how readily all the family would take to her.

The bitter irony was, of course, that Hubert did come back in February to see his mother - but only to find her seriously ill in hospital before she died.

Fanny's funeral service was arranged for Thursday 20th February at St. Paul's, the church where she and Geroge had married in 1898. But, before that, her body had to be brought back to Peterborough - a hazardous venture as the roads were thick with ice and so treacherous that the hearse twice skidded out of control. (There was no organized salting and gritting then!). In fact, fearing the body had been "disorganized" during the journey back, the undertaker took the decision not to open the coffin before the funeral.

In the Peterborough Standard, a weekly paper which came out every Friday, its report for February 21st gave the names of the mourners, as was the custom. The close family were all mentioned (except for Hubert who had probably had to return to the regiment in Germany) but it was noticeable that only three of those present were listed as "friends". One of these, Mr. Albert May, whose tailor's shop was at 423 Walpole Street (Kelly's Directory of 1940), was a close neighbor to the Moulds, living at a bungalow in Gilpin Street.

Although well known in the New England area for her part in running the dairy, Fanny could never be described as "sociable". She lived and worked for her family and "kept herself to herself". Even when she was younger, it seems she rarely went out, even to go shopping, and had few friends. She would probably have had few acquaintances either, had it not been for close neighbors and customers coming to the door.

According to the 1881 census (previously mentioned), the ten-year old Fanny had two brothers at home with her, William and Richard, and two sisters, Elizabeth and Daisy. With their parents, George and Mary Mills (n'ee Ives), they were living in one of the G.N.R. cottages, on Lincoln Road, quite close to Gilpin Street. The eldest daughter, Elizabeth, was two years older than Fanny, whilst the youngest child, Daisy, was eight years younger, aged two. (Unsurprisingly, since Mary was forty five at the time of the census, no more children were born.)

William, then eight, eventually married, moving with Ruby, his wife, to a small place called Holme outside Peterborough. (This brother was listed amongst the mourners at his sister's funeral.) Richard (or Dick) was known as the "bad boy of the family", according to Daisy's daughter, Dot Anderson, in Canada. Missing from the 1881 census was Mary's first child, Polly Ives, and half-sister to the other children. According to Guilf Mould, quite a mystery surrounded his Aunt Polly's origins and he related the following story concerning his maternal grandmother, Mary Ives: born around 1935/36 in London, she went into service straight from school at the age of thirteen or fourteen and later found employment with the Duke and Duchess of Buccleuch, as lady's maid to their daughters. Whilst in their service, she became pregnant and gave birth to a daughter out of wedlock early in 1862. Since the Duke and Duchess moved in royal circles, there was much speculation as to the identity of the father and whether Polly might have had "blue blood" in her veins! But, in any case, nothing in those days could remove the stigma attached to having a child outside of marriage.

A few months after the baby's birth, Mary married George Mills (from Kent) who was five years her junior. Their first child, Elizabeth, was born in Peterborough in 1868. Apart from census information from 1881, 1891 and 1901, little is known about Fanny's elder sister, but interestingly, she was still living at home in 1901, aged thirty two and unmarried .

As they grew up, Fanny and Daisy developed a close bond and, when her younger sister married the dashing Guy Wilders at Paston church in 1904, Fanny and George would surely have been present. The Wilders had four children - Ronald, Claude, Dorothy, and Jack, all similar in ages to the Mould children. (Guilford, especially remembered playing with Claude as a boy.) But when Guy and Daisy decided to emigrate to Canada with their family, the parting would undoubtedly have been very sad for the sisters. Daisy was stepping out into the unknown and uprooting herself from the town where she had grown up. Although she did return once to England with her daughter, it is certain that Fanny never ventured abroad. All that the two sisters could do was to correspond and they did.

By sad coincidence, Daisy learned of Fanny's death at about the time of her own birthday. She turned sixty-eight on the 19th February, 1947, the day before her sister's funeral.

Fanny's death obviously cast a pall of sadness over all the family, and especially at Rock House. The harshness of that winter did not help, of course, with the snow lingering on the ground from January until mid-March.

When, in August, Hubert came back to Peterborough with Ursula, his young German wife, Rock House came alive again. More cheering still, the following year Ursula gave birth to a baby boy - Laurence, George's ninth grandchild. There were now eight people living under one roof. With another year or so still to run, the dairy operation still engendered its normal bustle, making the house feel even more crowded.

It was during this period that Doris surprised everyone by taking on a new role as "nanny" to her small nephew. With everyone so busy, (not the least Ursula herself), Doris offered to take Laurence out in the pram, going so far as the town center where he was introduced to everyone at All Souls Church; then on to the cathedral - as well as to the shops, of course. His mother would bemoan the fact that she hardly saw her son, except to feed him and change his nappy (diaper). This task obviously suited Doris very well, with the added advantage of avoiding any involvement in the housework.

From Doris' point of view, there was another distinct advantage in taking her small nephew out for such nice long walks. It was a good opportunity to keep an eye on her father's movements. She knew that one favorite customer on his round was occupying ever more of his attention these days, now that he was a widower.

Early in 1951, Hubert and Ursula moved to their new home in Newark Avenue and were able to have their little son to themselves. Rock House returned more or less to how it had been in the summer of 1947, with George, his three daughters and Ernest in residence. But with the milk business having been sold the year before, the hustle and bustle had ceased, leaving the old home a quiet and dreary place, disturbed only by the sisterly bickering.

Doris must have missed Laurence terribly, especially at first, and would walk over to Hubert's as often as three times a day. Even she must have realized how busy they were, settling into their new house and trying to "get everything straight". On some occasions - though not all - Doris would drag poor Ernest along. Ursula recalls that these visits usually coincided with meal times, and wondered if Doris was checking that she was feeding her family properly. Ursula, of course, had never had the opportunity to demonstrate her culinary skills at Gilpin Street, apart from preparing the vegetables (before they were reduced to a pulp!) - but proved to be an excellent and adventurous cook. Not that her finicky sister-in-law, of all people, was in any position to judge!

Now mistress in her own home, Ursula was better able to limit these visits, as well as Lollie's outings with his eccentric aunt. The little boy had plenty of space at home to play with his toys and by the summer of 1952 he had been joined by a baby brother.

The following year was a momentous one for Doris and all of the Moulds. On the Easter Monday in April 1953 George married again, aged seventy-nine. His bride was Dorothy Ayres, from the tiny village of Broughton near Huntingdon and at fifty-two, twenty-seven years his junior. It must be said that this marriage met with considerable disapproval - and ridicule - from some of the family. Most had no desire to travel to Broughton for the wedding, which took place in the village church. Eric Mould's wife, Pollie, and their daughter Ann, then nineteen, did make the effort to be there. As to whether Doris attended is uncertain, but she would have hated to miss out on the conclusion to a romance she had followed so tenaciously.

Yes, this was the lady George had first met on his milk round some ten years before. At least, they had allowed a respectable amount of time to elapse following Fannie's death - six years in fact. But in light of subsequent events, they might have wished they had taken this bold step sooner.

Sadly, the marriage was only to last four days, since George never regained consciousness after falling from his bicycle near Broughton where the couple had set up home together.

Although virtually everyone in the Mould family knew Dorothy Ayres as the lady George Mould had married in the April of 1953, it soon became apparent that very little was known about her. They knew that she was from the small village of Broughton in Huntingdonshire and that George had met her whilst delivering milk to a family in Manor House Street, Peterborough, where Miss Ayres was working as housekeeper. This street - though some little distance from the dairy - was to the eastern side of Lincoln Road and therefore in the zone allocated to Rock House during WW2, according to the recollections of Olive Coleman. As also mentioned previously, from about the age of twelve, George's artistic granddaughter was regularly asked to paint a card 'for a special friend', so that, taken together, these two facts suggest that the friendship began in the early 1940's. Tragically, of course, their marriage was short-lived since, on the following day, George fell from his bicycle as the couple were descending Fenton Hill, outside Broughton, (where they had set up home together.) He died in Huntingdon Hospital two days later, without regaining consciousness.

Very aware of the controversy this romance had created from the beginning, Joan Bolton originally resisted the temptation to research her step-grandmother's story. She could remember meeting her on just one occasion, during the early summer of 1953, not long after she was widowed. Dorothy Mould called on Joan's parents at their house in Fulbridge Road, (whether by invitation or not is unknown.) She was offered a cup of tea and talked with Guilf and his wife, sitting at the dining-room table. Joan remembered their visitor as being dignified and quietly spoken, but even to the ten-year old girl looking on, this scene bore a touch of the surreal: here was Guilf, meeting for the first time his newly-widowed stepmother, (and only six years his senior!) What a strange mixture of emotions he must have felt, and Mary, too! In the end, their feelings of sympathy for Dorothy prevailed as they realised that her life had been turned upside down. With the benefit of hindsight, Joan reflected that not only was her visit a very brave move, but also a wise one.

It was at the beginning of 2007 that she finally decided to rise to the challenge and find out more about this lady. She wrote to two Huntingdon newspapers, The Hunts Post and The Town Crier, asking if they would publish an appeal for more information. Entitled **'Did you know Dorothy?'** the piece appeared in both publications in the April, fifty-four years after the ill-fated wedding. There were three responses: one gentleman who farmed near Abbots Ripton, phoned to say that, years ago, he had bought Rose Cottage in Broughton, where the Ayres family had lived, and demolished it in order to build a large bungalow on the site. It had later been enlarged, he said, and turned into a care home (actually named 'Rose Cottage Residential home.') But Joan was not entirely convinced this was the same site occupied by '3, Rose Cottages'. All the same, the caller was able to impart some most useful information, not least the names of the main families residing in Broughton. (Perhaps unsurprisingly, most of these were related.) All of these 'leads' were followed up.

There were also two letters. The first was from a lady in her 'eighties' - a Mrs. Joan Cade, nee Ayers, whose father, Percy James Ayres, was Dorothy's first cousin. (In fact, his signature as a witness appears on Dorothy's marriage certificate.) Joan Cade also revealed that Dorothy had a brother, Albert, and a sister, Maggie, who had never married. Albert, apparently, had married somewhat 'late in the day' and had two daughters, Christine and Ruby. Since the correspondent had given her telephone number, Joan wasted no time in contacting her. Amongst other things, she learned that Dorothy 's mother (whose Christian name she thought was Aggie) had gone to look after Joan and her four brothers and sisters when the child, Margot, was born in the 1920's. Joan Cade also told her that, at one stage, Albert had lived opposite her father (who was Albert's cousin) in Moot Way, in the village of Woodhurst near Huntingdon.

Over the next six months the two Joans spoke several times. Both agreed that the person who might be of most help would be Dorothy's niece, Ruby Green, who was thought to live in the Sapley area of Huntingdon. Thanks to these useful leads, Joan Bolton was eventually able to speak to Ruby in late October, (after a six-month search!) Immediately afterwards, she telephoned Mrs Cade to relate the good news - and, of course, to thank her.

The second letter was from the Secretary of the Huntingdonshire Family History Society, Mrs. Caroline Kesseler, who wrote: " I came across your letter in the 'Hunts Post' yesterday, 25th April, 2007...(etc.). I could not resist the challenge and decided to look for Dorothy on the 1901 Census for Broughton, Hunts." I found the following entry:

Edward AYRES, head of household, 32 years old, horse keeper on farm, born at Gt. Raveley, Hunts.

Betsy AYRES, wife, 25 years old, born at Sapley, Hunts.

Dorothy AYRES, daughter, 8 months old, born at Broughton, Hunts."

Mrs. Kesseler went on to say, "I thought she might have had brothers and sisters born after 1901." The timing of this letter was most fortuitous, arriving just minutes before Joan was due to drive to the Family History Centre in Dorchester, with the intention of searching for the Ayres family in the GRO records. This was an encouraging start! She duly found confirmation for most of what Joan Cade had told her, and quite a lot more besides.

There was another surprise at the end of the letter. Mrs. Kesseler continued, " From our list of members," she wrote, "I have found one who is researching the AYRES family of Broughton, and who lives in Peterborough. I have been given permission to pass on his contact details." The gentleman concerned was Mr. Shane Knighton who turned out to be a great nephew of Mrs Cade. A year before, (in 2006), he had been over to Huntingdon to 'interview' her as part of his research. Although Joan Bolton wrote to him straight away, she didn't receive a reply. However, by another strange coincidence, she discovered that he lived only a few doors away from some very good friends of hers. So, when Joan was invited to stay with them in Peterborough the following year, she seized the opportunity to knock on Mr. Knighton's door and introduce herself! She was invited in, and the two 'researchers' were able to exchange some valuable information during the course of their meeting. With so much help from different sources, she was able to build up a better picture of Dorothy and the Ayers family, although still far from complete.

Dorothy Ayres was born on July 20th, 1900, the eldest child of Edward James Ayres and his wife, Betsy, nee Woods. Her parents had married during the December quarter of 1898, (by coincidence, the same year that George and Fanny had married.) Edward Ayres was born in the September quarter of 1868 and, his wife who was seven years younger, (per the 1901 census), was born early in 1876. It is quite likely that Betsy's middle name was Agnes, since her great niece, Joan Cade, remembered her as 'Aggie'.

A son, Albert, arrived almost three years after Dorothy, in April 1903. Then followed two children who died in infancy: a son, Willie, born in June, 1906 and four years later, in the autumn of 1910, a baby daughter, Margery who died at four months. (Shane Knighton found evidence of these two babies from church burial records.) The Ayers' last child, a daughter they named Maggie, was born in May 1913, leaving a gap of thirteen years between the two sisters. Sadly, Joan could glean nothing about Dorothy's childhood, but one of her contacts from Broughton described the Ayres as 'a very private family who liked to keep themselves to themselves'.

It seems that Dorothy worked 'in service' in the Huntingdon area upon leaving school (i.e. from about 1915 onwards), and that her sister opted for similar employment in Huntingdon twelve years or so later. A member of the Castle family, who lived near to the Ayres, recalled that one of the sisters working as a house keeper for a Mr. Hall, a Huntingdon veterinary (or 'vet') in the 1920's or '30's. Ruby believed that her Aunt Maggie had been housekeeper to a lady called Mrs. Driver for quite a few years. What is not known is the year that Dorothy first moved to Peterborough and whether she had worked elsewhere in the city before taking up the post of housekeeper in Manor House Street. She was certainly living there by about 1940, and quite possibly earlier. This we know from the close friendship that developed between Dorothy and George Mould, already fully documented. How often did she manage to get back to Broughton and visit her parents? Living and working under the same roof, she would surely have looked forward to 'escaping' during her time off - especially in the early days.

It would also be interesting to know at which point Dorothy gave up her job in Peterborough in order to return to Broughton, and what prompted her to do so. Betsy, her mother, had died in early July 1946, aged seventy-one (seven months before Fanny Mould, in fact). Left a widower at seventy-seven Edward was fortunate to have his youngest daughter just a few miles away in Huntington, whilst Dorothy, presumably, would have gone over from Peterborough whenever she was free. However, her loyalties were being severely tested now that the friendship with George was deepening. How Dorothy's parents viewed this liaison we simply do not know - but it would not be difficult to guess. After all, her 'friend' was their age - only five years younger than Ted Ayers and two years older than Betsy.

During one of her visits to Dorchester, Joan managed to find the enry for Albert Ayres' marriage, though all she learned was that it had been registered during the fourth quarter of 1952. Ruby was the obvious person to tell her more - and did not disappoint. Yes, she confirmed, her parents had indeed married in 1952: on November 8th to be exact, a few months short of Albert's fiftieth birthday. His bride was May Louisa Wisdom from Doncaster; she was thirty-five and had lost her first husband in tragic circumstances. May had been in the A.T.S. (the Auxiliary Territorial Service, which was superceded by the WRAC, the Women's Royal Army Corps.) The wedding took place at St. Mathew's Church, St. Leonards-on-Sea, near Hastings - the same town where Doris and Ernest had married twenty years before!

Sadly, as we have seen, the groom's mother had died six years previously, and his father was probably not well enough to make the journey to Hastings. (He died the following February, in fact.) Whether George Mould had been invited to the wedding as Dorothy's 'escort', or had then found the courage to attend, is not known. What is certain though, is that George himself was very soon to forge a closer bond with the Ayers family.

Meanwhile, Albert and May set up home in Hastings where their two daughters, Christine and Ruby, were born in fairly quick succession. The girls were still small when, in 1957, the family moved to Stamford, about ten miles to the north of Peterborough, and there they lived for about eighteen months. But in 1958/59, Albert moved them all to Broughton and for a short time, they lived with his widowed sister, Dorothy ('Dorrie') Mould at 3, Rose Cottages - the home where he had been brought up fifty years before. Their next move was to the village of Woodhurst where they finally settled. (This was the period Joan Cade referred to when the two cousins, Percy and Albert, lived opposite one another in Moot Way.) Albert had various occupations over the years, including work in a Hastings gypsum mine and on the Railway.

Ted Ayers passed away on 27th February 1953, having outlived his wife by six-and-a-half years. Just five weeks later, Dorothy and George were married at Broughton church. Was the timing a coincidence, or did the first event prompt the second? Most conveniently, they were able to begin their married life in what had been the Ayers' family home. Any parental misgivings were no longer an obstacle, and Peterborough seemed worlds away as the newly-weds savoured their rural retreat; it was an idyllic start. Little did they imagine it would all end so soon.

On Thursday, 9th April, two days after the accident, Doris Maile and her niece, Olive Coleman, caught the bus to Huntingdon in order to visit George in hospital. Dorothy was awaiting them at the main entrance and told them that her husband was still in a coma. The outlook was not good, she said, before adding: "They say he's suffered brain damage so he will need constant care if he survives. But I am prepared to look after him." Sadly, he died an hour later. The funeral service took place the following Tuesday, 14th April, at St. Paul's Church, Peterborough, followed by interment at the Eastfield Cemetery. Here George was buried next to Fanny in the Mould family's plot.

It is hard to imagine the distress that his widow felt at this time; her emotions must have been in turmoil. She knew, though, that she would have to pick up the threads of her own life again and carry on. She remained in Broughton for a few more years and, as we know, was joined in the cottage for a time by Albert and his family in the late 1950's. It was not long after they left for their new home in Woodhurst that Dorothy decided to sell the house in Broughton, move to Huntingdon and look for some work. Maggie had managed to buy her own property there (27 Stukeley Road) so the sisters were able to be together. In fact, Ruby remembered seeing her "Aunt Dorrie' working as an orderly at the Huntingdon County Hospital in 1962, when she was admitted with a broken collarbone as a seven-year old. (Dorothy would then have been in her early sixties.)

During their first telephone conversation in the autumn of 2007, Ruby kindly offered to look out and send the only photograph of Dorothy she possessed. It turned out to be one of her own wedding to Ian Green in June 1980, which Dorothy had attended as a family guest. In the family group, flanking the bride and groom, were Ruby's older sister, Christine Foster, (who had married seven years before,) the best man, the bride's father, (Albert Ayers), and his two sisters. Maggie was standing to the far left and Dorothy on the far right, facing one another - and looking rather serious. Sadly, May Ayers had died two years before from multiple sclerosis, aged sixty-one. After his wife's death, Albert went to live with his sisters in Stukeley Road.

At the time of her niece's wedding, Dorothy was a few weeks short of her eightieth birthday. Four-and-a-half years later, on February 7th, 1985, Dorothy died at home aged eighty-four and was buried in the Primrose Lane Cemetery. The cause of death was given as 'Ischaemic Heart Disease'. Maggie survived her sister by almost six years dying in December 1990 aged seventy-seven. When Albert died in 1998, he had reached the grand old age of ninety-five.

Studying the wedding group photo again, Joan Bolton could not help feeling disappointed. One of her objectives in the 'search for Dorothy' had been to find a photograph - ideally, one of her own wedding, or perhaps one of herself, taken at about the time she first met George. Such photos must surely have existed. Sadly, however, with no children to treasure them, such mementoes could have been thrown away. As it was, the only photo that had come to light was one of her step grandmother towards the end of her life and as a guest at someone else's wedding. Furthermore, there was a strange irony here, for in I980 Dorothy was the same age as George had been on their wedding day, twenty-seven years before.

In July 2009, Joan decided to trouble Ruby yet again with some more questions - but this time by letter. Once again, she was happy to oblige (and with such full answers that another re-write was necessary!) Also enclosed was a small packet containing five photographs. They were of Dorothy, taken in the 1940's and '50's - and, yes, two of them were of herself and George on their wedding day! Ruby explained that they had been in an old photograph album in her sister's loft and were only discovered a few weeks before when the family moved house. Joan felt that her patience had been rewarded!

At the end of the newspaper appeal, Joan wrote the following: " I should really like to find out more about this lady, in recognition of the part she played in my grandfather's life." After all the researchy, her sincere hope now is that she has succeeded, and also done justice to Dorothy.

Four months after George's death, his middle daughter, Marjorie died, aged forty-three. She had already been diagnosed with cancer, but no one was in any doubt that the shock of losing her father so suddenly and in such a tragic fashion had contributed to her death.

The Gilpin Street household was now reduced to three. Unfortunately, Doris and Iris were the two sisters least capable of managing and most likely to fall out. Ernest always avoided any involvement in this verbal sparring but the unpleasantness made his lot harder to bear. On 3rd February 1957 he passed away, aged fifty-four.

It is hard to say how much Doris was affected by Ernest's death. From the day they first met, he had never been in robust health and no one knew how long he might be expected to live. Doris might have anticipated being a widow for a long time. In the end, she outlived him by thirty years. But she was never a typical caring wife, being constantly wrapped up in herself and her own interests.

Ursula told of a revealing incident that occurred during her own time at Gilpin Street, (between 1947 and 1951). One day Doris headed out to the Millfield shops via Lincoln Road, dragging poor Ernest along with her. They stopped for Doris to unwrap a toffee which she popped into Ernest's mouth before walking on. Because of his infirmity, he had limited control of his mouth and tongue, but Doris didn't concern herself about this. By the time they returned home, Ursula immediately realized that something was wrong. Ernest was blue in the face because the toffee was firmly stuck to his teeth and he couldn't breathe properly. Ursula promptly pried out the offending sweet and a major crisis was averted. Doris, of course, hadn't even noticed that anything was amiss!

After Ernest died, Doris and Iris were thrown together even more. "Chalk and cheese" only begins to describe how different and incompatible these two sisters were; Doris with her sharp brain (and tongue) and Iris seeming ever more slow by contrast. At least Iris had grown accustomed to carrying out a few tasks in the kitchen but Doris had never been known to do much, least of all the cooking. Even though she herself wanted little more than tea and biscuits, Doris was presumably prevailed upon to bring in cakes and savouries for her sister from Spires Bakery nearby. Since Iris hardly ever set foot outside the house, she was dependent on her sister for most of the groceries. Even when shops delivered to the house, which most did in those days, someone had to place the order and Iris would not have had the confidence to do this. They had no telephone at Rock House, of course.

Naturally, the brothers and their wives kept an eye on the two women, making sure they were alright. Also, their nephew, Dick Mould, lived behind them in Allen Road and his wife, Pat, used to call in regularly, often with a meal for the aunts.

But, whereas Iris hated to go out, Doris was hardly ever in. She continued going up to the Roman Catholic church for mass - mostly to All Souls in town, but occasionally to St. Oswald's at Walton if there was a special service.

One of the priests Doris found especially kind and helpful: he was Father Hignett. He had arrived in the city in 1948, initially to serve as an assistant priest at All Souls. Always a regular attendee at the services from the time of her conversion to Catholicism, Doris began to spend even more time there - to the extent that the family felt she "lived at the church". The fact that the priest's name cropped up in nearly every conversation suggested that she made a point of of seeking him out with her questions and concerns.

By 1962, the temporary church at Walton had been replaced with a new one - St. Oswald, King and Martyr. Built at the junction of Lincoln Road and Paston Lane, it was considerably closer to Gilpin Street than the main church (All Souls). But more significantly, perhaps, Father Hignett had been appointed as St. Oswald's first parish priest. These were two good reasons, then, for Doris to switch her allegiance to the Walton church.

As well as her visits to church, Doris liked to drop in on her relations. Most of the family tolerated such visits with a mixture of resignation and amusement, accepting Doris' eccentricities and feeling sorry for her. They knew hers was a sad existence - albeit mainly self-inflicted.

To be fair, away from Rock House, Doris could be pleasant company and quite entertaining. She had the Mould sense of humour, with a mischievous liking for gossip. (At times her stories bordered on the risqué!) But she seemed genuinely interested in all her brothers and their families, always inquiring how her nephews and nieces were getting on with their studies or at work. Melvin Mould turned to her for some help with his school homework on occasions. Doris always remembered birthdays and special anniversaries (more often than not, enclosing a gift of money in the envelope) and was grateful for kindnesses received. It was just a shame she could not "see eye to eye" with Iris.

Doubtless in the early years of being thrown together with her older sister, Iris would have felt a sense of relief when Doris went out. But as time went by, she came to feel increasingly isolated and depressed. She had no hobbies or interests and, after Marjorie died, no one to jolly her along. Apart from the radio, there was nothing to distract Iris from her morbid thoughts and, eventually, she reached breaking point. It was surely no coincidence that Iris carried out the supposed "suicide attempt" during the dismal month of November, 1964. It was thought that she swallowed some disinfectant while on her own and was then found by Doris who asked some neighbors to call for help.

Iris was taken to Rauceby Hospital near Sleaford in Lincolnshire where they specialized in mental disorders. The first course of action in such cases was to employ the stomach pump, which they did. Sadly, Iris did not survive. She died on Sunday 8th November, aged just fifty-one.

Joan Bolton, Guilf's daughter, can still remember her father's exasperation when, some years after the event, she asked him how his sister had died. Clearly he felt that much of the blame lay with Doris - on two counts: one, for contributing to Iris' unhappiness in the first place, and, two, for over-reacting at the time. Mary, his wife, had come to the same conclusion, maintaining that, even if her sister-in-law had drunk any of the disinfectant at all, (which was by no means clear,) it would not have been as harmful as the effects of the stomach pump. What looked outwardly like a suicide attempt was very probably a cry for help. This sad event bore echoes of Fanny Mould's death, also in a Lincolnshire hospital, almost eighteen years earlier.

Iris' death at the end of 1964 marked the beginning of a very difficult time for her sister. Doris now found herself completely alone at Gilpin Street, in a house that was too big for one person - especially for someone who had never liked housework at the best of times. Rock House was soon in a dreadful state and - even worse- Doris was seriously neglecting herself, giving cause for concern. Soon she had reached such a low point health-wise that she was on the verge of a breakdown.

It was in 1966 that she learned some news that hit her hard: Father Hignett was to leave the Peterborough Diocese to take up a post in Great Yarmouth, Norfolk, about a hundred miles away on the east coast. Doris felt she had built up a close rapport with the priest over the years, coming to rely on his advice and support during some very difficult times. She was devastated.

Olive was not the only member of the family, however, to wonder whether her aunt's "constant pestering" (as she put it) might have played some part in his departure. Whatever the case, seen from Doris' side, the loss of someone she regarded as a friend and mentor could only have added to her distress.

One thing that had become increasingly obvious to the Mould family, however, was that Doris could no longer remain at Gilpin Street - but there was another problem to resolve first. In their father's will, the family home had been left to the three daughters "for their lifetime". This arrangement might have been satisfactory had Marjorie not been the first to die. But once Doris and Iris were left to manage by themselves, Rock House became a "millstone around their necks".

The brothers met together and agreed to have the will altered so that the house could be sold. Dealing with the will was fairly straight-forward, but getting the house in order later was a challenge. It was a case of "all hands on deck" to spruce it up before putting it on the market and none of this could happen while Doris was living there.

Being curious to find out more about this dark chapter in her aunt's life, Joan decided to see if she could trace anyone who might remember Doris from the late 1960's. A telephone call to St. Oswald's Church resulted in her making contact with a Mr. Fitzgerald, who belonged to the Society of St. Vincent de Paul. Like all members of this organization, Michael Fitgerald was committed to visiting "the poor, the sick and the aged" in the Roman Catholic community and had visited Doris several times at the Gilpin Street home before she moved out in 1969. Although not poor or even elderly at the age of 68, she was very frail, having neglected herself over a long period. Doris had made quite an impression on him he said. In spite of her poor physical state, her mind was razor-sharp and her desire to discuss (and argue!) was as strong as ever.

Michael related how, on one of these visits, they had read the Bible together - at Doris' suggestion. The reading, which she had chosen beforehand, was from one of St. Paul's epistles (possibly 1 Corinthians 14:34 which reads, "Let your women keep silent in the churches." - not a message Doris would want to hear. Doris then asked her visitor what he thought of St. Paul. Though somewhat taken aback, he gave his opinion. She then astonished him with her forthright view: "Of course , St. Paul was a misogynist, wasn't he?"

Summing Doris up, Michael Fitzgerald described her as an intelligent, loquacious woman who loved an intellectual argument, but also someone who was spiritually vibrant.

He also revealed that, in fact, Doris did have some friends! Two of them lived nearby and were ladies she had met through the church. One was Mrs. Eileen Buckley, (the wife of Daniel Buckley) and the other was Mrs. Vines. Both lived in the GNR cottages on Lincoln Road. Apparently, all three would meet together in order to read and discuss the Bible.

The discovery of a third friend of Doris' was also thanks to Michael Fitzgerald - but there was an element of "happenchance" here. Enid Withers had saved a document on the history of the Roman Catholic church in Peterborough to show her cousin, Joan, when they had a reunion there in June 2007. It contained information on all the Peterborough churches, as well as references to Father Hignett. The author was Mr. Peter Waszak, the parish archivist and Michael Fitzgerald was able to put Joan in touch with him.

She contacted Peter on several occasions that summer and each time he generously shared information relevant to the "Aunt Doris Story". However, there was one thing he didn't know - something Joan discovered when she tried to phone him at his home in early October. A woman's voice came on the line, explaining that Mr. Waszak wasn't at home. It was Mary Waszak, Peter's mother. When Joan told her why she was calling and mentioned her aunt, there was a surprise in store. Not only did Mary remember Doris but they had been good friends over many years, up until her death in 1987, twenty years before. Not surprisingly, Mary was considerably younger than her friend - by seventeen and a half years in fact. (Mary confided that she had just celebrated her eighty ninth birthday the day before!) Her late husband, who was Polish, had died in 2002. They had three children, including Peter.

Mary told how she had visited Doris at Gilpin Street and The Peverels, as well as at Thorpe Hall, (where Doris was nursed back to health before being admitted to the residential home.) But her first memory was when, as a small girl, she had been given a new teddy bear by Doris. Mary felt that this kind gesture was typical of her friend.

So, how had the two first met? Almost certainly their first meeting was at the draper's shop at 349 Lincoln Road, Millfield because the owner, Miss Florence Wake, was linked to them both. Her shop was next door to the bus depot where Doris worked from about 1918, when she was seventeen and had been to secretarial college - the same year that Mary Watts was born. Unfortunately, (or so it seemed at the time), the Depot had no separate ladies "convenience" for Doris to use. When Miss Wake became aware of this problem, she allowed Doris to use her facilities. "Doris was a good customer," Mary explained, "especially at Christmas." Mary, (born Mary Watts), lived with her parents in nearby Windmill Street and was an only child. Owing to her mother's ill health, Mary spent much of her time with her maiden aunt, Florence Whitehead, (her mother's sister). Since both Florences shared the house at number 349, (behind and above the shop), Doris had most likely known Mary from infancy. Both Doris and Mary shared their Roman Catholic faith - another bond.

In October 2007, Mary and Peter Waszak wrote jointly to Joan, enclosing two fascinating items: one was a black and white photograph taken in the back garden of 349 Lincoln Road, (Miss Wake's shop), in about 1930. Standing at the back of the group is Doris, with Miss Wake in front of her on the left and Miss Whitehead on the right. At the very front, with long plaits, is an eleven-year-old Mary Watts.

The second item was a notelet which Doris sent to Mary, at Easter 1980, when Doris was seventy nine and living at The Peverels. The message in the notelet reads: ......I am still managing to keep mobile and help out in various ways......... The Reverend Dexter, vicar of Christ Church, Dogthorpe, (the local Anglican church).............informed me that Father Hignett was very ill, and would not write to his sister. He would seem to have become a complete introvert - desiring no contact with the world around him." There is a very nice follow-up to this story in Father Hignett's obituary which Peter Waszak sent Joan in October 2007. There we read that his only sister arrived back in England from the USA to visit her brother just as he was feeling much better and that "they were able to enjoy a happy reunion during those few days, before he unexpectedly died."

But now to return to the most pressing matter facing the Mould family: finding a suitable residential home for Doris and one that was prepared to take her. It is not known if she was presented with a selection of homes, or even if she had any say at all. But it certainly seemed that fate was smiling down on her because a new home called The Peverels had recently opened in the Dogsthorpe area, just off Welland Road and was happy to accept her. Doris moved there in 1969 and was one of their first residents.

By another stroke of good luck, a new Roman Catholic church, Our Lady of Lourdes, had been completed on Welland Road in 1965, four years before Doris' move. It could not have been more conveniently timed - or situated, being a mere "stone's throw" from The Peverels.

Doris would have known that Father Hignett had played a large part in the planning of this new Dogsthorpe church and, almost certainly, she would have attended the celebrations for its inauguration in 1965. But the nicest surprise for Doris in 1969 must have been to learn that Father Hignett was returning to the city and taking up the post of Parish Priest at the local church, after spending three years away in Norfolk. He would remain there until 1976, when he retired due to ill health, dying six years later in July 1982.

Did all of these factors come together purely by a happy coincidence? Or did the church/priest element influence Doris' choice of The Peverels in the first place? In any event, the move there proved a very positive one, heralding a new beginning for Doris. Although only sixty-eight - considerably younger than the average care home resident, she was not in the best of health after neglecting herself for so many years. (As we already know, Doris had to spend several weeks in the Thorpe Hall nursing home before she could be admitted to The Peverels.) But, in her new surroundings, she met with good care and kindness from the start. With encouragement to eat properly, Doris soon regained her health, energy and an interest in life. In spite of her reluctance to mix, she was gradually drawn into the various activities, and was soon doing jobs to help the staff, as well.

Being accepted at The Peverels brought another stroke of good fortune: Olive Coleman, her niece, was living just a few minutes walk away with husband, Frank, and their sixteen-year old daughter, Susan. When Olive went round to visit her aunt, after giving her time to settle in, she could scarcely believe her eyes. She wasn't in her room but in the dining room, laying the breakfast tables for the next morning! Doris was making herself useful at last and, more importantly, realizing that her efforts were appreciated. She had also undertaken another task - that of feeding the resident cat.

The Colemans welcomed Doris to their home on Eastern Avenue and generally kept an eye on her. After Olive's father, Cyril, died in 1978, Doris was often invited out on a Sunday afternoon for a ride in Frank's Robin Reliant van (a three wheeled vehicle), along with Beattie, Cyril's widow. Doris really enjoyed being with the Coleman family and, when Olive's first grandchild, Andrew, was born in 1971, she embraced the role of great-great aunt with enthusiasm.

Coming from a large family, Doris was never short of other relations to visit around Peterborough. Most were quite happy to listen to her tales over a cup of tea. For her part, Doris was grateful to escape from the Peverels for an hour or so, feeling she had little in common with most of the other occupants, and certainly not wishing to join them in the lounge watching endless television programs. They, of course, considered Doris to be the odd one out, and probably with good reason.....

The fact that she liked to make herself useful was probably welcomed by the staff, but served to distance Doris from her fellow residents. On the whole, though, whilst regarding her eccentric ways with mild amusement, both staff and residents liked and accepted her, and most were ready to share a joke or to pass the time of day. For her part, Doris seemed to be happier and more settled at The Peverels than she had been for a long time, even if she had no close friends there.

But eventually - and much to everyone's surprise - Doris found someone she could really relate to; he was a fellow resident by the name of Eric Buckley. A firm friendship developed between the pair and soon it was expected that Mr. Buckley would be included in any family invitations - and - vice-versa. And so it was that when Eric's son came to take his father to a cricket match, Doris went along too, suddenly acquiring an interest in the game as well as a knowledge of the rules.

One day when Olive went to visit her aunt at the home, Doris was nowhere to be found. She wasn't in her room, nor was she helping down in the dining room, and Olive knew for a fact that she would not be down in the television lounge. One of the staff suggested she try Mr. Buckley's room. Sure enough, there was Doris, lying on the bed with Eric beside her. There was nothing compromising about this episode, but Olive still felt uncomfortable.

Not long afterwards, Olive and Frank were invited to join Doris and Eric for a dinner at The Bluebell, a pub on Welland Road near The Peverels. Doris made it clear beforehand that Mr. Buckley had an announcement to make - the gist of which was as follows:

"My intentions towards Doris are entirely honorable and I should like to marry her. But unfortunately, I am not able to do so, since I have never been divorced from my first wife." Poor Olive and Frank didn't know where to look to hide their smiles of embarrassment!

Apparently, Eric had confided to Doris that, on his return to England after the Second World War, his wife had met him at the railroad station, only to announce that she wanted nothing more to do with him.

Really, very little is known about Eric Buckley. He was certainly well spoken, pleasant and polite and gave the impression that he had had a good job before retirement.

Guilf's wife, Mary, had always felt it was their duty to give Doris a break from the home and regularly invited her to their bungalow. When she became less agile, from the late 1970's, Guilf was sent to collect his sister in the car. Once Eric Buckley appeared on the scene, he was invited along too.

As Joan Mould soon realized, there was an advantage for her parents in ferrying these guests "to and fro" by car. When her mother felt they had stayed long enough, she would give Guilf a nod and say "Well, I expect you'll want to be getting back before it gets dark," or something similar. When Guilf returned, they usually watched a favorite television program in peace. Mary had no hesitation in asking Mr. Buckley about himself but even she was kept at arm's length by his somewhat guarded approach.

Doris always referred to her friend as Mr. Buckley, but whilst keeping up a front of formality, (as befitting the times), she was obviously pleased to have a man friend "in tow" and paying her attention. The Mould family played along with this, enjoying a few chuckles amongst themselves, needless to say. But all agreed that this unexpected friendship brought Doris contentment and companionship in this latter part of her life. It is believed that Eric died a year or so before Doris.

Doris passed away at The Peverels on Monday 19th October, 1987, after a short illness. All things considered, she had done very well to reach the age of eighty-six. Olive remembers that her body was taken to the Cooperative Society's Chapel of Rest, and the funeral took place at the nearby church, Our Lady of Lourdes, which Doris had attended from The Peverels.

Doris was laid to rest in the Mould family plot at Eastfield Cemetery, next to Ernest who had died thirty years earlier.

Cyril Eugene was Fanny and George's first son, born at Gunthorpe fourteen months after his sister. As a five-year old, he would have attended the school in Werrington, a half a mile walk across the fields. After the move to Gilpin Street in 1911 - the year Cyril turned nine - he would have transferred to the newly opened Lincoln Road School, along with Doris, aged ten, Bernard, eight, and six year old Eric. Depending on how eager these pupils were to get there, the walk from Rock House would have taken about five or six minutes, along Gilpin Street to Rock Road, then covering a short stretch of the Lincoln Road before turning into York Road where the school was. It is ironic that the new school replaced the old one in the very year that Fanny moved back to New England, so none of her children studied in the building where she had taught up to her marriage in 1898, thirteen years before.

Although the official school-leaving age was then fourteen, it is possible that Cyril left a year earlier in the summer of 1915 on turning thirteen. His father's milk business was established in the New England area by then and George would have found an extra pair of hands very useful.

Olive Coleman says that her father had recounted how, as a boy, he used to accompany his father on the horse and cart to collect the milk from Werrington.

Arthur Mould, Cyril's older son, says his father found employment at the Peter Brotherhood factory on Lincoln Road, Walton, where he worked on the shop floor. As young men were called up to fight in 1914, engineering jobs became vacant. Cyril may have been taken on around 1916/1917 as a fourteen or fifteen-year-old.

At some point, he was probably made redundant from Brotherhood's due to the slump, as was Bernard. (The careers of the two brothers did seem to run in parallel). But Cyril soon found work again, this time as a tram driver with the Peterborough Electric Traction Company. (If this was in 1921, Cyril would have been nineteen).

As the omnibus network expanded and more buses were acquired, Cyril could see that this was where the future lay. His sister Doris had already found employment in the bus depot offices at Millfield and could well have given her brothers prior warning of vacancies for drivers. Both Cyril and Bernard were taken on at the same time, in 1927.

The first buses they both drove had the engine protruding in front with the driver seated behind: they were known as bottle-nosed buses. The distinctive red double-deckers, very similar to the Routemasters still running in some British towns today, replaced them. Here the design was more compact and rectangular (viewed from the side). The driver's cab was to the right of the engine and raised for greater visibility. It was completely isolated from the main body of the vehicle. Passengers seated upstairs, right at the front, were immediately above the driver or the engine.

Passengers got on or off from the rear platform, which was rather high for some elderly folk, though the conductor often assisted them, also giving a hand to mothers with children and pushchairs. Unlike modern buses, there were no automatic doors; no doors at the back at all, in fact. Just plenty of bracing fresh air as the bus bowled along!

The main job of the conductor, of course, was to collect the fares and issue the tickets. If the conductor needed to speak to the driver, he, or she, could do so through a sliding glass panel behind the driver's seat.

Being a very reserved man, Cyril would not have minded being cocooned in his cab and cut off from all the chatter and activity inside the bus. In fact, he would have welcomed it. Knowing that her Uncle Cyril was far from being gregarious, Joan was intrigued to know how he had come to meet Beattie Ward, the pretty young woman who was to become his wife.

Olive did not know exactly how or when Cyril met her mother but did know she had been "in-service" with a Mrs. Neave who lived on Lincoln Road near Cobden Avenue. Straight after leaving school at fourteen, Beatrice had gone into service with a family in Crowland for a while, before moving to a similar job in Peterborough with a dentist and his family. So that, assuming Beattie started working for Mrs. Neave at the age of seventeen in 1923, Cyril could well have been working on the trams then. For the trams - and for the buses - Lincoln Road was one of the major routes, the depot being situated on Lincoln Road too, between Stone Lane and Oxford Road, Millfield.

It is not difficult to imagine how Beattie and Cyril's paths might have crossed: Cyril driving his tram along Lincoln Road, directly past the house where Beattie was employed and seeing her as she walked along to the town shops. By all accounts, she was a girl who turned heads! One lucky day, Cyril notices her climbing on board, watches for her to alight with his cab window wound down in readiness and manages to engage her in a brief conversation. The good-looking Cyril looks even more handsome in his uniform and sets her heart aflutter. On their next encounter, he will make sure he knows which film is showing at the New England cinema..........

Whatever the circumstances of their first meeting, the young couple fell in love, courted for several years and were married in the late summer of 1928, when Cyril was twenty-six and Beattie twenty-two. The ceremony took place at St. Mark's Church, Lincoln Road, at the early hour of eight o'clock in the morning. After honeymooning in Great Yarmouth, they set up home at 48 Silverwood Road. This was half way between the Neaves' house where Beattie had been working and Cyril's home in Gilpin Street. More importantly, Siverwood Road was only a five-minute cycle ride from the bus depot for Cyril.

The couple's first child, Olive, was born the following year, with Arthur arriving in 1931 and Harold (known as Dick) in 1933.

Cyril seemed to enjoy his work but, unfortunately, in 1946 after almost 20 years on the buses, he became very unwell. One evening in November of that year, Cyril collapsed in the kitchen after a day at work. The family doctor was called and attended immediately. After giving Cyril a thorough examination, he came to the conclusion that he was suffering from acute poisoning from the diesel fumes on the bus and told Cyril that on no account was he to go back.

Once recovered, Cyril soon found another job with a company called Grille Floors, in East Station Road just south of the Town Bridge. He worked for this firm for twenty-one years before taking retirement in 1967 aged sixty-five. Cyril lived to enjoy only eleven years of retirement, dying on November 17, 1978.

Joan has the impression that, of all of her father's brothers, Cyril was the one with whom Guilf had the least in common. There was very little social contact between the two families, even allowing for the fact that there was an age gap of almost fourteen years between Olive and Joan. Both Cyril and his wife seemed content to "keep themselves to themselves". Whereas Guilf always seemed to enjoy a chat and a joke, both at home and in company, brother Cyril gave the impression of being serious and reserved. But the brother Cyril was closest to was Hubert, who was almost fifteen years his junior. With Fanny working so hard in home and with the dairy, it must have been a tremendous boon to know that her eldest son would look after little Hubert, and keep him from constantly being "under her feet"!

It was Cyril who introduced Hubert to the pleasures of bird watching - an interest that Guilf also shared. It was obvious that George Mould was a nature-lover and would have pointed out the various animals and birds to his children. An opportune time for this would have been when one or other of his sons sat next to him on the cart as they fetched the churns of milk from Werrington. It was probably no coincidence that the hide Cyril and Hubert later set up was in Werrington.

By the time Hubert was eight in 1925, his older brother was nearly twenty-three and had already met Beattie. Unfortunately, Hubert had grown so accustomed to going everywhere with Cyril that he couldn't understand why his presence was unwelcome on these "dates". All the same, the brothers' common interest in bird-watching proved a binding force again after Cyril married. Olive claims that her father would occasionally join Hubert at the hide in Werrington where they could watch the birds and - in Hubert's case - photograph them, using a flashlight when it was dark.

Cyril Mould standing next to a bird-watching hide built by Hubert Mould

But now a word about the hide..... As a young lad, Hubert had become friendly with a Mr. and Mrs. Baker (Mr. Baker had worked at Brotherhoods) and they had welcomed Hubert into their cherry orchard where he was eventually allowed to construct his hide. According to Ursula, he had made himself useful, not only by picking cherries when they were ready but also by shinning up the walnut trees to harvest the nuts. These joint nocturnal adventures probably took place in the 1930's, continuing until Hubert was sent abroad with the army in 1942.

It seems that Hubert maintained contact with Cyril and family while away. Olive remembered him sending her some perfume as a present on one occasion and that her older cousin Eileen (Beattie's niece,) also received some. Hubert had met Eileen when she was staying with Beattie and, apparently, had been rather fond of her at the time.

In 1947 Hubert returned to Peterborough with Ursula, his German bride and renewed contact with Cyril. When he had his house built three years later, it was his older brother who offered to help with the painting.

Ursula relates how both couples would cycle out to Werrington on a fine spring afternoon, meeting up at the cherry orchard for a picnic, when Hubert's children were quite small. (By the end of 1956, Cyril and Beattie's family were all grown up and married.) While the two brothers looked for nests, the sisters-in-law enjoyed a chat, knowing that Laurence and Melvin could run about in the orchard without coming to any harm.

Both couples also got together regularly to play cards. This was usually at Newark Avenue so that Ursula and Hubert could keep an eye on their sons. One of their favorite card games was cribbage, where the score is kept on a special pegboard. Although Cyril and Beattie were generally good company, Cyril was definitely not a good loser! While he was winning, all was fine. But he soon became bad-tempered when the game wasn't going his way.

None of the Mould brothers (or, indeed sisters) could ever have been described as "the life and soul of the party"; far from it! Yet, Bernard, Eric, Guilf and Hubert all had a good sense of humor, if somewhat dry. By her own admission, Cyril was the uncle Joan knew least well, so she asked Olive how she would sum up her father. Olive agreed he was not very sociable, "keeping himself to himself", saying also that he could be moody - even sullen - at times. He was a jealous man and hated it if another man even looked at his wife, let alone spoke to her.

Years ago, Beattie told Olive of an incident during their courtship. The couple had attended the wedding of Beattie's oldest sister, Alethea, cycling the ten miles from Peterborough to Crowland. At the reception, Beattie had been drawn into conversation with a couple of men, who were family friends, which made Cyril jealous. By the time the young couple set off back to Peterborough it was dark. Beattie was cycling ahead of Cyril but, after a few minutes, realized he wasn't following. When she went back to look for him, she found him leaning against a gatepost "crying his eyes out". He explained he was upset because she had been laughing and talking to the other men and feared he might lose her.

After marriage, Beattie found Cyril very controlling. For instance, the obvious route into Peterborough town center if walking from Silverwood Road was along Lincoln Road. But because Cyril was concerned about potential male admirers, he told her to go down a quieter street, Cromwell Road, which ran parallel to Lincoln Road.

Certainly Cyril worked hard to provide for his family, but Olive tells a little story illustrating how the two women of the house looked after him too! When she arrived home from her junior school, aged about nine or ten, Beattie would sometimes ask Olive to take a flask of tea for her father if he was on one particular bus route: the 304 from the town center to Werrington, via Alexandra Road, St. Paul's Road and Fulbridge Road. Olive would take a short cut through the side streets in order to intercept the bus at a particular bus stop on Alexandra Road and hand Cyril the tea. This he would enjoy when he had his ten-minute break at the terminus on Werrington Green and had a read of his library books at the same time.

When Joan visited Peterborough in the spring of 2002, Olive related this intriguing story involving her mother. Once Cyril began courting Beattie, she became a regular visitor at Rock House, where she was often invited to stay for tea. (Olive says that her mother was "quite young", possibly about seventeen years of age when she first met Cyril, thus placing this story in about 1923.) On more than one occasion an eccentric aunt was present and sat beside Beattie. This lady tried to pass the young guest some money, which Beattie refused. The money was then placed in Beattie's lap: it was all very embarrassing. One of Cyril's sisters saw what was happening and told her mother. When Beattie learned (presumably through Cyril) that she was suspected of "taking money that didn't belong to her", she was so incensed that she never wanted to set foot in the house again.

Who this strange 'aunt' was or to whom she was related, no one seemed to know. It was a complete mystery! Instinctively, Joan felt this regular visitor was more likely to come from the Mills' side - Fanny's family. When Richard looked them up on the 1901 census, there were four of the family still living at the little house in New England: both parents, George and Mary Mills, their youngest daughter, Daisy, aged twenty-two (and a school teacher, like her married sister, Fanny) and, surprisingly, their elder daughter, Elizabeth. By this time thirty-two years old, she was still unmarried and had no 'occupation'. When Beattie was going to tea at Rock House, Elizabeth would have been in her mid fifties and could quite easily have been that 'eccentric aunt'!

After this unfortunate episode, Beattie stuck to her resolve to stay away from Gilpin Street, always sensing a certain coolness towards her from the women in the family.

Nevertheless all of this seems rather surprising and at odds with the easy-going attitude towards money which prevailed at Rock House. Olive clearly remembers that a communal pot of ready cash sat on the top shelf in the kitchen, seemingly for everyone in the household to dip into for various purposes. An errand boy would usually have a coin pressed into his hand, as would visiting children. The grandchildren, of course, never left empty handed. George was especially generous: some would have said profligate. Guilf's wife, Mary, thought her in-laws "had no idea how to run a business" and that there were "too many hangers-on"!

Happily, once Beattie and Cyril were married and their children born, there was a thawing of relations with the in-laws. By the summer of 1931, the young couple had presented Fanny and George with their first two grandchildren: Olive, born in 1929 and Arthur in 1931, with Harold - better known as Dick - completing the trio in September 1933. It was possibly round about the winter of 1935, then, that an invitation was issued for Cyril and Beattie's family to spend Christmas Day at Gilpin St. For several years this became an annual event, and, according to Olive, a happy occasion. (Sadly, Beattie's parents, the Wards, had both died before their daughter's wedding.)

The Moulds kept a "good table" at any time of year but the Christmas Day tea was special, of course. Olive recalls the "huge" cake her grandma had baked, using the oven next to the open fire. Afterwards, she remembers, the "men folk" went into the front room to play darts, while the women stayed in the dining room with the children. Grandma would ask Olive and her brothers how they were getting on at school and get them to sing nursery rhymes and recite poems.

Fanny's third child, Bernard, was born at Gunthorpe on 27 July 1903. His daughter, Enid, remembers him relating how, with the limitted accomodations at their cottage, the two older boys had to share a bed - and were later joined by Eric and Guilford! (In fact, these sleeping arrangements continued after the move to New England in 1911.) Bernard used to say that he and his brothers seemed to have "nine lives". On one occasion, they were all cycling down Castor Hill near Peterborough when they suddenly saw a farm vehicle and trailer across the road. As they had no brakes, they could only duck and hope they could ride under the vehicle without being decapitated. They all survived! Another time they were playing on the recreation ground in New England when one of the boys on a swing accidentally caught his brother with the swing and cut his head open.

Bernard worked at Brotherhoods engineering firm, first in the offices and then in the works until the "slump" when he was made redundant. He then worked as a tram driver and later on the buses. It was during this time that Bernard acquired the nickname "Joe": he was convinced that a boxer called Joe, (possibly Jersey Joe Walcott), was going to win a match. When the said boxer lost, Bernard's workmates forever teased him and said "Good Old Joe" and the name stuck. It was also during this time that he met Annie Louisa Green who was in service at a house in Eastfield Road. This was on one of the tram routes and Bernard would see Annie when she was out with the children of the family. After a four-year engagement, they married at the register office on 22nd August 1929 and spent their honeymoon at Gt. Yarmouth, on the Norfolk coast.

Bernard and Annie bought a house that was being built in Priory Road, in the West Town area of Peterborough. They spent their entire married lives there until Annie went into hospital and died on October 10, 1993. Bernard then spent the final two years of his life in a small residential home in Eastfield Road, curiously enough, just two doors from the house where Annie had been in service when they first met. When Bernard passed away on January 6, 1996 he was ninety-two; he had survived all of his siblings - and lived to be the oldest.

As a bus driver, Bernard had the advantage of not having to serve in the armed forces during WWII. However, he did serve in the Home Guard and loved to tell the story of one windy evening when his platoon was on parade and failed to hear one of the commands. They found themselves marching directly into a brick wall. Fortunately Bernard had a good sense of humor. There was a scare for Annie and the children one morning when Bernard had still not returned home from the previous day's late shift. The problem proved to be only a breakdown of the vehicle in the blacked-out countryside where Bernard had to walk to an isolated farmhouse to fetch help.

Bernard had probably been baptized as a baby in the Church of England but he was not confirmed until after he retired. He and Annie were active members of the Mission Church (now dedicated to St. Luke) in Mayor's Walk. This was a daughter church of St. John the Baptist Church in Cathedral Square. They were also members of the Over Sixties Club.

Bernard and Annie had several hobbies, and especially enjoyed gardening. Besides having a long garden with flowers, vegetables and fruit trees, they had an allotment where they grew more vegetables. In addition to gardening, Bernard was artistically talented and would probably have gone to art college if the family could have afforded to send him. He took ideas from postcards and pictures from tins, etc. and produced water-color paintings which his family still treasure.

The couple had two children. Enid, born February 3, 1937 and Derek, three and a half years later on August 7, 1940. Enid attended Peterborough County Grammar School for Girls and went on to obtain a BA honors degree in German from Leeds University in 1957. She then became a teacher and taught German at grammar schools in the Midlands for 13 years. In 1972, at the urging of a German friend, Enid went over to Düsseldorf in Germany where she taught English until her retirement in 1997. A couple of years afterwards, she returned to her roots in the Peterborough area.

Derek attended Deacon's Grammar School for Boys in Peterborough and lived at home until he was twenty eight. Since then, he and his Scottish wife, Joan have spent most of their working lives in Scotland. Derek worked as Manager of the Dunfermline Branch of the Halifax Building Society before taking early retirement and starting his own business. Derek and Joan have two sons, Simon born in 1975 and Christopher born in 1978.

George and Fanny's fourth child, Eric, was born on New Year's Day, 1905. Like his three older siblings, he would have attended primary school first in the Gunthorpe area (though probably only for a year), then transferring to the Infant Department of the Lincoln Road School after the move to Gilpin Street. Once there, he would have transferred to Lincoln Road School. Seeing that Eric was proving a good help at the dairy as a young lad, it is quite possible that George requested that his son be "released" before turning fourteen, in order to help (full time) with the milk business from the summer of 1918. Eric was allocated his round, and delivered the milk by bicycle, with a milk bucket on each handlebar. He continued working for the family business for over thirty years.

It was during his time at the dairy that Eric met the young woman who would become his wife. She was Mary Ethel Giddings from Blackheath in London. Born in July 1906, she was eighteen months younger than Eric - and known as Pollie.

After leaving school in London, Pollie went into service, working for a Mr. and Mrs. Meaker in Northampton. The family owned a chain of shops (bearing the Meaker name) and eventually moved to an impressive residence in Peterborough called Thorpe Hall. (This became the main maternity hospital for the Peterborough area in the 1940's.) It was situated on Thorpe Road, at Longthorpe. The building still exists and is now a residential care home.

Quite how Eric met Pollie is uncertain, but Ann, their daughter, thought that the Giddings had relatives in Gilpin Street, at the opposite end from Rock House. It is conceivable that Pollie was visiting her relatives on her day off, just as Eric was delivering the milk. However it was that they met, the two were soon going out together. They married in 1932 and their daughter (Rosita Ann) was born the following year, just the day after Pollie's twenty-seventh birthday. But Fanny Mould would persist in calling the baby "Rosie"; this so annoyed Pollie that she decided to call her daughter by her middle name of Ann.

So, within a short space of time, Pollie's life changed completely. The newly weds moved into their new home in Exeter Road and named the house "Blackheath", after the place where Pollie was born. Here she embraced her dual role of wife and mother whole-heartedly. Pollie was a natural home-maker. She liked cooking and baking, bottling fruit (much of it from their garden), she made jam and was very handy with a sewing machine too: all talents inherited by her daughter.

Just as Pollie's life had changed, so did her husband's when George Mould sold out to Brown's of Walton in 1950. Unlike his brother Guilf, Eric made the decision to work for Brown's as one of their roundsmen. There were two major differences , however: firstly, all of Brown's milk was in bottles and, secondly, Eric would have to deliver it by horse and cart.

Ann recalled how, on one occasion, the horse decided to take off by itself, with the cart behind, to make its own way back to the depot. This left Eric stranded - and with no milk to deliver. A treat for Ann, though, was accompanying her father to the farrier's when the horse required shoeing.

Eric had been with Brown's dairy for only a couple of years when it, too, was sold. He then experienced a complete life-change by going to work as a storeman at Brotherhood's Engineering factory, where he remained until retirement at sixty-five in 1970. But, unaccustomed to so much leisure, Eric found himself a part-time job at the Broadway Social Club where he worked until well into his eighties.

Holidays were virtually unknown whilst Eric worked for the Rock House Dairy. Ann claims that she was about sixteen before she and her parents were able to enjoy an annual family holiday, usually heading for the Norfolk coast. It was no coincidence that these holidays began after Eric's move to the larger dairy where the hours were more regular and holidays guaranteed. By contrast, the Rock House regime was hardly conducive to having any social life.

One of Eric's passions was cricket and, as a young man, he used to umpire matches in nearby villages, travelling either by bicycle or in a friend's car. Sadly, this all ended when Eric was forced to devote more time to "the day job". All the same, he did have several other interests. Eric was a life-long football fan. He was an ardent supporter of the Peterborough United football team (aka "The Posh"), cycling to the ground every Saturday afternoon, come rain or shine. When he had to give up cycling, he was taken to the matches by car.

As already mentioned, Eric enjoyed doing crosswords and was part of the Mould "team" when they entered competitions. He continued doing them for fun until shortly before his death and was also an avid reader.

Eric and Pollie were a devoted couple and went everywhere together, except for the football matches. They were lucky to have a son-in-law who found work as a librarian in such attractive places as Folkestone, Torquay and Jersey and enjoyed visiting their family for holidays.

In 1980, Pollie became ill and was diagnosed with terminal cancer. For the last few weeks before she died in the summer of 1981, the family were able to take advantage of a system being pioneered in Peterborough, called Hospital at Home, whereby terminally ill patients could be given round-the-clock care in their own home. Pollie passed away on July 30, the day before her 75th birthday. Eric survived her by fourteen years, living to the age of 90.

Guilford was born a month premature on 22 August 1906, "a poor little thing" and not expected to survive. His early arrival probably caught his parents off their guard because there was some confusion over the child's name. When George went to register the birth five weeks later, he spelled it as above - with one 'd', yet almost twenty-nine years later, on his marriage certificate, his name was spelt as "Guildford", the town in Surrey. Either way, it was certainly unusual! There was, however, an Earl of Guilford living in Kent at that time, so, bearing in mind that, <u>one</u>, George Mills, Fanny's father, had been born and bred near to Maidstone in Kent and, <u>two</u>, that he had probably met his wife, Mary, whilst she was in service with the aristocracy (as described earlier), it is entirely possible that Fannie had heard her parents mention the Earl and stored away the name for future use! The provenance of the name may be a matter for speculation, but the owner always answered to 'Guilf'.

Born in Gunthorpe, Guilf turned five in 1911, the year the family moved to New England. This meant that the upheaval in his young life was compounded by having to begin school in the September, although having three older brothers and a sister to accompany him would be of some consolation. He appeared to have an aptitude for maths as well as a facility with words and was able to put both gifts to good use after leaving school. But if Guilf had ever entertained any ambitions of continuing his education and entering a profession, he would have been disappointed: by the time he left Lincoln Road School in the spring of !920, his future was decided and he joined his father and brother Eric in the family business.

Guilf's daughters clearly remember their parents impressing on them how lucky they were to be able to stay on at school. (Both stayed on into the sixth form, going on to college at eighteen.) "Of course, in <u>our</u> day", they would say, "we had to leave school at fourteen and go out to work to earn some money."

Mary Joan Murden was born in the Huntingdonshire village of Alconbury Weston on 17 January 1912, five and a half years after Guilf. The twelfth of thirteen children, she too came into the world early, at seven months. By the time the Murden family moved to Peterborough in 1926, Mary was fourteen, had left school and was ready to go 'into service.' They settled into their new home in Scotney street, a road going off to the east of Lincoln Road, about half a mile north of New England.

It was probably during the Christmas season of 1929 that Mary first met Guilf, and, according to the Murden family folklore, it happened more or less as follows:- Just two years after George and Clara Murden's move to 83 Scotney Street, some new neighbours came to live at number 89, a Mr and Mrs Johnson from 56 Gilpin Street, (immediately opposite the Rock House Dairy.) The Johnsons had two daughters and an eighteen- year- old son named Sydney (or Syd, as he was known.) Although Guilf was four years older than Syd, they had become good friends as they grew up. Apparently, (or so the story goes...) the Johnsons thought it would be nice to have the piano played at their Christmas party and, aware that one of the Murden girls was a good pianist, asked Evelyn (Eva.) She agreed and took along her younger sister Mary. Syd's friend Guilf was also there and thus the seeds of a romance were sown! At the same party, Syd struck up what was to be a lasting friendship with Eva; they married in 1937.

However, when in 2006 Joan Bolton decided to check the accuracy of this story with her late uncle's sister, Audrey Johnson Flecknor, her account varied from 'the original version' in a couple of significant details. First of all, Audrey clearly recalled, the Christmas party was NOT held at her parents' house but at her aunt Emma (Aspittle's) place a few doors away at 75 Scotney Street, (Emma being her mother's sister.) Secondly, since Audrey's cousin, Jill Aspittle, was a good pianist, they did not actually need anyone to play the piano, but what they did need were more girls!

By 1931, Guilf and Mary's courtship was well established, as Mary's diary for that year reveals. She was working as cook for the Briggs family near Market Harborough in Leicestershire where her employers owned a shoe factory Most week-ends Guilf was cycling over from Peterborough to see his girlfriend on her day off. Mary's entry for February 14th reads: "Had a Valentine (card) from G.T.M. Felt quite happy about it." But, apparently, Guilf had asked one of his brothers to address the envelope in order to put her off the scent.

By the summer of 1933 the couple must have become engaged because in the September Guilf purchased a quarter acre plot of land in Fulbridge Road , Peterborough, where they would have their home built. He paid £150 for the land and the house cost £625 to build. The couple married at St. Paul's church on the 20th of May 1935 - a Monday. The event could scarcely have been more low-key: the bride wore a smart but simple day dress (in a dark coloured fabric, not the traditional white) and wore a hat. She carried a posy of lilies-of-the-valley and was attended by her youngest sister, Greta. A short honeymoon in Great Yarmouth followed before the newly-weds moved into their new home. The milkround awaited Guilf, but for Mary, marriage meant freedom from 'service' for other people and, although the new house and garden clamoured for her attention, she would now be working for herself.

There was something else that made Mary very proud. Number 97 was a double-fronted, detached house (of a symmetrical design, with the front door and porch in the centre), situated in a desirable neighbourhood. She was less pleased ten years later, however, when a row of pre-fabricated homes (or 'prefabs') sprang up along the adjacent Tennyson Road, ten of which backed on to their southern boundary.

It was because both Mary and Guilf were keen gardeners that they had saved hard for their plot of land. At the front there were lawns and flower beds, whilst at the rear of the house the larger area was for growing vegetables and for keeping chickens. Guilf made some extra income by selling cut flowers to his milk customers. These came from the garden (or from his allotment, before he married.) He grew tulips in April, peonies in May and gladioli in late summer.

Although Guilf and Mary were anxious to start a family, they had been married for seven-and-a-half years when Joan, their first child was born. (Their doctor, apparently, had told them that 'they weren't trying hard enough'!) Mary had had such a long and difficult home-labour the first time, that she booked into Thorpe Hall Maternity Home to have Alison four years later, in March 1947: this time all went smoothly.

There was, however, something which cast great sadness over what should have been a time of celebration. This, of course, was Fanny's death exactly two weeks before Alison's birth. (Although the funeral report listed both Mary and Guilf as being present, she did, in fact, stay at home. It was considered too risky to venture out in her condition, especially when roads and pavements were still treacherous with the lingering snow and ice.)

But the loss of Fanny had other consequences and was certainly a factor in her husband's decision to sell the business in 1950. Eric and Guilf knew they would have to find other work but, whilst his brother was content to continue with Brown's Dairy, Guilf wanted to preserve his independence. And so, with this in mind, he purchased a two-acre plot of land in July 1949, ('the field', as the family called it,) to run as a smallholding for keeping chickens and pigs. It was situated on the opposite side of Fulbridge Road to the house and about a hundred yards to the south. Doubtless, he hoped this would provide a good livelihood for his family, but he realised a lot of work would be required first to get the place "up and running," New chicken huts had to be set up and old ones repaired, while the four existing brick pigsties required considerable renovation.

There was an old boiler house with a large copper for cooking the 'pig potatoes' to feed to the pigs. Joan and Alison would often peel and eat one, pronouncing them 'quite tasty if you're hungry.' Behind the four pigsties, a storehouse was built to keep the sacks of poultry food, pig meal and so on. In the 1950's you could feed the pigs on 'pig swill'. This mainly consisted of what children left on their plates from school dinners and could be had for the asking, but Mary had to go round to the local schools in the afternoon to collect it. (You had to ensure there was no cutlery included if the children's plates had been scraped in a hurry, since pigs are not fussy eaters!)

One person who was always available to give the couple a hand from the very beginning was a young man called Peter Batchelor. Twenty years younger than Guilf, Peter had lost both his parents and a brother to tuberculosis at about the time the Moulds got married. They had first met him when, as an eight or nine-year-old, he used to visit his grandparents who lived at the bungalow next door. (Peter, too, had contracted the disease but had survived with one good lung and was cared for by his aunt.) Mary and Guilf soon befriended this very shy young lad. A clever boy, Peter was eventually taken on as an apprentice engineer at the Baker Perkins factory and became a skilled craftsman. Who better, then, to help and advise with the various challenges thrown up by the smallholding? One of Peter's first 'projects' was to help with the hen houses.

In the wonderfully evocative letter which George Mould wrote to his sister-in-law in the United States in February 1952, he made reference to his son's smallholding. On the last page he writes: 'Guilf is doing fairly well with his little holding. His pigs and poultry are doing well. The other week they had over a thousand eggs in, but the wintry weather this last week has pulled them in a bit.'

Whatever the weather, once this venture was begun, the work had to be done, day in and day out, with the pigs and poultry fed and cared for. It was obviously a tie for both Guilf and his wife. Fortunately, The Field was only a few minutes' walk from the house and Guilf did often walk, or took the car if there was a lot to carry.

But for Mary, it was very difficult to help with the work over there until both the girls had started at school. At the time the new venture began in 1950, Joan was seven and attending Fulbridge School, just ten minutes' walk away. But Alison was only three and would not start there until 1952. Once they were older, their mother would sometimes tell them she was 'just popping over to the field for a few minutes', leaving Joan in charge. She would go on her old racing bike, (the same one she had bought whilst in service in 1931,) cutting a strange figure in her overalls and with a bag or bucket suspended from each of the low handlebars!

Notice that in his letter George said only that Guilf was doing "fairly well" with his small holding, for by the mid-1950's he and Mary harbored serious doubts about the viability of their project. The profits from the pigs and poultry could never be great on such a small scale. Free-range chickens didn't produce as many eggs in the winter, for one thing. And for another, although the customers appreciated having eggs from free-range hens, they did not always want to pay more than for shop eggs. Mary did a weekly egg round in the car, while other customers called round to the house (and came to the bungalow after the move in 1960.)

As for the pigs, the price fetched at market fluctuated considerably. Farmers went in for pigs when the price was high, only to stop rearing them when the price fell. Joan Bolton remembers one occasion when the anticipated check arrived for one lot of pigs, sold a few days before at Peterborough market. After opening the envelope, Mary broke down in tears, disgusted at the low price they had fetched. The cost of the pig meal only went up, needless to say.

Joan also recalled that her parents had experienced a serious set-back during the early days of their new venture. It all started in the autumn of 1949 when Joan was nearly seven. Going into the kitchen of '97', she found a stranger on hands and knees by the back door, apparently mending the lock. Her mother explained: "This is Mr Oxley who is doing some work for us." The same man appeared at the house again on a couple of occasions, apparently doing odd jobs. Not long after this, there was great consternation in the household. All that Joan could gather in this highly charged atmosphere was that something had gone badly wrong and that money and pigs were involved. It was only when she spoke to Peter many years later - in 2007, in fact - that she was able to learn the full story.

It came as a revelation to learn that it was her mother, Mary, who wanted to keep pigs on the smallholding and not her father's wish at all. According to Peter, Guilf thought having chickens would be quite enough work. He knew his wife had always liked pigs, of course, since Peter had allowed her to keep one on the piece of land he owned a few doors from number 97 and which Guilf had used as his allotment. In addition, the field came complete with four brick pigsties already on it, albeit in need of some renovation. Mary was anxious to get started and fill them; then she could say they had a proper smallholding! The only problem was, she didn't know how to go about it, apart from the most obvious way of buying them at the Peterborough cattle market. But cattle markets were very much a man's domain in those days and were especially daunting for a novice and so she must have been relieved when Guilf told her of someone who might help.

During the previous autumn (of 1949), an acquaintance of Guilf's who had often brought the milk to Gilpin Street from Speechley's farm, called by at the smallholding to see if there was any work for him. Guilf did find him a few jobs and was glad of the help, especially as the man proved a good worker. Since her husband had never been handy around the house, Mary soon found Mr. Oxley some jobs inside as well. Realising that he had worked on a farm, the conversation soon turned to pigs and when George Oxley said he could get her some, the offer was eagerly accepted.

On Monday 13th February, Oxley took her to a farm and showed her some pigs that (he claimed) he had purchased for himself. Mary wanted ten of them and it was agreed that they would return to Fulbridge Road to find him the £65, (around a thousand pounds in today's money, and, back in 1950, it represented about eight weeks' wages!) Pocketing the cash, Oxley said he would be back with the pigs the next day. An empty promise! Mary and Guilf never saw him again; he had absconded with the money, of course. The police tracked him down in Essex and he was sent to prison for two years. At the trial, it emerged that Oxley had numerous previous convictions, including a five-year sentence for desertion in 1945!

Always so trustworthy themselves, Mary and Guilf thought everyone else was the same and had never thought to question the con man's background. Hearing the real facts about this fraud brought Joan another surprise: so it was her mother who had fallen for this 'scam' and not her father! And she had always thought that he was the gullible one whilst her mother was more shrewd.

But the whole sorry episode gave Joan pause for thought. She remembered something her parents had once told her when she was in her late teens: a woman had died in one of the pigsties and in somewhat bizarre circumstances. The story involved a couple who had been using the smallholding regularly for their nocturnal trysts. On this particular autumn night, it had all ended in tragedy. The man (who then owned the land) had placed an improvised heater in the pigsty - some coal in a perforated bucket - in order to keep them both warm. Unfortunately, there was no proper ventilation and the woman was asphyxiated, though the man survived.

Needless to say, this was a scandal that rocked the quiet market town, as well as being an enormous tragedy for the two families concerned. The victim left a husband and three children. "This sordid story" as the coroner described it, even found its way into the national papers with headlines such as "HAIRDRESSER'S SEAMY STORY OF PIGSTY LIAISON". It was hardly surprising that this land was up for sale within the year.

Knowing The Field's grim secret did not deter Guilf from buying it. In truth, its appearance on the market could not have been better timed in view of his personal circumstances. Nevertheless, this didn't alter the fact that they never seemed to have much luck with the pigs.

But even without such mishaps, the smallholding was proving to be an unreliable source of income for the family, so it was decided that Guilf would look for another job, whilst Mary managed the livestock by herself.

For a few months Guilf worked at the main Post Office, sorting the mail, but early in 1955 he heard that Frank Perkins Factory (or 'Perkins Diesel') on Eastfield Road was taking on workers and applied. He was taken on as a Progress Chaser, working on the shop floor. To begin a new job in a factory at the age of forty-eight must have been a huge upheaval, but his brother

Eric had led the way a couple of years before: Guilf knew he, too, would have to make the best of it. (In later years, the two brothers openly admitted that they would have done better to leave the milk business much sooner!)

One of Guilf's first discoveries was how down-to-earth life could be on the factory floor, with no room for any pretensions. Perhaps for the first time in his life, he became aware that his name could cause amusement and he was soon answering to his new name of 'Jeff.' His daughter recently dug out her School-Girl's Diary for 1955 and found the following entry for Saturday 9th of July: "Went to Perkins' "At Home Day". Saw the works." (ie the factory) "Had an iced lollie, drink, packed tea in a box. I didn't go on roundabouts." (Probably this was infra-dig. for a twelve-and-a-half year old!) But what stood out in her memory was the feeling of sadness that her father who was such an outdoor person - should be cooped up all day in such a soul-less place.

On the positive side, however, her father seemed to throw himself into his work as whole-heartedly as he could, making new friends and enjoying a laugh. Most days when he got home, he shared an amusing story with Mary about something that had happened at the factory. One good workmate was Eric Clarke (known as The Professor, since he had a beard) who seemed to feature in all the escapades. He and his wife, Gladys, became good friends with Mary and Guilf, going on several holidays together.

One advantage of the 'progress chasing' from Guilf's point of view was that it sent him all round the factory, meeting different people, as well as renewing acquaintance with former schoolmates and customers. All of this added variety to his day, as well as companionship. (By comparison, Guilf now realised how isolated he had been, working the smallholding.) But another bonus, of course, was receiving a regular wage each week: ten pounds was considered 'good money' in the 1950's and the couple's financial worries were eased. Guilf was still able to help Mary at the weekends and on summer evenings when he got home from work, so that there was some regular income from the eggs also.

Like most factories, Perkins allowed their employees two weeks' paid holiday in the summer and it was probably no coincidence that Joan and Alison's first recollections of family holidays dated back to this time. In late August 1955, for instance, their father drove the family to Cromer, a seaside resort on the Norfolk coast, for a week's holiday. There they stayed at a small Guest House, run by a landlady named Mrs. Makin. (The nearest equivalent today would be a very ordinary B&B with an evening meal provided.) They had booked a beach hut and the weather was so good that they were able to sunbathe every day. The following year, the family spent a pleasant week at Boscombe (near Bournemouth) on the south coast, where Mary's sister, Greta, and her husband Frank ran a small hotel. Modest though such holidays were, they seemed like heaven to Guilf and Mary after working so hard and for so many years without a break. They all returned to both Boscombe and Cromer on more than one occasion. Once their daughters left home, the couple grew more adventurous, going on organised holidays to Switzerland, Austria and the south of Spain.

It must have been soon after Guilf started working at Perkins that they made the decision to sell their house and have a bungalow built on the smallholding. They would then be on the spot instead of going to and fro. Also, a bungalow would be easier to heat in the winter and generally more convenient as they grew older. The plans were drawn up in the summer of 1958, the house was sold and the Moulds duly moved across the road to the new bungalow early in 1960. There was just about time to get everything 'ship-shape' before the Silver Wedding celebrations on the 20th of May.

But although everyone was in favour of the move, Guilf and Mary must have felt some disappointment over the bungalow itself. Its proportions were mean, and to describe it as unimpressive would be an understatement. The same well-respected builder, Cyril Arbon, who had designed their first home, had again been called on to draw up the plans for the bungalow. The only problem this time was finding the money! So, economies had to be made and corners cut: the couple had to accept that it would not be their 'dream home' and make the best of it. But they were well-practised at 'making the best of things'. Mary especially was a great optimist, given to 'counting her blessings' and ' looking on the bright side'. "We're quite content," she used to say, "just so long as we've got each other and so long as we've got our health and strength." (When Mary died in the summer of 1991, they had just celebrated their fifty-sixth wedding anniversary and over sixty years together.)

It was only when Alison and Joan had the task of sorting out their parents' possessions after their father died in 1992 that they learned of one cherished dream that had never been realised. They found an airmail letter from Aunt Daisy in Canada, written in early January 1957. (Daisy was Fanny Mould's sister and a favourite aunt, who had delighted the family by sending them food parcels during WW2.)

After the usual pleasantries, Daisy continues: "Well, my dears, I see you have a yearning for Canada." After conceding that "the country has many good points", she goes on to warn them of the 'down-side': the extremes of climate (and the warm clothing they would need), the ever-rising costs, (especially rents) and the difficulties involved in farming. She also felt obliged to point out that the education there did not compare with that in England. (Before she married, Daisy had been a teacher, quite probably at the same school as Fanny.)

Guilf and Mary had obviously sent their letter the previous month, (along with Christmas greetings and a picture calendar for 1957), which proves that, by the autumn of 1956, they were seriously considering emigrating to Alberta. By then, Guilf had been working at the factory for some eighteen months: could he still have felt so disillusioned? Or, as he reached the fifty-year milestone that August, did he want to take on one more challenge before it was too late? Daisy's reply seemed to resolve the matter and the family stayed in Peterborough. Looking again at the letter recently, Joan marvelled that all of their futures had hung on just one piece of thin blue paper. How differently their lives might have turned out! But it also then became clear why her parents had gone ahead with the bungalow project when they did. If Canada was not to be their 'land of milk and honey', they would have to do the best they could in Peterborough.

But life was not all disappointments by any means. At some point during the latter half of 1957, Guilf learned he had won first prize with his crossword entry - a cash prize sufficient to replace their old car. They bought a new Hillman Husky, an estate car which had obvious practical advantages, such as transporting sacks of pig meal or corn, as well as the eggs for Mary's customers.

Moving over to the bungalow in 1960 hailed a decade of changes for the family. Joan left for London University in 1961, with Alison also heading for the capital in 1965 to train as a teacher at Gypsy Hill College. Since Joan had obtained her first teaching post in Essex that same September, Mary and Guilf were effectively on their own again for the first time in twenty-three years. They were determined to make the most of their leisure time and amazed all the family by taking up ballroom dancing, with a view to socialising more. (By his own admission, Guilf had 'two left feet' and nobody had any doubt that this project was Mary's!)

There was another ambition she had long nurtured also. Since her faith was so important to her, Mary had urged her husband to be confirmed, thereby becoming a full member of the Anglican Church and able to join her for Holy Communion. Guilf agreed and was confirmed at Paston Church in the autumn of 1961 at the age of fifty-five. Considering that most candidates for confirmation are usually teenagers, this was a brave step for him to take.

Quite a few years later, in the mid 1980's, the couple made the decision to leave Paston Church and, instead, joined the congregation of St. Paul's, where they had been married. This move was prompted mainly by the changes in the road system, brought about by the growth of Greater Peterborough. The new Soke Parkway cut Fulbridge Road in half to the north of their home and Guilf resented having to negotiate what he called 'spaghetti junction' in order to get to church. In truth, St. Paul's 'high church' style of worship was not really their 'cup of tea', but the warm welcome they received there more than made up for this.

Mary and Guilf were taken aback in the spring of 1968 to learn that their older daughter's next teaching post would be considerably further away than Romford. Joan had accepted a three-year contract to teach Spanish in Jamaica, and would be sailing for Kingston that August. Although putting a brave face on it, her parents were clearly sad at the thought of her going so far away and for so long. One consolation was that their niece, Christine, (the only daughter of Mary's sister Evelyn,) had also decided to teach in Jamaica. (The two cousins taught at different schools but both in Brown's Town.)

In reality, Guilf and Mary should not have been surprised at all by their older daughter's desire to work abroad. From the time Joan opted to study modern languages at High School, it was clear that she would need to go on the school exchanges to France and Spain. Alison, too, was keen on languages and stayed with a German family one year and with a family in Barcelona the next. However difficult it might have been for the Moulds financially, they always managed to let the girls take part and, furthermore, always welcomed their European guests most warmly to Fulbridge Road.

There was something else too. During Joan's second year at university, where she was majoring in Spanish, she had a golden opportunity to spend the summer vacation of 1963 in North America and hoped to find work with Massey Ferguson in Toronto to fund her trip. When no job actually materialised, her parents generously offered her the trip as an early 21st birthday present! They knew that she had been awarded a place on the 'People to People Program' through which she would stay with several American host families but thought it would be even better if she could visit the American branches of the Mould family (in Oregon, California and South Dakota), as well as Aunt Daisy (Mills) and family in Canada.

Before his daughter's trip, though, Guilf had some research to do, if only to unearth some addresses for the American contingent. (His sister Doris was possibly useful here, being a good correspondent and having the time to keep in touch.) But he did far more than provide addresses; he wrote notes about his aunts, uncles and cousins, which would give Joan a most useful start with her research years later.

There was, however, one part of their daughter's tour that was of special interest to her parents: the trip to Alberta. The journey by Greyhound from Aberdeen, South Dakota, across the prairies to Calgary seemed never-ending, but the warm welcome by the Canadian cousins made up for it all. The highlight of the trip was the meeting with her great-aunt Daisy, by then eighty-four years old. Joan had been invited to stay with Daisey's youngest son, Jack and it was his family who drove her up to Edmonton for the reunion.

Mary and Guilf, of course, could hardly wait to hear how their daughter had got on in Canada. When they eventually learned of the wonderful welcome she had received, they felt encouraged to plan a trip of their own for the future.

But five years on in 1968, with Joan now in Jamaica, it was not too long before Mary and Guilf had something else to occupy their minds. Alison had graduated that summer and obtained her first teaching post at Weybridge in Surrey. It was through her new church there that she met her future husband, David Peters, whose parents had settled in the area after working in India. The young couple were married at Paston Church, Peterborough in August the following year.

Exactly two years later, Guilf retired aged sixty-five, having worked at Perkins for sixteen years; he was more than ready to take it easy. Always very fit physically, he had cycled the two or three miles to work each day, (come rain or shine,) ready to 'clock on' at 8am. Over his time on the shop floor, he had got on well with his workmates, who gave him a good 'send off '. Mary, naturally, organised a couple of informal gatherings at home for close friends and family. By happy coincidence, Joan's three- year contract in Jamaica also finished in the summer of 1971 and she returned to England in time for the celebrations.

A month later, she found a job in Peterborough, teaching English to the children of Asian immigrants and living at home again. The next two years proved to be very happy ones, both work-wise and socially.

It was during this time that Joan met Reg Bolton who was working as Agent for Peterborough's Member of Parliament, Sir Harmar Nicholls, and the two were soon courting seriously. But, it was very much a case of "love me, love my dog", she recalls. When asked if she liked dogs before her first visit to Reg's house, she replied in the affirmative, but was totally unprepared for the huge animal that came bounding out of the utility room, ending up with his two fore-feet on her shoulders! Bran was a Scottish deerhound (and big for his age) but Joan had passed 'the test' and would go on to welcome another dozen or so deerhounds over the years. Unfortunately, by the time the couple met, Reg had just been appointed to a new post in Shrewsbury, starting in the February of '73. This posed a slight problem, of course.

In the meantime, the family were awaiting a special event: Alison and David were expecting their first child - and a first grandchild for Guilf and Mary. Andrew was born in Lowestoft on Saturday, 9th June and joined by a sister, Catherine, just fifteen months later, in September 1974. Alison's parents seemed to revel in their new role and couldn't see enough of their grandchildren. In fact, they took to going on holiday together every year while the children were small, usually renting a cottage or an apartment so that they could cater for themselves. Mary delighted in taking two or three boxes full of produce from the garden since she begrudged spending money on meals out. "They only give you old frozen stuff," she would claim. It was certainly not a case of being mean. She was a most generous person, as was Guilf. But both remembered the hard times they had been through and couldn't 'break the habits of a lifetime'.

Going on holiday together, enabled Alison and David to appreciate at first hand how good the older couple were with children. Guilf was able to juggle with three (or even four) balls to amuse his grandchildren. Another 'party piece' was to walk about on a pair of home-made stilts. He was also an expert bird watcher, knowing all the birds by name. Being more fortunate with his health than Mary, he remained fit and energetic well into retirement. Alison clearly remembers her father climbing a tree to find an owl's nest when in his seventies.

Joan was delighted at becoming an 'auntie', as well as godmother to Andrew. The Friday after he was born, she asked her headmistress for the afternoon off in order to drive to Norfolk and give her sister a helping hand. (Mary and Guilf still had their livestock and didn't find it easy to get away.) A fortnight later, Joan made another trip. This time it was to Shrewsbury where she had an interview for a modern languages post at a small, private boarding school in the heart of the Shropshire countryside. Joan was appointed, starting in the September and shared a cottage in the school grounds. It was idyllic! The following June, Joan and Reg announced their engagement and married in Shrewsbury on 22nd July. They set up home in Montford Bridge and lived there for four years, before going up to Northumberland in1978 when Reg was appointed Conservative Agent to Geoffrey Rippon.

Soon after moving to their new home in Haydon Bridge, a few miles from Hexham, Joan learned that she was expecting her first baby for the following Easter. Unfortunately, the baby girl arrived in the January, three months early, and lived for only four days. It was especially sad for Joan's parents, since their daughter had been admitted to hospital just two days before Mary's birthday. Their initial optimism quickly turned to grief when they learned that their tiny granddaughter, christened Victoria Grace, had died in the premature baby unit at Newcastle General Infirmary.

Just over a year later, Joan returned to Hexham hospital where, on the 6th of February, she gave birth to a sturdy son - Maxwell James. This time, understandably, there was general rejoicing! Without any doubt, Guilf and Mary would have liked to see more of their third (and last) grandchild, but the sheer distance between Peterborough and Northumberland meant that get-togethers were bound to be limited. As things worked out, eighteen months later they would have this small grandson living under their roof for almost a year, but not before they had finally fulfilled a life-long ambition to visit Canada.

When Guilf and his wife flew out to Alberta in early June 1981 for a four-week visit, it was the furthest they had ever travelled and the longest they had ever been away from home: quite an adventure! Guilf's Aunt Daisy had died some fifteen years before, of course, but he had an emotional reunion with all four of his cousins, Ron, Claude, Dorothy, ('Dot') and Jack. The couple began their holiday as guests of Jack and Charlotte Wilders in the small town of Ponoka, in between Calgary and Edmonton, and then moved to Lacombe to stay with cousin Dot and her husband, Frank Adamson. From there, the Adamsons took their English guests for a week's trip into The Rockies and Banff National Park - a fitting conclusion to a memorable holiday.

They had been back in England for barely a week when Joan arrived with Maxwell - now seventeen months old. Alison and family were there for the weekend too and, like them, Joan wanted to hear all about the Canadian adventure. But, keen to get back to her teaching again, she was actually breaking her journey on her way to an interview in Yorkshire. It should perhaps be explained here that Reg's job in Northumberland had not turned out as he'd hoped, so that when his previous post (in Shrewsbury) unexpectedly became vacant again two and a half years later, he needed little persuasion to apply. But this time there were six of them making the journey back to Shropshire: Reg and Joan, Baby Maxwell (rather too 'chubby' for his eight months!) plus Bonnie the Deerhound with two of her year-old 'puppies'. Kate and Little Dog were now very much a part of the Bolton household - and already pretty huge!

Fast-forwarding again now to July 1981 and that interview (in Whitby) - where Joan was unsuccessful. She was, however, offered a teaching post in Peterborough a few days later. This then meant that she and Max would be living with her parents, whilst Reg soldiered on in Shrewsbury by himself. This was far from ideal, needless to say, even if the family did manage to get together for school holidays and some weekends. (After a year at the Peterborough school, it was back to Shropshire again, before Reg's last 'posting' took the Bolton trio to Dorset in the South West of England.)

But there was a positive aspect to all this upheaval. Mary and Guilf were able to form a close bond with their youngest grandchild during that year and all three seemed to have a great deal of fun in the process. Although they felt unable to look after Maxwell every day whilst their daughter was working, (a friend living nearby agreed to do this), the grandparents enjoyed amusing him for the rest of the time, often taking him for outings in the car. Both had a good sense of humour and were not above hoodwinking their small charge on occasions. Joan was intrigued, for instance, when Max told her that he had 'been to the beach' one afternoon and showed her his bucket and spade. "Oh, yes, and we had a lovely time, didn't we?" added Mary, with a wink in her daughter's direction. Once Max was in bed, Mary explained: they had driven all of five miles to a little place with a stream and some sandy soil on the bank, suitable for making 'sand' pies!

When their Golden Wedding came round in May 1985, Mary and Guilf invited about fifty friends and relatives to join in the celebrations at the Gordon Arms. It was a very happy occasion but, inevitably, also one that was tinged with nostalgia. In the press report for the local papers, the couple related how they had met and how Guilf had cycled to Leicestershire during their courtship. Not only did many of his former customers remember the energetic young man who had brought the milk to their doors (and sometimes flowers, too,) but several were also able to congratulate the couple in person, now that they were worshipping at St. Paul's in New England, the church where they had married.

It was towards the end of 1985 that a gentleman contacted the Moulds 'out of the blue', asking if he could come and see them. He was a land developer who had his eye on the bottom half of their holding, with a view to building a dozen houses on it, with access from Francis Gardens. Guilf was quite interested, especially since the smallholding now only supported a few chickens, whilst still requiring a lot of maintenance. After some discussion, he agreed to sell them one and a third acres, which would soon become Anthony Close. Most uncharacteristically for Guilford, (though most likely encouraged by Mary), he held out for the price he wanted and the deal was finalised in the May of 1987. The proceeds were certainly sufficient to have purchased a much smarter bungalow than they already had, (and even a Caribbean cruise, had they so wished!) But that was not their style and, after all, they were 'not getting any younger', as Guilf often chose to remind everyone in his later years. So instead, they opted to stay where they were and to 'help the family', though they did allow themselves a few 'treats', of course. This unexpected piece of good fortune was worth far more than all the crossword prizes put together and could be seen as a reward for all their hard work over the years. It was just a pity it had not come earlier, when they would have been better able to enjoy it.

On Sunday 16th June 1991, Mary and Guilf attended morning service at St. Paul's Church as usual. Then, after lunch, they walked over the road to the community centre in Beckett's Close for a concert put on by the Salvation Army. On their return, they had a light meal with a cup of tea before watching one of their favourite television programmes called 'Songs of Praise'. (Recorded from a different church each week, this programme featured well-known hymns sung by the congregation, with individual worshippers explaining why a particular hymn was special for them). Mary joined in the singing, as always. But after quite a busy day, she retired early.

Daughter Joan was also a fan of 'Songs of Praise' and had recorded it to watch later as she caught up with the ironing. It was well after midnight when she was interrupted by the telephone. It was her father, ringing in great distress, to tell them that Mary had been taken ill. He added, "I've dialled 999 and the medics are working on her now." But it was to no avail.

The Vicar of St. Paul's, Father Brian Secker, wrote the following tribute in the July magazine, headed **'In Memoriam: Mrs. Mary Mould:** Mrs. Mould, so full of life with energies that seemed inexhaustible, and such a good sense of humour. Her sudden death came as a stunning and almost unbelievable blow.

Was Mary not with us at Mass on Sunday 16th June? Then a full day, with an afternoon concert at Beckett's Close, and later joining in the hymns on Songs of Praise. And at the end of the day, the unexpected death. Somehow it all seems as if Mary would have wished it so, to die after an event-filled day. Not for her a long, lingering illness.

She will be much missed at St. Paul's, as a lady always buoyant and cheerful, and as a hard worker with her husband in fund raising. No-one having seen their garden produce stall will forget the fruit of her labours. May she rest in peace.'

Mary was seventy-nine when she died. Her funeral took place the following Friday, 21st June. She had well exceeded the biblical milestone she so often quoted - 'three score years and ten,' and enjoyed a good life, in every sense. But it was Guilf who was left to experience the 'labour and sorrow ' to which the psalmist referred. He had lost his companion of sixty years and felt desolate. Everyone rallied round to help and support him - friends, neighbours and family. He survived his wife by eighteen months and died at home in his sleep on Saturday, 5th December, 1992, aged eighty-six.

After Guilf's funeral service and cremation the following Friday, everyone gathered at the Loxley Community Centre in Werrington for a cup of tea and refreshments. (The caterers had, in fact, put on quite a spread, including a glass of sherry, something very much in keeping with the hospitable person Guilf had been.) By this time, all the decorations were up in readiness for Christmas, including at the Centre. As if suddenly aware of this, the Warden apologised profusely for not having taken them down. But Alison and Joan assured her there was no need, knowing their father wouldn't have minded at all. In fact, whilst planning the funeral, they had compiled a display of photos from the various stages of their parents' lives, as a reminder to everyone of the happy times they had enjoyed.

George and Fanny's second daughter was born on September 17, 1909, the last child to be born at the Gunthorpe home before the move to Gilpin Street in 1911. Although Marjorie seemed a happy, normal child in her early years, her parents must have been concerned when they noticed that their young daughter was developing a curvature of the spine. This became more pronounced as she grew older and was clearly disfiguring for a young woman. Apart from this, family photographs show Marjorie to have been quite nice looking with her long, dark hair.

Apparently, Fanny claimed that, Marjorie had been given a desk too small for her at school and this is what caused the problem. This explanation seems unlikely: for one thing, as a former teacher there herself, surely she could have complained about the desk and had something done about it. Far more likely is that the defect was there from

183

birth. Whether any remedial treatment was available (or considered, even) is not known.

Once again, it was Ursula who was able to give us a further picture of Marjorie from her three and a half years living at Rock House, between August 1947 and January 1951, and arriving back in Peterborough just six months after Fanny's death. "Marjorie used to do everything around the house - the cooking and the cleaning," Ursula recalled. She also acted as mediator between her bickering sisters, Doris and Iris. Of the three, Ursula had no doubt that "Marjorie was the nicest." She always seemed to have time for Ursula, making the effort to explain things and to help her German sister-in-law. Since neither sister had any friends - or, indeed, any life - outside of Rock House, Marjorie at least was probably pleased to have the diversion of a younger woman in the house, particularly since Ursula was not afraid to roll up her sleeves and help.

Another story told by Ursula may possibly throw a little light on Marjorie's demise, as well as illustrating her stubborn nature. (A trait shown by all the Mould siblings, in Joan Mould's view!) Ursula and Hubert's first child, Laurence, was born in November 1948, while they were still living at Gilpin Street. In those days mothers used toweling nappies (diapers) for their babies. After washing them out, Ursula asked Marjorie where she might hang them to dry and Marjorie said she would rig up the clothes line in the yard. Ursula said that she could do it but Marjorie ignored her offer. She carried a high, rickety chair from the kitchen into the yard so that she could attach the line to a post. Unfortunately, she fell off, breaking her collarbone in the process. The doctor put her arm in a sling, which put Marjorie out of action for several weeks. Ursula felt that her sister-in-law went downhill health-wise from that time.

Marjorie was the first of George and Fanny's children to die. She was a month short of her forty-fourth birthday when she passed away on the sixteenth of August in 1953. The death certificate gives cancer as the cause of death but how long she had suffered from the disease is not clear. In addition to the cancer, several other factors combined to make her later years unhappy. Her deformity, for one, must have caused her body extra stress. Also, the trauma of losing her mother in such tragic circumstances affected Marjorie deeply. Equally, she found it very difficult to come to terms with her father's second marriage - and to someone only nine years older than herself. This event, of course, was swiftly followed by her father's sudden death and could have been "the last straw". Five months later, she herself was dead. After the funeral, Marjorie was buried next to her parents' in the Eastfield Cemetery.

By the time the last daughter, Iris, was born in 1913, Fanny was forty two years old. She already had six children at home and was working hard at the dairy too. We can only imagine her feelings - surely of dismay - when, three years later she found she was "expecting" again at forty six. All the same, little Hubert, was doubtless welcomed and loved when he duly arrived on the last day of February 1917. George and Fanny's oldest child, Doris, was sixteen that same year and, although never considered home loving or maternal, she may well have helped her mother, if only by amusing her baby brother or taking him out in the pram.

Guilf had been the youngest son until Hubert's arrival but they were separated by a ten-and-a-half year age difference. In fact, it was the oldest boy, Cyril, Hubert's senior by fifteen years, who "took him under his wing" and was responsible for interesting his younger brother in bird watching. When Hubert was older, the two of them would go to a hide they had made in Werrington. So inseparable were these brothers that, when Cyril started courting Beattie, Hubert didn't understand why he wasn't welcome to go along too!

Brother Guilf was also interested in bird watching. Joan remembers some lovely outings to the woods on Sunday mornings in the spring. Quite often Guilf, Joan and Alison would meet up with Hubert and his sons, Laurence and Melvin. While the girls picked flowers, the others would search for nests. Hubert had a good collection of birds' eggs: in those days, it was not forbidden but the ground rule was to take only one egg from a nest. The main aim was to find a nest and to quietly watch the chicks.

As already mentioned, Hubert was also a keen photographer having improvised a small darkroom at Rock House and, later, had a purpose-built one at the family home in Newark Avenue. Combining these two interests, he took the photos for a book about kestrels, entitled," Kestrel Klee". The book's author Kenneth Richmond, was a friend of Hubert's who wrote several other bird books in which Hubert's photos were used.

Another of his hobbies was Meccano from which Hubert made some marvelous working models, including a train on its track, roundabouts, a crane and a four foot high windmill which he was working on just before he died. But then Hubert was always "good with his hands". For that reason becoming a joiner (carpenter) seemed the perfect choice of career. He left school at fourteen in 1931 and began a five year apprenticeship, probably continuing to work for the same firm for a year or so, after qualifying.

Ursula indicated that, in the early months of the war, Hubert began working for BTH, a company involved in war work in Fletton Avenue. (Hotpoint is now on this site). By so doing, he knew he would postpone his call up. Most young men of his age would have been called up by the summer of 1940, after Dunkirk. In fact, Hubert did not receive his papers until 1942, the year he turned twenty-five.

His regiment was the 11th Hussars which, as part of the 8th Army, from 1941 onwards became known as "the Desert Rats". Following the Allied landings in Europe in June and July of 1944, his regiment fought through Belgium and

Hubert Mould (on left) in World War II

Holland and into Germany, arriving in Berlin at the end of July 1945. Their base was in the regimental town of Spandau.

A few days later, on the 5th of August, a young woman was waiting for her cousin outside a local café and became aware that an English soldier was watching her. He spoke and the two were soon in conversation. The soldier was Hubert and the German girl was Ursula Oberländer.

In Berlin towards the end of the war, people were experiencing great hardship, Ursula's family included. There was a severe food shortage and Berliners risked Russian gunfire when they went on forays to find it. They had to cross a bridge over the River Havel and, on more than one occasion, Ursula remembered picking her way over bodies. One day she came across an abandoned van that had been fired on, carrying a load of cheeses wrapped in foil. Ursula gathered up as many as she could, delighted with her lucky find.

All of the Berliners had to potato pick for the Russians, and, in theory, were allowed to keep a bag for themselves. Often, however, the Russian guards would confiscate these at the border, so Ursula and her fellow pickers used to throw the bags into a ditch before reaching the border, returning to collect them the next day.

When they began courting, Hubert used to go to the Oberländers' garden which was separate from their house. Ursula often shared her bread ration with him to make a sandwich. Ursula's father who worked for the German Post Office, was most annoyed by this, since he knew Ursula was not eating properly. In fact, of course, Herr Oberländer was altogether displeased about Ursula befriending an English soldier, and on the army's side there was a "no fraternization" policy. But none of these considerations mattered to Hubert and Ursula once they were in love.

If Hubert's parents also had their misgivings about the romance (which would have been understandable) they did not let on. What we do know, however, is that once George Mould knew that his son's intentions were serious and honorable, he wrote a letter to the Oberländers. In it he assured Ursula's parents that she would be welcomed and well looked after with the family in Peterborough. "It was such a nice letter," says Ursula, "and after that Dad seemed happier".

For the first few months after the young couple met, Hubert was stationed in Spandau itself. His regiment then moved to the Harz Mountains and later to Jever in West Germany. By the spring of 1946 they were based in Delmenhorst, near Bremen in the north of Germany.

By this time they had been going out together for eight months or so and had become engaged. They were inseparable. Hubert asked Ursula if she was prepared to join him in West Germany and she agreed to go. This was very much against her parents' advice since they were only too aware of the danger involved. At least she didn't have to give up her job since she no longer had one.

Ursula had received a good education, having been through elementary school until the age of fourteen. She then passed the entry examination for commercial school where she had two years of secretarial training and also studied English (Little did she know how useful this would be five years later.) By the time she left commercial school at sixteen, it was late 1939 and the war had started. She found a job in the offices of the large Spreewerke factory which made parts for the U-boats. Ursula worked there for about four years. This industrial region was subjected to relentless bombing attacks. When Spreewerke was destroyed, her job also came to an end.

Therefore, Ursula had little to lose by following Hubert to Delmenhorst. Once there, he arranged for her to stay with the Meiers, a German couple who lived near the camp. Now promoted to the rank of Sergeant, Hubert gave the Meiers provisions by way of payment. These arrangements proved very satisfactory all around.

Ursula told Joan Bolton of a favorite rendezvous for her outings with Hubert. There was a nice restaurant by the river, meant only for soldiers. But Hubert would buy two meals, and then take them to an area at the back where the chairs were stored and where they would eat together, without attracting attention.

Plans were afoot for a wedding the following year. Ursula's father was adamant that this would take place in Berlin, not England. As a British citizen, Ursula would be able to travel out of Germany more easily and safely. Alongside this practical reason was a sentimental one; naturally the Oberländers wanted to see their daughter married amongst friends and family in Spandau. They did not know when they would see her again.

But in order to go along with these plans, Hubert's period of service had to be extended by six months. Whereas he had been due to be de-mobbed in February 1947, he would now stay on in Germany until the following August. This probably seemed a small sacrifice to make in order to satisfy his future in-laws, but what he could not have foreseen were the repercussions this decision might have back in Peterborough.

After Ursula had been in West Germany for several months, she wanted to return to Berlin to see her parents. This, of course, would involve going through the Russian-occupied zone. Hubert had managed to get four days leave and they had intended to travel together on the military train which was only for the use of military personnel. Ursula had to disguise herself to pass for a soldier, wearing an army cap and trench coat and was instructed only to go on board when Hubert gave the "all clear" signal. But, unfortunately, when Hubert glanced out of the window, Ursula mistook this for the signal and got on too soon. She sat quietly in the corner of the carriage with the collar of her coat turned up and her cap pulled well down. She forgot that her ears were still visible, complete with gold ear studs. When an officer looked into the carriage he noticed the strange figure in the corner and did a double take. Fortunately, he made no comment and took no action.

When they reached Charlottenburg Station in Berlin, Ursula waited until the soldiers had all gotten off, then climbed out of the carriage window and crossed over the lines to get to the street at the other side. She could then casually amble up to join Hubert before they took another train together for the short journey to Spandau.

The most daring journey Ursula made was in early June 1947 when she had to return to Berlin to make the final preparations for her wedding, set to take place on 18th June. Perhaps more importantly for Ursula, she had to ensure all her papers were in order before she traveled to England with Hubert. The route was the same as when they had traveled to Berlin to visit her parents, but this time Ursula was not on a military train and Hubert was not with her. He would follow a few days later and bring Ursula's luggage so she could travel unencumbered. Ursula made sure she always carried with her a good supply of cigarettes to serve as "sweeteners" when confronted by the East German and Russian officials along the way.

As she waited for the train on the first stage of the journey, Ursula noticed a young German who looked as though he too, might be planning to cross over the no-man's-land corridor into West Berlin. When she approached him, she found that her hunch had been correct. Furthermore, he knew of a good place to cross, so they joined forces. By the time they reached the crossing point, two or three others had joined them and they went to speak to the engine driver who was going up to the Russian border. When they reached the end of the Russian zone, they had to wait until the guards had disappeared before exiting the train. They were helped by the German staff who were "on the look out" for them and, since it was now night time, they had the cover of darkness. They made their way across the railway lines to the platform where the Berlin-bound goods train was expected. When it came in and the time was right, they went straight to the locomotive tender which the fireman had opened in readiness. The stowaways then had to lie face down in the space under the water tank for the twenty-minute journey across no-man's-land.

No doubt this hazardous stage of the journey seemed never-ending to Ursula and her companions. They had to keep very still and quiet, aware that, if they were discovered, they could be shot. Thankfully, all was well. Ursula not only survived to tell the tale but also to marry Hubert.

The marriage took place in Berlin at the British Army Church on Wednesday, 18th June 1947, with a ceremony conducted in English by the Army padre. Apparently, Doris Maile, her future sister-in-law, had been able to send Ursula a length of dress material, along with two lengths for a veil, as well as a series of food parcels. Ursula traveled to the church in a horse-drawn carriage with Herr Oberländer by her side. Sadly, no photos were taken of this. Hubert had arranged with one of his mates to be his best man, but, for some reason, he failed to show up. So Hubert had to go over to his old army base in Spandau to persuade someone to help him out. Jo filled the role very well - and ended up going out with one of Ursula's friends. After the ceremony, the Oberländers laid on a reception for about thirty people.

Two days after the church ceremony, Hubert and Ursula had to go through a civil ceremony at the Registrar's Office. For this, Ursula wore a simple suit. With these formalities, Ursula gave up her German nationality - something she regretted.

For the honeymoon, they were lucky enough to be accommodated for two days at the British Hotel in the center of Berlin where, Ursula said, the lovely food was much appreciated.

Hubert had been granted a week's leave for the nuptials, after which he had to return to the base in West Germany. Ursula went with him, of course, this time fully entitled to travel on the military train as a British citizen. Sad farewells were said as they left Spandau. Ursula would not see her parents again for almost four years.

Once in West Germany, Ursula was accommodated at a British hotel, along with other German girls who had also married British soldiers. Ursula claims they were "shabbily treated" by the British army wives and hotel staff and regularly insulted. The German girls responded in like fashion, so insults were soon flying in both directions! Typically, the British side was at more of a disadvantage language-wise since they couldn't understand the German brides when they grumbled amongst themselves. This problem was partially resolved when the Germans had their breakfast earlier than the others. When Ursula told Hubert how unpleasant the situation was, he again arranged for her to stay with the Meiers. There she remained until the end of July. Again, this proved to be a very happy solution and very convenient, too, since the hotel was in Oldenburg, a few miles from the camp, whereas the Meiers were situated next door.

Hubert and Ursula's journey to England finally began in early August when they took a British train bound for Holland. But, on arriving, there was a surprise in store for Ursula. They heard an announcement calling the soldiers to assemble separately in order to board an army boat (or "cattle ship" as it was known), so Ursula would have to sail by herself. Some consolation came with the discovery that she and her fellow passengers would be sailing for Harwich on the Arnhem, a brand new luxury liner. All the same, Ursula was apprehensive at the prospect of arriving in a strange country to confront the officialdom alone. But she needn't have worried: the army vessel overtook the Arnhem so that Hubert was on the quayside to welcome his young wife as she set foot on English soil for the first time. Two very eventful years had elapsed since their first encounter outside the café in August 1945.

They traveled from Harwich to Peterborough by train and then took a taxi to Gilpin Street. George Mould and his three daughters gave Ursula the warmest of welcomes to Rock House. Doris, who was back at Gilpin Street with her ailing husband, Ernest, took Ursula under her wing and would accompany her whenever she needed to go out. (It seems that Hubert was very protective of his German bride and thought it safer for her not to venture out unless accompanied.) Sister Iris mumbled away in typical Iris fashion but Marjorie was the nicest of all, Ursula thought. Sadly, Fanny, her mother-in-law, had died six months before.

On the positive side, however, the family had had some time to come to terms with Fanny's death. They would also quickly realize that their new sister-in-law was "not just a pretty face". No, Ursula was determined to throw in her lot with her new family and work alongside them. Soon she was washing out the milk churns (formerly Fanny's job) and helping in any way she could.

After the young couple's arrival, Hubert's brothers and their families came to Rock House to meet his new bride. Guilf and Mary took to Ursula right away. Mary had plenty in common with her, even if Ursula was twelve years younger. Both were interested in cooking and gardening and neither was afraid of hard work.

Soon after arriving back in England, Hubert had to go up to Yorkshire to be demobbed (de-mobilized) from the army. Ursula accompanied him and, while her husband went off to complete the formalities, Ursula spent the time looking around York.

At about this time, the couple were shopping in Peterborough town centre when they bumped into someone with whom Hubert had served his apprenticeship fifteen years before. Now a director of a building firm, this friend offered him a job. The Granville Building Company was where Hubert worked until he retired at 65 and where he, too, eventually became a director.

Very soon after arriving in Peterborough and moving in with his father, Hubert put his name on the council's housing list, but, somehow it never seemed to reach the top. As the weeks and months passed, he became tired of waiting and finally announced to Ursula:" We're going to build our own house!" This decision came as music to her ears. Their first child, Laurence, had been born in November 1948 and she could hardly wait for them all to have a place of their own. Hubert drew up the plans and submitted them. Then the waiting began all over again - until a useful contact emerged.

George Mould used to serve milk to many of the GNR cottages in New England. The then mayor of Peterborough, a Mr. Hall, lived in one of these terraced houses and was a customer. In the course of conversation with his milkman, the mayor had doubtless heard about Hubert's predicament. One day in March, 1950 he gave George a useful piece of information, "Tell your son", he said, "that he will get planning permission at the next meeting". On hearing the good news Hubert thought they had been waiting quite long enough and decided to "jump the gun". He and Ursula went over to the building plot on Newark Avenue and began to dig the foundations so that they would have a good start once the official permission came through ten days later. Hubert then completed the foundation work over the Easter holiday.

Although Hubert's firm did all the brickwork, he did all the carpentry himself. His brother, Cyril, did a lot of the painting and Ursula helped with the roof. Hubert was working full time so the house had to be built when he was free. During the summer he would get back to Gilpin Street after work, have a meal and go straight over to Newark Avenue to work on the house. Sometimes on weekends, Ursula would come with Laurence who was then about eighteen months old. By late autumn they had made tremendous progress. The house was not finished but it was habitable. As the days grew shorter, however, it was dark by the time Hubert had trekked over there and he decided it would be far easier to finish the remaining jobs (mostly inside) if they could move in. So, with one bedroom operational, a cooker in the kitchen and a working "loo", they moved in at the beginning of January 1951.

According to Ursula, the house resembled a builder's yard! The front room downstairs (designated as their lounge) was nothing more than a storeroom and instead of carpets there were wood shavings everywhere. In spite of this, their delight knew no bounds as they moved into their own home.

Ursula would be the first to say how welcoming and kind the family was at Gilpin Street but one can imagine the restrictions and frustrations of living under someone else's roof, with the resulting lack of privacy. Their only sanctuary was the bedroom. But understandably for someone like Ursula who enjoyed cooking, the greatest luxury of all was being mistress in her own kitchen.

It must have been a real race to get the house ready for their special visitors a few months after the move. But Ursula's parents had not seen their daughter for almost four years when they came over to England in the spring of 1951. Neither household had a telephone so that the only exchange of news had been through letters. They were delighted to find Ursula so happily settled in the new house their son-in-law had built and naturally were ecstatic to meet their little grandson for the first time. Laurence - or Lollie as he was called then - was two and a half.

On July 19th 1952, eighteen months after the move, their second son was born. They named him Melvin and the family was complete. All four were able to make their first visit to Berlin as a family in 1954. Returning to the city where they had met nearly a decade before must have triggered many memories and emotions for Hubert and Ursula.

Four years later, in 1958, Ursula's parents were preparing for a return visit to Peterborough. They were especially looking forward to seeing how their grandsons had changed since they'd last met. Herr Oberländer was at the doctor's for a routine visit before they traveled when he suddenly collapsed in the surgery and died. He was just 59 years old.

Although Hubert and Ursula both worked hard, they knew how to enjoy their leisure. They were a close-knit family and loved to get out and about together, especially when the boys were young. In the spring they enjoyed going bird watching in the woods, and in the summer, often headed for Brancaster on the Norfolk coast. At that time, they would travel in Hubert's works' van, until later when they had a car of their own.

In 1959 when Laurence and Melvin were established at school, Ursula found a job conveniently close to home - at the garage immediately next door in Newark Avenue. She worked there for six years and got on well. But Guilf and Mary, weren't the only one who felt Ursula's talents were wasted at the garage. By 1965, Guilf had been working at Perkins for about ten years (cycling past Hubert's house each day, in fact) and was aware that a works canteen had recently been opened. Having a sister-in-law who was such a good cook and so practical, It was hardly surprising that Mary and Guilf suggested she might be better off working there if an opportunity presented itself.

Always keen to help people, Mary thought she might even hurry the opportunity along. A woman named Vera, from the Paston area, worked in the offices at Perkins and came to the bungalow every week to fetch her eggs. By a happy coincidence, she called when Ursula was visiting and Mary introduced them. Vera told Ursula that a vacancy would be coming up and she said she would "put a word in" for her. Ursula applied, was interviewed and got the job. It was general work in the kitchen, working the day shift but only part-time. After doing this for a year, Ursula heard of a vacancy for a full-time cook on the night shift - from 10pm to 6am. Ursula had no objection to working nights realizing that working four nights (not Friday) would give her a long weekend. Another "plus" was the hourly rate of time-and-a-half. Only the chef, an Italian gentleman, was over her, but she was in charge of the cooking for the workers' canteen and supervised the girls under her. This was a job Ursula really enjoyed and she remained in the post for fourteen years.

In the late autumn of 1980, her eighty two year old mother left Berlin for good to live with Ursula and Hubert in Peterborough. Naturally Ursula wanted the freedom to enjoy her mother's company after being apart for so long and chose this moment to retire.

During her nine years at Newark Avenue, Frau Oberlander - or 'Oma' as she was generally known - was able to meet her first great grandson. Born on New Years Eve, 1978, Antony was almost two when she first came over and was joined by a sister, Clare, in December 1983. Oma also met Helen, Laurence's fiancée, but sadly died in the July of 1989 - a month short of her ninety-first birthday, and two months before her grandson's wedding.

Oma spoke hardly any English, so those who could speak some German felt obliged to make an effort to converse with her. Laurence had studied it to Advanced Level at Deacon's School and visited Germany several times. Having studied it to '0' level in only one year Joan struggled but managed with a few favorite phrases. (She had "invited herself" to stay with Oma in her Berlin apartment on her way back from a working holiday in Poland in August 1965 and, since that time, had always felt a special bond with her.) The real 'star', of course, was Bernard's daughter, Enid, who had studied German at Leeds University and taught in Germany for many years. As for Hubert, without any lessons, he had simply picked up 'the lingo' whilst over there and could "rattle away" fluently.

As related before, Hubert remained with the same firm until his retirement but when he was only fifty three years old he suffered a heart attack at work. Fortunately it was a mild one. He made a good recovery and went back to work for twelve more years before retiring in 1982.

In December 1994, Hubert fell ill again and was taken to Peterborough Hospital where he died shortly after. He was seventy-seven years old. At his cremation service three days before Christmas, the minister used the customary reading from John 14: "In my father's house are many mansions" which seemed entirely fitting for a man like Hubert who had built his own house! Toward the end of the service Joan Bolton remembers looking up at the winter sunshine coming through the chapel window, with a solitary robin perched on the ledge outside, as if to say its farewell. This was a poignant moment.

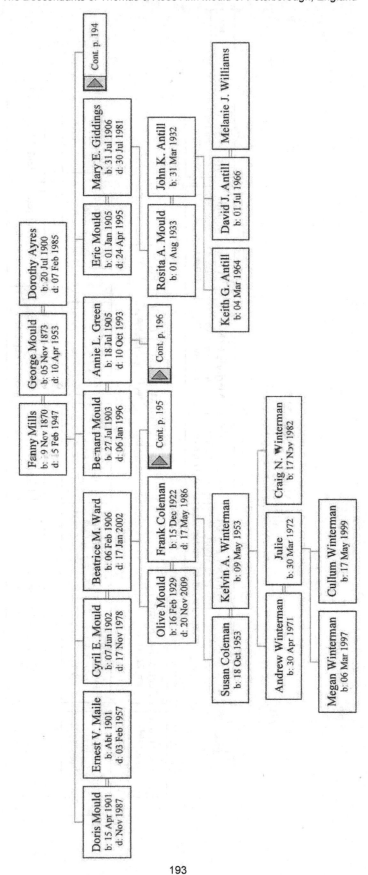

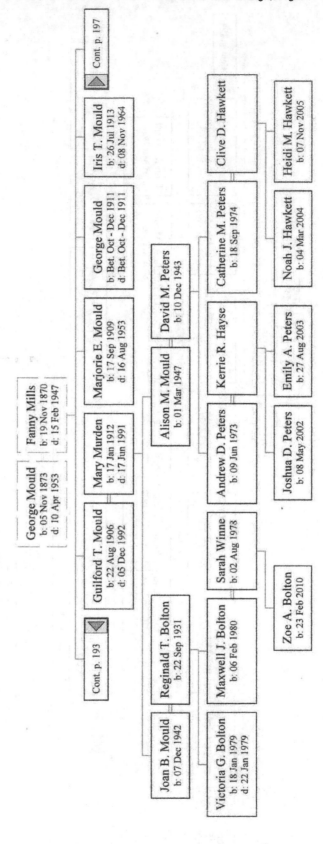

Cont. p. 197

George Mould
b: 05 Nov 1873
d: 10 Apr 1953

Fanny Mills
b: 19 Nov 1870
d: 15 Feb 1947

Iris T. Mould
b: 26 Jul 1913
d: 08 Nov 1964

George Mould
b: Bet. Oct - Dec 1911
d: Bet. Oct - Dec 1911

Marjorie E. Mould
b: 17 Sep 1909
d: 16 Aug 1953

Mary Murden
b: 17 Jan 1912
d: 17 Jun 1991

Guilford T. Mould
b: 22 Aug 1906
d: 05 Dec 1992

David M. Peters
b: 10 Dec 1943

Alison M. Mould
b: 01 Mar 1947

Clive D. Hawkett

Catherine M. Peters
b: 18 Sep 1974

Heidi M. Hawkett
b: 07 Nov 2005

Noah J. Hawkett
b: 04 Mar 2004

Kerrie R. Hayse

Andrew D. Peters
b: 09 Jun 1973

Emily A. Peters
b: 27 Aug 2003

Joshua D. Peters
b: 08 May 2002

Cont. p. 193

Reginald T. Bolton
b: 22 Sep 1931

Sarah Winne
b: 02 Aug 1973

Maxwell J. Bolton
b: 06 Feb 1980

Zoe A. Bolton
b: 23 Feb 2010

Joan B. Mould
b: 07 Dec 1942

Victoria G. Bolton
b: 18 Jan 1979
d: 22 Jan 1979

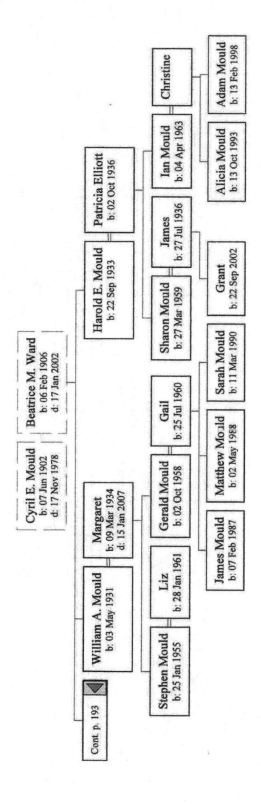

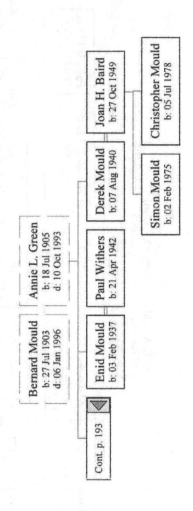

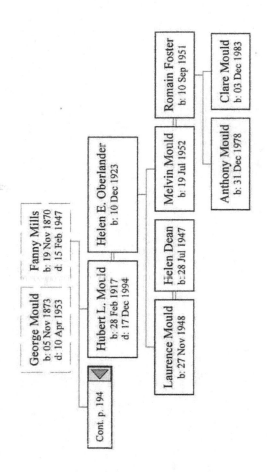

Chapter 11

Genealogy Descendant Report for Thomas Mould

Descendants of Thomas Mould

Generation No. 1

1. THOMAS[5] MOULD *(WILLIAM[4] MOLDS, WILLIAM[3], JOSEPH[2] MOULDS, THOMAS[1] MOULD)*[1,2,3] was born 08 Sep 1827 in Woodcroft, Northamptonshire England[4,5,6], and died 26 Jan 1906 in Gunthorpe, Northamptonshire, England[7,8]. He married ROSE ANN MACKNESS[9,10] 05 Apr 1852 in Etton Church near Peterborough, Northamptonshire, England[11,12], daughter of JABEZ MACKNESS and MARY WADE. She was born 20 Mar 1829 in Brigstock, Northamptonshire, England[13,14,15], and died 25 Jul 1908 in Rushden, Northamptonshire, England[16].

Notes for THOMAS MOULD:
    On July 26, 2000, a friend of Richard Klapper, Jayne Wright, who lives near Rushden, England, sent Richard an e-mail describing her chance meeting of a lovely lady named Miss Joan Mould who told her the following story about the sons of Thomas Mould. Miss Mould said"she was one of 8 children - mostly still alive in the area, and her father was one of about 8 children too. Her grandfather, Charles Mould was the youngest of 4 sons. Their father (Thomas) owned a small farm near or in Peakirk - which is just north of Peterborough. The farm was only large enough to provide work for sons. When the son "Jabe" was old enough to work, he was sent by train to Irthlingborough to find lodgings and work. He found work in a shoe factory. When the youngest, Charles, was old enough, he was sent to find work with his brother. "Uncle Jabe" subsequently emigrated to America and had at least 2 sons. Charles stayed in the area and married Emily Whitbread from Irthlingborough. She died in her 60s but her 2 sisters lived to be 100."
The above story has two correction that need to be made. Joan's grandfather Charles was not the youngest son - his brother George was younger than Charles. Also, Thomas' farm was a dairy farm near Gunthorpe.

Thomas and Rose Ann are buried in the same grave in Section B, grave 35 in the churchyard of All Saints Church in Paston, Northants, England. The headstone reads as follows: "In loving memory of Thomas Mould (of Gunthorpe). Who fell asleep January 26th 1906 aged 78 years. Also Rose Ann his beloved wife. Who fell asleep July 25th 1908 aged 79 years. Thanks be to God. Which giveth us the victory. Through our Lord Jesus Christ."

More About THOMAS MOULD:
Baptism: 21 Oct 1827, Etton, Northamptonshire, England[17,18]
Burial: 29 Jan 1906, Paston, Northants, England[19,20]
Cause of Death: Diarrhoea 4 days. Sudden Heart Failure.
Census: 1881, Paston, Northampton, England[21]
Occupation: 1881, Dairyman[22]
Residence: 31 Mar 1901, Rectory, Gunthorpe, Northants, England[23]

Notes for ROSE ANN MACKNESS:
Rose Ann lived in Gunthorpe with Thomas until his death in 1906. She must have then gone to Rushden to live with her daughter Mary Avery. I believe this because according to Rose Ann's death certificate she died in Rushden and her daughter M Avery was present at death. The burial record also notes she died in Rushden.

Thomas and Rose Ann are buried in the same grave in Section B, grave 35 in the churchyard of All Saints Church in Paston, Northants, England. The headstone reads as follows: "In loving memory of Thomas Mould (of Gunthorpe). Who fell asleep January 26th 1906 aged 78 years. Also Rose Ann his beloved wife. Who fell asleep July 25th 1908 aged 79 years. Thanks be to God. Which giveth us the victory. Through our Lord Jesus Christ."

More About ROSE ANN MACKNESS:
Baptism: 30 Aug 1829, Brigstock, Northamptonshire, England[24,25]
Burial: 28 Jul 1908, Paston, Northants, England[26,27]
Cause of Death: Hemiplegia, Cardiac Failure
Occupation: 30 Mar 1851, Servant[28]
Residence: 1841, Syke Row, Brigstock, England[29]

More About THOMAS MOULD and ROSE MACKNESS:
Marriage: 05 Apr 1852, Etton Church near Peterborough, Northamptonshire, England[50,51]

Children of THOMAS MOULD and ROSE MACKNESS are:
2.   i.   JANE[6] MOULD, b. 01 May 1853, Greatford, Lincolnshire, England; d. 01 Jul 1925, "Avonside", Lenham Road, Sutton, Surrey, England.
     ii.   BETSY MOULD[32,33], b. 19 Feb 1855, Gunthorpe, Northamptonshire, England[34,35,36]; d. 23 Nov 1928, 4 Liverton Road, Loftus, York, England[37,38]; m. JAMES MACKNESS[39,40,41], 16 Aug 1894, Peterborough Reg District, Parish church in Paston, Northants, England[42]; b. 29 Apr 1865, Port Mulgrave, Hinderwell, Yorkshire, England[43]; d. 04 Jan 1948, St. Lukes Hospital, Huddersfield, York, England[44].

Notes for BETSY MOULD:
Betsy married her cousin, James Mackness, and her sister Rebecca married James' cousin Joseph Mackness. Betsy and James had no children.

More About BETSY MOULD:
Baptism: 25 Mar 1855, Paston, Northants, England[45]
Burial: 26 Nov 1928, Loftus Cemetery (New Cemetery), Loftus, Yorks, England[46]
Cause of Death: 1a. heart failure, b. Peripheral neurites, c. senility[47]
Occupation: 1881, General servant for 2 older sisters[48]
Residence: Apr 1881, North Fen Lane, Glinton, Northampton, England[49]

More About JAMES MACKNESS:
Baptism: 05 May 1865, Hinderwell, Yorkshire, England[50]
Burial: 07 Jan 1948, Edgerton Cemetery, Huddersfield, York, England[51]
Cause of Death: Senility[52]
Occupation: 23 Nov 1928, Retired banksman at ironstone mine below ground[53]
Residence: 16 Aug 1894, Rushden, Northamptonshire, England[54]

More About JAMES MACKNESS and BETSY MOULD:
Marriage: 16 Aug 1894, Peterborough Reg District, Parish church in Paston, Northants, England[54]

    iii.   MARY MOULD[55], b. 08 Dec 1856, Gunthorpe, Northamptonshire, England[55,56,57]; d. 02 Mar 1941, Ellingson, Perkins County, South Dakota, USA[58,59,60]; m. JAMES EDWARD DALE AVERY[61,62], 02 Jun 1884, Parish church, Glinton, Northants, England[63]; b. 18 Jun 1859, Glinton, Northants, England[64,65]; d. 15 Feb 1915, Peakirk, Northants, England[66].

Notes for MARY MOULD:
Mary was called "Polly" and her husband died while they were in England. They never had children. Polly came to the US on September 18, 1921 and lived with her brother Jabez and his wife Sarah. Helen Klapper said she was a sweet and quiet woman who sat around the house and read her Bible a lot. Following the death(?) of Jabez, Polly moved to Ellingson, South Dakota to live with her sister Becky. They lived together until Polly's death.

More About MARY MOULD:
Burial: 06 Mar 1941, Ellingson, Perkins County, South Dakota, USA[67]
Cause of Death: Cerebral Hemorrhage[68]
Immigration: 18 Sep 1921, From England to U.S.[69]
Medical Information: Mary was 5'3" per the Ellis Island records.
Occupation: Apr 1881, Cook Domestic[70]
Residence: Apr 1881, Town Street, Glinton, Northampton, England[71]

Notes for JAMES EDWARD DALE AVERY:
James name history is unusual. In the 1881 census he is shown as James Dale the son of Edward and Rebecca Dale. On his marriage license (June 2, 1884) three years later, he was James Edward Dale Avery and his father was Edward Dale. His birth certificate cleared up the mystery. James was illegitimate. His mother Rebecca Avery gave birth to him 3 months before she married Edward Dale. James evidently took his fathers last name of Dale but later added Avery to the end. James couldn't read or write as he made his X on his marriage certificate.

More About JAMES EDWARD DALE AVERY:
Burial: 19 Feb 1915, Peakirk, Northants, England[72,73]
Cause of Death: Heart disease[74]

Medical Information: Mary was 5'3" per the arrival records at Ellis Island, New York.
Occupation: 1881, Farm labourer[75]
Residence: 02 Jun 1884, Glinton, Northants, England[76]

More About JAMES AVERY and MARY MOULD:
Marriage: 02 Jun 1884, Parish church, Glinton, Northants, England[76]

3. iv. ROSE MOULD, b. 02 Nov 1858, Gunthorpe, Northamptonshire, England; d. 25 Jun 1925, Peakirk, Northamptonshire, England.

    v. JABEZ A MOULD[77], b. 04 Oct 1860, Gunthorpe, Northamptonshire, England[77,78]; d. 14 Jan 1862[79].

        More About JABEZ A MOULD:
        Burial: 18 Jan 1862, Paston, Northants, England[80]
        Residence: 1861, Gunthorpe, Northants, England[81]

    vi. WILLIAM JABEZ MOULD[82], b. 06 Dec 1862, Gunthorpe, Northamptonshire, England[82,83]; d. 01 Jan 1863, Gunthorpe, Northamptonshire, England[84,85].

        More About WILLIAM JABEZ MOULD:
        Burial: 02 Jan 1863, Paston, Northants, England[86]
        Cause of Death: Whooping Cough

    vii. JOSEPH MOULD[87,88], b. 25 Apr 1864, Gunthorpe, Northamptonshire, England[89,90,91]; d. 31 Mar 1900, Gunthorpe, Northamptonshire, England[92,93].

        Notes for JOSEPH MOULD:
        On July 26, 2000, a friend of Richard Klapper, Jayne Wright, who lives near Rushden, England, sent Richard an e-mail describing her chance meeting of a lovely lady named Miss Joan Mould who told her the following story about the sons of Thomas Mould. Miss Mould said "she was one of 8 children - mostly still alive in the area, and her father was one of about 8 children too. Her grandfather, Charles Mould was the youngest of 4 sons. Their father (Thomas) owned a small farm near or in Peakirk - which is just north of Peterborough. The farm was only large enough to provide work for two sons. When the son "Jabe" was old enough to work, he was sent by train to Irthlingborough to find lodgings and work. He found work in a shoe factory. When Charles, was old enough, he was sent to find work with his brother. "Uncle Jabe" subsequently emigrated to America and had at least 2 sons. Charles stayed in the area and married Emily Whitbread from Irthlingborough. She died in her 60s but her 2 sisters lived to be 100."
        The above story has two correction that need to be made. Joan's grandfather Charles was not the youngest son - his brother George was younger than Charles. Also, Thomas' farm was a dairy farm near Gunthorpe.

        Joseph Mould committed suicide while living with his parents. He cut his throat. The depositions of the two witnesses in the coroner's investigation are as follows:

        The Liberty of the hundred of Nassaburg and Soke of Peterborough to wit:

        Deposition of witnesses taken for our Sovereign Lady the Queen at the house of Thomas Brown in the Parish of Gunthorpe within the said District this 31st day of March, One thousand and nine hundred, touching the death of Joseph Mould. Before me, John William Buckle, Coroner for the said Liberty.

        Thomas Mould sworn saith. I am a cottager and live at Gunthorpe. The body which the jury have just seen is that of my son Joseph. He was 35 years of age, a Bachelor and lived at home with me. He worked for William Rowe the Butcher. He was at work last a fortnight since having been since then at home ill with the influenza. He has been attended by Dr. Peach Hay about 3 times. The deceased went to the Dr. yesterday morning. He was very low spirited and has been for the last 4 or 5 days. I last saw him alive about 6:15 last night. He was then leaving the sitting room to go to his bed room. My wife and I went to our room. We neither heard anything of the deceased during the night - I went out this morning and about 20 to 6 this morning my wife came to me and asked if I knew anything of Joe meaning the deceased. She said
        T Mould
        (End of Page)

        I must come and I went directly. I found the deceased on the floor at the side of his bed in a pool of blood. He was quite dead then - I did not interfere with him there and sent my son George for the Police. My son George did not live with us - I never heard the deceased threaten to take his life. He has been queer in his mind at times. He was examined 20 years ago as to the state of his mind by Dr. Paley. He was at the Union Infirmary for one week. He was excited at times when the weather was hot. We thought it was ....(words missing from copy).

T Mould

Walter Knight sworn with. I am a Police Constable stationed at Werrington. About 6:30 this morning I was called by George Mould. He told me his Brother the deceased had killed himself. I went at once to Gunthorpe and found the deceased lying on the floor face downward in a pool of blood. I examined the body. He was dead, stiff and cold. I found a gash in his neck about 4 inches long cut deep. The wind pipe cut through. He had a razor in his right hand and a pocket knife lay under his face, small

Walter Knight

(End of Page)

blade open under his face - The bed clothes were turned down as if he had been to bed. He was undressed-There were no marks of any struggle. I think the injuries were self inflicted.

Walter Knight

Verdict

Suicide while temporarily insane - cutting his own throat

The foregoing testimony of Thomas Mould and Walter Knight were severally taken and deposited before me at the time and place aforesaid.

John William Buckle
Coroner for the hundred of Nassaburg

Joseph is buried in the churchyard of the All Saints Church in Paston, Northants, England in Section B, grave 29. The inscription on the headstone reads as follows: "In memory of Joseph. The beloved son of Thomas and Roseann Mould. Who died March 31st 1900 aged 35 years. Gone but not forgotten." As of October 2002 the headstone had been broken into many pieces.

More About JOSEPH MOULD:
Burial: 03 Apr 1900, Paston, Northants, England[94,95]
Cause of Death: Suicide whilst temporarily insane by cutting his throat
Medical Information: "(Death) Certificate received from J H Buckle, Coroner for the Hundred of Nassaburgh. Inquest held 31st March 1900.
Occupation: 31 Mar 1900, Builder's laborer[96]
Residence: 1881, Paston, Northants, England[97]

4.   viii.   JABEZ MOULD, b. 24 Dec 1865, Gunthorpe, Northants, England; d. 10 Jul 1936, Aberdeen, South Dakota, USA.

5.   ix.   REBECCA MOULD, b. 15 Feb 1868, Gunthorpe, Northamptonshire, England; d. 04 Jul 1946, Viking Township, Perkins County, South Dakota.

6.   x.   CHARLES MOULD, b. 15 Nov 1871, Gunthorpe, Northampton, England; d. 03 Mar 1945, 2 Grove Street, Higham Ferrers, Northamptonshire, England.

7.   xi.   GEORGE MOULD, b. 05 Nov 1873, Gunthorpe, Northants, England; d. 10 Apr 1953, County Hospital, Huntingdon, England.

Generation No. 2

2. JANE[6] MOULD (*THOMAS[5], WILLIAM[4] MOLDS, WILLIAM[3], JOSEPH[2] MOULDS, THOMAS[1] MOULD*)[98,99] was born 01 May 1853 in Greatford, Lincolnshire, England[100], and died 01 Jul 1925 in "Avonside", Lenham Road, Sutton, Surrey, England[101]. She married DEVEREUX HENRY JESSOP[102,103] 23 Oct 1878 in The Paston Parish Church, Northants, England[104], son of HENRY JESSOP. He was born Bet. Jan - Mar 1855 in Little Stonham, Suffolk, England[105,106], and died 08 Feb 1932 in 26 Wolverton Ave., Kingston, Surrey, England[107].

Notes for JANE MOULD:
An interesting piece of information on how Jane met Devereux is contained in the 1881 census information. Although Devereux was born in Stonehaven, Suffolk, his sister Rebecca was living with them in 1881 in Surrey. The census notes however, that Rebecca was born in Gunthorpe and was 13 years old. Jane and her parents lived in Gunthorpe so it appears that Although Devereux was born in Suffolk, he moved with his parents to Gunthorpe prior to 1868 and he met Jane there. They were married 10 years later in 1878.

More About JANE MOULD:
Burial: 06 Jul 1925, Section B, Grave 267, Sutton Cemetery, Sutton, London, England[108]
Cause of Death: 1) Myocardial Degeneration 2) Avicular Fibrillation Heart Failure[109]
Residence: Apr 1881, 55 Balham Grove, Streatham, Surrey, England[110]

More About DEVEREUX HENRY JESSOP:
Burial: 11 Feb 1932, Section B, Grave 267, Sutton Cemetery, Sutton, London, England[111]
Cause of Death: Myocardial Degeneration[112]
Occupation: Apr 1881, Plumber and Painter[113]
Residence: 23 Oct 1878, Clapham, Surrey, England[114]

More About DEVEREUX JESSOP and JANE MOULD:
Marriage: 23 Oct 1878, The Paston Parish Church, Northants, England[114]

Children of JANE MOULD and DEVEREUX JESSOP are:
8.   i.   NAOMI JANE[7] JESSOP, b. 19 Aug 1879, 5 Pickett Street, Tempesley Road, Clapham, Surrey, England; d. 12 Feb 1959, 27 Westbourne Villas, Aldrington, Hove, East Sussex, England.
9.   ii. DEVEREUX HENRY JESSOP, b. 16 Dec 1880, 55 Balham Road, Balham, Surrey, England; d. 12 Jun 1914, Driftway Road, Banstead, Surrey, England.
        iii. FREDERICK THOMAS JESSOP[115,116], b. 06 Apr 1882, 55 Balham Grove, Balham, Surrey, England[117,118]; d. 12 Aug 1953, Berrow Nursing Home, Carew Road, Eastbourne, County Borough of Eastbourne[119].

        Notes for FREDERICK THOMAS JESSOP:
        Per Virginia Manning, Frederick was called Bill. Also she indicated that he never married.

        Joan (Mould) Bolton Summarized the Will of Frederick Thomas Jessop below:
        The Last Will and Testament left by Frederick Thomas Jessop, (known as "Bill",) was drawn up on November 15th 1951, nearly two years before his death on 12th August 1953, aged 71. He died (of cancer) at the Berrow Nursing Home in Eastbourne but, at the time of writing this document, his address was given as 74 Vicarage Road, Sunbury-on-Thames, Middlesex, where, according to his great niece, Jane Baldwin, he was 'in lodgings'. (He begins: "I, Frederick Thomas Jessop, of 74 Vicarage Road....")
            In the Legacies section, the following Beneficiaries are listed:-
        (a) To my Great Niece – Mrs Virginia Manning of Dulwich College, London, the sum of £200.
        (b) To my Great Niece – Jane Baldwin of St Leonards, Ringwood, Hampshire, the sum of £200
        (c) To my Great Nephew – Christopher Baldwin (of the same address) the sum of £200
        (d) To my God Daughter – Ruth Young of 'Dikoya', Croft Drive, Caldy, Cheshire, the sum of £200
        (e) To my friend – Mrs Esme Green of 86 Surbiton Road, Kingston on Thames, the sum of £100 as a memento of her long friendship
        (f) To my friend – William Brown of the Old Coach House, Cailfail, Lewes, Sussex, the sum of £100 as a memento of his long friendship.

        After this, he continues: "All the residue of my estate... (etc.) I give and bequeath unto my Niece, Helena Joan Brushett of 'Avonside', 68 Lenham Road, Sutton, Surrey." (This was his sister Rose Brushett's only child, known as Joan, who remained single until she died in November 1996 aged eighty-six.)

        The two witnesses are:-(1) Alex Wilfred Ganley of 42, Zealand Avenue, Harmondsworth, West Drayton, Middlesex, described as a Chartered Mechanical Engineer, and

(2) L M Stovold of 74, Vicarage Road, Sunbury-on-Thames, a Housewife.

XXXXXXXXXXXXXXX

Joan Bolton feels that this Will raises some interesting questions. First and foremost, since the address of the second signatory, Mrs Stovold, was clearly where Bill Jessop was living at the time the document was written, was she his 'landlady', or was the relationship a closer one, perhaps? One of the Beneficiaries claimed there was a rumour circulating in the family to suggest that not only was there a romantic attachment between lodger and landlady but also a daughter!

(Memo: mention the places…Hove, Seaford, Lewes, Eastbourne….Also, how come Bill's address was 5, Milldown Road, Seaford at the time he died? Had he and Mrs S. bought a property (together?) on the south coast after his cancer was diagnosed? If so, why was she not mentioned in the Will? Unless, of course, he had helped her to buy 5 Milldown Road in her name? And, could Ruth Young conceivably be the DAUGHTER?)

More About FREDERICK THOMAS JESSOP:
Cause of Death: a) Secondary carcinomatosis b) Carcinoma of prostate[119]
Occupation: 1901, Commercial clerk[120]
Residence: 1901, 86 Balham High Road[120]

10.   iv. ROSE ANNA JESSOP, b. 24 Sep 1885, 55 Balham Grove, Surrey, England; d. 18 Apr 1968, 31 Worcester Road, Sutton, London, England.

3. ROSE[6] MOULD *(THOMAS[5], WILLIAM[4] MOLDS, WILLIAM[3], JOSEPH[2] MOULDS, THOMAS[1] MOULD)*[121] was born 02 Nov 1858 in Gunthorpe, Northamptonshire, England[122], and died 25 Jun 1925 in Peakirk, Northamptonshire, England[123]. She married JOHN WILLIAM PRENTICE[124,125,126] 07 Sep 1886 in Parish church in Paston, Northants, England[127], son of JOHN PRENTICE and SARAH. He was born 04 Nov 1858 in Peakirk, Northants, England[128,129], and died 26 Aug 1919 in Peakirk, Northants, England[130].

Notes for ROSE MOULD:
PEAKIRK LOSES A RESPECTED RESIDENT.

Death and Funeral of Mrs. John Prentice

We much regret to record that Mrs. Rose Prentice, widow of Mr. John William Prentice, on Friday, died (June 25th) after a long illness patiently borne. She had lived in Peakirk over 30 years, and was respected by all, and will be much missed.

The funeral service on Saturday was conducted by the Rev. Canon J.T. Nance. The body was placed in a polished oak coffin, with the inscription: "Rose Prentice, died June 25th, 1925, aged 66 years."

The mourners were: Mr. H. and Miss N. Prentice (son and daughter); Mr. F. and Miss L. Prentice (son and daughter); Mr. H.A. Baldwin (nephew), and Miss D. Prentice (daughter); Mr. And Mrs. C. Mould (brother and sister-in-law); Mr. G. Mould (brother), and Mrs. Blanchard (sister-in-law); Mr. G. Prentice and Mrs. French (brother-in-law and sister-in-law); Mr. G. Prentice (nephew); and Mrs. S. Prentice (sister-in-law); Mr. And Mrs. A. Mould (cousins); Mrs. Frost and Miss E. Mould (cousins); Mr. And Mrs. Lake, Mr. And Mrs. W.T. Welbourn, Mrs. Sisson, Mrs. A. Neaverson and Miss Pape.

Among those present in the church and at the graveside were Miss Ball, Miss Barron, Mr. And Mrs. W. Bodger, Mrs. Strange, Miss Bodger, Mrs. Lockyer, Miss G. Welbourn, Mrs. Legate, Miss Nix, Miss Morris, Mr. And Mrs. C. Neaverson, Miss L. Neaverson, Mrs. S. Neaverson, Mrs. Argent, Mrs. B. Smith, Mrs. L. Pearson, Mrs. Taylor, Mrs. Bates, Mrs. R. Neaverson, Miss O. Neaverson, Mr. And Mrs. Brewer, Mr. Harris, Mrs. Fickers, Mrs. Robinson, Mrs. Lewis Neaverson, Mr. And Mrs. W. Jones, etc.

THE WREATHS
The floral tributes were inscribed:
In loving memory of our dear Mother, from Nell, Lily, Harold and Dora.,
In ever loving memory, from Fred and Jesse
With deepest sympathy and affection, from Bert and Omy
In ever loving and affectionate memory of our beloved sister, from her deeply sorrowing sister and brother, Bessie and Jamie. At Rest. For ever with the Lord. Wherefore comfort one another with these words.
To our dearest aunt, from all at Old Fletton. "To one who lived for others but now 'Safe in the Arms of Jesus.'"

In loving memory, from Charlie and Emily and family. After pain, peace.
In deepest sympathy, from Fred, Rose and Joan [Brushett] "For so He giveth His beloved sleep."
In affectionate remembrance, from Mrs. W.T. Welbourn and family, Glinton.
In affectionate remembrance, from Mr. And Mrs. Strange and family.
In deep sympathy, from Mr. And Mrs. Brewer.
In loving memory of dear Rose, from all cousins at Maxey.
In loving memory, from George and Ellen, Arthur and Hannah.
With deepest sympathy, from Mr. And Mrs. C. Neaverson and family.
With deepest sympathy, from Mr. And Mrs. A. Neaverson and family.
With deepest sympathy, from Mr. And Mrs. Legate and family.
From Mrs. Lockyer.
With deepest sympathy and love, from Lizzie.
Love from Rowland.
Messrs. A. Neaverson and Sons were the undertakers.

The Peterborough & Hunts. Standard
July 3, 1925

Prentice – At Peakirk on June 25th 1925. Rose Prentice aged 66 years, widow of the late John William Prentice who died August 26, 1919, aged 60 years.
Acknowledgement (follows straight on): - The Family wish to thank all Friends for the kindness shown to their Mother during her long illness; and for expressions of sympathy extended to them in their sad bereavement; also for floral tributes.

Peterborough and Hunts Standard
Friday, 3rd July 1925

More About ROSE MOULD:
Burial: 27 Jun 1925, St. Pega's Church, Peakirk, Northamptonshire, England[131,132]
Cause of Death: (1) Carcinoma of Liver (2) Exhaustion   No P.M.
Medical Information: Rose died "after a long illness patiently borne".[133]
Occupation: Apr 1881, General servant[134]
Residence: Peakirk, Northants, England[135]

Notes for JOHN WILLIAM PRENTICE:
John Prentice's obituary reads as follows.
Mr. John William Prentice, sub-postmaster of Peakirk, was taken ill whilst on his rounds a week ago and rheumatic fever was followed by pneumonia and other complications, and he passed away on Tuesday afternoon.

The Peterborough Citizen
September 2, 1919   Page 4

Following the death of John W. Prentice in 1919, his estate had to be evaluated and a monetary value put on it to complete the settlement of the estate. The firm of Fox & Vergette, Licenced Valuers from Peterborough were hired to perform this function and develop a Valuation for Probate. Their report is reproduced below.

VALUATION OF LIVE & DEAD
FARMING STOCK, TENANT
RIGHT etc.
FARM & PREMISES at

PEAKIRK NORTHANTS

The property of the Executors of the late Mr. J.W. PRENTICE

Valuation of LIVE and DEAD FARMING STOCK, TENANT RIGHT and CORN And HAY in stock on the FARM & PREMISES at PEAKIRK , the property of the EXECUTORS of the late Mr. J.W. PRENTICE, taken the 22nd of SEPTEMBER 1919.
HORSES   Chestnut horse "Prince", Brown Mare "Bounce", Grey   Pony, Bay Mare "Lively", Bay Mare "Flower", Colt Foal,   Brown Mare "Beauty", Bay Mare "Blossom".

BEAST   4 Bullocks, Rearing calf

SHEEP   34 Ewes, 41 Lambs, 2 Barren Ewes, Hampshire Ram

Implements etc. 2 collars, 4 cow ties, pair reins, spring float, bridle, 2   hackbands, saddle, collar, old bin, weighing machine &   weights, sack elevator, barb wire, cutting knife, Bean mill,   Bamlett reaper, wood drag, shaft horse hoe, iron drag   harrows, barrel water cart, iron drag, turnip box, duckfoot   harrows, plough, turnip cutter, sheep wire & stakes, 10   sleepers etc., single horse hoe, stack pegs, odd wood,   steerage drill, flat roll, grass mower, wheelbarrow, 2   horse harrows, 1 horse harrow, 5 cart ropes, 2 skeps,   sundry tools, Hornsby Binder, Light cart & raves, Ash   screen, hay tedder, 2 drag rakes, 1/2 cwt. Binder string,   14 sheep troughs, 4 carts with raves, new wagon, gears   for 6 horses, horse rake, stack props etc., lever duckfoot,   6 ladders, 20 sheep trays, pulper, chaffcutter, corn bin,old   stackcloth, sack wheels, dressing machine, double furrow   plough, swell trees, 12 sleepers, loading ladder, sack   elevator, cake breaker, ridge plough, 3 scuttles, Ransome   cultivator, Martin cultivator, 2 single ploughs.

CORN   Stack of Peas, 3 stacks of Barley, 2 stacks of Wheat, 1   stack of Oats, 6 sacks of Peas, 16 sacks of light Oats, 2   cwt. Of condiment.

HAY   6 acres of Clover first and second crops, Stack of Hay,   stack of Wheat straw.

Quantity of Manure on the premises, allowing for the feeding stuiff therein.

5 acres young seeds, 5 acres Turnips, One & 1/2 acres   Mangolds, 10 acres & 4 1/2 acres, & 3 1/2 acres fallows.

We, the undersigned, have carefully estimated the matters herein do certify the value

Thereof at the sum of TWO THOUSAND FIVE HUNDRED & THIRTY-FOUR POUNDS, NINE SHILLINGS. (2,534 pounds, 9 shillings, 0 pence).

Mr. J.W. PRENTICE deceased

STATEMENT SHEWING ASSETS LESS VALUE OF Mrs. Prentice,s
SHARE AND COSTS OF PROBATE (taken from the Inland Revenue Affidavit)

Cash in hand   58:10:00
Cash in Barclay,s Bank   87:00:00
Book Debits   90:00:00
Prudential Insurance Policy   128:08:00
Household goods (bequeathed to Mrs. Prentice)   117:11:00
Stock in trade as per Messrs. Fox & Vergette,s
Valuation, annexed hereto   2225:09:00

          3936:18:00

PEAKIRK NORTHANTS

The property of the Executors of the late Mr. J.W. PRENTICE

Valuation of LIVE and DEAD FARMING STOCK, TENANT RIGHT and CORN And HAY in stock on the FARM & PREMISES at PEAKIRK , the property of the EXECUTORS of the late Mr. J.W. PRENTICE, taken the 22nd of SEPTEMBER 1919.
HORSES   Chestnut horse "Prince", Brown Mare "Bounce", Grey   Pony, Bay Mare "Lively", Bay Mare "Flower", Colt Foal,   Brown Mare "Beauty", Bay Mare "Blossom".

BEAST   4 Bullocks, Rearing calf

SHEEP   34 Ewes, 41 Lambs, 2 Barren Ewes, Hampshire Ram

Implements etc. 2 collars, 4 cow ties, pair reins, spring float, bridle, 2   hackbands, saddle, collar, old bin, weighing machine &   weights, sack elevator, barb wire, cutting knife, Bean mill,   Bamlett reaper, wood drag, shaft horse hoe, iron drag   harrows, barrel water cart, iron drag, turnip box, duckfoot   harrows, plough, turnip cutter, sheep wire & stakes, 10   sleepers etc., single horse hoe, stack pegs, odd wood,
          steerage drill, flat roll, grass mower, wheelbarrow, 2   horse harrows, 1 horse harrow, 5 cart ropes, 2
Enfranchisement & Conveyance   1612:13:06

          2324:04:06

Peterborough   21 June 1920

          Narrow Street
          Peterborough

Valuation for Probate

In the Estate of John William Prentice late of Peakirk in the County of Northampton made and taken 22nd. Day of September 1919.

Household goods, Pictures, China, Linen, Apparel.   117:11:Msrp
Stock in trade live and Dead Farming.   )   2225:9:-
)
Stock Implements of Husbandry   )

Other personal property not comprised under the
foregoing heads viz
          Tenant rights   250:-:-

          2593:-:-

We hereby certify that we have Appraised the whole
of the above mentioned at the sum of Two Thousand five hundred and ninety three pounds (2593)

          Fox & Vergette

Licenced Valuers.

George Prentice.   )
)   Executors
George Harold Prentice)

More About JOHN WILLIAM PRENTICE:
Burial: 29 Aug 1919, St. Pega's Church, Peakirk, Northamptonshire, England[136,137]
Occupation: Aug 1919, Baker and Grocer, Master[138]
Residence: 07 Sep 1886, Peakirk, Northamptonshire, England[139]

More About JOHN PRENTICE and ROSE MOULD:
Marriage: 07 Sep 1886, Parish church in Paston, Northants, England[140]

Children of ROSE MOULD and JOHN PRENTICE are:
  i. ELLEN[7] PRENTICE[141], b. 18 Mar 1888, Peakirk, Northants, England[142,143]; d. 11 Aug 1946, Peakirk, Northants, England[144].

      Notes for ELLEN PRENTICE:
      Before World War I Ellen Prentice went to Germany and taught English to German students. When the war broke out she was repatriated in exchange for Germans in England. In England she taught German in Nottingham until she had a stroke. She had the stroke when she was in her late 40's or early 50's. The stroke left her a partial invalid so she went to Bledington to stay with her brother Harold and his wife. She would occasionally go to Peakirk to stay with Dora for a month or two. It was on one of these trips to Peakirk that she died.
      Telephone interview with Sheila Rose - February 13, 2004

      More About ELLEN PRENTICE:
      Baptism: 15 Apr 1888, Peakirk, Northants, England[145]
      Burial: 14 Aug 1946, St. Pega's Church, Peakirk, Northamptonshire, England[146]
      Residence: 31 Mar 1901, The Vicarage, Peakirk, Northants, England[147]

  ii. LILIAN PRENTICE[148,149], b. 09 Mar 1889, Peakirk, Northants, England[150,151]; d. 16 Nov 1967, Peakirk, Northants, England[152,153].

      More About LILIAN PRENTICE:
      Baptism: 07 Apr 1889, Peakirk, Northants, England[154]
      Burial: 21 Nov 1967, St. Pega's Church, Peakirk, Northamptonshire, England[155]
      Cause of Death: 1a. Bronchopneumonia b. Right Hemiplagia c.Cerebral arterio schlerosis[156]
      Residence: 25 Jun 1925, 22 Ridley Road, Harlesden, London NW[157]

11.   iii. GEORGE HAROLD PRENTICE, b. 13 Jun 1890, Peakirk, Northamptonshire, England; d. 05 Apr 1975, Chipping Norton Memorial Hospital, Chipping Norton, Oxfordshire, England.
12.   iv. JOHN FREDERICK PRENTICE, b. 30 Jun 1893, Peakirk, Northamptonshire, England; d. 23 Jun 1969, 64 North Lane, East Preston, Sussex, England.
      v. DORA EVELYN PRENTICE[158,159,160,161], b. 02 Jan 1899, Peakirk, Northants, England[162,163]; d. 20 Dec 1965, Peterborough Memorial Hospital, Cambs, England[164,165,166].

      Notes for DORA EVELYN PRENTICE:
      Dora trained at the Pitman's College for Secretaries in London. She was a secretary for a solicitor in Peterborough for a number of years until he died. After he died she became secretary to the Dean of Peterborough Cathedral and was also the Treasurer of the Friends of Peterborough Cathedral which was an organization which raised money for the cathedral. She was very organized and efficient. Dora was very active in the Peakirk Church. She played the organ and was the Church Warden.
      Telephone interview of Sheila Rose - February 13, 2004

      On May 20, 2001, Ms. Freda Neaverson a churchwarden of St. Pega's Church, responsible for burial records for many years said, " The Blanchard's were bakers in the Nottingham area and Miss Dora Prentice, who worked so hard for St. Pega's church, was able to have cakes delivered from Blanchard's when food was strictly rationed to sell at the church bazaars. The company also supplied Marks and Spencer."

Dora Prentice - Suddenly on (Monday) Dec. 20th at Peterborough Memorial hospital, Dora aged 66 yrs. Funeral service at St. Pega's Peakirk, Thursday Dec. 23rd at 2pm followed by cremation at Marholm.

Peterborough Citizen and Advertiser
Friday December 24, 1965

Miss D. Prentice

Miss Dora Prentice, of Rectory Lane, Peakirk, died in Peterborough Memorial Hospital, the day after she had been playing the organ at St. Pega's Church, Peakirk, for the service of nine lessons and carols.
She was 66.
The funeral service was at St' Pega's, Peakirk, yesterday, conducted by the Rev. K. Sear, assisted by Archdeacon C.J. Grimes. The organist was Mr. Stanley Vann, director of music at the Peterborough Cathedral.
Apart from playing the organ in the church, Miss Prentice was a churchwarden for many years and had held the posts of secretary and treasurer of the Church Council. She was also a school manager.
She was well known in Peterborough having been a secretary in the Chapter office.
For many years she was a correspondent for the "Advertiser".
The Rev. K. Sear said of Miss Prentice: "It is with great sorrow that we have to report the death of Miss Prentice. For many years she had been people's warden, secretary and treasurer of the Church Council, organist and school manager as well as holding in the past many other positions and responsibilities in the Church and village, to which she gave much time and devotion. The Church at Peakirk and the Cathedral were her two great interests and she was for them an indefatigable worker."

Peterborough Citizen and Advertiser
December 24, 1965

Note: The full account of the funeral comes separately from page 14 of this same paper. See also copied article on p.6 of the Peterborough Citizen and Advertiser from the following Friday, Dec. 31, 1965.

Miss D. Prentice

The funeral service for Miss D. Prentice, Peakirk, whose sudden death was reported last week, was conducted at St. Pega's Church on December 23 by the Rev. R.K. Sear, assisted by Dr. C.J. Grimes. Mourners were: Mr. And Mrs. G.H. Prentice, Mr. J.F. Prentice (brothers and sister-in-law), Mr. John Prentice (nephew), Mr. And Mrs. Blanchard (cousins), Mrs. S. Rose (niece), Miss L. Prentice (sister) was unable to attend.
In church were the Archdeacon of Oakham (the Ven E.N. Millard), the Precenter Peterborough Cathedral (the Rev P.C. Nicholson), Mr. G. Elliott (Diocesan secretary), Mr. Brook (verger, Peterborough Cathedral), Mr. C.P. Tutt (representing Friends of the Cathedral), Miss M. Shipley Ellis, Mrs. Wood Canon H.G. Herklots, Canon and Mrs. J.C. Cartwright, Miss C. Gutteridge, Mr. And Mrs. S.E. Shearing, Mr. J.H. Woolgar, Mr. J.W.L. Samworth, Mr. J.G. Harrison (representing staff, John Lucas), Mrs. G.W. Wisbey (also representing Wisbey), Mrs. R.K. Sear, Mrs. H. Pearson, Mrs. Sibley, Miss M. Purcival, Mrs. C. Perrin, Mrs. E. Wilkinson, Mrs. H. Dudley, Mrs. Ewart, Miss L. Strange, Mr. P. Walker, Mr. And Mrs. J. Harris, Miss D. Neaverson, Mrs. H. Stimson (also representing Mrs. J. Pulley), Mrs. H. Wathen, Mrs. A Williams, Mrs. Palmer (representing the Wild Fowl Trust), Mr. And Mrs. G. Dunn, Miss Wheeler, Sister Sheila and Sister Jean, Mrs. E. Pearson (also representing Glinton Church Council), Mrs. C. Percival, Mrs. P. Noble (also representing Mr. Noble and the Village Hall Committee).
Mr. T. Neaverson, Miss F. Neaverson, Mr. and Mrs. C. Neaverson, Mr. and Mrs. A. Neaverson, (Mrs. Neaverson also representing the Women's Institute), Mr. E. Neaverson (representing Mrs. Neaverson), Mrs. Patterson, Mr. J. Patterson, Mr. Lang (representing Mrs. Lang and the Misses Welbon, Glinton), Miss Robinson, Mr. Wade, Peterborough, Mrs. N. Green, Mr. and Mrs. Lenton, Miss M. Sprigge (also representing Miss V. Sprigge), Mrs. C. Green, Mrs. O. Green.
Mr. Stanley Vann of Peterborough Cathedral, was organist.
There were many floral tributes from friends and organizations.

Peterborough Citizen and Advertiser
December 31, 1965

More About DORA EVELYN PRENTICE:
Baptism: 29 Jan 1899, Peakirk, Northants, England[167]
Burial: 24 Dec 1965, Ashes buried in St. Pega's Church, Peakirk, Northamptonshire, England[168]
Cause of Death: 1a. Cerebral haemorrhage b. Cerebrovascular disease[169]
Cremation: 23 Dec 1965, Marholm, near Peterborough, Cambs, England[170]
Residence: 31 Mar 1901, The Vicarage, Peakirk, Northants, England[171]

4. JABEZ[6] MOULD *(THOMAS[5], WILLIAM[4] MOLDS, WILLIAM[3], JOSEPH[2] MOULDS, THOMAS[1] MOULD)*[172,173] was born 24 Dec 1865 in Gunthorpe, Northants, England[174,175], and died 10 Jul 1936 in Aberdeen, South Dakota, USA[176]. He married SARAH ANN COX 04 Jun 1885 in Register office, Wellingborough, Northampton,England[177,178], daughter of ELIZABETH COX. She was born 12 Jan 1867 in Union Workhouse, Kettering, Northamptonshire, England[179,180], and died 07 Nov 1957 in Daughter Rose's house, San Ysidro, California[181,182].

Notes for JABEZ MOULD:
    On July 26, 2000, a friend of Richard Klapper, Jayne Wright, who lives near Rushden, England, sent Richard an e-mail describing her chance meeting of a lovely lady named Miss Joan Mould who told her the following story about the sons of Thomas Mould. Miss Mould said"she was one of 8 children - mostly still alive in the area, and her father was one of about 8 children too. Her grandfather, Charles Mould was the youngest of 4 sons. Their father (Thomas) owned a small farm near or in Peakirk - which is just north of Peterborough. The farm was only large enough to provide work for two sons. When the son "Jabe" was old enough to work, he was sent by train to Irthlingborough to find lodgings and work. He found work in a shoe factory. When Charles was old enough, he was sent to find work with his brother. "Uncle Jabe" subsequently emigrated to America and had at least 2 sons. Charles stayed in the area and married Emily Whitbread from Irthlingborough. She died in her 60s but her 2 sisters lived to be 100."
The above story has two correction that need to be made. Joan's grandfather Charles was not the youngest son - his brother George was younger than Charles. Also, Thomas' farm was a dairy farm near Gunthorpe.

Jabez was the "Jabe" referred to above. While in England he was a member of the Rushden City Council and was presented a walking cane with a silver plaque on it in appreciation of his service. He married Sarah Ann Cox and emigrated to the U.S. and settled in Aberdeen, South Dakota. When asked why Jabez and Sarah came to the US, Jabez' grandson, Alfred Bull, said it was for economic reasons. Jabez' son George had come to the US earlier in 1906 and 1911 and was doing very well in his creamery business. He was making lots of money and paid for his sister Annie to come to the US the next year in 1912. George later talked his parents into coming to the US and paid for their trip. They arrived at Ellis Island on the ship Orduna on December 24, 1919. They ran a small grocery store in the front of their house at 111 8th Ave. S.W. in Aberdeen which George helped them set up. George also gave them the milk and cream to sell in their little store. George and his wife went to New York to meet them when their ship came in. Jabez had a handlebar mustache and George told him " We're going to have to get you de horned since those aren't too popular over here."
In 1928, Jabez and Sarah went back to England when their daughter Annie and her son Alfred. Annie and Alfred traveled around England visiting relatives for about 6 months. Jabez and Sarah did not come back to the US with Annie and Alfred. They stayed in England for several years before returning to the US.
 A year before his death, Jabez and Sarah celebrated their 50th anniversary. Jabez died a year later in the upstairs bedroom of his house. Helen Klapper, Hazel Ritter and Don Mould all indicated to Richard Klapper their memories of how unbearably hot it was in that upstairs bedroom. The funeral was also unbearably hot. Jabez's death certificate even indicates he died of heat stroke.

More About JABEZ MOULD:
Burial: 12 Jul 1936, Aberdeen, South Dakota, USA, Riverside Cemetary[183,184]
Cause of Death: Heat stroke
Emigration: 24 Dec 1919, To the USA[185]
Medical Information: Jabez was 5'6" per the Ellis Island records.
Naturalization: Naturalized citizen[186]
Occupation: 04 Jun 1885, Shoe finisher[187]

Residence: 27 Jul 1912, 13 Westfield Ave., Higham Ferrers, Northants, England[188]

Notes for SARAH ANN COX:
There is a discrepancy between the cemetery records and the grave headstone on the date of birth for Sarah. The headstone gives the date of birth as January 12, 1867 while the cemetery records give it as January 12, 1866. Her birth certificate indicates the date was January 12, 1867. The 1881 census in England gives the 1867 date. According to Helen Klapper her grandmother Sarah Mould was illegitimate. Her father was a Jewish man who didn't marry her mother. According to Hazel Ritter, Sarah's father was a Jewish musician from London. He was planning to marry Sarah's mother but he died of TB. This appears to be verified by her birth certificate which lists no father and notes that her mother gave birth to her in the Union Workhouse in Kettering. She was raised by her Uncle and Aunt, Rowland and Mary A. Cox. Sarah told stories to her granddaughter, Helen Bull, of her aunt making her stand on a box to wash dishes when she was 4 years old. Sarah married Jabez Mould in England and they emigrated to America, arriving at Ellis Island, New York on the ship Orduna on December 24, 1919. They settled in Aberdeen, South Dakota with their grown children. Sarah ran a small grocery store in the front of her house at 111 8th Ave. S.W. Her husband died and Sarah eventually moved to Chula Vista, California to live near her children George and Rose. She is buried in California which caused some concern among some of her descendants who felt she should have been buried back in Aberdeen, South Dakota with her husband.

More About SARAH ANN COX:
Burial: Glen Abby Memorial Park - Bonita, California[189]
Immigration: 24 Dec 1919, To US from England[190]
Medical Information: Sarah was 5'2" tall per the Ellis Island records.
Naturalization: Naturalized citizen[191]
Occupation: Apr 1881, Shoe fitter[192]
Residence: 27 Jul 1912, 13 Westfield Ave., Higham Ferrers, Northants, England[193]

Marriage Notes for JABEZ MOULD and SARAH COX:
Jabez Mould and Sarah Ann Cox were married in the Register Office in Wellingborough, Northampton, England. The two witnesses were Bowland Cox and Mary Mould (most likely the sister of the groom).

More About JABEZ MOULD and SARAH COX:
Marriage: 04 Jun 1885, Register office, Wellingborough, Northampton, England[194,195]

Children of JABEZ MOULD and SARAH COX are:
13.   i.   ROSE MARION[7] MOULD, b. 01 Jan 1885, Rushden, England; d. 26 Jan 1973, Chula Vista, California.
14.   ii. GEORGE EWART MOULD, b. 15 Oct 1887, Rushden, England; d. 07 Oct 1965, Hospital in San Diego, California.
          iii. BESSIE LILIAN MOULD[196,197], b. Bet. Jan - Mar 1890, Rushden, Northampton, England[198,199,200]; d. Feb 1894, Rushden, Northampton, England[201].

          More About BESSIE LILIAN MOULD:
          Burial: 19 Feb 1894, Rushden, Northamptonshire, England[202]
          Residence: Apr 1891, Lancaster Street, Rushden, Northants, England[203]

15.   iv. ANNIE BEATRICE MOULD, b. 06 Oct 1891, Rushden, Northamptonshire, England; d. 16 Mar 1974, St. Luke's Hospital, Aberdeen, SD USA.
          v.   THOMAS ROWLAND MOULD[204,205], b. Dec 1899, Rushden, Northamptonshire, England[206]; d. Dec 1899, Rushden, Northamptonshire, England.

          More About THOMAS ROWLAND MOULD:
          Burial: 30 Dec 1899, Rushden, Northamptonshire, England[207]

5. REBECCA[6] MOULD *(THOMAS[5], WILLIAM[4] MOLDS, WILLIAM[3], JOSEPH[2] MOULDS, THOMAS[1] MOULD)*[208] was born 15 Feb 1868 in Gunthorpe, Northamptonshire, England[208,209], and died 04 Jul 1946 in Viking Township, Perkins County, South Dakota[210,211,212]. She married JOSEPH THOMAS MACKNESS[213,214,215,216,217] 28 May 1890 in Paston, Northamptonshire, England[218], son of WILLIAM MACKNESS and REBECCA BLAND. He was born 03 Dec 1865 in Brigstock, Northamptonshire, England[219,220,221], and died 23 May 1938 in Viking Township, Perkins County, South Dakota[222,223].

Notes for REBECCA MOULD:
Rebecca married her cousin Joseph Thomas Mackness. Rebecca's sister Betsy married Joseph's cousin James.

More About REBECCA MOULD:
Burial: 09 Jul 1946, Ellingson, Perkins County, South Dakota[224]
Cause of Death: Arterial Schlerosis[225]
Immigration: 16 Oct 1906, England to U.S.[226]
Medical Information: Rebecca was 5'4" per Ellis Island records.
Naturalization: Unknown, Became a US citizen[227,228]
Residence: 28 May 1890, Gunthorpe, Northamptonshire, England[229]

Notes for JOSEPH THOMAS MACKNESS:
Joseph and his wife Rebecca Mould lived in Oregon when the first came to the U.S. but their house burned down and Joseph moved the family to South Dakota where he homesteaded on the South Dakota/North Dakota border. From Marge Redford - 2001
When Frank and his mother Rebecca came to the US on October 16, 1906, Joseph was already living at 1006 ??? St., Aberdeen according to the ship's manifest. Obviously, Joseph came to the USA before his wife and son. Since I haven't been able to find his arrival in the Ellis Island files I suspect he came into the USA through another port.

More About JOSEPH THOMAS MACKNESS:
Burial: 26 May 1938, Ellingson, Perkins County, South Dakota[230]
Cause of Death: Carcinoma gastrica[231]
Immigration: 1906, From England to US[232]
Naturalization: Unknown, Became a US citizen[233]
Occupation: 1881, Shoe Finisher[234]
Residence: 1890, Rushden[235]

More About JOSEPH MACKNESS and REBECCA MOULD:
Marriage: 28 May 1890, Paston, Northamptonshire, England[236]

Children of REBECCA MOULD and JOSEPH MACKNESS are:
16.   i.   FRANK[7] MACKNESS, b. 09 Jul 1891, Northamptonshire, England; d. 1971, Portland, Oregon.
         ii. NELLIE MACKNESS[237], b. Jan 1894[237]; d. May 1895.

              More About NELLIE MACKNESS:
              Burial: 21 May 1895, Newton Road Cemetery, Rushden, Northamptonshire, England[237]

6. CHARLES[6] MOULD *(THOMAS[5], WILLIAM[4] MOLDS, WILLIAM[3], JOSEPH[2] MOULDS, THOMAS[1] MOULD)*[238,239] was born 15 Nov 1871 in Gunthorpe, Northampton, England[240,241,242], and died 03 Mar 1945 in 2 Grove Street, Higham Ferrers, Northamptonshire, England[243]. He married EMILY JANE WHITBREAD[244,245] 05 Jul 1891 in Parish Church, Rushden, Northants, England[246], daughter of GEORGE WHITBREAD and ELIZABETH GADSBY. She was born 18 Aug 1872 in Rushden, Northamptonshire, England[247,248,249,250], and died 21 Apr 1942 in 2 Grove Road, Higham Ferrers, Northants, England[251].

Notes for CHARLES MOULD:
     On July 26, 2000, a friend of Richard Klapper, Jayne Wright, who lives near Rushden, England, sent Richard an e-mail describing her chance meeting of a lovely lady named Miss Joan Mould who told her the following story about the sons of Thomas Mould. Miss Mould said"she was one of 8 children - mostly still alive in the area, and her father was one of about 8 children too. Her grandfather, Charles Mould was the youngest of 4 sons. Their father (Thomas) owned a small farm near or in Peakirk - which is just north of Peterborough. The farm was only large enough to provide work for two sons. When the son "Jabe" was old enough to work, he was sent by train to Irthlingborough to find lodgings and work. He found work in a shoe factory. When the youngest, Charles, was old enough, he was sent to find work with his brother. "Uncle Jabe" subsequently emigrated to America and had at least 2 sons. Charles stayed in the area and married Emily Whitbread from Irthlingborough. She died in her 60s but her 2 sisters lived to be 100."
The above story has two correction that need to be made. Joan's grandfather Charles was not the youngest son -

his brother George was younger than Charles. Also, Thomas' farm was a dairy farm near Gunthorpe.

Charles Mould's obituary reads as follows.

Mr. C. Mould, Higham Ferrers

The death occurred on Saturday of Mr. Charles Mould, of 2, Grove-street, Higham Ferrers. He had been in Northampton General Hospital for 14 weeks and had been home for a fortnight before his death.

Aged 73 years, Mr. Mould was born at Peterborough, came to Higham Ferrers as a boy, and spent his working life in the boot trade, retiring three years ago. For some years he was a Sunday School teacher and superintendent of the Band of Hope at the Methodist Church, but in recent years had attended the Milton Hall Chapel.

A daughter, Mrs. I. Lovell, had been living with him. His wife died three years ago, and two sons, six daughters and 12 grandchildren are left.

The funeral took place on Tuesday, and the service was conducted at the home by the Rev. T.S. Kee, of the Rushden Independent Wesleyan Church, before interment at the Higham Ferrers cemetery. Mourners were : Mr. and Mrs. C. Headland, Rushden, Mr. and Mrs. J.W. Barrett, Northampton, Mr. and Mrs. R.E. Roberts, Higham Ferrers, Mr. and Mrs. J. Sharp, Rushden, Gnr. H. Eaton and Mrs. Eaton, Souldrop, (sons-in-law and daughters), Mr. and Mrs. B. Mould (son and daughter-in-law), Mr. and Mrs. A.T. Lovell (son-in-law and daughter), Mr. and Mrs. P. Mould (son and daughter-in-law), Mr. G. Mould (brother), Mrs. E. Mould (niece), Mrs. H. Durham, Mrs. W. Hensman (sisters-in-law), Mrs. E. Wrighton (cousin), and Mrs. Firkins (friend). Several friends of the Milton Chapel attended, these including Mr. L. Bradshaw, Mr. J. Lynn and Mr. W. Marriott.

Messrs. T. Swindall and Sons were the undertakers.

Rushden Echo & Argus
Friday, March 9, 1945   Page 2

More About CHARLES MOULD:
Burial: 06 Mar 1945, Higham Ferrers, Northampton, England[252,253,254]
Cause of Death: 1) a Bronchial pneumonia b) Cystatoning? c) Enlarged prostate
Census: 1881, Paston, Northampton, England[255]
Occupation: 03 Mar 1945, Boot finisher[256]
Residence: 24 Dec 1919, 2 Grove St., Higham Ferrers, Northants, England[257]
Retirement: 1942, Retired 3 years before his death in 1945[258]

Notes for EMILY JANE WHITBREAD:
Emily Mould's obituary reads as follows.

Mrs. E. J. Mould, Higham Ferrers

Mrs. Emily Jane Mould (69) of 2, Grove-street, Higham Ferrers, who had been in failing health for about a year although she had only been seriously ill for about 17 weeks, passed away on Tuesday. Mrs. Mould was born at Rushden and went to live at Higham at the time of her marriage. She had been associated with the Rushden Salvation Army Corps and more recently with the Higham Ferrers Baptist Mission. Her husband, who, until he retired, was employed as a finisher by Messrs. B. Ladds, of Rushden, six daughters and two sons survive.

Rushden Echo and Argus
Friday, April 24, 1942   Page 9

More About EMILY JANE WHITBREAD:
Burial: Higham Ferrers, Northants, England[259]
Cause of Death: 1) a Cerebral Thrombosis[260]
Occupation: 05 Jul 1891, Machinist[261]
Residence: 05 Jul 1891, Rushden, Northants, England[261]

More About CHARLES MOULD and EMILY WHITBREAD:
Marriage: 05 Jul 1891, Parish Church, Rushden, Northants, England[261]

215

Children of CHARLES MOULD and EMILY WHITBREAD are:

    i.   EMILY MAY[7] MOULD[262], b. Apr 1892[263]; d. May 1892[264].

        More About EMILY MAY MOULD:
        Burial: 24 May 1892, Rushden, Northampton, England[265]

    ii. ELSIE MAY MOULD[266,267], b. 23 May 1893, Rushden, Northants, England[267,268]; d. 03 Jan 1984[268,269]; m. CHARLES HEADLAND[270], 26 Sep 1931, Independent Wesleyan Chapel, Rushden, Northants, England[271]; b. Bet. Apr - Jun 1871[272]; d. Bet. Oct - Dec 1953[273].

        Notes for ELSIE MAY MOULD:
        Per Trevor Mould, Elsie and Charles had no children.

        More About ELSIE MAY MOULD:
        Burial: Cremated[274]
        Cremation: 11 Jan 1984, Kettering Crematorium, Kettering, Northants, England[275]
        Occupation: 26 Sep 1931, Commercial clerk[276]
        Residence: 31 Mar 1901, Westfields, Higham Ferrers, Northants, England[277]

        More About CHARLES HEADLAND:
        Burial: Orlingbury Churchyard, Northants, England[278]
        Cremation: 08 Oct 1953, Kettering Crematorium, Kettering, Northants, England[279]
        Occupation: 26 Sep 1931, Leather dresser[280]
        Residence: 26 Sep 1931, 43 Queen Street, Rushden, Northants, England[280]

        More About CHARLES HEADLAND and ELSIE MOULD:
        Marriage: 26 Sep 1931, Independent Wesleyan Chapel, Rushden, Northants, England[280]

    iii. JESSIE MOULD[281], b. 22 Oct 1895, Higham Ferrers, Northamptonshire, England[282,283,284]; d. 02 Jul 1977, St. Edmund's Hospital, Northampton, Northants, England[285]; m. JOHN WILLIAM J. BARRETT[286,287,288], Bet. Apr - Jun 1937[289]; b. Bet. Sep - Dec 1883[290]; d. 09 May 1957, Northampton General Hospital, Northampton, Northants, England[291].

        Notes for JESSIE MOULD:
        Per Trevor Mould, Jessie and John had no children.

        More About JESSIE MOULD:
        Burial: 08 Jul 1977, Cremated and ashes buried in parents' grave, Higham Ferrers, Northants, England[292,293]
        Residence: 31 Mar 1901, Westfields, Higham Ferrers, Northants, England[294]

        Notes for JOHN WILLIAM J. BARRETT:
        John Barrett's obituary reads as follows.
        Barrett – On May 9, after a short illness, at Northampton General Hospital, John William James, aged 73, of 118, St. Jame's Park-road. Beloved husband of Jessie, and dear brother of Ivy. Resting in the Lord. Funeral service, Monday, May 13, at 1:45pm at Princes-street Baptist Church. No flowers please.

        (Northampton Chronicle and Echo
        Friday May 10, 1957   Page 12

        More About JOHN WILLIAM J. BARRETT:
        Cause of Death: 1a Cerebro-vascular Episode with (L) hemiplegia 1b Parkinson's Disease[295]
        Occupation: 1957, Boot and shoe operative[295]
        Residence: 09 May 1957, 118 St. James Park Road, Northampton, Northants, England[296]

        More About JOHN BARRETT and JESSIE MOULD:
        Marriage: Bet. Apr - Jun 1937[297]

17.   iv. VIOLET MOULD, b. 23 Nov 1897, Higham Ferrers, Northamptonshire, England; d. 08 Jan 1982, The Poplars Thrapston Road, Finedon, Northants, England.

      v.   DAISY MOULD[298], b. Bet. Apr - Jun 1900, Rushden, Northamptonshire, England[299,300]; d. 29 Jan 1995, Fairlawns Nursing Home, Higham Road, Rushden, Northants, England[301,302]; m. ALFRED JAMES

SHARP[303,304], Bet. Apr - Jun 1927[305]; b. Bet. Jan - Mar 1899[306,307]; d. 14 Nov 1948, Northampton General Hospital, Northampton, Northants, England[308,309].

Notes for DAISY MOULD:
Per Trevor Mould, Daisy and Jim had no children.

More About DAISY MOULD:
Burial: Higham Ferrers, Northants, England[310]
Residence: 31 Mar 1901, Westfields, Higham Ferrers, Northants, England[311]

Notes for ALFRED JAMES SHARP:
Alfred Sharp's obituary reads as follows.

Funeral of Mr. A. J. Sharp

The funeral of Mr. Alfred James Sharp, of 19, Wentworth Road, Rushden, who died in the Northampton General Hospital, took place on November 18, the service being conducted by the Rev. John Renison at the Independent Wesleyan Church.
Mr. C. Headland (brother-in-law) at the organ accompanied the hymns "Jesu, Lover of my Soul" and "In Heavenly Love Abiding" and played "O Rest in the Lord" and Handel's "Largo".
The coffin was draped with the Union Jack and among those present were representatives of the Independent Wesleyan Women's Auxiliary, the C.W.S. Boot Works (clicking department), the British Legion and Messrs. W. Sargent (closing department).
Mourners were: Mrs. D. Sharp (widow), Mr. And Mrs. W. Sharp (father and mother), Mr. And Mrs. P. Sturgess (brother-in-law and sister), Mr. And Mrs. C. Headland, Mrs. J. Barrett, Northampton, Mr. And Mrs. J.E. Roberts, Mr. And Mrs. H. Eaton, Mr. And Mrs. B. Mould, Mr. And Mrs. A.T. Lovell, and Mr. And Mrs. P. Mould (brothers-in-law and sisters-in-law), Messrs. P. Sturgess, N. Mould, P. Mould and P. Eaton (nephews), and Miss P. Roberts and Miss D. Lovell (nieces). Mrs. Firkins, Souldrop, and Mr. T. Wright (friends).
The interment was at the Higham Ferrers Cemetery.

Rushden Echo and Argus and Northampton Advertiser Higham Ferrers, Irthlingborough and Raunds Free Press
Friday November 26, 1948   Page 9

More About ALFRED JAMES SHARP:
Burial: 18 Nov 1948, Higham Ferrers, Northants, England[312,313]
Residence: 14 Nov 1948, 19 Wentworth Road, Rushden, Northants, England[314]

More About ALFRED SHARP and DAISY MOULD:
Marriage: Bet. Apr - Jun 1927[315]

18.   vi.   LILY MOULD, b. 09 Mar 1902, Higham Ferrers, Northants, England; d. 01 Mar 1988, The Poplars Marshalls Road, Raunds, Northants, England.
19.   vii.   BERNARD WILLIAM MOULD, b. 20 Aug 1905, Higham Ferrers, Northants, England; d. 19 Feb 1982, Isebrook Hospital, Wellingborough, Northants, England.
20.   viii.   IVY DOREEN MOULD, b. Bet. Oct - Dec 1907; d. 01 Apr 1999, Nursing home, Irchester, Northants, England.
21.   ix.   PERCY WHITBREAD THOMAS MOULD, b. Bet. Apr - Jun 1910; d. 31 Oct 1983, Wellingborough Hospital, Wellingborough, Northants, England.

7. GEORGE[6] MOULD (THOMAS[5], WILLIAM[4] MOLDS, WILLIAM[3], JOSEPH[2] MOULDS, THOMAS[1] MOULD)[316,317] was born 05 Nov 1873 in Gunthorpe, Northants, England[318,319,320], and died 10 Apr 1953 in County Hospital, Huntingdon, England[321]. He married (1) FANNY MILLS[322,323] 10 Aug 1898 in Church of St. Paul, Peterborough, Northants, England[324], daughter of GEORGE MILLS and MARY IVES. She was born 19 Nov 1870 in G.N.R. Cottage, Peterborough, Northants, England[325,326], and died 15 Feb 1947 in Bracebridge Heath Hospital, Rauceby, near Sleaford, Lincolnshire, England[327,328,329]. He married (2) DOROTHY AYRES[330,331] 06 Apr 1953 in Rose Cottages, Broughton, Hunts, England[332]. She was born 20 Jul 1900 in Broughton, Cambs, England[333], and died 07 Feb 1985 in 27 Stukeley Road, Huntingdon, Cambridgeshire, England[333].

Notes for GEORGE MOULD:

On July 26, 2000, a friend of Richard Klapper, Jayne Wright, who lives near Rushden, England, sent Richard an e-mail describing her chance meeting of a lovely lady named Miss Joan Mould who told her the following story about the sons of Thomas Mould. Miss Mould said"she was one of 8 children - mostly still alive in the area, and her father was one of about 8 children too. Her grandfather, Charles Mould was the youngest of 4 sons. Their father (Thomas) owned a small farm near or in Peakirk - which is just north of Peterborough. The farm was only large enough to provide work for two sons. When the son "Jabe" was old enough to work, he was sent by train to Irthlingborough to find lodgings and work. He found work in a shoe factory. When the youngest, Charles, was old enough, he was sent to find work with his brother. "Uncle Jabe" subsequently emigrated to America and had at least 2 sons. Charles stayed in the area and married Emily Whitbread from Irthlingborough. She died in her 60s but her 2 sisters lived to be 100."

The above story has two correction that need to be made. Joan's grandfather Charles was not the youngest son - his brother George was younger than Charles. Also, Thomas' farm was a dairy farm near Gunthorpe.

From an article in a newspaper in April 1953:
"Mr. George Mould, aged 79 of 30(?) Gilpin-street, was married at Broughton Hunts on Monday, to Miss Dorothy Ayres, of Rose Cottages, Broughton. The following day he was involved in an accident while out cycling and now lies dangerously ill in Huntingdon Hospital with a suspected fracture of the skull. It is thought that the accident occurred when Mr. Mould lost control of his cycle. A native of Gunthorpe where he lived for 37 years, Mr. Mould started work in his father's milk business when he was eight years old. He took over the business in 1898(?) and in 1911moved to Gilpin-street. The business was sold to Brown and Sons of Walton, in 1950(?) and Mr. Mould officially "retired" though he still insisted on accompanying his son on the milk round every morning. Mr. Mould has been unconscious since he was admitted to hospital. Yesterday it was stated that there is no change in his condition." George died within a few days of this article.

More About GEORGE MOULD:
Burial: 14 Apr 1953, Eastfield Cemetery, Peterborough, Northants, England[334,335]
Cause of Death: Fracture of the base of the skullsustained when he fell from his pedal cycle.
Census: 1881, Paston, Northampton, England[336]
Medical Information: Accident certificate received Philip Davies Coroner of Huntingdon. Inquest held 11th April 1953.
Occupation: 10 Apr 1953, Retired dairyman[337]
Residence: 10 Apr 1953, 3 Rose Cottages, Broughton St. Ives RD[338]

Notes for FANNY MILLS:
From Fanny's obituary we learn the following. ".....she was born in one of the G.N.R. Cottages, and for 13 years in Canon Ball's time, was a teacher at New England Church schools."

Death of Mrs. F. Mould

Mrs. Fannie Mould, wife of Mr. Geo Mould, 59, Gilpin-st., died at Bracebridge Hospital, Lincoln, on Saturday, aged 76. Formerly Miss Mills, she was born in one of the G.N.R. Cottages, and for 13 years, in Canon Ball's time, was a teacher at New England Church schools. Mr. And Mrs. Mould were married at St. Paul's 48 years ago, and Mr. Mould has been a dairyman nearly 60 years, carrying on the business started by his father, Mr. Thomas mould at Gunthorpe. Five sons and three daughters survive. Mr. C. Mould, 48, Silverwood-rd; Mr. B. Mould, 19, Priory-rd; Mr. E. Mould, 65, Exeter-rd; Mr. G.T. Mould, 97,Fulbridge-rd; Sgt. H. Mould, with the 11th ?????in Germany; Mrs. D. Maile, Gilpin-st; Miss M. Mould and Miss I. Mould, Gilpin-st. The funeral yesterday at St. Paul's was conducted by the Vicar, and the mourners were Mr. G. Mould (husband); Mr. And Mrs. C. Mould, Mr. And Mrs. B. Mould, Mr. And Mrs. E. Mould, Mr. And Mrs. G.T. Mould (sons and daughters-in-law); Mr. And Mrs. E. Maile, Miss M. Mould, Miss I. Mould (son-in-law and daughters); Mr. W. Mills, Holme (brother); Miss O. Mould, Miss A. Mould (grand-daughters); Mr. A. May, Mr. C. Butler and Mrs. Patchett (friends).

Peterborough Standard
Friday, February 21, 1947   Page 8

More About FANNY MILLS:
Burial: 20 Feb 1947, Eastfield Cemetery, Peterborough, Northants, England[339]
Cause of Death: Broncho Pneumonia, Arterio Sclerosis, Senility[340]
Occupation: 10 Aug 1898, School Teacher at New England Church schools[341,342]
Residence: 31 Mar 1901, Rectory, Gunthorpe, Northants, England[343]

More About GEORGE MOULD and FANNY MILLS:
Marriage: 10 Aug 1898, Church of St. Paul, Peterborough, Northants, England[344]

More About DOROTHY AYRES:
Burial: Feb 1985, Primrose Lane Cemetery, Huntingdon, Cambridgeshire, England[345]
Cause of Death: Ischaemic heart disease[346]
Residence: 07 Feb 1985, 27 Stukeley Road, Huntingdon, Cambridgeshire, England[346]

More About GEORGE MOULD and DOROTHY AYRES:
Marriage: 06 Apr 1953, Rose Cottages, Broughton, Hunts, England[347]

Children of GEORGE MOULD and FANNY MILLS are:

     i.   DORIS[7] MOULD[348,349], b. 15 Apr 1901, Peterborough, Northants, England[349,350]; d. Nov 1987, Peterborough, Northants, England[350]; m. ERNEST VICTOR MAILE[351,352], 20 Jun 1932[353]; b. Abt. 1901, Peterborough, Northants, England[354,355,356]; d. 03 Feb 1957, St. John's Hospital, Peterborough, Northants, England[357,358,359,360].

        More About DORIS MOULD:
        Burial: Eastfield Cemetery, Peterborough, England[361]
        Occupation: Bet. 1932 - 1941, Ran a newsagent's and tobacconist's shop[362]
        Residence: Feb 1947, Gilpin St., Peterborough, Cambridgeshire, England[363]

        Notes for ERNEST VICTOR MAILE:
        Ernest Maile's obituary reads as follows.
        Mr. E. V. Maile – After a long illness Mr. Ernest Victor Maile, 59 Gilpin-street, died in St. John's Hospital on Sunday at the age of 56. Born in Peterborough Mr. Maile was the eldest son of the late Mr. And Mrs. J. T. Maile and for some years worked in the oven shop of Baker Perkins Ltd. Twenty-five years ago he married Miss Doris Irene Mould, of St. Leonard's-on-Sea, and, for some years he and his wife kept a newsagent's and tobacconist's shop in the town returning to Peterborough about 16 years ago. The funeral took place at All Soul's yesterday.

        Peterborough Standard
        Friday February 8, 1957   Page 10

        More About ERNEST VICTOR MAILE:
        Burial: 07 Feb 1957, Eastfield Cemetery, Peterborough, England[364,365]
        Occupation: Bet. 1932 - 1941, Owned a newsagent's and tobacconist's shop in St. Leonards-on-Sea[366]
        Residence: Feb 1947, SGilpin Street, Cambridgeshire, England[367]

        More About ERNEST MAILE and DORIS MOULD:
        Marriage: 20 Jun 1932[368]

22.   ii.   CYRIL EUGENE MOULD, b. 07 Jun 1902, Gunthorpe, Northants, England; d. 17 Nov 1978, Peterborough, Cambridgeshire, England.
23.   iii.   BERNARD MOULD, b. 27 Jul 1903, Gunthorpe, Northants, England; d. 06 Jan 1996, Peterborough, England.
24.   iv.   ERIC MOULD, b. 01 Jan 1905, Gunthorpe, Northants, England; d. 24 Apr 1995, Peterborough Cambs, England.
25.   v.   GUILFORD THOMAS MOULD, b. 22 Aug 1906, Gunthorpe, Northants, England; d. 05 Dec 1992, Home in Peterborough, Cambridgeshire, England.
     vi.   MARJORIE EDNA MOULD[369,370], b. 17 Sep 1909, Peterborough, Northants, England[371,372,373]; d. 16 Aug 1953, Peterborough, Northants, England[374,375].

        Notes for MARJORIE EDNA MOULD:
        Per Joan Bolton, Marjorie never married.

More About MARJORIE EDNA MOULD:
Burial: Eastfield Cemetery, Peterborough, England[376]
Residence: Feb 1947, Gilpin Street, Peterborough, Cambridgeshire, England[377]

   vii.   GEORGE MOULD[378], b. Bet. Oct - Dec 1911[378]; d. Bet. Oct - Dec 1911[379].
   viii.   IRIS THERESA MOULD[380,381,382], b. 26 Jul 1913, Peterborough, Northants, England[383,384,385]; d. 08 Nov 1964, Peterborough, Northants, England[386,387].

   Notes for IRIS THERESA MOULD:
   Per Joan Bo;ton, Iris never married.

   More About IRIS THERESA MOULD:
   Burial: Eastfield Cemetery, Peterborough, England[387]
   Residence: Feb 1947, Gilpin St., Peterborough, Cambridgeshire, England[388]

26.   ix.   HUBERT LAWRENCE MOULD, b. 28 Feb 1917, Peterborough, Northants, England; d. 17 Dec 1994, Peterborough, Cambridge, England.

Generation No. 3

8. NAOMI JANE[7] JESSOP (*JANE[6] MOULD, THOMAS[5], WILLIAM[4] MOLDS, WILLIAM[3], JOSEPH[2] MOULDS, THOMAS[1] MOULD*)[389,390,391] was born 19 Aug 1879 in 5 Pickett Street, Tempesley Road, Clapham, Surrey, England[392,393], and died 12 Feb 1959 in 27 Westbourne Villas, Aldrington, Hove, East Sussex, England[394]. She married HERBERT ALPHONSUS BALDWIN[395] 23 May 1904 in Victoria Baptist Chapel, Wandsworth Road, District of Wandsworth, County of London, England[396], son of PHILLIP BALDWIN and H.. He was born Bet. Oct - Dec 1878 in Camberwell, England[397,398,399], and died 15 Apr 1938 in Jumped off a ferry in Engish Channel[400].

More About NAOMI JANE JESSOP:
Burial: Cremated in Brighton Crematorium, Brighton, East Sussex, England[401]
Cause of Death: 1a. Cerebral hoemorrhage, b. Hypertension[402]
Occupation: 1901, Cashier[403]
Residence: 23 May 1904, 86 High Road, Balham, England[404]

Notes for HERBERT ALPHONSUS BALDWIN:
   Herbert was a butcher and had a large and very successful shop in Epsom High Street. He made a fortune As a young girl, Naomi worked as the cashier in the butcher shop. She was very good at mental arithmetic. Having made money, they moved to a large house in Kingswood, Surrey and later back to Epsom. Herbert had a Bentley automobile and Muriel was taught to drive in it at age 17. He also had horses and used to hunt. He sustained several serious falls and at least one concussion.
   Herbert was a conscientious objector in World War I and was imprisoned in Dartmoor Prison. Somehow Naomi managed to visit him although no females were allowed in there in those days. It was said she was the only female to have gotten inside to visit.
   After the war, in 1923 and 1924 Herbert ran for Parliament as the Labor Party candidate in Acton (West London). He was unsuccessful both times.
   When it became apparent to him that there was going to be another major war, Herbert became very depressed. He committed suicide by jumping overboard from a ferry in the English Channel. The boat was the night ship Paris which was travelling between Newhaven and Dieppe. Herbert and Naomi were living in Goring next to Worthing in Sussex when he committed suicide.
A brief newspaper article on his suicide can be found in the newspaper The Daily Mirror on page 5 of the Monday, April 18, 1938 issue. The article reads as follows.

KISSED HIS WIFE FAREWELL, DROWNED
   "It's no good. I have come to the end of my tether. Since boyhood days I have been battling with a frail body."
   That letter was written to his wife by a man who despaired in the struggle with life, Mr. Herbert A. Baldwin of Epsom, Surrey, a retired business man, aged fifty-nine.
   He is reported to have fallen overboard soon after the night boat PARIS, left Newhaven for Dieppe on Good Friday.

Tears filled the eyes of his wife as she quoted parts of the letter to the Daily Mirror yesterday in her daughter's home at Alleyn Road, Dulwich.

"He has been kissing me good-bye for weeks past," she said, "and we could not understand the pathetic farewells. I thought he might be thinking he would die within a short time."

Mr. Baldwin's brother, Mr. B. J. Baldwin, told the Daily Mirror: "He had a severe breakdown after receiving head injuries while riding a horse at Epsom two years ago and after that he seemed to go to pieces."

More About HERBERT ALPHONSUS BALDWIN:
Burial: Body never recovered[405]
Occupation: 23 May 1904, Butcher (Master)[406]
Residence: 23 May 1904, 73 Honeybrook Road, Clapham[406]

More About HERBERT BALDWIN and NAOMI JESSOP:
Marriage: 23 May 1904, Victoria Baptist Chapel, Wandsworth Road, District of Wandsworth, County of London, England[407]

Children of NAOMI JESSOP and HERBERT BALDWIN are:
27.   i.   MURIEL NAOMI[8] BALDWIN, b. 26 Mar 1905, 151 High St., Sutton, Surrey, England; d. Apr 1993.
28.   ii. DOUGLAS HERBERT BALDWIN, b. 23 Nov 1908, 151 High Street, Epsom, Sutton, Surrey, England; d. 08 Sep 1971, Hospital in Bournmouth, Dorset, England.
        iii. JOHN RUPERT BALDWIN[408], b. 25 Aug 1916, Epson, Surrey, England[409]; d. Jul 1924, Reigate, Surrey, England[409].

9. DEVEREUX HENRY[7] JESSOP *(JANE[6] MOULD, THOMAS[5], WILLIAM[4] MOLDS, WILLIAM[3], JOSEPH[2] MOULDS, THOMAS[1] MOULD)*[410,411] was born 16 Dec 1880 in 55 Balham Road, Balham, Surrey, England[412,413], and died 12 Jun 1914 in Driftway Road, Banstead, Surrey, England[414]. He married JESSIE ANSCOMBE[415] 13 Sep 1910 in Baptist Church, Epsom, England[416,417], daughter of JOSEPH ANSCOMBE and ELIZA. She was born Bet. 1889 - 1890 in Southwark, London, England[417,418].

Notes for DEVEREUX HENRY JESSOP:
Per his death certificate a certificate was received from Gilbert H. White, coroner for West Surrey. The inquest was held 12th June 1914 and by adjournment on the 24th June 1914.

On June 12, 1914, Jane (Mould) Jessop's son, Devereux Henry , was killed when a motorcycle he was driving ran into a tree killing him instantly. His brother-in-law, Herbert Baldwin, was riding behind him and although thrown to the ground, was not seriously injured. Devereux's wife, Jesse, was riding in a side car and was seriously injured. An inquest was held and the death was ruled an accident.

The accident was written up in a couple of newspaper articles and these are written up below.

Banstead
        Motor Fatality
        The Adjourned Inquest

The inquest on Mr. Henry Jessop (32) of High-street, Epsom, partner in the firm of Messrs. Baldwin Bros., on Wednesday afternoon before Mr. Gilbert White. The only witness called was Mr. Herbert Baldwin, brother-in-law of deceased, of Dulverton, Holland-avenue, Sutton, who was riding at the back of deceased's motor-cycle on the day of the accident. He said that deceased called at his house with his wife to discuss business matters and witness returned with him. They went along Banstead-road into Drift Way-road. After passing the Kensington and Chelsea Schools there was a slight gradient, and at the bottom of it a large beech tree and a turning to the left. Deceased had complained about the controls of his machine not being efficient, and witness was of opinion that something went wrong with them on this occasion. Deceased was unable to turn the corner at a sharp enough angle. They were travelling at a fair pace, and the machine dashed into the tree, killing deceased instantly and throwing both witness and deceased's wife, who was in the side car, on to the ground.
The jury returned a verdict of accidental death, and on the Coroner's suggestion recommended that a warning signal should be near the spot. Sympathy was also expressed for the widow and relatives of deceased. Mr. Baldwin said that Mrs. Jessop, who was seriously injured, was progressing favourably.

The Surrey Advertiser And ??

> Epsom
>> Motor Cycle Fatality

On Wednesday evening Mr. Jessop, manager of Messrs. Baldwin Bros., butchers, High-street, Epsom, was motor cycling along the Banstead-road with his wife, who was in a side-car, when the machine by some means got out of control and ran into a tree. Both Mr. Jessop and his wife were thrown out, the former being killed instantly, whilst his wife was seriously hurt. Mr. Jessop was a brother-in-law of Mr. Baldwin, one of the members of the firm of Baldwin Bros.
The inquest was opened at the Banstead Institute yesterday (Friday). Evidence of identification having been taken, the inquiry was adjourned. Mrs. Jessop, who was taken to Holland-avenue, Sutton, is stated to be progressing favourably.

Unknown newspaper

More About DEVEREUX HENRY JESSOP:
Burial: 16 Jun 1914, Section B, Grave 267, Sutton Cemetery, Sutton, London, England[419]
Cause of Death: Thrown from a motorcycle he was driving and instantly killed.[420]
Occupation: 1901, Groom/worker[421]
Residence: 1901, 86 Balham High Road, Surrey, England[421]

More About DEVEREUX JESSOP and JESSIE ANSCOMBE:
Marriage: 13 Sep 1910, Baptist Church, Epsom, England[422,423]

Child of DEVEREUX JESSOP and JESSIE ANSCOMBE is:
29.   i.   DEVEREUX FREDERICK[8] JESSOP, b. 25 Jun 1911; d. 17 Aug 2004, Wimbledon, England.

10. ROSE ANNA[7] JESSOP (JANE[6] MOULD, THOMAS[5], WILLIAM[4] MOLDS, WILLIAM[3], JOSEPH[2] MOULDS, THOMAS[1] MOULD)[424,425] was born 24 Sep 1885 in 55 Balham Grove, Surrey, England[426,427], and died 18 Apr 1968 in 31 Worcester Road, Sutton, London, England[428]. She married FREDERICK THOMAS BRUSHETT[429,430,431] 21 Sep 1908 in St. Peters Presbyterian Church of England, Wandsworth, Surrey, England[432], son of FREDERICK WILLIAM BRUSHETT. He was born Bet. 1879 - 1880 in Holborn, Middlesex, England[433], and died 24 Aug 1968 in Sutton General Hospital, Sutton, England[434,435].

More About ROSE ANNA JESSOP:
Cause of Death: 1a. Cardiac failure b. Myocardial degeneration[436]
Medical Information: Rose Anna was slightly swarthy in color.[437]
Residence: Bef. 1946, Avonside, 62 Lenham Rd., Sutton, Surrey, England[438]

Notes for FREDERICK THOMAS BRUSHETT:
"Her father Frederick Thomas Brushett was the son of a cheesemonger and worked for his father when young. He later became a butcher (employed) and my husband's family shopped with his employer. During the war when we had rationing you would register with a butcher as your sole supplier. The same thing for grocery."
E-mail from Eileen Adkins to Richard Klapper, April 7, 2006

".....we checked where Frederick Brushett worked and it was a butcher shop called Henry in Sutton High Street. Philip's mother would have patronized this shop from the middle 1930's when the Adkins moved to Carshalton. This shop was just a short walk from Lenham Road in Sutton where the Brushetts lived."
E-mail from Eileen Adkins to Richard Klapper, April 10, 2006

More About FREDERICK THOMAS BRUSHETT:
Cause of Death: 1a: Acute left ventricular failure, b: Ischaemic heart disease[439]
Occupation: 21 Sep 1908, Cheesemongers Asst.[440]
Residence: 1881, 150 Lambeth Walk, Lambeth, Surrey, England[441]

More About FREDERICK BRUSHETT and ROSE JESSOP:
Marriage: 21 Sep 1908, St. Peters Presbyterian Church of England, Wandsworth, Surrey, England[442]

Child of ROSE JESSOP and FREDERICK BRUSHETT is:
    i.   HELENA JOAN[8] BRUSHETT[443], b. 11 Oct 1910, 254 Upper Tooting Road, Streatham, London, England[443]; d. 04 Nov 1996[444,445].

Notes for HELENA JOAN BRUSHETT:
"Joan adopted my mother-in-law as a sort of surrogate mother after her parents died and particularly after my father-in-law died."
E-mail from Eileen Adkins to Richard Klapper, April 7, 2006

"She (Joan) was very fond of her parents and when they had to give up their home she moved into the care home with them. .... After they both died within weeks of each other in 1968 she found herself a flat and that is when Dorothy (Eileen's sister-in-law) and she became close as she needed some help with decorations, etc. She moved twice more and each time Dorothy helped and so did we."
E-mail from Eileen Adkins to Richard Klapper, April 10, 2006

"HELLENA (sp) JOAN BRUSHETT   Always known to us as JOAN
Mother's maiden name JESSOPP.
Educated at GPDST (Girls' Public Day School Trust) High School for Girls, SUTTON Surrey.
Almoner & Dispenser at Sutton & Cheam General Hospital. (see photo in lab: coat)

Her parents and mine were friends so my sisters and I knew her from the late 1930's until she died in 1996.

My younger sister who died in February this year was Joan's executrix. Joan was a very kindly and likable person, somewhat Edwardian in outlook & dress. Was always considerate of and sympathetic with the elderly. I guess her experience in her work at the hospital would encourage this apart from her innate character she used to visit my mother regularly, she lived to be 98.
After retirement Joan lived with her parents in rooms at a Care Home and at their demise she moved to her own flat in Sutton and then to a Wardened apartment leaving there she bought a bungalow in the grounds of the Care Home where she was living at the time of her death.

She was very studious indeed bookish, her parent's home contained a considerable collection of books, I have tried to think if I knew what she did at home but I believe she was committed to her work and Bible study. She had interests in many charities, one I remember particularly was the Church Mission to the Jews. I don't recall that any time in our life she had taken an interest in a sport.
A passion for English Royalty did occupy her and she had a large collection of books and photographs on the subject.

Joan never married. We thought of her being so involved with her hospital work that she would not have time for any other activity. So it was to our great surprise and I guess delight that in the early 1940's we discovered that she was being 'courted by a soldier .... said to be a Vicar! I was a teenager at the time and my detective instincts were immediately aroused as soon as I knew.... I didn't like the fellow!! He was in fact a patient at a local psychiatric unit masquerading as a chaplain with shell shock. To my amazement he had insinuated himself into the Bretheren community who had been completely taken in. Poor Joan was his prey he had only one thing in mind, unsuspecting she looked so happy to start with......I could have killed him. I alerted my father as soon as I had the information but was told I shouldn't even suggest such things. Joan went away for a holiday for a while, and we didn't see her for some time. I was in disgrace! After this life went on as normal and we all saw each other often."

Written by Philip Adkins of Alresford, Hampshire, England   June 2006

More About HELENA JOAN BRUSHETT:
Burial: 13 Nov 1996, Sutton Cemetery, Sutton, Surrey, England[445]
Education: Sutton High School, Sutton, Surrey, England[446]
Medical Information: Joan was slightly swarthy in skin color.[447]
Occupation: Medication dispenser at Sutton & Cheam Hospital, Sutton, England[448,449]

Residence: 12 Aug 1953, 68 Lenham Road, Sutton, Surrey[450]

11. GEORGE HAROLD[7] PRENTICE *(ROSE[6] MOULD, THOMAS[5], WILLIAM[4] MOLDS, WILLIAM[3], JOSEPH[2] MOULDS, THOMAS[1] MOULD)*[451,452] was born 13 Jun 1890 in Peakirk, Northamptonshire, England[453,454,455], and died 05 Apr 1975 in Chipping Norton Memorial Hospital, Chipping Norton, Oxfordshire, England[456,457]. He married LILLIAN LAKE[458] 07 Jul 1919 in Peakirk, Northamptonshire, England[459], daughter of WILLIAM LAKE. She was born 01 Mar 1893 in Deeping St. James, Lincolnshire, England[460,461], and died 01 Mar 1984 in Y Gorlan, Cross Inn, Llandyssul, Wales[462,463].

Notes for GEORGE HAROLD PRENTICE:
George Harold Prentice prior to World War I helped his father farm. During the war, George Harold was in the army (Royal Horse Artillery). He served in France. After the war he came home and in 1919 when John William died, Harold took over the farm. In 1923 or 1924 George left Peakirk and moved to Cold Ashby, Northants to have more land to farm. England went through the depression and it became very difficult to continue farming. Finally in 1935 or 1936 Harold gave up farming and moved his family to Bledington which is on the border of Oxfordshire and Gloucestershire. Harold became an Air Ministry Warder which was a policeman job. Harold and Lillian stayed there until they retired and were getting up in years. In about 1970, George and Lillian moved to the farm of their daughter Sheila and Dick Rose (Churchill Heath Farm) and stayed in a cottage on their farm. George died there in 1975. In about 1983, Dick and Sheila gave up farming and moved to Wales to be near a cousin of Sheila's. They took Lillian with them. Lillian died the next year there in Wales and in 1985 Dick had an operation for cancer. Following the operation, Dick felt they should move back to where they came from so they moved back to Oxfordshire.
Telephone interview of Sheila Rose February 13, 2004

More About GEORGE HAROLD PRENTICE:
Baptism: 13 Jul 1890, Peakirk, Northants, England[464]
Burial: Cremated, Ashes buried in Churchill, Oxfordshire, England[465,466]
Occupation: Farmer[467]
Residence: 31 Mar 1901, The Vicarage, Peakirk, Northants, England[468]

More About LILLIAN LAKE:
Burial: Cremated, Ashes buried in Churchill, Oxfordshire, England[469,470]

More About GEORGE PRENTICE and LILLIAN LAKE:
Marriage: 07 Jul 1919, Peakirk, Northamptonshire, England[471]

Children of GEORGE PRENTICE and LILLIAN LAKE are:
30.   i.   JOHN TREVOR[8] PRENTICE, b. 25 Apr 1920, Peakirk, Northamptonshire, England.
31.   ii. SHEILA MARGARET PRENTICE, b. 03 Sep 1921, Peakirk, Northants, England.

12. JOHN FREDERICK[7] PRENTICE *(ROSE[6] MOULD, THOMAS[5], WILLIAM[4] MOLDS, WILLIAM[3], JOSEPH[2] MOULDS, THOMAS[1] MOULD)*[472,473] was born 30 Jun 1893 in Peakirk, Northamptonshire, England[474,475], and died 23 Jun 1969 in 64 North Lane, East Preston, Sussex, England[476]. He married JESSIE EDITH SMELLIE[477] 11 Apr 1925 in Bounds Green, North London, England[478], daughter of ROBERT GEORGE SMELLIE. She was born 21 Feb 1902 in North London, (Bounds Green?) England[479,480], and died 18 Oct 1983 in St. Barnabas(Nursing home), Columbia Drive, Worthing, England[481,482,483].

More About JOHN FREDERICK PRENTICE:
Baptism: 06 Aug 1893, Peakirk, Northants, England[484]
Burial: Buried Worthing Crematorium[485]
Cause of Death: 1a. haemorrhage b. burst aorta (thoric) 11 generalised arteriosclerosis[486]
Graduation: Aug 1913, Certified teacher from London Chelsea St. Marks Training College[487]
Occupation: School teacher in London[488]
Residence: 31 Mar 1901, The Vicarage, Peakirk, Northants, England[489]

More About JESSIE EDITH SMELLIE:

Burial: Buried Worthing Crematorium[490]
Cause of Death: 1a. Carcinomatosis   b. Carcinoma of rectum[491]
Occupation: 11 Apr 1925, Civil Servant[492]
Residence: 11 Apr 1925, 35 West(?)bury Road, Bounds Green, Middlesex, England[492]

More About JOHN PRENTICE and JESSIE SMELLIE:
Marriage: 11 Apr 1925, Bounds Green, North London, England[493]

Children of JOHN PRENTICE and JESSIE SMELLIE are:
32.   i.   JOHN ROBERT[8] PRENTICE, b. 16 May 1926, Bowes Rd. Palmers Green, North London, England.
33.   ii.   MICHAEL PRENTICE, b. 1928; d. 1992.

13. ROSE MARION[7] MOULD *(JABEZ[6], THOMAS[5], WILLIAM[4] MOLDS, WILLIAM[3], JOSEPH[2] MOULDS, THOMAS[1] MOULD)*[494] was born 01 Jan 1885 in Rushden, England[495,496], and died 26 Jan 1973 in Chula Vista, California[497,498]. She married GEORGE HENRY LOVELL[499,500] 08 May 1911 in Aberdeen, Brown County, South Dakota[501,502], son of ARTHUR LOVELL and JANE BAILEY. He was born 09 Nov 1884 in Higham Ferrers, Northampton, England[503,504], and died 09 Feb 1959 in At home in San Ysidro, California[505,506].

Notes for ROSE MARION MOULD:
Rose was born in England and did some singing in her younger days. She came to the U.S., arriving at Ellis Island on May 1, 1911 on the ship Baltic. She settled in Aberdeen, South Dakota and married George Lovell. They ran the Cottage grocery store on 7th Ave. S.E. next to the Wilcox Apartments. They retired in 1946 and turned their grocery over to their son Jim Lovell. They moved to Chula Vista, California where they lived the rest of their lives.

More About ROSE MARION MOULD:
Burial: Glen Abby Memorial Park - Bonita, California[507,508]
Immigration: 01 May 1911, From England to the USA on the ship Baltic[509]
Naturalization: Unknown, Naturalized US citizen[510]
Occupation: 31 Mar 1901, Boot closer[511]
Residence: 31 Mar 1901, 4 Station Rd, Rushden, Northants, England[511]
Social Security Number: 564-80-8921[512]

Notes for GEORGE HENRY LOVELL:
George was born in England and came to the U.S., arriving at Ellis Island on March 24, 1906 on the ship Cedric. He settled in Aberdeen, South Dakota. He lived at 918 South Lloyd Street and on August 25, 1912 there was an article in the Aberdeen newspaper on George and how he had lived in Aberdeen for 6 years and had not been downtown in 5 years. It noted how he was amazed at how much the city had grown. He was the chief engineer at the city pumping station and worked from midnight to noon. He had married Rose Mould and they later owned the Cottage grocery store on 7th Ave. S.E. next to the Wilcox Apartments. They retired in 1946, turned their store over to their son, Jim, and moved to Chula Vista, California. George was a Mason, however, he had a heart condition and the Dr. told him that if he felt he was having an attack he should sit down and rest. The Masons didn't think this was proper so they really didn't really want him in the Masons.

More About GEORGE HENRY LOVELL:
Burial: Glen Abby Memorial Park - Bonita, California[513]
Immigration: 24 Mar 1906, England to the US on the ship Cedric[514]
Naturalization: Unknown, Naturalized US citizen[515,516]
Occupation: 07 Jan 1920, Storekeeper - groceries[517]
Organization: Masons[518]
Residence: 07 Jan 1920, Seventh Ave. SE, Aberdeen, Brown County, South Dakota[519]

More About GEORGE LOVELL and ROSE MOULD:
Marriage: 08 May 1911, Aberdeen, Brown County, South Dakota[520,521]

Children of ROSE MOULD and GEORGE LOVELL are:
            i.   HAZEL CONSTANCE[8] LOVELL[522], b. 06 Mar 1913, Aberdeen, South Dakota[523]; d. 05 Oct 2002, Hospital in

Chula Vista, California[524]; m. CLARENCE ALVA RITTER[525], 23 Dec 1942, Methodist Parsonage, Chula Vista, Sn Diego County, California[526]; b. 05 Jun 1915, Calexico, California[527,528,529]; d. 06 Mar 1981, Hospital in Chula Vista, California[530,531,532].

More About HAZEL CONSTANCE LOVELL:
Burial: Glen Abby Memorial Park, Bonita, California[533]
Cause of Death: antibiotic resistant bacteria in colon[534]
Occupation: 09 Apr 1930, Grocery clerk[535]
Residence: 07 Jan 1920, Seventh Ave. SE, Aberdeen, Brown County, South Dakota[536]
Social Security Number: 504-14-0104[537]

More About CLARENCE ALVA RITTER:
Burial: 10 Mar 1981, Glen Abby Memorial Park - Bonita, California[538,539]
Social Security Number: 553-24-3746[540]

More About CLARENCE RITTER and HAZEL LOVELL:
Marriage: 23 Dec 1942, Methodist Parsonage, Chula Vista, Sn Diego County, California[541]

34.   ii.   JAMES ARTHUR LOVELL, b. 10 Jun 1922, Aberdeen, South Dakota; d. 13 Aug 1993, Grants Pass, Oregon.

14. GEORGE EWART[7] MOULD *(JABEZ[6], THOMAS[5], WILLIAM[4] MOLDS, WILLIAM[3], JOSEPH[2] MOULDS, THOMAS[1] MOULD)[542]* was born 15 Oct 1887 in Rushden, England[542,543], and died 07 Oct 1965 in Hospital in San Diego, California[544,545]. He married KATE FREEMAN[546] 14 Feb 1914 in Aberdeen, Brown County, South Dakota[547,548], daughter of CHARLES FREEMAN and ELLEN SKINNER. She was born 10 Jul 1882 in Rushden, England[549,550], and died 06 Mar 1947 in Home in National City, California[551,552].

Notes for GEORGE EWART MOULD:
George Mould was born in England and his middle name (Ewart) was copied from a famous English lawyer. He later emigrated to the U.S. He made at least 2 trips to the U.S. He arrived at Ellis Island on the ship Oceanic on June 13, 1906. He next arrived at Ellis Island with his sister Rose on May 1, 1911 on the ship Baltic. He settled in Aberdeen, South Dakota and married Kate Freeman. He opened a creamery in Aberdeen where farmers brought him milk and he processed and bottled it and took it to grocery stores. He made a lot of money at a relatively young age. He sold his creamery for $35,000 in 1932 or 1933. He moved to Chula Vista, California. He didn't work until about 1940 when he opened a delicatessen which he owned for about 3 years until the bank expanded and took over his building. He then worked as a checker in a grocery store. George and Kate lived in Chula Vista until their deaths.

More About GEORGE EWART MOULD:
Burial: Glen Abby Memorial Park - Bonita, California[553]
Emigration: 13 Jun 1906, To USA[554]
Naturalization: Unknown, Naturalized US citizen[555]
Occupation: 31 Mar 1901, Boot builder[556]
Organization: Masons[557]
Residence: 24 Dec 1919, 8 Third Ave., Aberdeen, South Dakota[558]
Social Security Number: 566-20-8171[559]

Notes for KATE FREEMAN:
There is a discrepancy on Kate's date of birth. The cemetery records indicate she was born on July 10, 1883 but the grave headstone indicates 1882.

More About KATE FREEMAN:
Burial: Glen Abby Memorial Park - Bonita, California[560]
Residence: 08 Jan 1920, Ninth Ave. SW, Aberdeen, Brown County, South Dakota[561]

More About GEORGE MOULD and KATE FREEMAN:
Marriage: 14 Feb 1914, Aberdeen, Brown County, South Dakota[562,563]

Children of GEORGE MOULD and KATE FREEMAN are:

      i.   CONSTANCE DOREEN[8] MOULD[564], b. 06 Jan 1915, Aberdeen, Brown County, South Dakota[564,565,566]; d. 26 Jun 1997, National City, California[567,568]; m. THOMAS HARRY LARGE[569], 30 May 1936, Glen Abby Chapel of the Roses, Bonita, California[570,571]; b. 22 Mar 1911, Cincinnati, Ohio[572,573]; d. 12 Jan 1972, San Diego area, California[574,575].

           More About CONSTANCE DOREEN MOULD:
           Burial: Glen Abby Memorial Park - Bonita, California[576]
           Residence: 08 Jan 1920, Ninth Ave. SW, Aberdeen, Brown County, South Dakota[577]
           Social Security Number: 561-01-4181[578]

           More About THOMAS HARRY LARGE:
           Burial: Glen Abby Memorial Park - Bonita, California[579]
           Social Security Number: 557-03-6852[580]

           More About THOMAS LARGE and CONSTANCE MOULD:
           Marriage: 30 May 1936, Glen Abby Chapel of the Roses, Bonita, California[581,582]

     ii.   STILLBORN INFANT MOULD[583], b. 24 Jun 1919, Aberdeen, Brown County, South Dakota[583]; d. 24 Jun 1919, Aberdeen, Brown County, South Dakota[583].

           More About STILLBORN INFANT MOULD:
           Burial: 24 Jun 1919, Riverside Cemetery, Aberdeen, South Dakota[584]
           Cause of Death: Stillborn asphasia

    iii.   IRENE MARGUERITE MOULD[585], b. 23 Jan 1921, Aberdeen, Brown County, South Dakota[586]; d. 28 Aug 2003[587].

           More About IRENE MARGUERITE MOULD:
           Social Security Number: 571-22-0900[588]

35.   iv.   DONALD THOMAS MOULD, b. 15 May 1925, Aberdeen, Brown County, South Dakota.

15. ANNIE BEATRICE[7] MOULD (*JABE[6], THOMAS[5], WILLIAM[4] MOLDS, WILLIAM[3], JOSEPH[2] MOULDS, THOMAS[1] MOULD)[589]* was born 06 Oct 1891 in Rushden, Northamptonshire, England[590,591,592], and died 16 Mar 1974 in St. Luke's Hospital, Aberdeen, SD USA[593]. She married FRED ALBERT BULL[594] 11 Jul 1915 in Aberdeen, Brown County, South Dakota[595], son of GEORGE BULL and DEBORAH WRIGHTON. He was born 10 May 1890 in Rushden, Northamptonshire, England[596,597], and died 24 Nov 1982 in At home, Aberdeen, South Dakota USA[598].

Notes for ANNIE BEATRICE MOULD:
Annie attended school only through the third or fourth grade and quit when she kept fainting. The doctor said she would have to be outside and not inside a school building. She emigrated to the USA and arrived in the port of New York, NY, from Liverpool, on July 26, 1912 on the ship Baltic. She settled in Aberdeen, South Dakota and married Fred Bull on July 11, 1915. She became a naturalized citizen on February 24, 1925 receiving Naturalization Certificate # 2119517 from the Circuit Court, Brown County, Aberdeen, S.D. In 1928 she took her son, Alfred back to England to see family. She kept a daily diary which mentions all the family members she visited. She and Fred ran a dairy until World War II when they sold their dairy and moved to Chula Vista, California and a couple of years later to Denver, Colorado where Fred was a blood technician at Fitzsimmons Army Hospital until his retirement. They then moved back to Aberdeen where their son Alfred lived. Annie died in Aberdeen in 1974 and was buried in Riverside Cemetery.
An interesting story concerned Annie and her young daughter, Helen. They went to see President Franklin Roosevelt when he visited Aberdeen. He came in on the train and then rode in a car down Main St. Helen recalls how surprised they all were to find that President Roosevelt was wheelchair bound and had to be helped off the train and into the car. There was no TV in those days and people only heard him on the radio so many, if no most people, had no idea that Roosevelt was handicapped!
Annie Bull's obituary reads as follows.

Mrs. Bull

Mrs. Fred A. (Annie Beatrice) Bull, 82, of 207 4th Ave. N.E., died Saturday night at St. Lukes's Hospital. Services will be at 2 p.m. Tuesday at the Gates-Vik Funeral Home with the Rev. Robert Brown of the First

United Methodist Church officiating. Burial will be in Riverside Memorial Park Cemetery.

Visitation will begin Monday night and continue until the time of the service.

Annie Beatrice Mould was born Oct. 6, 1891 at Rushden-North Hamptonshire, England. She came with her family to Aberdeen in 1912. She married Fred A. Bull on July 11, 1915 at Aberdeen. They moved to Denver, Colo. in 1941 and then returned to Aberdeen in 1961.

She was baptized in the Wesleyan Methodist Church in England and was a member of the Friendly Neibors Club and of the Royal Neighbors of America.

Survivors include her husband; one son, Alfred, of Aberdeen; one daughter, Mrs. Richard (Helen) Klapper, Borger, Tex; and four grandchildren.

Aberdeen American News - March 18, 1974
Reproduced with permission

More About ANNIE BEATRICE MOULD:
Burial: 19 Mar 1974, Aberdeen, South Dakota - Riverside Memorial Park[599]
Immigration: 27 Jul 1912, Arrived at Ellis Island from Liverpool, England[600]
Medical Information: Annie was 5'6" tall per Ellis Island records.
Naturalization: 24 Feb 1925, Circuit Court, Brown County, Aberdeen, S.D.[601]
Occupation: 27 Jul 1912, Milliner[602]
Residence: 31 Mar 1901, 4 Station Rd, Rushden, Northants, England[603]
Social Security Number: 503-62-4843

Notes for FRED ALBERT BULL:
Fred A. Bull was one of the most memorable of the grandchildren of James and Eliza Bull. This was due to the fact that he had an outgoing personality, a photographic memory and was a truly memorable storyteller. No one who ever met him forgot him and his reputation for storytelling is renown throughout the family. Fred was born the youngest of 5 sons in Rushden, Northamptonshire, England. His father had built 2 houses next door to each other on Harborough Road in the 1889 and 1890 time frame. The two houses were still there in 2000 and were 72 and 74 Harborough Road. Fred was born in 1890 in the new house at 72 Harborough Road. It is interesting to note that his aunt Deborah Bull, wife of John Bull was living in 74 Harborough Road when she died in 1935. Fred's father, George, was a famous professional cricket player who contracted TB at about the time of Fred's birth. He died in 1993 when Fred was very young, leaving his wife, Deborah, with 5 sons to raise. Deborah earned money to support the 5 boys by doing piece work for a shoe factory two doors down on Harborough Road. The factory was owned by Deborah's brother, Ebeneezer Wrighton. There was still a factory at this same location in 2000. She worked in a little shed at the back of her house. Her sons all went to work in the same shoe factory as they became old enough. The working conditions in the factories were crowded and cramped and because of this TB was prevalent since at that time it was not understood how it was spread. In 1901 one of Fred's older brothers, George Herbert (Bert), contracted TB and died. Following this Fred's oldest brother, Harry, decided that he wasn't going to stay in England and die of TB. He wanted to take the family to America to start a new life. If the family didn't want to go, he at least wanted to take little Fred so he wouldn't catch the disease. Harry made a trip to America with a friend arriving at Ellis Island on April 10, 1905 on the ship Coronia. He returned to England to marry his girlfriend Bertha Shorely and he convinced his entire family to return to America with him. Deborah Bull, her sons Harry, Horace, Arthur and Fred and Harry's wife Bertha arrived at Ellis Island from Liverpool, England on March 24, 1906 on the ship Cedric. A friend, George Henry Lovell travelled with them also. Fred and George later married sisters Annie and Rose Mould. On the voyage to America which took about a week, The women travelled first or second class while the men and boys travelled third class. The provisions and food in third class were spartan and the men survived by eating a ham which George Lovell had strapped to the outside of his suitcase. The women leaned over the deck and threw rolls down to the men on a lower deck. After landing in New York, they made their way to Aberdeen, South Dakota where Fred got a job delivering groceries in a wagon. In 1910, the four brothers went together and began a dairy called the Bull Brothers Dairy, first on S. Lloyd St. and later on Main St. In 1913, they built a huge barn which was so large it was written up in the Aberdeen paper on July 13, 1913. If it were laid out straight, the barn would have been a city block long. It was laid out in an L shape and was 245 feet long and 36 feet wide. It had a concrete floor. It had 125 stalls and could hold 150 head of cattle. It was the largest structure of its kind in South Dakota. The dairy grew to be one of the largest in the northwest part of South Dakota. The Aberdeen newspaper on June 25, 1917 carried an article written by the Bull brothers which laid out their reasoning for why they would not allow their

228

cattle to be tested for tuberculosis. They said that the tests were not very accurate and if positive would require an expensive cow to be killed. They noted that some of their dairy cows cost as much as $1200 which in 1917 was a tremendous amount of money. Ripley's "Believe It or Not" had a cartoon which said you could buy a quart of Bull's milk at Steer's Grocery in Aberdeen, South Dakota. In 1924, the barn and the two huge silos burned. Fred married Annie Beatrice Mould on July 11, 1915. Annie and her family were from Rushden, England but they had never met until they both immigrated to America. Fred became a naturalized citizen on October 4, 1924 in Circuit Court of Brown County in Aberdeen, South Dakota. His naturalization Certificate was # 2125961. Fred had earlier split from his brothers and started his own dairy which was called Willow Home Dairy. His dairy was near Riverside Cemetery. He worked the dairy until World War II made it impossible to find help. He then sold his dairy and moved to Chula Vista and worked in an airplane factory for about 2 years. His daughter, Helen asked her parents if they would be interested in moving to Denver, Colorado if she took a job and moved there. They agreed and the 3 of them moved to Denver. He and Annie bought the house at 1459 Milwaukee St. He became a blood technician at Fitzsimmons Army Hospital where he drew blood for many years until his retirement. After retiring, he and his wife moved back to Aberdeen to live out their lives at 207 4th Ave. N.E. Annie died in 1974 and Fred continued to live by himself in his house. In 1981, Fred had a heart attack from which he recovered. That same year, Richard, Linda, Helen and Fred Klapper took Fred back to England . Fred had not been back in 75 years so it was an exciting trip for Fred. He went back to Rushden and pointed out his old house, school, shoe factory where he and his family had worked, etc. The young couple who currently owned the house where Fred had been born, invited the group in and listened enthralled as Fred told them stories of their house and what it had been like to live there 80 years before. Fred died in his home 2 years later.

Fred's obituary reads as follows.

Fred Bull – Aberdeen

Fred Bull, 92, of 207 4th Ave. N.E., died of a heart attack Wednesday, Nov. 24, at his home.

Services will be 2 p.m. Saturday, Nov. 27, at the Gates-Vik Funeral Home, 320 6th Ave. S.E., with the Rev. Allen Lang of the Plymouth Congregational United Church of Christ officiating.

Burial will be in Riverside Memorial Park.

Visitation will be Friday evening and until the service Saturday at the funeral home.

The family prefers memorials to the Senior Citizens Center.

Fred Albert Bull was born May 10, 1890, at Rushden, Northamptonshire, England. He attended school there and in 1906 came to the U.S. where he joined in the operation of the Bull Brothers Dairy. He married Annie Mould July 11, 1915, at Aberdeen. In 1944 they moved to Denver, Colo., where he was a technician in the blood bank of the Fitzsimmons Army Hospital. They retired in 1960 and returned to Aberdeen where he has since resided. Mrs. Bull died in 1974.

Survivors include one son, Alfred, Aberdeen; one daughter, Mrs. William (Helen) Klapper, Borger, Texas; and four grandchildren.

He was preceded in death by his wife and four brothers.

Casket bearers will be Willard Ellis, Ray Stewart, Leslie Zumm, R.N. Fossum, Howard Frolland and Joseph Leon. Larry Arndt will be the soloist and Mrs. John Evens will be the organist.

Aberdeen American News - November 26, 1982   page 5
Reproduced by permission

More About FRED ALBERT BULL:
Burial: 27 Nov 1982, Aberdeen, South Dakota - Riverside Memorial Park[604]
Immigration: 24 Mar 1906, Arrived on ship "Cedric" at Ellis Island[605]
Naturalization: 04 Oct 1924, Circuit Court, Brown County, Aberdeen, S.D.[606]
Occupation: 31 Mar 1901, Clicker[607]
Residence: 31 Mar 1901, 72 Harboro Rd., Northants, England[607]
Social Security Number: 548-30-3145

More About FRED BULL and ANNIE MOULD:
Marriage: 11 Jul 1915, Aberdeen, Brown County, South Dakota[608]

Children of ANNIE MOULD and FRED BULL are:
36.   i.   ALFRED MOULD[8] BULL, b. 16 Oct 1916, Aberdeen, South Dakota, USA; d. 04 Aug 2009, Minneapolis,

Minnesota.

37.   ii.   HELEN WRIGHTON BULL, b. 26 Mar 1921, Aberdeen, SD USA.

16. FRANK[7] MACKNESS *(REBECCA[6] MOULD, THOMAS[5], WILLIAM[4] MOLDS, WILLIAM[3], JOSEPH[2] MOULDS, THOMAS[1] MOULD)[609]* was born 09 Jul 1891 in Northamptonshire, England[610], and died 1971 in Portland, Oregon[610]. He married ESTHER MARY PRESTON[610] 10 Dec 1918[610]. She was born 29 Aug 1900 in South Dakota[610], and died Aug 1972 in Torrence, California[611].

Notes for FRANK MACKNESS:

Frank Mackness worked for Woolworth from early on in his career. He met his wife there since she worked in Woolworth as well. He transferred around to several places working for Woolworth from Omaha to Huron. In 1930 he left Woolworth because they wanted to transfer him again and he and Esther didn't want to move from Huron. He went into business for himself selling insurance but eventually went bankrupt. When he was in Lead, South Dakota and Portland, Oregon he demoed Electrolux vacuum cleaners part time. He did this at Moreland Hardware in Portland and while there he reorganized their window displays and in-store displays and they were so impressed they hired him full time. He worked there until he retired when he was in his mid-70s. He retired because Esther was not in good health and he needed to take care of her. Frank was a very kind and gentle man. He and his wife played bridge.

More About FRANK MACKNESS:
Burial: Portland, Oregon[612]
Immigration: 16 Oct 1906, From Liverpool, England to the U.S.[613]
Medical Information: Frank was 4'9" tall at 15 years old per Ellis Island records.
Naturalization: 01 Oct 1918, Brown County, South Dakota, USA[614,615]
Occupation: 16 Oct 1906, Grocer[616]
Residence: 31 Mar 1901, York Rd, Rushden, Northants, England[617]

Notes for ESTHER MARY PRESTON:
For most of her married life Esther stayed home and took care of the kids. When the kids were grown and after Frank and Esther had moved to Portland, she worked for a paper box company. She did their cost accounting and later did estimating for them. She was very good with numbers. Esther wrote but was never published. She and her husband played bridge.

More About ESTHER MARY PRESTON:
Burial: Portland, Oregon[618]
Residence: 1943, Lead, South Dakota[619]

More About FRANK MACKNESS and ESTHER PRESTON:
Marriage: 10 Dec 1918[620]

Children of FRANK MACKNESS and ESTHER PRESTON are:
38.   i.   ROBERT[8] MACKNESS, b. 19 Dec 1922, Omaha, Nebraska; d. 15 Jul 2000, Sierra Madre, California.
39.   ii.   MARJORIE MACKNESS, b. 25 May 1926, Huron, South Dakota.

17. VIOLET[7] MOULD *(CHARLES[6], THOMAS[5], WILLIAM[4] MOLDS, WILLIAM[3], JOSEPH[2] MOULDS, THOMAS[1] MOULD)[621]* was born 23 Nov 1897 in Higham Ferrers, Northamptonshire, England[622,623,624,625], and died 08 Jan 1982 in The Poplars Thrapston Road, Finedon, Northants, England[626,627]. She married ROBERT EDWARD ROBERTS[628,629] Bet. Oct - Dec 1920 in Methodist Church, Higham Ferrers, Northants, England[630,631]. He was born 24 May 1897 in Ruthin, Wales[632,633], and died 12 Feb 1971 in General Hospital, Kettering, Northants, England[634,635,636].

More About VIOLET MOULD:
Burial: Higham Ferrers, Northants, England[637]
Cause of Death: 1a Congestive cardiac failure b Myocardial Ischaemia c Coronary atherosclerosis[638]
Residence: 31 Mar 1901, Westfields, Higham Ferrers, Northants, England[639]

More About ROBERT EDWARD ROBERTS:

Burial: 17 Feb 1971, Higham Ferrers, Northants, England[640,641]
Occupation: 1971, Farmer[642]

More About ROBERT ROBERTS and VIOLET MOULD:
Marriage: Bet. Oct - Dec 1920, Methodist Church, Higham Ferrers, Northants, England[643,644]

Children of VIOLET MOULD and ROBERT ROBERTS are:
     i.   JEFFREY DAVID[8] ROBERTS[645,646], b. 10 Oct 1925, Higham Ferrers, Northants, England[647,648]; d. 2007[649].

          Notes for JEFFREY DAVID ROBERTS:
          Per Trevor Mould, Jeffrey never married. Jeffrey was the house master at a public school.

          More About JEFFREY DAVID ROBERTS:
          Residence: 08 Jan 1982, 23 Ascot Road, Gravesend, Kent, England[650]

     ii. PAULINE HILDA MAY ROBERTS[651,652], b. 15 Jul 1927, Higham Ferrers, Northants, England[653,654]; m. ROBERT SPILLER[655], 24 Dec 1958, Souldrop, Bedfordshire, England[656]; b. , Sommerset, England[656]; d. , Kettering Hospital, Northants, England[656].

          Notes for PAULINE HILDA MAY ROBERTS:
          Per Trevor Mould, Pauline and Robert had no children.

          More About PAULINE HILDA MAY ROBERTS:
          Residence: 02 Jul 1977, Corner House, Keyston, Huntingdon, Cambs, England[657]

          More About ROBERT SPILLER:
          Burial: Keystone Churchyard, Northants, England[658]

          More About ROBERT SPILLER and PAULINE ROBERTS:
          Marriage: 24 Dec 1958, Souldrop, Bedfordshire, England[658]

40.   iii. JOHN ROBERTS, b. 22 Oct 1930, Higham Ferrers, Northants, England; d. Bef. 2002, Souldrop, Bedfordshire, England.

18. LILY[7] MOULD *(CHARLES[6], THOMAS[5], WILLIAM[4] MOLDS, WILLIAM[3], JOSEPH[2] MOULDS, THOMAS[1] MOULD)*[659] was born 09 Mar 1902 in Higham Ferrers, Northants, England[660,661,662], and died 01 Mar 1988 in The Poplars Marshalls Road, Raunds, Northants, England[663]. She married HUBERT JIM EATON[664,665] Bet. Oct - Dec 1929[666]. He was born 12 Apr 1909[667], and died Bet. Oct - Dec 1981[667].

More About LILY MOULD:
Cause of Death: 1a Bronchopneumonia[668]
Residence: 01 Mar 1988, 20 Commercial Street, Higham Ferrers, Northants, England[668]

More About HUBERT JIM EATON:
Occupation: 1981, Boot and shoe clicker (retired)[669]

More About HUBERT EATON and LILY MOULD:
Marriage: Bet. Oct - Dec 1929[670]

Child of LILY MOULD and HUBERT EATON is:
     i.   PETER[8] EATON[671], b. Bet. Oct - Dec 1931[672].

          Notes for PETER EATON:
          Per Trevor, Peter has been married and divorced.

          More About PETER EATON:
          Immigration: From England to Australia[673]

19. BERNARD WILLIAM[7] MOULD *(CHARLES[6], THOMAS[5], WILLIAM[4] MOLDS, WILLIAM[3], JOSEPH[2] MOULDS, THOMAS[1]*

MOULD)[674,675,676] was born 20 Aug 1905 in Higham Ferrers, Northants, England[677,678,679], and died 19 Feb 1982 in Isebrook Hospital, Wellingborough, Northants, England[680]. He married JANE MARGARETTA MAYCOCK[681] 09 Oct 1926 in Silver Street Methodist Church, Kettering, England[682]. She was born 27 Jun 1906 in Kettering, Northants, England[683], and died 08 Jan 1986 in Wymington Road Hospital, Rushden, Northants, England[683].

More About BERNARD WILLIAM MOULD:
Burial: Cremated in Kettering, Northamptonshire, England[684]
Cause of Death: (1) Myocardial Infarction (2) Left Hemiplegia[685]
Occupation: 19 Feb 1982, Lime Yard Manager (Tannery), Retired[685]
Residence: 19 Feb 1982, 34 Handerors(?) Way, Higham Ferrers, Northants, England[685]

More About JANE MARGARETTA MAYCOCK:
Burial: Cremated[686]
Cause of Death: 1a) Broncho pneumonia b) Progressive Cerebrial Vascular disease[687]
Occupation: 08 Jan 1986, 34 Handcross Way, Higham Ferrers, Northants, England[687]

More About BERNARD MOULD and JANE MAYCOCK:
Marriage: 09 Oct 1926, Silver Street Methodist Church, Kettering, England[688]

Children of BERNARD MOULD and JANE MAYCOCK are:
    i.   JOAN MARGARETTA[8] MOULD[689,690,691], b. 17 Apr 1927, Kettering, Northants, England[691]; d. 22 Mar 2002, Kettering General Hospital, Kettering, Northants, England[692,693,694].

        Notes for JOAN MARGARETTA MOULD:
        Joan went to church in Higham Ferrers and as she was going in the door, someone came out and knocked her down. She hit her head and was unconscious. An ambulance took her to the hospital emergency room where she was treated and released. She went to her home and died there from a brain hemorrhage. Joan had never married.

        More About JOAN MARGARETTA MOULD:
        Burial: Cremated in Kettering, Northants, England[695,696]

41.   ii.   NORMAN WILLIAM MOULD, b. 30 Nov 1928, Kettering, Northants, England.
     iii.   PHILLIP MOULD[697,698], b. 25 Nov 1930, Higham Ferrers, Northants, England[699,700,701].

        Notes for PHILLIP MOULD:
        Per Trevor Mould, Philip never married.

     iv.   MARY GILLIAN MOULD[702,703], b. 31 Dec 1932, Higham Ferrers, Northants, England[704,705]; m. ARTHUR JOSEPH FAREY[706,707], 01 Apr 1961, Methodist Church, Higham Ferrers, Northants, England[707]; b. 05 Aug 1937, Wellingborough, Northants, England[707].

        Notes for MARY GILLIAN MOULD:
        Mary and Arthur had no children per Trevor Mould.

        More About ARTHUR FAREY and MARY MOULD:
        Marriage: 01 Apr 1961, Methodist Church, Higham Ferrers, Northants, England[707]

42.   v.   TREVOR GILBERT MOULD, b. 17 Apr 1939, Higham Ferrers, Northants, England.
43.   vi.   JOYCE IRENE MOULD, b. 12 Oct 1934, Higham Ferrers, Northants, England.
44.   vii.   MARGARET ANN MOULD, b. 22 Dec 1940, Higham Ferrers, Northants, England.
45.   viii.   JANET ELIZABETH MOULD, b. 19 Mar 1947; d. 11 Feb 2001, Northampton, Northants, England.

20. IVY DOREEN[7] MOULD *(CHARLES[6], THOMAS[5], WILLIAM[4] MOLDS, WILLIAM[3], JOSEPH[2] MOULDS, THOMAS[1] MOULD)*[708,709] was born Bet. Oct - Dec 1907[710,711], and died 01 Apr 1999 in Nursing home, Irchester, Northants, England[712,713]. She married ARCHIBALD THOMAS LOVELL[714] Bet. Jul - Sep 1931[715]. He was born Bet. Oct - Dec 1907[716], and died 03 Mar 1965 in 40 High Street South, Rushden, Northants, England[717,718].

More About IVY DOREEN MOULD:
Burial: Cremated in Kettering[719]

Residence: 07 Jun 1932, 27 St. Mays Road, Peckham, S.E.15[720]

More About ARCHIBALD THOMAS LOVELL:
Burial: Cremated - Wall plaque at Rushden Cemetery, Northants, England[721]
Cremation: 05 Mar 1965, Kettering Crematorium, Kettering, Northants, England[722]
Occupation: Hairdresser[723]

More About ARCHIBALD LOVELL and IVY MOULD:
Marriage: Bet. Jul - Sep 1931[724]

Child of IVY MOULD and ARCHIBALD LOVELL is:
46.   i.   DOREEN[8] LOVELL, b. 07 Jun 1932, 70 High St., Rushden, Northants, England; d. 15 Mar 1978, Kettering General Hospital, Kettering, Northants, England.

21. PERCY WHITBREAD THOMAS[7] MOULD (*CHARLES[6], THOMAS[5], WILLIAM[4] MOLDS, WILLIAM[3], JOSEPH[2] MOULDS, THOMAS[1] MOULD*)[725,726,727,728] was born Bet. Apr - Jun 1910[729], and died 31 Oct 1983 in Wellingborough Hospital, Wellingborough, Northants, England[730,731]. He married ELIZABETH WINIFRED FIRKINS[732,733,734,735] 29 Jul 1933 in Parish Church, Souldrop, Bedfordshire, England[735], daughter of JOHN FIRKINS and CORBY. She was born Bet. Jul - Sep 1911[736], and died 23 May 1982[737].

More About PERCY WHITBREAD THOMAS MOULD:
Cremation: 03 Nov 1983, Kettering Crematorium, Kettering, Northants, England[737]
Residence: 03 Mar 1945, 5 Lime Street, Rushden[738]

More About ELIZABETH WINIFRED FIRKINS:
Cremation: 26 May 1982, Kettering Crematorium, Kettering, Northants, England[739]

More About PERCY MOULD and ELIZABETH FIRKINS:
Marriage: 29 Jul 1933, Parish Church, Souldrop, Bedfordshire, England[740]

Child of PERCY MOULD and ELIZABETH FIRKINS is:
          i.   ANTHONY[8] MOULD[741], b. Bet. Apr - Jun 1935[742]; d. Bet. Apr - Jun 1938[743].

              Notes for ANTHONY MOULD:
              Per Trevor Mould, Anthony died in infancy.

              More About ANTHONY MOULD:
              Burial: Souldrop Churchyard, Northants, England[744]

22. CYRIL EUGENE[7] MOULD (*GEORGE[6], THOMAS[5], WILLIAM[4] MOLDS, WILLIAM[3], JOSEPH[2] MOULDS, THOMAS[1] MOULD*)[745,746,747] was born 07 Jun 1902 in Gunthorpe, Northants, England[748,749], and died 17 Nov 1978 in Peterborough, Cambridgeshire, England[750]. He married BEATRICE MARY WARD[751] Sep 1928 in St Pauls Church, New England, Peterborough, Northants, England[752]. She was born 06 Feb 1906 in Stickney, near Baston, Lincolnshire, England[752], and died 17 Jan 2002 in Peterborough, Cambridgeshire, England[753].

More About CYRIL EUGENE MOULD:
Burial: Cremated at Marholm Crematorium, Peterborough, Cambridgeshire[753,754]
Residence: Feb 1947, 48 Silverwood Road, Peterborough, Cambridgeshire, England[755]

More About BEATRICE MARY WARD:
Burial: Cremated at Marholm Crematorium, Peterborough, Cambridgeshire[756,757]
Residence: Feb 1947, 48 Silverwood Road, Peterborough, Cambridgeshire, England[758]

More About CYRIL MOULD and BEATRICE WARD:
Marriage: Sep 1928, St Pauls Church, New England, Peterborough, Northants, England[759]

Children of CYRIL MOULD and BEATRICE WARD are:

47.   i.   OLIVE[8] MOULD, b. 16 Feb 1929, 48 Silverwood Rd. Millfield, Peterborough, Cambridgeshire, England; d. 20 Nov 2009, Peterborough Hospital, Peterborough, England.

48.   ii.   WILLIAM ARTHUR MOULD, b. 03 May 1931.

49.   iii. HAROLD EDWARD MOULD, b. 22 Sep 1933.

23. BERNARD[7] MOULD *(GEORGE[6], THOMAS[5], WILLIAM[4] MOLDS, WILLIAM[3], JOSEPH[2] MOULDS, THOMAS[1] MOULD)*[760] was born 27 Jul 1903 in Gunthorpe, Northants, England[761], and died 06 Jan 1996 in Peterborough, England[761]. He married ANNIE LOUISA GREEN[761] 22 Aug 1929 in Peterborough Registration Office, Northants, England[761]. She was born 18 Jul 1905 in Crowland, Northants, England[761], and died 10 Oct 1993 in Fenland Wing, Peterborough Hospital, Peterborough, England[761,762].

Notes for BERNARD MOULD:
Alfred Bull in Aberdeen, South Dakota has two paintings of birds which were done by Bernard Mould. The wording on the back of the paintings says Bernard Mould in Peterborough painted this for Uncle Jabez's birthday in 1922 in the USA. Although Jabez had two nephews named Bernard this Bernard lived in Peterborough while the other one (son of Charles Mould) lived in Higham Ferrers. Joan Bolton said her uncle Bernard copied pictures from postcards so her father, Guilford, was always somewhat dismissive of Bernard's efforts but he did really good work.

More About BERNARD MOULD:
Burial: Cremated in Peterborough, Northants, England[763]
Residence: Feb 1947, 19 Priory Road, Peterborough, Cambridgeshire, England[764]

More About ANNIE LOUISA GREEN:
Burial: Cremated in Peterborough, Northants, England[765]
Cremation: 15 Oct 1993[766]
Residence: Feb 1947, 19 Priory Road, Peterborough, Cambridgeshire, England[767]

More About BERNARD MOULD and ANNIE GREEN:
Marriage: 22 Aug 1929, Peterborough Registration Office, Northants, England[768]

Children of BERNARD MOULD and ANNIE GREEN are:

      i.   ENID[8] MOULD[769], b. 03 Feb 1937, Peterborough, Northants, England[769]; m. PAUL WITHERS[770], 27 Feb 1965, Wolverhamton, England[770]; b. 21 Apr 1942[770].

             More About ENID MOULD:
             Divorced: Jul 1971, Marriage dissolved - no children[770]

             More About PAUL WITHERS and ENID MOULD:
             Marriage: 27 Feb 1965, Wolverhamton, England[770]

50.   ii.   DEREK MOULD, b. 07 Aug 1940.

24. ERIC[7] MOULD *(GEORGE[6], THOMAS[5], WILLIAM[4] MOLDS, WILLIAM[3], JOSEPH[2] MOULDS, THOMAS[1] MOULD)*[771,772] was born 01 Jan 1905 in Gunthorpe, Northants, England[773,774], and died 24 Apr 1995 in Peterborough Cambs, England[775]. He married MARY ETHEL GIDDINGS[776,777] 07 Dec 1932 in Longthorpe Church, Peterborough, Northants, England[778]. She was born 31 Jul 1906 in Blackheath, London[778], and died 30 Jul 1981 in 65 Exeter Road, Peterborough, Cambridgeshire, England[778,779].

More About ERIC MOULD:
Cremation: 01 May 1995[780]
Occupation: Dairy farmer[781]
Residence: Feb 1947, 65 Exeter Road, Peterborough, Cambridgeshire, England[782]

More About MARY ETHEL GIDDINGS:
Baptism: All Saints Church, Blackheath, London, England[783]

Burial: Cremated in Peterborough, Northants, England[784]
Residence: Feb 1947, 65 Exeter Road, Peterborough, Cambridgeshire, England[785]

More About ERIC MOULD and MARY GIDDINGS:
Marriage: 07 Dec 1932, Longthorpe Church, Peterborough, Northants, England[786]

Child of ERIC MOULD and MARY GIDDINGS is:
51. i. ROSITA ANN[8] MOULD, b. 01 Aug 1933, 65 Exeter Road, Peterborough, Northamptonshire, England.

25. GUILFORD THOMAS[7] MOULD *(GEORGE[6], THOMAS[5], WILLIAM[4] MOLDS, WILLIAM[3], JOSEPH[2] MOULDS, THOMAS[1] MOULD)*[787,788] was born 22 Aug 1906 in Gunthorpe, Northants, England[789,790], and died 05 Dec 1992 in Home in Peterborough, Cambridgeshire, England[791,792]. He married MARY MURDEN 20 May 1935 in St. Paul's Church, Peterborough, England[792]. She was born 17 Jan 1912 in Alconbury, Weston, Huntingdonshire, England[792], and died 17 Jun 1991 in Home in Peterborough, Cambridgeshire, England[792,793].

More About GUILFORD THOMAS MOULD:
Burial: Cremated[794]
Residence: Feb 1947, 97 Fulbridge Road, Peterborough, Cambridgeshire, England[795]

More About MARY MURDEN:
Burial: Cremated[796]
Residence: Feb 1947, 97 Fulbridge Road, Peterborough, Cambridgeshire, England[797]

More About GUILFORD MOULD and MARY MURDEN:
Marriage: 20 May 1935, St. Paul's Church, Peterborough, England[798]

Children of GUILFORD MOULD and MARY MURDEN are:
52. i. JOAN BARBARA[8] MOULD, b. 07 Dec 1942, Peterborough, England.
53. ii. ALISON MARY MOULD, b. 01 Mar 1947, Peterborough, England.

26. HUBERT LAWRENCE[7] MOULD *(GEORGE[6], THOMAS[5], WILLIAM[4] MOLDS, WILLIAM[3], JOSEPH[2] MOULDS, THOMAS[1] MOULD)*[799,800] was born 28 Feb 1917 in Peterborough, Northants, England[801,802,803], and died 17 Dec 1994 in Peterborough, Cambridge, England[804,805]. He married HELEN EMMA AUGUSTA OBERLANDER[806] 18 Jun 1947 in Berlin, Germany[806]. She was born 10 Dec 1923 in Berlin, Spandau, Germany[806].

More About HUBERT LAWRENCE MOULD:
Burial: Cremated
Military service: Feb 1947, SGt. in the 11th Hussars in Germany
Residence: Feb 1947, Germany[807]

More About HUBERT MOULD and HELEN OBERLANDER:
Marriage: 18 Jun 1947, Berlin, Germany[808]

Children of HUBERT MOULD and HELEN OBERLANDER are:
  i. LAURENCE[8] MOULD[809,810], b. 27 Nov 1948, Peterborough, Northants, England[811]; m. HELEN DEAN[811], 30 Sep 1989, Peterborough, Northants, England[811]; b. 28 Jul 1947, Peterborough, England[811].

  Notes for LAURENCE MOULD:
  Laurence a Buildings Quantity Surveyor, the oldest of Hubert's children married Helen a divorcee with two children in 1989. They had no further children. Laurence has a keen interest in home improvements, game fishing, pigeon shooting and ornithology.
  E-mail from Helen Mould (wife of Lawrence) 16 Nov 2006

  Laurence was born 27 November 1948 and spent his first two years at Rock House in Gilpin Street. As a small baby, he caused great concern: he could not keep his milk down and obviously wasn't thriving. After an operation to clear the duct leading from his stomach, all was well.
  For the two years he was at the dairy, there were seven adults living there: his parents, grandfather, and three

aunts, Doris, Marjorie and Iris, as well as Ernest Maile, Doris' husband.

Doris was the least domesticated inhabitant of Rock House. (Some would say she seemed to live on another planet.) But she was besotted with little 'Lollie' and took him out for walks in his pram nearly every day. Since Doris loved going to the Catholic Church Lollie had to go too. Some days Ursula would hardly see her son but it meant that Ursula could get on with the tasks she had undertaken knowing that Laurence was well looked after.

Aged eleven, Laurence passed the entrance examination for a grammar school and opted for the Deacon's School, (just as his cousin, Derek, had done, though they did not overlap.)

After doing well in his '0' level examinations, Laurence entered the sixth form to study for his 'A' levels, one subject being German. He left school in July 1966 aged eighteen and then went to the Peterborough Technical College ("The Tech") where took his exams to qualify as a quantity surveyor.

His first job was at Henry Firman's on Oxney Road where he stayed until the company went into liquidation around 1971. He moved to Mitchells Construction in the center of Peterborough, but when firm required Laurence to go abroad for them he felt this would 'get in the way of his fishing' and resigned. Then followed a period 'on the dole' before meeting up one day with an ex-colleague – another quantity surveyor from the time at Firman's. Laurence says: "This chap was working for a firm based in Lincolnshire, called Eccleshore. He told me he would be in charge of a new branch soon to open in Peterborough and suggested I come and work for him – so I did."

This firm, sited in Prince Street, later became Princebuild where Laurence has remained ever since, becoming a director in 1990.

Laurence's chief 'passion' for a long time was his fishing. This lead to a real life drama in September of 1964 when, as a fifteen-year-old Deacon's Schoolboy, he and a friend went to work a major angling contest in Worcester, on the River Severn. While walking along the bank of the river with a friend, Laurence heard an angler shout that someone was in trouble. Laurence stripped off his outer clothes and jumped into the river and was carried downstream of the boy who had disappeared. The river's current was very strong. When he finally made it to the spot where the boy had disappeared, Laurence could only see bubbles and the boy's hair. Laurence grabbed the hair and towed the unconscious boy to the bank. The bank was steep and Laurence had a difficult time getting the unconscious youth out of the water but finally made it. The youth regained consciousness and recovered. In the meantime, Laurence's friend had run to the nearby race course and fetched an ambulance. A passing boat was flagged down and took Laurence and the boy across the river to the waiting ambulance.

In recognition of his courageous deed, Laurence was awarded a Royal Humane Society testimonial by the Mayor, Councillor George Bradley. Following this award, the boy's father presented Laurence with an inscribed fishing rod in appreciation of his actions. The rod had an inscription, which said, "(he) landed a 140 pounder."

Laurence was a most reluctant hero, doing his best to avoid the press and any praise. When asked why he was not keen for people to hear about it, he said, with typical modesty "Well it's just something you do in the situation, isn't it?"

It was not until September 1989 that he married Helen. He was forty. On an earlier occasion when Joan knowingly asked him how a good-looking chap like him had avoided matrimony, he put it down to his obsession with fishing, often a nocturnal occupation when others were socializing.

Helen is an accomplished artist who paints on commission. She also had her own gallery.

Writeup by Joan (Mould) Bolton in February 2007 after talking to Laurence

More About LAURENCE MOULD and HELEN DEAN:
Marriage: 30 Sep 1989, Peterborough, Northants, England[811]

54.   ii.   MELVIN MOULD, b. 19 Jul 1952, Peterborough, England.

Generation No. 4

27. MURIEL NAOMI[8] BALDWIN (*NAOMI JANE[7] JESSOP, JANE[6] MOULD, THOMAS[5], WILLIAM[4] MOLDS, WILLIAM[3], JOSEPH[2] MOULDS, THOMAS[1] MOULD*)[812] was born 26 Mar 1905 in 151 High St., Sutton, Surrey, England[812], and died Apr 1993[813]. She married ERIC PARSLEY[814] 25 Jul 1925 in St. George's Hanover Square, London, England[815,816]. He was born Bet. Jul - Sep 1900[817], and died Jul 1972[818].

More About MURIEL NAOMI BALDWIN:
Burial: Cremated Luton, Hertfordshire, England[818]

Residence: 18 Apr 1938, Alleyn Road, Dulwich[819]

Notes for ERIC PARSLEY:
Eric taught at Keble College, Oxford from 1919 - 1923. In 1923, he was appointed Master in Charge of French at Dulwich College. From 1933 to 1946 he was Head of the Modern Side. He also was House master of Blew House at the college. From May 1954 to his retirement in July 1960 he was President of the Common Room. Eric was in a second-hand book store one day and found and purchased a First Edition of Racine. He gave it to France and they bestowed on him the Legion d' Honor. It was noted that Eric proudly wore the ribbon.

More About ERIC PARSLEY:
Burial: Cremated Cambridge, England[820]
Occupation: Bet. 1919 - 1923, Teaching at Keble College at Oxford, England[821]

More About ERIC PARSLEY and MURIEL BALDWIN:
Marriage: 25 Jul 1925, St. George's Hanover Square, London, England[822,823]

Children of MURIEL BALDWIN and ERIC PARSLEY are:
      i.   DAVID[9] PARSLEY[824], b. 13 Oct 1927, Camberwell, London, England[824,825]; d. 05 Jul 1949[826,827].
55.   ii. VIRGINIA PARSLEY, b. 24 Nov 1928, Camberwell, London, England.

28. DOUGLAS HERBERT[8] BALDWIN *(NAOMI JANE[7] JESSOP, JANE[6] MOULD, THOMAS[5], WILLIAM[4] MOLDS, WILLIAM[3], JOSEPH[2] MOULDS, THOMAS[1] MOULD)*[828] was born 23 Nov 1908 in 151 High Street, Epsom, Sutton, Surrey, England[829], and died 08 Sep 1971 in Hospital in Bournmouth, Dorset, England[830,831,832]. He married MONA WINIFRED SKELTON[833,834,835] 08 Nov 1934 in Epsom, Surrey, England[835,836]. She was born 19 Aug 1909 in Epsom, Surrey, England[837,838,839].

More About DOUGLAS HERBERT BALDWIN:
Burial: Cremated in Bournmouth Crematorium, Bournmouth, Dorset, England[839]

More About DOUGLAS BALDWIN and MONA SKELTON:
Marriage: 08 Nov 1934, Epsom, Surrey, England[840,841]

Children of DOUGLAS BALDWIN and MONA SKELTON are:
56.   i.   JANE[9] BALDWIN, b. 05 Dec 1935, Epsom, Surrey, England.
57.   ii. CHRISTOPHER BALDWIN, b. 01 Mar 1937, Cheam, Surrey, England.

29. DEVEREUX FREDERICK[8] JESSOP *(DEVEREUX HENRY[7], JANE[6] MOULD, THOMAS[5], WILLIAM[4] MOLDS, WILLIAM[3], JOSEPH[2] MOULDS, THOMAS[1] MOULD)*[842] was born 25 Jun 1911[843,844], and died 17 Aug 2004 in Wimbledon, England[844]. He married (1) KATHLEEN MARY WEEKS[845] 23 Jul 1939 in St. Paul's Church, Clapham, Surrey, England[846], daughter of WILLIAM HENRY WEEKS. She was born Bet. 1915 - 1916[846]. He married (2) NURIA RIBERA MARIMON[847] 1963[847]. She was born 09 May 1928 in Igualada, Catalonia, Spain (near Barcelona)[847].

More About DEVEREUX FREDERICK JESSOP:
Burial: 25 Aug 2004, Merton & Sutton Cemetery, Sutton, England[847]
Occupation: 23 Jul 1939, Shop proprietor[848]
Residence: 23 Jul 1939, 88 Edgeley Road, Clapham, Surrey, England[848]

More About KATHLEEN MARY WEEKS:
Occupation: 23 Jul 1939, Secretary[848]
Residence: 23 Jul 1939, 88 Edgeley Road, Clapham, Surrey, England[848]

More About DEVEREUX JESSOP and KATHLEEN WEEKS:
Marriage: 23 Jul 1939, St. Paul's Church, Clapham, Surrey, England[848]

More About DEVEREUX JESSOP and NURIA MARIMON:
Marriage: 1963[849]

Children of DEVEREUX JESSOP and NURIA MARIMON are:
      i.   MICHAEL DEVEREUX[9] JESSOP[849], b. 29 Feb 1968[849].
     ii.   MARK FREDERICK JESSOP[849], b. 12 Jan 1973[849].

30. JOHN TREVOR[8] PRENTICE *(GEORGE HAROLD[7], ROSE[6] MOULD, THOMAS[5], WILLIAM[4] MOLDS, WILLIAM[3], JOSEPH[2] MOULDS, THOMAS[1] MOULD)[850]* was born 25 Apr 1920 in Peakirk, Northamptonshire, England[851]. He married MOLLY MARY MARK[852] 02 Apr 1945 in Bishops, Stortford, Essex[853]. She was born 11 Feb 1917 in Mill Farm, Thorpe Abbotts, Diss, Norfolk[854].

Notes for JOHN TREVOR PRENTICE:
    "Our daughter Jane married Rodney Gordon, a New Zealander in 1976 and went to live there. In 1986 we went on a 2 months holiday and were very impressed with the wide open spaces, the scenery and the friendliness of the New Zealand people. Also, the Country which is 1/6 larger than Britain in area, had a population of less than 4 million people. When we got home we decided that we would like to spend our retirement years in New Zealand and in 1948 we applied to and got approval to become permanent residents. We eventually arrived here in November 1988 and have never regretted making the decision."
E-mail from John Trevor Prentice to Richard Klapper on April 5, 2004

More About JOHN TREVOR PRENTICE:
Immigration: 26 Nov 1988, From England to New Zealand[855]
Military: Jan 1936, Joined RAF [856]
Military service: Bet. Jan 1936 - Jan 1971, RAF[856]

Notes for MOLLY MARY MARK:
    "She has always been known as Molly. Before the War she became a Red Cross nurse and continued nursing until the latter part of 1945. She was a nurse in the Norfolk and Norwich Hospital and the Bishop Stortford General Hospital where we met in November 1944.
    When we bought our first house in a village called Bloxham which is about 3 miles from the Market town of Banbury in Oxfordshire, she ran the Meals on Wheels Service for some 10 years until we left to live in Moreton on Lugg near Hereford. .... Our daughter Jane married Rodney Gordon, a New Zealander in 1976 and went to live there. In 1986 we went on a 2 months holiday and were very impressed with the wide open spaces, the scenery and the friendliness of the New Zealand people. Also, the Country which is 1/6 larger than Britain in area, had a population of less than 4 million people. When we got home we decided that we would like to spend our retirement years in New Zealand and in 1948 we applied to and got approval to become permanent residents. We eventually arrived here in November 1988 and have never regretted making the decision."
E-mail from John Trevor Prentice to Richard Klapper on April 5, 2004

More About MOLLY MARY MARK:
Immigration: 26 Nov 1988, Immigrated to New Zealand[857]

More About JOHN PRENTICE and MOLLY MARK:
Marriage: 02 Apr 1945, Bishops, Stortford, Essex[858]

Children of JOHN PRENTICE and MOLLY MARK are:
58.   i.   JANE ANN ELIZABETH[9] PRENTICE, b. 13 Jan 1946, Chipping Norton Memorial Hospital, Chipping Norton, Oxfordshire, England.
59.   ii.   MARGARET PRISCILLA INGRID PRENTICE, b. 20 Jan 1948, Changi Hospital, Singapore.

31. SHEILA MARGARET[8] PRENTICE *(GEORGE HAROLD[7], ROSE[6] MOULD, THOMAS[5], WILLIAM[4] MOLDS, WILLIAM[3], JOSEPH[2] MOULDS, THOMAS[1] MOULD)[859]* was born 03 Sep 1921 in Peakirk, Northants, England[859,860]. She married RICHARD ROSE[861] 27 Dec 1941 in Bledington Church, Bledington, Gloucestershire, England[862]. He was born 12 Aug 1917 in Churchill Heath Farm, Kingham, Oxford[862], and died 05 Feb 2003.

More About RICHARD ROSE and SHEILA PRENTICE:
Marriage: 27 Dec 1941, Bledington Church, Bledington, Gloucestershire, England[862]

Children of SHEILA PRENTICE and RICHARD ROSE are:
60.   i.   RICHARD[9] ROSE, b. 22 Feb 1943, Chipping Norton, Oxfordshire, England.
61.   ii.   DAVID ROSE, b. 04 Feb 1945, Hospital in Chipping Norton, Oxford, England.

32. JOHN ROBERT[8] PRENTICE *(JOHN FREDERICK[7], ROSE[6] MOULD, THOMAS[5], WILLIAM[4] MOLDS, WILLIAM[3], JOSEPH[2] MOULDS, THOMAS[1] MOULD)*[863] was born 16 May 1926 in Bowes Rd. Palmers Green, North London, England[863,864]. He married VIVIENNE ROSEMARY ROSE[865] 18 Apr 1949 in Churchill Church, Oxfordshire, England[866]. She was born 26 Apr 1927 in Churchill Heath Farm, Kingham,, Oxfordshire, England[867,868].

More About JOHN PRENTICE and VIVIENNE ROSE:
Marriage: 18 Apr 1949, Churchill Church, Oxfordshire, England[868]

Children of JOHN PRENTICE and VIVIENNE ROSE are:
62.   i.   MARY[9] PRENTICE, b. 21 Jul 1950, Hillingdon Hospital, Hillingdon, Middlesex, England.
63.   ii.   MICHAEL PRENTICE, b. 24 Nov 1952, Farnborough, Hampshire, England.
64.   iii. ROBERT DAVID PRENTICE, b. 26 May 1956, Farnborough, Hampshire, England.
65.   iv. LESLEY ANNE PRENTICE, b. 30 Dec 1962, Hillingdon Hospital, Hillingdon, Middlesex, England.

33. MICHAEL[8] PRENTICE *(JOHN FREDERICK[7], ROSE[6] MOULD, THOMAS[5], WILLIAM[4] MOLDS, WILLIAM[3], JOSEPH[2] MOULDS, THOMAS[1] MOULD)*[869] was born 1928[869], and died 1992[869]. He married CLAIRE ANDERSON[869] Abt. 1961 in E. Preston, Sussex, England[870].

More About MICHAEL PRENTICE and CLAIRE ANDERSON:
Marriage: Abt. 1961, E. Preston, Sussex, England[870]

Children of MICHAEL PRENTICE and CLAIRE ANDERSON are:
        i.   MICHAEL KEITH[9] PRENTICE[871,872], b. 1962[873].
66.   ii.   ADRIENNE PRENTICE.
        iii. STEPHEN PRENTICE[873], m. ANN[873].

34. JAMES ARTHUR[8] LOVELL *(ROSE MARION[7] MOULD, JABEZ[6], THOMAS[5], WILLIAM[4] MOLDS, WILLIAM[3], JOSEPH[2] MOULDS, THOMAS[1] MOULD)*[874] was born 10 Jun 1922 in Aberdeen, South Dakota[875], and died 13 Aug 1993 in Grants Pass, Oregon[876,877]. He married MARTHA MAY HETTICH[878,879] May in Aberdeen, Brown County, South Dakota[880]. She was born in Kulm, Norht Dakota[881], and died 01 Sep 2000 in Chula Vista, California[882].

Notes for JAMES ARTHUR LOVELL:
At some point during his life James went back to England and during WWII he talked airplanes in for landing.

More About JAMES ARTHUR LOVELL:
Burial: Cremated
Residence: 09 Apr 1930, 312 Seventh Ave., Aberdeen, Brown County, South Dakota[883]
Social Security Number: 503-18-7657[884]

More About MARTHA MAY HETTICH:
Social Security Number: 503-26-0315[884]

More About JAMES LOVELL and MARTHA HETTICH:
Marriage: May, Aberdeen, Brown County, South Dakota[885]

Children of JAMES LOVELL and MARTHA HETTICH are:
        i.   DAVID GEORGE[9] LOVELL[886], b. 18 Feb 1947, Aberdeen, Brown County, South Dakota[886].
        ii.   JAMES WINSTON LOVELL[887], b. 28 Dec 1950, Chula Vista, California[888]; m. VIRGINIA LYON[889,890], 20 Sep 1997, San Diego, California[891,892].

            More About JAMES LOVELL and VIRGINIA LYON:

Marriage: 20 Sep 1997, San Diego, California[893,894]

iii.   GEORGE HENRY LOVELL[895], b. 09 Feb 1953, Chula Vista, California[895].

35. DONALD THOMAS[8] MOULD *(GEORGE EWART[7], JABEZ[6], THOMAS[5], WILLIAM[4] MOLDS, WILLIAM[3], JOSEPH[2] MOULDS, THOMAS[1] MOULD)*[896] was born 15 May 1925 in Aberdeen, Brown County, South Dakota[896]. He married (1) LOIS ELLEN ONCLEY[896] 15 Jun 1946 in Glen Abbey, Little Church of the Roses, Bonita, California[896]. She was born 22 Dec 1926 in Lincoln Park, Michigan[896], and died 20 Sep 1980 in Los Angeles, California[896]. He married (2) EDIE CORRINE BILLINGS[896] 14 Feb 1982 in Lutherin Church in Anaheim Hills, California[896]. She was born 11 Jul 1929 in Nashville, Arkansas[896].

More About LOIS ELLEN ONCLEY:
Burial: Cremated - Ashes scattered from a plane[896]

More About DONALD MOULD and LOIS ONCLEY:
Marriage: 15 Jun 1946, Glen Abbey, Little Church of the Roses, Bonita, California[896]

More About DONALD MOULD and EDIE BILLINGS:
Marriage: 14 Feb 1982, Lutherin Church in Anaheim Hills, California[896]

Children of DONALD MOULD and LOIS ONCLEY are:
     i.   GARY THOMAS[9] MOULD[896], b. 24 Sep 1947, National City, California[896,897]; m. (1) SHARON ALEXANDER[898,899]; m. (2) JODI[900]; m. (3) RITA[900].
     ii.   DENNIS LLOYD MOULD[900], b. 13 Jul 1950, National City, California[900,901]; m. TINA SORRONSON[902].
67.   iii.   TIMOTHY STEVEN MOULD, b. 18 Mar 1955, Whittier, California.

36. ALFRED MOULD[8] BULL *(ANNIE BEATRICE[7] MOULD, JABEZ[6], THOMAS[5], WILLIAM[4] MOLDS, WILLIAM[3], JOSEPH[2] MOULDS, THOMAS[1] MOULD)*[903] was born 16 Oct 1916 in Aberdeen, South Dakota, USA[904], and died 04 Aug 2009 in Minneapolis, Minnesota[905]. He married LOIS ELIZABETH FRAD 26 May 1940 in Faulkton, Faulk County, South Dakota[906], daughter of WILLIAM FRAD and LULU PICKLER. She was born 17 Oct 1914 in Faulkton, Faulk County, South Dakota[906], and died 02 Jan 2004 in North Memorial Hospital, Robinsdale, Minnesota[907].

Notes for ALFRED MOULD BULL:
Alfred Bull was born in Aberdeen, South Dakota and lived there for most of his life. When he was 12 years old, he went back to England with his mother to visit the family members there. They were in England for 6 months from May until October of 1928. His mother kept a diary which noted their daily activities and the various family members they met and stayed with. While in England, They went to a birthday party for Eliza Bull, Alfred's great grandmother who was in her late 90s. He remembers she was feeble and bedridden. Alfred married Lois Frad and they honeymooned in the Black Hills. He went into the Navy in 1944. He was a civilian radio teacher for the Army in Souix Falls, S. D. He later took a test and went to radio school in Chicago and then was assigned to Ward Island, near Corpus Christi, Texas as a radar technician. During his time at Ward Island, Lois lived in a place called Perry Place where the wives stayed. Alfred never went overseas during the war. He went back to Aberdeen after the war and taught high school science for many years until retiring. He continued to live in Aberdeen until the death of Lois, at which time his daughter moved him to an assisted living facility in Anoka, Minnesota. As his health deteriorated Marily moved him to a skilled nursing facility closer to where she lived in Blaine, Minnesota. Alfred died at this facility. The funeral was held in Aberdeen and he was buried in Faulkton, South Dakota next to his wife Lois in her family plot.

The following information was provided by Alfred Bull and updated after Lois' death by their daughter Marilyn (Bull) Pash.

My Parents
... came from the shoe manufacturing town in the English midlands called Rushden. My paternal grandfather was a professional Cricket and football player and coach. He contracted T.B. (tuberculosis) and spent a year in Australia. My father and three brothers came to the United States about 1906 and settled in Aberdeen. My mother came from Rusden and about 1913 met my father here (in the U.S). They were married in 1915.

I was born in Aberdeen in 1916. My father had a small dairy farm and ran a milk route in Aberdeen. Our farm was just west of the Aberdeen city limits about 5 blocks (approximately 12th Avenue west and south 16th street. I remember helping my father pedal milk.
At that time there were practically no houses west of south 12th street. I also remember there were approximately 5 different movie theaters when I was growing up as a child in Aberdeen.

Since we were outside of the city limits. I attended Riverside rural school which was located about 4 blocks west of Riverside Cemetery close to where Highway 281 and Melgaard Road now intersect. Riverside was a demonstration school for the Normal and we usually had about six practice teachers. Julia Finley was my grade school teacher from the 2nd through the 8th grade. We had a YCL organization and I attended the state meeting as representative from Brown county. I went to Simmons school for the 9th grade.

1916 Born in Aberdeen on October 16.
1921 Started education at Riverside School.
1928 Went to England with my mother from May until September and stayed with my mother's friends and relations all over England. We visited many historic sights, museums, and art galleries, (e.g. Sulgrave Manor, Shakespeare's home, Westminster Abbey, the seashore.)
1931 - 1934 Attend Central High school which consisted of 3 separate buildings.
1934 - 1938 Attend Northern States Teachers College and earned a Bachelor of Science degree. Taught in Warner.
1938 Took a teaching job at Bonilla high school.
1940 Married Lois Frad.
(In 1941, for our honeymoon, we went to San Diego, CA with Dean and Edith for a couple of weeks. We visited relatives and ended (the trip) in L.A. and then went home.)
1941 - 1942 We lived during the 1941-42 school years in Bonilla. Lois was a high school English, Social Science and vocal music teacher. The summer of 1941 we to the University of Colorado with Dean and Edith Meyer, and I started work on my Master's degree .
1942 Taught in spring at Bonilla, spent the summer in Colorado and fall at Nebraska. World War II started in November.
1943 Went to Sioux Falls to Teach radio and electronics at the Army Air Force base.
1944 My son Richard was born in Sioux Falls on July 17.
1945 Enlisted in the US Navy Radar Electronics program and trained at the Great Lakes Naval Station and (at) Corpus Christie, Texas.
1946 Discharged from the Navy and took a teaching job at Highmore High School in South Dakota.
1946 Changed jobs to Faulkton High School. We owned a small house there, and I taught at Faulkton 9 years. (1947-1955)
1950 My daughter Marilyn was born on June 15 in Faulkton.
1955 Took a position as a Chemistry teacher with Aberdeen Public High School. Attended the University of Colorado during the summer for 5 years.
1958 - 1959 Took a leave of absence and got my MA in chemistry and Zoology in 1959.
1955 – 1982 Taught at Aberdeen Central High Schools for 27 years. (Primarily taught physics and chemistry but also taught biology, geometry and trigonometry.)
1982 Retired in the spring of the year
1982-2004 Lived with my wife Lois and helped care for her. (She had diabetes and congestive heart trouble.) We also were active in a variety of civic, academic, and social organizations, e.g. Retired Teachers, Shakespeare Club, The Westerner Club, SD Historical Society, etc.)
2004 Lois died on January 2, 2004.
2004 – Present Moved to the Twin Cities where my daughter could help care for me. Entered Assisted Living at Walker Plaza, Anoka MN in May of 2004 and Comforts of Home Assisted Living in December of 2007.

More About ALFRED MOULD BULL:
Burial: 08 Aug 2009, Faulkton Cemetery, Faulkton, South Dakota[908]
Residence: 26 Jan 1920, Farm, Aberdeen, Brown County, South Dakota, USA[909]

Notes for LOIS ELIZABETH FRAD:

Lois (Frad) Bull was born in Faulkton, South Dakota in the front room of the house known as the Pickler Mansion. Her maternal grandparents were John Alfred Pickler and Alice Mary (Alt) Pickler, one of the leading families in South Dakota in the mid-1800s. John Played a significant role in the early west and was Commissioner of Indian Affairs. He opened the Oklahoma Territory in 1899 by firing the gun which started the wagons racing into Oklahoma to homestead land and settle the country. John was the first member elected to the U.S. House of Representatives from South Dakota. The Picklers were big advocates of the women's suffrage movement. John introduced the first women's suffrage bill in the U.S. Congress but it didn't pass. Julia Ward Howe visited the Picklers in the Faulkton house and Susan B. Anthony stayed at the house for 6 weeks while she was planning her campaign in the area. Susan was 70 years old when she was there. Alice Mary went on tours with Susan B. Anthony. In the library of the house is a picture of Susan B. Anthony and another of the assembled 54th U.S. House of Representatives with John Pickler in it. The house also contains a painting of the war chief Red Cloud on leather which was presented to John Pickler by the Souix tribe. Lois's mother, Lulu, was the daughter of John and Alice Mary and she attended 5 presidential inaugural balls including Cleveland, McKinley on down to her last one which was that of Teddy Roosevelt. Most all of John Alfred's papers and letters are now in the historical center at Pierre, South Dakota.

The Pickler Mansion was passed down to Lois' mother upon the death of her parents and Lois was born in the front room of the house. She grew up there and was married to Alfred Bull in the library of the mansion. Their daughter Marilyn was brought home from the hospital to the house and was the last baby brought home to this house. In 1945, their son Richard Bull stayed in the mansion because his parents thought he would be safer there from the polio which was spreading all over. Upon her mother's death, the house passed to Lois and she donated it to a historical society in Faulkton which has begun restoration work. In May 2000, on their 60th wedding anniversary, Alfred and Lois and their families went to Faulkton to visit the house and sit in the library where they had been married. In addition to their two children, there was Alfred's sister Helen (Bull) Klapper and her son, Richard and his wife Linda. They were met by the people from the historical society who toured them through the old house to show the progress of the restoration. Lois and Alfred currently live in Aberdeen.
Richard Klapper - October 25, 2001

More About LOIS ELIZABETH FRAD:
Burial: 08 Jan 2004, Faulkton, Faulk County, South Dakota[910]

More About ALFRED BULL and LOIS FRAD:
Marriage: 26 May 1940, Faulkton, Faulk County, South Dakota[911]

Children of ALFRED BULL and LOIS FRAD are:
   i.   RICHARD ALBERT[9] BULL[912], b. 17 Jul 1944, Sioux Falls, South Dakota[913]; m. (1) TARA[914]; m. (2) CHRISTINE DRAEGER, 14 Jan 1968, First Congregational Church, Sioux Falls, South Dakota[915]; m. (3) BETTY ANN BEATTIE[916], Jul 1972, Sioux Falls, South Dakota[916]; b. 05 Aug 1944, Toronto, Canada[916]; m. (4) LINDA KATHERINE MENDELSON[917], 29 Jul 1979, Palo Alto, California[917]; b. 05 Feb 1957[917].

        More About RICHARD BULL and CHRISTINE DRAEGER:
        Marriage: 14 Jan 1968, First Congregational Church, Sioux Falls, South Dakota[918]

        More About RICHARD BULL and BETTY BEATTIE:
        Marriage: Jul 1972, Sioux Falls, South Dakota[919]

        More About RICHARD BULL and LINDA MENDELSON:
        Marriage: 29 Jul 1979, Palo Alto, California[920]

   ii. MARILYN JEAN BULL[921], b. 15 Jun 1950, Faulkton, South Dakota[921]; m. PETER PAUL PASH[921], 06 Oct 1973, Minneapolis, Minnesota - St. John's Episcopal Church[921]; b. 24 May 1942, Minneapolis, Minnesota[921].

        More About PETER PASH and MARILYN BULL:
        Marriage: 06 Oct 1973, Minneapolis, Minnesota - St. John's Episcopal Church[921]

37. HELEN WRIGHTON[8] BULL *(ANNIE BEATRICE[7] MOULD, JABEZ[6], THOMAS[5], WILLIAM[4] MOLDS, WILLIAM[3], JOSEPH[2] MOULDS, THOMAS[1] MOULD)*[922] was born 26 Mar 1921 in Aberdeen, SD USA[922]. She married WILLIAM RICHARD KLAPPER[923,924] 10 May 1946 in Denver, Colorado USA[925], son of ERNEST JR and BRUNETTA VARNER. He was born 13 Aug 1920 in Coleman, Coleman County, TX USA[925,926,927], and died 30 Dec 1975 in Borger, Hutchinson County, TX USA[928,929].

Notes for HELEN WRIGHTON BULL:
Helen (Bull) Klapper Personal History
As Told to Richard Klapper on 10/6/2005

Helen Wrighton Bull was born in Aberdeen, South Dakota in the house on her parent's dairy farm. Her middle name was taken from her paternal grandmother's maiden name. The day before she was born her mother had been planting flowers in her flower bed because the weather was very nice. Suddenly the weather changed and by the time Helen was born, there was a raging blizzard. Dr. King came out to their farm to deliver her during the storm. Helen and her brother had bedrooms on the second floor. One day when she was just a toddler she crawled out of her upstairs bedroom window and on to the roof over their porch. The neighbor who lived across the road from the farm called Helen's mother and asked if she knew her baby was sitting on the roof. Her mother stood under Helen to catch her if she fell, while her father went upstairs and quietly crawled out the window to grab her. Everything worked out fine and she was nabbed before she fell off the roof.

She attended school in a small school house about a mile from the farm. Students from 1st-8th grade were taught together by Miss Julia Finley. It was named Riverside School. She walked the mile to school each day. When Helen was in about fourth or fifth grade they built a new school which was about one-half mile further away from the farm so Helen had to walk farther to school. It was still called Riverside School and it was the largest of 4 or 5 country schools in Aberdeen. One day there was such a bad dust storm that you couldn't' see outside. The dust was so bad they finally let out school and had the parents come get their children. Helen's mother was concerned about the long walk each day so when Helen finished seventh grade she encouraged her to take a test which would allow her to skip the eighth grade and go directly to the ninth grade. This would allow her to go to the Simmons Junior High School for ninth grade which was a shorter walk. Helen was sick on the day of the test but she managed to pass it and skip the eighth grade. For the 10th – 12th grades she walked to Central High School. She graduated from high school and went to business school in Aberdeen. At about the time she graduated from high school Helen's brother, Alfred, who had been helping their dad run the dairy, had left to take a job teaching. Her dad didn't' think women should have to work in the barn but he needed help so Helen learned to milk and began helping him. When the man who ran the business school came out to interview Helen he found her wearing a pair of boots and carrying buckets of milk. Since she had taken all the basic courses in high school she only needed finishing courses in the business school. Following completion of that she worked as a secretary for a man who made loans. Her boss had been a prize fighter and had two men who collected loans. He was a low class character who cussed out the two collectors every morning before sending them out to collect overdue loans. Helen went to California to visit her Uncle George Mould and her boss replaced her while she was gone so when she got back Helen went to work for an insurance company in Aberdeen. She passed the federal test and accepted a job as a secretary with the Federal Agriculture Dept. in Washington, D.C. The federal job paid more. She reported to work in Washington on September 2 of 1941. Her mother and her cousin Hazel drove her to Washington. While in Washington, she attended the Presbyterian Church in which the famous pastor Peter Marshall preached. She attended a party and shook hands with Admiral King of the Navy. About a year later she accepted a transfer within the Agriculture Dept. to Denver and after a year the Denver office was closed. During her stay in Washington Helen's dad sold his dairy because he couldn't' get any help to run it. The war was on and most of the young men were getting drafted so he kept losing his help. They bought a small travel trailer and moved to the San Diego, California area where all their Aberdeen relatives had moved. Her dad took a job in a defense plant. Helen wrote her parents and asked them if they would move to Denver if she transferred there from Washington D.C. and they did. Helen lived with her parents while working in Denver. She then transferred to New York City to work for the Treasury Dept. for about 8 months but she didn't like riding the subway. She managed to get a transfer within the Treasury Dept. back to Denver. While working in Denver, Colorado the first time, she met William Richard Klapper, her future husband, who was in the Army and stationed at Fitzsimmons Army Hospital there in Denver. The husband of one of Helen's bosses was in the military. He was over some soldiers who were being trained in Denver. The military sponsored a dance and they needed girls to go with the soldiers. Helen's boss asked some of the girls who worked for her if they would go to the dance with some of the soldiers. They put the names of all the girls in a sack and the soldiers each drew the name of one of the girls. Dick drew Helen's name and they got along well. They dated quite a bit while they were both in Denver going to concerts in the park, etc. When she was in New York City she saw Dick again before he boarded a ship for England and the war. Helen married him when he returned from serving in the war in Europe. Upon Dick's return from the war he went back to his hometown of Coleman, Texas and then went to Denver to take a short term job. He went to an employment agency in Denver and applied for a job in Borger, Texas with Phillips Petroleum Co. and was accepted. He moved to Borger to work for Phillips. He lived in a company men's dorm. He applied for company housing but that was reserved for married employees. He called Helen and told her they would have to get married if he was to get a decent place to live! They were married in Denver and took a train to Colorado Springs for their honeymoon. The train was very crowded and Helen rode the entire way sitting on her suitcase. They stayed at the Antlers Hotel but Dick told their friends they were going to the Biltmore and sure enough they called the Biltmore looking for them. They returned to Borger after their marriage. Phillips owned and operated several chemical plants and carbon black plants in the area of Borger. Near their plants they built "camps" which consisted of apartments and 1, 2 or 3 bedroom houses for their employees. For the first year or two they lived in a small apartment but then were eligible to move into a 2 bedroom house in Bunavista which was a Phillips camp about 3 miles outside Borger. They lived in this house together at 401 Dolomita for nearly 30 years until Dick's death in 1975. In the late 1950's or early 1960's Phillips sold the house to Dick and Helen and they added on to the house. They added a living room, kitchen and a basement. Helen is still living there currently in 2005. They had two sons and the family attended the First Christian Church in Borger. Their first son, Richard James, was born in the hospital in Borger. Their second son, Fred William, was born in Denver. Dick had positive blood and Helen had negative blood and this could lead to the baby's and mother's blood being positive and negative respectively which could cause complications for the baby requiring a complete blood change out at the time of birth. If this condition arose in Borger they would have to send to Amarillo, 50 miles away, for the replacement blood. In Denver if this problem arose they had the blood right there in the same hospital which improved the chances of the baby's survival. For this reason Helen went to Denver to stay with her parents and have her baby in Denver. It turned out that the birth went smoothly with no problems so the trip to Denver for the birth was not necessary after all. Helen and her husband lived in Borger until his death and Helen continued to live there until July 2009 when she moved to an assisted living facility in Estes Park, Colorado to be near her son Richard.

More About HELEN WRIGHTON BULL:
Residence: 02 Apr 1930, Dairy farm, Aberdeen, Brown County, South Dakota[930]

Notes for WILLIAM RICHARD KLAPPER:
William Richard "Dick" Klapper was born in Coleman, Texas. He graduate from Coleman High School and attended Howard Payne College in Brownwood, Texas. He would not have been able to afford to go to college without the help of his uncle and aunt, Charles and Amelia Klapper, who lived in Brownwood and let him stay with them to reduce expenses. He graduated from Howard Payne with a degree in Chemistry and he and his entire graduating class enlisted in the Army since the war had begun. He trained at Fitzsimmons Army Hospital in Denver Colorado as an Army medic. There he met his future wife, Helen Bull. He shipped overseas to England and was part of the Allied buildup there. He went ashore in France at Omaha Beach on D-Day. He went through the rest of the war through France and Germany. He served under General Patton and his outfit liberated Buchenwald Concentration Camp on April 11, 1945. He described the scene as "bodies stacked like cordwood as far as you could see". He and his fellow soldiers threw their rations over the fence to some of the survivors who looked like scarecrows. He didn't talk much about his war experiences although he did mention delivering a French woman's baby in a ditch by the side of the road. He was in Germany when the war ended and was shipped back home in 1945. He married Helen and got a job with Phillips Petroleum Co. in Borger, Texas. Borger was a "Phillips town", meaning that Phillips had several chemical plants and refineries there and was the main support for the town. Phillips built camps of apartments and houses for their employees near their plants and Dick and Helen lived in one of these camps called Bunavista which is about 3 miles outside Borger. For the first year or two they lived in a small apartment but then qualified to move into a 2 bedroom house at 401 Dolomita where they lived together until Dick's death in 1975. Helen is currently still living in there in 2001. Dick worked at Phillips' Butadiene Plant and later at their Copolymer Plant, both of which are near Bunavista. The family were active members of the First Christian Church of Borger. In about 1972, Dick began having problems with his colon which the family doctor mis-diagnosed as diverticulitis. The problem persisted for about a year and Dick finally went to Temple, Texas to the Scott & White Clinic where it was discovered that he had colon cancer and they operated to remove a large tumor. The cancer had spread to his liver and he lived two years before dying at home. He was taken to Coleman, Texas and buried in the family plot along with his parents and grandparents.

More About WILLIAM RICHARD KLAPPER:
Burial: 03 Jan 1976, Coleman, Coleman County, Tx USA[931]

Cause of Death: Colon cancer which spread to liver
Degree: BS-Chemistry, Howard Payne University, Brownwood, Brown County, Texas[932]
Military service: Bet. 21 Aug 1942 - 27 Oct 1945, U.S. Army - WWII[933,934]
Occupation: Bet. 1948 - 1975, Chemical engineer, Phillips Petroleum Co.[935]
Religion: Bet. 1948 - 1975, Disciples of Christ (First Christian Church)[935]
Residence: Bet. 1949 - 1975, 401 Dolomita, Borger, Hutchinson County, Texas[935]
Social Security Number: 451-12-6819[936]

More About WILLIAM KLAPPER and HELEN BULL:
Marriage: 10 May 1946, Denver, Colorado USA[937]

Children of HELEN BULL and WILLIAM KLAPPER are:
   i.   RICHARD JAMES[9] KLAPPER[938], b. 20 Sep 1948, North Plains Hospital, Borger, Hutchinson Co., TX USA[939]; m. LINDA RUTH URSELL[940], 27 May 1972, Boerne, Kendall County, TX USA[941]; b. 03 Feb 1950, San Antonio, Bexar County, Texas[942].

   Notes for RICHARD JAMES KLAPPER:
   HISTORY OF RICHARD JAMES KLAPPER
   (Written August 4, 2009)

   I was born on September 20, 1948 in Borger, Hutchinson County, Texas in High Plains Hospital. I was the oldest of two children born to William Richard Klapper and Helen Wrighton Bull Klapper. My younger brother Fred William Klapper was born approximately 2-1/2 years later on February 3, 1951. My dad worked for Phillips Petroleum Company from the the time he got out of the Army after returning from World War II where he served in Europe. We lived in a house at 401 Dolomita in Bunavista which is a small community outside Borger built by Phillips for employees who worked in one of their several plants around Borger. During this time I earned my Eagle Scout and God and Country award on September 23, 1962. I lived in Bunavista until I graduated from Borger High School in May 1967. I left that fall to enroll at Texas A&M University. My parents continued to live in Borger. My father died in 1975 and my mother continues to live there today in the same house in Bunavista where she has lived since I was 2 years old.
   In 1971 I graduated with a B.S. in Nuclear Engineering from A&M and began graduate school there. I earned a black belt in karate and was the instructor of the A&M Karate club during graduate school. A year later, on May 27, 1972, I married Linda Ruth Ursell from Boerne, Kendall County, Texas. We honeymooned in Colorado where we spent time backpacking in the mountains and to old ghost towns.
   In August of 1972 I graduated with a Master of Engineering degree in Nuclear Engineering and accepted a job with Houston Lighting & Power Company in Houston, Texas. We moved there and I began a career with that company which has lasted until today. In 1979 we built a new house in the small town of Alvin which is about 30 miles south of Houston and are still living there. Our house is at 3116 Skyranch Dr.
   In 1976 we took a trip to Europe and became hooked on foreign travel. Since then we have traveled in over 40 countries. In addition to foreign travel, in our early married years, Linda and I hunted big game in various places in North America. We hunted in Texas, New Mexico, Colorado, Montana and Alaska. In the late 1970s we flew to Alaska and took a charter flight north of the Arctic Circle. A bush pilot dropped us off in the wilderness about 200 miles north of Ft. Yukon and returned for us a week later. Linda killed a moose with 48" wide antlers. I returned to Alaska several years later with a friend and had a bush pilot drop us off for a week about 200 miles southwest of Anchorage on Whitefish lake. I killed a small caribou.
   In November 1993, Linda and I were in Jerusalem and went into a small shop in the Old City. We had gotten to know the owner who sold ancient oil lamps. I had done him a favor the day before. While we were looking at lamps, an old Bedouin man came in and tried to sell the owner some coins he had found. The owner knew the old man well and asked if we would like to have him take our picture with the old Bedouin. It turned out that the old man was Mohammed-ed-Dibb, the Bedouin, who, 50 years ago, had found the Dead Sea Scrolls. We had our picture taken with him and after he left the shop owner told us several stories the Bedouin had told him about the finding of the scrolls.
   In November 1989, Linda and I travelled to Germany and made our first trip to Berlin. The trip had been planned 6 months in advance and shortly before we left for Germany several Eastern Bloc countries began loosening their border controls. Things were getting rather tense behind the iron curtain and we debated whether we should skip Berlin. We finally decided to go and this turned out to be the best decision we ever made. As we were arriving in Berlin the infamous Berlin Wall began coming down and for three days we were in the middle of one of the most historic events of the 20th century. We participated in the huge celebrations at Brandenburg Gate and watched as sections of the wall were lifted out and East Berliners were allowed to cross into West Berlin for the first time in 30 years. We were a part of history and revelled in every second of it!

In 1995, I made my fourth trip to Israel and worked for a week on an archaeological dig at Bethsaida. In the early 1990s, I began collecting ancient teracotta oil lamps and to date have a collection of approximately 80 lamps. They range in age from 1200 to 4000 years old. I have lectured on oil lamps several times at the Houston Theological College, at a special Alvin Library League presentation and at several churches. On November 16, 2002 I retired from Houston Lighting & Power Co. after 30 years of service. Linda "semi-retired" from BACH where she had worked for over 25 years. She began working for them part time as a contractor. This allowed her to work whenever she wanted but also allowed us to travel anytime we wanted. After retirement we purchased a summer home in Estes Park, Colorado and lived in Alvin during the winter and spring and lived in Colorado during the summer and fall.

Richard James Klapper

More About RICHARD JAMES KLAPPER:
Degree: 1971, BS-Nuclear Engineering, Texas A&M University[943]
Residence: 31 Jul 1974, 10627 Sagewind, Houston, Harris County, Texas[944]
Retirement: 16 Nov 2002, Retired from Centerpoint Energy[945]

Notes for LINDA RUTH URSELL:
 HISTORY OF LINDA RUTH URSELL KLAPPER
     (Written July 5, 2000)

I was born on February 3, 1950 in San Antonio, Bexar County, Texas in Nix Hospital. I was the second of five children born to Milton Charles Ursell and Dorothy Mae Short Ursell. For the first years of my life we lived at 1032 Gibbs St. in San Antonio. I attended St. Lutheran School until the fifth grade. When I was about 8 years old my parents bought a 3500 acre ranch just outside Toponas, Colorado but since the extremely harsh winters would have kept us from getting to school, we continued to live in San Antonio and spent the summers at the ranch in Colorado. When I was in the sixth grade, my parents sold the ranch in Colorado and bought a 510 acre ranch about 5 miles outside Boerne, Kendall County, Texas. I then went to the sixth grade in Comfort, Texas and continued in the Comfort school system until I graduated from Comfort High School as Salutatorian in May, 1968. That fall I enrolled at Texas Women's University majoring in Physical Therapy. In May, 1972 I graduated with a B.S. in Physical Therapy and with a double minor in Biology and Psychology.
On May 27, 1972 I married Richard James Klapper who was a graduate student at Texas A&M University. Prior to his graduation in August, I worked at St. Joseph's Hospital in Bryan, Texas as a physical therapist. When Richard graduated in August 1972 and accepted a position with Houston Lighting & Power Co. we moved to Houston, Harris County, Texas. I got a job as a physical therapist at Jeff Davis Rehab Hospital where I worked until February 1976. At that time I accepted the position as Chief Therapist at a new rehab center for handicapped children in Angleton, Texas called Brazoria County Association for Children with Handicaps (Bach). I have worked there developing their program until the present time. In 1978 we built a new house at 3116 Skyranch Dr. in Alvin, Brazoria County, Texas which is about 30 miles south of Houston. We moved there since it was approximately half way between Richard's work in Houston and my job in Angleton.
In 1976, Richard and I began traveling overseas and it became a lifelong hobby. We travel the world every year and have been in more than 40 countries to date. In addition to foreign travel, in our early married years, Richard and I hunted big game in various places in North America. We hunted in Texas, Colorado, Montana and Alaska. In the late 1970s we flew to Alaska and took a charter flight north of the Arctic Circle. A bush pilot dropped us off in the wilderness about 200 miles north of Ft. Yukon and returned for us a week later. I killed a moose with 48" wide antlers.
In November 1989, Richard and I travelled to Germany and made our first trip to Berlin. The trip had been planned 6 months in advance and shortly before we left for Germany several Eastern Bloc countries began loosening their border controls. Things were getting rather tense behind the iron curtain and we debated whether we should skip Berlin. We finally decided to go to Berlin and this turned out to be the best decision we ever made. As we were arriving in Berlin the infamous Berlin Wall began coming down and for three days we were in the middle of one of the most historic events of the 20th century. We participated in the huge celebrations at Brandenburg Gate and watched as sections of the wall were lifted out and East Berliners were allowed to cross into West Berlin for the first time in 30 years. We were a part of history and revelled in every second of it!
 In addition to traveling, I paint ceramics and have painted many Santa Claus figures for Christmas presents. My main hobby however, is working in my yard.

Linda Ruth Klapper

More About LINDA RUTH URSELL:
Retirement: Jun 2002, Retired from Brazoria County Assn. for Citizens with Handicaps[946]

More About RICHARD KLAPPER and LINDA URSELL:
Marriage: 27 May 1972, Boerne, Kendall County, TX USA[947]

68.   ii.   FRED WILLIAM KLAPPER, b. 03 Feb 1951, Denver, CO USA.

38. ROBERT[8] MACKNESS *(FRANK[7], REBECCA[6] MOULD, THOMAS[5], WILLIAM[4] MOLDS, WILLIAM[3], JOSEPH[2] MOULDS, THOMAS[1] MOULD)*[948] was born 19 Dec 1922 in Omaha, Nebraska[949], and died 15 Jul 2000 in Sierra Madre, California. He married LORRAINE BUCHNEL?[950] Abt. 10 Dec 1951[950].

Notes for ROBERT MACKNESS:
According to his sister, Marge, Robert went out to Ellingson, South Dakota every summer to help his grandparents with their farm.

More About ROBERT MACKNESS:
Burial: Near Pasadena, California[951]
Residence: Bet. 02 - 03 Apr 1930, 580 Montana, Huron, Beadle, South Dakota[952]

More About LORRAINE BUCHNEL?:
Burial: Near Pasadena, California[953]

More About ROBERT MACKNESS and LORRAINE BUCHNEL?:
Marriage: Abt. 10 Dec 1951[954]

Children of ROBERT MACKNESS and LORRAINE BUCHNEL? are:
    i.   NOLAN[9] MACKNESS[954].
    ii.   MICHAEL D. MACKNESS[955].
    iii.   JOE MACKNESS[955].

39. MARJORIE[8] MACKNESS *(FRANK[7], REBECCA[6] MOULD, THOMAS[5], WILLIAM[4] MOLDS, WILLIAM[3], JOSEPH[2] MOULDS, THOMAS[1] MOULD)*[956] was born 25 May 1926 in Huron, South Dakota[956]. She married ED REDFORD[956] 01 Jan 1947 in Portland, Oregon[957]. He was born 24 Jan 1926 in Pendleton, Oregon[958], and died 29 Oct 1996 in Mountain View, Arkansas[958].

More About MARJORIE MACKNESS:
Residence: Bet. 02 - 03 Apr 1930, 580 Montana, Huron, Beadle, South Dakota[959]

More About ED REDFORD:
Burial: Cremated in Mountain View, Arkansas[960]

More About ED REDFORD and MARJORIE MACKNESS:
Marriage: 01 Jan 1947, Portland, Oregon[961]

Children of MARJORIE MACKNESS and ED REDFORD are:
69.   i.   MARGO ESTHER[9] REDFORD, b. 04 May 1948, Portland, Oregon.
70.   ii.   ROBERT EDGAR REDFORD, b. 21 Mar 1949, Portland, Oregon.
71.   iii.   NICHOLAS FRANK REDFORD, b. 17 Jul 1955, Honolulu, Hawaii.

40. JOHN[8] ROBERTS *(VIOLET[7] MOULD, CHARLES[6], THOMAS[5], WILLIAM[4] MOLDS, WILLIAM[3], JOSEPH[2] MOULDS, THOMAS[1] MOULD)*[962] was born 22 Oct 1930 in Higham Ferrers, Northants, England[963,964], and died Bef. 2002 in Souldrop, Bedfordshire, England[965]. He married (1) DOREEN[966]. He married (2) JANE HUGHES[967].

More About JOHN ROBERTS:
Burial: Sharnbrook, Bedfordshire, England[968]

Child of JOHN ROBERTS and DOREEN is:
   i. CAROLINE[9] ROBERTS[969].

    Notes for CAROLINE ROBERTS:
    Per Jeffrey Roberts John had a daughter named Caroline who would probably be in her 30's as of 2004. She
    married a Canadian man and now lives in Canada but contact has been lost with her.

41. NORMAN WILLIAM[8] MOULD *(BERNARD WILLIAM[7], CHARLES[6], THOMAS[5], WILLIAM[4] MOLDS, WILLIAM[3], JOSEPH[2] MOULDS, THOMAS[1] MOULD)[970,971]* was born 30 Nov 1928 in Kettering, Northants, England[972,973]. He married JOYCE MARGARET BATES[974,975] 22 Apr 1950 in All Hallows Church, Wellingborough, Northants, England[975]. She was born 20 Nov 1928 in Wellingborough, Northants, England[975], and died Mar 2005[976].

More About NORMAN WILLIAM MOULD:
Residence: 19 Feb 1982, 7 Abbey Way, Rushden, Northants, England[977]

More About NORMAN MOULD and JOYCE BATES:
Marriage: 22 Apr 1950, All Hallows Church, Wellingborough, Northants, England[978]

Children of NORMAN MOULD and JOYCE BATES are:
72.	i.	CHRISTINE ANN[9] MOULD, b. 09 Feb 1952, Wellingborough, Northants, England.
73.	ii.	STUART NORMAN MOULD, b. 29 Aug 1954, Wellingborough, Northants, England.
74.	iii.	DIANE CAROL MOULD, b. 17 Sep 1956, Higham Ferrers, Northants, England.
	iv.	IAN PAUL MOULD[979,980], b. 29 Jul 1958, Wellingborough, Northants, England[980].
75.	v.	LINDA JANE MOULD, b. 17 Jul 1960, Wellingborough, Northants, England.

42. TREVOR GILBERT[8] MOULD *(BERNARD WILLIAM[7], CHARLES[6], THOMAS[5], WILLIAM[4] MOLDS, WILLIAM[3], JOSEPH[2] MOULDS, THOMAS[1] MOULD)[981,982]* was born 17 Apr 1939 in Higham Ferrers, Northants, England[983,984]. He married JOYCE WEBB[985] 10 Sep 1960 in Methodist Church, Higham Ferrers, Northants, England[986]. She was born 21 Jul 1930 in Higham Ferrers, Northants, England[986].

More About TREVOR MOULD and JOYCE WEBB:
Marriage: 10 Sep 1960, Methodist Church, Higham Ferrers, Northants, England[986]

Children of TREVOR MOULD and JOYCE WEBB are:
76.	i.	RALPH[9] MOULD, b. 07 Feb 1954, Romford, Essex.
77.	ii.	ROBERT JAMES MOULD, b. 30 Apr 1956, Billericay, Essex, England.
78.	iii.	NEIL MOULD, b. 04 Oct 1963, St. Mary's Hospital, Kettering, Northants, England.
79.	iv.	SCOTT MOULD, b. 05 Oct 1966, St. Mary's Hospital, Kettering, Northants, England.

43. JOYCE IRENE[8] MOULD *(BERNARD WILLIAM[7], CHARLES[6], THOMAS[5], WILLIAM[4] MOLDS, WILLIAM[3], JOSEPH[2] MOULDS, THOMAS[1] MOULD)[987,988]* was born 12 Oct 1934 in Higham Ferrers, Northants, England[989,990]. She married TERRENCE WILLIAM KING[991,992] 16 Jul 1955 in Methodist Church, Higham Ferrers, Northants, England[992]. He was born 19 Jun 1927 in Irthlingborough, Northants, England[992].

More About TERRENCE KING and JOYCE MOULD:
Marriage: 16 Jul 1955, Methodist Church, Higham Ferrers, Northants, England[992]

Children of JOYCE MOULD and TERRENCE KING are:
80.	i.	RUTH GILLIAN[9] KING, b. 17 Jun 1956, Wellingborough, Northants, England.
81.	ii.	VICKY ALISON KING, b. 21 Apr 1961, Northampton, Northants, England.
82.	iii.	SANDRA MAUREEN KING, b. 13 Mar 1965, Northampton, Northants, England.

44. MARGARET ANN[8] MOULD *(BERNARD WILLIAM[7], CHARLES[6], THOMAS[5], WILLIAM[4] MOLDS, WILLIAM[3], JOSEPH[2] MOULDS, THOMAS[1] MOULD)[993,994]* was born 22 Dec 1940 in Higham Ferrers, Northants, England[994]. She married JOHN WALTER RICHARDSON[995,996] 23 Dec 1961 in Methodist Church, Higham Ferrers, Northants, England[996]. He was born 19 Aug 1939 in Rushden, Northants, England[996].

More About JOHN RICHARDSON and MARGARET MOULD:
Marriage: 23 Dec 1961, Methodist Church, Higham Ferrers, Northants, England[996]

Children of MARGARET MOULD and JOHN RICHARDSON are:
83.   i.   JOANNE ELIZABETH[9] RICHARDSON, b. 09 Nov 1966, Wellingborough, Northants, England.
84.   ii.   ANDREW JAMES RICHARDSON, b. 21 Jul 1971, Wellingborough, Northants, England.

45. JANET ELIZABETH[8] MOULD *(BERNARD WILLIAM[7], CHARLES[6], THOMAS[5], WILLIAM[4] MOLDS, WILLIAM[3], JOSEPH[2] MOULDS, THOMAS[1] MOULD)*[997,998] was born 19 Mar 1947[999,1000], and died 11 Feb 2001 in Northampton, Northants, England[1001,1002]. She married ROBERT DAVID SEAMAN[1003,1004] 24 Apr 1989 in Registry Office, Wellingborough, Northants, England[1004]. He was born 22 Oct 1960 in Amersham, Buckinghamshire, England[1004].

More About ROBERT SEAMAN and JANET MOULD:
Marriage: 24 Apr 1989, Registry Office, Wellingborough, Northants, England[1004]

Child of JANET MOULD and ROBERT SEAMAN is:
        i.   ELIZABETH JAYNE[9] SEAMAN[1005,1006], b. 18 Oct 1989, Kettering, Northants, England[1007,1008].

46. DOREEN[8] LOVELL *(IVY DOREEN[7] MOULD, CHARLES[6], THOMAS[5], WILLIAM[4] MOLDS, WILLIAM[3], JOSEPH[2] MOULDS, THOMAS[1] MOULD)*[1009] was born 07 Jun 1932 in 70 High St., Rushden, Northants, England[1010,1011,1012,1013], and died 15 Mar 1978 in Kettering General Hospital, Kettering, Northants, England[1014,1015]. She married BERNARD WILLIAM RAWLINS[1016,1017] 02 Jun 1952 in Rushden Methodist Church, Rushden, Northants, England[1018,1019]. He was born 23 Sep 1929 in Podington, Bedfordshire, England[1019,1020], and died 27 Mar 1985 in Rushden, Northants, England[1021].

More About DOREEN LOVELL:
Burial: Cremated in Kettering Crematorium and ashes scattered wall plaque at Rushden cemetery, Northants, England[1021,1022]

More About BERNARD WILLIAM RAWLINS:
Burial: Cremated at Kettering Crematorium, Kettering, Northants, England; ashes buried in Rushden Cemetery by his mother's grave[1023]
Occupation: Builder[1024]

More About BERNARD RAWLINS and DOREEN LOVELL:
Marriage: 02 Jun 1952, Rushden Methodist Church, Rushden, Northants, England[1025,1026]

Children of DOREEN LOVELL and BERNARD RAWLINS are:
85.   i.   HEATHER[9] RAWLINS, b. 10 Aug 1954, Northampton General Hospital, Northampton, Northants, England.
86.   ii.   PAUL RAWLINS, b. 29 Dec 1956, Wellingborough, Northants, England.

47. OLIVE[8] MOULD *(CYRIL EUGENE[7], GEORGE[6], THOMAS[5], WILLIAM[4] MOLDS, WILLIAM[3], JOSEPH[2] MOULDS, THOMAS[1] MOULD)*[1027] was born 16 Feb 1929 in 48 Silverwood Rd. Millfield, Peterborough, Cambridgeshire, England[1027,1028], and died 20 Nov 2009 in Peterborough Hospital, Peterborough, England[1029]. She married FRANK COLEMAN[1030] 03 Jan 1953 in All Saints Church, Park Road, Peterborough, Cambridgeshire, England[1030,1031]. He was born 15 Dec 1922 in Peterborough, England[1032], and died 17 May 1986 in Peterborough, England[1032].

Notes for OLIVE MOULD:
    Olive Mould was born at home in Silverwood Road on 16 February 1929. After attending Queen's Drive Infants School until the age of seven and All Saints Junior School until eleven, she went on to Beech Avenue Secondary School. It was apparent from an early age that Olive had a talent for painting and was generally

creative and artistic. Her grandfather, George, admired her work so much that he used to "commission" her to paint greeting cards for special occasions.

When she was at the Beech Avenue Secondary School, she made friends with Celia Anton whose father had set up a group called the Antonian Concert Party. They put on entertainments, including tap dancing, and Olive joined them. Fortunately Beattie was a good dressmaker and the various costumes required kept her busy. Olive inherited her mother's talent.

On leaving school in 1943 aged fourteen, she decided to train as a tailoress and went to the Peterborough Cooperative Society, a large, countrywide, chain of stores (known as "The Coop" for short) to serve a seven-year apprenticeship. Most of this time, Olive was employed making men's suits and at the end of the training, she completed three years "improving".

In January 1953, Olive married Frank Coleman, at All Saints Church on Park Road. Susan, their daughter, was born in October of that year and Olive left work to spend a few years at home.

In 1960, she was ready to return to work and joined a small team of tailoresses at a men's outfitters in Peterborough called Ellis Bell. There her main job was alterations. She remained there until Christmas 1980 when the business closed down rather unexpectedly.

Not long afterwards Olive was contracted by one of the former Ellis Bell directors, Paul Rochnan, for whom she had worked. He was planning to set up his own bespoke tailoring shop in Stamford, about eight miles from Peterborough, and wanted Olive to join him. Olive agreed – even though some traveling was involved – and stayed until 1995 when she retired.

Very sadly, her husband, Frank, died of cancer in May 1986 aged only sixty-three, not living to enjoy retirement.

More About OLIVE MOULD:
Cremation: 07 Dec 2009, Peterborough Crematorium, Peterborough, England[1033]

More About FRANK COLEMAN:
Burial: Cremated at Marholm Crematorium, Peterborough, Cambridgeshire[1034]

More About FRANK COLEMAN and OLIVE MOULD:
Marriage: 03 Jan 1953, All Saints Church, Park Road, Peterborough, Cambridgeshire, England[1035,1036]

Child of OLIVE MOULD and FRANK COLEMAN is:
87.   i. SUSAN[9] COLEMAN, b. 18 Oct 1953, The Gables Maternity Hospital, Peterborough, Cambridgeshire, England.

48. WILLIAM ARTHUR[8] MOULD (CYRIL EUGENE[7], GEORGE[6], THOMAS[5], WILLIAM[4] MOLDS, WILLIAM[3], JOSEPH[2] MOULDS, THOMAS[1] MOULD)[1037,1038] was born 03 May 1931[1039]. He married MARGARET[1039] 19 Aug 1950[1040]. She was born 09 Mar 1934[1040], and died 15 Jan 2007[1041].

Notes for WILLIAM ARTHUR MOULD:
Arthur was born on 3 May 1931, two years after his sister. On leaving secondary school aged fourteen, he went to work in the stores at Frank Perkins' factory, then situated in Queen Street, close to the town center. When the stores were transferred to Manchester, Arthur moved to the main Eastfield factory where he trained as an engineer. He took retirement in 1996.

When asked what he remembered best about life at Gilpin Street, it was the "bickering", especially over the crossword competitions they used to enter!

Arthur married his wife, Margaret, in August 1950 when both were in their "teens" (Margaret was sixteen, Arthur nineteen). Margaret died on 15 January 2007 after a long battle with cancer. She was seventy-two.

They had two sons, Stephen and Gerald, and three grandchildren.

Written by Joan (Mould) Bolton in March 2007 after talking with Arthur.

More About MARGARET:
Cause of Death: Cancer[1041]

More About WILLIAM MOULD and MARGARET:
Marriage: 19 Aug 1950[1042]

Children of WILLIAM MOULD and MARGARET are:
  i. STEPHEN[9] MOULD[1043], b. 25 Jan 1955[1044]; m. LIZ[1044], 02 Apr 1983[1044]; b. 28 Jan 1961[1044].

      More About STEPHEN MOULD and LIZ:
      Marriage: 02 Apr 1983[1044]

88.   ii. GERALD MOULD, b. 02 Oct 1958.

49. HAROLD EDWARD[8] MOULD *(CYRIL EUGENE[7], GEORGE[6], THOMAS[5], WILLIAM[4] MOLDS, WILLIAM[3], JOSEPH[2] MOULDS, THOMAS[1] MOULD)*[1045,1046] was born 22 Sep 1933[1047]. He married PATRICIA ELLIOTT[1047,1048] 15 Dec 1956[1049]. She was born 02 Oct 1936[1049].

Notes for HAROLD EDWARD MOULD:
    Cyril and Beattie's third child was born on 22 September 1933, two years after his brother. On leaving school, he managed to get a full-time job as a projectionist at the New England Cinema in Occupation Road and stayed there for three years. The films changed twice a week, with a special program for children on Saturday afternoons. When Dick wasn't showing the films, he had to go all around Peterborough on his bike delivering publicity leaflets to promote the films.
    When Dick was eighteen he went into the RAF for three years, as a mechanic. He was based at Odium, in Hampshire, and Tangner.
    After coming out of the forces at twenty-one, his brother, Arthur, told him about an engineering job at Perkins' Queen Street factory. Dick got the job and worked there for a couple of years in the engine-rebuild department.
    He then moved on to work in the Railway stores, sending equipment round the region. After two or three years with the railway, Dick realized that "the money was better" at Frank Perkins and went back, this time to the Eastfield factory where the work was then concentrated.
    By this time Dick was a married man with two young children, having married Patricia ('Pat) Elliot in December 1956. Their daughter, Sharon, was born in 1959 and son, Ian, in 1963.
    Dick stayed at Perkins until his retirement in 1998.

Written by Joan (Mould) Bolton in March 2007 after talking to Dick

More About HAROLD MOULD and PATRICIA ELLIOTT:
Marriage: 15 Dec 1956[1049]

Children of HAROLD MOULD and PATRICIA ELLIOTT are:
89.   i. SHARON[9] MOULD, b. 27 Mar 1959.
90.   ii. IAN MOULD, b. 04 Apr 1963.

50. DEREK[8] MOULD *(BERNARD[7], GEORGE[6], THOMAS[5], WILLIAM[4] MOLDS, WILLIAM[3], JOSEPH[2] MOULDS, THOMAS[1] MOULD)*[1050] was born 07 Aug 1940[1050]. He married JOAN HARVEY BAIRD[1051] 19 Jun 1971 in Falkirk, Scotland[1052]. She was born 27 Oct 1949[1052].

More About DEREK MOULD and JOAN BAIRD:
Marriage: 19 Jun 1971, Falkirk, Scotland[1052]

Children of DEREK MOULD and JOAN BAIRD are:
  i. SIMON[9] MOULD[1053], b. 02 Feb 1975, Cleethorpes, England[1054].
  ii. CHRISTOPHER MOULD[1055], b. 05 Jul 1978, Dunfermline, Scotland[1056].

51. ROSITA ANN[8] MOULD *(ERIC[7], GEORGE[6], THOMAS[5], WILLIAM[4] MOLDS, WILLIAM[3], JOSEPH[2] MOULDS, THOMAS[1]*

MOULD)[1057,1058] was born 01 Aug 1933 in 65 Exeter Road, Peterborough, Northamptonshire, England[1059,1060,1061]. She married JOHN KENNETH ANTILL[1062,1063] 22 Jun 1957 in All Saints Church, Park Road, Peterborough, Northants, England[1064]. He was born 31 Mar 1932 in Ashey Road, Loughborough, Leics, England[1064,1065].

More About JOHN ANTILL and ROSITA MOULD:
Marriage: 22 Jun 1957, All Saints Church, Park Road, Peterborough, Northants, England[1066]

Children of ROSITA MOULD and JOHN ANTILL are:
  i. KEITH GRAHAME[9] ANTILL[1066,1067], b. 04 Mar 1964, Torquay Hospital, Devonshire, England[1068,1069].
  ii. DAVID JOHN ANTILL[1070], b. 01 Jul 1966, Totnes Cottage Hospital, Devon, Dorsetshire, England[1070,1071]; m. MELANIE JANE WILLIAMS[1071], 30 Nov 2002, Norfolk, England[1071].

      More About DAVID ANTILL and MELANIE WILLIAMS:
      Marriage: 30 Nov 2002, Norfolk, England[1071]

52. JOAN BARBARA[8] MOULD *(GUILFORD THOMAS[7], GEORGE[6], THOMAS[5], WILLIAM[4] MOLDS, WILLIAM[3], JOSEPH[2] MOULDS, THOMAS[1] MOULD)[1072,1073]* was born 07 Dec 1942 in Peterborough, England[1074,1075]. She married REGINALD THOMAS BOLTON[1076,1077] 22 Jul 1974 in Greenfields Methodist Chapel, Shrewsbury, Shropshire, England[1077]. He was born 22 Sep 1931 in York, England[1077].

More About JOAN BARBARA MOULD:
Residence: 2000, 139 West Bay Rd., Bridport, Dorset, England[1078]

More About REGINALD BOLTON and JOAN MOULD:
Marriage: 22 Jul 1974, Greenfields Methodist Chapel, Shrewsbury, Shropshire, England[1079]

Children of JOAN MOULD and REGINALD BOLTON are:
  i. VICTORIA GRACE[9] BOLTON[1080], b. 18 Jan 1979, Newcastle Hospital, Northumberland[1080]; d. 22 Jan 1979, Newcastle Hospital, Northumberland[1080].

      More About VICTORIA GRACE BOLTON:
      Burial: Newcastle, Northumberland[1080]

91.   ii. MAXWELL JAMES BOLTON, b. 06 Feb 1980, Hesham, Northumberland, England.

53. ALISON MARY[8] MOULD *(GUILFORD THOMAS[7], GEORGE[6], THOMAS[5], WILLIAM[4] MOLDS, WILLIAM[3], JOSEPH[2] MOULDS, THOMAS[1] MOULD)[1081,1082,1083]* was born 01 Mar 1947 in Peterborough, England[1084,1085]. She married DAVID MICHAEL PETERS[1086,1087] 23 Aug 1969 in All Saints Church, Paston, Peterborough, England[1088]. He was born 10 Dec 1943 in Bombay, India[1089].

Notes for ALISON MARY MOULD:
Alison's Memories

I had a very happy childhood in Peterborough with my parents and sister, Joan. After leaving the County Grammar School for Girls I went to Gipsy Hill College of Education in Kingston upon Thames from 1965 – 1968 to train to be a Junior School teacher. I had always wanted to teach and many of my childhood games involved pretending to be a teacher - my friends were cajoled into being pupils!

My first teaching post was at St Pauls, Addlestone, Surrey where I stayed 2 years. I enjoyed it and it was far less stressful than teaching today. We were still allowed to 'smack' a child on the legs and discipline was not a problem. It was during this time that I met my husband, David, at St Michaels Church, Weybridge. We were married in 1969 and decided to move to a cheaper part of the UK to buy a house in 1970.

Our first house, a new 3 bedroom detached in Oulton Broad, Suffolk, cost £3995 but we struggled to pay the mortgage on our low pay! David trained to be a psychiatric nurse in Norwich and when our 2 children were born in 1973 and 1974 we had to manage on David's nursing salary.

We moved house again to a 4 bedroom terraced house on the sea front in Lowestoft as we needed more space. It was there that we got our taste for living by the sea and David bought his first fishing boat!

I had a break from teaching until our daughter Catherine went to Nursery School. I did some supply teaching, part time Youth Work and TEFL teaching in Suffolk but didn't teach full-time again till 1978 when we moved to Lancashire. David worked as a Social Worker and I changed to Special Education, teaching at the Adolescent Unit at Prestwich Hospital, Manchester. I completed a One Year full time Diploma in Special Education and was promoted to deputy at a small special school in Rawtenstall, Lancashire where we lived.

In 1986 we moved south again to Hastings, East Sussex and I taught at Saxon Mount Special School. This was a sideways move for me and I had no responsibilities at the school, which I found frustrating. David was finding social work very stressful and in 1988 I started a flights business from home. I had been looking into running my own business for a while and liked the idea of being my own boss.

However, neither of us had any business background or training and we soon hit problems after the first Gulf War, when nobody flew etc. .We had bought a flat near Barcelona in 1988 and we rented out and used it for our holidays. I enjoy speaking Spanish and we sold a lot of flights to Spain. The final straw came when we realised that we were losing money every year so we closed the business in 1996.

I had been teaching again but always on short-term contracts in a variety of schools in Hastings. Our children worked hard at school and our son, Andrew, studied Civil Engineering at Warwick University. Catherine studied Sociology at Bristol University.

I had no health problems till 1999 when I was diagnosed with cancer and was treated at the Royal Marsden Hospital in London. I recovered well till I had an infection in my right hip in 2000 resulting in a hip replacement. All went well till 2001 when another infection started near the hip. Finally, in 2003 I had to have the artificial hip removed in a Girdlestone procedure, leaving me with no right hip and shorter leg. I can actually walk quite well, amazingly, and now I am in good health.

Our children married in 2000 and we have 4 grandchildren, who give us much pleasure. Andrew lives near Sydney but Catherine lives near Basingstoke. In 2004 we decided to leave Hastings and the sea and move to Chineham, Basingstoke to be closer to Catherine and family. I still do supply teaching and David did social work till this October.

We enjoy living in Chineham but it was more expensive to live here so our flat in Spain was sold to finance our new house. We enjoy gardening and have a vegetable plot and green house in our small back garden.

I like to think that I have a good sense of humour and I particularly revel in April Fool's Day! My children have received a number of my hoax letters, which cause great hilarity!

My Christian faith has enabled me to cope with all the ups and downs of life.

Written by Alison Mary (Mould) Peters in November 2006

More About DAVID PETERS and ALISON MOULD:
Marriage: 23 Aug 1969, All Saints Church, Paston, Peterborough, England[1090]

Children of ALISON MOULD and DAVID PETERS are:
92.   i.   ANDREW DAVID[9] PETERS, b. 09 Jun 1973, Gt. Yarmouth, Norfolk, England.
93.   ii.   CATHERINE MARY PETERS, b. 18 Sep 1974, Gt. Yarmouth, Norfolk, England.

54. MELVIN[8] MOULD (*HUBERT LAWRENCE*[7], *GEORGE*[6], *THOMAS*[5], *WILLIAM*[4] *MOLDS*, *WILLIAM*[3], *JOSEPH*[2] *MOULDS*, *THOMAS*[1] *MOULD*)[1091] was born 19 Jul 1952 in Peterborough, England[1092]. He married ROMAIN FOSTER[1092] 12 May 1973 in Longthorpe, Peterborough, Northants, England[1092]. She was born 10 Sep 1951 in Bedford,

England[1092].

Notes for MELVIN MOULD:
Melvin, a carpenter, married Romaine, they have two children, Anthony, an environmental biologist, and Clare, a social work assistant. Clare will marry 28th December 2006 and is expecting the first of the next Mould generation in May 2007. Melvin has a keen interest in ornithology, bird nesting in particular and has passed these loves onto Anthony who is a keen ornithologist helps to protect endangered bird's nests and also does a lot of volunteer work with bats.
E-mail from Helen Mould (wife of Lawrence) 16 Nov 2006

More About MELVIN MOULD and ROMAIN FOSTER:
Marriage: 12 May 1973, Longthorpe, Peterborough, Northants, England[1092]

Children of MELVIN MOULD and ROMAIN FOSTER are:
    i.   ANTHONY[9] MOULD[1093,1094], b. 31 Dec 1978, Peterborough, England[1095].

        Notes for ANTHONY MOULD:
        Melvin, a carpenter, married Romaine, they have two children, Anthony, an environmental biologist, and Clare, a social work assistant. Clare will marry 28th December 2006 and is expecting the first of the next Mould generation in May 2007. Melvin has a keen interest in ornithology, bird nesting in particular and has passed these loves onto Anthony who is a keen ornithologist helps to protect endangered bird's nests and also does a lot of volunteer work with bats.
        E-mail from Helen Mould (wife of Lawrence) 16 Nov 2006

    ii.   CLARE MOULD[1096], b. 03 Dec 1983, Peterborough, England[1097].

        Notes for CLARE MOULD:
        Melvin, a carpenter, married Romaine, they have two children, Anthony, an environmental biologist, and Clare, a social work assistant. Clare will marry 28th December 2006 and is expecting the first of the next Mould generation in May 2007.
        E-mail from Helen Mould (wife of Lawrence) 16 Nov 2006

Generation No. 5

55. VIRGINIA[9] PARSLEY *(MURIEL NAOMI[8] BALDWIN, NAOMI JANE[7] JESSOP, JANE[6] MOULD, THOMAS[5], WILLIAM[4] MOLDS, WILLIAM[3], JOSEPH[2] MOULDS, THOMAS[1] MOULD)*[1098] was born 24 Nov 1928 in Camberwell, London, England[1099,1100]. She married JOHN ERNEST MANNING[1101,1102] Bet. Jul - Sep 1949 in Camberwell, London, England[1103]. He was born 20 Apr 1922[1104], and died Oct 2001[1105].

More About JOHN MANNING and VIRGINIA PARSLEY:
Marriage: Bet. Jul - Sep 1949, Camberwell, London, England[1106]

Children of VIRGINIA PARSLEY and JOHN MANNING are:
94.   i.   BELINDA[10] MANNING, b. Bet. Oct - Dec 1952, Lambeth.
95.   ii.   JOHN MARK MANNING, b. 1954.
96.   iii. HILLARY MANNING, b. Bet. Jan - Mar 1956, Hatfield, Hertfordshire, England.
97.   iv. KATHARINE MANNING, b. Bet. Jan - Mar 1956, Hartfield, Hertfordshire, England.

56. JANE[9] BALDWIN *(DOUGLAS HERBERT[8], NAOMI JANE[7] JESSOP, JANE[6] MOULD, THOMAS[5], WILLIAM[4] MOLDS, WILLIAM[3], JOSEPH[2] MOULDS, THOMAS[1] MOULD)*[1107] was born 05 Dec 1935 in Epsom, Surrey, England[1108,1109]. She married (1) NEIL MCROBERT[1110] 21 Nov 1955 in St. Leonards, Dorset, England[1110,1111]. He was born 08 Aug 1933 in Fife, Scotland[1112]. She married (2) JOHN ROGER FLETCHER[1113] 27 Nov 1972 in Ringwood Registry Office, Ringwood, Hampshire, England[1113,1114].

More About NEIL MCROBERT and JANE BALDWIN:
Marriage: 21 Nov 1955, St. Leonards, Dorset, England[1115,1116]

More About JOHN FLETCHER and JANE BALDWIN:

Marriage: 27 Nov 1972, Ringwood Registry Office, Ringwood, Hampshire, England[1117,1118]

Children of JANE BALDWIN and NEIL MCROBERT are:
98. i. SARAH JANE[10] MCROBERT, b. 26 Jun 1957, Mona Baldwin's house in St. Leonards, Dorset, England.
99. ii. MONA MCROBERT, b. 10 May 1959, Mona Baldwin's house, Ringwood, Hampshire, England.

57. CHRISTOPHER[9] BALDWIN *(DOUGLAS HERBERT[8], NAOMI JANE[7] JESSOP, JANE[6] MOULD, THOMAS[5], WILLIAM[4] MOLDS, WILLIAM[3], JOSEPH[2] MOULDS, THOMAS[1] MOULD)*[1119] was born 01 Mar 1937 in Cheam, Surrey, England[1120,1121]. He married PATRICIA ANN CHILDS[1122] 24 Sep 1960 in Ellingham Church, Ellingham (near Ringwood), Hampshire, England[1123,1124]. She was born 26 Nov 1940 in Ringwood, Hampshire, England[1125,1126].

More About CHRISTOPHER BALDWIN and PATRICIA CHILDS:
Marriage: 24 Sep 1960, Ellingham Church, Ellingham (near Ringwood), Hampshire, England[1127,1128]

Children of CHRISTOPHER BALDWIN and PATRICIA CHILDS are:
   i. MARK[10] BALDWIN[1129], b. 18 Jul 1961, Fordingbridge, Hampshire, England[1129,1130]; m. AMANDA BELL[1131], 02 Nov 2002[1131]; b. 30 Nov 1964, Great Yarmouth, Norfolk, England[1132].

      More About MARK BALDWIN and AMANDA BELL:
      Marriage: 02 Nov 2002[1133]

100. ii. KEITH BALDWIN, b. 25 Mar 1965, Fordingbridge, Hampshire, England.

58. JANE ANN ELIZABETH[9] PRENTICE *(JOHN TREVOR[8], GEORGE HAROLD[7], ROSE[6] MOULD, THOMAS[5], WILLIAM[4] MOLDS, WILLIAM[3], JOSEPH[2] MOULDS, THOMAS[1] MOULD)*[1134] was born 13 Jan 1946 in Chipping Norton Memorial Hospital, Chipping Norton, Oxfordshire, England[1134]. She married (1) DAVID SMITH[1135] 1965 in Church on Royal Air Force, Bruggen, Germany[1135]. She married (2) RODNEY HEATON GORDON[1136] 04 Jun 1976 in Bodicote, Banbury, Oxfordshire, England[1136]. He was born in New Zealand[1136].

More About DAVID SMITH and JANE PRENTICE:
Marriage: 1965, Church on Royal Air Force, Bruggen, Germany[1137]

More About RODNEY GORDON and JANE PRENTICE:
Marriage: 04 Jun 1976, Bodicote, Banbury, Oxfordshire, England[1138]

Children of JANE PRENTICE and DAVID SMITH are:
   i. NICHOLAS CHARLES[10] SMITH[1139], b. 11 Jan 1967, Chipping Norton Memorial Hospital, Chipping Norton, Oxfordshire, England[1139].

      Notes for NICHOLAS CHARLES SMITH:
      Per John Trevor Prentice on January 31, 2002, Nicholas changed his name by Deed poll to Nicholas Gordon, after his mother divorced his father and remarried Rodney Heaton Gordon.

   ii. JAMES DAVID SMITH[1139], b. 13 May 1968, Chipping Norton Memorial Hospital, Chipping Norton, Oxfordshire, England[1139].

      Notes for JAMES DAVID SMITH:
      James had his surname changed from Smith to Gordon after his parents were divorced and his mother remarried Rodney Heaton Gordon. In 1999, James returned to England and shortly thereafter changed his name back to Smith.

Children of JANE PRENTICE and RODNEY GORDON are:
   iii. GEORGE HEATON[10] GORDON[1140], b. 15 Oct 1977, Lower Hutt, New Zealand[1140].
   iv. GRACE JANE GORDON[1140], b. 08 Dec 1979, Hastings, New Zealand[1140].

59. MARGARET PRISCILLA INGRID[9] PRENTICE *(JOHN TREVOR[8], GEORGE HAROLD[7], ROSE[6] MOULD, THOMAS[5],*

WILLIAM⁴ MOLDS, WILLIAM³, JOSEPH² MOULDS, THOMAS¹ MOULD)¹¹⁴¹ was born 20 Jan 1948 in Changi Hospital, Singapore¹¹⁴¹. She married PETER FLYNN¹¹⁴² May 1966 in Haslinton, Lancastershire, England¹¹⁴³.

More About MARGARET PRISCILLA INGRID PRENTICE:
Divorced: Abt. 1992, Had not remarried by 2002¹¹⁴⁴

More About PETER FLYNN and MARGARET PRENTICE:
Marriage: May 1966, Haslinton, Lancastershire, England¹¹⁴⁵

Children of MARGARET PRENTICE and PETER FLYNN are:
  i. JOHN PATRICK¹⁰ FLYNN¹¹⁴⁶, b. 08 Dec 1966, Wegberg Military Hospital, West Germany¹¹⁴⁶.
  ii. ANNEMARIE FLYNN¹¹⁴⁶, b. 12 May 1968, Wegberg Military Hospital, West Germany¹¹⁴⁶.
  iii. NINA VICTORIA FLYNN¹¹⁴⁶, b. 09 Sep 1974, Hanover British Army Hospital, West Germany¹¹⁴⁶.

60. RICHARD⁹ ROSE *(SHEILA MARGARET⁸ PRENTICE, GEORGE HAROLD⁷, ROSE⁶ MOULD, THOMAS⁵, WILLIAM⁴ MOLDS, WILLIAM³, JOSEPH² MOULDS, THOMAS¹ MOULD)¹¹⁴⁷* was born 22 Feb 1943 in Chipping Norton, Oxfordshire, England¹¹⁴⁷,¹¹⁴⁸. He married CHRISTINE COPLEY¹¹⁴⁸ 27 Mar 1965 in Shipton Under Wychwood, Oxford, England¹¹⁴⁸. She was born 01 Dec 1942 in Bristol, England¹¹⁴⁸,¹¹⁴⁹.

More About RICHARD ROSE and CHRISTINE COPLEY:
Marriage: 27 Mar 1965, Shipton Under Wychwood, Oxford, England¹¹⁵⁰

Children of RICHARD ROSE and CHRISTINE COPLEY are:
101.   i. JONATHAN¹⁰ ROSE, b. 08 Jun 1966, Chipping Norton, Oxfordshire, England.
102.   ii. JULIAN ROSE, b. 19 Jun 1968, Chipping Norton, Oxfordshire, England.
       iii. EDWARD ROSE¹¹⁵¹, b. Chipping Norton, Oxfordshire, England¹¹⁵².

           Notes for EDWARD ROSE:
           As of September 7, 2002, Edward had not married.

61. DAVID⁹ ROSE *(SHEILA MARGARET⁸ PRENTICE, GEORGE HAROLD⁷, ROSE⁶ MOULD, THOMAS⁵, WILLIAM⁴ MOLDS, WILLIAM³, JOSEPH² MOULDS, THOMAS¹ MOULD)¹¹⁵³* was born 04 Feb 1945 in Hospital in Chipping Norton, Oxford, England¹¹⁵³,¹¹⁵⁴. He married (1) MARSHA ELIZABETH LEWIS¹¹⁵⁴,¹¹⁵⁵ Mar 1966 in Churchill, Oxfordshire, England¹¹⁵⁵. He married (2) JULIA KEIGHTLEY¹¹⁵⁶,¹¹⁵⁷ 07 Apr 1972 in Melton Mowbray, Leicestershire, England¹¹⁵⁷.

More About DAVID ROSE and MARSHA LEWIS:
Marriage: Mar 1966, Churchill, Oxfordshire, England¹¹⁵⁷

More About DAVID ROSE and JULIA KEIGHTLEY:
Marriage: 07 Apr 1972, Melton Mowbray, Leicestershire, England¹¹⁵⁷

Child of DAVID ROSE and MARSHA LEWIS is:
103.   i. AMANDA¹⁰ ROSE, b. 21 Mar 1968, Chipping Norton, Oxfordshire, England.

Children of DAVID ROSE and JULIA KEIGHTLEY are:
  ii. TANIA¹⁰ ROSE¹¹⁵⁸, b. 14 Aug 1973, Chipping Norton, Oxfordshire, England¹¹⁵⁹; m. GARETH BROWN¹¹⁵⁹, 27 Apr 2002, Churchill Church, Oxfordshire, England¹¹⁵⁹; b. 27 Dec 1974, Sunderland, England¹¹⁶⁰.

      More About GARETH BROWN and TANIA ROSE:
      Marriage: 27 Apr 2002, Churchill Church, Oxfordshire, England¹¹⁶¹

  iii. CHARLES ROSE¹¹⁶², b. 09 Aug 1975, Chipping Norton, Oxfordshire, England¹¹⁶³.

      Notes for CHARLES ROSE:
      As of September 7, 2002, Charles had not married.

More About CHARLES ROSE:
Twin: Twin to Elaine[1164]

iv.   ELAINE ROSE[1164], b. 09 Aug 1975, Chipping Norton, Oxfordshire, England[1165].

Notes for ELAINE ROSE:
As of September 7, 2002 Elaine had not married.

More About ELAINE ROSE:
Twin: Twin to Charles[1166]

62. MARY[9] PRENTICE *(JOHN ROBERT[8], JOHN FREDERICK[7], ROSE[6] MOULD, THOMAS[5], WILLIAM[4] MOLDS, WILLIAM[3], JOSEPH[2] MOULDS, THOMAS[1] MOULD)[1166]* was born 21 Jul 1950 in Hillingdon Hospital, Hillingdon, Middlesex, England[1166,1167]. She married PATRICK EDGINTON[1168] 01 Sep 1974 in Church in Milton Under Wychwood, Oxfordshire, England[1169]. He was born 1946[1170].

More About PATRICK EDGINTON and MARY PRENTICE:
Marriage: 01 Sep 1974, Church in Milton Under Wychwood, Oxfordshire, England[1171]

Children of MARY PRENTICE and PATRICK EDGINTON are:
  i.   GEORGE[10] EDGINTON[1171], b. 26 Dec 1976, Chipping Norton, Oxfordshire, England[1171].
  ii. ALEX EDGINTON[1171], b. 11 Jun 1981, Chipping Norton Memorial Hospital, Chipping Norton, Oxfordshire, England[1171].

63. MICHAEL[9] PRENTICE *(JOHN ROBERT[8], JOHN FREDERICK[7], ROSE[6] MOULD, THOMAS[5], WILLIAM[4] MOLDS, WILLIAM[3], JOSEPH[2] MOULDS, THOMAS[1] MOULD)[1172]* was born 24 Nov 1952 in Farnborough, Hampshire, England[1172,1173]. He married ANNE BANBURY[1174] 25 May 1974 in Ruislip, Middlesex, England[1175].

More About MICHAEL PRENTICE and ANNE BANBURY:
Marriage: 25 May 1974, Ruislip, Middlesex, England[1175]

Children of MICHAEL PRENTICE and ANNE BANBURY are:
  i.   JAMES[10] PRENTICE[1176], b. 1977[1176].
  ii. CLARE PRENTICE[1176], b. 1980[1176].
  iii. KATE PRENTICE[1176], b. 1982[1176].

64. ROBERT DAVID[9] PRENTICE *(JOHN ROBERT[8], JOHN FREDERICK[7], ROSE[6] MOULD, THOMAS[5], WILLIAM[4] MOLDS, WILLIAM[3], JOSEPH[2] MOULDS, THOMAS[1] MOULD)[1176,1177]* was born 26 May 1956 in Farnborough, Hampshire, England[1178,1179]. He met SHARON FUTTER[1180,1181].

Children of ROBERT PRENTICE and SHARON FUTTER are:
  i.   LOUISE[10] PRENTICE[1182], b. 1980[1182].
  ii. DAVID PRENTICE[1182], b. 1983[1182].
  iii. ROSE PRENTICE[1182], b. 1991[1182].

65. LESLEY ANNE[9] PRENTICE *(JOHN ROBERT[8], JOHN FREDERICK[7], ROSE[6] MOULD, THOMAS[5], WILLIAM[4] MOLDS, WILLIAM[3], JOSEPH[2] MOULDS, THOMAS[1] MOULD)[1182,1183]* was born 30 Dec 1962 in Hillingdon Hospital, Hillingdon, Middlesex, England[1184]. She married GUY CANNING[1185] 07 Jul 1990 in Shipton Under Wychwood, Oxford, England[1185].

More About GUY CANNING and LESLEY PRENTICE:
Marriage: 07 Jul 1990, Shipton Under Wychwood, Oxford, England[1185]

Children of LESLEY PRENTICE and GUY CANNING are:
  i.   TOM[10] CANNING[1186], b. 1994[1186].
  ii. JOE CANNING, b. 1997.

66. ADRIENNE[9] PRENTICE *(MICHAEL[8], JOHN FREDERICK[7], ROSE[6] MOULD, THOMAS[5], WILLIAM[4] MOLDS, WILLIAM[3], JOSEPH[2] MOULDS, THOMAS[1] MOULD)[1186]*. She married HERB PROUST[1186].

Child of ADRIENNE PRENTICE and HERB PROUST is:
   i.   ANNA[10] PROUST[1186].

67. TIMOTHY STEVEN[9] MOULD *(DONALD THOMAS[8], GEORGE EWART[7], JABEZ[6], THOMAS[5], WILLIAM[4] MOLDS, WILLIAM[3], JOSEPH[2] MOULDS, THOMAS[1] MOULD)[1187]* was born 18 Mar 1955 in Whittier, California[1187,1188]. He married LORI ANN RICHARDSON[1189].

Children of TIMOTHY MOULD and LORI RICHARDSON are:
   i.   ASHLEY ELLEN[10] MOULD[1189], b. Dec 1981, San Diego, California[1189,1190].
   ii. MATTHEW VAN ERIN MOULD[1191], b. Oct 1984, San Diego, California[1191,1192].

68. FRED WILLIAM[9] KLAPPER *(HELEN WRIGHTON[8] BULL, ANNIE BEATRICE[7] MOULD, JABEZ[6], THOMAS[5], WILLIAM[4] MOLDS, WILLIAM[3], JOSEPH[2] MOULDS, THOMAS[1] MOULD)[1193,1194]* was born 03 Feb 1951 in Denver, CO USA[1195,1196]. He married PAMELA ANN WOLNY[1197] 26 Jul 1986 in First Christian Church, Borger Texas USA[1197,1198], daughter of VALENTINE WOLNY and MARY McMAHON. She was born 30 Aug 1951 in Pittsburg. Allegheny County, PA USA[1199].

Notes for FRED WILLIAM KLAPPER:
Although his parents were living in Borger, Texas, Fred was born in Denver, Colorado in Mercy Hospital. This was because his father had Rh+ blood while his mother had Rh- blood. This blood combination sometimes caused severe problems in the second child of a couple requiring a complete change out of the blood. Helen was not comfortable having Fred in Borger so she went to Denver and stayed with her parents until Fred was born. Fred grew up in Bunavista, outside Borger, Texas and graduated from Borger High School. He attended Frank Phillips Jr. College in Borger for 2 years before completing his degree at Texas Tech in Lubbock. He went to work at Panhandle Bank & Trust in Borger and worked his way up to the position of Vice-President. He married Pamela Wolny. The bank was taken over by another bank and Fred was laid off. He moved to Spartanburg, South Carolina and went to work for the New York Times newspaper.

More About FRED WILLIAM KLAPPER:
Baptism: 03 Feb 1963, First Christian Church, Borger, Hutchinson, Texas[1200]
Religion: Disciples of Christ (First Christian Church)[1201]

More About PAMELA ANN WOLNY:
Occupation: Bef. 2000, Human Resources Supervisor[1202]
Religion: Catholic[1203]

More About FRED KLAPPER and PAMELA WOLNY:
Marriage: 26 Jul 1986, First Christian Church, Borger Texas USA[1204,1205]

Child of FRED KLAPPER and PAMELA WOLNY is:
   i.   ANDREW FREDERICK[10] KLAPPER[1206,1207], b. 15 Jul 1992, Spartanburg, Spartanburg County, South Carolina[1208,1209].

       More About ANDREW FREDERICK KLAPPER:
       Baptism: 15 Nov 1992, Church of Jesus, Our Risen Savior, Spartanburg, South Carolina[1210]

69. MARGO ESTHER[9] REDFORD *(MARJORIE[8] MACKNESS, FRANK[7], REBECCA[6] MOULD, THOMAS[5], WILLIAM[4] MOLDS, WILLIAM[3], JOSEPH[2] MOULDS, THOMAS[1] MOULD)[1211]* was born 04 May 1948 in Portland, Oregon[1212]. She married BILL SCHARLACH[1213,1214]. He was born 06 Aug 1946[1214].

Children of MARGO REDFORD and BILL SCHARLACH are:

i. DOMINIC[10] SCHARLACH[1215], b. 10 Apr 1970[1216]; Adopted child.
ii. AMY ESTHER SCHARLACH[1217], b. 12 Feb 1971[1218].
iii. DEBORAH SCHARLACH[1219], b. 10 Jun 1976[1220].

70. ROBERT EDGAR[9] REDFORD (*MARJORIE*[8] *MACKNESS, FRANK*[7], *REBECCA*[6] *MOULD, THOMAS*[5], *WILLIAM*[4] *MOLDS, WILLIAM*[3], *JOSEPH*[2] *MOULDS, THOMAS*[1] *MOULD*)[1221] was born 21 Mar 1949 in Portland, Oregon[1221]. He married SHERRILYN PELIQUIN[1222] 08 Apr 1967[1222]. She was born 30 Jun 1951[1222].

More About ROBERT REDFORD and SHERRILYN PELIQUIN:
Marriage: 08 Apr 1967[1222]

Children of ROBERT REDFORD and SHERRILYN PELIQUIN are:
104.   i. TRACY LYNN[10] REDFORD, b. 02 Oct 1967.
105.   ii. ERIC REDFORD, b. 09 Dec 1969.

71. NICHOLAS FRANK[9] REDFORD (*MARJORIE*[8] *MACKNESS, FRANK*[7], *REBECCA*[6] *MOULD, THOMAS*[5], *WILLIAM*[4] *MOLDS, WILLIAM*[3], *JOSEPH*[2] *MOULDS, THOMAS*[1] *MOULD*)[1223] was born 17 Jul 1955 in Honolulu, Hawaii[1224]. He married (1) WIFE ONE. He married (2) GINA[1225]. She was born 02 Apr 1959[1226].

Children of NICHOLAS REDFORD and WIFE ONE are:
i. JASON[10] REDFORD, b. 21 Jul 1980.
ii. NICHOLAS REDFORD, b. 04 Feb 1982.

Children of NICHOLAS REDFORD and GINA are:
iii. IAN[10] REDFORD[1227], b. 21 Oct 1993[1227].
iv. GILIAN REDFORD[1227], Adopted child.
v. KADI REDFORD[1227], Adopted child.
vi. SYDNI REDFORD[1227], Adopted child.

72. CHRISTINE ANN[9] MOULD (*NORMAN WILLIAM*[8], *BERNARD WILLIAM*[7], *CHARLES*[6], *THOMAS*[5], *WILLIAM*[4] *MOLDS, WILLIAM*[3], *JOSEPH*[2] *MOULDS, THOMAS*[1] *MOULD*)[1228,1229] was born 09 Feb 1952 in Wellingborough, Northants, England[1229]. She married PETER JAMES DRUCE[1230,1231] 11 Mar 1972 in Park Road Methodist Church, Rushden, England[1231]. He was born 15 Jul 1950 in Finedon, Northants, England[1231].

More About PETER DRUCE and CHRISTINE MOULD:
Marriage: 11 Mar 1972, Park Road Methodist Church, Rushden, England[1231]

Children of CHRISTINE MOULD and PETER DRUCE are:
106.   i. SUZANNE ELIZABETH[10] DRUCE, b. 16 Aug 1972, Northampton, Northants, England.
ii. SIMON DRUCE[1232,1233], b. 01 Jul 1976, Northampton, Northants, England[1233]; m. TAMMY MEARS[1233], 20 Sep 2003, Plan to Marry in Gosport, England[1233]; b. 29 Apr 1975.

More About SIMON DRUCE and TAMMY MEARS:
Marriage: 20 Sep 2003, Plan to Marry in Gosport, England[1233]

73. STUART NORMAN[9] MOULD (*NORMAN WILLIAM*[8], *BERNARD WILLIAM*[7], *CHARLES*[6], *THOMAS*[5], *WILLIAM*[4] *MOLDS, WILLIAM*[3], *JOSEPH*[2] *MOULDS, THOMAS*[1] *MOULD*)[1234,1235] was born 29 Aug 1954 in Wellingborough, Northants, England[1235]. He married JENNIFER MARY DUMMER[1236,1237] 18 Jul 1981 in Carey Baptist Church, Kettering, Northants, England[1237]. She was born 13 Mar 1958 in Hemel Hempstead, Herts, England.

More About STUART MOULD and JENNIFER DUMMER:
Marriage: 18 Jul 1981, Carey Baptist Church, Kettering, Northants, England[1237]

Children of STUART MOULD and JENNIFER DUMMER are:
i. EMMA LOUISE[10] MOULD[1238], b. 24 Apr 1982[1239].

    ii.   JAMES STUART MOULD[1240,1241], b. 15 Dec 1984[1241]; d. 12 Sep 1990[1242,1243].
   iii.   LAURA ANN MOULD[1244,1245], b. 13 Jul 1990[1245].
   iv.   CHRISTOPHER JAMES MOULD[1246,1247], b. 30 Jan 1993[1247].

74. DIANE CAROL[9] MOULD *(NORMAN WILLIAM[8], BERNARD WILLIAM[7], CHARLES[6], THOMAS[5], WILLIAM[4] MOLDS, WILLIAM[3], JOSEPH[2] MOULDS, THOMAS[1] MOULD)*[1248,1249] was born 17 Sep 1956 in Higham Ferrers, Northants, England[1249]. She married ROBIN WILLIAM KIRTON[1250,1251] 19 Sep 1975 in St Marys Church, Rushden, Northants, England[1251]. He was born 01 Sep 1953 in Addington, Northants, England[1251].

More About ROBIN KIRTON and DIANE MOULD:
Marriage: 19 Sep 1975, St Marys Church, Rushden, Northants, England[1251]

Children of DIANE MOULD and ROBIN KIRTON are:
    i.   AMY LOUISE[10] KIRTON[1252,1253], b. 15 Dec 1982[1253].
   ii.   GEMMA MICHELLE KIRTON[1254,1255], b. 23 Aug 1985[1255].

75. LINDA JANE[9] MOULD *(NORMAN WILLIAM[8], BERNARD WILLIAM[7], CHARLES[6], THOMAS[5], WILLIAM[4] MOLDS, WILLIAM[3], JOSEPH[2] MOULDS, THOMAS[1] MOULD)*[1256,1257] was born 17 Jul 1960 in Wellingborough, Northants, England[1257]. She married PETER JOHN HOLT[1258,1259] 19 Jul 1980 in St Marys Church, Rushden, Northants, England[1259]. He was born 01 Jan 1957 in Finedon, Northants, England[1259].

More About PETER HOLT and LINDA MOULD:
Marriage: 19 Jul 1980, St Marys Church, Rushden, Northants, England[1259]

Children of LINDA MOULD and PETER HOLT are:
    i.   WILLIAM JOHN[10] HOLT[1260,1261], b. 16 Feb 1987[1261].
   ii.   CHARLOTTE LOUISE HOLT[1262,1263], b. 16 May 1989[1263].
   iii.   SAMUEL JAMES HOLT[1264,1265], b. 23 Feb 1993[1265].

76. RALPH[9] MOULD *(TREVOR GILBERT[8], BERNARD WILLIAM[7], CHARLES[6], THOMAS[5], WILLIAM[4] MOLDS, WILLIAM[3], JOSEPH[2] MOULDS, THOMAS[1] MOULD)*[1266] was born 07 Feb 1954 in Romford, Essex[1267]. He married CLAIRE WELLS[1268] 16 Oct 1982 in Wellingborough Registry Office, Northants, England[1269]. She was born 27 Aug 1962 in Northampton, Northants, England[1269].

More About RALPH MOULD:
Divorced: Ralph and Claire were divorced[1270]

More About RALPH MOULD and CLAIRE WELLS:
Divorce: Unknown, Ralph and Claire divorced[1271]
Marriage: 16 Oct 1982, Wellingborough Registry Office, Northants, England[1271]

Children of RALPH MOULD and CLAIRE WELLS are:
    i.   MATTHEW JAMES[10] MOULD[1272,1273], b. 28 May 1986, Kettering Hospital, Kettering, Northants, England[1274,1275].
   ii.   GEMMA MOULD[1276], b. 01 Aug 1983, Park Hospital, Wellingborough, Northants, England[1277].

77. ROBERT JAMES[9] MOULD *(TREVOR GILBERT[8], BERNARD WILLIAM[7], CHARLES[6], THOMAS[5], WILLIAM[4] MOLDS, WILLIAM[3], JOSEPH[2] MOULDS, THOMAS[1] MOULD)*[1278,1279] was born 30 Apr 1956 in Billericay, Essex, England[1279]. He married ELAINE SUSAN HANGER[1279] 28 Aug 1982 in Wellingborough Registry Office, Northants, England[1279]. She was born 01 Jun 1957 in Park Hospital, Wellingborough, Northants, England[1279].

More About ROBERT MOULD and ELAINE HANGER:
Marriage: 28 Aug 1982, Wellingborough Registry Office, Northants, England[1279]

Children of ROBERT MOULD and ELAINE HANGER are:

    i.   KAYLEIGH[10] MOULD[1280], b. 25 Feb 1986, Kettering Hospital, Kettering, Northants, England[1281].

    ii. VERITY MOULD[1282], b. 01 May 1989, Kettering Hospital, Kettering, Northants, England[1283].

78. NEIL[9] MOULD *(TREVOR GILBERT[8], BERNARD WILLIAM[7], CHARLES[6], THOMAS[5], WILLIAM[4] MOLDS, WILLIAM[3], JOSEPH[2] MOULDS, THOMAS[1] MOULD)[1284]* was born 04 Oct 1963 in St. Mary's Hospital, Kettering, Northants, England[1285]. He married ELLEN ELIZA SMITH[1285] 14 Jun 1997 in St. Peter's Catholic Church, Rushden, Northants, England[1285]. She was born 18 Feb 1974 in Grantham, Lincs, England[1285].

More About NEIL MOULD and ELLEN SMITH:
Marriage: 14 Jun 1997, St. Peter's Catholic Church, Rushden, Northants, England[1285]

Child of NEIL MOULD and ELLEN SMITH is:

    i.   SEAN DARREN[10] MOULD[1285], b. 01 Apr 2000, Kettering Hospital, Kettering, Northants, England[1285].

79. SCOTT[9] MOULD *(TREVOR GILBERT[8], BERNARD WILLIAM[7], CHARLES[6], THOMAS[5], WILLIAM[4] MOLDS, WILLIAM[3], JOSEPH[2] MOULDS, THOMAS[1] MOULD)[1286]* was born 05 Oct 1966 in St. Mary's Hospital, Kettering, Northants, England[1287]. He married CLAIRE AMANDA MOBBS[1287]. She was born 11 Oct 1969 in Lee-on-Solent, Hampshire, England[1287].

Child of SCOTT MOULD and CLAIRE MOBBS is:

    i.   ARCHIE ELLIOT[10] MOULD[1287], b. 17 Feb 2001, Worcester Hospital, Worcestershire, England[1288].

80. RUTH GILLIAN[9] KING *(JOYCE IRENE[8] MOULD, BERNARD WILLIAM[7], CHARLES[6], THOMAS[5], WILLIAM[4] MOLDS, WILLIAM[3], JOSEPH[2] MOULDS, THOMAS[1] MOULD)[1288,1289]* was born 17 Jun 1956 in Wellingborough, Northants, England[1289]. She married DAVID DOUGLAS BASSON[1290,1291] 15 Mar 1975 in Methodist Church, Higham Ferrers, Northants, England[1291]. He was born 09 Apr 1948 in Hail Weston, Huntingdon, England[1291].

More About DAVID BASSON and RUTH KING:
Marriage: 15 Mar 1975, Methodist Church, Higham Ferrers, Northants, England[1291]

Children of RUTH KING and DAVID BASSON are:

107.   i.   CLAIRE LOUISE[10] BASSON, b. 30 Nov 1978, Kettering, Northants, England.

         ii. REBECCA AIMEE BASSON[1292,1293], b. 09 Oct 1981, Kettering, Northants, England[1293]; m. MATTHEW JONATHON ODELL[1293], 20 Jul 2002, All Saints Church, Earls Barton, Northants, England[1293]; b. 18 May[1293].

            More About MATTHEW ODELL and REBECCA BASSON:
            Marriage: 20 Jul 2002, All Saints Church, Earls Barton, Northants, England[1293]

81. VICKY ALISON[9] KING *(JOYCE IRENE[8] MOULD, BERNARD WILLIAM[7], CHARLES[6], THOMAS[5], WILLIAM[4] MOLDS, WILLIAM[3], JOSEPH[2] MOULDS, THOMAS[1] MOULD)[1294,1295]* was born 21 Apr 1961 in Northampton, Northants, England[1295]. She married ROBIN FRANK PIGGOTT[1296,1297,1298] 23 Apr 1983 in St. Peters Church, Irthlingborough, Northants, England[1298]. He was born 29 Mar 1956 in Kettering, Northants, England[1298].

More About ROBIN PIGGOTT and VICKY KING:
Marriage: 23 Apr 1983, St. Peters Church, Irthlingborough, Northants, England[1298]

Children of VICKY KING and ROBIN PIGGOTT are:

    i.   MARCUS ROBIN[10] PIGGOTT[1299], b. 17 Jun 1987, Kettering, Northants, England[1300].

    ii. LUCY VICTORIA PIGGOTT[1301,1302], b. 08 Feb 1990, Kettering, Northants, England[1302].

82. SANDRA MAUREEN[9] KING *(JOYCE IRENE[8] MOULD, BERNARD WILLIAM[7], CHARLES[6], THOMAS[5], WILLIAM[4] MOLDS, WILLIAM[3], JOSEPH[2] MOULDS, THOMAS[1] MOULD)[1303,1304]* was born 13 Mar 1965 in Northampton, Northants, England[1304]. She married COLIN SMITH[1305] 18 Oct 1986 in St. Mary's Church, Rushden, Northants, England[1306]. He was born 16 Oct 1958 in Rintein, West Germany[1306].

More About COLIN SMITH and SANDRA KING:
Marriage: 18 Oct 1986, St. Mary's Church, Rushden, Northants, England[1306]

Child of SANDRA KING and COLIN SMITH is:
     i. KARL ALEXANDRA[10] SMITH[1307,1308], b. 12 Jan 1991, Bury St Edmonds, Suffolk, England[1308].

83. JOANNE ELIZABETH[9] RICHARDSON *(MARGARET ANN[8] MOULD, BERNARD WILLIAM[7], CHARLES[6], THOMAS[5], WILLIAM[4] MOLDS, WILLIAM[3], JOSEPH[2] MOULDS, THOMAS[1] MOULD)[1309,1310]* was born 09 Nov 1966 in Wellingborough, Northants, England[1310]. She married NIGEL AUSTIN STEELE[1311,1312] 29 Apr 1989 in Methodist Church, Higham Ferrers, Northants, England[1312]. He was born 31 Jul 1965 in Wellingborough, Northants, England[1312].

More About NIGEL STEELE and JOANNE RICHARDSON:
Marriage: 29 Apr 1989, Methodist Church, Higham Ferrers, Northants, England[1312]

Children of JOANNE RICHARDSON and NIGEL STEELE are:
     i. GABRIELLE ELIZABETH[10] STEELE[1313,1314], b. 07 Sep 1999, Kettering, Northants, England[1315,1316].
     ii. HENRY JAMES STEELE[1317], b. 26 Mar 2003[1317].

84. ANDREW JAMES[9] RICHARDSON *(MARGARET ANN[8] MOULD, BERNARD WILLIAM[7], CHARLES[6], THOMAS[5], WILLIAM[4] MOLDS, WILLIAM[3], JOSEPH[2] MOULDS, THOMAS[1] MOULD)[1318,1319]* was born 21 Jul 1971 in Wellingborough, Northants, England[1319]. He married TANYA CLOREY[1320,1321] 24 Jul 1993 in St Peters Church, Raunds, Northants, England[1321]. She was born 28 Sep 1971 in Wellingborough, Northants, England[1321].

More About ANDREW RICHARDSON and TANYA CLOREY:
Marriage: 24 Jul 1993, St Peters Church, Raunds, Northants, England[1321]

Children of ANDREW RICHARDSON and TANYA CLOREY are:
     i. CAMERON JOHN[10] RICHARDSON[1322,1323], b. 29 Sep 1999, Kettering, Northants, England[1324,1325].
     ii. BROMWYN ANNE RICHARDSON[1326,1327], b. 07 Sep 2001, Kettering, Northants, England[1328,1329].

85. HEATHER[9] RAWLINS *(DOREEN[8] LOVELL, IVY DOREEN[7] MOULD, CHARLES[6], THOMAS[5], WILLIAM[4] MOLDS, WILLIAM[3], JOSEPH[2] MOULDS, THOMAS[1] MOULD)[1330]* was born 10 Aug 1954 in Northampton General Hospital, Northampton, Northants, England[1331,1332,1332]. She married PAUL MACKNESS[1333] 01 Sep 1973 in Wellingborough Road Wesleyan Reform Mission Church, Rushden, Northants, England. He was born 27 Aug 1948 in Rushden, Northants, England[1334].

Notes for HEATHER RAWLINS:
I am currently living at Ickwell Bury a very old large country house, you'd love it. I work here for the Yoga for Health Foundation, I'm a yoga instructor. We run
courses on yoga for people with MS, ME., Parkinson's Disease, Breathing
Disorders, Cancer, Stress and Arthritis and off course general courses for
people who are not ill.
From an e-mail from Heather to Richard Klapper - October 29, 2002

More About PAUL MACKNESS and HEATHER RAWLINS:
Marriage: 01 Sep 1973, Wellingborough Road Wesleyan Reform Mission Church, Rushden, Northants, England

Children of HEATHER RAWLINS and PAUL MACKNESS are:
     i. HELEN ANNE[10] MACKNESS[1335,1336], b. 25 Aug 1976, Northampton General Hospital, Northampton, Northants, England[1337,1338].
     ii. ANNA DOREEN MACKNESS[1339,1340], b. 15 Sep 1978, Kettering General Hospital, Kettering, Northants, England[1341,1342].
     iii. KAREN HAZEL MACKNESS[1343,1344], b. 15 Nov 1980, Hitchin Hospital, Hertfordshire, England[1345,1346].

86. PAUL[9] RAWLINS *(DOREEN[8] LOVELL, IVY DOREEN[7] MOULD, CHARLES[6], THOMAS[5], WILLIAM[4] MOLDS, WILLIAM[3], JOSEPH[2] MOULDS, THOMAS[1] MOULD)[1347]* was born 29 Dec 1956 in Wellingborough, Northants, England[1348,1349]. He married WENDY ANNE BELDHAM[1350,1351] 18 Oct 1980 in All Saints Church, Mickelover, Derbyshire, England[1352]. She was born 24 Nov 1958 in Beeston, Nottinghamshire, England[1353,1354].

More About PAUL RAWLINS and WENDY BELDHAM:
Marriage: 18 Oct 1980, All Saints Church, Mickelover, Derbyshire, England[1354]

Children of PAUL RAWLINS and WENDY BELDHAM are:
  i.   JONATHAN[10] RAWLINS[1355], b. 22 Feb 1983, Kettering, Northants, England[1355,1356].
  ii. MATHEW RAWLINS[1357], b. 22 Jan 1985, Kettering, Northants, England[1357,1358].

87. SUSAN[9] COLEMAN *(OLIVE[8] MOULD, CYRIL EUGENE[7], GEORGE[6], THOMAS[5], WILLIAM[4] MOLDS, WILLIAM[3], JOSEPH[2] MOULDS, THOMAS[1] MOULD)[1359,1360]* was born 18 Oct 1953 in The Gables Maternity Hospital, Peterborough, Cambridgeshire, England[1361,1362]. She married KELVIN ARTHUR WINTERMAN[1363,1364] 30 Aug 1975 in All Saints Church, Park Road, Peterborough, Cambridgeshire, England[1365,1366]. He was born 09 May 1953 in The Gables Maternity Hospital, Peterborough, Cambridgeshire, England[1367,1368].

More About KELVIN WINTERMAN and SUSAN COLEMAN:
Marriage: 30 Aug 1975, All Saints Church, Park Road, Peterborough, Cambridgeshire, England[1369,1370]

Children of SUSAN COLEMAN and KELVIN WINTERMAN are:
108. i.   ANDREW[10] WINTERMAN, b. 30 Apr 1971.
      ii. CRAIG NEIL WINTERMAN[1371], b. 17 Nov 1982, Maternity Unit, Aldermans Drive, Peterborough, Cambridshire, England[1371,1372].

88. GERALD[9] MOULD *(WILLIAM ARTHUR[8], CYRIL EUGENE[7], GEORGE[6], THOMAS[5], WILLIAM[4] MOLDS, WILLIAM[3], JOSEPH[2] MOULDS, THOMAS[1] MOULD)[1373]* was born 02 Oct 1958[1374]. He married GAIL[1374]. She was born 25 Jul 1960[1374].

Children of GERALD MOULD and GAIL are:
  i.   JAMES[10] MOULD[1374], b. 07 Feb 1987[1374].
  ii.   MATTHEW MOULD[1374], b. 02 May 1988[1374].
  iii. SARAH MOULD[1374], b. 11 Mar 1990[1374].

89. SHARON[9] MOULD *(HAROLD EDWARD[8], CYRIL EUGENE[7], GEORGE[6], THOMAS[5], WILLIAM[4] MOLDS, WILLIAM[3], JOSEPH[2] MOULDS, THOMAS[1] MOULD)[1375]* was born 27 Mar 1959[1376]. She married JAMES[1376]. He was born 27 Jul 1936[1376].

Child of SHARON MOULD and JAMES is:
  i.   GRANT[10,1377], b. 22 Sep 2002[1378].

90. IAN[9] MOULD *(HAROLD EDWARD[8], CYRIL EUGENE[7], GEORGE[6], THOMAS[5], WILLIAM[4] MOLDS, WILLIAM[3], JOSEPH[2] MOULDS, THOMAS[1] MOULD)[1379]* was born 04 Apr 1963[1380]. He married CHRISTINE[1380].

More About IAN MOULD:
Divorced: 1999[1380]

Children of IAN MOULD and CHRISTINE are:
  i.   ALICIA[10] MOULD[1380], b. 13 Oct 1993[1380]; Adopted child.
  ii. ADAM MOULD[1380], b. 13 Feb 1998[1380]; Adopted child.

91. MAXWELL JAMES[9] BOLTON *(JOAN BARBARA[8] MOULD, GUILFORD THOMAS[7], GEORGE[6], THOMAS[5], WILLIAM[4]*

MOLDS, WILLIAM[3], JOSEPH[2] MOULDS, THOMAS[1] MOULD)[1381,1382,1383] was born 06 Feb 1980 in Hesham, Northumberland, England[1383]. He married SARAH WINNE[1384] 14 Jul 2006 in Methodist Church, Bournemouth, Hampshire, England[1384]. She was born 02 Aug 1978[1384].

More About MAXWELL BOLTON and SARAH WINNE:
Marriage: 14 Jul 2006, Methodist Church, Bournemouth, Hampshire, England[1384]

Child of MAXWELL BOLTON and SARAH WINNE is:
    i. ZOE ANNABELLE[10] BOLTON[1385], b. 23 Feb 2010[1385].

92. ANDREW DAVID[9] PETERS (ALISON MARY[8] MOULD, GUILFORD THOMAS[7], GEORGE[6], THOMAS[5], WILLIAM[4] MOLDS, WILLIAM[3], JOSEPH[2] MOULDS, THOMAS[1] MOULD)[1386,1387] was born 09 Jun 1973 in Gt. Yarmouth, Norfolk, England[1387]. He married KERRIE RAE HAYSE[1388,1389] 04 Nov 2000 in St. Peter's Church, Southport, Queensland, Australia[1389].

More About ANDREW PETERS and KERRIE HAYSE:
Marriage: 04 Nov 2000, St. Peter's Church, Southport, Queensland, Australia[1389]

Children of ANDREW PETERS and KERRIE HAYSE are:
    i. JOSHUA DAVID[10] PETERS[1390,1391], b. 08 May 2002, Wollongong, Australia[1392,1393].
    ii. EMILY ALISON PETERS[1394], b. 27 Aug 2003, Wollongong, Australia[1394].

93. CATHERINE MARY[9] PETERS (ALISON MARY[8] MOULD, GUILFORD THOMAS[7], GEORGE[6], THOMAS[5], WILLIAM[4] MOLDS, WILLIAM[3], JOSEPH[2] MOULDS, THOMAS[1] MOULD)[1395,1396] was born 18 Sep 1974 in Gt. Yarmouth, Norfolk, England[1396]. She married CLIVE DAVID HAWKETT[1397,1398] 22 Jul 2000 in All Saints Church, Hillingdon, Middlesex, England[1398].

More About CLIVE HAWKETT and CATHERINE PETERS:
Marriage: 22 Jul 2000, All Saints Church, Hillingdon, Middlesex, England[1398]

Children of CATHERINE PETERS and CLIVE HAWKETT are:
    i. NOAH JOHN[10] HAWKETT[1399], b. 04 Mar 2004, Basingstoke, Hampshire, England[1399,1400].
    ii. HEIDI MIA HAWKETT[1401], b. 07 Nov 2005, Basingstoke, Hampshire, England[1401].

Generation No. 6

94. BELINDA[10] MANNING (VIRGINIA[9] PARSLEY, MURIEL NAOMI[8] BALDWIN, NAOMI JANE[7] JESSOP, JANE[6] MOULD, THOMAS[5], WILLIAM[4] MOLDS, WILLIAM[3], JOSEPH[2] MOULDS, THOMAS[1] MOULD)[1402] was born Bet. Oct - Dec 1952 in Lambeth[1403]. She married NEIL SUMNER[1404].

Children of BELINDA MANNING and NEIL SUMNER are:
    i. JAMIE[11] SUMNER[1404], b. Mar 1988[1405].
    ii. ROBERT SUMNER[1406], b. Jul 1993[1407].

95. JOHN MARK[10] MANNING (VIRGINIA[9] PARSLEY, MURIEL NAOMI[8] BALDWIN, NAOMI JANE[7] JESSOP, JANE[6] MOULD, THOMAS[5], WILLIAM[4] MOLDS, WILLIAM[3], JOSEPH[2] MOULDS, THOMAS[1] MOULD)[1408] was born 1954[1409]. He married SUSAN[1410].

Children of JOHN MANNING and SUSAN are:
    i. VICTORIA[11] MANNING[1410], b. Sep 1980[1410].
    ii. LUCY MANNING[1410], b. Jan 1982[1410].

96. HILLARY[10] MANNING (VIRGINIA[9] PARSLEY, MURIEL NAOMI[8] BALDWIN, NAOMI JANE[7] JESSOP, JANE[6] MOULD, THOMAS[5], WILLIAM[4] MOLDS, WILLIAM[3], JOSEPH[2] MOULDS, THOMAS[1] MOULD)[1411] was born Bet. Jan - Mar 1956 in

Hatfield, Hertfordshire, England[1412]. She married STUART F. GUYTON[1413] Bet. Jul - Sep 1977[1414].

More About HILLARY MANNING:
Twin: 1956, Twin to Kathryn[1415]

More About STUART GUYTON and HILLARY MANNING:
Marriage: Bet. Jul - Sep 1977[1416]

Children of HILLARY MANNING and STUART GUYTON are:
    i.   NEIL FIRTH[11] GUYTON[1417], b. Jul 1980[1417].
    ii. EMILY GUYTON[1417]. b. Mar 1982[1417].
    iii. ELIZABETH GUYTON[1417], b. May 1984[1417].

97. KATHARINE[10] MANNING *(VIRGINIA[9] PARSLEY, MURIEL NAOMI[8] BALDWIN, NAOMI JANE[7] JESSOP, JANE[6] MOULD, THOMAS[5], WILLIAM[4] MOLDS, WILLIAM[3], JOSEPH[2] MOULDS, THOMAS[1] MOULD)*[1418] was born Bet. Jan - Mar 1956 in Hartfield, Hertfordshire, England[1418]. She married PATRICK R. BROOKER[1419] Bet. Jul - Sep 1977[1420].

More About PATRICK BROOKER and KATHARINE MANNING:
Marriage: Bet. Jul - Sep 1977[1420]

Children of KATHARINE MANNING and PATRICK BROOKER are:
    i.   SALLY JO[11] BROOKER[1421], b. Jul 1980[1421].
    ii. NICHOLAS PATRICK BROOKER[1421]. b. Jul 1982[1421].
    iii. AMY ROSE BROOKER[1421], b. Aug 1984[1421].

98. SARAH JANE[10] MCROBERT *(JANE[9] BALDWIN, DOUGLAS HERBERT[8], NAOMI JANE[7] JESSOP, JANE[6] MOULD, THOMAS[5], WILLIAM[4] MOLDS, WILLIAM[3], JOSEPH[2] MOULDS, THOMAS[1] MOULD)*[1422] was born 26 Jun 1957 in Mona Baldwin's house in St. Leonards, Dorset, England[1423,1424]. She married (1) MARK GERALD JARVIS[1425] 10 Aug 1977 in Near Ringwood, Hampshire, England[1425,1426]. She married (2) JOHN HIGBEE[1427] 10 Sep 1995 in Rustington, Sussex, England[1427,1428].

More About MARK JARVIS and SARAH MCROBERT:
Marriage: 10 Aug 1977, Near Ringwood, Hampshire, England[1429,1430]

More About JOHN HIGBEE and SARAH MCROBERT:
Marriage: 10 Sep 1995, Rustington, Sussex, England[1431,1432]

Children of SARAH MCROBERT and MARK JARVIS are:
109.   i.   REBECCA EVELYN[11] JARVIS, b. 21 Dec 1983, Hospital in Yeovil, Sommerset, England.
         ii. ROBERT STEPHEN JARVIS[1433,1434], b. 07 May 1986, Hospital in Yeovil, Sommerset, England[1435,1436].

99. MONA[10] MCROBERT *(JANE[9] BALDWIN, DOUGLAS HERBERT[8], NAOMI JANE[7] JESSOP, JANE[6] MOULD, THOMAS[5], WILLIAM[4] MOLDS, WILLIAM[3], JOSEPH[2] MOULDS, THOMAS[1] MOULD)*[1437] was born 10 May 1959 in Mona Baldwin's house, Ringwood, Hampshire, England[1438]. She married (1) DONALD POUNDS[1439] 05 Jun 1978 in Parish Church, Ringwood, Hampshire, England[1439,1440]. She married (2) WLADEK KAYWICZANIN[1441] 22 Jul 1995 in Registry Office, Ringwood, Hampshire, England[1441,1442].

More About DONALD POUNDS and MONA MCROBERT:
Marriage: 05 Jun 1978, Parish Church, Ringwood, Hampshire, England[1443,1444]

More About WLADEK KAYWICZANIN and MONA MCROBERT:
Marriage: 22 Jul 1995, Registry Office, Ringwood, Hampshire, England[1445,1446]

Children of MONA MCROBERT and DONALD POUNDS are:
    i.   MICHAEL JOHN[11] POUNDS[1447], b. 28 Jul 1981, Hospital in Odstock, near Salsbury, Wiltshire, England[1447,1448].

ii.   DAVID NEIL POUNDS[1449], b. 22 May 1983, Hospital in Odstock, near Salsbury, Wiltshire, England[1449,1450].

100. KEITH[10] BALDWIN *(CHRISTOPHER[9], DOUGLAS HERBERT[8], NAOMI JANE[7] JESSOP, JANE[6] MOULD, THOMAS[5], WILLIAM[4] MOLDS, WILLIAM[3], JOSEPH[2] MOULDS, THOMAS[1] MOULD)* was born 25 Mar 1965 in Fordingbridge, Hampshire, England[1451]. He met LOUISE ROLL[1452].

Child of KEITH BALDWIN and LOUISE ROLL is:
i.   KIMBERLY[11] ROLL-BALDWIN[1452], b. 11 May 1996, Salisbury, Wiltshire, England[1452,1453].

101. JONATHAN[10] ROSE *(RICHARD[9], SHEILA MARGARET[8] PRENTICE, GEORGE HAROLD[7], ROSE[6] MOULD, THOMAS[5], WILLIAM[4] MOLDS, WILLIAM[3], JOSEPH[2] MOULDS, THOMAS[1] MOULD)[1454]* was born 08 Jun 1966 in Chipping Norton, Oxfordshire, England[1455]. He married RUBY GILBERT[1455,1456] 18 Dec 1993 in St. Andrews Methodist Church, Filton, Bristol[1456]. She was born 27 Feb 1966 in Bristol, England[1456].

More About JONATHAN ROSE and RUBY GILBERT:
Marriage: 18 Dec 1993, St. Andrews Methodist Church, Filton, Bristol[1456]

Children of JONATHAN ROSE and RUBY GILBERT are:
i.   DANIEL[11] ROSE[1457], b. 21 Nov 1994, Bristol, Gloucestershire, England[1458].
ii.   SCOTT ROSE[1459], b. 11 Jul 1996, Bristol, Gloucestershire, England[1460].
iii.   SOPHIE ROSE[1461], b. 25 Apr 1998, Bristol, Gloucestershire, England[1462].

102. JULIAN[10] ROSE *(RICHARD[9], SHEILA MARGARET[8] PRENTICE, GEORGE HAROLD[7], ROSE[6] MOULD, THOMAS[5], WILLIAM[4] MOLDS, WILLIAM[3], JOSEPH[2] MOULDS, THOMAS[1] MOULD)[1463]* was born 19 Jun 1968 in Chipping Norton, Oxfordshire, England[1464,1465]. He married JO-ANNE BLAKE[1466,1467] 01 Aug 1992 in Burford Church, Burford, Oxfordshire, England[1468,1469]. She was born 12 Jun 1968 in Wolverhampton, England[1469].

More About JULIAN ROSE and JO-ANNE BLAKE:
Marriage: 01 Aug 1992, Burford Church, Burford, Oxfordshire, England[1470,1471]

Child of JULIAN ROSE and JO-ANNE BLAKE is:
i.   ALEXANDRA[11] ROSE[1472], b. 28 Aug 1999, Glouchester Royal Hospital, England[1473,1474].

103. AMANDA[10] ROSE *(DAVID[9], SHEILA MARGARET[8] PRENTICE, GEORGE HAROLD[7], ROSE[6] MOULD, THOMAS[5], WILLIAM[4] MOLDS, WILLIAM[3], JOSEPH[2] MOULDS, THOMAS[1] MOULD)[1475]* was born 21 Mar 1968 in Chipping Norton, Oxfordshire, England[1476]. She met STEPHEN DAVIS[1476,1477] 1986[1478,1479].

More About STEPHEN DAVIS and AMANDA ROSE:
Partners: 1986[1480,1481]

Child of AMANDA ROSE and STEPHEN DAVIS is:
i.   TOM[11] DAVIS[1482,1483,1484], b. 12 Apr 1988, Cheltenham, Glouchestershire, England[1484].

104. TRACY LYNN[10] REDFORD *(ROBERT EDGAR[9], MARJORIE[8] MACKNESS, FRANK[7], REBECCA[6] MOULD, THOMAS[5], WILLIAM[4] MOLDS, WILLIAM[3], JOSEPH[2] MOULDS, THOMAS[1] MOULD)[1485]* was born 02 Oct 1967[1485].

Child of TRACY LYNN REDFORD is:
i.   ROBERT[11][1486], b. 24 Jul 1990[1486].

105. ERIC[10] REDFORD *(ROBERT EDGAR[9], MARJORIE[8] MACKNESS, FRANK[7], REBECCA[6] MOULD, THOMAS[5], WILLIAM[4] MOLDS, WILLIAM[3], JOSEPH[2] MOULDS, THOMAS[1] MOULD)[1487]* was born 09 Dec 1969[1487]. He married (1) JESSICA[1488]. He married (2) AMY[1488].

Child of ERIC REDFORD and JESSICA is:

i. CRYSTAL[11] REDFORD[1488].

Child of ERIC REDFORD and AMY is:

ii. SABRA[11] REDFORD[1488], b. 20 Jul 1990[1488].

106. SUZANNE ELIZABETH[10] DRUCE *(CHRISTINE ANN[9] MOULD, NORMAN WILLIAM[8], BERNARD WILLIAM[7], CHARLES[6], THOMAS[5], WILLIAM[4] MOLDS, WILLIAM[3], JOSEPH[2] MOULDS, THOMAS[1] MOULD)*[1489,1490] was born 16 Aug 1972 in Northampton, Northants, England[1490]. She married ANDREW CASWELL[1491,1492] 31 May 2003 in Plan to Marry Wellingborough Registry Office, Northants, England[1492]. He was born 14 Jun 1958 in Fulham, London, England[1492].

More About ANDREW CASWELL and SUZANNE DRUCE:
Marriage: 31 May 2003, Plan to Marry Wellingborough Registry Office, Northants, England[1492]

Children of SUZANNE DRUCE and ANDREW CASWELL are:

i. EMILY MAY-LEAN[11] CASWELL[1493,1494], b. 13 Aug 2000[1495,1496].

ii. THOMAS NORMAN CASWELL[1496], b. 14 Sep 2002[1496].

107. CLAIRE LOUISE[10] BASSON *(RUTH GILLIAN[9] KING, JOYCE IRENE[8] MOULD, BERNARD WILLIAM[7], CHARLES[6], THOMAS[5], WILLIAM[4] MOLDS, WILLIAM[3], JOSEPH[2] MOULDS, THOMAS[1] MOULD)*[1497,1498] was born 30 Nov 1978 in Kettering, Northants, England[1498]. She married NAYTHAN JAMES BELLAMY[1499,1500] 25 May 1997 in All Hallows Church, Wellingborough, Northants, England[1500]. He was born 13 Sep 1973 in Wellingborough, Northants, England[1500].

More About NAYTHAN BELLAMY and CLAIRE BASSON:
Marriage: 25 May 1997, All Hallows Church, Wellingborough, Northants, England[1500]

Children of CLAIRE BASSON and NAYTHAN BELLAMY are:

i. WILLIAM ALAN[11] BELLAMY[1501,1502], b. 23 Oct 1999, Kettering, Northants, England[1503,1504].

ii. SOPHIE RUTH BELLAMY[1505,1506], b. 20 Jan 2002, Kettering, Northants, England[1507,1508].

108. ANDREW[10] WINTERMAN *(SUSAN[9] COLEMAN, OLIVE[8] MOULD, CYRIL EUGENE[7], GEORGE[6], THOMAS[5], WILLIAM[4] MOLDS, WILLIAM[3], JOSEPH[2] MOULDS, THOMAS[1] MOULD)*[1509] was born 30 Apr 1971[1509]. He married JULIE[1509] 25 Jul 1992[1509]. She was born 30 Mar 1972[1509].

More About ANDREW WINTERMAN and JULIE:
Marriage: 25 Jul 1992[1509]

Children of ANDREW WINTERMAN and JULIE are:

i. MEGAN[11] WINTERMAN[1509], b. 06 Mar 1997[1509].

ii. CULLUM WINTERMAN[1509], b. 17 May 1999[1509].

Generation No. 7

109. REBECCA EVELYN[11] JARVIS *(SARAH JANE[10] MCROBERT, JANE[9] BALDWIN, DOUGLAS HERBERT[8], NAOMI JANE[7] JESSOP, JANE[6] MOULD, THOMAS[5], WILLIAM[4] MOLDS, WILLIAM[3], JOSEPH[2] MOULDS, THOMAS[1] MOULD)*[1510] was born 21 Dec 1983 in Hospital in Yeovil, Sommerset, England[1510]. She married NEILL ROBERT NORTHCOTT. He was born 02 Jan 1974 in Portsmouth, England[1511].

Child of REBECCA JARVIS and NEILL NORTHCOTT is:

i. FRANCES JANE SASHA[12] NORTHCOTT[1511], b. 01 Dec 2004, Portsmouth, England[1511].

Endnotes

1. Jabez Mould death certificate, B5, P171, B-1789.
2. Interview with Fred Albert Bull and Helen (Bull) Klapper.
3. Census - 1881, Paston, Northampton, England, FHL Film 1341381, PRO Ref: RG11, Piece 1592, Folio: 48, Page 18., Thomas Moulds, Relationship: Head, Married, Age: 53, Sex: M, Birthplace: Woodcroft, Northampton, England, Occupation: Dairyman.
4. Census - 1881, Paston, Northampton, England, FHL Film 1341381, PRO Ref: RG11, Piece 1592, Folio: 48, Page 18., Thomas Moulds, Relationship: head, married, Age: 53 years, Sex: M, Birthplace: Woodcroft, Northampton, England. Occupation: Dairyman.
5. Interview with Fred Albert Bull and Helen (Bull) Klapper.
6. Family tree created by Guilford Mould, son of George Mould., "Thomas mould was born at Woodcroft (nr. Maxey, Northants.) on September 8th 1827."
7. E-mail from Marjorie Redford to Richard James Klapper, December 31, 2000.
8. Death certificate - Thomas Mould, Peterborough registration district, sub-district of Peterborough, Counties of Hunts and Peterborough, England, No. 272.
9. Interview with Fred Albert Bull and Helen (Bull) Klapper.
10. Census - 1881, Paston, Northampton, England, FHL Film 1341381, PRO Ref: RG11, Piece: 1592, Folio: 48, Page 18, Roseann Moulds, Rel: Wife, Married, Age:52, Sex: F, Birthplace: Brigstock, Northampton, England.
11. Interview with Fred Albert Bull and Helen (Bull) Klapper.
12. Marriage license - Thomas Moulds/Rose Ann Mackness, Peterborough Registration District, Parish of Etton, Northampton, England, No. 17.
13. Interview with Fred Albert Bull and Helen (Bull) Klapper.
14. Census - 1881, Paston, Northampton, England, FHL Film 1341381, PRO RG11, Piece: 1592, Folio: 48, Page 48, Roseann Moulds, Rel: Wife, Married, Age: 52, Sex: F, Brigstock, Northampton, England.
15. Family tree created by Guilford Mould, son of George Mould., "Married Rose Ann Mackness on 5th April 1852. R.A.M. born at Brigstock (Northants) 20th March 1829."
16. Death certificate - Rose Ann Mould, Wellingborough registration district, Sub-district of Higham Ferrers, Counties of Northampton and Bedford, England, No. 321.
17. *Parish Registers - Etton, Northamptonshire*, Baptism records, "Thomas Mole was baptised at Etton on 21 October 1827, the son of William and Edith Mole of Woodcroft, labourer."
18. Bishop's Transcripts - Etton, Northants, England, Baptism registers, October 21, 1827 Thomas son of William & Edith Mole of Woodcroft.
19. *Diary of Annie Beatrice Mould Bull's 6 month trip to England in 1928*, August 14, 1928, "...in the afternoon we walked over to Gunthorpe through Paston, looked around the church - visited my grandparents graves - also Uncle Joe's..."
20. Burial records - Paston Northants, England, Parish registers - burial - 1896-1934, page 18, No. 141.
21. Census - 1881, Paston, Northampton, England, Film 1341381, RG11, Piece 1592, Folio 48, Page 18.
22. Census - 1881, Rushden, Northampton, England.
23. Census - 1901, Gunthorpe, Northants, England, RG13, 1466, 88, 23, Sched.#151, "Thomas Mould, Head, Male, married, 73, Birthplace: Norths Woodcroft, Address: Rectory, Occ: Dairymen."
24. *Parish Registers for Brigstock, Northants, England*, "....and Rose Ann (baptised May 30, 1829)." E-mail from Samantha Thomson to Richard Klapper - June 23, 2001.
25. *Parish Registers for Brigstock, Northants, England*, Baptism Registers - 1829, I personally looked at the parish registers on microfische on October 30, 2002 and the baptism was on August 30 - not May 30 as indicated by Samantha Thompson.
26. *Diary of Annie Beatrice Mould Bull's 6 month trip to England in 1928*, August 14, 1928, "...in the afternoon we walked over to Gunthorpe through Paston, looked around the church - visited my grandparents graves - also Uncle Joe's..."
27. Burial records - Paston Northants, England, Parish registers - burials - 1896-1934, page 24, No. 188, The burial entry notes that Rose Ann was living in Rushden when she died.
28. Census - 1851, Deepingate, Lincolnshire, England, Deepingate, Maxey.
29. E-mail from Samantha Thompson, March 24, 2002, 1841 census has the following information: "Syke Row Brigstock Jabez Mackeniss 45 Agricultural Labourer Syke Row Brigstock Mary Mackeniss 40 Syke Row Brigstock Elizabeth Mackeniss 14 Syke Row Brigstock Roseann Mackeniss 12 Syke Row Brigstock Jabez Mackeniss 10 Syke Row Brigstock Nathaniel Mackeniss 8 Syke Row Brigstock Joseph Mackeniss 1."
30. Interview with Fred Albert Bull and Helen (Bull) Klapper.
31. Marriage license - Thomas Moulds/Rose Ann Mackness, Peterborough Registration District, Parish of Etton, Northampton, England, No. 17.
32. Interview with Fred Albert Bull and Helen (Bull) Klapper.
33. Marriage license - James Mackness/Betsy Mould, Peterborough Reg Dist, Parish Church, Parish of Paston, Northants, England.
34. Interview with Fred Albert Bull and Helen (Bull) Klapper.
35. Census - 1881, Glinton, Northamptonshire, England, FHL Film 1341383, PRO Ref: RG11, Piece 1598, Folio 29, page 7, "Betsy Mould ....26 years old,......Birthplace: Gunthorpe, Northampton, England.

36. Birth certificate - Betsy Mould, Peterborough Registration District, Subdistrict of Peterborough, Counties of Northampton, Huntingdon & Cambridge, England No. 279.

37. E-mail from Derek Mackness to Richard Klapper, April 21, 2002.

38. Death certificate - Betsy Mackness, Died 23rd November 1928 at 4 Liverton Road, Loftus, Betsy Mackness, female, 73 years, wife of James Mackness, banksman at ironstone mine below ground (retired), cause of death: 1a. heart failure, b. peripheral neurites, c. senility, no P.M., informant and residence: J. Mackness, widower of deceased, present at the death, 4 Liverton Road, Loftus.

39. E-mail from Marjorie Redford to Richard James Klapper, December 31, 2000.

40. Letter from Joan (Mould) Bolton to Richard James Klapper, January 9, 2001.

41. Census - 1881, Lofthouse, York, England, FHL Film 1342165, PRO Ref: RG11, Piece 4838, Folio 19, Page 32, "James Mackness, son, 15 years old, male, Birthplace: Hinderwell, York, England, Occ: Ironstone Miner, Dwelling: 6 St. Hildes Terrace."

42. Marriage license - James Mackness/Betsy Mould, Peterborough Reg Dist, Parish Church, Parish of Paston, Northants, England.

43. Birth certificate - James Mackness, Whitby Registration District, Lythe district, York County, England.

44. Death certificate - James Mackness, Huddersfield, England.

45. *Parish Registers - Paston, Northants, England*, Baptism Records, March 25, 1855, Betsy, daughter of Thomas & Rose Ann Moulds of Gunthorpe, a labourer.

46. Loftus Cemetery Records, Loftus, Yorks, England, Book 5, 1928, Betsy Mackness, 73 years, 4 Liverton Road, November 26, 1928, grave # 4103, Unconsecrated ground : A - F/26.

47. Death certificate - Betsy Mackness, Died 23rd November 1928 at 4 Liverton Road, Loftus, Betsy Mackness, female, 73 years, wife of James Mackness, banksman at ironstone mine below ground (retired), cause of death: 1a. heart failure, b. peripheral neurites, c. senility, no P.M., informant and residence: J. Mackness, widower of deceased, present at the death, 4 Liverton Road, Loftus.

48. Census - 1881, Glinton, Northamptonshire, England, FHL Film 1341383, PRO Ref: RG11, Piece 1598, Folio 29, Page 7, "Betsy Mould.......Occupation: General servant."

49. Census - 1881, Glinton, Northamptonshire, England, FHL Film 1341383, PRO Ref: RG11, Piece 1598, Folio 29, Page 7, "Betsy Mould.......Dwelling: North Fen Lane, Census Place: Glinton, Northampton, England."

50. E-mail from Derek Mackness to Richard Klapper, Aprill 11, 2002.

51. Edgerton Cemetery Records, Huddersfield, York, England, Page 423, No. 36740, January 7 (or 8), 1948, James Mackness, 82 years, Retired, Abode: 17 Poplar Street, Moldgreen, Huddersfield,   Section 27, Grave no. 128.

52. Death certificate - James Mackness, Huddersfield, England.

53. Death certificate - Betsy Mackness, Died 23rd November 1928 at 4 Liverton Road, Loftus, Betsy Mackness, female, 73 years, wife of James Mackness, banksman at ironstone mine below ground (retired), cause of death: 1a. heart failure, b. peripheral neurites, c. senility, no P.M., informant and residence: J. Mackness, widower of deceased, present at the death, 4 Liverton Road, Loftus.

54. Marriage license - James Mackness/Betsy Mould, Peterborough Reg Dist, Parish Church, Parish of Paston, Northants, England.

55. Interview with Fred Albert Bull and Helen (Bull) Klapper.

56. Census - 1881, Glinton, Northamptonshire, England, FHL Film 1341383, PRO Ref: RG11, Piece 1598, Folio 30, Page 10, "Mary Mould.......24 years old, Birthplace: Gunthorpe, Northampton, England."

57. Birth certificate - Mary Mould, Peterborough registration district, sub-district of Peterborough, Counties of Northampton, Huntingdon & Cambridge, England, No. 325.

58. E-mail from Marjorie Redford to Richard James Klapper, December 31, 2000.

59. E-mail from Marjorie Redford to Richard James Klapper, April 13, 2001, "They both died on the farm, the nearest town in South Dakota being Lemmon, but the closest town to them was Hettinger, North Dakota. Their farm was right near the North Dakota/South Dakota border. I think it was in Perkins County."

60. Death certificate - Mary Avery, Perkins County, South Dakota, State File # 199343, Register # D-14.

61. Interview with Fred Albert Bull and Helen (Bull) Klapper.

62. Marriage license - James Edward Dale Avery/Mary "Polly" Mould.

63. Marriage license - James Edward Dale Avery/Mary "Polly" Mould, Peterborough Reg Dist., Parish Church, Parish of Glinton, Northants, county, England, no. 116.

64. Census - 1881, Glinton, Northamptonshire, England, FHL Film 1341383, PRO Ref RG11, Piece 1598, Folio 30, Page 10, "James Dale, wife, unmarried, 22 years, male, Beirthplace: Glinton, Northampton, England, Occ: Farm Labourer, Dwelling: Town Street."

65. Birth certificate - James Edward Avery, Reg. Dist. Peterborough, sub-dist. of Crowland, counties of Lincoln and Northampton.

66. Death certificate - James Edward Dale Avery, Peterborough Reg Dist, Sub-dist of Crowland, counties of Lincoln and Northampton.

67. Death certificate - Mary Avery, Perkins County, South Dakota, State Registration # 199342, Registered # D-14, Buried in Ellingson, South Dakota on March 6, 1941. Undertaker: H. C. Kern, Hettinger, North Dakota.

68. Death certificate - Mary Avery, Perkins County, South Dakota, State file # 230182.

69. Ellis Island Arrival Records, May Avery, "May Avery, Arrived September 18, 1921 in Ellis Isalnd from Southampton, England on the ship Berengaria. She was 64 years old, a widow and her place of residence was Peakirk, England."

70. Census - 1881, Glinton, Northamptonshire, England, FHL Film 1341383, PRO Ref: RG11, Piece 1598, Folio 30, Page 10, "Mary Mould .....Occ: Cook Domestic."

71. Census - 1881, Glinton, Northamptonshire, England, FHL Film 1341383, PRO Ref: RG11, Piece 1598, Folio 30, Page 10, "Mary Mould......Dwelling: Town Street, Glinton, Northampton, England."

72. Letter from Joan (Mould) Bolton to Richard James Klapper, January 9, 2001.

73. *Parish Registers - Peakirk, Northants, England*, Burial Records, "James Edward Dale Avery, Peakirk, 19 Feb 1915, 56 years."

74. Death certificate - James Edward Dale Avery, Peterborough Reg Dist, Sub-dist of Crowland, counties of Lincoln and Northampton.

75. Census - 1881, Glinton, Northamptonshire, England, FHL Film 1341383, PRO Ref RG11, Piece 1598, Folio 30, Page 10, "James Dale, wife, unmarried, 22 years, male, Beirthplace: Glinton, Northampton, England, Occ: Farm Labourer, Dwelling: Town Street."

76. Marriage license - James Edward Dale Avery/Mary "Polly" Mould, Peterborough Reg Dist., Parish Church, Parish of Glinton, Northants, county, England, no. 116.

77. Interview with Fred Albert Bull and Helen (Bull) Klapper.

78. Birth certificate - Jabez A. Mould, Peterborough Registration District, Peterborough sub-district, Counties of Northampton, Huntingdon & Cambridge, England, no. 186.

79. Interview with Fred Albert Bull and Helen (Bull) Klapper.

80. Burial records - Paston Northants, England, 1862 - Page 32, No. 253, "Jabez Mould, Abode: Gunthorpe, January 18, 15 months."

81. Census - 1861, Gunthorpe, Northants, England, Jabez Mould, son, 6 months old, born: Gunthorpe, Northants .

82. Interview with Fred Albert Bull and Helen (Bull) Klapper.

83. Birth certificate - William Jabez Mould, Peterborough registration district, Sub-district of Peterborough, Counties of Northampton, Huntingdon & Cambridge, England, No. 90.

84. Interview with Fred Albert Bull and Helen (Bull) Klapper.

85. Death certificate - William Jabez Mould, Peterborough Registration district, Sub-district of Peterborough, Counties of Northampton, Huntingdon & Cambridge, England, No. 349.

86. Burial records - Paston Northants, England, 1863 - Page 35, No. 277, "Jabez William Mould, Abode: Gunthorpe, January 2, infant."

87. Interview with Fred Albert Bull and Helen (Bull) Klapper.

88. Census - 1881, Paston, Northampton, England, FHL Film 1341381, PRO Ref: RG11, Piece: 1592, Folio: 48, Page 18, Joseph Moulds, Rel: Son, Unmarried, Age: 16, Sex: M, Birthplace: Gunthorpe, Northampton, England, Occ: Agricultural Laborer.

89. Interview with Fred Albert Bull and Helen (Bull) Klapper.

90. Census - 1881, Paston, Northampton, England, FHL Film 1341381, PRO Ref: RG11, Piece: 1592, Folio: 48, Page 18., Joseph Moulds, Rel: Son, Occ: Agricultural Laborer, Unmarried, Age: 16 years, Sex: M, Birthplace: Gunthorpe, Northamptonshire, England.

91. Birth certificate - Joseph Mould, Peterborough registration district, Sub-district of Peterborough, Counties of Northampton, Huntingdon & Cambridge, England, No. 74.

92. Interview with Fred Albert Bull and Helen (Bull) Klapper.

93. Death certificate - Joseph Mould, Peterborough registration district, Sub-district of Peterborough, Counties of Hunts and Peterborough, England, No.236.

94. *Diary of Annie Beatrice Mould Bull's 6 month trip to England in 1928*, August 14, 1928, "....in the afternoon we walked over to Gunthorpe through Paston, looked around the church - visited my grandparents graves - also Uncle Joe's..."

95. Burial records - Paston Northants, England, Parish registers, 1896-1934, Page 8, No. 61.

96. Death certificate - Joseph Mould, Peterborough registration district, Sub-district of Peterborough, Counties of Hunts & Peterborough.

97. Census - 1881, Paston, Northampton, England, FHL Film 1341381, RG11, 1592, 48, 18, "Joseph Moulds, son, unmarried, 16, male, Born Gunthorpe, Northampton, England, Ag Lab."

98. Interview with Fred Albert Bull and Helen (Bull) Klapper.

99. Birth certificate - Jane Mould, Peterborough Reg. Dist, Barnack Sub-district, Northants, Rutland, Lincoln and Huntington Counties, 1853, Last name was spelled Mowls.

100. Birth certificate - Jane Mould, Peterborough Reg. Dist., Barnack sub-dist, counties of Northampton, Rutland, Lincoln, Huntington, 1853, # 405, "First May 1853, born in Greatford" Note that Rose Ann Mould's maiden name is incorrect on the birth certificate. It says Rose Ann Wade instead of Rose Ann Mackness. Wade is Rose Ann's mother's maiden name (Mary Wade).

101. Death certificate - Jane Jessop, Epsom Reg. Dist., Carshalton sub-dist, County of Surrey.

102. E-mail from Marjorie Redford to Richard James Klapper, December 31, 2000.

103. Census - 1881, Streatham, Surry, England, FHL Film: 1341154, PRO Ref: RG11, Piece 00664, Folio 116, Page 34, "Deveroux Jessop, Rel: Head, married, 26 years old, Male, Birthplace: Stonehaven, Suffolk, England, Occ: Plumber and painter, Dwelling: 55 Balham Grove."

104. Marriage license - Devereux Henry Jessop/Jane Mould, Peterborough registration district, parish of Paston, Northants, England.

105. Census - 1881, Streatham, Surry, England, FHL Film: 1341154, Pro Ref: RG11, Piece: 0664, Folio: 116, Page 34,

"Deveroux Jessop, Rel: Head, married, 26 years old, Male, Birthplace: Stonehaven, Suffolk, England, Occ: Plumber and painter, Dwelling: 55 Balham Grove."

106. *GRO birth index for England*, 1st Q 1855.

107. Death certificate - Devereux Henry Jessop, Kingston Reg. Dist., Kingston Sub-district, County of Surrey.

108. Cemetery records, Sutton Cemetery, Sutton, London, England, The records show that Jane Jessop is buried in the same grave as her husband Devereux and her son Devereux. Jane was buried on July 6, 1925.

109. Death certificate - Jane Jessop, Epsom Reg. Dist., Carshalton sub-dist, County of Surrey.

110. Census - 1881, Streatham, Surry, England, FHL Film: 1341154, PRO Ref: RG11, Piece 0664, Folio 116, Page 34., "Jane Jessop, wife, married, 27 years old, female, Birthplace: Greatford, Lincolnshire, England, Dwelling: 55 Balham Grove."

111. Cemetery records, Sutton Cemetery, Sutton, London, England, The records show that Jane Jessop is buried in the same grave as her husband Devereux and her son Devereux. Devereux was buried February 11, 1932.

112. Death certificate - Devereux Henry Jessop, Kingston Reg. Dist., Kingston Sub-district, County of Surrey.

113. Census - 1881, Streatham, Surry, England, FHL Film: 1341154, PRO Ref: RG11, Piece: 0664, Folio: 116, Page 34, "Deveroux Jessop, Rel: Head, married, 26 years old, Male, Birthplace: Stonehaven, Suffolk, England, Occ: Plumber and painter, Dwelling: 55 Balham Grove."

114. Marriage license - Devereux Henry Jessop/Jane Mould, Peterborough registration district, parish of Paston, Northants, England.

115. Census - 1901, Balham, England, "Fred D. Jessop, son, single, 18, Occ: Commercial clerk, Birthplace: Surrey Balham, Dwelling: 86 Balham High road."

116. *GRO birth index for England*.

117. Census - 1901, Balham, England, "Fred D. Jessop, son, single, 18, Occ: Commercial clerk, Birthplace: Surrey Balham, Dwelling: 86 Balham High road."

118. Birth Certificate - Devereux Henry Jessop, Wandsworth Reg Dist, Streatham Sub-dist, County of Surrey, England, Frederick Thomas Jessop, born April 6, 1882, father: Devereux Henry Jessop, mother: Jane Jessop formerly Mould, father a plumber, informant: Jane Jessop Mother 55 Balham Grove.

119. Death certificate - Frederick Thomas Jessop, Reg Dist of Eastbourne, Sub-dist of Eastbourne, County Borough of Eastbourne.

120. Census - 1901, Balham, England, RG13, 474, 82, 6, Sched.# 29, "Fred D. Jessop, son, single, 18, Occ: Commercial clerk, Birthplace: Surrey Balham, Dwelling: 86 Balham High road."

121. Interview with Fred Albert Bull and Helen (Bull) Klapper.

122. Birth certificate - Rose Mould, Peterborough registration district, Sub-registration district of Peterborough, Counties of Northampton, Huntingdon and Cambridge, England, no. 458.

123. Death certificate - Rose Prentice, Peterborough registration district, Sub-district of Crowland, Counties of the Soke of Peterborough, England, No. 388.

124. Interview with Fred Albert Bull and Helen (Bull) Klapper.

125. Burial records - St. Pega's Church, Peakirk, Northamptonshire, England, "John William Prentice   4.11.1858   26.8.1919."

126. Marriage license - John William Prentice/Rose Mould, Peterborough Reg Dist, Paston Parish, Northants County, England, 1886, #340.

127. Marriage license - John William Prentice/Rose Mould, Peterborough Reg Dist, Paston Parish, Northants, England, 1886, #340.

128. Burial records - St. Pega's Church, Peakirk, Northamptonshire, England, "John William Prentice   4.11.1858   26.8.1919."

129. Census - 1901, Peakirk, Northants, England, RG13, 1467, 46, 5, 30, John W. Prentice, Where born: Northampton Peakirk.

130. Church records - St. Pegas, Peakirk, Northants, England, "John William Prentice   4.11.1858   26.8.1919."

131. *Diary of Annie Beatrice Mould Bull's 6 month trip to England in 1928*, August 16, 1928, "....Alfred and I went over to Peakirk and saw my cousins Lily and Dora and visited the graves of Uncle Jim and Aunt Rose and Uncle John."

132. *Parish Registers - Peakirk, Northants, England*, Burial records, Page 61, No. 481, Rose Prentice of Peakirk, buried June 27, 1925, 66 years old.

133. Obituary - Rose Mould, The Peterborough & Hunts. Standard, July 3, 1925, ".........on Friday, died (June 25th) after a long illness patiently borne."

134. Census - 1881, Hampstead, London, Middlesex, England, FHL Film 1341036, PRO Ref: RG11, Piece 0168, Folio 13, Page 19, "Rose Mould........Occupation: General Serv."

135. Letter from Joan (Mould) Bolton to Richard James Klapper, January 9, 2001.

136. *Diary of Annie Beatrice Mould Bull's 6 month trip to England in 1928*, August 16, 1928, ".....Alfred and I went over to Peakirkand saw my cousins Lily and Dora and visited the graves of Uncle Jim and Aunt Rose and Uncle John."

137. *Parish Registers - Peakirk, Northants, England*, Burial records, Page 57, No. 451, John William Prentice of Peakirk, buried 29th August 1919, 60 years old.

138. Death certificate - Rose Prentice, Peterborough registration district, Sub-district of Crowland, Counties of the Soke of Peterborough, England, No.388.

139. Marriage license - John William Prentice/Rose Mould, Peterborough Reg Dist, Paston Parish Church, Northants, County, England, 1886, #340.

140. Marriage license - John William Prentice/Rose Mould, Peterborough Reg Dist, Paston Parish, Northants, England,

1886, #340.

141. Information from Freda Neaverson, May 20, 2001 e-mail from Graham Garrett, "Freda also adds the following comments: ' I knew Misses Ellen, Lilian and Dora also Frederick and Harold.' ."

142. Burial records - St. Pega's Church, Peakirk, Northamptonshire, England, "Ellen Prentice   18.3.1888   11.8.1946."

143. Census - 1901, Peakirk, Northants, England, RG13, 1467, 46, 5, Sched.# 30.

144. Church records - St. Pegas, Peakirk, Northants, England, "Ellen Prentice   18.3.1888   11.8.1946."

145. *Parish Registers - Peakirk, Northants, England*, Baptism records, Page 65, No. 518, April 15, 1888, Ellen, daughter of John William and Rose Prentice of Peakirk, a baker.

146. *Parish Registers - Peakirk, Northants, England*, Burial records, Page 71, No.561, Ellen Prentice, Peakirk, Buried August 14, 1946, 58 years old.

147. Census - 1901, Peakirk, Northants, England, RG13, 1467, 46,5, Sched.# 30.

148. Letter from Joan (Mould) Bolton to Richard James Klapper, January 9, 2001.

149. *Telephone call between Joan Bolton and Richard Klapper*, May 12, 2001.

150. Burial records - St. Pega's Church, Peakirk, Northamptonshire, England, "Lilian Prentice   9.3.1889   16.11.1967."

151. Census - 1901, Peakirk, Northants, England, RG13, 1467, 46, 5, Sched.# 30.

152. Church records - St. Pegas, Peakirk, Northants, England, "Lilian Prentice   9.3.1889   16.11.1967."

153. Death certificate - Lilian Prentice, Reg. Dist. of Peterborough, sub-dist. of Peterborough, county of Huntingdon and Peterborough.

154. *Parish Registers - Peakirk, Northants, England*, Baptism records, page 66, No. 525, April 7, 1889, Lilian, daughter of John William and Rose Prentice of Peakirk, a baker.

155. *Parish Registers - Peakirk, Northants, England*, Burial records, Lilian Prentice, 1 Rectory Lane, Peakirk, buried 21st November 1967, 78 years old.

156. Death certificate - Lilian Prentice, Reg. Dist. of Peterborough, sub-dist. of Peterborough, county of Huntingdon and Peterborough.

157. Death certificate - Rose Prentice, Peterborough registration district, Sub-district of Crowland, Counties of the Soke of Peterborough, England, No. 388.

158. Letter from Joan (Mould) Bolton to Richard James Klapper, January 9, 2001.

159. *Telephone call between Joan Bolton and Richard Klapper*, May 12, 2001.

160. Burial records - St. Pega's Church, Peakirk, Northamptonshire, England, May 20, 2001, "Dora Evelyn   1898."

161. *Parish Registers - Peakirk, Northants, England*, Baptism records, January 29, 1899, Dora Evelyn, John William and rose Prentice of Peakirk, a baker.

162. Burial records - St. Pega's Church, Peakirk, Northamptonshire, England, "Dora Prentice   2.1.1899   20.12.1927."

163. Census - 1901, Peakirk, Northants, England, RG13, 1467, 46, 5, Sched.# 30.

164. Church records - St. Pegas, Peakirk, Northants, England, "Dora Prentice   2.1.1899   20.12.1965."

165. Death certificate - Dora Evelyn Prentice, Reg. Dist. of Peterborough, sub-dist. of Peterborough, county of Huntingdon and Peterborough.

166. Obituary - Dora Prentice, Peterborough Citizen and Advertiser, December 24, 1965, "Dora Prentice - Suddenly on December 20th at Peterborough Memorial Hospital, Dora aged 66 years. Funeral service at St. Pega's Peakirk, Thursday Dec 23rd at 2pm followed by cremation at Marholm."

167. *Parish Registers - Peakirk, Northants, England*, Baptism records, January 29, 1899, Dora Evelyn, John William and rose Prentice of Peakirk, a baker.

168. *Parish Registers - Peakirk, Northants, England*, Burial records, page 78, No. 622, Dora Evelyn Prentice, 1 Rectory Lane, Peakirk. 24th December 1965, 66 years old.

169. Death certificate - Dora Evelyn Prentice, Reg. Dist. of Peterborough, sub-dist. of Peterborough, county of Huntingdon and Peterborough.

170. Obituary - Dora Prentice, Peterborough Citizen and Advertiser, December 24, 1965, "Dora Prentice - Suddenly on December 20th at Peterborough Memorial Hospital, Dora aged 66 years. Funeral service at St. Pega's Peakirk, Thursday Dec 23rd at 2pm followed by cremation at Marholm."

171. Census - 1901, Peakirk, Northants, England, RG13, 1467, 46,5, Sched.# 30.

172. Jabez Mould death certificate, B5, P171, B-1789.

173. Interview with Fred Albert Bull and Helen (Bull) Klapper.

174. Jabez Mould obituary in Aberdeen, South Dakota newspaper, July 11, 1936.

175. Birth certificate - Jabez Mould, Peterborough registration district, Sub-district of Peterborough, Counties of Northampton, Huntingdon & Cambridge, England, No. 206.

176. Jabez Mould death certificate, B5, P171, B-1789.

177. Jabez Mould/Sarah Mould 50th anniversary newspaper article - Aberdeen, S.D., June 6, 1935.

178. Marriage license - Jabez Mould/Sarah Ann Cox, Wellingborough Registration Office, 1885, No. 177, Marriage solemnized at the register office, district of Wellingborough, June 4, 1885.

179. Grave headstone - Sarah Ann Mould, June 26, 2000.

180. Birth certificate - Sarah Ann Cox, Kettering Reg. Dist., Kettering Sub-district, Northamptonshire, England, No. 202, When and where born: Twelfth January 1867, Union Workhouse Kettering.

181. Grave headstone - Sarah Ann Mould, June 26, 2000.

182. *Telephone interview of Hazel Ritter by Richard Klapper*, August 17, 2002.

183. Jabez Mould obituary in Aberdeen, South Dakota newspaper, July 15, 1936.

184. Grave headstone - Jabez Mould, Riverside Cemetery, Aberdeen, South Dakota.

185. Ellis Island Arrival Records, December 24, 1919, Jabez arrived at Ellis Island, NY on December 24, 1919 on the ship Orduna from Liverpool, England with his wife Sarah.

186. *US Census - 1930, Aberdeen, Brown County, South Dakota*, Enumeration district 7-10, sheet # 18A.

187. Marriage license - Jabez Mould/Sarah Ann Cox, Wellingborough Registration District, 1885, No. 177.

188. Ellis Island Arrival Records, Jult 27, 1912, Annie Bull arrived at Ellis Island on the ship Baltic and listed her mother, S. A. Mould as living at 13 Westfield Ave., Higham Ferrers.

189. Grave headstone - Sarah Ann Mould, June 26, 2000, Glen Abby Memorial Park, Bonita, California - Section 71, Block 68, Lot 3.

190. Ellis Island Arrival Records, December 24, 1919, Sarah arrived at Ellis Island, NY on December 24, 1919 on the ship Orduna from Liverpool, England with her husband Jabez.

191. *US Census - 1930, Aberdeen, Brown County, South Dakota*, Enumeration district 7-10, sheet # 18A, Sara A Mould, wife, female, white, 62, married, first married at 17, born: England, immigrated to US in 1919, naturalized citizen, saleslady in grocery store, residence: 111 Eighth Ave.

192. Census - 1881, Rushden, Northampton, England, FHL Film 1341377, PRO Ref RG11, Piece 1569, Folio 14, Page 21, Sarah A. Cox, Niece, unmarried, 14 years old, female, Birthplace: Kettering, Northamptonshire, England, Occupation: shoe fitter, Dwelling: Duck Street.

193. Ellis Island Arrival Records, July 27, 1912, Annie Bull arrived at Ellis Island on the ship Baltic and listed her mother, S. A. Mould as living at 13 Westfield Ave., Higham Ferrers.

194. Jabez Mould/Sarah Mould 50th anniversary newspaper article - Aberdeen, S.D., June 6, 1935.

195. Marriage license - Jabez Mould/Sarah Ann Cox, Wellingborough Registration Office, 1885, No. 177, Marriage solemnized at the register office, district of Wellingborough, June 4, 1885.

196. *Rushden, Northamptonshire, England cemetery records at the Rushden Center*, Rushden Cemetery Records, Book 1, Entry No. 560., Annie Lilian Mould, Daughter of Jabez and Sarah Ann Mould, age 4 years, buried February 19, 1894. Plot 303a.

197. *GRO birth index for England*, The GRO birth indexes show her name as Bessie Lilian as opposed to the Rushden Cemetery records which listed as Annie Lillian.

198. *Rushden, Northamptonshire, England cemetery records at the Rushden Center*, Rushden Cemetery Records - Book 1, Entry No. 560., Annie Lilian Mould, daughter of Jabez and Sarah Ann Mould, age 4 years. Buried February 19, 1894. Plot 303a.

199. Richard Klapper assumption, Since Bessie was the 3rd of 5 children and and the other 4 were born in Rushden, it is logical to assume that Bessie was also born in Rushden.

200. *GRO birth index for England*, 1 Q 1890.

201. *Rushden, Northamptonshire, England cemetery records at the Rushden Center*, Rushden Cemetery Records - Book 1, Entry No. 560., Annie Lilian Mould, daughter of Jabez and Sarah Ann Mould, age 4 years. Buried February 19, 1894. Plot 303a.

202. *Rushden, Northamptonshire, England cemetery records at the Rushden Center*, Rushden Cemetery Records - Book 1, Entry no. 560., Annie Lilian Mould, daughter of Jabez and Sarah Ann Mould, age 4 years, buried February 19, 1894. Plot 303a.

203. Census - 1891, Rushden, Northants, England, Bessie L. Mould, daughter, 1, born: Rushden, Northants, dwelling: Lancaster Street.

204. *Rushden, Northamptonshire, England cemetery records at the Rushden Center*, Book 1, Entry no. 1445., Thomas Roland Mould, son of Jabez and Sarah Anne Mould, age 5 days, buried December 30, 1899. Plot 761a.

205. *GRO birth index for England*, The GRO index spells Thomas' middle name as Rowland as opposed to Roland in the Rushden Cemetery records.

206. *Rushden, Northamptonshire, England cemetery records at the Rushden Center*, Book 1, Entry no. 1445., Thomas Roland Mould, son of Jabez and Sarah Anne Mould, age 5 days, buried December 30, 1899. Plot 1445.

207. *Rushden, Northamptonshire, England cemetery records at the Rushden Center*, Book 1, Entry no. 1445., Thomas Roland Mould, son of Jabez and Sarah Anne Mould, age 5 days, buried December 30, 1899. Plot 761a.

208. Interview with Fred Albert Bull and Helen (Bull) Klapper.

209. Birth certificate - Rebecca Mould, Peterborough registration district, Sub-district of Peterborough, Counties of Northampton, Huntingdon & Cambridge, England, No. 295.

210. Interview with Fred Albert Bull and Helen (Bull) Klapper.

211. E-mail from Marjorie Redford to Richard James Klapper, April 13, 2001, "They both died on the farm, the nearest town in South Dakota being Lemmon, but the closest town to them was Hettinger, North Dakota. Their farm was right near the South Dakota North Dakota border. I think it was in Perkins county."

212. Death certificate - Rebecca Mackness, Perkins County, South Dakota, State file # 230182, Registered # D34.

213. Interview with Alfred and Lois Bull, May 26, 2000.

214. E-mail from Marjorie Redford to Richard James Klapper, December 30, 2000.

215. *Aberdeen American News article on the death of John Mackness*, September 14, 1935.

216. *Aberdeen newspaper article on the golden anniversary of Mr. and Mrs John Mackness*, March 14, 1925.

217. Death certificate - Rebecca Mackness, Perkins County, South Dakota, State file # 230182, Registered # D-34.

218. Marriage license - Joseph Thomas Mackness/Rebecca Mould, Parish Church in Parish of Paston, Northamptonshire, England, Page 178.

219. E-mail from Marjorie Redford to Richard James Klapper, January 2, 2001, "He was 24 years old when he and grandma were married. They were married in 1890,....."

220. Census - 1881, Rushden, Northampton, England, FHL Film 1341377, PRO Ref: RG11, Piece 1569, Folio 7, Page 8., Joseph Mackness, Son, Unmarried, 15 years old, Male, Birthplace: Brigstock, Northampton, England, Dwelling: High Street.

221. Death certificate - Joseph T. Mackness, Dept. of Health, State of South Dakota, Reg. No. D-18, "Date of Birth: December 3, 1865   Birthplace: Brigstock, England."

222. E-mail from Marjorie Redford to Richard James Klapper, January 2, 2001, "I don't know the exact date of Grandpa's death except that he died when my brother was in high school and I think it was 1938 when he died on the farm in South Dakota of stomach cancer."

223. Death certificate - Joseph T. Mackness, Dept. of Health, State of South Dakota, Reg. No. D-18.

224. Death certificate - Rebecca Mackness, Perkins County, South Dakota, State File # 230182, Registered # D34, Buried in Ellingson, South Dakota, July 9, 1946. Undertaker: Barklay in Hettinger, North Dakota.

225. Death certificate - Rebecca Mackness, Perkins County, South Dakota, State file # 230182, Registered # D-34.

226. Ellis Island Arrival Records, Rececca Mackness, "Reccecca Mackness arrived 16 Oct 1906 at Ellis Island from Liverpool, England on the Carmania. She was married and 38 yers old and resided in Rushden, England."

227. *Telephone interview of Marge Redford by Richard Klapper*, October 19, 2003, Marge said that Joseph Thomas and his son Frank both became US citizens and she has the papers for Frank. She also believed her grandmother, Rebecca Mackness became a US citizen also but Marge doesn't have any papers on that.

228. *US Census - 1930, Viking Township, Perkins County, South Dakota*, Enumeration district 53-49, sheet # 1B, Rebecca Mackness, wife, lives on a farm, female, white, 62, married, 22 at first marriage, able to read and write, born: England, immigrated to US in 1906, naturalized citizen.

229. Marriage license - Joseph Thomas Mackness/Rebecca Mould, Parish Church, parish of Paston, Northamptonshire, England, Page 178.

230. Death certificate - Joseph T. Mackness, Dept. of Health, State of South Dakota, Reg. No. D-18, "Burial, cremation or removal: Place: Ellingson, S. Dakota   Date: May 26, 1938."

231. Death certificate - Joseph T. Mackness.

232. *US Census - 1930, Viking Township, Perkins County, South Dakota*, Enumeration district 53-49, sheet # 1B, Joseph Mackness, head, owns home, lives on a farm, male, white, 64, married, age at first marriage: 24, able to read and write, born: England, immigrated to US in 1906, naturalized citizen, able to read and write, farmer.

233. *Telephone interview of Marge Redford by Richard Klapper*, October 19, 2003, Marge said that Joseph Thomas and his son Frank both became US citizens and she has the papers for Frank. She also believed her grandmother, Rebecca Mackness became a US citizen also but Marge doesn't have any papers on that.

234. Census - 1881, Rushden, Northampton, England, FHL Film 1341377, PRO Ref: RG11, Piece 1569, Folio 7, Page 8., Joseph Mackness, Son, Unmarried, 15 years old, Male, Birthplace: Brigstock, Northampton, England, Occupation: Shoe Finisher.

235. E-mail from Marjorie Redford to Richard James Klapper, January 2, 2001, ".....they were married in 1890, according to the marriage register of the parish of Paston on the 28th day of May. His residence was in Rushden..."

236. Marriage license - Joseph Thomas Mackness/Rebecca Mould, Parish Church in Parish of Paston, Northamptonshire, England, Page 178.

237. *Rushden, Northamptonshire, England cemetery records at the Rushden Center*, Book 1, Entry # 741, "Mackness, Nellie, Buried May 21, 1895, 16 months of age, Daughter of Joseph and Rebecca Mackness."

238. Interview with Fred Albert Bull and Helen (Bull) Klapper.

239. Census - 1881, Paston, Northampton, England, FHL Film 1341381, PRO Ref: RG11, Piece: 1592, Folio: 48, Page 18., Charles Moulds, Rel: Son, Age: 9 years, Sex: M, Birthplace: Gunthorpe, Northampton, England, Occ: Scholar.

240. Interview with Fred Albert Bull and Helen (Bull) Klapper.

241. Census - 1881, Paston, Northampton, England, FHL Film 1341381, PRO Ref: RG11, Piece: 1592, Folio: 48, Page 18., Charles Moulds, Rel: Son, Age: 9 years, Sex: M, Birthplace: Gunthorpe, Northampton, England, Occ: Scholar.

242. Birth certificate - Charles Mould, Peterborough registration district, Sub-district of Peterborough, Counties of Northampton, Huntingdon & Cambridge, England, No. 418.

243. Death certificate - Charles Mould, Wellingborough registration district, Sub-district of Rushden, County of Northamptonshire, England, No. 417.

244. E-mail from Jayne Wright of Rushden,Northampton, England, July 26, 2000, An old lady named Miss Mould (Joan) came in. Her grandfather Charles Mould was the youngest of 4 sons. Charles stayed in the (Rushden) area and married Emily Whitbread from Irthlingborough. She died in her sixties, but her two sisters lived to see 100.

245. Census - 1901, Higham Ferrers, England, RG13, 1440, 46, 46, Sched. # 296, "Emily J. Mould, wife, female, married, 28, Born: Northants, Rushden, Address: Westfields."

246. Marriage license - Charles Mould/Emily Jane Whitbread, Wellingborough Reg. Dist., Parish of Rushden, County of Northants, England.

247. E-mail from Jayne Wright of Rushden,Northampton, England, July 26, 2000, A Miss Mould (Joan) came in. Her grandfather Charles Mould was the youngest of 4 sons. Charles stayed in the area and married Emily Whitbread from Irthlingborough. She died in her 60s but her 2 sisters lived to see 100.

248. Marriage license - Charles Mould/Emily Jane Whitbread, Wellingborough Reg. Dist., Parish of Rushden, County of Northants, England.

249. Census - 1901, Higham Ferrers, England, RG13, 1440, 46, 46, Sched. # 296, "Emily J. Mould, wife, female, married,

28, Born: Northants, Rushden, Address: Westfields."

250. Birth certificate - Emily Jane Whitbread, Wellingborough Reg Dist, Higham Ferrers Sub-dist, Counties of Northampton and Bedford.

251. Death certificate - Emily Jane Mould, Wellingborough Reg Dist, Rushden Sub-dist, County of Northampton.

252. Interview with Joan Mould, September 16, 2000, When I told Joan that we had walked the cemetery in Higham Ferrers but didn't find any Moulds she said we missed some because Charles is buried there.

253. Grave headstone - Charles and Emily Mould, Higham Ferrers Cemetery, Northants, England.

254. Obituary - Charles Mould, Rushden Echo and Argus, Friday March 9, 1945, page 2, The funeral took place on Tuesday, and the service was conducted at the home by the Rev. T.S. Kee, of the Rushden Independent Wesleyan Church, before interment at the Higham Ferrers cemetery.

255. Census - 1881, Paston, Northampton, England, FHL Film 1341381, RG11, 1592, 48, 18.

256. Death certificate - Charles Mould, Wellingborough registration district, Sub-district of Rushden, County of Northampton, England, No. 417.

257. Ellis Island Arrival Records, December 24, 1919, ship manifest for ship Orduna, Jabez Mould listed his brother Charles' address in the ship's manifest.

258. Obituary - Charles Mould, Rushden Echo and Argus, Friday March 9, 1945, page 2, Aged 73 years, Mr. Mould was born at Peterborough, came to Higham Ferrers as a boy, and spent his working life in the boot trade, retiring three years ago.

259. Grave headstone - Charles and Emily Mould, Higham Ferrers Cemetery, Northants, England.

260. Death certificate - Emily Jane Mould, Wellingborough Reg Dist, Rushden Sub-dist, County of Northampton.

261. Marriage license - Charles Mould/Emily Jane Whitbread, Wellingborough Reg. Dist., Parish of Rushden, County of Northants, England.

262. *Rushden, Northamptonshire, England cemetery records at the Rushden Center*, Book 1, entry # 380, Emily May Mould, buried May 24, 1892, 1 month old, grave # 180a, daughter of Charles and Emily Mould.

263. *Rushden, Northamptonshire, England cemetery records at the Rushden Center*, Book 1, entry # 380, Emily May Mould, buried 5/24/1892, 1 month old, grave # 180a, daughter of Charles and Emily Mould.

264. *Rushden, Northamptonshire, England cemetery records at the Rushden Center*, Book 1, Entry # 380, Emily May Mould, buried 5/24/1892, 1 month old, grave 180a, daughter of Charles and Emily Mould.

265. *Rushden, Northamptonshire, England cemetery records at the Rushden Center*, Book 1, entry # 380, Emily May Mould, buried 5/24/1892, 1 month old, grave 180a, daughter of Charles and Emily Mould.

266. Letter from Joan (Mould) Bolton to Richard James Klapper, January 9, 2001.

267. *GRO birth index for England*, Elsie May Mould 2 Q 1893.

268. GRO death index for England, First quarter 1984, The death index gives the date of birth as well as the month and year of death. The death index for Elsie gives her death date as January 1984 and her birth date as May 23, 1893.

269. E-mail from Jayne Blanchard of Kettering Crematorium to Richard Klapper, October 27, 2006, "Elsie May Headland died on 3.1.1984 and was cremated here on 11.1.1984."

270. Family tree by Trevor Mould, May 16, 2002.

271. Marriage Certificate - Charles Headland/Elsie May Mould, Independent Wesleyan Chapel, Rushden, District of Wellingborough in county of Northampton, September 26, 1931, Charles Headland, 60 years, widower, leather dresser, living at 43 Queen Street, Rushden, father: John Thomas Headland, leather dresser (deceased) married Elsie May Mould, 38 years, spinster, a Commercial clerk, living at 70 High Street, Rushden, father: Charles Mould, shoe trade.

272. *GRO birth index for England*, 2 Q 1871.

273. GRO death index for England, 4Q 1953.

274. *Telephone interview of Philip Mould by Richard Klapper*, February 23, 2004, "Elsie was a widow for a long time. She died when she was in her 80's or almost 90. Elsie was cremated.

275. E-mail from Jayne Blanchard of Kettering Crematorium to Richard Klapper, October 27, 2006, "Elsie May Headland died on 3.1.1984 and was cremated here on 11.1.1984."

276. Marriage Certificate - Charles Headland/Elsie May Mould, Independent Wesleyan Chapel, Rushden, District of Wellingborough in county of Northampton, September 26, 1931, Charles Headland, 60 years, widower, leather dresser, living at 43 Queen Street, Rushden, father: John Thomas Headland, leather dresser (deceased) married Elsie May Mould, 38 years, spinster, a Commercial clerk, living at 70 High Street, Rushden, father: Charles Mould, shoe trade.

277. Census - 1901, Higham Ferrers, England, RG13, 1440, 46, 46, Sched.# 296.

278. *Telephone interview of Philip Mould by Richard Klapper*, February 23, 2004, Philip indicated that Charles was married to another wife before Elsie. Charles' first wife died and was buried in the Orlingbury Churchyard. When Charles died he was buried with his first wife in Orlingbury Churchyard.

279. E-mail from Jayne Blanchard of Kettering Crematorium to Richard Klapper, October 27, 2006, "Charles Headland was cremated here on 8.10.1953. His date of death would be on our old written records that are held in the basement at the Council offices."

280. Marriage Certificate - Charles Headland/Elsie May Mould, Independent Wesleyan Chapel, Rushden, District of Wellingborough in county of Northampton, September 26, 1931, Charles Headland, 60 years, widower, leather dresser, living at 43 Queen Street, Rushden, father: John Thomas Headland, leather dresser (deceased) married Elsie May Mould, 38 years, spinster, a Commercial clerk, living at 70 High Street, Rushden, father: Charles Mould, shoe trade.

281. Letter from Ernest James Klapper to Charles James Klapper, January 9, 2001.

282. Census - 1901, Higham Ferrers, England, RG13, 1440, 46, 46, Sched.# 296.

283. *GRO birth index for England.*

284. Death certificate - Jessie Barrett, Northampton reg dist, Northampton sub-dist, Northants, England, Jessie Barrett died on July 2, 1977 in St. Edmund's Hospital, Northampton, Northants. She was born October 22, 1894 in Higham Ferrers, Northant. She was the widow of John Barrett a boot and shoe operative. She lived at 118 St. James Park Road, Northampton. The informant was Pauline Hilda May Spiller, her niece who lived at Corner House, Keyston, Huntingdon, Cambs. Cause of death: 1a Cerebro-vascular Episode with (L) hemiplegia 1b Parkinson's Disease Note: This birth date doesn't agree with the GRO birth index which shows 1895.

285. Death certificate - Jessie Barrett, Northampton reg dist, Northampton sub-dist, Northants, England, Jessie Barrett died on July 2, 1977 in St. Edmund's Hospital, Northampton, Northants. She was born October 22, 1894 in Higham Ferrers, Northant. She was the widow of John Barrett a boot and shoe operative. She lived at 118 St. James Park Road, Northampton. The informant was Pauline Hilda May Spiller, her niece who lived at Corner House, Keyston, Huntingdon, Cambs. Cause of death: 1a Cerebro-vascular Episode with (L) hemiplegia 1b Parkinson's Disease.

286. Family tree by Trevor Mould, May 16, 2002.

287. *GRO marriage index for England*, 2Q 1937, Barrett, John W. J.   Mould   Wellingbro'   3b 311.

288. *GRO birth index for England*, 2Q 1883, Barrett, John William J.   Northampton   3b 82.

289. *GRO marriage index for England*, 2Q 1937, Barrett, John W. J.   Mould   Wellingbro'   3b 311.

290. *GRO birth index for England*, 4Q 1883, Barrett, John William J.   Northampton   3b 82.

291. Obituary - John William James Barrett, Northampton Chronicle and Echo, Friday May 10, 1957, page 12, Barrett – On May 9, after a short illness, at Northampton General Hospital, John William James, aged 73, of 118, St. Jame's Park-road. Beloved husband of Jessie, and dear brother of Ivy. Resting in the Lord. Funeral service, Monday, May 13, at 1:45pm at Princes-street Baptist Church. No flowers please.

292. Interview with Joyce King, March 2003.

293. Obituary - Jessie Barrett, Northampton Chronicle and Echo, July 5, 1977, page 2, "Service at Kettering Crematorium on Friday 8th July at 3pm."

294. Census - 1901, Higham Ferrers, England, RG13, 1440, 46, 46, Sched.# 296.

295. Death certificate - Jessie Barrett, Northampton reg dist, Northampton sub-dist, Northants, England, Jessie Barrett died on July 2, 1977 in St. Edmund's Hospital, Northampton, Northants. She was born October 22, 1894 in Higham Ferrers, Northant. She was the widow of John Barrett a boot and shoe operative. She lived at 118 St. James Park Road, Northampton. The informant was Pauline Hilda May Spiller, her niece who lived at Corner House, Keyston, Huntingdon, Cambs. Cause of death: 1a Cerebro-vascular Episode with (L) hemiplegia 1b Parkinson's Disease.

296. Obituary - John William James Barrett, Northampton Chronicle and Echo, Friday, May 10, 1957, page 12, Barrett - On May 9, after a short illness, at Northampton General Hospital, John William James, aged 73, of 118, St. Jame's Park-road.

297. *GRO marriage index for England*, 2Q 1937, Barrett, John W. J.   Mould   Wellingbro'   3b 311.

298. Letter from Joan (Mould) Bolton to Richard James Klapper, January 9, 2001.

299. Census - 1901, Higham Ferrers, England, RG13, 1440, 46, 46, Sched.# 296.

300. *GRO birth index for England*.

301. Grave headstone - Daisy Sharp, March 2003, Beloved Husband Of / Daisy Sharp / Died Nov. 14th 1948, Age 49 / Also His Dear Wife / Daisy, / Died Jan. 29th 1995. Age 94. / Reunited.

302. *Telephone interview of Jeffrey Roberts*, February 2004, Daisy died in Fairlawns Nursing Home in Higham Road, Rushden.

303. Family tree by Trevor Mould, May 16, 2002.

304. Grave headstone - Alfred James Sharp, March 2003, Jim and Daisy are buried next to her parents. Headstone inscription: In / Loving Memory of / Alfred James / The Beloved Husband Of / Daisy Sharp / Died Nov. 14th 1948, Age 49 / Also His Dear Wife / Daisy, / Died Jan. 29th 1995. Age 94. / Reunited

305. *GRO marriage index for England*, 2Q 1927, Sharp, Alfred J.   Mould   Wellingbro'   3b 370.

306. Grave headstone - Alfred James Sharp, March 2003, Beloved Husband Of / Daisy Sharp / Died Nov. 14th 1948, Age 49 / Also His Dear Wife / Daisy, / Died Jan. 29th 1995. Age 94. / Reunited.

307. *GRO birth index for England*, 1 Q 1899, 1 Q 1899   Sharp, Alfred James   Welligbro'   3 b 138.

308. Grave headstone - Alfred James Sharp, March 2003, Beloved Husband Of / Daisy Sharp / Died Nov. 14th 1948, Age 49 / Also His Dear Wife / Daisy, / Died Jan. 29th 1995. Age 94. / Reunited.

309. Obituary - Alfred James Sharp, Rushden Echo and Argus, Friday November 26, 1948 page 9, "The funeral of Mr. Alfred James Sharp, of 19, Wentworth Road, Rushden, who died in the Northampton General Hospital, took place on November 18, ..."

310. Grave headstone - Daisy Sharp, March 2003, Beloved Husband Of / Daisy Sharp / Died Nov. 14th 1948, Age 49 / Also His Dear Wife / Daisy, / Died Jan. 29th 1995. Age 94. / Reunited.

311. Census - 1901, Higham Ferrers, England, RG13, 1440, 46, 46, Sched.# 296.

312. Grave headstone - Alfred James Sharp, March 2003, Beloved Husband Of / Daisy Sharp / Died Nov. 14th 1948, Age 49 / Also His Dear Wife / Daisy, / Died Jan. 29th 1995. Age 94. / Reunited.

313. Obituary - Alfred James Sharp, Rushden Echo and Argus, Friday November 26, 1948 page 9, "The funeral of Mr. Alfred James Sharp, of 19, Wentworth Road, Rushden, who died in the Northampton General Hospital, took place on November 18, ..."

314. Obituary - Alfred James Sharp, "The funeral of Mr. Alfred James Sharp, of 19, Wentworth Road, Rushden, who died in the Northampton General Hospital, took place on November 18, ..."

315. *GRO marriage index for England*, 2Q 1927, Sharp, Alfred J.   Mould   Wellingbro'   3b 370.

316. Interview with Fred Albert Bull and Helen (Bull) Klapper.

317. Census - 1881, Paston, Northampton, England, FHL Film 1341381, PRO Ref: RG11, Piece: 1592, Folio: 48, Page 18., George Moulds, Rel: Son, Age: 7 years, Sex: Male, Birthplace: Gunthorpe, Northampton, England, Occ: Scholar.

318. Interview with Fred Albert Bull and Helen (Bull) Klapper.

319. Census - 1881, Paston, Northampton, England, FHL Film 1341381, PRO Ref: RG11, Piece: 1592, Folio: 48, Page 18., George Moulds, Rel: Son, Age: 7years, Male, Birthplace: Gunthorpe, Northampton, England, Occ: Scholar.

320. Birth certificate - George Mould, Peterborough registration district, Sub-district of Peterborough, Counties of Northampton, Huntingdon & Cambridge, England, No. 19.

321. Death certificate - George Mould, Huntingdon reg dist, Huntingdon sub-registration district, Huntingdon England, No. 309, 1953.

322. *Diary of Annie Beatrice Mould Bull's 6 month trip to England in 1928*, August 13, 1928, "Left Higham for Peterboro about 10:30- arrived about 1:00 o'clock - Uncle George met us with a car - soon home - met Aunt Fanny and all the family...."

323. Letter from Joan (Mould) Bolton to Richard James Klapper, January 9, 2001.

324. Marriage license - George Mould/Fanny Mills, Peterborough Reg. Dist., Peterborough Parrish, Northants, England, No. 318.

325. Birth certificate - Fanny Mills, Peterborough Reg. Dist., Sub-district of Peterborough, Northants, England, 1870, No. 28.

326. Obituary - Fannie Mould, Peterborough Standard, Friday, February 21, 1947, "Formerly Miss Mills, she was born in one of the G.N.R. Cottages and for 13 years , in Canon Ball's time, was a teacher at New England Church schools."

327. Letter from Joan (Mould) Bolton to Richard James Klapper, January 9, 2001.

328. Letter from Joan (Mould) Bolton to Richard James Klapper, February 4, 2002, "Died at Rauceby, nr Sleaford, Lincs. Rauceby Hospital on 15.2.1947."

329. Death certificate - Fannie Mould, Lincoln Reg Dist, North Kesteven sub-dist, Lincoln county, 1947, #87.

330. Newspaper article about George Mould's cycle accident, April 1953, "Mr. George Mould, aged 79, formerly of 28(?) Gilpin-street, was married at Broughton Hunts on Monday, to Miss Dorothy Ayres of Rose Cottages, Broughton."

331. Death certificate - Dorothy Ayers Mould, Reg dist: Huntingdon, Sub-dist: Huntingdon, County of Cambridgeshire, Date and place of death:Feb 7, 1985 at 27 Stukeley Road Huntingdon, Name of deceased: Dorothy Mould, female, Maiden name: Ayers, born: 20th July 1900 at Broughton, Cambs, widow of George mould a Dairyman, address: 27 Stukeley Road, Huntingdon, Cambs, Informant: Maggie Ayers-sister, Informant's address: 27 Stukeley Road, Huntingdon, Cambs, Cause of death: Ischaemic heart disease (certified by Paul Petty Coroner for the District of Huntingdon after post mortem with inquest.

332. Letter from Muriel Hind to Richard Klapper.

333. Death certificate - Dorothy Ayers Mould, Reg dist: Huntingdon, Sub-dist: Huntingdon, County of Cambridgeshire, Date and place of death:Feb 7, 1985 at 27 Stukeley Road Huntingdon, Name of deceased: Dorothy Mould, female, Maiden name: Ayers, born: 20th July 1900 at Broughton, Cambs, widow of George mould a Dairyman, address: 27 Stukeley Road, Huntingdon, Cambs, Informant: Maggie Ayers-sister, Informant's address: 27 Stukeley Road, Huntingdon, Cambs, Cause of death: Ischaemic heart disease (certified by Paul Petty Coroner for the District of Huntingdon after post mortem with inquest.

334. Letter from Joan (Mould) Bolton to Richard James Klapper, February 4, 2002, "Buried in Peterborough Eastfield Cemetery (alongside 1st wife Fanny 'Mills).'."

335. Bulletin from funeral of George Mould, Card notes he was interred in Rastfield Cemetery, April 14, 1953.

336. Census - 1881, Paston, Northampton, England, FHL Film 1341381, RG11, 1592, 48, 18.

337. Death certificate - George Mould, Huntingdon reg dist, Huntingdon sub-registaration dist, Huntingdon, England, No. 309, 1953.

338. Death certificate - George Mould, Huntingdon reg dist, Huntingdon sub-reg dist, Huntingdon, England, no. 309, 1953.

339. Letter from Joan (Mould) Bolton to Richard James Klapper, February 4, 2002, "Buried in Peterborough's Eastfield Cemetery (George bought a family plot....)" .

340. Death certificate - Fannie Mould, Lincoln Reg dist, North Kesteven sub-dist, Lincoln County, 1947, # 87.

341. Marriage license - George Mould/Fanny Mills, Peterborough Reg. Dist., Peterborough Parrish, Northants, England, No. 318.

342. Obituary - Fannie Mould, Peterborough Standard, Friday, February 21, 1947, "Formerly Miss Mills, she was born in one of the G.N.R. Cottages and for 13 years , in Canon Ball's time, was a teacher at New England Church schools."

343. Census - 1901, Gunthorpe, Northants, England, RG13, 1466, 88, 23, Sched.# 152.

344. Marriage license - George Mould/Fanny Mills, Peterborough Reg. Dist., Peterborough Parrish, Northants, England, No. 318.

345. Telephone call between Joan Bolton and Ruby Green, Autumn 2007, ".......on February 7, 1985, Dorothy died at home aged eighty-four and was buried in the Primrose Lane Cemetery."

346. Death certificate - Dorothy Ayers Mould, Reg dist: Huntingdon, Sub-dist: Huntingdon, County of Cambridgeshire, Date and place of death:Feb 7, 1985 at 27 Stukeley Road Huntingdon, Name of deceased: Dorothy Mould, female, Maiden name: Ayers, born: 20th July 1900 at Broughton, Cambs, widow of George mould a Dairyman, address: 27 Stukeley Road, Huntingdon, Cambs, Informant: Maggie Ayers-sister, Informant's address: 27 Stukeley Road, Huntingdon, Cambs, Cause of death: Ischaemic heart disease (certified by Paul Petty Coroner for the District of Huntingdon after post mortem with inquest.

347. Letter from Muriel Hind to Richard Klapper.

348. *Diary of Annie Beatrice Mould Bull's 6 month trip to England in 1928*, August 13, 1928, "Uncle George met us with a car - soon home - met Aunt Fanny and all the family, Doris, Cyril, Bernard, Eric, Guildford, Marjorie, Iris, Hubert...."

349. Letter from Joan (Mould) Bolton to Richard James Klapper, January 9, 2001.

350. *Telephone call between Joan Bolton and Richard Klapper*, October 6, 2002.

351. Letter from Joan (Mould) Bolton to Richard James Klapper, January 9, 2001, Headstone inscription Memories / In The Most holy Name of / Jesus pray for the repose of the soul / of Ernest Victor Maile / who departed this life February 3rd 1957 / aged 54 years / RIP.

352. Grave headstone - Ernest Maile, March 2003.

353. Letter from Joan (Mould) Bolton to Richard James Klapper, February 4, 2002.

354. Letter from Joan (Mould) Bolton to Richard James Klapper, February 4, 2002, "E. born 1903(?) D. 1957 (Age 54)."

355. *Telephone call between Joan Bolton and Richard Klapper*, October 6, 2002.

356. Obituary - Ernest Victor Maile, Peterborough Standard Friday February 8, 1957 Page 10 , Mr. E. V. Maile – After a long illness Mr. Ernest Victor Maile, 59 Gilpin-street, died in St. John's Hospital on Sunday at the age of 56. Born in Peterborough Mr. Maile was the eldest son of the late Mr. And Mrs. J. T. Maile and for some years worked in the oven shop of Baker Perkins Ltd.

357. Letter from Joan (Mould) Bolton to Richard James Klapper, February 4, 2002, "E. born 1903(?) D. 1957 (Age 54)."

358. *Telephone call between Joan Bolton and Richard Klapper*, October 6, 2002.

359. Grave headstone - Ernest Maile, March 2003, Headstone inscription Memories / In The Most holy Name of / Jesus pray for the repose of the soul / of Ernest Victor Maile / who departed this life February 3rd 1957 / aged 54 years / RIP.

360. Obituary - Ernest Victor Maile, Peterborough Standard, Friday February 8, 1957, page 10, After a long illness Mr. Ernest Victor Maile, 59 Gilpin-street, died in St. John's Hospital on Sunday at the age of 56.

361. Interview of Olive Coleman by Richard Klapper, March 2003, Olive told me that Doris Maile was buried in the plot next to her husband Ernest. She then took me to Eastfield cemetery to show me the headstone of Ernest Maile and pointed out the unmarked grave next to it which is Doris'.

362. Obituary - Ernest Victor Maile, Peterborough Standard, Friday February 8, 1957, page 10, Twenty-five years ago he married Miss Doris Irene Mould, of St. Leonard's-on-Sea, and, for some years he and his wife kept a newsagent's and tobacconist's shop in the town returning to Peterborough about 16 years ago.

363. *Obituary - Fanny Mould*, February 1947.

364. Grave headstone - Ernest Maile, March 2003, Headstone inscription Memories / In The Most holy Name of / Jesus pray for the repose of the soul / of Ernest Victor Maile / who departed this life February 3rd 1957 / aged 54 years / RIP.

365. Obituary - Ernest Victor Maile, Peterborough Standard, Friday February 8, 1957, page 10, The funeral took place at All Soul's yesterday.

366. Obituary - Ernest Victor Maile, Peterborough Standard, Friday February 8, 1957, page 10, Twenty-five years ago he married Miss Doris Irene Mould, of St. Leonard's-on-Sea, and, for some years he and his wife kept a newsagent's and tobacconist's shop in the town returning to Peterborough about 16 years ago.

367. *Obituary - Fanny Mould*, February 1947.

368. Letter from Joan (Mould) Bolton to Richard James Klapper, February 4, 2002.

369. *Diary of Annie Beatrice Mould Bull's 6 month trip to England in 1928*, August 13, 1928, Uncle George met us with a car - soon home - met Aunt Fanny and all the family, Doris, Cyril, Bernard, Eric, Guildford, Marjorie, Iris, Hubert..."

370. Letter from Joan (Mould) Bolton to Richard James Klapper, February 4, 2002, "Marjorie Edna, 17th Sept. 1909 Enid phoned me from Germany - her Mum had them in a cooking book!!"

371. Letter from Joan (Mould) Bolton to Richard James Klapper, January 9, 2001.

372. Letter from Joan (Mould) Bolton to Richard James Klapper, February 4, 2002, "Marjorie Edna, 17th Sept. 1909 Enid phoned me from Germany - her Mum had them in a cooking book!!"

373. *Telephone call between Joan Bolton and Richard Klapper*, October 6, 2002.

374. Letter from Joan (Mould) Bolton to Richard James Klapper, January 9, 2001.

375. *Telephone call between Joan Bolton and Richard Klapper*, October 6, 2002.

376. Grave headstone - Marjorie Mould, March 2003, Marjorie is buried in the family plot with her sister Iris and her parents. The headstone inscription says: In / Loving memory of / Marjorie Edna / Mould / Called To Rest / August 16th 1953 / Aged 43 years.

377. *Obituary - Fanny Mould*, February 1947.

378. *GRO birth index for England*.

379. GRO death index for England.

380. *Diary of Annie Beatrice Mould Bull's 6 month trip to England in 1928*, August 13, 1928, Uncle George met us with a car - soon home - met Aunt Fanny and all the family, Doris, Cyril, Bernard, Eric, Guildford, Marjorie, Iris, Hubert..."

381. Letter from Joan (Mould) Bolton to Richard James Klapper, January 9, 2001.

382. Letter from Joan (Mould) Bolton to Richard James Klapper, February 4, 2002, "Iris Theresa, 26 July 1914 Enid phoned from Germany - her Mum had them in a cooking book!!"

383. Letter from Joan (Mould) Bolton to Richard James Klapper, January 9, 2001.

384. Letter from Joan (Mould) Bolton to Richard James Klapper, February 4, 2002, "Iris Theresa, 26 July 1914 Enid phoned from Germany - her Mum had them in a cooking book!!"

385. *Telephone call between Joan Bolton and Richard Klapper*, October 6, 2002.

386. Letter from Joan (Mould) Bolton to Richard James Klapper, January 9, 2001.

387. Grave headstone - Iris Teresa Mould, March 2003, Iris is buried in the family plot with her sister Marjorie and her parents. Headstone inscription says: Also of / Iris Teresa / Mould / Called to Rest / Nov. 8th 1964 / Aged 61 Years / R. I. P.

388. *Obituary - Fanny Mould*, February 1947.

389. Letter from Joan (Mould) Bolton to Richard James Klapper, January 9, 2001.

390. Census - 1881, Streatham, Surry, England, FHL Film: 1341154, PRO Ref: RG11, Piece 0664, Folio 116, Page 34,

"Naomi Jessop, daughter, 1 year old, female, Birthplace: Balham, Surrey, England, Dwelling: 55 Balham Grove."

391. Interview of Shiela Rose by Joan Bolton, March 2002, Shiela indicated that Naomi's middle name was Jane. She said Naomi married an English member of Parliament. Her husband committed suicide and was lost at sea so he must have jumped overboard. They had a daughter named Barbara.

392. Census - 1881, Streatham, Surry, England, FHL Film: 1341154, PRO Ref: RG11, Piece 0664, Folio 116, Page 34, "Naomi Jessop, daughter, 1 year old, female, Birthplace: Balham, Surrey, England, Dwelling: 55 Balham Grove."

393. Birth Certificate - Naomi Jane Jessop, Wandsworth Reg Dist, Clapham Sub-dist, County of Surrey, Naomi Jane Jessop, born August 19, 1879 at 5 Pickett Street, father: Devereux Henry Jessop, mother: Jane Jessop formerly Mould, father: painter, Informant: Devereux H. Jessop, father 5 Pickett Street, Temperley Road, Clapham.

394. Death certificate - Naomi Jane Baldwin, Hove Reg. Dist., Hove Sub-dist., County of East Sussex.

395. Marriage license - Herbert Alphonsus Baldwin/Naomi Jane Jessop, Victoria Baptist Chapel, Wandsworth Road, District of Wandsworth, County of London, England.

396. Marriage license - Herbert Alphonsus Baldwin/Naomi Jane Jessop, Victoria Baptist Chapel, Wandsworth Road, District of Wandsworth, County of London, England, May 23, 1904, Herbert Alphonsus Baldwin/Naomi Jane Jessop, 25 years/24 years, bachelor/spinster, butcher (master)/none, 73 Honeybrook Road, Clapham/86 High Road, Balham, Father: Philip James Baldwin/Devereux Henry Jessop, Profession: Joiner (journeyman)/Builder (master), Witnesses: D H Jessop, P J Baldwin, M Jones, J Jessop.

397. Marriage license - Herbert Alphonsus Baldwin/Naomi Jane Jessop, Victoria Baptist Chapel, Wandsworth Road, District of Wandsworth, County of London, England.

398. Census - 1881 Newington, Surrey, England, FHL Film 1341123, PRO Ref RG11, Piece 0541, Folio 31, Page 18, "Herbert A. Baldwin, son, unmarried, 2 years old, male, Birthplace: Camberwell, Dwelling: 3 Palmerston St."

399. *GRO birth index for England*, 4th Quarter 1878, San Salvior, South London, England.

400. Family Bible in possession of Jane Baldwin, October 2003, Jane has a family Bible which indicates Herbert died on April 15, 1938. April 15 was Good Friday in 1938 so according to this he died on Good Friday.

401. *Telephone interview of Mona Baldwin by Richard Klapper*, December 21, 2003.

402. Death certificate - Naomi Jane Baldwin, Hove Reg. Dist., Hove Sub-dist., County of East Sussex.

403. Census - 1901, Balham, England, "Naino Jessop, Daughter, single, 20, Occ: cashier, Birthplace: Surrey, Balham, Dwelling: 86 Balham High Road."

404. Marriage license - Herbert Alphonsus Baldwin/Naomi Jane Jessop, Victoria Baptist Chapel, Wandsworth Road, District of Wandsworth, County of London, England.

405. Interview of Mona Baldwin by Joan Bolton, September 2003.

406. Marriage license - Herbert Alphonsus Baldwin/Naomi Jane Jessop, Victoria Baptist Chapel, Wandsworth Road, District of Wandsworth, County of London, England.

407. Marriage license - Herbert Alphonsus Baldwin/Naomi Jane Jessop, Victoria Baptist Chapel, Wandsworth Road, District of Wandsworth, County of London, England, May 23, 1904, Herbert Alphonsus Baldwin/Naomi Jane Jessop, 25 years/24 years, bachelor/spinster, butcher (master)/none, 73 Honeybrook Road, Clapham/86 High Road, Balham, Father: Philip James Baldwin/Devereux Henry Jessop, Profession: Joiner (journeyman)/Builder (master), Witnesses: D H Jessop, P J Baldwin, M Jones, J Jessop.

408. E-mail from Kate Brooker to Richard Klapper, May 14, 2003, "Muriel Naomi ....she had two brothers. John died in infancy and Douglas died between the age 50-60."

409. Family Bible in possession of Jane Baldwin, November 5, 2003.

410. Census - 1881, Streatham, Surry, England, FHL Film: 1341154, PRO Ref: RG11, Piece 0664, Folio 116, Page 34, "Deveroux Jessop, son, 3 months old, male, Birthplace: Balham, Surrey, England, Dwelling: 55 Balham Grove."

411. *GRO birth index for England*, 1881 Mar Q, Wandsworth,.

412. Census - 1881, Streatham, Surry, England, FHL Film: 1341154, PRO Ref: RG11, Piece 0664, Folio 116, Page 34, "Deveroux Jessop, son, 3 months old, male, Birthplace: Balham, Surrey, England, Dwelling: 55 Balham Grove."

413. Birth Certificate - Devereux Henry Jessop, Wandsworth Reg. Dist, Streatham Sub-dist, County of Surrey, England, Devereux Henry Jessop, born on December 16, 1880 at 55 Balham Grove, father: Devereux Henry Jessop, mother: Jane Jessop formerly Mould, father is a plumber, informant: Devereux Henry Jessop father 55 Balham Grove.

414. Death certificate - Devereux H. Jessop, Epsom Reg. Dist., Carshalton Sub-dist., Surrey, England, "1914 June 12th. Driftway Road in the Parish of Banstead Surrey"   "The deceased was thrown from motor bicycle driven by himself and instantly killed - misadventure."   "Certificate received from Gilbert H. White Coroner for West Surrey. Inquest held 1?th June 1914 and by adjournment on the 24th June 1914."

415. Marriage Certificate - Devereux Jessop/Jesse Anscombe.

416. *GRO marriage index for England*, 1910, 3 Q 1910.

417. Marriage Certificate - Devereux Jessop/Jesse Anscombe.

418. Census - 1901, New Windsor, Berkshire, England, RG13, 1168, 111, 19, Sched # 145, Jessie Anscombe, daughter, unmarried, 12, female, born: Southwark, London, Dwelling: 23 Dagmar Rd.

419. Cemetery records, Sutton Cemetery, Sutton, London, England, The records show that Jane Jessop is buried in the same grave as her husband Devereux and her son Devereux Henry. Devereux Henry was buried June 16, 1914.

420. Death certificate - Devereux Henry Jessop, Epsom Reg. Dist., Carshalton Sub-dist., Surrey, England, "The deceased was thrown from motor bicycle driven by himself and instantly killed - misadventure."

421. Census - 1901, Balham, England, RG13, 474, 82, 6, Sched.# 29, "Deveroux H. Jessop, son, single, Occ: groom/worker, Birthplace: Surrey, Balham, Dwelling: 86 Balham High Road."

422. *GRO marriage index for England*, 1910, 3 Q 1910.

423. Marriage Certificate - Devereux Jessop/Jesse Anscombe.

424. Letter from Joan (Mould) Bolton to Richard James Klapper, January 9, 2001.

425. *GRO birth index for England*, 1885 Dec Q, Wandsworth.

426. Census - 1901, Balham, England, "Rose A. Jessop, Daughter, single, 15, Birthplace: Surrey, Balham, Dwelling: 86 Balham High Road."

427. Birth Certificate - Rose Anna Jessop, Wandsworth Reg. Dist, Streatham Sub-dist, County of Surrey, England, Rose Anna Jessop, born September 24, 1885 at 55 Balham Grove, father: Devereux Henry Jessop, mother: Jane Jessop formerly Mould, father is a house decorator, informant: Jane Jessop mother 55 Balham Grove Balham.

428. Death certificate - Rose Anna Brushett, Sutton Reg Dist, Sutton and Cheam sub dist, London Borough of Sutton, April 18, 1968, Rose Anna Brushett died at 31 Worcester Road, Sutton, female, 82 years old, Lived at 68 Lenham Road, Sutton. Wife of Frederick Brushett an insurance agent (retired). Cause of death: 1a. Cardiac failure, b. myocardial degeneration. Informant: J. Barnes occupier 31 Worcester Road, Sutton, Registered: April 19, 1968.

429. *GRO marriage index for England*, 1908 Sept Q, Wandsworth, Surrey, England.

430. Census - 1881, Lambeth, Surrey, England, FHL Film 1341136, RG11, 0596, 34, 10.

431. Census - 1901, London, England, RG13, 248, 6, 4, Sched. #33, Frederick Thomas Brushett, son, single, male, 21, Birthplace: London Holborn, Occ: Cheesemonger Asst, Address: 12 Leather Lane.

432. Marriage certificate - Frederick Thomas Brushett/Rose Anna Jessop, Wandsworth Reg. Dist., County of London, St. Peters Presbyterian Church of England, Wandsworth, Surrey, England.

433. Census - 1881, Lambeth, Surrey, England, FHL Film 1341136, RG11, 0596, 34, 10.

434. GRO death index for England.

435. Death certificate - Frederick Thomas Brushett, Sutton Reg Dist, Sutton and Cheam Sub-dist, London, England, Frederick Thomas Brushett died August 24, 1968 in Sutton General Hospital. Male, 88 years old, retired insurance official, lived at 68 Lenham Road, Sutton. Cause of death: 1a: Acute left ventricular failure, 1b: Ischaemic heart disease. Informant: H.J. Brushett, daughter of 31 Worcester Road, Sutton.

436. Death certificate - Rose Anna Brushett, Sutton reg dist, Sutton and Cheam sub dist, London borough of Sutton, April 18, 1968, Rose Anna Brushett died at 31 Worcester Road, Sutton, female, 82 years old, Lived at 68 Lenham Road, Sutton. Wife of Frederick Brushett an insurance agent (retired). Cause of death: 1a. Cardiac failure, b. myocardial degeneration. Informant: J. Barnes occupier 31 Worcester Road, Sutton, Registered: April 19, 1968.

437. E-mail from Eileen Adkins to Richard Klapper, April 10, 2006, "The other story about Mrs. Brushett's family was that she had some Spanish blood. She and Joan were slightly swarthy in skin colour as the Spanish are."

438. Address book of Rebecca (Mould) Mackness, Before 1946, Rebecca Mould who died in 1946 had the following entry in her address book: Mrs. Fred Brushett, Avonside, 62 Lenham Road, Sutton, Surrey, England.

439. Death certificate - Frederick Thomas Brushett, Sutton Reg dist, Sutton and Cheam sub-dist, London, England, Frederick Thomas Brushett died August 24, 1968 in Sutton General Hospital. Male, 88 years old, retired insurance official, lived at 68 Lenham Road, Sutton. Cause of death: 1a: Acute left ventricular failure, 1b: Ischaemic heart disease. Informant: H.J. Brushett, daughter of 31 Worcester Road, Sutton.

440. Marriage certificate - Frederick Thomas Brushett/Rose Anna Jessop, Wandworth Reg. Dist., County of London, St. Peters Presbyterian Church of England, Wandsworth, Surrey, England.

441. Census - 1881, Lambeth, Surrey, England, FHL Film 1341136, RG11, 0596, 34, 10.

442. Marriage certificate - Frederick Thomas Brushett/Rose Anna Jessop, Wandsworth Reg. Dist., County of London, St. Peters Presbyterian Church of England, Wandsworth, Surrey, England.

443. Birth certificate - Helena Joan Brushett, Wandsworth Reg. District, Streatham Sub-dist., County of London.

444. GRO death index for England, November 1996, "Brushett, Joan Helena   Reg. Dist. Sutton   1996   November Dist# 2541B   Reg# B7B   Entry# 270   Dor 1196."

445. Newspaper obituary - Joan Brushett, Unknown newspaper but most likely the local Sutton, Surrey, England newspaper, BRUSHETT – On November 4, 1996 HELENA JOAN. Service at Cheam Road Hall, 14 Cheam Road, Sutton, Surrey on Wednesday November 13, 1996 at 12.30 p.m. followed by interment at Sutton Cemetery at 1.30 p.m. Donations, if desired, to The Trinitarian Bible Society, Tyndale House, Dorset Road, London 3NN or flowers to W.A. Truelove & Son, 118 Carshalton Road, Sutton, Surrey.   "With Christ" Philippians 1-23. .

446. E-mail from Eileen Adkins to Richard Klapper, April 10, 2006, "It was always thought that Mrs. Brushett had money - this was because Joan was sent to a private school, Sutton High School. For a butcher's employee to afford private school fees was quite unusual."

447. E-mail from Eileen Adkins to Richard Klapper, April 10, 2006, "The other story about Mrs. Brushett's family was that she had some Spanish blood. She and Joan were slightly swarthy in skin colour as the Spanish are."

448. E-mail from Eileen Adkins to Richard Klapper, April 6, 2006, "My husban's family had friends called Brushett who lived in Lenham Road, Sutton. Their daughter who was born in 1910 was a dispenser at the local hospital and became a friend, although a good bit older than she, of my husband's sister."

449. E-mail from Eileen Adkins to Richard Klapper, April 7, 2006, "As you've guessed a dispenser dispenses medicines. We aren't sure whether Joan would have had any college training or whether she learnt on the job. The latter is I think more likely. It couldn't happen today but she probably left school on the middle 1920s, more than 20 years before the National Health came into being. Sutton & Cheam Hospital where she worked was originally founded by subscription from wealthy local folk and it provided a very good service. It is still going today."

450. Death certificate - Frederick Thomas Jessop, Reg Dist of Eastbourne, Sub-dist of Eastbourne, County Borough of

Eastbourne, Informant information: "N.T. Brushett, niece, 68 Lenham Road, Sutton, Surrey" Note: It is virtually certain that the N.T. Brushett should be H. J. Brushett. I am certain that the H.J. was incorrectly typed on the death cert copy and was mis-read from the writing on the original.

451. *Record book kept in late 1800s by Rector of St. Pega's Church, Peakirk, Northamptonshire, England*, "Sec Harold 11890."

452. Family tree by Sheila Rose, July 2001.

453. *Record book kept in late 1800s by Rector of St. Pega's Church, Peakirk, Northamptonshire, England*, "Sec Harold 1893" (probably baptism).

454. E-mail from John Trevor Prentice to Richard Klapper, February 12, 2002, "My father George Harold Prentice, who was always known as Harold was born on 13th July, 1890." NOTE: This is incorrect. Sheila Rose later said Harold was born June 13 not July 13. It didn't make sense that Harold was born and baptised on the same day.

455. *Telephone interview of Sheila Rose by Richard Klapper*, February 20, 2004, Sheila said her brother was wrong about her father's birthday. Harold was born on June 13, 1890 - not July 13.

456. Family tree by Sheila Rose, July 2001.

457. E-mail from John Trevor Prentice to Richard Klapper, February 12, 2002, "He died on 5th April 1975, in Chipping Norton Memorial Hospital. He was buried with my mother in Churchill."

458. Family tree by Sheila Rose, July 2001.

459. *Parish Registers - Peakirk, Northants, England*, Marriage records.

460. Family tree by Sheila Rose, July 2001.

461. E-mail from John Trevor Prentice to Richard Klapper, January 31, 2002, "My Mother was born on 1st March 1893 in Deeping St. James, Lincolnshire. She died on 1st March 1984 at Y Gorlan, Cross Inn, Llandyssul, Wales, and was buried in Churchill Oxfordshire."

462. Family tree by Sheila Rose, July 2001.

463. E-mail from John Trevor Prentice to Richard Klapper, January 31, 2002, "My Mother was born on 1st March 1893 in Deeping St. James, Lincolnshire. She died on 1st March 1984 at Y Gorlan, Cross Inn, Llandyssul, Wales, and was buried in Churchill Oxfordshire."

464. *Parish Registers - Peakirk, Northants, England*, Baptism records, page 67, No. 533, July 13, 1890, George Harold son of John William and Rose Prentice of Peakirk, a baker.

465. E-mail from John Trevor Prentice to Richard Klapper, February 12, 2002, "He died on 5th April 1975, in Chipping Norton Memorial Hospital. He was buried with my mother in Churchill."

466. *Telephone interview of Sheila Rose by Richard Klapper*, February 20, 2004, Sheila expanded on the information I received from her brother. She said her parents were cremated and their ashes were buried in Churchill. They are buried next to each other and each has a flat headstone. The cemetery they are buried in is not the churchyard at All Saints Church. They are in the cemetery in town which was an old churchyard but the church is no longer there.

467. Family tree by Sheila Rose, July 2001.

468. Census - 1901, Peakirk, Northants, England, RG13, 1467, 46,5, Sched.# 30.

469. E-mail from John Trevor Prentice to Richard Klapper, January 31, 2002, "My Mother was born on 1st March 1893 in Deeping St. James, Lincolnshire. She died on 1st March 1984 at Y Gorlan, Cross Inn, Llandyssul, Wales, and was buried in Churchill Oxfordshire."

470. *Telephone interview of Sheila Rose by Richard Klapper*, February 20, 2004, Sheila expanded on the information I received from her brother. She said her parents were cremated and their ashes were buried in Churchill. They are buried next to each other and each has a flat headstone. The cemetery they are buried in is not the churchyard at All Saints Church. They are in the cemetery in town which was an old churchyard but the church is no longer there.

471. *Parish Registers - Peakirk, Northants, England*, Marriage records.

472. Information from Freda Neaverson, May 20, 2001 e-mail from Graham Garrett to Richard Klapper, "Freda also adds the following comments "I knew Misses Ellen, Lilian and Dora also Frederick and Harold.'"

473. Birth certificate - John Frederick Prentice, Peterborough reg. dist., Crowland sub-dist, counties of Lincoln and Northampton, England, June 30, 1893, no.112.

474. *Record book kept in late 1800s by Rector of St. Pega's Church, Peakirk, Northamptonshire, England*, " Jn Frederick 1893" (probably baptism).

475. Birth certificate - John Frederick Prentice, Crowland Sub-district, England.

476. Death certificate - John Frederick Prentice, Worthing Reg Dist., Littlehampton Sub-dist., West Sussex County, England.

477. Family tree by Sheila Rose, July 2001.

478. Marriage Certificate - John Frederick Prentice/Jessie Smellie, April 11, 1925.

479. Family tree by Sheila Rose, July 2001.

480. Birth certificate - Jessie Edith Smellie, Highbury Sub-district, England.

481. Family tree by Sheila Rose, July 2001.

482. Letter from John Robert Prentice, February 20, 2002.

483. Death certificate - Jessie Prentice, Worthing Reg. Dist., Worthing Sub-dist., West Sussex, England.

484. *Parish Registers - Peakirk, Northants, England*, Baptism registers, page 71, No. 561, Aug 6, 1893, John Frederick son of John William and Rose Prentice of Peakirk, a baker.

485. Letter from John Robert Prentice, February 20, 2002.

486. Death certificate - John Frederick Prentice, Worthing Reg. Dist., Littlehampton Sub-dist., West Sussex County, England.

487. *Telephone interview of John Robert Prentice by Richard Klapper*, February 20, 2004, John found a certificate which indicated that Frederick graduated from London Chelsea St. Marks Training College and became a certified teacher in August 1913. There is also a certificate which indicates that Frederick completed one year of service on January 14, 1915.
488. Family tree by Sheila Rose, July 2001.
489. Census - 1901, Peakirk, Northants, England, RG13, 1467, 46,5, Sched.# 30.
490. Letter from John Robert Prentice, February 20, 2002.
491. Death certificate - Jessie Prentice, Worthing Reg. Dist., Worthing Sub-dist., West Sussex, England.
492. Marriage Certificate - John Frederick Prentice/Jessie Smellie, Bounds Green, Middlesex, England.
493. Marriage Certificate - John Frederick Prentice/Jessie Smellie, April 11, 1925.
494. Cemetery records - Glen Abby Memorial Park, Bonita, California, June 26, 2000.
495. *Rose Lovell Obituary in Aberdeen, South Dakota newspaper*, January 30, 1973.
496. Cemetery records - Glen Abby Memorial Park, Bonita, California, June 26, 2000.
497. *Rose Lovell Obituary in Aberdeen, South Dakota newspaper*, January 30, 1973.
498. Cemetery records - Glen Abby Memorial Park, Bonita, California, June 26, 2000.
499. Grave headstone - George Henry Lovell, June 26, 2000.
500. Census - 1891, Higham Ferrers, Northampton, England, Hind Stile, Higham Ferrers, enumeration dist 6, page 17., George Lovell, son, 5 years old, scholar, Birthplace: Higham Ferrers.
501. Interview letter with Hazel Ritter, July 5, 2000.
502. Marriage license - George H. Lovell/Rose Mould, Aberdeen, Brown County, South Dakota.
503. Cemetery records - Glen Abby Memorial Park, Bonita, California, June 26, 2000.
504. Census - 1891, Higham Ferrers, Northampton, England, Hind Stile, Higham Ferrers, enumeration dist 6, page 17., George Lovell, son, 5 years old, scholar, Birthplace: Higham Ferrers.
505. Cemetery records - Glen Abby Memorial Park, Bonita, California, June 26, 2000.
506. *Telephone interview of Hazel Ritter by Richard Klapper*, August 17, 2002.
507. *Rose Lovell Obituary in Aberdeen, South Dakota newspaper*, January 30, 1973.
508. Grave headstone - Rose Lovell, June 26, 2000, Glen Abby Memorial Park, Bonita, California - Section 74, Block 68, Lot 6.
509. Ellis Island Arrival Records, May 1, 1911 - ship: Baltic.
510. *US Census - 1930, Aberdeen, Brown County, South Dakota*, Enumeration district 7-8, sheet # 12A, Rose M Lovell, wife, female, white, 44, married, 25 at time of first marriage, able to read and write, born: England, immigrated to the US in 1911, naturalized citizen, Residence: 312 Seventh Ave.
511. Census - 1901, Rushden, Northants, England, RG13, 1440, 124, 35, Sched.# 228.
512. *Social Security Death Index*.
513. Grave headstone - George Henry Lovell, June 26, 2000, Glen Abby Memorial Park, Bonita, California - Section 74, Block 68. Lot 5.
514. Ellis Island Arrival Records, March 24, 1906 on the ship Cedric.
515. *US Census - 1910, Aberdeen, Brown County, South Dakota*, Enumeration district 53, sheet # 2A, George Lovell, lodger, male, white, 26, single, born: England, immigrated to US in 1906, naturalized citizen, city engineer, able to read and write.
516. *US Census - 1930, Aberdeen, Brown County, South Dakota*, Enumeration district 7-8, sheet # 12A, George H Lovell, head, owns home worth $5,000 and owns a radio, male, white, 45, married, 26 when first married, able to read and write, born: England, immigrated to US in 1906, a naturalized citizen, grocery storekeeper, not a US veteran, residence: 312 Seventh Ave.
517. *US Census - 1920, Aberdeen, Brown County, South Dakota*, Enumeration District 44, Sheet # 6B, George H Lovell, head, owns house, male, white, 35, married, immigration to US 1906, naturalized citizen in 1913, can read and write, born: England, Storekeeper (groceries), Residence: Seventh Ave SE.
518. Grave headstone - George Henry Lovell, The Masonic emblem is on George's headstone.
519. *US Census - 1920, Aberdeen, Brown County, South Dakota*, Enumeration District 44, Sheet # 6B, George H Lovell, head, owns house, male, white, 35, married, immigration to US 1906, naturalized citizen in 1913, can read and write, born: England, Storekeeper (groceries), Residence: Seventh Ave SE.
520. Interview letter with Hazel Ritter, July 5, 2000.
521. Marriage license - George H. Lovell/Rose Mould, Aberdeen, Brown County, South Dakota.
522. Interview with Don Mould and Hazel Ritter, June 26, 2000.
523. Interview letter with Hazel Ritter, July 5, 2000.
524. *Telephone call between Richard Klapper and George Mould (Hazel Ritter's nephew)*, January 4, 2003.
525. Grave headstone - Clarence Alva Ritter, June 26, 2000.
526. Interview with Don Mould and Hazel Ritter, June 26, 2000.
527. Grave headstone - Clarence Alva Ritter, June 26, 2000.
528. Cemetery records - Glen Abby Memorial Park, Bonita, California, June 26, 2000.
529. *Telephone interview of Hazel Ritter by Richard Klapper*, August 17, 2002.
530. Grave headstone - Clarence Alva Ritter, June 26, 2000.
531. Cemetery records - Glen Abby Memorial Park, Bonita, California, June 26, 2000.
532. *Telephone interview of Hazel Ritter by Richard Klapper*, August 17, 2002.
533. *Telephone call between Richard Klapper and George Mould (Hazel Ritter's nephew)*, January 4, 2003, George indicated that Hazel is not buried next to her husband Alva but about 6 or 8 graves away.

534. *Telephone call between Richard Klapper and George Mould (Hazel Ritter's nephew)*, January 4, 2003, George indicated that Hazel had a heart pacemaker put in and while in the hospital she caught an antibiotic resistant bacteria in her colon. She had bad diarrhea for weeks before she died.

535. *US Census - 1930, Aberdeen, Brown County, South Dakota*, Enumeration district 7-8, sheet # 12A, Hazel C Lovell, daughter, female, white, 19, single, able to read and write, born: South Dakota, clerk in a grocery store, residence: 312 Seventh Ave.

536. *US Census - 1920, Aberdeen, Brown County, South Dakota*, Enumeration District 44, Sheet # 6B, Hazel C Lovell, daughter, female, white, age:?, single, born: South Dakota, Residence: Seventh Ave. SE.

537. *Social Security Death Index.*

538. Cemetery records - Glen Abby Memorial Park, Bonita, California, June 26, 2000, Glen Abby Memorial Park, Bonita, California - Section 10, Block 76, Lot 4.

539. Grave headstone - Clarence Alva Ritter, June 26, 2000.

540. *Social Security Death Index.*

541. Interview with Don Mould and Hazel Ritter, June 26, 2000.

542. Grave headstone - George Ewart Mould, June 26, 2000.

543. Interview with Don Mould and Hazel Ritter, June 26, 2000.

544. Grave headstone - George Ewart Mould, June 26, 2000.

545. *Telephone interview of Don Mould by Richard Klapper*, August 17, 2002.

546. Infant son of George E. Mould death certificate, B2, P127, No. 3666.

547. Interview with Don Mould and Hazel Ritter, June 26, 2000.

548. Interview letter with Hazel Ritter, July 5, 2000.

549. Grave headstone - Kate Mould, June 26, 2000, Glen Abby Memorial Park, Bonita, California - Section 79A, Block 68, Lot 1 Cemetery records differ from headstone saying the date of birth was July 10, 1883.

550. Interview with Don Mould and Hazel Ritter, June 26, 2000.

551. Grave headstone - Kate Mould, June 26, 2000.

552. *Telephone interview of Don Mould by Richard Klapper*, August 17, 2002.

553. Grave headstone - George Ewart Mould, June 26, 2000, Glen Abby Memorial Park, Bonita, California - Section 79A, Block 68, Lot 2.

554. Ellis Island Arrival Records, June 14, 1906, George came to the US on the ship Oceanic which arrived in New York on June 14, 1906 from Liverpool, England.

555. *US Census - 1910, Aberdeen, Brown County, South Dakota*, Enumeration district 53, sheet # 2A, George Mould, lodger, male, white, 24, single, born: England, immigrated to US in 1906, naturalized citizen, delivery driver, able to read and write.

556. Census - 1901, Rushden, Northants, England, RG13, 1440, 124, 35, Sched.# 228.

557. E-mail from Melinda Pendered Wade.

558. Ellis Island Arrival Records, December 24, 1919, ship manifest for ship Orduna, Jabez Mould listed on the ship's manifest his son George who lived at 8 Third Ave., Aberdeen, South Dakota.

559. *Social Security Death Index.*

560. Grave headstone - Kate Mould, June 26, 2000, Glen Abby Memorial Park, Bonita, California - Section 79A, Block 68, Lot 1.

561. *US Census - 1920, Aberdeen, Brown County, South Dakota*, Enumeration District 46, Sheet # 8A, Kate Mould, wife, female, white, 37, married, immigrated to US in 1911, can read and write, born: England, residence: Ninth Ave. SW.

562. Interview with Don Mould and Hazel Ritter, June 26, 2000.

563. Interview letter with Hazel Ritter, July 5, 2000.

564. Grave headstone - Constance Doreen Large, June 26, 2000.

565. Interview with Don Mould and Hazel Ritter, June 26, 2000.

566. Interview letter with Hazel Ritter, July 5, 2000.

567. Grave headstone - Constance Doreen Large, June 26, 2000.

568. *Telephone interview of Don Mould by Richard Klapper*, August 17, 2002.

569. Grave headstone of Thomas Harry Large, June 26, 2000.

570. Interview with Don Mould and Hazel Ritter, June 26, 2000.

571. Interview letter with Hazel Ritter.

572. Grave headstone of Thomas Harry Large, June 26, 2000.

573. *Telephone interview of Don Mould by Richard Klapper*, August 17, 2002.

574. Grave headstone of Thomas Harry Large, June 26, 2000.

575. *Telephone interview of Don Mould by Richard Klapper*, August 17, 2002.

576. Grave headstone - Constance Doreen Large.

577. *US Census - 1920, Aberdeen, Brown County, South Dakota*, Enumeration District 46, Sheet # 8A, Doreen Mould, daughter, female, white, 4, born: South Dakota, residence: Ninth ave. SW.

578. *Social Security Death Index.*

579. Grave headstone of Thomas Harry Large.

580. *Social Security Death Index.*

581. Interview with Don Mould and Hazel Ritter, June 26, 2000.

582. Interview letter with Hazel Ritter.

583. Infant son of George E. Mould death certificate, B2, P127, No. 3666.

584. *Riverside Memorial Park Cemetery records*, June 5, 2000, Block 60, Lot 47.

585. Interview with Don Mould and Hazel Ritter, June 26, 2000.

586. Interview with Don Mould and Hazel Ritter.

587. *Telephone interview of Don Mould by Richard Klapper*, August 28, 2003, Don called Helen Klapper and told her Marguerite had died today. Helen Klapper called me to relay the message.

588. *Social Security Death Index*.

589. Interview with Helen Bull Klapper.

590. *Postcard to W.R. Klapper from Fred and Annie Bull*, June 18, 1958.

591. *Aberdeen S.D. newspaper article on the death of Annie Beatrice Bull*, March 18, 1974.

592. Birth certificate - Annie Beatrice Bull, February 26, 2004, Joan Bolton called the County Registrar's Office and they looked at the birth certificate and indicated to Joan that the place of birth for Annie was Rushden - not Higham Ferrers.

593. *Aberdeen S.D. newspaper article on the death of Annie Beatrice Bull*, March 18, 1974.

594. Interview with Helen Bull Klapper.

595. *Aberdeen, S.D. newspaper article on death of Fred Albert Bull*, November 26, 1982.

596. Funeral bulletin for Fred A. Bull, November 27, 1982.

597. *Postcard to W.R. Klapper from Fred and Annie Bull*, June 18, 1958.

598. Funeral bulletin for Fred A. Bull, November 27, 1982.

599. *Aberdeen S.D. newspaper article on the death of Annie Beatrice Bull*, March 18, 1974.

600. Ellis Island Arrival Records, July 27, 1912, Arrived on the ship Baltic.

601. *Postcard from Fred Bull to William R. Klapper*, June 18, 1958.

602. Ellis Island Arrival Records, July 27, 1912, When Annie arrived at Ellis Island on the Baltic she listed her occupation as milliner.

603. Census - 1901, Rushden, Northants, England, RG13, 1440, 124, 35, Sched.# 228.

604. Funeral bulletin for Fred A. Bull, November 27, 1982.

605. Ellis Island Arrival Records, Ship manifest for Cedric, Arrived: March 24, 1906, from Liverpool, England, Bull, Fred Albert, Male, 15 years 9 Months, Single, England, English, Place of origin: Rushden.

606. *Postcard from Fred Bull to William R. Klapper*, June 18, 1958.

607. Census - 1901, Rushden, Northants, England, PG13, 1441, 88, 23, Sched.#139.

608. *Aberdeen, S.D. newspaper article on death of Fred Albert Bull*, November 26, 1982.

609. Interview with Alfred and Lois Bull, May 26, 2000.

610. E-mail from Marjorie Redford to Richard James Klapper, January 2, 2001.

611. *Telephone interview of Marge Redford by Richard Klapper*, October 19, 2003, Marge said her Mother died in Marge's home in torrence, CA. Marge was the one who found her. Marge had her mother sent back to Portland, Oregon to be buried in the same mausoleum as Esther's husband Frank.

612. *Telephone interview of Marge Redford by Richard Klapper*, October 19, 2003, Marge said that her father Frank and her mother Esther were both buried in a mausoleum in Portland, Oregon.

613. Ellis Island Arrival Records, October 16, 1906, Frank Mackness arrived Ellis Island from Liverpool, England on the ship Carmania on October 16, 1906.

614. *Telephone interview of Marge Redford by Richard Klapper*, October 19, 2003, Marge said that Joseph Thomas and his son Frank both became US citizens and she has the papers for Frank. She also believed her grandmother, Rebecca Mackness became a US citizen also but Marge doesn't have any papers on that.

615. E-mail from Marjorie Redford to Richard James Klapper, December 1, 2003.

616. Ellis Island Arrival Records, October 16, 1906, ship manifest for the ship Carmania, Frank listed his occupation as grocer in the ship's manifest.

617. Census 1891 - Rushden, Northamptonshire, England, RG13, 1441, 80, 8,Sched.# 49.

618. *Telephone interview of Marge Redford by Richard Klapper*, October 19, 2003, Marge said that her father Frank and her mother Esther were both buried in a mausoleum in Portland, Oregon.

619. *Telephone interview of Marge Redford by Richard Klapper*, October 19, 2003, Marge said her parents moved from Lead, SD to Ellensburg, Washington in 1943 and lived there for about a year and then moved to Portland, Oregon in 1944 to follow Marge who had moved there to work.

620. E-mail from Marjorie Redford to Richard James Klapper, January 2, 2001.

621. Letter from Joan (Mould) Bolton to Richard James Klapper, January 9, 2001.

622. Census - 1901, Higham Ferrers, England, RG13, 1440, 46, 46, Sched.# 296.

623. *GRO birth index for England*.

624. *Telephone interview of Jeffrey Roberts*, February 28, 2004, "Violet was born 23, Nov 1897" NOTE: Jeffrey is very certain of Violet's birth date. The GRO Index indicates that Violet was born 1Q 1898 which would mean she was not registered for a couple of months after her birth.

625. Death certificate - Violet Roberts, Wellingborough reg dist, Wellingborough sub-dist, Northants, England, Violet Roberts died on January 8, 1982 in The Poplars, Thrapston Road, Finedon, Northants, England. She was born November 23, 1897 in Higham Ferrers, Northants, England. She lived at 50 Wellingborough Road, Rushden, Northants. The informant was Jeffrey David Roberts a son who lives at 23 Ascot Road, Gravesend, Kent. Cause of death: 1a Congestive Cardiac Failure 1b Myocardial Ischaemia 1c Coronary Atherosclerosis.

626. GRO death index for England, 1 Q 1982, Roberts, Violet 23 NO 1897 Wellingboro 7 3169.

627. Death certificate - Violet Roberts, Wellingborough reg dist, Wellingborough sub-dist, Northants, England, Violet Roberts died on January 8, 1982 in The Poplars, Thrapston Road, Finedon, Northants, England. She was born November 23, 1897 in Higham Ferrers, Northants, England. She lived at 50 Wellingborough Road, Rushden, Northants. The informant was Jeffrey David Roberts a son who lives at 23 Ascot Road, Gravesend, Kent. Cause of death: 1a Congestive Cardiac Failure 1b Myocardial Ischaemia 1c Coronary Atherosclerosis.

628. Family tree by Trevor Mould, May 16, 2002.

629. Grave headstone - Robert Edward Roberts, April 2003, Headstone inscription in Higham Ferrers Cemetery in Higham Ferrers, Northants, England says "IN LOVING MEMORY OF / ROBERT EDWARD ROBERTS. / BELOVED WIFE OF VIOLET / DIED 12th FEBRUARY 1971 / AGED 73 YEARS."

630. *Telephone interview of Pauline Spiller and Jeffrey Roberts by Richard Klapper*, February 24, 2004, Jeffrey said Robert and Violet were married in 1921 or 1922 in the Methodist Chapel in Higham Ferrers. NOTE: A picture of Robert and Violet's wedding is labeled 1920 so that is the date I've used.

631. *GRO marriage index for England*, 4 Q 1920, 4 Q 1920 Violet Mould married Roberts Wellingbro' 3 b 437.

632. Grave headstone - Robert Edward Roberts, April 2003, Headstone inscription in Higham Ferrers Cemetery in Higham Ferrers, Northants, England says "IN LOVING MEMORY OF / ROBERT EDWARD ROBERTS. / BELOVED WIFE OF VIOLET / DIED 12th FEBRUARY 1971 / AGED 73 YEARS."

633. *Telephone interview of Jeffrey Roberts*, February 28, 2004.

634. Grave headstone - Robert Edward Roberts, April 2003, Headstone inscription in Higham Ferrers Cemetery in Higham Ferrers, Northants, England says "IN LOVING MEMORY OF / ROBERT EDWARD ROBERTS. / BELOVED HUSBAND OF VIOLET / DIED 12th FEBRUARY 1971 / AGED 73 YEARS."

635. *Telephone interview of Jeffrey Roberts*, February 28, 2004.

636. Obituary - Bob Roberts, The Wellingborough News, Friday, February 19, 1971, page 2, "Suddenly on Feb. 12 1971 at the General Hospital, kettering, Robert Edward aged 73 yeqrs, ..."

637. *Telephone interview of Jeffrey Roberts*, February 28, 2004, "Violet is buried in an unmarked grave just a few steps from her husband Robert. Violet made sure they put a headstone on her husbands grave but there is not a headstone on her grave. There was a problem so she could not be buried in the same grave as her husband so she was buried close by."

638. Death certificate - Violet Roberts, Wellingborough reg dist, Wellingborough sub-dist, Northants, England, Violet Roberts died on January 8, 1982 in The Poplars, Thrapston Road, Finedon, Northants, England. She was born November 23, 1897 in Higham Ferrers, Northants, England. She lived at 50 Wellingborough Road, Rushden, Northants. The informant was Jeffrey David Roberts a son who lives at 23 Ascot Road, Gravesend, Kent. Cause of death: 1a Congestive Cardiac Failure 1b Myocardial Ischaemia 1c Coronary Atherosclerosis.

639. Census - 1901, Higham Ferrers, England, RG13, 1440, 46, 46, Sched.# 296.

640. Grave headstone - Robert Edward Roberts, April 2003, Headstone inscription in Higham Ferrers Cemetery in Higham Ferrers, Northants, England says "IN LOVING MEMORY OF / ROBERT EDWARD ROBERTS. / BELOVED WIFE OF VIOLET / DIED 12th FEBRUARY 1971 / AGED 73 YEARS."

641. Obituary - Bob Roberts, The Wellingborough News, Friday, February 19, 1971, page 2, "Interred at Higham Ferrers on Wednesday."

642. Death certificate - Violet Roberts, Wellingborough reg dist, Wellingborough sub-dist, Northants, England, Violet Roberts died on January 8, 1982 in The Poplars, Thrapston Road, Finedon, Northants, England. She was born November 23, 1897 in Higham Ferrers, Northants, England. She lived at 50 Wellingborough Road, Rushden, Northants. The informant was Jeffrey David Roberts a son who lives at 23 Ascot Road, Gravesend, Kent. Cause of death: 1a Congestive Cardiac Failure 1b Myocardial Ischaemia 1c Coronary Atherosclerosis.

643. *Telephone interview of Pauline Spiller and Jeffrey Roberts by Richard Klapper*, February 24, 2004, Jeffrey said Robert and Violet were married in 1921 or 1922 in the Methodist Chapel in Higham Ferrers. NOTE: A picture of Robert and Violet's wedding is labeled 1920 so that is the date I've used.

644. *GRO marriage index for England*, 4 Q 1920, 4 Q 1920 Violet Mould married Roberts Wellingbro' 3 b 437.

645. Family tree by Trevor Mould, May 16, 2002.

646. Death certificate - Violet Roberts, Wellingborough reg dist, Wellingborough sub-dist, Northants, England, Violet Roberts died on January 8, 1982 in The Poplars, Thrapston Road, Finedon, Northants, England. She was born November 23, 1897 in Higham Ferrers, Northants, England. She lived at 50 Wellingborough Road, Rushden, Northants. The informant was Jeffrey David Roberts a son who lives at 23 Ascot Road, Gravesend, Kent. Cause of death: 1a Congestive Cardiac Failure 1b Myocardial Ischaemia 1c Coronary Atherosclerosis.

647. *Telephone interview of Pauline Spiller and Jeffrey Roberts by Richard Klapper*, February 24, 2004, Jeffrey said his date of birth was October 10, 1925.

648. *Telephone interview of Jeffrey Roberts*, February 28, 2004, "Jeffrey, Pauline and John were all born in Higham Ferrers."

649. Telephone call between Joan Bolton and Joyce King, November 2007.

650. Death certificate - Violet Roberts, Wellingborough reg dist, Wellingborough sub-dist, Northants, England, Violet Roberts died on January 8, 1982 in The Poplars, Thrapston Road, Finedon, Northants, England. She was born November 23, 1897 in Higham Ferrers, Northants, England. She lived at 50 Wellingborough Road, Rushden, Northants. The informant was Jeffrey David Roberts a son who lives at 23 Ascot Road, Gravesend, Kent. Cause of death: 1a Congestive Cardiac Failure 1b Myocardial Ischaemia 1c Coronary Atherosclerosis.

651. Family tree by Trevor Mould, May 16, 20022.

652. Death certificate - Jessie Barrett, Northampton reg dist, Northampton sub-dist, Northants, England, Jessie Barrett died on July 2, 1977 in St. Edmund's Hospital, Northampton, Northants. She was born October 22, 1894 in Higham Ferrers,

Northant. She was the widow of John Barrett a boot and shoe operative. She lived at 118 St. James Park Road, Northampton. The informant was Pauline Hilda May Spiller, her niece who lived at Corner House, Keyston, Huntingdon, Cambs. Cause of death: 1a Cerebro-vascular Episode with (L) hemiplegia   1b Parkinson's Disease.

653. *Telephone interview of Pauline Spiller and Jeffrey Roberts by Richard Klapper*, February 24, 2004, Pauline said she was born on July 15, 1927.

654. *Telephone interview of Jeffrey Roberts*, February 28, 2004, "Jeffrey, Pauline and John were all born in Higham Ferrers."

655. Family tree by Trevor Mould, May 16, 2002.

656. *Telephone interview of Jeffrey Roberts*, February 28, 2004.

657. Death certificate - Jessie Barrett, Northampton reg dist, Northampton sub-dist, Northants, England, Jessie Barrett died on July 2, 1977 in St. Edmund's Hospital, Northampton, Northants. She was born October 22, 1894 in Higham Ferrers, Northant. She was the widow of John Barrett a boot and shoe operative. She lived at 118 St. James Park Road, Northampton. The informant was Pauline Hilda May Spiller, her niece who lived at Corner House, Keyston, Huntingdon, Cambs. Cause of death: 1a Cerebro-vascular Episode with (L) hemiplegia   1b Parkinson's Disease.

658. *Telephone interview of Jeffrey Roberts*, February 28, 2004.

659. Letter from Joan (Mould) Bolton to Richard James Klapper, January 9, 2001.

660. *GRO birth index for England.*

661. GRO death index for England, March 1988 death index, Eaton, Lily   9 March 1902   Wellingboro   1988 March Vol. No. 7, Page No. 3112, Reg. No. 388 The death index entry gives Lily's exact birth date.

662. Death certificate - Lily Eaton, Wellingborough reg dist, Wellingborough sub-dist, Northants, Lily Eaton died March 1, 1988 at The Poplars Marshalls Road, Raunds, Northants, England. Born: 9th March 1902 in Higham Ferrers, Northants, she was the widow of Hubert Jim Eaton, a boot and shoe clicker (retired) and she lived at 20 Commercial Street, Higham Ferrers, Northants. The informant was Ivy Doreen Lovell, her sister, who lived at 1 Glassbrook Road, Rushden, Northants. Cause of death: 1a Bronchopneumonia.

663. Death certificate - Lily Eaton, Wellingborough reg dist, Wellingborough sub-dist, Northants, England, Lily Eaton died March 1, 1988 at The Poplars Marshalls Road, Raunds, Northants, England. Born: 9th March 1902 in Higham Ferrers, Northants, she was the widow of Hubert Jim Eaton, a boot and shoe clicker (retired) and she lived at 20 Commercial Street, Higham Ferrers, Northants. The informant was Ivy Doreen Lovell, her sister, who lived at 1 Glassbrook Road, Rushden, Northants. Cause of death: 1a Bronchopneumonia.

664. Family tree by Trevor Mould, May 16, 2002.

665. GRO death index for England, 4Q 1981, Eaton, Hubert Jim   12 April 1909   Wellingboro   7 2876.

666. *GRO marriage index for England*, 4Q 1929, Eaton, Hubert J.   Mould   Wellingbro'   3b 367.

667. GRO death index for England, 4Q 1981, Eaton, Hubert Jim   12 April 1909   Wellingboro   7 2876.

668. Death certificate - Lily Eaton, Wellingborough reg dist, Wellingborough sub-dist, Northants, Lily Eaton died March 1, 1988 at The Poplars Marshalls Road, Raunds, Northants, England. Born: 9th March 1902 in Higham Ferrers, Northants, she was the widow of Hubert Jim Eaton, a boot and shoe clicker (retired) and she lived at 20 Commercial Street, Higham Ferrers, Northants. The informant was Ivy Doreen Lovell, her sister, who lived at 1 Glassbrook Road, Rushden, Northants. Cause of death: 1a Bronchopneumonia.

669. Death certificate - Lily Eaton, Wellingborough Reg dist, Wellingborough sub-dist, Northants, Lily Eaton died March 1, 1988 at The Poplars Marshalls Road, Raunds, Northants, England. Born: 9th March 1902 in Higham Ferrers, Northants, she was the widow of Hubert Jim Eaton, a boot and shoe clicker (retired) and she lived at 20 Commercial Street, Higham Ferrers, Northants. The informant was Ivy Doreen Lovell, her sister, who lived at 1 Glassbrook Road, Rushden, Northants. Cause of death: 1a Bronchopneumonia.

670. *GRO marriage index for England*, 4Q 1929, Eaton, Hubert J.   Mould   Wellingbro'   3b 367.

671. Family tree by Trevor Mould, May 16, 2002.

672. *GRO birth index for England*, 4Q 1931, Eaton, Peter   Mould   Wellingbro'   3b 158.

673. *Telephone interview of Philip Mould by Richard Klapper*, February 23, 2004, "He (Peter) married in England and had several children. He and his wife divorced and he immigrated to Australia. He took two of his sons with him. The oldest son was electrocuted on a farm in Australia."

674. Interview with Joan Mould, September 16, 2000, " Bernard, my father, was one of 8 children (6 daughters and 2 sons) of Charles Mould. Bernard, his wife and his brother were cremated at the crematorium at Kettering and are in the Book of Rememberances there at the crematorium." Bernard and his wife are in the Book of Rememberances at the Methodist Church in Higham Ferrers also."

675. Letter from Joan (Mould) Bolton to Richard James Klapper, January 9, 2001.

676. Letter from Trevor Gilbert Mould to Joan Bolton, December 2002.

677. *GRO birth index for England.*

678. *Phone call between Trevor Mould and Joan (Mould) Bolton*, November 2002, Trevor's wife indicated that Bernard's birthday was August 20.

679. Letter from Trevor Gilbert Mould to Joan Bolton. December 2002.

680. Death certificate - Bernard William Mould, Wellingborough Reg. Dist., Wellingborough Sub-dist., Northants, County.

681. Death certificate - Jane Margaretta Mould, Wellingborough Reg. Dist., Wellingborough Sub-dist., Northants, County.

682. Family tree by Trevor Mould, May 16, 2002.

683. Death certificate - Jane Margaretta Mould, Wellingborough Reg. Dist., Wellingborough Sub-dist., Northants, County.

684. Interview with Joan Mould, September 16, 2000, " My father, Bernard, and his wife were cremated in the crematorium in Kettering. His brother was also cremated there. They are in the Book of Rememberances at the crematorium. My parents

are also in the Book of Rememberances in the Methodist Church in Higham Ferrers."

685. Death certificate - Bernard William Mould, Wellingborough Reg. Dist., Wellingborough Sub-dist., Northants, County.

686. Letter from Trevor Gilbert Mould to Joan Bolton, December 2002.

687. Death certificate - Jane Margaretta Mould, Wellingborough Reg. Dist., Wellingborough Sub-dist., Northants, County.

688. Family tree by Trevor Mould, May 16, 2002.

689. Interview with Joan Mould, September 16, 2000, "I am the oldest of Bernard's 8 children".

690. Letter from Trevor Gilbert Mould to Joan Bolton. December 2002.

691. Letter from Joyce King to Richard Klapper, February 24, 2003.

692. *Phone call between Trevor Mould and Joan (Mould) Bolton*, April 2, 2002.

693. Family tree by Trevor Mould, May 16, 2002.

694. Letter from Joyce King to Richard Klapper, February 24, 2003.

695. Letter from Trevor Gilbert Mould to Joan Bolton, December 2002.

696. Letter from Joyce King to Richard Klapper, February 24, 2003.

697. *Telephone interview with Trevor Mould by Joan Bolton*, July 2001.

698. Letter from Joyce King to Richard Klapper, February 24, 2003.

699. Family tree by Trevor Mould, May 16, 2002.

700. Letter from Trevor Gilbert Mould to Joan Bolton, December 2002.

701. Letter from Joyce King to Richard Klapper, February 24, 2003.

702. *Telephone call between Joan Bolton and Richard Klapper*, July 2001, "Mary (m. Farey)."

703. Letter from Joyce King to Richard Klapper, February 24, 2003.

704. Family tree by Trevor Mould, May 16, 2002.

705. Letter from Joyce King to Richard Klapper, February 24, 2003.

706. Family tree by Trevor Mould, May 16, 2002.

707. Letter from Joyce King to Richard Klapper, February 24, 2003.

708. Letter from Joan (Mould) Bolton to Richard James Klapper, January 9, 2001.

709. Birth certificate - Doreen Lovell, Wellingborough Reg Dist, Higham Ferrers Sub-dist, Northampton and Bedford Counties, Name of mother: Ivy Doreen Lovell formerly Mould.

710. Letter from Ann Antill to Joan Bolton, 2002.

711. *GRO birth index for England*.

712. Letter from Ann Antill to Joan Bolton, 2002.

713. *E-mail from Heather Mackness to Richard Klapper*, February 26, 2004, "My grandmother Ivy Doreen Lovell died on 1st April 1999....."

714. Birth certificate - Doreen Lovell, Wellingborough Reg. Dist., Higham Ferrers Sub-dist, Northampton and Bedford Counties, Father's name: Archibald Thomas Lovell.

715. *GRO marriage index for England*, 3Q 1931, 3Q 1931 Lovell, Archibald T., Mould Wellingbro' 3b 395.

716. *GRO birth index for England*, 4Q 1907, 4 Q 1907 Lovell, Archibald Thomas Wellingbro' 3b 130.

717. *E-mail from Heather Mackness to Richard Klapper*, February 26, 2004, ".......his full name was Archibald Thomas Lovell he died in the year I was either 10 or 11 so that would be 1964/65."

718. Obituary - Bob Lovell, Northamptonshire Advertiser, March 5, 1965, "On March 3rd 1965 at 40 High Street South, Rushden, Archibald Thomas (Bob) Lovell,....... Cremation at Kettering today (5th March)."

719. *E-mail from Heather Mackness to Richard Klapper*, February 27, 2004, "Both [of my grandparents] were cremated, my nan was cremated at Kettering, they both have wall plaques at Rushden Cemetery along with my mother."

720. Birth certificate - Doreen Lovell, Wellingborough Reg Dist, Higham Ferrers Sub-dist, Northampton and Bedford Counties, Signature and residence of informant: Ivy D. Lovell, Mother, 27 St. Mays Road, Peckham, S.E. 15.

721. *E-mail from Heather Mackness to Richard Klapper*, February 27, 2004, "Both [of my grandparents] were cremated, my nan was cremated at Kettering, they both have wall plaques at Rushden Cemetery along with my mother."

722. Obituary - Bob Lovell, Northamptonshire Advertiser, March 5, 1965 , "On March 3rd 1965 at 40 High Street South, Rushden, Archibald Thomas (Bob) Lovell,....... Cremation at Kettering today (5th March)."

723. Letter from Ann Antill to Joan Bolton, 2002.

724. *GRO marriage index for England*, 3Q 1931, 3Q 1931 Lovell, Archibald T., Mould Wellingbro' 3b 395.

725. Letter from Joan (Mould) Bolton to Richard James Klapper, January 9, 2001.

726. Death certificate - Charles Mould, Wellingborough registration district, Sub-district of Rushden, County of Northampton, England, No. 417, Signature, description, and residence of informant: Percy W T Mould, son, present at the death, 5 Lime Street, Rushden.

727. *GRO birth index for England*, Percy Whitbread T. Mould born 2Q 1910.

728. *Marriage license, Percy ThomasWhitbread Mould/Elizabeth Winifred Firkins*, July 29, 1933, Percy Thomas Whitbread Mould, 23, bachelor, motor driver of Rushden, father: Charles Mould a boot operator, married Elizabeth Winifred Firkins, 22, spinster, of Souldrop, father: John Thomas Firkins, a gamekeeper. Witnesses: Charles Mould and Kate Firkins.

729. *GRO birth index for England*, Percy Whitbread T. Mould born 2Q 1910.

730. Letter from Joyce King to Richard Klapper, September 28, 2006, "We have been trying to find out about Uncle Percy. He died in Wellingborough Hospital, we think in 1984 and cremated at Kettering."

731. E-mail from Jayne Blanchard of Kettering Crematorium to Richard Klapper, October 24, 2006, ""Percy Whitbread Thomas Mould died on 31.10.1983 and was cremated on 3.11.1983. Elizabeth Winifred Mould died on 23.5.1982 and was cremated on 26.5.1982 as far as I can tell there are no memorials for either of them."

732. Family tree by Trevor Mould, May 16, 2002, Joan Bolton called Richard Klapper and indicated that she found the marriage of Percy Mould to Elizabeth W. Firkins in the 3Q 1933 in Bedford.

733. *Telephone interview of Philip Mould by Richard Klapper*, February 23, 2004, "Betty's last name was Firkins and she was from Bozeat, Northants. Her father was a gamekeeper and her mother was headmistress of Bozeat school."

734. *GRO marriage index for England*, 3Q 1933, Joan Bolton called Richard Klapper and indicated that she found the marriage of Percy Mould to Elizabeth W. Firkins in the 3Q 1933 in Bedford.

735. *Marriage license, Percy ThomasWhitbread Mould/Elizabeth Winifred Firkins*, July 29, 1933, Percy Thomas Whitbread Mould, 23, bachelor, motor driver of Rushden, father: Charles Mould a boot operator, married Elizabeth Winifred Firkins, 22, spinster, of Souldrop, father: John Thomas Firkins, a gamekeeper. Witnesses: Charles Mould and Kate Firkins.

736. *GRO birth index for England*, 3 Q 1911, 3 Q 1911, Elizabeth W. Firkins, Seversaks, Kent, Ref: 2a 1592.

737. E-mail from Jayne Blanchard of Kettering Crematorium to Richard Klapper, October 24, 2006, ""Percy Whitbread Thomas Mould died on 31.10.1983 and was cremated on 3.11.1983. Elizabeth Winifred Mould died on 23.5.1982 and was cremated on 26.5.1982 as far as I can tell there are no memorials for either of them."

738. Death certificate - Charles Mould, Wellingborough registration district, Sub-district of Rushden, County of Northampton, England, No. 417, Signature, description, and residence of informant: Percy W T Mould, son, present at the death, 5 Lime Street, Rushden.

739. E-mail from Jayne Blanchard of Kettering Crematorium to Richard Klapper, October 24, 2006, ""Percy Whitbread Thomas Mould died on 31.10.1983 and was cremated on 3.11.1983. Elizabeth Winifred Mould died on 23.5.1982 and was cremated on 26.5.1982 as far as I can tell there are no memorials for either of them."

740. *Marriage license, Percy ThomasWhitbread Mould/Elizabeth Winifred Firkins*, July 29, 1933, Percy Thomas Whitbread Mould, 23, bachelor, motor driver of Rushden, father: Charles Mould a boot operator, married Elizabeth Winifred Firkins, 22, spinster, of Souldrop, father: John Thomas Firkins, a gamekeeper. Witnesses: Charles Mould and Kate Firkins.

741. *Telephone interview of Philip Mould by Richard Klapper*, February 23, 2004, Percy and Betty were living in Lime Street in Rushden when their son Anthony died at 3 years of age of meningitis. This was in the late 1930's or early 1940's. Anthony was buried in Souldrop Churchyard.

742. *GRO birth index for England*, 2Q 1935, Mould, Anthony J. Firkins Northampton 3 b 57.

743. GRO death index for England, 2 Q 1938, Mould, Anthony J. 3 Northampton 3 b 85.

744. *Telephone interview of Philip Mould by Richard Klapper*, February 23, 2004, Percy and Betty were living in Lime Street in Rushden when their son Anthony died at 3 years of age of meningitis. This was in the late 1930's or early 1940's. Anthony was buried in Souldrop Churchyard.

745. *Diary of Annie Beatrice Mould Bull's 6 month trip to England in 1928*, August 13, 1928, Uncle George met us with a car - soon home - met Aunt Fanny and all the family, Doris, Cyril, Bernard, Eric, Guildford, Marjorie, Iris, Hubert....."

746. Letter from Joan (Mould) Bolton to Richard James Klapper, January 9, 2001.

747. Letter from Olive (Mould) Coleman, March 4, 2002.

748. Letter from Joan (Mould) Bolton to Richard James Klapper, January 9, 2001.

749. Letter from Olive (Mould) Coleman, March 4, 2002.

750. Letter from Joan (Mould) Bolton to Richard James Klapper, January 9, 2001.

751. Letter from Olive (Mould) Coleman, March 4, 2002.

752. Letter from Olive (Mould) Coleman to Richard Klapper, March 13, 2003.

753. Letter from Olive (Mould) Coleman, March 4, 2002.

754. Letter from Olive (Mould) Coleman to Richard Klapper, March 13, 2003.

755. *Obituary - Fanny Mould*, February 1947.

756. Letter from Olive (Mould) Coleman, March 4, 2002.

757. Letter from Olive (Mould) Coleman to Richard Klapper, March 13, 2003.

758. *Obituary - Fanny Mould*, February 1947.

759. Letter from Olive (Mould) Coleman to Richard Klapper, March 13, 2003.

760. *Diary of Annie Beatrice Mould Bull's 6 month trip to England in 1928*, August 13, 1928, "Uncle George met Aunt Fanny and all the family, Doris, Cyril, Bernard, Eric, Guildford, Marjorie, Iris, Hubert..."

761. Letter from Joan (Mould) Bolton to Richard James Klapper, February 4, 2002, Information provided to Joan by her cousin Enid.

762. Obituary - Annie Louisa Mould, Peterborough Evening Telegraph, October 13, 1993, "MOULD - Peacefully at Fenland Wing on 10th October, Annie Louisa of Priory Road, Peterborough aged 88 years. .... Funeral service at St. John's Church Peterborough on Friday 15th October at 2:15pm followed by cremation."

763. Letter from Joan (Mould) Bolton to Richard James Klapper, February 4, 2002, Information provided to Joan by her cousin Enid.

764. *Obituary - Fanny Mould*, February 1947.

765. Letter from Joan (Mould) Bolton to Richard James Klapper, February 4, 2002, Information provided to Joan by her cousin Enid.

766. Obituary - Annie Louisa Mould, Peterborough Evening Telegraph, October 13, 1993, "MOULD - Peacefully at Fenland Wing on 10th October, Annie Louisa of Priory Road, Peterborough aged 88 years. .... Funeral service at St. John's Church Peterborough on Friday 15th October at 2:15pm followed by cremation."

767. *Obituary - Fanny Mould*, February 1947.

768. Letter from Joan (Mould) Bolton to Richard James Klapper, February 4, 2002, Information provided to Joan by her cousin Enid.

769. Letter from Joan (Mould) Bolton to Richard James Klapper, January 9, 2001.
770. Letter from Joan (Mould) Bolton to Richard James Klapper, February 4, 2002, Information provided to Joan by her cousin Enid.
771. Interview with Joan Mould, September 16, 2000, " George had a son named Eric who was a dairy farmer the same as his dad. Eric had a daughter named Ann who is still living."
772. *Diary of Annie Beatrice Mould Bull's 6 month trip to England in 1928*, August 13, 1928, "Uncle George met us with a car - soon home - met Aunt Fanny and all the family, Doris, Cyril, Bernard, Eric, Guildford, Marjorie, Iris, Hubert..."
773. Letter from Joan (Mould) Bolton to Richard James Klapper, January 9, 2001.
774. Letter from Joan (Mould) Bolton to Richard James Klapper, February 4, 2002, Joan received this information from her cousin, Ann Antill.
775. Letter from Joan (Mould) Bolton to Richard James Klapper, January 9, 2001.
776. Letter from Joan (Mould) Bolton to Richard James Klapper, February 4, 2002, Joan received this information from her cousin, Ann Antill.
777. Letter from Ann Antill to Richard Klapper, October 21, 2002.
778. Letter from Joan (Mould) Bolton to Richard James Klapper, February 4, 2002, Joan received this information from her cousin, Ann Antill.
779. Letter from Ann Antill to Richard Klapper, October 21, 2002.
780. Obituary - Eric Mould, Peterborough Evening Telegraph, April 27, 1995, "On 24th April, Eric aged 90 years,........Funeral service at St. Paul's Church on Monday 1st May, followed by cremation."
781. *Telephone call between Joan Bolton and Richard Klapper*, September 16, 2000, "George had a son named Eric who was a dairy farmer also."
782. *Obituary - Fanny Mould*, February 1947.
783. Letter from Ann Antill to Richard Klapper, October 21, 2002.
784. Letter from Joan (Mould) Bolton to Richard James Klapper, February 4, 2002, Joan received this information from her cousin, Ann Antill.
785. *Obituary - Fanny Mould*, February 1947.
786. Letter from Joan (Mould) Bolton to Richard James Klapper, February 4, 2002, Joan received this information from her cousin, Ann Antill.
787. *Diary of Annie Beatrice Mould Bull's 6 month trip to England in 1928*, August 13, 1928, "Uncle George met us with a car - soon home - met Aunt Fanny and all the family, Doris, Cyril, Bernard, Eric, Guildford, Marjorie, Iris, Hubert...."
788. Telephone call between Richard Klapper and Joan Bolton, December 8, 2004, "My father's middle name was Thomas."
789. Letter from Joan (Mould) Bolton to Richard James Klapper, January 9, 2001.
790. *Telephone call between Joan Bolton and Richard Klapper*, September 8, 2002.
791. Letter from Joan (Mould) Bolton to Richard James Klapper, January 9, 2001.
792. *Telephone call between Joan Bolton and Richard Klapper*, September 8, 2002.
793. Telephone call between Richard Klapper and Joan Bolton, December 8, 2004.
794. *Telephone call between Joan Bolton and Richard Klapper*, September 8, 2002.
795. *Obituary - Fanny Mould*, February 1947.
796. *Telephone call between Joan Bolton and Richard Klapper*, September 8, 2002.
797. *Obituary - Fanny Mould*, February 1947.
798. *Telephone call between Joan Bolton and Richard Klapper*, September 8, 2002.
799. *Diary of Annie Beatrice Mould Bull's 6 month trip to England in 1928*, August 13, 1928, "Uncle George met us with a car - soon home - met Aunt Fanny and all the family, Doris, Cyril, Bernard, Eric, Guildford, Marjorie, Iris, Hubert..."
800. Letter from Joan (Mould) Bolton to Richard James Klapper, February 4, 2002, Joan received this information from her aunt Ursula, Hubert's wife.
801. Letter from Joan (Mould) Bolton to Richard James Klapper, January 9, 2001.
802. Letter from Joan (Mould) Bolton to Richard James Klapper, February 4, 2002, Joan received this information from her aunt Ursula, Hubert's wife.
803. *Telephone call between Joan Bolton and Richard Klapper*, October 6, 2002.
804. Letter from Joan (Mould) Bolton to Richard James Klapper, January 9, 2001.
805. *Telephone call between Joan Bolton and Richard Klapper*, October 6, 2002.
806. Letter from Joan (Mould) Bolton to Richard James Klapper, February 4, 2002, Joan received this information from her aunt Ursula, Hubert's wife.
807. *Obituary - Fanny Mould*, February 1947.
808. Letter from Joan (Mould) Bolton to Richard James Klapper, February 4, 2002, Joan received this information from her aunt Ursula, Hubert's wife.
809. Letter from Joan (Mould) Bolton to Richard James Klapper, January 9, 2001.
810. E-mail from Helen Mould to Richard Klapper, November 16, 2006, "I keep noticing Richard that you have the wrong spelling for Laurence. There are two ways of spelling it and his is spelt Laurence." .
811. Letter from Joan (Mould) Bolton to Richard James Klapper, February 4, 2002, Joan received this information from her aunt Ursula, Hubert's wife.
812. Birth certificate - Muriel Naomi Baldwin.
813. Family tree created by Joan Bolton from info from Mona Baldwin, 2003.
814. *GRO marriage index for England*, Marriage of Eric Parsley and Eric Parsley.

815. *GRO marriage index for England.*

816. Family tree created by Joan Bolton from info from Mona Baldwin, December 2003.

817. *GRO marriage index for England,* Marriage of Eric Parsley and Muriel Naomi Baldwin.

818. E-mail from Kate Brooker to Richard Klapper, May 14, 2003.

819. *The Dily Mirror newspaper,* Monday, April 18, 1938   Page 5, An article on the suicide of Herbert A. Baldwin. "Tears filled the eyes of his wife as she quoted parts of the letter to the Daily Mirror yesterday in her daughter's home at Alleyn Road, Dulwich."

820. E-mail from Kate Brooker to Richard Klapper, March 14, 2003.

821. *Tribute to Eric Parsley on his retirement from Dulwich College,* 1960 article in unknown publication, "in 1923, having just come from Keble College, Oxford." "......he first came to Dulwich in 1923 after four years at Oxford......."

822. *GRO marriage index for England.*

823. Family tree created by Joan Bolton from info from Mona Baldwin, December 2003.

824. *GRO birth index for England.*

825. Family tree created by Joan Bolton from info from Mona Baldwin, December 2003.

826. *Telephone call between Katharine Brooker and Richard Klapper,* May 11, 2003, Katharine indicated that her uncle, David Parsley died in a plane crash on his way to her mother, Virginia Parsley's wedding in 1949.

827. Family tree created by Joan Bolton from info from Mona Baldwin, December 2003.

828. E-mail from Kate Brooker to Richard Klapper, May 14, 2003, "Muriel Naomi ....she had two brothers. John died in infancy and Douglas died between the age 50-60."

829. Birth Certificate - Douglas Herbert Baldwin, Reg District of Epsom, Sub-district of Cashalton, Surrey, England.

830. Letter from Virginia Manning to Joan Bolton, July 28, 2003, Letter says date of death was 1972.

831. Family tree created by Joan Bolton from info from Mona Baldwin, December 2003.

832. *Telephone interview of Mona Baldwin by Richard Klapper,* December 21, 2003.

833. Letter from Virginia Manning to Joan Bolton, July 28, 2003.

834. *Telephone interview of Mona Baldwin by Joan Bolton,* August 2003.

835. Family tree created by Joan Bolton from info from Mona Baldwin, December 2003.

836. *Telephone interview of Mona Baldwin by Richard Klapper,* December 21, 2003.

837. *Telephone interview of Mona Baldwin by Joan Bolton,* August 2003.

838. Family tree created by Joan Bolton from info from Mona Baldwin, December 2003.

839. *Telephone interview of Mona Baldwin by Richard Klapper,* December 21, 2003.

840. Family tree created by Joan Bolton from info from Mona Baldwin, December 2003.

841. *Telephone interview of Mona Baldwin by Richard Klapper,* December 21, 2003.

842. *GRO birth index for England,* 3Q 1911, Jessop, Deveroux F., Anscombe, Epsom 5, 2, a, 52. The spelling of this name in various documents is inconsistent. It is spelled Deveraux on his marriage certificate but I am convinced that the name is spelled Devereux like his grandfather, father and son. .

843. *GRO birth index for England,* 3Q 1911, Jessop, Deveroux F., Anscombe, Epsom 5, 2, a, 52.

844. Interview of Nuria Jessop by Joan Bolton, October 11, 2006.

845. *GRO marriage index for England,* 3 Q 1939.

846. Marriage Certificate - Deveraux Frederick Jessop/Kathleen Mary Weeks, St. Paul's Church, Clapham, County of Surrey, England.

847. Interview of Nuria Jessop by Joan Bolton, October 11, 2006.

848. Marriage Certificate - Deveraux Frederick Jessop/Kathleen Mary Weeks, St. Paul's Church, Clapham, County of Surrey, England.

849. Interview of Nuria Jessop by Joan Bolton, October 11, 2006.

850. Family tree by Sheila Rose, July 2001.

851. E-mail from John Trevor Prentice to Richard Klapper, January 31, 2002, ".....and I was born on 25th April, 1920 in Peakirk, Northamptonshire."

852. E-mail from John Trevor Prentice to Richard Klapper, January 31, 2002, "My wife's maiden name was Molly Mary Mark."

853. E-mail from John Trevor Prentice to Richard Klapper, January 31, 2002, "We were married on 2nd April, 1945, in Bishops Stortford, Essex."

854. E-mail from John Trevor Prentice to Richard Klapper, January 31, 2002, "She was born at Mill Farm, Thorpe Abbotts, Diss, Norfolk on the 11th February, 1917."

855. E-mail from John Trevor Prentice to Richard Klapper, January 31, 2002, "We emigrated to New Zealand on 26th November, 1988."

856. E-mail from John Trevor Prentice to Richard Klapper, January 31, 2002, "I joined the Royal Air Force in January 1936 as an aircraft apprentice on a 3 year training course. In September 1940 I transferred to aircrew as a Flight Engineer on Sterling Bombers when they came into service with the RAF. I was one of the first 3 Flight Engineers in the RAF and stayed on Sterlings until the war in Europe ended. I retired from the RAF in January 1971 after 35 years service, as a Wing Commander."

857. E-mail from John Trevor Prentice to Richard Klapper, January 31, 2002.

858. E-mail from John Trevor Prentice to Richard Klapper, January 31, 2002, "We were married on 2nd April, 1945, in Bishops Stortford, Essex."

859. Family tree by Sheila Rose, July 2001.

860. *Telephone interview of Sheila Rose by Richard Klapper*, September 7, 2002.
861. Family tree by Sheila Rose, July 2001.
862. *Telephone interview of Sheila Rose by Richard Klapper*, September 7, 2002.
863. Family tree by Sheila Rose, July 2001.
864. Letter from John Robert Prentice, February 20, 2002.
865. Family tree by Sheila Rose, July 2001.
866. Letter from John Robert Prentice, February 20, 2002.
867. Family tree by Sheila Rose, July 2001.
868. Letter from John Robert Prentice, February 20, 2002.
869. Family tree by Sheila Rose, July 2001.
870. Letter from John Robert Prentice, March 1, 2004, A photo of Michael and Claire's wedding was enclosed with the letter which indicated the approximate date and the location of their wedding.
871. Family tree by Sheila Rose, July 2001.
872. Letter from John Robert Prentice, March 1, 2004, A photo with the letter gave Michael Keith Prentice as his full name.
873. Family tree by Sheila Rose, July 2001.
874. Interview with Don Mould and Hazel Ritter, June 26, 2000.
875. *Telephone interview of Hazel Ritter by Richard Klapper*, August 17, 2002.
876. Interview with Don Mould and Hazel Ritter, June 26, 2000.
877. Interview letter with Hazel Ritter, July 5, 2000.
878. Interview with Don Mould and Hazel Ritter, June 26, 2000.
879. Interview letter with Hazel Ritter, July 5, 2000.
880. Interview letter with Hazel Ritter.
881. *Telephone interview of Hazel Ritter by Richard Klapper*, August 17, 2002.
882. Helen Klapper postcard to Richard Klapper, September 3, 2000, HAZEL rITTER   "Hazel Ritter (my cousin) called this afternoon to tell me her brother's wife--Martha Lovell (was Jim's wife) died Friday from the leukemia."   .
883. *US Census - 1930, Aberdeen, Brown County, South Dakota*, Enumeration district 7-8, sheet # 12A, James A Lovell, son, male, white, 7, single, able to read and write, born: South Dakota, residence: 312 Seventh Ave.
884. *Social Security Death Index*.
885. Interview letter with Hazel Ritter.
886. Interview letter with Hazel Ritter, July 5, 2000.
887. Interview with Don Mould and Hazel Ritter, June 26, 2000.
888. Interview letter with Hazel Ritter, July 5, 2000.
889. Interview with Don Mould and Hazel Ritter, June 26, 2000.
890. *Telephone interview of Hazel Ritter by Richard Klapper*, August 17, 2002.
891. Interview with Don Mould and Hazel Ritter, June 26, 2000.
892. *Telephone interview of Hazel Ritter by Richard Klapper*, August 17, 2002.
893. Interview with Don Mould and Hazel Ritter, June 26, 2000.
894. *Telephone interview of Hazel Ritter by Richard Klapper*, August 17, 2002.
895. Interview letter with Hazel Ritter, July 5, 2000.
896. Interview with Don Mould and Hazel Ritter, June 26, 2000.
897. *Telephone interview of Don Mould by Richard Klapper*, August 17, 2002.
898. Interview with Don Mould and Hazel Ritter, June 26, 2000.
899. *Telephone interview of Don Mould by Richard Klapper*, August 17, 2002.
900. Interview with Don Mould and Hazel Ritter, June 26, 2000.
901. *Telephone interview of Don Mould by Richard Klapper*, August 17, 2002.
902. Interview with Don Mould and Hazel Ritter, June 26, 2000.
903. Alfred Mould Bull birth certificate, File # 140-1916-138415.
904. Alfred Mould Bull birth certificate, File # 140-1916-138415.
905. *Telephone call between Richard Bull and Richard Klapper*, August 4, 2009, Richard Bull called to inform me that his dad, Alfred Bull, died this morning at about 6am. He died peacefully after suffering from pneumonia for about a week. The arrangements have not been finalized but he anticipates that the funeral will be either Friday or Saturday in Aberdeen, South Dakota.
906. Geneology book of Catherine Schilder of Faulkton, S.D..
907. *Telephone call between Richard Bull and Richard Klapper*, January 2, 2004, Richard indicated that Lois went into the hospital last Monday (December 29). She died at 1pm on January 2. Lois and Alfred were visiting Marilyn for Christmas and New Years. Her son Richard and his wife Linda were there as well.
908. Obituary - Alfred M. Bull, August 6, 2009 Aberdeen, South Dakota newspaper.
909. *US Census - 1920, Aberdeen, Brown County, South Dakota*, Enumeration District 47, Sheet number 1A, Alfred Mould Bull, son, male, white, 3, single, born: South Dakota, Residence: farm.
910. *Telephone call between Peter Pash and Richard Klapper*, January 10, 2004, Peter indicated that Lois' funeral was held on Wednesday, January 7 in the First Methodist Church in Aberdeen, S.D. and the burial was in Faulkton, S.D. the next day, Thursday, January 8, 2004.
911. Geneology book of Catherine Schilder of Faulkton, S.D..
912. Marilyn Jean Pash interview, May 16, 2000.

913. Geneology book of Catherine Schilder of Faulkton, S.D..
914. Marilyn Jean Pash interview, May 28, 2000.
915. *Richard Bull Interview*, May 27, 2000.
916. Catherine Schilder Family History - Faulkton, S.D., June 2000.
917. Interview with Linda Katherine Bull, May 27, 2000.
918. *Richard Bull Interview*, May 27, 2000.
919. Catherine Schilder Family History - Faulkton, S.D., June 2000.
920. Interview with Linda Katherine Bull, May 27, 2000.
921. Marilyn Jean Pash interview, May 16, 2000.
922. Helen Wrighton Bull birth certificate, File # 140-1921-203056.
923. Interview with Helen Bull Klapper.
924. Birth certificate - William Richard Klapper, Coleman County, Texas.
925. Interview with Helen Bull Klapper.
926. Grave headstone - William Richard Klapper.
927. Birth certificate - William Richard Klapper, Coleman County, Texas.
928. Interview with Helen Bull Klapper.
929. Grave headstone - William Richard Klapper.
930. *US Census - 1930, Aberdeen, Brown County, South Dakota*, Enumeration district 7-12, sheet 2A, Helen W Bull, daughter, female, white, 9, single, able to read and write, born: South Dakota, residence: dairy farm.
931. *Obituary - William Richard Klapper*, Coleman County Chronicle - January 2, 1976.
932. *Personnal knowledge - Richard J. Klapper*.
933. *Personnal knowledge - Richard J. Klapper*, Dad served in the Army as a medic in WWII and then served in the US Army Reserves until his retirement.
934. Enlisted Record and Report of Separation - Honorable Discharge, William R. Klapper, Army Serial #: 18 126 311, Arm or service: MD, Component: A US, Organization: Co B 94th, Med Gas Trt Bn, Date of separation: October 27, 1945, Place of separation: Cp Sibert Sep Cp Sibert Ala, Permanent address: 300 E. Walnut St Coleman Coleman Tex, date of birth: 13 Aug 20, Place of birth: Coleman, Tex, Blue eyes, Blond hair, 5'11", 139 pounds, white, single, US citizen. ---Military History--- Military occupation specialty and No.: First Sgt   502, Battles and campaigns: Northern France, Rhineland, Central Europe,   WD GO 33-45,   Decorations and citations: Good conduct Med AR 600-68   EA METO Med Wounds received in action: None ----Total Length of service---- Continental service: 1 year, 11 months, 21 days Foreign service: 1 year, 2 months, 16 days Highest grade held: 1st Sgt ---Service outside continental US and return--- Departed 12 May 44 Destination: EA Meto Date of arrival: 25 May 44 Return: date of departure: 19 July 45 Destination: US Date of arrival: 27 Jul 45 Service schools attended: Grad Pharmacy Techn Course Fitzsimmons Gen Hosp Denver Colo 3 Feb 43.
935. *Personnal knowledge - Richard J. Klapper*.
936. *Social Security Death Index*.
937. Interview with Helen Bull Klapper.
938. Birth certificate for Richard James Klapper, September 20, 1948, Richard James Klapper was born at North Plains Hospital at 2:10am, September 20, 1948. Father: William Richard Klapper, Residence: Box 2625 Philrich, Borger, Texas , Father's birthplace: Texas - August 13, 1920, Mother's maiden name: Helen Wrighton Bull, Birthplace: South Dakota - March 26, 1921. NOTE: Box 2625 was a post office box in the small community of Bunavista just outside Borger, Texas. We were actually living in a Phillips Petroleum Co. apartment when I was born.
939. Birth certificate for Richard James Klapper, September 20, 1948, Richard James Klapper was born at North Plains Hospital at 2:10am, September 20, 1948. Father: William Richard Klapper, Residence: Box 2625 Philrich, Borger, Texas , Father's birthplace: Texas - August 13, 1920, Mother's maiden name: Helen Wrighton Bull, Birthplace: South Dakota - March 26, 1921. NOTE: Box 2625 was a post office box in the small community of Bunavista just outside Borger, Texas.
940. Interview with Richard James Klapper, 7/9/2000.
941. *Personnal knowledge - Richard J. Klapper*.
942. Interview with Richard James Klapper, July 9, 2000.
943. *Personnal knowledge - Richard J. Klapper*.
944. *Personnal knowledge - Richard J. Klapper*, Linda and Richard Lived in this house until August 1978 when we moved to 3116 Skyranch Drive, Alvin, Brazoria County, Texas.
945. *Personnal knowledge - Richard J. Klapper*, I retired from Centerpoint Energy which had previously been Houston Lighting & Power Co. I had 30 years of service.
946. *Personnal knowledge - Richard J. Klapper*, Linda retired in June 2002 but continued to work as a contractor to BACH 1 or 2 days per month.
947. *Personnal knowledge - Richard J. Klapper*.
948. E-mail from Marjorie Redford to Richard James Klapper, January 2, 2001.
949. E-mail from Marjorie Redford to Richard James Klapper, January 10, 2001.
950. E-mail from Marjorie Redford to Richard James Klapper, January 2, 2001.
951. *Telephone interview of Marge Redford by Richard Klapper*, October 19, 2003, Marge said her brother Robert was buried next to his wife in a cemetery near Pasadena, California.
952. *US Census - 1930, Huron, Beadle County, South Dakota*, Enumeration district 3-24, sheet # 2B, Robert F. Mackness, son, male, white, 8, single, able to read and write, residence: 580 Montana.
953. *Telephone interview of Marge Redford by Richard Klapper*, October 19, 2003, Marge said her brother Robert was

buried next to his wife in a cemetery near Pasadena, California.

954. E-mail from Marjorie Redford to Richard James Klapper, January 2, 2001.
955. *Telephone interview of Marge Redford by Richard Klapper*, October 19, 2003, Marge said her brother had three sons; Nolan, the oldest, Michael D. and Joe, the youngest.
956. E-mail from Marjorie Redford to Richard James Klapper, January 2, 2001.
957. E-mail from Marjorie Redford to Richard James Klapper, February 11, 2001.
958. E-mail from Marjorie Redford to Richard James Klapper, January 2, 2001.
959. *US Census - 1930, Huron, Beadle County, South Dakota*, Enumeration district 3-24, sheet # 2B, Marjorie E. Mackness, daughter, female, white, 3-10/12, single, residence: 580 Montana.
960. E-mail from Marjorie Redford to Richard James Klapper, January 2, 2001.
961. E-mail from Marjorie Redford to Richard James Klapper, February 11, 2001.
962. Family tree by Trevor Mould, May 16, 2002.
963. *Telephone interview of Pauline Spiller and Jeffrey Roberts by Richard Klapper*, February 24, 2004, Jeffrey and Pauline said John was born on October 22, 1930.
964. *Telephone interview of Jeffrey Roberts*, February 28, 2004, "Jeffrey, Pauline and John were all born in Higham Ferrers."
965. *Telephone interview of Jeffrey Roberts*, February 28, 2004, "John died in Souldrop and is buried in Sharnbrook, Beds which is the next largest town to Souldrop."
966. *Telephone interview of Pauline Spiller and Jeffrey Roberts by Richard Klapper*, February 24, 2004, Pauline said John's first wife was named Doreen. She couldn't remember her maiden name. They were divorced.
967. *Telephone interview of Pauline Spiller and Jeffrey Roberts by Richard Klapper*, February 24, 2004, Pauline and Jeffrey said John remarried a woman named Jane Hughes.
968. *Telephone interview of Jeffrey Roberts*, February 28, 2004, "John died in Souldrop and is buried in Sharnbrook, Beds which is the next largest town to Souldrop."
969. *Telephone interview of Jeffrey Roberts*, February 28, 2004.
970. *Telephone interview with Trevor Mould by Joan Bolton*, July 2001, "Norman (18 years younger) (than Joan)."
971. Letter from Joyce King to Richard Klapper, February 24, 2003.
972. Family tree by Trevor Mould, May 16, 2002.
973. Letter from Joyce King to Richard Klapper, February 24, 2003.
974. Family tree by Trevor Mould, May 16, 2002.
975. Letter from Joyce King to Richard Klapper, February 24, 2003.
976. Letter from Joyce King to Richard Klapper, September 28, 2006, "Unfortunately Norman lost his wife Joyce, March 2005."
977. Death certificate - Bernard William Mould, Wellingborough Reg. Dist., Wellingborough, Northants, England, Norman was the informant for his father's death certificate.
978. Letter from Joyce King to Richard Klapper, February 24, 2003.
979. Family tree by Trevor Mould, May 16, 2002.
980. Letter from Joyce King to Richard Klapper, February 24, 2003.
981. *Telephone interview with Trevor Mould by Joan Bolton*, July 2001, "Trevor m. to Joyce (4 sons) (62 years old, still working)."
982. Letter from Trevor Gilbert Mould to Joan Bolton, December 2002.
983. Family tree by Trevor Mould, May 16, 2002.
984. Letter from Trevor Gilbert Mould to Joan Bolton, December 2002.
985. Family tree by Trevor Mould, May 16, 2002.
986. Letter from Trevor Gilbert Mould to Joan Bolton, December 2002.
987. *Telephone interview with Trevor Mould by Joan Bolton*, July 2001, "Joyce m. King."
988. Letter from Joyce King to Richard Klapper, February 24, 2003.
989. Family tree by Trevor Mould, May 16, 2002.
990. Letter from Joyce King to Richard Klapper, February 24, 2003.
991. Family tree by Trevor Mould, May 16, 2002.
992. Letter from Joyce King to Richard Klapper, February 24, 2003.
993. *Telephone interview with Trevor Mould by Joan Bolton*, July 2001, "Margaret m. Richardson."
994. Letter from Joyce King to Richard Klapper, February 24, 2003.
995. Family tree by Trevor Mould, May 16, 2002.
996. Letter from Joyce King to Richard Klapper, February 24, 2003.
997. *Telephone interview with Trevor Mould by Joan Bolton*, July 2001.
998. Letter from Joyce King to Richard Klapper, February 24, 2003.
999. Family tree by Trevor Mould, May 16, 2002.
1000. Letter from Joyce King to Richard Klapper, February 24, 2003.
1001. Family tree by Trevor Mould, May 16, 2002.
1002. Letter from Joyce King to Richard Klapper, February 24, 2003.
1003. Family tree by Trevor Mould, May 16, 2002.
1004. Letter from Joyce King to Richard Klapper, February 24, 2003.
1005. Family tree by Trevor Mould, May 16, 2002.
1006. Letter from Joyce King to Richard Klapper, February 24, 2003.

1007. Family tree by Trevor Mould, May 16, 2002.

1008. Letter from Joyce King to Richard Klapper, February 24, 2003.

1009. Family tree by Trevor Mould, May 16, 2002.

1010. Letter from Ann Antill to Joan Bolton, July 2002, Doreen born June 1931/32.

1011. *E-mail from Heather Mackness to Richard Klapper*, October 29, 2002.

1012. *E-mail from Heather Mackness to Richard Klapper*, December 18, 2002.

1013. Birth certificate - Doreen Lovell, Wellingborough Reg. Dist., Higham Ferrers sub-district, Northampton and Bedford Counties.

1014. Letter from Ann Antill to Joan Bolton, July 2002, Doreen died March 1978.

1015. *E-mail from Heather Mackness to Richard Klapper*, October 29, 2002.

1016. Family tree by Ann Anthill, July 2002.

1017. *E-mail from Heather Mackness to Richard Klapper*, October 29, 2002.

1018. Letter from Ann Antill to Joan Bolton, July 2002.

1019. *E-mail from Heather Mackness to Richard Klapper*, October 29, 2002.

1020. *E-mail from Heather Mackness to Richard Klapper*, December 18, 2002.

1021. *E-mail from Heather Mackness to Richard Klapper*, October 29, 2002.

1022. *E-mail from Heather Mackness to Richard Klapper*, February 27, 2004, "Both [of my grandparents] were cremated, my nan was cremated at Kettering, they both have wall plaques at Rushden Cemetery along with my mother."

1023. *E-mail from Heather Mackness to Richard Klapper*, October 29, 2002.

1024. Letter from Ann Antill to Joan Bolton, 2002.

1025. Letter from Ann Antill to Joan Bolton, July 2002.

1026. *E-mail from Heather Mackness to Richard Klapper*, October 29, 2002.

1027. Letter from Joan (Mould) Bolton to Richard James Klapper, January 9, 2001.

1028. Letter from Olive (Mould) Coleman to Richard Klapper, March 13, 2003.

1029. *Telephone call between Joan Bolton and Richard Klapper*, December 10, 2009, Joan called to let me know that Olive died last week on November 20. She died in Peterborough Hospital and was cremated on Joan's birthday on December 7, 2009 in Peterborough Crematorium. .

1030. Letter from Olive (Mould) Coleman, March 4, 2002.

1031. Letter from Olive (Mould) Coleman to Richard Klapper, March 13, 2003.

1032. Letter from Olive (Mould) Coleman, March 4, 2002.

1033. *Telephone call between Joan Bolton and Richard Klapper*, February 1, 2010, Joan indicated that Olive had been cremated on December 7, 2009. Joan said she remembers because Olive was cremated on Joan's birthday, December 7. .

1034. Letter from Olive (Mould) Coleman to Richard Klapper, March 13, 2003.

1035. Letter from Olive (Mould) Coleman, March 4, 2002.

1036. Letter from Olive (Mould) Coleman to Richard Klapper, March 13, 2003.

1037. Letter from Joan (Mould) Bolton to Richard James Klapper, January 9, 2001.

1038. Letter from Joan (Mould) Bolton to Richard James Klapper, March 2007, History of "William Arthur Mould (Arthur)."

1039. Letter from Joan (Mould) Bolton to Richard James Klapper, January 9, 2001.

1040. Letter from Olive (Mould) Coleman, March 4, 2002.

1041. Letter from Joan (Mould) Bolton to Richard James Klapper, March 2007, "Margaret died on 15th January 2007 after a long battle with cancer."

1042. Letter from Olive (Mould) Coleman, March 4, 2002.

1043. Letter from Joan (Mould) Bolton to Richard James Klapper, January 9, 2001.

1044. Letter from Olive (Mould) Coleman, March 4, 2002.

1045. Letter from Joan (Mould) Bolton to Richard James Klapper, January 9, 2001.

1046. Letter from Joan (Mould) Bolton to Richard James Klapper, March 2007, History of "Harold Edward Mould ('Dick')."

1047. Letter from Joan (Mould) Bolton to Richard James Klapper, January 9, 2001.

1048. Letter from Joan (Mould) Bolton to Richard James Klapper, March 2007, "By this time Dick was a married man with two young children, having married Patricia (Pat) Elliott in December 1956."

1049. Letter from Olive (Mould) Coleman, March 4, 2002.

1050. Letter from Joan (Mould) Bolton to Richard James Klapper, January 9, 2001.

1051. Letter from Joan (Mould) Bolton to Richard James Klapper, February 4, 2002.

1052. Letter from Joan (Mould) Bolton to Richard James Klapper, February 4, 2002, Information provided to Joan by her cousin Enid.

1053. Letter from Joan (Mould) Bolton to Richard James Klapper, January 9, 2001.

1054. Letter from Joan (Mould) Bolton to Richard James Klapper, February 4, 2002, Information provided to Joan by her cousin Enid.

1055. Letter from Joan (Mould) Bolton to Richard James Klapper, January 9, 2001.

1056. Letter from Joan (Mould) Bolton to Richard James Klapper, February 4, 2002.

1057. Interview with Joan Mould, September 16, 2000, "Jabez's brother, George, was a dairy farmer near Peterborough. He had a son named Eric who was a dairy farmer too. Eric had a daughter named Ann who is still living."

1058. Letter from Joan (Mould) Bolton to Richard James Klapper, February 4, 2002, Joan received this information from her cousin, Ann Antill.

1059. Letter from Joan (Mould) Bolton to Richard James Klapper, January 9, 2001.

1060. Letter from Joan (Mould) Bolton to Richard James Klapper, February 4, 2002, Joan received this information from her cousin, Ann Antill.

1061. Letter from Ann Antill to Richard Klapper, October 21, 2002.

1062. Letter from Joan (Mould) Bolton to Richard James Klapper, February 4, 2002, Joan received this information from her cousin, Ann Antill.

1063. Letter from Ann Antill to Richard Klapper, October 21, 2002.

1064. Letter from Joan (Mould) Bolton to Richard James Klapper, February 4, 2002, Joan received this information from her cousin, Ann Antill.

1065. Letter from Ann Antill to Richard Klapper, October 21, 2002.

1066. Letter from Joan (Mould) Bolton to Richard James Klapper, February 4, 2002, Joan received this information from her cousin, Ann Antill.

1067. Letter from Ann Antill to Richard Klapper, October 21, 2002.

1068. Letter from Joan (Mould) Bolton to Richard James Klapper, February 4, 2002, Joan received this information from her cousin, Ann Antill.

1069. Letter from Ann Antill to Richard Klapper, October 21, 2002.

1070. Letter from Joan (Mould) Bolton to Richard James Klapper, February 4, 2002, Joan received this information from her cousin, Ann Antill.

1071. Letter from Ann Antill to Richard Klapper, October 21, 2002.

1072. Letter from Joan (Mould) Bolton to Helen Klapper, December 1999.

1073. Letter from Joan (Mould) Bolton to Richard James Klapper, February 4, 2002.

1074. Letter from Joan (Mould) Bolton to Richard James Klapper, January 9, 2001.

1075. Letter from Joan (Mould) Bolton to Richard James Klapper, February 4, 2002.

1076. Letter from Joan (Mould) Bolton to Helen Klapper, December 1999.

1077. Letter from Joan (Mould) Bolton to Richard James Klapper, February 4, 2002.

1078. Joan Mould Christmas card to Helen Klapper, December 2000.

1079. Letter from Joan (Mould) Bolton to Richard James Klapper, February 4, 2002.

1080. Letter from Joan (Mould) Bolton to Richard James Klapper, February 4, 2002, "Victoria Grace (b. 13 weeks premature ie. at 27 weeks) on 18/1/1979 in Hershan, Northumberland D. on 22/1/1979 in Newcastle Hospital Northumberland (premature baby unit) Lived 4 days. Buried in Newcastle."

1081. Letter from Joan (Mould) Bolton to Helen Klapper, December 1999.

1082. Letter from Joan (Mould) Bolton to Richard James Klapper, January 9, 2001.

1083. E-mail from David Peters to Richard Klapper, January 20, 2002, "Alison Mary Peters Born Peterborough 1st March 1947."

1084. Letter from Joan (Mould) Bolton to Richard James Klapper, January 9, 2001.

1085. E-mail from David Peters to Richard Klapper, January 20, 2002, "Alison Mary Peters Born Peterborough 1st March 1947."

1086. Letter from Joan (Mould) Bolton to Richard James Klapper, January 9, 2001.

1087. E-mail from David Peters to Richard Klapper, January 20, 2002, "David Michael Peters Born Bombay, India 10th Dec. 1943."

1088. E-mail from David Peters to Richard Klapper, January 20, 2002, "Alison Mary Peters Born Peterborough 1st March 1947 Married 23 Aug 1969, All Saints Church, Paston, Peterborough."

1089. E-mail from David Peters to Richard Klapper, January 20, 2002, "David Michael Peters Born Bombay, India 10th Dec. 1943."

1090. E-mail from David Peters to Richard Klapper, January 20, 2002, "Alison Mary Peters Born Peterborough 1st March 1947 Married 23 Aug 1969, All Saints Church, Paston, Peterborough."

1091. Letter from Joan (Mould) Bolton to Richard James Klapper, January 9, 2001.

1092. Letter from Joan (Mould) Bolton to Richard James Klapper, February 4, 2002, Joan received this information from her aunt Ursula, Hubert's wife.

1093. Letter from Joan (Mould) Bolton to Richard James Klapper, January 9, 2001.

1094. E-mail from Helen Mould to Richard Klapper, 16 Nov 2006, Melvin, a carpenter, married Romaine, they have two children, Anthony, an environmental biologist, and Clare, a social work assistant. Clare will marry 28th December 2006 and is expecting the first of the next Mould generation in May 2007. Melvin has a keen interest in ornithology, bird nesting in particular and has passed these loves onto Anthony who is a keen ornithologist helps to protect endangered bird's nests and also does a lot of volunteer work with bats. E-mail from Helen Mould (wife of Lawrence) 16 Nov 2006.

1095. Letter from Joan (Mould) Bolton to Richard James Klapper, February 4, 2002, Joan received this information from her aunt Ursula, Hubert's wife.

1096. Letter from Joan (Mould) Bolton to Richard James Klapper, January 9, 2001.

1097. Letter from Joan (Mould) Bolton to Richard James Klapper, February 4, 2002, Joan received this information from her aunt Ursula, Hubert's wife.

1098. *GRO birth index for England.*

1099. *GRO birth index for England*, Shows birth date of 1Q 1929.

1100. Family tree created by Joan Bolton from info from Mona Baldwin, December 2003.

1101. *GRO marriage index for England*, 3 Q 1949.

1102. GRO death index for England, October 2001, "Manning, John Ernest   DOB 20 April 1922   Reg Dist Hitch&Steven   October 2001   Dist# 5341A   Reg# 13A   Entry# 118   Dor 1001."

1103. *GRO marriage index for England*, 3 Q 1949.

1104. GRO death index for England, November 2001, "Manning, John Ernest   DOB 20 April 1922   Reg Dist Hitch&Steven   October 2001   Dist# 5341A   Reg# 13A   Entry# 118   Dor 1001."

1105. GRO death index for England, October 2001, "Manning, John Ernest   DOB 20 April 1922   Reg Dist Hitch&Steven   October 2001   Dist# 5341A   Reg# 13A   Entry# 118   Dor 1001."

1106. *GRO marriage index for England*, 3 Q 1949.

1107. Letter from Virginia Manning to Joan Bolton, July 28, 2003.

1108. Family tree created by Joan Bolton from info from Mona Baldwin, December 2003.

1109. *Telephone interview of Mona Baldwin by Richard Klapper*, December 21, 2003.

1110. Family tree created by Joan Bolton from info from Mona Baldwin, December 2003.

1111. *Telephone interview of Jane Fletcher by Richard Klapper*, December 21, 2003.

1112. E-mail from Jane Fletcher to Richard Klapper, March 4, 2009, "My first husband, the father of my two daughters was Neil McRobert born 8th August 1933 in Fife in Scotland."

1113. Family tree created by Joan Bolton from info from Mona Baldwin, December 2003.

1114. *Telephone interview of Jane Fletcher by Richard Klapper*, December 21, 2003.

1115. Family tree created by Joan Bolton from info from Mona Baldwin, December 2003.

1116. *Telephone interview of Jane Fletcher by Richard Klapper*, December 21, 2003.

1117. Family tree created by Joan Bolton from info from Mona Baldwin, December 2003.

1118. *Telephone interview of Jane Fletcher by Richard Klapper*, December 21, 2003.

1119. Letter from Virginia Manning to Joan Bolton, July 28, 2003.

1120. Family tree created by Joan Bolton from info from Mona Baldwin, December 2003.

1121. *Telephone interview of Mona Baldwin by Richard Klapper*, December 21, 2003.

1122. Letter from Joan (Mould) Bolton to Richard James Klapper, October 9, 2003.

1123. Family tree created by Joan Bolton from info from Mona Baldwin, December 2003.

1124. *Telephone interview of Mona Baldwin by Richard Klapper*, December 21, 2003.

1125. Family tree created by Joan Bolton from info from Mona Baldwin, December 2003.

1126. E-mail from Christopher Baldwin to Richard Klapper, January 21, 2004.

1127. Family tree created by Joan Bolton from info from Mona Baldwin, December 2003.

1128. *Telephone interview of Mona Baldwin by Richard Klapper*, December 21, 2003.

1129. Family tree created by Pat Baldwin, December 2003.

1130. E-mail from Christopher Baldwin to Richard Klapper, January 21, 2004.

1131. Family tree created by Pat Baldwin, December 2003.

1132. E-mail from Christopher Baldwin to Richard Klapper, January 21, 2004.

1133. Family tree created by Pat Baldwin, December 2003.

1134. E-mail from John Trevor Prentice to Richard Klapper, January 31, 2002, "Our daughter Jane whose maiden was Jane Ann Elizabeth Prentice was born in Chipping Norton Memorial Hospital, Oxfordshire, on 13th January 1946."

1135. E-mail from John Trevor Prentice to Richard Klapper, January 31, 2002, "Jane was married the first time to David Smith in the Church on Royal Air Force, Bruggen, Germany in 1965. They had two sons. Nicholas Charles Smith was born in Chipping Norton Hospital on 11th January 1967 and James David Smith was born in the same Hospital on 13th May 1968."

1136. E-mail from John Trevor Prentice to Richard Klapper, January 31, 2002, "Jane was subsequently divorced and remarried Rodney Heaton Gordon a New Zealander on 4th June 1976 in Bodicote, Banbury, Oxford."

1137. E-mail from John Trevor Prentice to Richard Klapper, January 31, 2002, "Jane was married the first time to David Smith in the Church on Royal Air Force, Bruggen, Germany in 1965. They had two sons. Nicholas Charles Smith was born in Chipping Norton Hospital on 11th January 1967 and James David Smith was born in the same Hospital on 13th May 1968."

1138. E-mail from John Trevor Prentice to Richard Klapper, January 31, 2002, "Jane was subsequently divorced and remarried Rodney Heaton Gordon a New Zealander on 4th June 1976 in Bodicote, Banbury, Oxford."

1139. E-mail from John Trevor Prentice to Richard Klapper, January 31, 2002, "Jane was married the first time to David Smith in the Church on Royal Air Force, Bruggen, Germany in 1965. They had two sons. Nicholas Charles Smith was born in Chipping Norton Hospital on 11th January 1967 and James David Smith was born in the same Hospital on 13th May 1968."

1140. E-mail from John Trevor Prentice to Richard Klapper, January 31, 2002, "They have a son George Heaton Gordon who was born on 15th October 1977 in Lower Hutt, New Zealand and a daughter Grace Jane Gordon who was born on 8th December 1979 in Hastings, New Zealand."

1141. E-mail from John Trevor Prentice to Richard Klapper, January 31, 2002, "Our other daughter Margaret Priscilla Ingrid was born in Singapore, at the RAF Changi Hospital on 20th January 1948."

1142. E-mail from John Trevor Prentice to Richard Klapper, January 31, 2002.

1143. E-mail from John Trevor Prentice to Richard Klapper, January 31, 2002, "She was married to Peter Flynn in Haslinton, Lancastershire in May 1966."

1144. E-mail from John Trevor Prentice to Richard Klapper, January 31, 2002, "Our daughter Margaret was divorced about 10 years ago and has not remarried."

1145. E-mail from John Trevor Prentice to Richard Klapper, January 31, 2002, "She was married to Peter Flynn in Haslinton, Lancastershire in May 1966."

1146. E-mail from John Trevor Prentice to Richard Klapper, January 31, 2002.

1147. Family tree by Sheila Rose, July 2001.
1148. *Telephone interview of Sheila Rose by Richard Klapper*, September 7, 2002.
1149. Letter from Sheila Rose to Richard Klapper, October 3, 2002.
1150. *Telephone interview of Sheila Rose by Richard Klapper*, September 7, 2002.
1151. Family tree by Sheila Rose, July 2001.
1152. Letter from Sheila Rose to Richard Klapper, October 2, 2002.
1153. Family tree by Sheila Rose, July 2001.
1154. *Telephone interview of Sheila Rose by Richard Klapper*, September 7, 2002.
1155. Letter from Sheila Rose to Richard Klapper, October 2, 2002.
1156. *Telephone interview of Sheila Rose by Richard Klapper*, September 7, 2002.
1157. Letter from Sheila Rose to Richard Klapper, October 2, 2002.
1158. Family tree by Sheila Rose, July 2001.
1159. *Telephone interview of Sheila Rose by Richard Klapper*, September 7, 2002.
1160. Letter from Sheila Rose to Richard Klapper, October 2, 2002.
1161. *Telephone interview of Sheila Rose by Richard Klapper*, September 7, 2002.
1162. Family tree by Sheila Rose, July 2001.
1163. *Telephone interview of Sheila Rose by Richard Klapper*, September 7, 2002.
1164. Family tree by Sheila Rose, July 2001.
1165. *Telephone interview of Sheila Rose by Richard Klapper*, September 7, 2002.
1166. Family tree by Sheila Rose, July 2001.
1167. Letter from John Robert Prentice, February 20, 2002.
1168. Family tree by Sheila Rose, July 2001.
1169. Letter from John Robert Prentice, February 20, 2002.
1170. Family tree by Sheila Rose, July 2001.
1171. Letter from John Robert Prentice, February 20, 2002.
1172. Family tree by Sheila Rose, July 2001.
1173. Letter from John Robert Prentice, February 20, 2002.
1174. Family tree by Sheila Rose, July 2001.
1175. Letter from John Robert Prentice, February 20, 2002.
1176. Family tree by Sheila Rose, July 2001.
1177. Letter from John Robert Prentice, February 20, 2002.
1178. Family tree by Sheila Rose, July 2001.
1179. Letter from John Robert Prentice, February 20, 2002.
1180. Family tree by Sheila Rose, July 2001.
1181. Letter from John Robert Prentice, February 20, 2002.
1182. Family tree by Sheila Rose, July 2001.
1183. Letter from John Robert Prentice, February 20, 2002.
1184. Family tree by Sheila Rose, July 2001.
1185. Letter from John Robert Prentice, February 20, 2002.
1186. Family tree by Sheila Rose, July 2001.
1187. Interview with Don Mould and Hazel Ritter, June 26, 2000.
1188. *Telephone interview of Don Mould by Richard Klapper*, August 17, 2002.
1189. Interview with Don Mould and Hazel Ritter, June 26, 2000.
1190. *Telephone interview of Don Mould by Richard Klapper*, August 17, 2002.
1191. Interview with Don Mould and Hazel Ritter, June 26, 2000.
1192. *Telephone interview of Don Mould by Richard Klapper*, August 17, 2002.
1193. Interview with Fred William Klapper.
1194. Birth certificate - Fred William Klapper, Mercy Hospital, Denver, Colorado   Feb 3, 1951.
1195. Interview with Fred William Klapper, December 19, 2000.
1196. Birth certificate - Fred William Klapper, Mercy Hospital, Denver, Colorado   Feb 3, 1951.
1197. Interview with Fred William Klapper, December 19, 2000.
1198. Marriage license - Fred William Klapper/Pamela Ann Wolny, Hutchinson County, Texas   July 26, 1986.
1199. Interview with Fred William Klapper, December 19, 2000.
1200. Baptismal certificate - Fred William Klapper, February 3, 1963   First Christian Church, Borger, Texas.
1201. *Personnal knowledge - Richard J. Klapper*.
1202. Interview with Pamela Ann Klapper.
1203. Interview with Fred William Klapper.
1204. Interview with Fred William Klapper, December 19, 2000.
1205. Marriage license - Fred William Klapper/Pamela Ann Wolny, Hutchinson County, Texas   July 26, 1986.
1206. Interview with Fred William Klapper, December 19, 2000.
1207. Birth certificate - Andrew Frederick Klapper, July 15, 1992, Spartanburg Regional Medical Center, Spartanburg, South Carolina.
1208. Interview with Fred William Klapper.
1209. Birth certificate - Andrew Frederick Klapper, July 15, 1992, Spartanburg Regional Medical Center, Spartanburg,

South Carolina.
1210. Baptism certificate - Andrew Frederick Klapper, November 15, 1992   Church of Jesus, Our Risen Savior, Spartanburg, South Carolina.
1211. E-mail from Marjorie Redford to Richard James Klapper, January 2, 2001, "We have three children,Margo Esther...."
1212. E-mail from Marjorie Redford to Richard James Klapper, January 2, 2001, "...Margo Esther, born May 4th, 1948 in Portland, Oregon..."
1213. E-mail from Marjorie Redford to Richard James Klapper, January 2, 2001.
1214. E-mail from Marjorie Redford to Richard James Klapper, February 11, 2001.
1215. E-mail from Marjorie Redford to Richard James Klapper, January 2, 2001, "Margo has 3 (children), Dominic Scharlach (can't remember his middle name, he was adopted)...."
1216. E-mail from Marjorie Redford to Richard James Klapper, January 2, 2001, "....Dominic Scharlach....born April 10, 1970..."
1217. E-mail from Marjorie Redford to Richard James Klapper, January 2, 2001, "...Amy Esther Scharlach, born Feb. 12, 1971..."
1218. E-mail from Marjorie Redford to Richard James Klapper, January 2, 2001, "....Amy Esther Scharlach, born Feb. 12, 1971..."
1219. E-mail from Marjorie Redford to Richard James Klapper, January 2, 2001, "....Margo has three (children), ...Deborah..."
1220. E-mail from Marjorie Redford to Richard James Klapper, January 2, 2001, "....Deborah, born June 10, 1976."
1221. E-mail from Marjorie Redford to Richard James Klapper, January 2, 2001.
1222. E-mail from Marjorie Redford to Richard James Klapper, February 11, 2001.
1223. E-mail from Marjorie Redford to Richard James Klapper, January 2, 2001, "We have three children...Nicholas Frank..."
1224. E-mail from Marjorie Redford to Richard James Klapper, January 2, 2001, ".....Nicholas Frank, born July 17, 1955 in Honolulu, Hawaii."
1225. E-mail from Marjorie Redford to Richard James Klapper, January 2, 2001.
1226. E-mail from Marjorie Redford to Richard James Klapper, February 11, 2001.
1227. E-mail from Marjorie Redford to Richard James Klapper, January 2, 2001.
1228. Family tree by Trevor Mould, May 16, 2002.
1229. Letter from Joyce King to Richard Klapper, February 24, 2003.
1230. Family tree by Trevor Mould, May 16, 2002.
1231. Letter from Joyce King to Richard Klapper, February 24, 2003.
1232. Family tree by Trevor Mould, May 16, 2002.
1233. Letter from Joyce King to Richard Klapper, February 24, 2003.
1234. Family tree by Trevor Mould, May 16, 2002.
1235. Letter from Joyce King to Richard Klapper, February 24, 2003.
1236. Family tree by Trevor Mould, May 16, 2002.
1237. Letter from Joyce King to Richard Klapper, February 24, 2003.
1238. Family tree by Trevor Mould, May 16, 2002.
1239. Letter from Joyce King to Richard Klapper, February 24, 2003.
1240. Family tree by Trevor Mould, May 16, 2002.
1241. Letter from Joyce King to Richard Klapper, February 24, 2003.
1242. Family tree by Trevor Mould, May 16, 2002.
1243. Letter from Joyce King to Richard Klapper, February 24, 2003.
1244. Family tree by Trevor Mould, May 16, 2002.
1245. Letter from Joyce King to Richard Klapper, February 24, 2003.
1246. Family tree by Trevor Mould, May 16, 2002.
1247. Letter from Joyce King to Richard Klapper, February 24, 2003.
1248. Family tree by Trevor Mould, May 16, 2002.
1249. Letter from Joyce King to Richard Klapper, February 24, 2003.
1250. Family tree by Trevor Mould, May 16, 2002.
1251. Letter from Joyce King to Richard Klapper, February 24, 2003.
1252. Family tree by Trevor Mould, May 16, 2002.
1253. Letter from Joyce King to Richard Klapper, February 24, 2003.
1254. Family tree by Trevor Mould, May 16, 2002.
1255. Letter from Joyce King to Richard Klapper, February 24, 2003.
1256. Family tree by Trevor Mould, May 16, 2002.
1257. Letter from Joyce King to Richard Klapper, February 24, 2003.
1258. Family tree by Trevor Mould, May 16, 2002.
1259. Letter from Joyce King to Richard Klapper, February 24, 2003.
1260. Family tree by Trevor Mould, May 16, 2002.
1261. Letter from Joyce King to Richard Klapper, February 24, 2003.
1262. Family tree by Trevor Mould, May 16, 2002.
1263. Letter from Joyce King to Richard Klapper, February 24, 2003.

1264. Family tree by Trevor Mould, May 16, 2002.
1265. Letter from Joyce King to Richard Klapper, February 24, 2003.
1266. Family tree by Trevor Mould, May 16, 2002.
1267. Letter from Trevor Gilbert Mould to Joan Bolton, December 2002.
1268. Family tree by Trevor Mould, May 16, 2002.
1269. Letter from Trevor Gilbert Mould to Joan Bolton, December 2002.
1270. Family tree by Trevor Mould, May 16, 2002.
1271. Letter from Trevor Gilbert Mould to Joan Bolton, December 2002.
1272. Family tree by Trevor Mould, May 16, 2002.
1273. Letter from Trevor Gilbert Mould to Joan Bolton, December 2002.
1274. Family tree by Trevor Mould, May 16, 2002.
1275. Letter from Trevor Gilbert Mould to Joan Bolton, December 2002.
1276. Family tree by Trevor Mould, May 16, 2002.
1277. Letter from Trevor Gilbert Mould to Joan Bolton, December 2002.
1278. Family tree by Trevor Mould, May 16, 2002.
1279. Letter from Trevor Gilbert Mould to Joan Bolton, December 2002.
1280. Family tree by Trevor Mould, May 16, 2002.
1281. Letter from Trevor Gilbert Mould to Joan Bolton, December 2002.
1282. Family tree by Trevor Mould, May 16, 2002.
1283. Letter from Trevor Gilbert Mould to Joan Bolton, December 2002.
1284. Family tree by Trevor Mould, May 16, 2002.
1285. Letter from Trevor Gilbert Mould to Joan Bolton, December 2002.
1286. Family tree by Trevor Mould, May 16, 2002.
1287. Letter from Trevor Gilbert Mould to Joan Bolton, December 2002.
1288. Family tree by Trevor Mould, May 16, 2002.
1289. Letter from Joyce King to Richard Klapper, February 24, 2003.
1290. Family tree by Trevor Mould, May 16, 2002.
1291. Letter from Joyce King to Richard Klapper, February 24, 2003.
1292. Family tree by Trevor Mould, May 16, 2002.
1293. Letter from Joyce King to Richard Klapper, February 24, 2003.
1294. Family tree by Trevor Mould, May 16, 2002.
1295. Letter from Joyce King to Richard Klapper, February 24, 2003.
1296. Family tree by Trevor Mould, May 16, 2002.
1297. E-mail from Vicky Piggott to Richard Klapper, February 22, 2003, "My surname has two T's - Piggott." .
1298. Letter from Joyce King to Richard Klapper, February 24, 2003.
1299. Family tree by Trevor Mould, May 16, 2002.
1300. Letter from Joyce King to Richard Klapper, February 24, 2003.
1301. Family tree by Trevor Mould, May 16, 2002.
1302. Letter from Joyce King to Richard Klapper, February 24, 2003.
1303. Family tree by Trevor Mould, May 16, 2002.
1304. Letter from Joyce King to Richard Klapper, February 24, 2003.
1305. Family tree by Trevor Mould, May 16, 2002.
1306. Letter from Joyce King to Richard Klapper, February 24, 2003.
1307. Family tree by Trevor Mould, May 16, 2002.
1308. Letter from Joyce King to Richard Klapper, February 24, 2003.
1309. Family tree by Trevor Mould, May 16, 2002.
1310. Letter from Joyce King to Richard Klapper, February 24, 2003.
1311. Family tree by Trevor Mould, May 16, 2002.
1312. Letter from Joyce King to Richard Klapper, February 24, 2003.
1313. Family tree by Trevor Mould, May 16, 2002.
1314. Letter from Joyce King to Richard Klapper, February 24, 2003.
1315. Family tree by Trevor Mould, May 16, 2002.
1316. Letter from Joyce King to Richard Klapper, February 24, 2003.
1317. Letter from Joyce King to Richard Klapper, March 27, 2003.
1318. Family tree by Trevor Mould, May 16, 2002.
1319. Letter from Joyce King to Richard Klapper, February 24, 2003.
1320. Family tree by Trevor Mould, May 16, 2002.
1321. Letter from Joyce King to Richard Klapper, February 24, 2003.
1322. Family tree by Trevor Mould, May 16, 2002.
1323. Letter from Joyce King to Richard Klapper, February 24, 2003.
1324. Family tree by Trevor Mould, May 16, 2002.
1325. Letter from Joyce King to Richard Klapper, February 24, 2003.
1326. Family tree by Trevor Mould, May 16, 2002.
1327. Letter from Joyce King to Richard Klapper, February 24, 2003.

1328. Family tree by Trevor Mould, May 16, 2002.
1329. Letter from Joyce King to Richard Klapper, February 24, 2003.
1330. Family tree by Trevor Mould, May 16, 2002.
1331. Family tree by Ann Anthill, July 2002.
1332. *E-mail from Heather Mackness to Richard Klapper*, October 29, 2002.
1333. Family tree by Ann Anthill, July 2002.
1334. *E-mail from Heather Mackness to Richard Klapper*, October 29, 2002.
1335. Family tree by Ann Anthill, July 2002.
1336. *E-mail from Heather Mackness to Richard Klapper*, October 29, 2002.
1337. Family tree by Ann Anthill, July 2002.
1338. *E-mail from Heather Mackness to Richard Klapper*, October 29, 2002.
1339. Family tree by Ann Anthill, July 2002.
1340. *E-mail from Heather Mackness to Richard Klapper*, October 29, 2002.
1341. Family tree by Ann Anthill, July 2002.
1342. *E-mail from Heather Mackness to Richard Klapper*, October 29, 2002.
1343. Family tree by Ann Anthill, July 2002.
1344. *E-mail from Heather Mackness to Richard Klapper*, October 29, 2002.
1345. Family tree by Ann Anthill, July 2002.
1346. *E-mail from Heather Mackness to Richard Klapper*, October 29, 2002.
1347. Family tree by Trevor Mould, May 16, 2002.
1348. Family tree by Ann Anthill, July 2002.
1349. E-mail from Paul Rawlins to Richard Klapper, December 10, 2002.
1350. Family tree by Ann Anthill, July 2002.
1351. E-mail from Paul Rawlins to Richard Klapper, December 10, 2002.
1352. E-mail from Paul Rawlins to Richard Klapper, January 29, 2003.
1353. E-mail from Paul Rawlins to Richard Klapper, December 10, 2002.
1354. E-mail from Paul Rawlins to Richard Klapper, January 29, 2003.
1355. Family tree by Ann Anthill, July 2002.
1356. E-mail from Paul Rawlins to Richard Klapper, December 10, 2002.
1357. Family tree by Ann Anthill, July 2002.
1358. E-mail from Paul Rawlins to Richard Klapper, December 10, 2002.
1359. Letter from Olive (Mould) Coleman, March 4, 2002.
1360. Letter from Olive (Mould) Coleman to Richard Klapper, March 13, 2003.
1361. Letter from Olive (Mould) Coleman, March 4, 2002.
1362. Letter from Olive (Mould) Coleman to Richard Klapper, March 13, 2003.
1363. Letter from Olive (Mould) Coleman, March 4, 2002.
1364. Letter from Olive (Mould) Coleman to Richard Klapper, March 13, 2003.
1365. Letter from Olive (Mould) Coleman, March 4, 2002.
1366. Letter from Olive (Mould) Coleman to Richard Klapper, March 13, 2003.
1367. Letter from Olive (Mould) Coleman, March 4, 2002.
1368. Letter from Olive (Mould) Coleman to Richard Klapper, March 13, 2003.
1369. Letter from Olive (Mould) Coleman, March 4, 2002.
1370. Letter from Olive (Mould) Coleman to Richard Klapper, March 13, 2003.
1371. Letter from Olive (Mould) Coleman, March 4, 2002.
1372. Letter from Olive (Mould) Coleman to Richard Klapper, March 13, 2003.
1373. Letter from Joan (Mould) Bolton to Richard James Klapper, January 9, 2001.
1374. Letter from Olive (Mould) Coleman, March 4, 2002.
1375. Letter from Joan (Mould) Bolton to Richard James Klapper, January 9, 2001.
1376. Letter from Olive (Mould) Coleman, March 4, 2002.
1377. Letter from Joan (Mould) Bolton to Richard James Klapper, January 9, 2001.
1378. Letter from Olive (Mould) Coleman, March 4, 2002.
1379. Letter from Joan (Mould) Bolton to Richard James Klapper, January 9, 2001.
1380. Letter from Olive (Mould) Coleman, March 4, 2002.
1381. Letter from Joan (Mould) Bolton to Helen Klapper, December 1999.
1382. Letter from Joan (Mould) Bolton to Richard James Klapper, January 9, 2001.
1383. Letter from Joan (Mould) Bolton to Richard James Klapper, February 4, 2002.
1384. *Telephone call between Joan Bolton and Richard Klapper*, July 3, 2008, "My son Maxwell was married to Sarah Winne on July 14, 2006 in the Methodist Church in Bournemouth, Hampshire, England. Sarah was born on August 2, 1978."
1385. *Telephone call between Joan Bolton and Richard Klapper*, March 9, 2010.
1386. Letter from Joan (Mould) Bolton to Richard James Klapper, January 9, 2001.
1387. E-mail from David Peters to Richard Klapper, January 20, 2002, "Andrew David Peters Born 9th June 1973, Gt Yarmouth, Norfolk Married Kerrie Rae Hayse 4th Nov 2000, St. Peters Church, Southport, Queensland, Australia Baby due May 2002."
1388. Letter from Joan (Mould) Bolton to Richard James Klapper, January 9, 2001.

1389. E-mail from David Peters to Richard Klapper, January 20, 2002, "Andrew David Peters Born 9th June 1973, Gt Yarmouth, Norfolk Married Kerrie Rae Hayse 4th Nov 2000, St. Peters Church, Southport, Queensland, Australia Baby due May 2002."

1390. Letter from Joan (Mould) Bolton to Richard James Klapper, November 11, 2002, "Andrew and Carrie had a son Joshua in May 2002."

1391. E-mail from Alison Peters to Richard Klapper, July 27, 2008, "Joshua David Peters was born 8th May 2002 in Wollongong, Australia."

1392. Letter from Joan (Mould) Bolton to Richard James Klapper, November 4, 2002, "Andrew and Carrie had a son Joshua in May 2002."

1393. E-mail from Alison Peters to Richard Klapper, July 27, 2008, "Joshua David Peters was born 8th May 2002 in Wollongong, Australia."

1394. E-mail from Alison Peters to Richard Klapper, July 27, 2008, "Emily Alison Peters 27th Aug 2003, Wollongong."

1395. Letter from Joan (Mould) Bolton to Richard James Klapper, January 9, 2001.

1396. E-mail from David Peters to Richard Klapper, January 20, 2002, "Catherine Mary Peters Born 18 September 1974 Gt. Yarmouth, Norfolk, England Married Clive David Hawkett 22nd July 2000 All Saints Church, Hillingdon, Middlesex."

1397. Letter from Joan (Mould) Bolton to Richard James Klapper, January 9, 2001.

1398. E-mail from David Peters to Richard Klapper, January 20, 2002, "Catherine Mary Peters Born 18 September 1974 Gt. Yarmouth, Norfolk, England Married Clive David Hawkett 22nd July 2000 All Saints Church, Hillingdon, Middlesex."

1399. *Telephone call between Joan Bolton and Richard Klapper*, March 9, 2004.

1400. E-mail from Alison Peters to Richard Klapper, July 27, 2008, "Noah was born in Basingstoke, Hampshire."

1401. E-mail from Alison Peters to Richard Klapper, July 27, 2008, "Do you have Heidi Mia Hawkett 7th November 2005, Basingstoke?"

1402. *GRO birth index for England*, 4 Q 1952.

1403. *GRO birth index for England.*

1404. E-mail from Kate Brooker to Richard Klapper, June 5, 2003.

1405. E-mail from Kate Brooker to Richard Klapper, June 5, 2003, I am not completely sure about these dob's.

1406. E-mail from Kate Brooker to Richard Klapper, June 5, 2003.

1407. E-mail from Kate Brooker to Richard Klapper, June 5, 2003, I am not completely sure about these dob's.

1408. E-mail from Kate Brooker to Richard Klapper, May 14, 2003, "....... there is my brother John Mark Manning born 1954."

1409. E-mail from Kate Brooker to Richard Klapper, 1954.

1410. E-mail from Kate Brooker to Richard Klapper, June 5, 2003.

1411. *Telephone call between Katharine Brooker and Richard Klapper*, May 11, 2003, Katharine confirmed that Hillary was her twin sister. Joan Bolton had already found this information in the GRO Indexes.

1412. *GRO birth index for England*, 1 Q 1956.

1413. E-mail from Kate Brooker to Richard Klapper, June 5, 2003.

1414. *GRO marriage index for England.*

1415. *Telephone call between Katharine Brooker and Richard Klapper*, May 11, 2003, Kathryn confirmed the GRO data that Hillary was her twin.

1416. *GRO marriage index for England.*

1417. E-mail from Kate Brooker to Richard Klapper, June 5, 2003.

1418. *GRO birth index for England*, 1 Q 1956.

1419. *GRO marriage index for England.*

1420. Family tree created by Joan Bolton from info from Mona Baldwin, December 2003, Kate and twin Hilary had a double wedding.

1421. E-mail from Kate Brooker to Richard Klapper, June 5, 2003.

1422. Family tree created by Joan Bolton from info from Mona Baldwin, December 2003.

1423. *Telephone interview of Jane Fletcher by Richard Klapper*, December 21, 2003.

1424. E-mail from Jane Fletcher to Richard Klapper, December 23, 2003.

1425. Family tree created by Joan Bolton from info from Mona Baldwin, December 2003.

1426. *Telephone interview of Jane Fletcher by Richard Klapper*, December 21, 2003.

1427. Family tree created by Joan Bolton from info from Mona Baldwin, December 2003.

1428. *Telephone interview of Jane Fletcher by Richard Klapper*, December 21, 2003.

1429. Family tree created by Joan Bolton from info from Mona Baldwin, December 2003.

1430. *Telephone interview of Jane Fletcher by Richard Klapper*, December 21, 2003.

1431. Family tree created by Joan Bolton from info from Mona Baldwin, December 2003.

1432. *Telephone interview of Jane Fletcher by Richard Klapper*, December 21, 2003.

1433. Family tree created by Joan Bolton from info from Mona Baldwin, December 2003.

1434. *Telephone interview of Jane Fletcher by Richard Klapper*, December 21, 2003.

1435. Family tree created by Joan Bolton from info from Mona Baldwin, December 2003.

1436. *Telephone interview of Jane Fletcher by Richard Klapper*, December 21, 2003.

1437. Family tree created by Joan Bolton from info from Mona Baldwin, December 2003.

1438. *Telephone interview of Jane Fletcher by Richard Klapper*, December 21, 2003.

1439. Family tree created by Joan Bolton from info from Mona Baldwin, December 2003.

1440. *Telephone interview of Jane Fletcher by Richard Klapper*, December 21, 2003.
1441. Family tree created by Joan Bolton from info from Mona Baldwin, December 2003.
1442. *Telephone interview of Jane Fletcher by Richard Klapper*, December 21, 2003.
1443. Family tree created by Joan Bolton from info from Mona Baldwin, December 2003.
1444. *Telephone interview of Jane Fletcher by Richard Klapper*, December 21, 2003.
1445. Family tree created by Joan Bolton from info from Mona Baldwin, December 2003.
1446. *Telephone interview of Jane Fletcher by Richard Klapper*, December 21, 2003.
1447. Family tree created by Joan Bolton from info from Mona Baldwin, December 2003.
1448. *Telephone interview of Jane Fletcher by Richard Klapper*, December 1, 2003.
1449. Family tree created by Joan Bolton from info from Mona Baldwin, December 2003.
1450. *Telephone interview of Jane Fletcher by Richard Klapper*, December 21, 2003.
1451. E-mail from Christopher Baldwin to Richard Klapper, January 21, 2004.
1452. Family tree created by Pat Baldwin, December 2003.
1453. E-mail from Christopher Baldwin to Richard Klapper, January 21, 2004.
1454. Family tree by Sheila Rose, July 2001.
1455. *Telephone interview of Sheila Rose by Richard Klapper*, September 7, 2002.
1456. Letter from Sheila Rose to Richard Klapper, October 3, 2002.
1457. Family tree by Sheila Rose, July 2001.
1458. *Telephone interview of Sheila Rose by Richard Klapper*, September 7, 2002.
1459. Family tree by Sheila Rose, July 2001.
1460. *Telephone interview of Sheila Rose by Richard Klapper*, September 7, 2002.
1461. Family tree by Sheila Rose, July 2001.
1462. *Telephone interview of Sheila Rose by Richard Klapper*, September 7, 2002.
1463. Family tree by Sheila Rose, July 2001.
1464. *Telephone interview of Sheila Rose by Richard Klapper*, September 7, 2002.
1465. Letter from Sheila Rose to Richard Klapper, October 2, 2002.
1466. *Telephone interview of Sheila Rose by Richard Klapper*, September 7, 2002.
1467. Letter from Sheila Rose to Richard Klapper, October 2, 2002.
1468. *Telephone interview of Sheila Rose by Richard Klapper*, September 7, 2002.
1469. Letter from Sheila Rose to Richard Klapper, October 2, 2002.
1470. *Telephone interview of Sheila Rose by Richard Klapper*, September 7, 2002.
1471. Letter from Sheila Rose to Richard Klapper, October 2, 2002.
1472. Family tree by Sheila Rose, July 2001.
1473. *Telephone interview of Sheila Rose by Richard Klapper*, September 7, 2002.
1474. Letter from Sheila Rose to Richard Klapper, October 2, 2002.
1475. Family tree by Sheila Rose, July 2001.
1476. *Telephone interview of Sheila Rose by Richard Klapper*, September 7, 2002.
1477. Letter from Sheila Rose to Richard Klapper, October 2, 2002.
1478. *Telephone interview of Sheila Rose by Richard Klapper*, September 7, 2002.
1479. Letter from Sheila Rose to Richard Klapper, October 2, 2002.
1480. *Telephone interview of Sheila Rose by Richard Klapper*, September 7, 2002.
1481. Letter from Sheila Rose to Richard Klapper, October 2, 2002.
1482. Family tree by Sheila Rose, July 2001.
1483. *Telephone interview of Sheila Rose by Richard Klapper*, September 7, 2002.
1484. Letter from Sheila Rose to Richard Klapper, October 2, 2002.
1485. E-mail from Marjorie Redford to Richard James Klapper, January 2, 2001.
1486. E-mail from Marjorie Redford to Richard James Klapper, February 11, 2001.
1487. E-mail from Marjorie Redford to Richard James Klapper, January 2, 2001.
1488. E-mail from Marjorie Redford to Richard James Klapper, February 11, 2001.
1489. Family tree by Trevor Mould, May 16, 2002.
1490. Letter from Joyce King to Richard Klapper, February 24, 2003.
1491. Family tree by Trevor Mould, May 16, 2002.
1492. Letter from Joyce King to Richard Klapper, February 24, 2003.
1493. Family tree by Trevor Mould, May 16, 2002.
1494. Letter from Joyce King to Richard Klapper, February 24, 2003.
1495. Family tree by Trevor Mould, May 16, 2002.
1496. Letter from Joyce King to Richard Klapper, February 24, 2003.
1497. Family tree by Trevor Mould, May 16, 2002.
1498. Letter from Joyce King to Richard Klapper, February 24, 2003.
1499. Family tree by Trevor Mould, May 16, 2002.
1500. Letter from Joyce King to Richard Klapper, February 24, 2003.
1501. Family tree by Trevor Mould, May 16, 2002.
1502. Letter from Joyce King to Richard Klapper, February 24, 2003.
1503. Family tree by Trevor Mould, May 16, 2002.

1504. Letter from Joyce King to Richard Klapper, February 24, 2003.

1505. Family tree by Trevor Mould, May 16, 2002.

1506. Letter from Joyce King to Richard Klapper, February 24, 2003.

1507. Family tree by Trevor Mould, May 16, 2002.

1508. Letter from Joyce King to Richard Klapper, February 24, 2003.

1509. Interview of Olive Coleman by Richard Klapper, March 2003.

1510. Family tree created by Joan Bolton from info from Mona Baldwin, December 2003.

1511. E-mail from Jane Fletcher to Richard Klapper, March 4, 2009, My Great Grandaughter is Frances Jane Sasha Northcott born 1 December 2004 in Portsmouth. Her father is Neill Robert Northcott born on 2nd January 1974 also in Portsmouth.

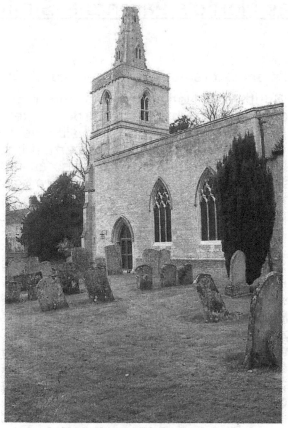

Southwick, Northants parish church where Thomas
Mould's grandparents were married and Thomas' father was
baptised.

Appendix I

Ancestors and Relatives
of Thomas Mould

Thomas Mould's Parents & Siblings

Thomas Mould's ancestors appear to have come from the Wood Newton/Apethorpe/Southwick, Northants area and migrated to the small villages around Peterborough such as Gunthorpe, Maxey, Etton, Glinton, Peakirk, Helpstone, etc. Thomas' parents' and siblings' identifications are pretty certain but earlier generations are less certain in that they are pieced together from parish data from nearby villages so assumptions have been made. Thomas was the seventh of ten children born to William and Mary Edith Molds. William was baptized in the parish church of Southwick on April 1, 1792. Mary Mould (nee Pick) was born about 1792 according to her death certificate. According to the 1841 census, Mary was born in Essendine, Northants. She is referred to in various records as Mary, Edith, Mary Edith and Ann. William and Mary Edith were married November 25, 1816 in Uffington, Lincolnshire but all ten children were baptized in Etton so that is probably where they set up housekeeping shortly after their marriage. William was an agricultural labourer. Mary Edith died at fifty-five on January 12, 1847. According to her death certificate she died of "apoplexy". William died at seventy years of age on December 20, 1862 of an "abscess". Both William and Mary Edith were buried in the Etton churchyard.

Thomas' oldest sister was named Sarah. She was baptized at Etton on April 27, 1817. It doesn't appear that Sarah ever married. In the 1851 census Sarah was listed as thirty-three years old and still single. She was a housekeeper and living with her father and siblings. No death or burial information for Sarah has been found.

Thomas' brother, William, was baptized at Etton on October 25, 1818. William never married and lived with his father until his father's death and then he lived with his brother John. The only time William was listed with an occupation was in the 1861 census when he was listed as a cow tender. In the 1871 census, William was listed as an imbecile. Wlliam died in 1880 and was buried in Etton with his family. At the time of his death, William was living in Peterborough, probably in a home of some kind.

Thomas' brother, John, was baptized in Etton on March 5, 1820. He married Elizabeth Marshall Taylor and they had two daughters. Apparently Elizabeth died because twenty one years later he married Susannah Panter and they had seven children. The first three children were born in Woodcroft but then they moved to Maxey where their remaining four children were born. John was a farmer. His wife, Susannah, died in 1880 and John died in 1893. They were both buried in Maxey.

Thomas' twin sisters, Elizabeth and Mary, were baptized in Etton on April 28, 1822. Eizabeth was a servant in Peakirk when she married John Day, a labourer on November 5, 1844 in Peakirk. John and Eizabeth had five children and John was a farmer until 1891 when the census listed him as the postmaster of Peakirk. Elizabeth died in October 1884 and John died in October 1891. They were both buried in Peakirk. Eizabeth's twin, Mary, was still living at home on January 2, 1843 when she married a labourer from Helpstone named John Fisher. They were married In Etton and then moved to Helpstone where John was an agricultural labourer for the remainder of his life. John and Mary had one daughter. John died on April 17, 1887 and Mary died in February 1889. Both of them were buried in Helpstone.

Thomas' brother, Joseph, was baptized in Etton on May 9, 1824. He moved to Peakirk and on June 18, 1849 married Martha Hall of Peakirk. Joseph was an agricultural labourer his entire life. He and Martha had eight children. By 1871 they had moved to Glinton. Martha died May 23, 1891 and Joseph died January 5, 1894. They were buried in Glinton.

Thomas' twin sisters, Ann and Jane, were baptized October 21, 1832 in Etton. We assume that Ann and Jane were twins since in the 1841 census they were both listed as 9 years old. In 1841 they were both living in Woodcroft with their parents. Ann was present at the death of her mother in January 1847 and was the informant for the death certificate. She had a son, James, out of wedlock in 1856. Ann appears never to have married since in the 1901 census an Ann Mould who was 68 years old was a servant in Spalding, Lincolnshire. She is listed as being single - not widowed. This is most likely the correct Ann Mould since she is the correct age and was born in "Woodcroft, North Hants". Jane was single and living with her father in Woodcroft in 1861. Later, in 1861, Jane had a daughter, Emily, who was born out of wedlock and was baptized on September 1. In 1871, Emily was living with her uncle and aunt, John and Elizabeth Day. No more information has been found on Jane so it is not known if Jane died during this period or if she was working as a servant and had to have her daughter raised by her older sister. In 1881, Emily was living in Broughton and was working as the cook for the Rector of Broughton.

Thomas' sister, Susannah, was baptized in Etton on May 17, 1839. In 1841 she was living with her parents in Woodcroft. In 1851 she was living with her father in Woodcroft. Susannah had two sons out of wedlock. Joseph was baptized May 4, 1856 and Arthur was baptized September 25, 1859. In 1861 she was living with her father and was working as a housekeeper. In 1869, Susannah married Luke Mandeville in Newark District. Susannah and Luke moved to Bradford, West Yorks and lived there the rest of their lives. They had four children. Susannah died in 1900 in Bradford.

Thomas Mould's Grandparents, Uncles & Aunts

Thomas' grandparents (William Mould's parents) were William Molds and Elizabeth Cox. William was born about 1761 per the Southwick parish records. The burial record for William dated October 5, 1816 indicates his age to be 56 years old. There is no baptisimal record of any Moulds in Southwick according to the baptismal records that are held in Northamptonshire. However, there was a William Moulds baptised August 16, 1761 in Wood Newton, 4.2 kms away by road. (Note: More work needs to be done to verify that this is the correct William although it is most likely correct.)

Elizabeth was born about 1761 in Northants. Wliam and Elizabeth were married in Southwick, Northants on November 15, 1784. Banns for the marriage were read in the church at Southwick on the three Sundays of October 31, November 7 and 14. In the marriage record William was listed as a bachelor and Elizabeth was a spinster. Both were living in Southwick at that time. In the various records William's name is spelled Mould, Moulds, Moules and Molds. William was a witness at the wedding of John Sewell and Mary Wight in Southwick in February 1796. William and Elizabeth had six children including Thomas' father William, all of whom were baptized in Southwick. William died in Southwick and was buried there on October 5, 1816 at the age of fifty-six years. Elizabeth lived to a ripe old age and in the 1841 census she was living in Southwick at the age of eighty. Her burial record has not been found. It appears that the children moved away from Southwick since none of their burials have been found there. The reason Elizabeth's burial has not been found in Southwick even though she was living there in 1841 at the age of eighty may be that she had to move to where one of her children were living and was buried there.

William and Elizabeth's first child was a son named Oliver Cox Mould who was baptized on August 19, 1785 in Southwick. No further information has been found on Oliver.

William and Eizabeth's second child was Joseph who was baptized on July 22, 1787 in Southwick. No further information has been found on Joseph.

William and Elizabeth's third child was Mary who was baptized on October 4, 1789. No further information has been found on Mary.

William and Elizabeth's fourth child was William (Thomas' father) who is discussed in detail above.

William and Elizabeth's fifth child was Henry who was baptized on April 5, 1795 in Southwick. It is believed that Henry has been found in the 1871 census as a publican living in Kirkby la Thorpe in Lincolnshire. The person found is the right age and is a widower who is noted to have been born in Southwark, Northamptonshire which should probably be Southwick since there only appears to be a Southwark in Surrey but none in Northants.

William and Elizabeth's sixth and final child was John who was baptized in Southwick on February 13, 1801. John was an agricultural labourer. In the mid-1820s he married Sarah Wright. John and Sarah had eight children. Sometime before their first child was born in 1828, John and Sarah had moved to Helpstone and lived there for the rest of their lives. Only a couple of months after the birth in the first quarter of 1846 of her last child (a daughter named Edith Mary), Sarah died on June 6, 1846. This left John alone with eight children, all under 16 years of age, including one newborn girl. It may not be all that surprising then that the little infant died only eight months later at the age of ten months. Surprisingly, John did not remarry for seven years. On August 1, 1853 he married Elizabeth Parish. John died about four years later on May 8, 1857. He and Sarah along with little Edith Mary are buried in Helpston churchyard.

Thomas Mould's Great-Grandparents

If the William Mould born in Wood Newton is indeed Thomas' grandfather, then Thomas' great grandparents (William's parents) were

Joseph Moulds and Sarah or Elizabeth Askew. Joseph's baptism in Wood Newton occured in 1724. Joseph and Mary Elizabeth were married in Wood Newton on October 2, 1748. They had ten children, all baptised in Wood Newton. The children and their baptism dates were: Henry (July 2,1749), Joseph (January 13, 1751), William (March 1753), Mary (February 27, 1754), John (April 10, 1757), Elizabeth (June 19, 1759), William (August 16, 1761), Sarah September 26, 1762, Mary (June 10, 1764 and Thomas (December 27, 1767).

Thomas Mould's G-G-Grandparents

Thomas Mould's g-g-grandparents (Joseph's parents) were Thomas Mould and his second wife, Mary (maiden name not known).Thomas was born between 1675 and 1680 and Mary was born about 1695. They had five children baptised in Wood Newton, Northants. Their children and dates of baptism are: Elizabeth Moulds (1715), Thomas Moulds (1718), William Moulds (1721), Joseph Moulds (about 1724) (died: December 1790 in Wood Newton) and Henry Moulds (1728) (died: August 1846 in Wood Newton).

Thomas apparently had a wife (unidentified) prior to his marriage to Mary (?). His first marriage produced five children as well. Their names and baptism dates in Wood Newton are: Thomas Mould (1704) (died: 1718 in Wood Newton), Mary Mould (1705) (died: 1771 in Wood Newton), John Mould (1708), William Mould (1711) and Susannah (1712).

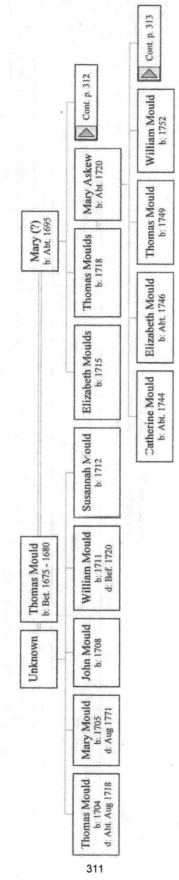

Cont. p. 313

Cont. p. 312.

William Mould
b: 1752

Thomas Mould
b: 1749

Elizabeth Mould
b: Abt. 1746

Catherine Mould
b: Abt. 1744

Mary Askew
b: Abt. 1720

Thomas Moulds
b: 1718

Elizabeth Moulds
b: 1715

Susannah Mould
b: 1712

William Mould
b: 1711
d: Bef. 1720

John Mould
b: 1708

Mary Mould
b: 1705
d: Aug 1771

Thomas Mould
b: 1704
d: Abt. Aug 1718

Mary (?)
b: Abt. 1695

Thomas Mould
b: Bet. 1675 - 1680

Unknown

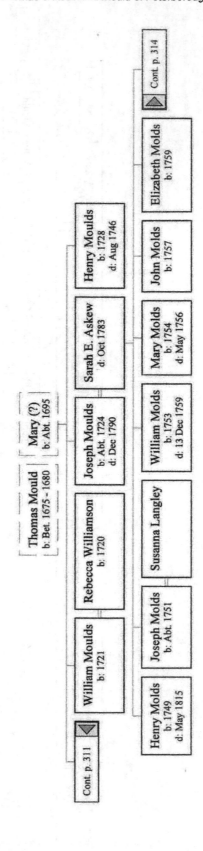

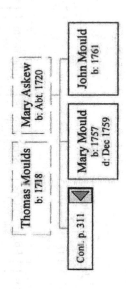

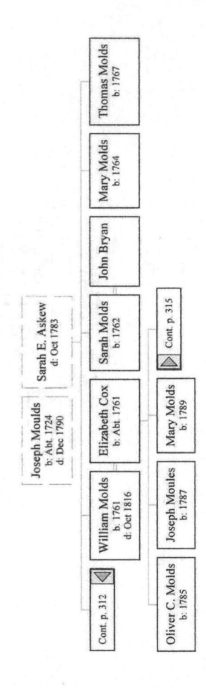

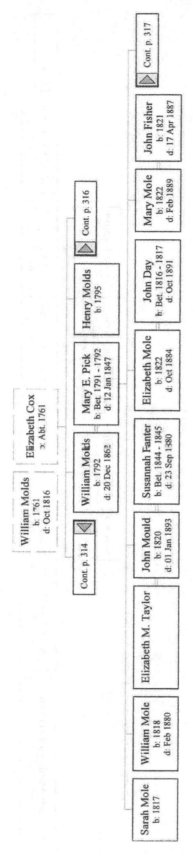

Cont. p. 317

John Fisher
b: 1821
d: 17 Apr 1887

Mary Mole
b: 1822
d: Feb 1889

Cont. p. 316

Henry Molds
b: 1795

John Day
b: Bet. 1816 - 1817
d: Oct 1891

Elizabeth Mole
b: 1822
d: Oct 1884

Mary E. Pick
b: Bet. 1791 - 1792
d: 12 Jan 1847

William Molds
b: 1761
d: Oct 1816

Elizabeth Cox
x: Abt. 1761

William Molds
b: 1792
d: 20 Dec 1862

Susannah Fanter
b: Bet. 1844 - 1845
d: 23 Sep 1880

Cont. p. 314

John Mould
b: 1820
d: 01 Jan 1893

Elizabeth M. Taylor

William Mole
b: 1818
d: Feb 1880

Sarah Mole
b: 1817

315

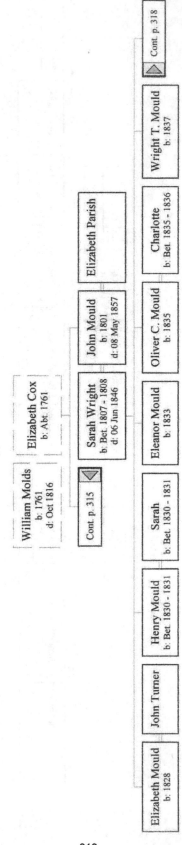

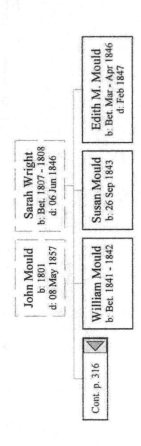

Brigstock, Northants parish church where Rose Ann
Mould's parents, Jabez and Mary Mackness are buried.
Author Richard Klapper is shown standing next to their
headstone.

Appendix II

Ancestors and Relatives
of Rose Ann Mould

Rose Ann Mould was born Rose Ann Mackness the fifth of nine children born to Jabez and Mary Mackness in Brigstock, Northants. According to the 1851 census and his grave headstone, Jabez was born in Higham Ferrers about 1793. His wife Mary Wade was born in Weldon about 1799. The 1799 date comes from the inscription on her grave headstone but the 1851 census indicates she was born about 1797. Jabez and Mary were married in Brigstock on October 12, 1820 and lived the rest of their lives there. Jabez was a farm laborer.

As noted above they had nine children of which three died as infants and six lived to adulthood. All nine children were baptised in the parish church in Brigstock. Their first child was a daughter they named Jane. She was baptised March 4, 1821 but died eighteen months later from smallpox. She was buried October 1, 1822 in Brigstock churchyard.

Jabez and Mary's second child was another daughter they again named Jane. She was baptized October 5, 1823 but again, died as an infant in July of the next year. Jane was buried in Brigstock churchyard August 1, 1824.

Their third child was a son they named William. William was the first of their children not to die in infancy. He was born November 7, 1824 and was baptised March 13, 1825. He married Rebecca Bland on October 16, 1846 in the area of Thrapston, Northants. He and Rebecca had at least five children - Mary born April 24, 1848, William born December 26, 1849, John born November 8, 1851, Eva born about 1853 and Joseph Thomas born December 3, 1865. Joseph Thomas married his cousin Rebecca Mould (daughter of Thomas and Rose Ann) and is discussed in detail in Chapter 8. Three of these children emigrated to the United States and settled in South Dakota and Montana. William and Rebecca were both buried in Rushden's Newton Road Cemetery.

Jabez and Mary's fourth child was a daughter named Elizabeth baptised February 10, 1827. She appears to have never married since in the 1891 census she was in Rushden and listed as single working as a domestic servant and living with her brother Joseph Thomas' wife. Elizabeth died in Rushden, Northants and was buried there October 29, 1894.

The fifth child was a daughter named Rose Ann who is one of the main characters of this book and is discussed in detail in Chapter 1.

Jabez and Mary's sixth child was a son they named Jabez and who was baptised June 5, 1831. Jabez married Anne Stonehouse during the fourth quarter of 1860 in Lythe, Whitby, Yorks. Jabez died in Huddersfield, Yorks on March 14, 1906. The date and location of Anne's death are unknown. They had six children. The first two were daughters who must have been twins born in early 1861 and who died within three months. The third child was another daughter who was named Mary born December 1861 in Whitby, Yorkshire. Unfortunately, this daughter only lived about a half year and died in the third quarter of 1862. A fourth daughter was born in the

320

third quarter 1863 Hinderwell, Yorks. This daughter survived childhood as she has been found in the 1881 census as a 17 year old living with her parents in Hinderwell. The fifth child was a son, James, born April 29, 1865 in Hinderwell, Yorks. James married his cousin, Betsy Mould and they are discussed in detail in Chapter 3. The sixth and last child was a son, William, born 1867 in Hinderwell. William married Mary Ann Hill, date and place unknown.

Jabez and Mary's seventh child was a son, Nathaniel, born 1833. In the second quarter 1875 he married Ann (last name unknown). Nathaniel died in Marske (Guisboro), Yorkshire in the fourth quarter 1897. No details on Ann's death have been found. They had two children - Hannah Elizabeth, born about 1886 in Guisboro and Thomas William, born second quarter 1880 in Guisboro. Thomas William married Ethel Thomlinson in 1906 and they had two children.

Jabez and Mary's eighth child was a son, Joseph, born 1837. Joseph only lived about a year and died in 1838.

Jabez and Mary's ninth and final child was another son named Joseph. He was born October 1839. He married Ann Bagshaw Adams, May 6, 1858 in Brigstock. Joseph and Ann moved to Rushden in about 1869 and lived there for many years where Joseph supported the family as a shoemaker.

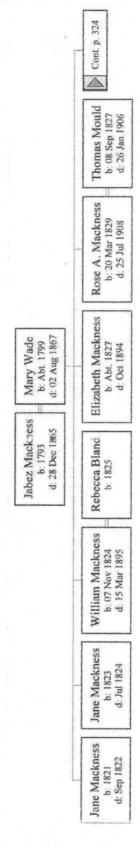

Jabez Mackness
b: 1793
d: 28 Dec 1865

Mary Wade
b: Abt. 1799
d: 02 Aug 1867

Jane Mackness
b: 1821
d: Sep 1822

Jane Mackness
b: 1823
d: Jul 1824

William Mackness
b: 07 Nov 1824
d: 15 Mar 1895

Rebecca Bland
b: 1825

Elizabeth Mackness
b: Abt. 1827
d: Oct 1894

Rose A. Mackness
b: 20 Mar 1829
d: 25 Jul 1908

Thomas Mould
b: 08 Sep 1827
d: 26 Jan 1906

Cont. p. 324

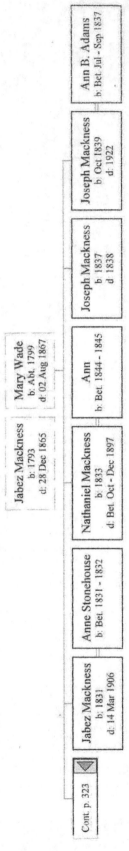

Jabez Mackness
b: 1793
d: 28 Dec 1865

Mary Wade
b: Abt. 1799
d: 02 Aug 1867

Jabez Mackness
b: 1831
d: 14 Mar 1906

Anne Stonehouse
b: Bet. 1831 - 1832

Nathaniel Mackness
b: 1833
d: Bet. Oct - Dec 1897

Ann
b: Bet. 1844 - 1845

Joseph Mackness
b: 1837
d: 1838

Joseph Mackness
b: Oct 1839
d: 1922

Ann B. Adams
b: Bet. Jul - Sep 1837

Cont. p. 323

Appendix III

Directions to Ellingson, South Dakota Cemetery

Ellingson, South Dakota as a town no longer exists. It was always very small and only consisted of a church, store/post office and a school. The buildings are now gone and all that remains is the cemetery which was once next to the church. The town has been gone since at least before the early 1970s. The easiest way to drive to Ellingson cemetery is to start in Hettinger, North Dakota. The directions from Hettinger to Ellingson cemetery, as of 2003, are as follows.

From Hettinger, North Dakota take Highway 8/75 south two miles towards Lodgepole. After two miles there is an old metal sign on the right in the shape of a buffalo. It is very old.

At the buffalo sign turn right (west) onto a well maintained dirt road. Follow this road for twelve miles and you will come to a bridge over the Grand River.

After crossing the river the road curves to the left (south). Continue following the road for three and seven-tenths miles. After three and seven-tenths miles there is a two track trail going to the right (west).

Follow this trail for one-half mile up the hill and the Ellingson Zion Cemetery is on top of the hill on the right.

It is a small cemetery with about forty graves inside a barbed wire fence. It has a brick sign with the name of the cemetery in the middle of the cemetery.

The Descendants of Thomas & Rose Ann Mould of Peterborough, England

Burial record of Joseph Mould in Paston Parish Churchyard

Appendix IV

Coroner's Report on Death of Joseph Mould

On March 31, 1900, Joseph Mould was found dead in his bedroom by his father, Thomas. Thomas sent his son George (Joseph's brother) to report the finding to the police. The Coroner, John William Buckle, held an inquest on that same day. The jury was composed of Thomas Brown, John Laxton, George Lawson, Frederick Techell, James Garner, William Fox, Robert Hadman, George William Tywell, John Barnes, James Harlock, Charles Brown, Joseph White and John William Dexter. There were only two witnesses called to testify - Thomas Mould and Walter Knight, a policeman from Werrington. After listening to the testimony of the witnesses the Coroner and jury ruled "......the said Joseph Mould committed suicide whilst temporarily insane cutting his own throat."

The testimony of the two witnesses and the coroner's findings are as follows:

The Liberty of the hundred of Nassaburg and Soke of Peterborough to wit:

Deposition of witnesses taken for our Sovereign Lady the Queen at the house of Thomas Brown in the Parish of Gunthorpe within the said District this 31st day of March, One thousand and nine hundred, touching the death of Joseph Mould. Before me, John William Buckle, Coroner for the said Liberty.

Thomas Mould sworn saith. I am a cottager and live at Gunthorpe. The body which the jury have just seen is that of my son Joseph. He was 35 years of age, a Bachelor and lived at home with me. He worked for William Rowe the Butcher. He was at work last a fortnight since having been since then at home ill with the influenza. He has been attended by Dr. Peach Hay about 3 times. The deceased went to the Dr. yesterday morning. He was very low spirited and has been for the last 4 or 5 days. I last saw him alive about 6:15 last night. He was then leaving the sitting room to go to his bed room. My wife and I went to our room. We neither heard anything of the deceased during the night I went out this morning and about 20 to 6 this morning my wife came to me and asked if I knew anything of Joe meaning the deceased. She said
                    T Mould
                    (End of Page)

I must come and I went directly. I found the deceased on the floor at the side of his bed in a pool of blood. He was quite dead then. I did not interfere with him there and sent my son George for the Police. My son George did not live with us. I never heard the deceased threaten to take his life. He has been queer in his mind at times. He was examined 20 years ago as to the state of his mind by Dr. Paley. He was at the Union Infirmary

330

for one week. He was excited at times when the weather was hot. We thought it was ....(words missing from copy).
　　　　T Mould

Walter Knight sworn with. I am a Police Constable stationed at Werrington. About 6:30 this morning I was called by George Mould. He told me his Brother the deceased had killed himself. I went at once to Gunthorpe and found the deceased lying on the floor face downward in a pool of blood. I examined the body. He was dead, stiff and cold. I found a gash in his neck about 4 inches long cut deep. The wind pipe cut through. He had a razor in his right hand and a pocket knife lay under his face, small
　　　　Walter Knight
　　　　(End of Page)

blade open under his face The bed clothes were turned down as if he had been t bed. He was undressed- There were no marks of any struggle. I think the injuries were self inflicted.
　　　　Walter Knight

Verdict

Suicide while temporarily insane cutting his own throat

The foregoing testimony of Thomas Mould and Walter Knight were severally taken and deposited before me at the time and place aforesaid.

　　　　John William Buckle
　　　　Coroner for the hundred of Nassaburg

Appendix V

Thomas & Rose Ann Pictures

Thomas Mould

Rose Ann Mould

Family tea with Thomas in white hat and Rose Ann in black hat.

Thomas and Rose Ann Mould and two daughters

4 Generations L-R: Jane Jessop, Rose Ann Mould
(holding baby Muriel Baldwin), Naomi Baldwin

Appendix VI

Jane Jessop Descendant Pictures

Jane Jessop

Baby Muriel Baldwin with L-R: Jane Jessop, Rose Anr Mould and Naomi Baldwin

Standing: Herbert and Naomi Baldwin. Seated: Frederick Thomas "Bill" Jessop with Muriel and Douglas Baldwin on his knees.

Naomi Jane Baldwin at 63 years old.

Herbert Alphonsus Baldwin

Herbert and Naomi Baldwin at wedding of Eric and
Muriel Parsley in 1925.

4 Generations: L-R: Katharine Manning held by Muriel
Parsley, Naomi (Jessop) Baldwin, Virginia Manning
holding Hillary Manning. Front L-R: John Mark Manning
and Belinda Manning.

Eric Parsley at Christ's Hospital School

Eric Parsley/Muriel Baldwin wedding (1925)

Eric Parsley (1960)

David Parsley (in 1946)

Douglas Herbert and Mona Baldwin

John Rupert Baldwin who died at 8 years of age.

Devereux Henry Jessop II who was killed in a motorcycle accident in 1914.

Jesse (Anscombe) Jessop wife of Devereux Henry Jessop II who was injured in the motorcycle accident which killed her husband.

Jesse Anscombe Jessop and her son Devereux Frederick Jessop

Jesse (Anscombe) Jessop in her later years

Devereux Frederick Jessop (November 1934)

Devereux Frederick Jessop (1940's)

Rose Anna (Jessop) Brushett

Frederick Thomas and Rose Anna Brushett with daughter Helena Joan.

Joan Brushett with unknown child

Appendix VII

Polly Avery Pictures

L-R: Mary "Polly Avery, Jabez Mould, Sarah Ann Mould

Mary "Polly" Avery

Wedding in Everard family. Mary "Polly" Avery is in chair on far left front. Man behind her is Joseph Mackness.

Appendix VIII

Rose Prentice Descendant Pictures

John William Prentice

George Harold Prentice with his mother Rose Prentice

John William Prentice

Ellen "Nellie" Prentice in 1906

L-R: Ellen "Nellie" Prentice and Lily Prentice in 1933

Lilian Prentice

Lilian Lake and George Harold Prentice in 1917

Lily and Geroge Harold Prentice in the early 1950's

L-R: John Trevor Prentice, Sheila (Prentice) Rose, Lily (Lake) Prentice, Molly Mary (Marck) Prentice holding baby Jane Prentice and George Harold Prentice in 1946.

Harold and Lily Prentice in 1962

Wedding picture of John Frederick Prentice and Jessie Edith Smellie on April 11, 1925.

John Frederick and Jessie Prentice in Torquay in 1939.

John Frederick Prentice

Dora Prentice

Dora Prentice with Trevor and Sheila Prentice

L-R: Sheila (Prentice) Rose and Dora Prentice

Appendix IX

Jabez Mould
Descendant Pictures

Jabez and Sarah Ann Mould

Jabez Mould in 1928

Jabez and Sarah Ann Mould

Sarah Ann (Cox) Mould in her medical uniform in England

354

Sarah Ann Mould

L-R: Annie (Mould) Bull, Sarah Mould, Helen (Bull)
Klapper holding Richard James Klapper,

Four generations: L-R: Sarah Mould, Annie (Mould)
Bull, Alfred Bull and son Richard Bull in 1944/1945

George Mould and his mother Sarah Mould in front of her grocery
store called the 8th Avenue Grocery in Aberdeen, South Dakota

Rose Marion Mould in the late 1880's

Rose Marion Mould

L-R: Annie (Mould) Bull, George Mould, Rose (Mould) Lovell in November 1949.

Rose and George Lovell and their daughters Hazel (left) and Irene Marguerite (right)

Rose (Mould) Lovell

Standing L-R: Annie Mould, George Lovell, George Mould. Seated: Rose (Mould) Lovell holding daughter Hazel

L-R: Irene Marguerite Mould, George Mould, George Lovell

George Mould

L-R: Helen Bull, Tom Large, Doreen Large, Lois and Alfred Bull, Kate and George Mould. In front: Irene Marguerite Mould in 1940.

357

Wedding of Fred Bull and Annie Mould

Fred and Annie (Mould) Bull with children Alfred and Helen in 1922/1923.

Fred and Annie (Mould) Bull

Fred and Annie Bull on their 50th anniversary on July 11, 1965

Annie (Mould) Bull and son Alfred in 1917

Annie Mould in 1904

Annie Mould in 1905. Note: She was known as Nancy.

Appendix X

Rebecca Mackness Descendant Pictures

Joseph and Rebecca (Mould) Mackness

Thomas and Rebecca (Mould) Mackness in August 1921.

Joseph Thomas Mackness

Rebecca (Mould) Mackness

Rebecca (Mould) Mackness with son Frank in August 1921.

Frank Mackness in August 1921.

L-R: Esther Mackness, Nick Redford, Frank Mackness in 1963.

Appendix XI

Charles Mould Descendant Pictures

Charles Mould

Wedding of Robert Lovell/Ivy Mould in 1931.

Wedding of Bob Roberts/Violet Mould in 1920. L-R: Charles Headland, Elsie Headland, Bob Roberts, Violet (Mould) Roberts, Jessie Mould, Charles Mould, Emily Mould.

Bernard and Jane Mould in March 1975.

Bernard and Jane Mould and their eight children taken in September 1960. L-R: Margaret, Joan, Norman, Bernard, Phillip, Jane, Trevor, Janet, Mary and Joyce.

Appendix XII

George Mould Descendants

George Mould

George Mould with children L-R: Doris, Cyril (seated),
Bernard

Fanny Mould with children. L-R: Doris (partially cut
off), Cyril, Fanny holding Guilford, Bernard and Eric in
1906/1907.

Back row L-R: Hubert Mould, Doris Mould, Bernard
Mould, Marjorie Mould, Cyril Mould. Front row L-R:
Fanny Mould, Iris Mould, George Mould. Picture taken at
59 Gilpin Street in 1927.

Back row L-R: Hubert Mould, Kate (Freeman) Mould, Doris Mould,
Bernard Mould, Marjorie Mould, Cyril Mould and Doreen Mould.
Front L-R: Fanny Mould, Irene Marguerite Mould, Iris Mould,
George Mould. Picture taken by George Ewart Mould in 1927.

George Mould with granddaughter Olive at
her wedding on January 3, 1953.

Doris Mould in 1903/1904.

Cyril and Beattie Mould on their honeymoon in Great
Yarmouk

Ernest Maile

L-R: Cyril and Bernard Mould.

Beatrice (Ward) Mould

Cyril Mould

Eric Mould. Picture taken April 21, 1995 - three days before his death.

L-R: Guilford, Mary, and Joan Mould in May 1973.

Guilford and Mary Mould

Guilford Mould and Marge (Mackness) Redford (granddaughter of Joseph and Rebecca Mackness) next to grave of Rose Ann (Mackness) Mould's parents in Brigstock in 1990

L-R: Marjorie and Iris Mould in 1927.

Wedding picture of Hubert Lawrence Mould/Ursula Oberlander in Berlin, Germany on June 18, 1947.

Ursula and Hubert Mould in May 1973.

Dorothy Ayers (undated photo)

George Mould and Dorothy Ayers on their wedding day,
April 6, 1953.

L-R: Romain Mould, Melvin Mould, Ursula Mould's
mother, Hubert Mould, Ursula Mould

Iris Mould (about 1930)

Fanny Mould (about 1930)

Wedding of Doris Mould/Ernest Maile on June 20, 1932. L-R: Iris Mould, Best Man Harold Toyne, Ernest Maile, unknown woman, Doris Mould, two unknown ladies, Marjorie Mould, unknown man, George Mould (on end). Unknown child in front.

L-R: Hubert, Bernard, Eric and Guilford Mould in May 1973.

L-R: Kate Mould, Irene Marguerite Mould and Doreen Mould at the grave of Thomas and Rose Ann Mould in 1927

Appendix XIII

Family Grave
Headstone Pictures

Grave on left is John Mould; grave on right is Sarah and Edith Mary Mould - John was Thomas Mould's uncle and Sarah was John's wife and Mary Edith was their daughter; Helpston, England

Jabez and Mary Mackness - parents of Rose Ann Mould; Brigstock, England

William Mould - brother of Thomas Mould; Etton, England

John and Susannah Mould - John was Thomas Mould's brother; Maxey, England

John and Mary (Mould) Fisher - Mary was Thomas Mould's
sister; Helpston, England

Joseph and Martha Mould - brother of Thomas
Mould; Glinton, England

Susannah Marshall Mould - Daughter of Thomas
Mould's brother John Mould and his first wife Elizabeth
; Etton, England

Robert Day - son of Thomas Mould's sister Elizabeth;
Peakirk, England

Joseph and Betsy Day - son of Thomas Mould's sister
Elizabeth; Peakirk, England

John and John Joseph Day - John was the son of Thomas
Mould's sister Elizabeth; Peakirk, England

Jessie Day - Granddaughter of Thomas Mould's sister
Elizabeth; Glinton, England

Thomas and Rose Ann Mould; Paston, England

Thomas and Rose Ann Mould - Paston, England
(Grave as it appeared in May 1939)

Devereux Henry Jessop, Jane Jessop & Devereux Henry
Jessop II; Sutton, England

Mary (Mould) Avery; Elligson, South Dakota

James Edward Dale Avery; Peakirk, England

John William and Rose Prentice; Peakirk, England

Joseph Mould's broken headstone; Paston, England

Jabez Mould; Aberdeen, South Dakota

Sarah Ann Mould; Bonita, California

Rebecca (Mould) Mackness; Ellingson, England

Joseph Thomas Mackness; Ellingson, South Dakota

Charles and Emily Mould; Higham Ferrers,
England

George and Fanny Mould and Marjorie and Iris Mould;
Peterborough, England

Ellen, Lillian and Dora Prentice; Peakirk, England

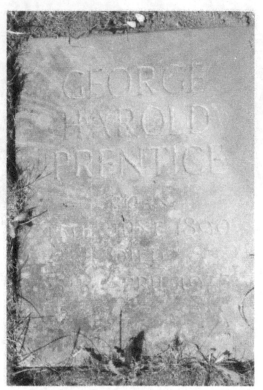

George Harold Prentice: Churchill, Oxfordshire, England

Lily Prentice: Churchill, Oxfordshire, England

Rose Marion (Mould) Lovell; Bonita, California

George Henry Lovell; Bonita California

George Ewart Mould; Bonita, California

Kate Mould; Bonita, California

Fred and Annie (Mould) Bull; Aberdeen, South Dakota

Clarence Alva Ritter; Bonita, California

Constance Doreen (Mould) Large; Bonita, California

Thomas Harry Large; Bonita, California

James and Daisy Sharpe; Higham Ferrers, England

William Richard Klapper; Coleman, Texas

Alfred and Lois Bull - Falkton, South Dakota
(Picture taken prior to Alfred's death)

Eric Parsley

Appendix XIV

Finding of Rare Manuscript by Eric Parsley

In 1947, the husband of one of Jane (Mould) Jessop's granddaughters, Eric Parsley, found a rare and very valuable first edition manuscript of the play "Athalie" by the seventeenth century French writer, Jean Racine. Eric donated the manuscript to the French and was awarded the Feuilles Academiques in 1950 and the Order of Chevalier des Artes et Letters, for services to French literature. Below is the story in Eric's own words of his locating and obtaining the manuscript.

Survival Story

This account of the adventures of a book begins at Versailles in 1691 and ends here in our own days; some parts of the book's history over the intervening two and a half centuries must be supplied by well-founded conjecture, but the story of its surviving the London blitz, its rescue from the pulping mill, and its restoration to its proper home, is exact in every verifiable detail.

Jean Racine had ceased to write for the theater several years before Louis XIV took to wife the widow Scarron, the discreet, wise and pious governess of his bastards by Madame de Montespan. The disreputable name of Scarron had been effaced by the lady's elevation to the marquisate of Maintenon. Whatever drawbacks her promotion had for her - and there were many - she was at least excellently placed for furthering the interests of the school for girls she had founded, and which she was now able, with the king's help, to establish in the New Buildings at Saint Cyr, a very few miles from Versailles. To the wise government of this Foundation Madame de Maintenon devoted every moment she could spare from the Court; to Saint Cyr she withdrew immediately after Louis' death, and there she herself died and was buried.

The curriculum at Saint Cyr was not so austere as to exclude play-acting; the difficulty was to find suitable material which was morally acceptable without being insipid. Madame appealed to Racine, now well established in the Royal favour and holding an official post at the Court. She asked him to compose a moral or historical poem for the girls to perform. It was a great deal to ask, and Racine had many misgivings; but the dramatic genius which had been acquiescent for a dozen years rose far above the occasion and produced the play "Esther", a pretty faithful dramatisation (sic) of the Bible Story. The girls gave a number of performances of "Esther" in 1689, before very select audiences, including the King himself, and, once, the English refugee James II and his Queen. (Madame de Sevigne was invited to the final performance of the 'run', on February 19th, and sat in the front row just behind all the royalties. "It is so beautiful that it makes one weep"

390

she wrote; and she was greatly envied because the King had quite a conversation with her about the play. It was, however, too much of a success, and quite turned the heads of some of the girls, who even stopped singing in the Chapel for fear of tiring their voices. Madame determined it should not happen again. But the girls were not wholly to be deprived of their chance of showing how well they could act, and in 1691 Racine gave them "Athalie" the tremendous story of the overthrow of the usurping Queen Athaliah by the high priest Jehoiada.

The tragedy which Voltaire was later to call "the masterpiece of the human spirit" seems startlingly unsuitable for a performance by a cast of young girls; and it is impossible not to believe that the author was carried away by his own genius, or at least had one eye on posterity.

The author was, however, never to see an adequate production of his great play, for he was dead years before it had its first public performance. He only saw it given privately in Madame's apartments at Versailles, before the King, the Dauphin and the exiled English royalties; and there were neither costumes or scenery, nor any of that exiting audience from the Court which had made Madame de Lafayette write, doubtless with an implication quite undeserved, "It is unreasonable to imagine that three hundred girls and the young men of the Court can be so near to each other without the walls being scaled."

"Athalie" was printed in the spring of 1691 by Denys Thierry of the Rue Saint Jacques in Paris, and the first copies were sent round to Racine's house.

Madame de Maintenon may well have bidden him send her a printed copy as soon as it was available; at all events the author selected one, wrote the words "A Madame de Maintenon" across the title page, and sent or took it to her at Versailles. This is the copy whose fortunes we are now following; it was, and is, a quarto volume bound in full calf, printed in a great variety of elegant fonts, with wood-cut decorations wherever a title, change of act or scene gives the opportunity. Madame de Maintenon passed the book to her librarian at Saint Cyr, who pasted the schools bookplate inside the front cover. It is a large handsome plate, leaving only a narrow margin of the marbled lining paper shewing; the engraved device shews the arms of Saint Cyr, a wreath of palm-leaves and flowers enclosing a cross with a crown and fleur-de-lis, and a scroll beneath with the words "De la Bibliotheque de la Maison Roiale de St. Louie a S. Cyr".

The long reign had ended gloomily in 1715, and Madame de Maintenon herself had died in 1719, aged 83; her last years had been clouded by anxiety for her beloved foundation; the new King was a little boy and the Regent had soon diverted to his own needs the endowment and the special grants which maintained St. Cyr. Security was restored by 1720 by the personal intervention of the young King Louis 15th and the traditions of the school were faithfully carried on by the admirable Superior, Madame de Glapion.

The memory of "Madame" was hallowed, her room with her furniture, books and needlework kept as it had been when she was still there, and her body lay in a vault near the altar in the Chapel.

Our book stood on its shelf through what proved for Saint Cyr a prosperous eighteenth century. The royal protection was continued and indeed increased, royal visits and royal "pensionnaires" and royal bounty enhanced the prestige of the House, until, with the Revolution the fatal day came when the immensely wealthy foundation fell victim to the confiscatory zeal of the National Assembly. After the abortive flight to Varennes, the rumour that Marie Antoinette had deposited her jewels at the school dealt the final blow; the staff and pupils were dispersed to their homes, every vestige of royalty was effaced. The Republic was at war and the great building was gutted and fitted out as an army hospital; by the autumn of 1794 there were nearly two thousand wounded lodged there. Later, the premises were used for a college which developed Napoleon into the officers training establishment which the name of Saint Cyr connotes still.

When the Peace of Amiems re-opened the Channel ports to English tourists in 1802, among early visitors to Paris were Lord and Lady Holland and their kinsman, Charles James Fox. The Hollands met Lafayette and Talleyrand, were presented to Napoleon and Josephine, and later dined with them. "Long talk with Bony, he talked almost all. Was presented to Madame. Liked her very much". (Though Lady Holland, while conceding Josephine's perfect figure and taste in dress, described her face as "ghastly, shocking, disgusting, a worn out hag"). But the real purpose of this trip to Paris was to collect certain material for Lord Holland's history of the early part of the reign of James II, the work was published in 1808. Now James II, in exile at the French Court, had been present at the exceedingly private first performance of Racine's "Athalie" in 1691. At some moment at the beginning of the 19th Century the copy of that play in which we are interested, passed into the hands of Lord Holland. The conjecture imposes itself that it was acquired amongst the "certain material" pertaining to James II, in 1802. At that precise time, of course, English collectors were busily acquiring all kinds of objects d'art, pictures, books, etc., which only The Revolution could have made available and many were the great English houses whose galleries and libraries were so enriched when their owners returned from the first visit to France that had been possible for a dozen years or more.

At all events, the library at Holland House in London acquired Madame de Maintenon's own copy of "Athalie", and the librarian affixed his lordship's bookplate inside the cover, but right at the top so as to avoid overlaying any part of the design of the Saint Cyr plate.

So our book kept its place on the shelves of the great Holland House library for the next century and a half of its life, until another great Continental upheaval came to disturb it. Holland House, the 1st great country house in London, was bombed beyond repair in the London blitz; its ruins still stand in Holland Park. The library suffered greatly. When the debris was sorted out after the War, part of the contents which did not seem worth retaining was sent to be sold at auction, and at some stage, and in spite of the express instructions of Lord Ilchester, the present head of the Holland family, that no "inscribed book" should be sold, "Athalie" though undamaged and intact, found its way into a stack of old books which was knocked down to a junk dealer for ten shillings. As he drove his horse and cart down through South London - perhaps on his way to sell his old paper to some Kentish papermill - the dealer looked into one of his sacks and found that it contained a number of books in a fair state of preservation. His way lay through old Dulwich where Charles Salkeld, one of the most sagacious of antiquarian booksellers, keeps his shop. The cart pulled up, and the dealer declaring that "This lot looks more in your line than mine, guv'nor" turned over the sack of books to Mr. Salkeld at a rewarding figure, and "Athalie" fell into the hands of a new proprietor, and one who knew what he had acquired. Indeed it was just in time to be included in the winter catalogue which Mr. Salkeld was preparing to send out to his customers.

As well as a second-hand bookshop, some elegant Georgian houses, and the most beautiful picture gallery in Europe, Dulwich contains a famous College for boys. There the present writer was employed, and the chief part of his duties to teach some of the older boys what they need to know about French literature. For the summer Examination of 1948 these boys had to prepare among other texts, the "Athalie" of Racine; but text books were at the time in short supply, and "Athalie" was not yet available, although expected any day. So one Saturday morning late in the Michaelmas term 1947 I was introducing the Sixth Form to the play, and telling them how Madame de Maintenon had been concerned in the matter. As I spoke to them I had in my hand Mr. Salkeld's winter catalogue, which had come by post that morning and had been waiting for me in the Masters Common Room. Reprehensibly - for one should do nothing, they say, to distract the attention of one's pupils - I opened the pamphlet as I stood talking, and looking down it, I read the words: Racine, J. "Athalie", Tragedie de l'Ecriture Sainte, Paris, 1691. First edition, inscribed on the title page 'A Madame de Maintenon, etc. Incredulously I communicated the thing to the class who were good enough to be almost as excited as I was myself. They insisted that I must run down the road at once and secure the book for the modest guinea indicated. The mid-morning "break" came, and I got on my bicycle - it was one of those periods when we had no petrol for private cars - and was soon asking Mr. Salkeld whether he still had No. 471 in his current catalogue. He had; it was just as he had described it, no page was torn or missing, though it was far from being a 'mint' copy; the lower half of some pages was stained by water from the fireman's hoses, after the bombing raid. But there was the great bookplate of the "Maison Royale de Saint Cyr", with the small one of Holland House superimposed at the top; and there too was the bold inscription across the title page - A Madame de Maintenon - in a clear firm hand that seemed to convey a quiet conviction of authenticity; as it well might, for the experts of the Bibliotheque Nationale have since accepted it as Racine's own. I rode back to the College ....(unreadable).......... best guinea's worth I have ever bought. I learned afterwards that I had no sooner left the shop than Mr. Selkeld's telephone signalled the first of a large number of calls from all over the country as customers opened their catalogues which had reached them by the second post; mine had reached me, not half-a-mile away, by the first post, and I had not been allowed to waste time. Dulwich College is well known to possess a number of manuscripts of particular value to Shakespearan (sic) students, which came to the College through its founder, the actor Edward Alleyn, the Henslowe Diary and a first Folio are the most important. Every year on Founders Day, the College librarian arranges a small exhibition of items of interest from the treasures of the library. In June 1948 the usual exhibitor was projected, and the librarian asked me to lend the "Athalie" for the interest of the visitors. At the same time there was being prepared in London an infinitely more important exhibition, devoted to French manuscripts, First Editions and Bindings, which was to be called "A thousand years of French books", and to be displayed at the National Book League in Albermarle street in the autumn of the same year. Mr. Desmond Flower, the distinguished organiser (sic), wishing to borrow from the Dulwich College Gallery the portraits of Boileau and Buffon to decorate the walls of the exhibition rooms, happened to visit the College on Founders Day and was extremely surprised to see displayed this indisputable Racine first edition with its startling inscriptions. Indeed, to have seen it before, one would have needed to have the entree to Holland House and to have run it to earth in a library which contained, even in the time of the third Lord Holland who acquired the Racine, over thirteen thousand books. Naturally Mr. Flower lost little time in inviting me to lend the 'Athalie' for inclusion in his exhibition. When it opened the book attracted particular attention even amongst so glittering a collection of rareties (sic), and it was selected for special mention in the principal reviews of the Exhibition on both sides of the Channel; which was all very exciting for me.

When Mr. Desmond Flower brought the "Athalie" back to me in Dulwich he very kindly asked me to luncheon, to meet the Cultural Counsellor at the French Embassy, M. Rene Varin. This meeting was one of the most rewarding of the experiences which have resulted from my finding this book. In the course of an excellent luncheon at Boulestin's I learned with enormous interest that the authorities at Versailles were at present engaged in reconstituting the apartments, in the palace, of Madame de Maintenon. Some of the original furnishings and carpets were finding their way back to Versailles from all over the world. M. Varin, whose house is at Versailles and who was a personal friend of the then Conservateur-en-Chef, the late M. Beaupre, was closely concerned with the reconstitution. What was lacking it seemed, was any of the lady's books, of which a number had been destroyed in the Allied bombing during 1944. Well, it was very flattering to find oneself in a position to restore to France something which belonged there and which France wanted; the Conservateur-en-Chef at Versailles was pleased to accept the book, and it was soon lodged prominently in Madame de Maintenon's own room in the Chateau, were (sic) it remains. My wife and I were invited to Versailles, at Easter 1949, to see the installation, and were most hospitably entertained in the Grand Trianon, and shown many things and places which do not meet the eye of the ordinary visitor. It was our good fortune to watch the functionary who attends to the Palace clocks at works: Louis XIV's great clock, as big as and rather like a sedan chair, had just been put in order after three years work, and one of Marie Antoinette's clocks was made to play the tinkling tunes of Gretry in which she delighted. The tapestry expert, who had succeeded his father in the post, and who remembered being dandled by Queen Victoria at Windson when his father had been called in for consultation there, took down from its oval frame over a door a portrait of the Archduke Joseph, Marie Antoinette's brother, and opened the back to investigate the ravages of the years; on the back of the canvas was scrawled in brown paint the name of the sitter and the note that it had been painted in the presence of his sisters. Had any other eyes seen that since, say 1770?

There is a tail-piece to this story which one must not allow oneself to call sad. Two years later my friend John Cruesmann was on holiday in Paris. He was entertained by a French bibliophile who has a notable collection of XVII century first editions, especially Racine. He listened incredulously to the story of my "Athalie" and would not be satisfied short of driving out to Versailles to see it with his own eyes. When he stood before the case he said, shaking his head sadly " If I had known that book was in the market, I would have given up to ten million francs for it".

Eric Parsley.

Eric Parsley died in 1972. He was awarded the Feuilles Academiques in 1950 and the Order of Chevalier des Artes et Lettres, for services to French literature. (This final note was added by an unknown person to the bottom of the story written by Eric Parsley.)

Reproduced by permission.

Annie and Alfred Bull. Picture taken in
Northamptonshire during 1928 trip to England.

Appendix XV

Diary of 1928 Trip to England by Annie (Mould) Bull

Thomas and Rose Ann's son Jabez and his family emigrated to America. In 1928 Jabez, his wife, Sarah and his daughter, Annie Beatrice Bull, the wife of Fred A. Bull, took a four and a half month trip back to her native England. Annie took her son, Alfred. Annie's husband Fred had to stay home and run the family dairy business and their seven year old daughter, Helen, stayed with her father. Annie's diary of the trip covers from May 19 through October 12, 1928. The diary is included in this book since it mentions numerous members of the Mould family. The Bulls mentioned are relatives of Annie's husband. The diary was handwritten and was later typed by Annie's daughter Helen Klapper in 2001. It was this typed version which has been copied for this book. Comments or clarifications by the author are noted in square brackets [ ].

May 19, 1928 Left Aberdeen, So Dakota 12:30 by train
Bigstone Lake 3:45 Terribly dusty all through Dakota and part of Minnesota crops all look just about the same. They haven't had any rain, but we are past Montividio now and the country is more hilly and the grass lots longer and lots of trees quite pretty in fact. Illinois looks quite nice as though they had plenty of rain. Arrived in Chicago at 9:00. Len [**Charles Leonard Bull**] met us at the depot just the same old Len had his pipe on. He took us to breakfast then home to wash up then out to Jackson Park a very big park and down to the shore of lake Michigan. There was a beautiful breeze and hundreds of people on the beach just like the seaside. Alfred paddled some- then we went and had chicken dinner at restaurant. Then we went on a sight seeing bus for miles came back had ice cream and went to the Chicago Theater had a lunch then home to bed tired out. **Monday** we went to the Field Museum. It was a wonderful place, and will be more so when it is finished. They are all the time working on it. We didn't see all of it as we wanted to go to Lincoln Park. When we got there we went and saw the animals and the fish, but we didn't get to see all of them as it was 5:00 o'clock and they were closing up, so we walked around the park some, which is very beautiful then we had supper went for another bus ride went out on the north side of Chicago then we went down town to another show the Reniora(?) then home, tired again. **Tuesday**: Len and Alfred went to meet Mum and Dad, and I fixed dinner for them then we went down the loop and out on a bus and looked at the shops had ice cream and came back home and Mom & Dad had a sleep. Len and Alfred and I went shopping and back and I fixed supper then sat around and talked with the folks until train time then Len took us to the depot and saw us on the train en route for Buffalo where we went to bed. In the morning we woke just outside Cleveland. The country from there on was very pretty, especially through Pennsylvania and along by Lake Erie. The farms are very prettily situated. They grow lots of grapes (concord) here. The soil is sandy here. We arrived in New York at 9:10 went to the hotel in a taxi. No one met us, but it was not far from the depot. We then had a bath got cleaned

398

up and went to the Bronx Park where we looked at the animals and walked around a bit came back had supper and went to the picture show and to bed. **Friday** Alfred and I went to the aquarium and the Natural History Museum then home to rest awhile. Then Dad, Alfred and I went out for supper and a shopping expedition then back to the Hotel and got Mum and went to the Roxy Theatre, came back and had a lunch.. met an interesting young Scotchman talked for awhile and then to bed. Morning Saturday packed up went down to the ship got acquainted with a few nice people went below unpacked. Then ate lunch, after which I went on deck, but came down pretty quick as I got sick and stayed that way until the next Friday. Almost all the time after that I was lots better and chummed around with a girl named Bina Finnigan. The boat fare was pretty good, but our cabin was too low down. Alfred enjoyed himself immensely on the boat he was not at all sick. Mum was just the same as me. We arrived in Queenstown on Sunday afternoon at 3 and were there until nearly ____(?). My friend left us there. We reached Liverpool Monday June 4 at about 11:00 o'clock, but we didn't get by the Doctor and Customs until about half past 1:00 o'clock when my Aunt Mary met us then we went on to Upton for dinner then we went for a walk in the evening with my cousin Elsie who had come over to see us. **Tuesday** we went to Liverpool where I bought a warmer dress had tea then went to a picture show then home.
Wednesday I went to Arthur's to dinner and Tea and saw a wedding in the afternoon June 6. We also went to Moreton Hoylake and West Kirby by car a young man named Fred Thomas. **Thursday June 7** we all went Heswell to my cousin Elsie's had a nice time, but it rained which kind of spoiled things. **Friday, 8th**, we went to Bulls for tea and Alfred and I went to B.head [Birkenhead] and bought each of us a raincoat. Then we went to the Avenue Theatre then home again. **Sat. June 9**. We went to Chester Dad, Uncle George, Alfred and I and had a very pleasant time. **Sunday June 10** we all went to tea to a lady's named Mrs. Lynet, a place called Greasby. Then we came back and went to a lady's named Moore for supper where Mum and Dad had a room. **Mon. June 11** Alfred and I went to Liverpool to see Mum and Dad off for Upton then we went with Mrs. Thomson's daughter around the Liverpool Museum. Then we had a lunch then out to her place in Boolte where she got us a very nice tea then we came back to Liverpool, did some shopping and came home.**Tue. June 12**, we went again to Heswell, went down to the shore...Where Alfred had a fine time paddling, etc. then we went home and had supper then back to Upton. **Wed. June 13.** Alfred and I went to B.port(?) Sunlight and had a very interesting trip. Also went Moro(?) Grove Sunlight Art Gallery had tea in Birkenhead went to the Pictures and home again. Thursday June 14 stayed home while Alfred went to Hoylake School for the day with Miss B. Jones to study their system of schools. Aunt Mary and I went to a lady named Mrs. Grady's for tea and went to Mrs. Moore's again in the evening. **Friday June 15**: Aunt Mary, Alfred, and I went to Llanndudno by bus. Had very nice time trip but not much time in Llanndudno. **Sat. June 16** Alexandra Day and I went to Liverpool and made arrangements for my passage home on the Baltic. Took in the Liverpool art gallery and attended to some other business. Alfred went to Moreton(?) with Mrs. Moore and her little boy and had quite a good time. **Sun. June 17**. Went down to Arthur's

in the morning. In the afternoon Elsie & her husband had Mrs. Moore & son
Stevie come to tea in the evening we went to Moore's and heard the radio.
Mon. June 18 Helped Aunt Mary. Walked to Moreton with Mrs. Moore to
meet her sister Mrs. Sales and went with Mrs. Moore and her sister to
Pictures in Burkenhead. **Tues. June 19** went to Southport Alfred and I had
a lovely time very pretty. **Wednesday June 20**. Aunt Mary, Alfred and I
went to Winderemere had very enjoyable time went rowing on the lake.
Thurs. June 21. Went walking with Mrs. Moore to her sister's Mrs. Sales
had a lovely time although it rained and we did not get to New Brighton.
Fri. June 22. Left Liverpool. Arrived in Northampton at 4:00 o'clock went
up to Aunt Lizzie's had tea went to Annie's where Alfred and I are staying.
Sat. June 23 Met Harold down at Aunt Lizzie's . went down to the market
in the afternoon and evening. **Sun. June 24**. went around the race course
and then Mum and Dad and Aunt Lizzie came to tea at Annie's in the
evening. Harry took us for a lovely drive. **Monday, June 25**. I went over to
Rushden had tea with Mrs. Dawks then went up to see poor Grandma Bull
[Eliza Bull wife of James] from there over to Uncle Charlie's [Charles
Mould brother of Jabez] then stopped a minute at Priss's then home to
Northampton in Harry's car then bed. **Tue. June 26** did some mending
and went with Annie to my cousin's Bill and Lil for tea. Alfred went with
Harry to Rolverton where he has a studio back to Annie's for supper. Then
to bed. **June 27, Wed**. Went down to the market with Aunt Lizzie and
Annie. Came back had tea, then Harry took us out to Melton where they
played tennis. Had a nice time then home again supper and bed. **Thurs.
June 28**. Alfred and I went down to the depot to see about getting our
things to the depot back to Aunt Lizzie's for tea. After went to the
Exchange Cinema. Then home in Harry's car. Supper. Bed. Wireless. **Friday
June 29**. went in the morning to see my cousin George and his wife had a
nice little visit. Back to dinner. Then down to Station. Then on to Higham to
Uncle Charlie's where I met Mum and Dad just leaving for Peterboro via
Yorkshire. Had a nice evening talking over old time's. Went to bed . **Sat.
June 30**. Went up to see Uncle Ebb [Ebinezer Wrighton] and Aunt Eva
called on Priss & Tom. Met Charles Edward Troome. Had tea and supper
with my cousin Urie(?) **Sun. July 1**. Had dinner with Uncle Charlie and
went to old Mr. and Mrs. Lovells [Arthur and Jane Lovell] for tea. Then went
to chapel with Priss. After that went for a walk. Met Agnes and Naomi Tye.
Had quite a long chat then met Aunt Rea [Rebecca (Wrighton) White] and
Annie Wiggington. Another chat then on home. **Mon. July 2**. went
shopping called on Willie Cox and wife. Howard Lovell and wife. Mr. and
Mrs. Quincy. Then on to Lily Emery. Mrs. Dawkes. Then to the Palace. Then
home. **Tues. July 3** went over to Rushden spent the day with Agnes. She
took me up to Gert and Annie Freeman's had tea. Then back up Queen St.
had some more tea. Met Mr. and Mrs. Harrod. Then back to Higham on the
bus. **Wed. July 4**. went down to Mrs. Wapplington's to tea. In the evening
went walking with Aggie Curtis had a nice time. **Thurs. July 5**. got a bike
went round Saunders Lod, called at Aunt Eve's [Eve Wrighton] then on to
Grandma Bull's to celebrate her 96 Birthday. Met Flo [Florence Knight],
Ethel [Stapleton], Mr. and Mrs. Ambridge. Rode home in the evening. **Fri.
July 6**. went to Desboro. Had a lovely time with old friend , Mr. and Mrs.
Clark [possibly daughter of Eb Wrighton] and Edna Tumell and her husband

and Mabel Lee Curtis, and Mabel Crabb, Ethel Cox and others. . **Sat. July 7**. Alfred and I biked around Chelveston Kinabation(?). back to Swinshead and Yelden. Back home. Washed up and had tea. Then called on Willie Quincey and his wife and Mr. J & Mrs. Then over to Rushden met a lot of old friends Rollie Cox [Rowland ?] and wife, Walter Wood, Mrs. Ablett and wife [probably husband], then Horace [Bull] who walked home with us. He was going camping next day. **Sunday July 8** Alfred and I went over to Aunt Rea's for dinner and tea in the evening we called on Mr./Mrs. Joe Knight and Mrs. Shoreley had very enjoyable day... **Mon. July 9** I went over to Mrs. Dawkes. Mailed my pictures to you. Mum and Dad came over in the evening we had a nice chat then Dad and I walked up to Uncle Ebb's, had a visit. Then to bed at Mrs. Dawkes. **Tuesday July 10.** Went up to Aunt Eva's for tea. Had a nice time. **Wed. July 11** (my wedding anniversary) called on Mrs. Denton then up to Mrs. Joe Knight's had tea. Watched them play tennis putting(?) game with Joe Knight. Very enjoyable time. **Thursday July 12**. went up to see grandma [Eliza Bull]in the morning. Called by Aunt Rea's left each a picture. Then met Priss talked a few minutes. Then by bus to Higham to Uncle Charlie's for dinner and tea in the evening. We all went first to London then to Bedford by bus. **Friday July 13** Stayed with Mrs. Dawkes nearly all day. Went to see Ollie's mother a few minutes then went to Camfuer(?) for tea. in the evening went over to Higham to Uncle Charlie's. then to Mrs. Wagstaffs to see Mum and Dad. Then back to Mrs. Dawkes for supper. **Sat. July 14**. Left Mrs. Dawkes at 10:30 for Northampton, stopped at Eaton and visited Allwyn's father and mother. Then on to Northampton. Had dinner with Aunt Lizzie. Met Elsie and husband Fred Jones. Then down town to catch bus for Cold Ashby. Harold [Harold Prentice] and the children met us there then over the field to the house. Met Lily, Harold's wife and their Aunt Emily [John William Prentice's younger sister?]and youngest son. Had tea chatted 'till bedtime. **Sunday July 15** Aunt Emily's oldest son and young lady came over in a car also Jesse Mould and her young lady friend Miss Webb came over on their bikes from Northampton. We had dinner and tea on the lawn. Had thorough good old fashioned English country Sunday a day of rest. In the evening Aunt Emily, her eldest son and his young lady went back to Nottingham. Left the youngest he was lots of company for Alfred. Then Jesse and her friend left. **Mon. July 16-Tue. July 17**. passed quietly reading, writing and sewing. **Wed. July 18** Lily and I went to Liecester by bus. Had a very enjoyable day. Returned home about 5:45. found Mum and Dad waiting with the tea all set. Then we had a nice long chat and enjoyed the radio. Then bed. **Thurs. July 19**: We left Cold Ashby for Northampton. Had tea with Aunt Lizzie. Then on again to Higham to Uncle Charlie's for the night. **Fri. July 20**. We left Uncle Charlie's early in the morning for Hunstanton where we arrived about 11:30. found rooms. Went shopping. Had dinner. Then onto the beach. **Sat. July 21**. Spent the day on the shore. In the evening Mr. & Mrs. Wagstaff came down on their motor so we spent a very pleasant time. **Sun. July 22**. we went along the shore to old Hunstanton with Mr. & mrs. Wagstaff . then back to dinner. After dinner a walk on the shore, tea. Mr. & Mrs. left. We also met Annie & Harry Leeson & cousin Phil down on the shore, but they all went back in the evening. **Mon. July 23**. Spent the day on the shore. In the evening went to concert(?) on the pier(?). **Tues. July 24**. Looking for a letter none for nearly three weeks. Came Friday. Went up town and done some shopping got caught up on my diary. **Wed. July 25**. Sandringham Flower show. All around Sandringham kitchen gardens also flower show and church. There were thousands here. Had a very nice time from then until **Aug. 3rd** at Hunstanton very quiet but enjoyable time. **Fri. Aug. 3rd** left for Northampton. Stayed at Annie's. **Sat. Aug. 4th** Morning went down to bank and shopping. Left for Birmingham in the afternoon. Arrived in Birmingham met Mrs. Pendrey went round the store's market. Then on to Erdington. **Sun. Aug. 5th** Quiet with Mrs. Pendrey and family. **Mon. Aug. 6th**. Visited Aston Hall fine old place of historical interest, beautiful grounds, etc. Went on to Birmingham had tea of a sort. Took in a show then home. Tue. **Aug. 7th**. Visited Warick Castle and town via Coventry, Scanigton(?), Kinilworth a very fine old castle beautifully situated and furnished partly occupied by rich American. **Wed. August 8th** visited Birmingham Art gallery and museum a very wonderful collection. **Thurs. Aug. 9th** Stratford-on-Avon Shakespeare's birth place and residence also library and Ann Hathaway's cottage. Came back through WarickLeann(?). Stopped at Kenilworth Castle. Went all around the ruins. Then on to Coventry and back to Birmingham a most enjoyable day outing **Friday Aug. 10** did my washing went to Mrs. Wittons to tea spent the evening music and singing. **Sat. August 11** left Birmingham for Northampton via Higham on the bus arrived about 8:30. **Sun. Aug. 12th** had tea with Priss and Tom [Lovell], Horace and Joe Tompkins had a very pleasant time had supper home to Uncle Charlie's and to bed. **Mon. Aug. 13th** Left Higham for Peterboro about 10:30- arrived about 1:00 o'clock Uncle George met us with a car soon home met Aunt Fanny and all the family, Doris, Cyril, Bernard, Eric, Guildford, Marjorie, Iris, Hubert went for a walk with some of them. In the evening went to a picture show-saw Jack Mulhall in The Poor Nut. **Tue Aug. 14th** in the morning I wrote a letter to Fred [Fred Bull, her husband] in the afternoon we walked over to Gunthorpe through Paston, looked around the church visited my grandparents graves [Thomas & Rose Ann Mould] also Uncle Joe's [Joseph Mould, buried about 20 feet from his parents, Thomas and Rose Ann Mould] then on to Mrs. Harlachs where we had tea and spent a most enjoyable time. Mrs. Harlach is 83 years old and a very intelligent woman, well ahead of her time and able to talk on (missing). We also visited the cottage where my grandparents [Thomas and Rose Ann Mould] spent the last years of their lives. Then in the evening we walked back to Peterboro through the fields. **Wed. Aug. 15th** We went to Crowland Abby, a very interesting old place partly in good repair and part in ruin. The town also is very old contains a very quaint old bridge called the "three-way" with a man in one corner holding a loaf we had dinner at Bernard's girls home in Crowland and had a very nice time returning home in time for tea spent a quiet evening at home with Aunt Fanny [wife of George Mould]. **Thursday Aug. 16th** I washed-in the afternoon we visited Peterboro Cathedral a very beautiful old building, the original being built about the fifth century It has three different styles of architecture and was burned down twice and rebuilt. I believe I saw Ols Scarlet's picture stand on Hye with visage grim, but it was very dark there and I could not decipher it very plainly then we came home again. In the evening Uncle George,

Alfred and I went over to Peakirk and saw my cousins Lily and Dora [Prentice] and visited the graves of Uncle Jim [James D. Avery, husband of Mary "Polly" Avery nee Mould] and Aunt Rose [Rose Prentice nee Mould, wife of John Prentice] and Uncle John [John Prentice]. Dora and Lily wanted us to go over again on the Friday, so we promised to do so and rode home again. On **Friday Aug. 17th** I went into Peterboro to the bank and also visited the bank also visited the museum, a small but very interesting place with many things there that can be found nowhere else, such as pictures of straw work one of Peterboro Cathedral, a very beautiful piece of work looked like gold. Then there was a splendid collection of work done from bones that the French soldiers did in the time of Napoleon when they were in prison from the bone they were given their meat on one was a ship, a fine piece of work and many others too numerous to mention. Then Alfred and I biked over to Peakirk again to tea and had a very enjoyable time then rode back again in the evening. **Sat. Aug. 18th**-Bernard's girl, Annie, saw us off for London where we arrived about 2:00 o'clock. Mrs. Lingard met us at the Kings Cross Station and took us home and we had a very nice tea in the evening we went down the Ridley Road Market it's a very interesting place where they sell things very cheap there(?) Alfred and I went to the Pictures at the Colosium while Mrs. Lingard was busy in the shop. **Sunday Aug. 19th** Mrs. Lingard took us to Westminster Bridge and all around the Tower of London and then on to St. Paul's Cathedral then down Fleet Street Then down Thread needle SSt. Where the mint and bank are. Fleet Street is all newspaper offices then down Grays Inn Rd. where all the lawyers have their offices then back to dinner after dinner we had a rest and in the evening we went to the embankment and all around Westminster Abbey and Houses of Parliament on the outside then down White Hall by the place where the mounted guards are then on down to Piccadilly Trafalgar Square and the Strand then by bus back home tired out. **Mon. Aug. 20th** Mrs. Lingard took us to the Crystal Palace it's quite aways from London a very fine place somewhat neglected of late fine statuary and fine old stone work from various places quite a lot. concert and organ recital it is a tremendous place and the grounds are very nice. There are also quite a number of paintings by old masters. **Tues. Aug. 21st** We visited Madam Tussauds and the Zoo. **Wed. Aug. 22nd**. We went down Oxford Street and Regent Street shopping. **Thurs. Aug. 23rd** We went to the British Museum then on to the Strand to the Duke of York's Theatre where we saw a revue of which I did not think so much. **Friday Aug. 24th** Alfred and I went to Westminster Abbey and went all over it. It's a fine old place. Saw the tombs of numerous famous people. **Sat. Aug. 25th** Alfred and I left for Bournmouth, but stopped off at Guildford where there is a fine old castle ruin and the grounds are laid out all around it with a nice War Memorial and is well worth a visit. Then we went on to Winchester 9:30 got a room and some supper then went to bed. **Sunday Aug. 26th** We looked around the Cathedral (as fine as any of those I have seen) and attended part of a service then on by Charabac to Bournmouth through quite a part of the new Forest. We arrived in Bournmouth and it was raining hard I soon got a room then dinner and in the afternoon we went to visit Mr. & Mrs. Clark had tea with them. Then came back and read awhile then went to bed. On **Mon., Aug. 27th** we went around the town and down on the shore in the afternoon. We went on Charabac trip to a place called Lulworth Cove, a very beautiful place and the road lay through the heart of Thomas Hardy's country. **Tues. Aug. 28th** we went to Swanage by boat visited the Tilly Whim Caves and the Globe saw the light house met some very nice people named Nichols from London. **Wed. Aug. 29th**- We went on a trip around the Isle of White by Charabac, Boat and Rail. It was a lovely trip. Started at 7:30 returned to Bournmouth 9:00 at night. **Thurs. Aug. 30** we spent the morning on the shore and in the afternoon we went on a trip to Milton Abbey(?) a very old and interesting church set around the beautiful scenery of Dorsetshire. We also visited a place called Bere(?) Regis a very pretty place also a church, then too went through Blanford where the King and Queen go to church when they visit the Marquis. On **Friday, Aug. 31st** we left Bournmouth by coach for Oxford through the new Forest to Lyndehurst-Basingstoke, Brockhurst Southampton Winchester on to Reading through the Berkshire Hills to the beautiful Thames Valley through Shillingford bridge and Munham and Dorchester to Oxford where we arrived about 2:10 found Mrs. Weaver had dinner then chatted 'till tea time. After tea we visited Magdalen College a little then on to Christ Church College where there was a big dinner in progress and all the nationalities of different countries were represented we watched them arrive. Then home to supper and bed. Here endeth August 31st. **Sept. 1st Sat.** went shopping in the morning a little wrote letters and post cards in the afternoon. Mr. Weaver, Mary, Alfred and I went in Magdalen College where the Prince of Wales was educated. Visited the Cathedral and the Cloisters there is a pulpit in stone above the Cloisters from where a sermon is preached to the students the 7th of May each year. We also saw the deer in the park surrounding the college where they get venison from for the college. Then we visited the Botanical Gardens and saw the walk where the students go down to river to train for their boat races. From there we went to Christ Church College went through the quad(?) and the dining hall where so many of England's great men were educated and where they ate and where their pictures still hang. Alfred and the others went up into the Tower called Big Tom and where there is a big bell of that name which strikes 101 times every night at nine o'clock. From there we went to new college. All Souls and all Saints and By Brazenose and several others. After that we went home to tea. After tea May and I went up to the Morris Cowley Motor Works then went by bus to Connor Hill and tried to find Connor Place where Amy Robsart was imprisoned and killed, but didn't quite make it as it was three miles from where the bus stopped and it got quite dark before we had gone two miles so we had to turn back. Home & to supper and bed, but better luck next time. **Sunday Sept. 2**. Went to Deddington to visit Mr. & Mrs. Dawes. Had a very nice time. In the evening we went on a nice walk through the fields met Mr. Weaver's son. When we came back a very clever old gentleman who does this old woodcarving by hand, an art almost extinct now**. Mon. Sept. 3**. we went back to Oxford for St. Giles Fair. Quite celebrated affair and certainly an awful big crowd. When we had English production of which I do not recall the name. Then home to Mrs. Weaver to bed. In the morning **Tues. Sept. 4** we left Oxford for Banbury and Sulgrave. We first arrived in Banbury from where I hired a taxi to take us to Sulgrave about 7-1/2 miles. In Banbury we went all over the Old Manor

404

and grounds and also the church it is a very pretty and interesting old place and I quite enjoyed looking over it. Then we went back to Banbury and had a good look around the town and St. Mary's Churcha very beautiful old church with some interesting round stained glass windows a church of very unusual style of architecture. Then we examined the cross where statues to Queen Victoria, King Edward and King George have been erected three generations. From there we went and did a little shopping bought some Banbury cakes. Had dinner. Then left for Northampton by bus through some very pretty country and quaint old towns and villages. Arrived in Northampton about 4:30 at Aunt Lizzie's where I saw Mum & Dad and had a little chat. Then on again by bus to Higham to Priss's and to bed of which I was very glad as my head was full of wheels from riding so much. On **Wed. Sept. 5th** I visited with Priss did my washing, wrote letters, went down to Aunt Emily's then went to tea with Mrs. Quincey, then took a walk with Priss in the evening. On **Thurs. Sept. 6th** I ironed and mended in the morning. In the afternoon I went over to Grandma Bull's [Eliza Bull]. Also called on Uncle Ebb. I stayed there until about 8:30. then home to bed. **Fri. Sept. 7** I went down to Aunt Emm's and the bank. In the afternoon I went to George's mother with Priss to tea where we stayed until quite late. I also called on Emily, Howard's wife. On **Sat. Sept. 8th** it was hospital day in Higham so everyone was busy. In the afternoon I went with Priss to Willie Cox's and had tea. Had a very nice time. Then in the evening I left Priss's for Uncle Ebb's [Ebinezer Wrighton] where we arrived about 8:30. had a chat with them. Then supper and bed. **Sunday morning Sept. 9th** Aunt Eva had her pork pie for breakfast which we enjoyed very much. Then Uncle Ebb went to Sunday School so Alfred and I went to visit grandma [Eliza Bull] and Mrs. Dawke's. then on the way home I called on Bennet, a lady I used to know when she was a little girl named Annie Dawkins of Desboro. She wanted me to go again and I had intended doing so but after events made this impossible, from there we went back to Uncle ebb's to dinner and as it was raining the rest of the day, we spent indoors visiting very pleasantly in the evening. Mrs. Gray told me the story of early adventures in South Dakota. She is very frail now she is 81 yrs. of age and that was about 48 years ago. It hardly seems possible as one looks around now that such things could have been. **Mon. Sept. 10th** We spent with Frances and Cecil [Frances Clark nee Wrighton; Ebb's daughter] we had a most enjoyable time, they are both full of fun. In evening Frances and I took a walk down town while Alfred and Keith played together. Then back to supper and the radio, which was certainly very fine. After which or before supper I should have said, Willie Wrighton and Sis came in and we all visited together and had quite a time. Uncle Ebb was there too. It was the first time I had met Willie. They asked me to go up the next day. **Tues. Sept. 11**. In the morning I went up to Miss Greens then on up to Ray Bull's where I met Eva and saw the baby, but she was asleep. Eva is very nice and asked me to come again but I told her I hadn't much time or I would have done. I did not see Ray there as he was out working. They have a very nice home. Ray came up to Uncle Ebb's to see me afterwards he seems a very nice fellow and was sorry I couldn't get to spend more time with them. In the afternoon I went to Will & Sis for tea and had a very enjoyable time with them. In the evening Herbert Boswell came in and we had quite a talk and it turned out that he had married Jessie Desborough an old friend of mine and they have one boy and live in Wymington, but she was in Rushden, so he went and fetched her and we had supper and quite a jolly time going over old times. Then Sis had a friend of theirs take me home in a Saloon car**. Wed. Sept. 12th**. In the morning I visited Mrs. Joe Knight and had a chat with her while she did her washing. Then in the afternoon we went out to Fred Wrighton's to tea as it was Lorna's birthday and we had a very nice time there. Also went to Aunt Rea to dinner and Mrs. Linnett's funeral. **Thurs. Sept. 13**. I left Uncle Ebb's for Mrs. Dawkes where I arrived about 11:30 after visiting Mrs. Shorley and Aunt Rea. In the afternoon I went over to Aunt Emm's [Emily, wife of Charles Mould] as Uncle George from Peterboro came up to see us again. We all had tea together. Then in the evening I went over to Rushden again to Sis's and we walked over to Wymington to visit Jessie D. and her hubby and Mr. & Mrs. Desborough. Had quite a nice time. Then back to Mrs. Dawkes. Oh I met Horace and he walked down with us and met Mrs. Dawkes. **Friday, Sept. 14th** I had a bad cold didn't go far. Met a lady from Canada at Mrs. Dawkes for tea in the evening. I visited Grandma Bull. Then home to bed. **Sat. Sept. 15th** I went up to Sis's and she went with me to Mrs. Freemans where we had tea. Then I went and bought some flowers and took them to grandma's [Eliza Bull]. Then Sis and I went by bus to Wellingboro where we went around the market and looked around the town. Then we went back to Sis's had supper. Then I went on to Higham to Uncle Charlie's and to bed. **Sun. Sept 16** I had quite a cold and didn't go far. Sat around, talked, and wrote and then Aunt Emm had all of them for tea after that I walked over to Sis's and we went for a walk. Then I came back had supper and went to bed. **Mon. Sept. 17** I went around Higham Church and went up to my cousin Violet's [Violet Roberts] for the day, but didn't feel very good. Had a nice time. Went and looked at Bob's [Bob Roberts] chickens very nice ones. Then home to supper and bed. **Tues. Sept. 18** had a letter from Dad in London saying Mrs. Lingard's dog had bitten Mum right through her chin and they had had to take her to the hospital. It upset me terrible. I went over to Rushden to see if Willie didn't have to work if he could take us up in his car, but he had got to work so Horace said to leave Alfred with him as he would like to have him, so we left Dick too and Sis went to London with me as Bill had to go on the Thurs. and said he would bring us both back. Then we arrived at Mrs. Lingards and found Mum was progressing quite good with regards to the bite, which was a very bad one. Then Dad took us to St. Paincras[?] where we got the underground for Sutton and my cousin Rosies[?] Brushelts[Rose Brushett] where we arrived about 9:30 and soon had supper and chatted awhile and went to bed. **Wed Sept 19th**. In the morning we looked around Sutton quite a nice little town. In the afternoon we went to London by bus. We went through Mitcham by the place where Nelson used to live and by the common where they play Cricket. Then to the National Art Gallery, where we spent about 2-1/2 hours. Very interesting. Then had tea at Mrs. Lyons. Then back to Sutton by bus had a pleasant evening chatting. **Thur. Sept. 20** We left Sutton for Mrs. Lingards via Westminster Bridge. Arrived there about 1 o'clock Willie Wrighton, Alfred, and Dick came soon after. Then we had dinner and left for Rushden with Bill and Sis in the car. Stopped for supper near Hitchen and arrived at Uncle Charlies about 9:30 after a pleasant time. **Friday Sept. 21** Went all around saying goodbye in Higham and Rushden then left for Northampton in the evening where we arrived at Aunt Lizzie's about 8:30. Talked awhile had supper and bed tired out. **Sat. Sept. 22** Went downtown and did some shopping. Then came back to dinner said goodbye. Then left on the 1:40 train for Birmingham. Arrived there about 3:15. Looked around. Tried to do some business, but the places were closed. So got the car to Erdinyeon(?). Arrived about 4:30. Mrs. Pendrey surprised but pleased to see us. Had tea. Chatted awhile. Went to pictures saw Adolph Menjou in "A Gentleman of Paris". Home and supper and bed. **Sunday Sept. 23.** Spent the day resting and talking with Mrs. P., Alfred, and Edith P. also Mrs. Shelley-Edith's mother. **Mon. Sept. 24** Mrs. P. and Edith saw us off at New Street for Matlock where we arrived shortly after ten. Looked around. Visited the petrifying well also the Cumberland Caverns and walked around the Heights of Abraham. Back into town. Shopped a little. Then went on to Matlock Bridge. Ate dinner. Then took the bus to Bakewell via Haddon Hall, Chatsworth House. Stayed in Bakewell ¾ of an hour. Looked around the church and the village. It was market day. Bought some Bakewell tarts and some P.C. and caught the bus to Buxton a lovely ride through the Cheddar gorge arrived in Buxton about 4:30 looked around. A very pretty town worthy of a longer stay. Then on to Manchester and Liverpool. Arrived there. Went on to Upton and reached Aunt Mary's about 9:30 tired out. **Tues. Sept. 25th** In the morning I washed and in the afternoon Aunt Mary, Alfred and I went to Liverpool did some shopping. Had tea saw the Illuminations went to a show. Then Home. **Wed. Sept. 26th**. Wrote letters visited around. In the afternoon went to meet Mum & Dad at Woodside Ferry. Mum looked pretty sick came back to Aunt Mary's where we had tea and chatted until bedtime. **Thurs. Sept. 27**. Dad, Uncle George, Alfred and I went on a Chara trip to Blackpool had a lovely ride went through Preston. Arrived in Blackpool. Had dinner. Walked along the front. Went to the Lower Theatre saw a wonderful show midgets and acrobats and swimming. Saw a young lady who swam the Channel and another who nearly swam the Irish Sea, but failed within about a mile. After the show we had tea. Then took in the sights and the Illuminations miles of them very beautiful. Blackpool is a very lively town and interesting-would like a week there. Then back to Liverpool by Chara. Home about 12 o'clock. **Friday Sept. 28th**. A busy time saying goodbye packing etc. Elsie and her husband came over. We had tea at Arthur's in the evening. Bill came up to Aunt Mary's we had a nice time. In the afternoon Dad, Alfred, and I went over to Liverpool to the Shipping office, etc. and also visited Liverpool Cathedral a massive pile. To me not as appealing as some of the older ones. **Sat. Sept. 29th** the end of the visit a few more goodbyes. Mum & Dad and Aunt Mary came with us to the boat. Arthur took us with our trunks to Woodside where we said goodbye. Then by Ferry to the other side where we got on the Baltic and left the folks at three o'clock and pulled out into the Mersey down by New Brighton where we waited for the tide to turn until 9 o'clock when we got underway properly. **Sun. Sept. 30th**. In the morning I wrote a letter in the afternoon I got sick. **Monday Oct. 1st** SICK. **Tues. Oct. 2nd** a little better. In the morning got acquainted with a few nice people on the ship. In the afternoon a terrible storm came up, and I was sick again it lasted all day. **Wed. Oct. 3rd and part of Thurs. Oct. 4. Friday morning Oct. 5** It was a bit better and I was able to do a little in my diary but in the afternoon it was rough again and I had sickness and diarrhea and didn't get up again until **Sat. even Oct. 6th**, my Birthday, and there was a masquerade ball in the lounge so the evening was pleasantly spent. **Sunday Oct. 7th** I am feeling some better. The sea is like a big lake and I am writing this in my diary Sunday morning it is nearly dinner time I have not much appetite. Had dinner rested awhile. Went up to the lounge listened to the music. Had supper music bed. **Mon. Oct. 8th** felt sick. Bot up on deck, wrote P.C.'s. Had dinner. Packed. Went to the lounge for music and tea. Children had a party in the evening a concert. Bed. **Tues. Oct. 9th** Land, about 9:30. Got through the customs after a struggle. Took a taxi to the B.J.O. Depot boarded a boat then a Saloon coach. Arrived at New Jersey Depot. Boarded train for Washington. Arrived there 4:20. Sent telegram to Len, attended to Pullman for next night. Got tickets. Then located the Hotel Plaza got washed up. Sent off some P.C.'s then started after a meal which we ate at the Park Lunch, a very good one. Met an interesting lady there talked awhile looked around the town a bit. Also rested awhile by the Capital. A beautiful building from the outside. Then we came back to the hotel. I washed my hair. Alfred was so tired so he went to bed. Then I am writing in my diary so goodnight. **Wed., Oct. 10th** had breakfast. Took a coach tour to the most interesting places the Pan American Building, The Printing and Engraving Bureau where all currency, stamps, etc. are made. It takes 30 days to make a dollar bill and 3 days for a postage stamp. Then to the White House, a magnificent building. Then Smithsonian Institute saw Lindberg's plane and many things of interest as the evolution of the sewing machine, the car, phonograph, and many others. Then on to the Capital a wonderful work of art. The Freize around the interior of the Dome is beautiful, representing many incidents of American History, such as Landing of the Pilgrims, the Baptism of Pocahontos, Washington crossing the Delaware, etc. then the Senate and the Congressional Hall and the Halls of Presidents and statues presented by the different states. South Dakota is not there yet. From there to the basement where there is a statue of white marble representing the three pioneers of the Women's Suffrage movement; also a very fine monument in Plaster Paris of the Capital which was shown at the Centenial in Philadelphia and was being restored before being sent on to Paris. From the Capitol we went to the Congressional Library, a marvel in marble and mosaic, a thing of great beauty therefore a joy forever. Then back to dinner, a rest, then the train again en route for Chicago. Arrived in Chicago at the Grand Central at 9 o'clock. **Thursday morning October 11th** Len met us. Took us to breakfast. Then to the house for a general clean up. Then to the Field Museum and Lincoln Park where he and Alfred visited the bird house. Then downtown again for supper. Then we went into the Free Library. Then to a picture show. Saw Edmund Lowe in the Wizard. From there we went and had a little lunch. Then back to Len's place a little while. Then he took us to Milwaukee Depot saw us on the train said goodbye. We then went to bed, and woke up **Friday morning October 12th** nearing Minneapolis. Met a few interesting people on the train, a Mr. Jurgens from Milbank an implement dealer, gave him a message for Bob [Robert Bull]; also met a lady from Oregon. Arrived in Aberdeen at 8:20 and that is the end of the trip.

Paston Parish Church. Picture taken in May, 1939.

Appendix XVI

Maps of Paston Churchyard Burials

Mr. Alan J. Marks of Paston, England has performed a survey
of the grave headstones in the All Saints Church in Paston in which he
mapped individual headstones and transcribed each headstone inscription.
He has graciously allowed the use of two of his survey maps in this book for
the purpose of showing the location of the graves of Thomas and Rose Ann
Mould and their son Joseph. All three are buried in Plot B. Thomas and Rose
Ann are buried in grave 35 and Joseph is buried in grave 29.

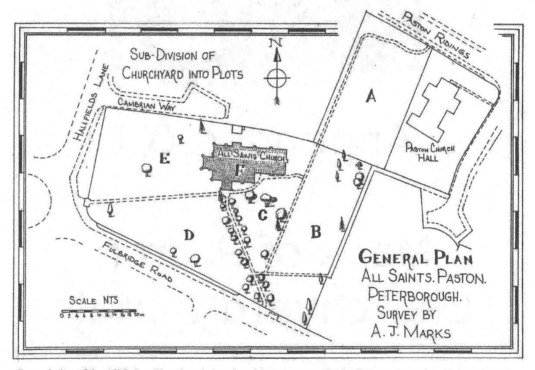

General plan of the All Saints Church and churchyard in Paston, England. The survey was done by A. J. Marks.

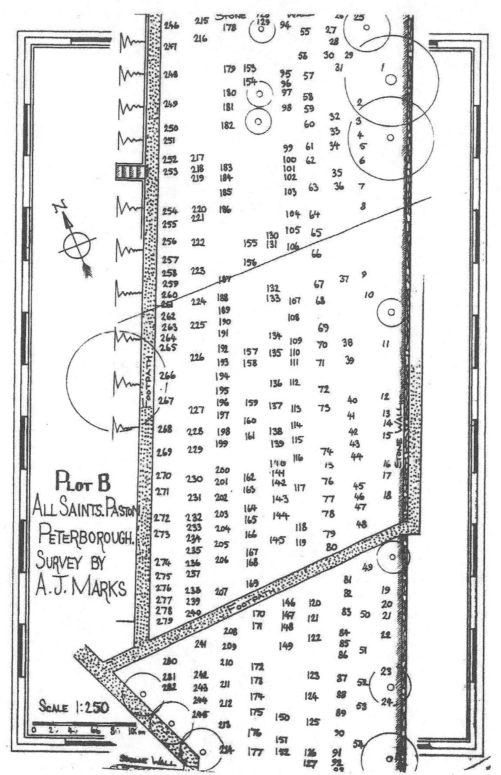

Plan of Plot B of All Saints Churchyard in Paston, England. Survey done by A. J. Marks.

John William Prentice

Appendix XVII

Valuation of John William Prentice Estate

Following the death of John W. Prentice in 1919, his estate had to be evaluated and a monetary value put on it to complete the settlement of the estate. The firm of Fox & Vergette, Licenced Valuers from Peterborough were hired to perform this function and develop a Valuation for Probate. Their report is reproduced below.

VALUATION OF LIVE & DEAD
FARMING STOCK, TENANT
RIGHT etc.
FARM & PREMISES at
PEAKIRK NORTHANTS

The property of the Executors of the late Mr. J.W. PRENTICE

Valuation of LIVE and DEAD FARMING STOCK, TENANT RIGHT and CORN

And HAY in stock on the FARM & PREMISES at PEAKIRK , the property of the EXECUTORS of the late Mr. J.W. PRENTICE, taken the 22nd of SEPTEMBER 1919.

HORSES	Chestnut horse "Prince", Brown Mare "Bounce", Grey Pony, Bay Mare "Lively", Bay Mare "Flower", Colt Foal, Brown Mare "Beauty", Bay Mare "Blossom".
BEAST	4 Bullocks, Rearing calf
SHEEP	34 Ewes, 41 Lambs, 2 Barren Ewes, Hampshire Ram
Implements etc.	2 collars, 4 cow ties, pair reins, spring float, bridle, 2 hackbands, saddle, collar, old bin, weighing machine & weights, sack elevator, barb wire, cutting knife, Bean mill, Bamlett reaper, wood drag, shaft horse hoe, iron drag harrows, barrel water cart, iron drag, turnip box, duckfoot harrows, plough, turnip cutter, sheep wire & stakes, 10 sleepers etc., single horse hoe, stack pegs, odd wood, steerage drill, flat roll, grass mower, wheelbarrow, 2 horse harrows, 1 horse harrow, 5 cart ropes, 2 skeps, sundry tools, Hornsby Binder, Light cart & raves, Ash screen, hay tedder, 2 drag rakes, 1/2 cwt. Binder string, 14 sheep troughs, 4 carts with raves, new wagon, gears for 6 horses, horse rake, stack props etc., lever duckfoot, 6 ladders, 20 sheep trays, pulper, chaffcutter, corn bin,old stackcloth, sack wheels, dressing machine, double furrow plough, swell trees, 12 sleepers, loading ladder, sack elevator, cake breaker, ridge plough, 3 scuttles, Ransome

416

cultivator, Martin cultivator, 2 single ploughs.

CORN   Stack of Peas, 3 stacks of Barley, 2 stacks of Wheat, 1 stack of Oats, 6 sacks of Peas, 16 sacks of light Oats, 2 cwt. Of condiment.

HAY   6 acres of Clover first and second crops, Stack of Hay, stack of Wheat straw.

Quantity of Manure on the premises, allowing for the feeding stuiff therein.

5 acres young seeds, 5 acres Turnips, One & 1/2 acres Mangolds, 10 acres & 4 1/2 acres, & 3 1/2 acres fallows.

We, the undersigned, have carefully estimated the matters herein do certify the value

Thereof at the sum of TWO THOUSAND FIVE HUNDRED & THIRTY-FOUR POUNDS, NINE SHILLINGS. (2,534 pounds, 9 shillings, 0 pence).

Mr. J.W. PRENTICE deceased

STATEMENT SHEWING ASSETS LESS VALUE OF Mrs. Prentice,s
SHARE AND COSTS OF PROBATE (taken from the Inland Revenue Affidavit)

Cash in hand	58:10:00
Cash in Barclay,s Bank	87:00:00
Book Debits	90:00:00
Prudential Insurance Policy	128:08:00
Household goods (bequeathed to Mrs. Prentice)	117:11:00
Stock in trade as per Messrs. Fox & Vergette,s Valuation, annexed hereto	2225:09:00
	3936:18:00

DEDUCT

Household goods bequeathed to Mrs. Prentice	117:11:00
Stock in trade in shop, bequeathed to Mrs. Prentice to the value of	200:00:00
Debts & proportions of rents To date of death	681:02:09
Funeral expenses	18:07:06
Dwellinghouse shop & cottage adjoining bequeathed to Mrs. Prentice	460:00:00
Estate duty & other payments (per Messr. Mellow & Sons account)	104:14:00

Messr. Mellow & Sons charges re
Probate   18:18:00
Estimated cost of admission to
Copyhold property   12:00:00

Fox & Vergette charges. Cost of
Enfranchisement & Conveyance   1612:13:06

                                                                2324:04:06

Peterborough   21 June 1920

                                                        Narrow Street
                                                        Peterborough

                        Valuation for Probate

In the Estate of John William Prentice late of Peakirk in the County of
Northampton made and taken 22nd. Day of September 1919.

Household goods, Pictures, China, Linen, Apparel.   117:11:Msrp
Stock in trade live and Dead Farming.   )   2225:9:-
)
Stock Implements of Husbandry   )

Other personal property not comprised under the
foregoing heads viz
            Tenant rights   250:-:-

                                                              2593:-:-

We hereby certify that we have Appraised the whole
of the above mentioned at the sum of Two Thousand five hundred and
ninety three pounds (2593)

                                Fox & Vergette
                                Licenced Valuers.

            George Prentice.   )
)   Executors
            George Harold Prentice   )

Paston Churchyard

Appendix XVIII

Family Burial Locations

This chapter, which contains the burial locations of the first three generations of Thomas and Rose Ann's descendants, is provided to facilitate look-ups of burials.

First Generation
Thomas Mould
> All Saints Churchyard, Paston, England, Section B, Grave 35

Rose Ann Mould
> All Saints Churchyard, Paston, England, Section B, Grave 35

Second Generation
Jane Jessop
> Sutton Cemetery, Sutton, London, England, Section B, Grave 267

Devereux Henry Jessop
> Sutton Cemetery, Sutton, London, England, Section B, Grave 267

Betsy Mackness
> Loftis Cemetery (new cemetery), Loftis, Yorks, England, A-F/26, Grave # 4103

James Mackness
> Edgerton Cemetery, Huddersfield, York, England, Section 27, Grave # 128

Mary Avery
> Ellingson Zion Cemetery, Ellingson, South Dakota, USA

James Edward Dale Avery
> St. Pega's Churchyard, Peakirk, Northants, England

Rose Prentice
> St. Pega's Churchyard, Peakirk, Northants, England

John William Prentice
> St. Pega's Churchyard, Peakirk, Northants, England

Jabez A. Mould
> All Saints Churchyard, Paston, Northants, England

William Jabez Mould
> All Saints Churchyard, Paston, Northants, England

Joseph Mould
> All Saints Churchyard, Paston, Northants, England, Section B, Grave 29

Jabez Mould
> Riverside Cemetery, Aberdeen, South Dakota, USA, Block 86, Lot 33

Sarah Ann Mould
> Glen Abby Memorial Park, Bonita, California, USA, Section 71, Block 68, Lot 3

Rebecca Mackness
> Ellingson Zion Cemetery, Ellingson, South Dakota, USA

Joseph Thomas Mackness
> Ellingson Zion Cemetery, Ellingson, South Dakota, USA

Charles Mould
> Higham Ferrers Cemetery, Higham Ferrers, Northants, England

Emily Jane Mould
> Higham Ferrers Cemetery, Higham Ferrers, Northants, England

George Mould
> Eastfield Cemetery, Peterborough, Northants, England

Fanny Mould
> Eastfield Cemetery, Peterborough, Northants, England

Third Generation

Naomi Jane Baldwin
> Cremated in Brighton Crematorium, Brighton, East Sussex, England

Herbert Alphonsus Baldwin
> Lost at sea

Frederick Thomas Jessop
> Unknown

Devereux Henry Jessop
> Sutton Cemetery, Sutton, London, England, Section B, Grave 267

Jesse Jessop
> Unknown

Henry Victor Jessop
> Unknown

Rose Anna Brushett
> Unknown

Frederick Thomas Brushett
> Unknown

Ellen Prentice
> St. Pega's Churchyard, Peakirk, Northants, England

Lilian Prentice
>St. Pega's Churchyard, Peakirk, Northants, England - same grave as Ellen

George Harold Prentice
>Cremated, Ashes buried in Churchill, Oxfordshire, England (Not the All Saints Churchyard but the cemetery not associated with any church.)

Lillian Prentice
>Cremated, Ashes buried in Churchill, Oxfordshire, England (Not the All Saints Churchyard but the cemetery not associated with any church.)

John Frederick Prentice
>Cremated - ashes buried at Worthing Crematorium

Jesse Edith Prentice
>Cremated - ashes buried at Worthing Crematorium

Dora Evelyn Prentice
>Cremated - ashes buried at St. Pega's Churchyard, Peakirk, Northants, England - same grave as Ellen and Lilian

Rose Marion Lovell
>Glen Abby Memorial Park, Bonita, California, USA, Section 74, Block 68, Lot 6

George Henry Lovell
>Glen Abby Memorial Park, Bonita, California, USA, Section 74, Block 68, Lot 5

George Ewart Mould
>Glen Abby Memorial Park, Bonita, California, USA, Section 79A, Block 68, Lot 2

Kate Mould
>Glen Abby Memorial Park, Bonita, California, USA, Section 79A, Block 68, Lot 1

Bessie Lilian Mould
>Newton Road Cemetery, Rushden, Northants, England, Plot 303A

Annie Beatrice Bull
>Riverside Memorial Park, Aberdeen, South Dakota, USA, Block D, Lot 247

Fred Albert Bull
>Riverside Memorial Park, Aberdeen, South Dakota, USA, Block D, Lot 247

Thomas Rowland Mould
>Newton Road Cemetery, Rushden, Northants, England, Plot 761A

Frank Mackness
>Mausoleum in Portland, Oregon

Esther Mary Mackness
>Mausoleum in Portland, Oregon

Nellie Mackness
    Newton Road Cemetery, Rushden, Northants, England

Emily May Mould
    Newton Road Cemetery, Rushden, Northants, England, Plot 180A

Elsie May Headland
    Unknown
Charles Headland
    Unknown

Jesse Barrett
    Cremated and ashes buried in parents' grave in Higham Ferrers
    Cemetery, Northants, England
John Barrett
    Unknown

Violet Roberts
    Higham Ferrers Cemetery, Higham Ferrers, Northants, England, in an
    unmarked grave just a few steps from her husband Robert's grave.
Robert Edward Roberts
    Higham Ferrers Cemetery, Higham Ferrers, Northants, England

Daisy Sharpe
    Higham Ferrers Cemetery, Higham Ferrers, Northants, England
Alfred James Sharpe
    Higham Ferrers Cemetery, Higham Ferrers, Northants, England

Lily Eaton
    Unknown
Hubert Eaton
    Unknown

Bernard William Mould
    Cremated Kettering, Northants, England
Jane Margaretta Mould
    Cremated

Ivy Doreen Lovell
    Unknown
Archibald Thomas Lovell
    Unknown

Doris Maile
    Unmarked grave next to the grave of her husband (marked) in
     Eastfield Cemetery, Peterborough, Cambridgeshire, England
Ernest Victor Maile
    Eastfield Cemetery, Peterborough, Cambridgeshire, England

Cyril Eugene Mould
> Cremated at Marholm Crematorium, Peterborough, Cambridgeshire, England

Beatrice Mary Mould
> Cremated at Marholm Crematorium, Peterborough, Cambridgeshire, England

Bernard Mould
> Cremated - Peterborough, Cambridgeshire, England

Annie Louisa Mould
> Cremated - Peterborough, Cambridgeshire, England

Eric Mould
> Unknown

Mary Ethel Mould
> Cremated - Peterborough, Cambridgeshire, England

Guilford Mould
> Cremated

Mary Mould
> Cremated

Marjorie Edna Mould
> Family plot with parents and sister Iris - Eastfield Cemetery, Peterborough, Cambridgeshire, England

George Mould
> Unknown

Iris Theresa Mould
> Family plot with parents and sister Marjorie - Eastfield Cemetery, Peterborough, Cambridgeshire, England

Hubert Lawrence Mould
> Cremated

Appendix XIX

U.S. Arrival Information

Several of the descendants of Thomas and Rose Ann emigrated to the United States for various reasons. The information on their descendants who emigrated, their spouses and children (if applicable) is listed below.

Mary (Mould) Avery arrived at Ellis Island, New York on the ship Berengaria from Southampton on September 18, 1921.

Jabez Mould arrived at Ellis Island, New York on the ship Orduna from Liverpool on December 24, 1919.

Sarah Ann Mould (wife of Jabez) arrived at Ellis Island, New York on the ship Orduna from Liverpool on December 24, 1919.

Rose (Mould) Lovell arrived at Ellis Island, New York on the ship Baltic on May 1, 1911.

George Henry Lovell (husband of Rose) arrived at Ellis Island, New York on the ship Cedric on March 24, 1906. He returned to England and returned to the U.S. and arrived at Ellis Island, New York on the ship Mauretania on August 28, 1908.

George Ewart Mould arrived at Ellis Island, New York on the ship Oceanic from Liverpool on June 14, 1906. He returned to England and returned again to the U.S. arriving at Ellis Island, New York on the ship Baltic from Liverpool on May 1, 1911.

Kate (Freeman) Mould (wife of George Ewart) - no arrival information available.

Annie Beatrice (Mould) Bull arrived at Ellis Island, New York on the ship Baltic from Liverpool on July 27, 1912.

Fred Albert Bull (husband of Annie Beatrice) arrived at Ellis Island, New York on the ship Cedric from Liverpool on March 24, 1906.

Rebecca (Mould) Mackness arrived at Ellis Island, New York on the ship Carmania from Liverpool on October 16, 1906.

Joseph Thomas Mackness (husband of Rebecca) arrived in the U.S. in 1906. No further information available.

Frank Mackness (son of Rebecca) arrived at Ellis Island, New York on the ship Carmania from Liverpool on October 16, 1906.

Rebecca Mould

Appendix XX

Rebecca Mackness' Address Book

Rebecca Mackness had an address book which we have included in this appendix to aid future researchers. Most of the names are of family members and give a researcher an idea of where these people were living at this time. The address book has to predate July 9, 1946 since that is when Rebecca died. It is most likely the address book she was using at the time of her death. Clarifying information added by the authors is in parentheses ().

W.J. Everard
Route 1
Missula, Montana

Mrs. Fred Brushett (Rose Jessop, daughter of Jane [Mould] Jessop)
Avonside
62 Lenham Road
Sutton
Surrey, England

Mrs. J.E. Hayes
Route 3, Box 166
Eugene, Oregon

Mrs. J. Mould (Sarah Ann Mould - wife of Jabez)
111 8th Ave. S.W.
Aberdeen, South Dakota

Mrs. Brackley
1 Woodbine Villa
Leveralie Avenue
Chesham
Bucks, England

Mrs. Burton
c/o Mrs. P. Denton
9 King Road
Rushden, Northants, England

Mr. C. Mould (Rebecca's brother Charles)
No. 2 Grove St.
Higham Ferrers, Northants, England

Mr. G. Mould (Rebecca's brother George)
Rock House
59 Gilpin St.
Peterborough, Northants, England

Mr. H.R. Bull (Horace Bull - brother-in-law of Annie [Mould] Bull)
814 8th Ave. S.E.
Aberdeen, So. Dakota

Mrs. Mark Keith
321 Center St.
Maukato, Minn

Miss Florence Keith
371 E. Main
Worthville, Michigan

Mrs. A.F. Bertapelle
2107 J 7th St. W
Missoula, Montana

Miss Dora Prentice (Rebecca's niece)
Peakirk
Peterborough, Northants, England

Mrs. A. Johnson
906 So. Penn Street
Aberdeen, S. Dakota

Mrs. G. French
803 9th Ave. SE
Aberdeen, SD

Mr. H. Prentice (Rebecca's nephew)
Dubuque Villas
Station Road
Bledington
Kingham
Oxfordshire

Mrs. Fred Bull (Rebecca's niece Annie [Mould] Bull)
1459 Milwauke St.
Denver, CO

Miss Margreat Plondke
2615 S. Wayne St.
Arlington, VA

Mrs. Eb Wrighton
257 Wellingboro Rd.
Rushden, Northants, England

Mrs. E.H. Chelstron
3134 Cleveland St. NE
Minneapolis, MN

Mrs. Walt Keith
#507 2nd Ave NE
St. Cloud, MN

Mrs. J. Barrett (Jesse [Mould] Barrett - niece of Rebecca)
118 St. James Park Rd
Northampton, England

Mrs. C. Wheeler
c/o Mrs. Philips
4 BClurement Clure
Bath
Somerset, England

J. Mackness (James Mackness - husband of Rebecca's sister Betsy)
17 Poplar St.Mold Green
Teivenment
Huddersfield, England

H.A. Baldwin (Rebecca's sister Jane's daughter Naomi's husband Herbert)
27 Bigwood Avenue
Hove 4
Sussex, England

Mrs. John Rowland
12 North 2nd
Loftus, Yorks (Loftus is where Rebecca's sister Betsy died in 1928)
England

EPSOM.
(See also Page 6).

MOTOR CYCLE FATALITY.

On Wednesday evening Mr. Jessop, manager of Messrs. Baldwin Bros., butchers, High-street, Epsom, was motor cycling along the Banstead road with his wife, who was in a side-car, when the machine by some means got out of control and ran into a tree. Both Mr. Jessop and his wife were thrown out, the former being killed instantly, whilst his wife was seriously hurt. Mr. Jessop was a brother-in-law of Mr. Baldwin, one of the members of the firm of Baldwin Bros.

The inquest was opened at the Banstead Institute yesterday (Friday). Evidence of identification having been taken, the inquiry was adjourned. Mrs. Jessop, who was taken to Holland-avenue, Sutton, is stated to be progressing favourably.

Account of the death of Devereux Henry Jessop in a motorcycle accident in an unknown newspaper in 1914

THE SURREY ADVERTISER AND

BANSTEAD.

MOTOR FATALITY.

THE ADJOURNED INQUEST.

The inquest on Mr. Henry Jessop (32), of High-street, Epsom, partner in the firm of Messrs. Baldwin Bros., butchers, of Sutton and Epsom, was resumed at the Banstead Institute on Wednesday afternoon before Mr. Gilbert White.—The only witness called was Mr. Herbert Baldwin, brother-in-law of deceased, of Dulverton, Holland-avenue, Sutton, who was riding at the back of deceased's motor-cycle on the day of the accident. He said that deceased called at his house with his wife to discuss business matters, and witness returned with him. They went along Banstead-road into Drift Way-road. After passing the Kensington and Chelsea Schools there was a slight gradient, and at the bottom of it a large beech tree and a turning to the left. Deceased had complained about the controls of his machine not being efficient, and witness was of opinion that something went wrong with them on this occasion. Deceased was unable to turn the corner at a sharp enough angle. They were travelling at a fair pace, and the machine dashed into the tree, killing deceased instantly and throwing both witness and deceased's wife, who was in the side car, on to the ground.

The jury returned a verdict of accidental death, and on the Coroner's suggestion recommended that a warning signal should be erected near the spot. Sympathy was also expressed for the widow and relatives of deceased. Mr. Baldwin said that Mrs. Jessop, who was seriously injured, was progressing favourably.

Account of the death and coroner's inquest of Devereux Henry Jessop in 1914.

Appendix XXI

Motorcycle Death of Devereux Jessop in 1914

On June 12, 1914, Jane (Mould) Jessop's son, Devereux Henry , was killed when a motorcycle he was driving ran into a tree killing him instantly. His brother-in-law, Herbert Baldwin, was riding behind him and although thrown to the ground, was not seriously injured. Devereux's wife, Jesse, was riding in a side car and was seriously injured. An inquest was held and the death was ruled an accident.

The accident was written up in a couple of newspaper articles and these are reproduced below.

Banstead
Motor Fatality
The Adjourned Inquest

The inquest on Mr. Henry Jessop (32) of High-street, Epsom, partner in the firm of Messrs. Baldwin Bros., on Wednesday afternoon before Mr. Gilbert White. The only witness called was Mr. Herbert Baldwin, brother-in-law of deceased, of Dulverton, Holland-avenue, Sutton, who was riding at the back of deceased's motor-cycle on the day of the accident. He said that deceased called at his house with his wife to discuss business matters and witness returned with him. They went along Banstead-road into Drift Way-road. After passing the Kensington and Chelsea Schools there was a slight gradient, and at the bottom of it a large beech tree and a turning to the left. Deceased had complained about the controls of his machine not being efficient, and witness was of opinion that something went wrong with them on this occasion. Deceased was unable to turn the corner at a sharp enough angle. They were travelling at a fair pace, and the machine dashed into the tree, killing deceased instantly and throwing both witness and deceased's wife, who was in the side car, on to the ground.

The jury returned a verdict of accidental death, and on the Coroner's suggestion recommended that a warning signal should be near the spot. Sympathy was also expressed for the widow and relatives of deceased. Mr. Baldwin said that Mrs. Jessop, who was seriously injured, was progressing favourably.

The Surrey Advertiser And ??

Epsom
Motor Cycle Fatality

On Wednesday evening Mr. Jessop, manager of Messrs. Baldwin Bros., butchers, High-street, Epsom, was motor cycling along the Banstead-road with his wife, who was in a side-car, when the machine by some means got out of control and ran into a tree. Both Mr. Jessop and his wife were thrown out, the former being killed instantly, whilst his wife was seriously hurt. Mr. Jessop was a brother-in-law of Mr. Baldwin, one of the members of the firm of Baldwin Bros.

The inquest was opened at the Banstead Institute yesterday (Friday). Evidence of identification having been taken, the inquiry was adjourned. Mrs. Jessop, who was taken to Holland-avenue, Sutton, is stated to be progressing favourably.

Unknown newspaper

Article in the Acton Gazette and Express concerning
Herbert Baldwin's candidacy for the Labor Party
candidate for Parliament.

Appendix XXII

Herbert Baldwin's Campaign for Parliament

In 1923 and 1924 Herbert Baldwin, son-in-law of Devereux and Jane Jessop, stood for election to Parliament as a Labour Party candidate. He lost both elections. Details of his campaigns along with election results are included in this appendix.

In a November 11, 1923 newspaper article: H. Baldwin, of "Chalcots" Lower Kingswood, Reigate at election time he agreed to act as Labour candidate for the December 1923 election. A rumor circulated that Mr. Baldwin was "the Prime Minister's socialist son" - there was no truth in it. He was adopted as the candidate and described as "a popular and wealthy businessman". He criticized "the unscrupulous Lloyd George and the fire-eating Churchill".

The results of the 1923 election were as follows:

Total voters = 31,394   Turn-out = 63.5%

Sir H. E. Brittain	C	8,943	44.9%
H. A. Baldwin	Lab	6,069	30.5%
B. A. Levinson	Lib	4,909	24.6%

In a March 7, 1924 newspaper article: At a meeting he spoke of "the oppression of shop assistants; he had been one once and it had been purgatory to him. Prisons should be abolished since no one in England was bad enough to go to prison." There was a dispute between Mr. Baldwin and Miss Mary R. Richardson for the Labour candidacy at the 1924 election. He offered to "clear out" if independent arbitration could be found. There was a split in the local Labour party in Acton and Miss Richardson (ex-suffragette) came in as a left wing candidate with Communist party support.

The results of the 1924 election were as follows:

Total voters = 31,999   Turn-out = 72.6%

Sir H. E. Brittain	C	12,799	55.2%
H. A. Baldwin	Lab	5,583	24%
B. A. Levinson	Lib	3,074	13.2%
Miss H. R. Richardson	Ind. Lab	1,775	7.6%

In an article in the Friday, October 17, 1924, Acton Gazette and Express, the following information on the Labour party and Herbert Baldwin's positions was noted.

Labour
Mr. Baldwin Unanimously "Adopted"
Split Deplored and then Ignored

"The fight is between the workers and the capitalist class, who form the party of privilege, position and power which they are anxious to maintain," declared Mr. F. G. Armey, president of the Acton Labour Party, at a crowded meeting held in the Priory Schools on Monday night to adopt a candidate.

The Labour Party was, he said, out for the workers all the time, and they should therefore always vote Labour (applause). Carson and Birkenhead had said worse things than Campbell, who had been used as an excuse for bringing about a dissolution by people alarmed at the success of Labour and the prospect of another popular Labour budget (applause). A vote against Baldwin was a vote for their traditional enemies (loud applause).

Mr. H. A. Baldwin, who was received with loud cheers said he was not concerned for the moment with the Communist prosecution, Free Trade or the Russian Treaty so much as with the fact that, though he was a stranger to them at that time last year he was now a friend amongst friends (applause0. He was not going to discuss the "split" (hear, hear). Those present were a united party (applause). Others who thought differently from them had left them for good or ill, and there he would leave it without any personal allusion (hear, hear). It was refreshing to come from a place where he was surrounded by Tories (though even there a young man had come forward to challenge Tory supremacy) to hold a heart to heart communion with those who, like Christian in the House Beautiful, looked across the Slough of Despond and the tangle of difficulties, to the things beyond which were worth all their best efforts (applause). It was the Labour movement that mattered. The movement needed them, and they needed the movement. The other parties had money, place, power and wonderful organizations. Their party was evidence of the revolt against things as they were, standing for the inherent revolt against that type of civilization which had inflicted evil on all of them. Everyone present could tell a tale of personal suffering, such as he himself had borne when young as a shop assistant, and it was for them to see that their children did not go through similar torture. Sooner or later the Conservatives and Liberals were bound to draw together in order to prevent Labour from consolidating the position which it had gained by forming a Government of which every Britisher might be proud (applause). Some of them had come out from Liberalism, and there were others in the left wing of that party who would never be happy until they found their natural home with their prodigal son (loud laughter).

They had to win through in spite of their difficulties. He was sure that, but for the split in their ranks, they could have won Acton quite reasonably (hear, hear). No one deplored that split more than he did, but in the Labour party they could not submit to dictation by anybody (hear, hear). They would ignore the split, feeling sure that the support of reasonable public opinion at the poll would give them the victory which they would do their best to merit (applause).

They were face to face with a period of depression, during which there would be a steady relentless rise in food prices. There was also a steady pressure to place the burden of the war debt more and more on the workers, who had to be spared from bearing more than their proper proportion of it (hear, hear).

If political action were to prove futile he did not know what would save them, but he did not think it would prove futile if they returned a strong, healthy, forceful Labour party to power (loud applause).

On the motion of Mr. Brickley, seconded by Mr. Bishop, the vote of adoption was unanimously carried.

Mr. O'Day, propaganda secretary, declared that they were out to win, though he had heard of one man who declined to vote for them this time because there was too much comradeship in the Labour party (laughter).

The meeting closed with the singing of 'The Red Flag'.

An Earl To Speak

Clr. Spencer, Labour agent, announced that the Liberals had this time captured the only available vacant date at the Acton Baths, but that Labour could do without baths.

Deprived of halls the party would tour a separate district each night with a motor van and have chats at street corners. They would let Mr. Baldwin have a holiday until Sunday, and after that he would be speaking every day.

Unable to get anything else, they had rented the Horn-lane cinema for mass meetings on two successive Sunday evening meetings after church, viz, 8pm.

Earl De La Warr had promised to speak next Sunday.

They had got the Central Hall for the eve of the poll.

Three motor-cycles, with side-cars, which have been lent to the Labour Party during the election, will be used for the conveyance of instructions and literature to the party canvassers.

Clr. Spencer asks Labour supporters to keep away from their opponents' meetings and attend to their own work.

If they have any complaints to make they should be made direct to him. They want, he says, no grumbling.

Clr. Spencer At Work

On being appointed agent, Clr. Spencer hunted for committee-rooms and halls. Everywhere he found "the bar up".

He had to be content with 19, Park-road-east, off Church-road, which is fairly central. Ward committee-rooms were obtained rent free from members.

Every worker for the party under Clr. Spencer is an unpaid volunteer. Clr. Spencer himself will be paid a small fee for his time.

The reason for Clr. Spencer's appointment is that Mr. C. O'Day can no longer spare the time. Mr. O'Day at the adoption meeting, appealed for help for Mr. Spencer and the cause.

In another 1924 article in The Acton Gazette and Express (exact date unknown), Herbert's campaign was again discussed. The article read in part as follows.

Ill Advised Oratory.
Rival Anthem Sung

Mr. H. A. Baldwin, the Labour candidate, displayed some lack of tact in holding an open-air meeting outside the Priory Constitutional Club soon after the crowd had poured out of the Conservative meeting in the Baths. It was understood to be a response to the Conservative habit of distributing literature outside Labour meetings.

The din was almost continuous, and Mr. Baldwin had to reply to a series of personal questions in his capacity as an employer of labour. He stated that he himself had founded a branch of the Shop Assistants' Union in his district, but that it had collapsed owing to the workers' own apathy. He accused several of his interrupters of being Tories posing as supporters of Miss Richardson. He was not afraid to risk his capital under a Socialist regime.

Sir Harry Brittain was afterwards seen coming out of the club, and a section of the crowd began singing "The Red Flag". To this the Conservatives responded with "Hearts of Oak", "Rule Britannia" and the National Anthem.

To make matters worse, Miss Richardson's illuminated car appeared at the end of the street.

The noise swelled to a crescendo of discord, but a strong force of police succeeded in preventing noise from degenerating into violence, though the situation was at times threatening.

Frederick Thomas Jessop with Muriel and Douglas
Baldwin on his knees and Herbert and Naomi Baldwin
behind him

Appendix XXIII

Will of Frederick Thomas Jessop

J oan (Mould) Bolton has summarized the will of Frederick Thomas (Bill) Jessop and this summary is shown below.

The Last Will and Testament left by Frederick Thomas Jessop, (known as "Bill",) was drawn up on **November 15th 1951**, nearly two years before his death on **12th August 1953**, aged 71. He died (of cancer) at the Berrow Nursing Home in Eastbourne but, at the time of writing this document, his address was given as 74 Vicarage Road, Sunbury-on-Thames, Middlesex, where, according to his great niece, Jane Baldwin, he was 'in lodgings'. (He begins: "I, Frederick Thomas Jessop, of 74 Vicarage Road....")

In the Legacies section, the following Beneficiaries are listed:-
(a)   To my Great Niece - Mrs Virginia Manning of Dulwich College, London, the sum of £200.
(b)   To my Great Niece - Jane Baldwin of St Leonards, Ringwood, Hampshire, the sum of £200
(c)   To my Great Nephew - Christopher Baldwin (of the same address) the sum of £200
(d)   To my God Daughter - Ruth Young of 'Dikoya', Croft Drive, Caldy, Cheshire, the sum of £200
(e)   To my friend - Mrs Esme Green of 86 Surbiton Road, Kingston on Thames, the sum of £100 as a memento of her long friendship
(f) To my friend - William Brown of the Old Coach House, Cailfail, Lewes, Sussex, the sum of £100 as a memento of his long friendship.

After this, he continues: "All the residue of my estate... (etc.) I give and bequeath unto my Niece, Helena Joan Brushett of 'Avonside', 68 Lenham Road, Sutton, Surrey." (This was his sister Rose Brushett's only child, known as Joan, who remained single until she died in November 1996 aged eighty-six.)

The two witnesses are:-(1) Alex Wilfred Ganley of 42, Zealand Avenue, Harmondsworth, West Drayton, Middlesex, described as a Chartered Mechanical Engineer, and
(2) L M Stovold of 74, Vicarage Road, Sunbury-on-Thames, a Housewife.

XXXXXXXXXXXXXXX
Joan Bolton feels that this Will raises some interesting questions. First and foremost, since the address of the second signatory, Mrs Stovold, was

clearly where Bill Jessop was living at the time the document was written, was she his 'landlady', or was the relationship a closer one, perhaps? One of the Beneficiaries claimed there was a rumour circulating in the family to suggest that not only was there a romantic attachment between lodger and landlady but also a daughter!

Sat. 11 July 1936 p3 AER

JABEZ MOULD, 70, TAKEN BY DEATH

Jabez Mould, 70, 111 Eighth avenue southwest, a grocer in this city for the past 17 years, died at his residence Friday evening.

He was born at Gunthorpe, Northants, England, Dec. 24, 1865. He came to this country in 1919 from England, settling in Aberdeen.

He is survived by his widow, one son, George E., San Diego, Calif., two daughters, Mrs. George Lovell and Mrs. Fred A. Bull, both of Aberdeen, two sisters, Mrs. Polly Avery, Aberdeen, and Mrs. Rebecca Mackness, Ellingson, and one brother, Charles Mould, who is now residing in England.

Funeral arrangements will be made later.

Appendix XXIV

Obituaries

Ｏne of the best sources of information on distant ancestors is their newspaper obituary if it can be found. These obituaries often give interesting details of the ancestor's life and provide a wonderful source of facts for the genealogist. They often mention friends and associates of the deceased and are one of the best sources for the deceased relatives both living and dead. This chapter includes obituaries for twenty-five of the Mould descendants. These obituaries are provided in generational order. Unfortunately, no obituary has been found for either Thomas or Rose Ann Mould.

Rose Prentice

Prentice - At Peakirk on June 25th 1925. Rose Prentice aged 66 years, widow of the late John William Prentice who died August 26, 1919, aged 60 years.
Acknowledgement (follows straight on): - The Family wish to thank all Friends for the kindness shown to their Mother during her long illness; and for expressions of sympathy extended to them in their sad bereavement; also for floral tributes.

Peterborough and Hunts Standard
Friday, 3rd July 1925

Also see page 7 of the same paper which contains the obituary for Rose.

Second Obituary for Rose Prentice

Rose Prentice

PEAKIRK LOSES A RESPECTED RESIDENT.

Death and Funeral of Mrs. John Prentice

We much regret to record that Mrs. Rose Prentice, widow of Mr. John

William Prentice, on Friday, died (June 25th) after a long illness patiently borne. She had lived in Peakirk over 30 years, and was respected by all, and will be much missed.

The funeral service on Saturday was conducted by the Rev. Canon J.T. Nance. The body was placed in a polished oak coffin, with the inscription: "Rose Prentice, died June 25th, 1925, aged 66 years."

The mourners were: Mr. H. and Miss N. Prentice (son and daughter); Mr. F. and Miss L. Prentice (son and daughter); Mr. H.A. Baldwin (nephew), and Miss D. Prentice (daughter); Mr. and Mrs. C. Mould (brother and sister-in-law); Mr. G. Mould (brother), and Mrs. Blanchard (sister-in-law); Mr. G. Prentice and Mrs. French (brother-in-law and sister-in-law); Mr. G. Prentice (nephew); and Mrs. S. Prentice (sister-in-law); Mr. and Mrs. A. Mould (cousins); Mrs. Frost and Miss E. Mould (cousins); Mr. and Mrs. Lake, Mr. and Mrs. W.T. Welbourn, Mrs. Sisson, Mrs. A. Neaverson and Miss Pape.

Among those present in the church and at the graveside were Miss Ball, Miss Barron, Mr. and Mrs. W. Bodger, Mrs. Strange, Miss Bodger, Mrs. Lockyer, Miss G. Welbourn, Mrs. Legate, Miss Nix, Miss Morris, Mr. And Mrs. C. Neaverson, Miss L. Neaverson, Mrs. S. Neaverson, Mrs. Argent, Mrs. B. Smith, Mrs. L. Pearson, Mrs. Taylor, Mrs. Bates, Mrs. R. Neaverson, Miss O. Neaverson, Mr. and Mrs. Brewer, Mr. Harris, Mrs. Fickers, Mrs. Robinson, Mrs. Lewis Neaverson, Mr. and Mrs. W. Jones, etc.

THE WREATHS

The floral tributes were inscribed:
In loving memory of our dear Mother, from Nell, Lily, Harold and Dora.
In ever loving memory, from Fred and Jesse
With deepest sympathy and affection, from Bert and Omy
In ever loving and affectionate memory of our beloved sister, from her deeply sorrowing sister and brother, Bessie and Jamie. At Rest. For ever with the Lord. Wherefore comfort one another with these words.
To our dearest aunt, from all at Old Fletton. "To one who lived for others but now 'Safe in the Arms of Jesus.'"
In loving memory, from Charlie and Emily and family. After pain, peace.
In deepest sympathy, from Fred, Rose and Joan [Brushett] "For so He giveth His beloved sleep."
In affectionate remembrance, from Mrs. W.T. Welbourn and family, Glinton.
In affectionate remembrance, from Mr. And Mrs. Strange and family.
In deep sympathy, from Mr. and Mrs. Brewer.
In loving memory of dear Rose, from all cousins at Maxey.
In loving memory, from George and Ellen, Arthur and Hannah.
With deepest sympathy, from Mr. and Mrs. C. Neaverson and family.
With deepest sympathy, from Mr. and Mrs. A. Neaverson and family.
With deepest sympathy, from Mr. and Mrs. Legate and family.
From Mrs. Lockyer.
With deepest sympathy and love, from Lizzie.
Love from Rowland.

Messrs. A. Neaverson and Sons were the undertakers.

The Peterborough & Hunts. Standard
July 3, 1925

John William Prentice

Mr. John William Prentice, sub-postmaster of Peakirk, was taken ill whilst on his rounds a week ago and rheumatic fever was followed by pneumonia and other complications, and he passed away on Tuesday afternoon.

The Peterborough Citizen
September 2, 1919   Page 4

Jabez Mould

Jabez Mould , 70, Taken By Death

Jabez Mould, 70, 111 Eighth avenue southwest, a grocer in this city for the past 17 years, died at his residence Friday evening.

He was born at Gunthorpe, Northants, England Dec. 24, 1865. He came to this country in 1919 from England, settling in Aberdeen.

He is survived by his widow, one son, George E., San Diego, Calif., two daughters, Mrs. George Lovell and Mrs. Fred A. Bull, both of Aberdeen, two sisters, Mrs. Polly Avery, Aberdeen, and Mrs. Rebecca Mackness, Ellingson, and one brother, Charles Mould, who is now residing in England.

Funeral arrangements will be made later.

Aberdeen South Dakota newspaper
July 11, 1936   page 3

Second Obituary For Jabez Mould

Mould

Funeral services for Jabez Mould, 70, 111 Eighth avenue southwest, Aberdeen, grocer, were held in the Wilson Funeral home Sunday at 4p.m. with the Rev. Earl Gulbranson officiating. Burial was in Riverside cemetery.

Pall bearers were George Finch, Syril Allen, Fred McNames, Alwyne Johnon, Charles Freeman and W. Drage.

Mr. Mould was born in Gunthorpe, Northants, England, Dec. 24, 1865. He came to this country in 1919, settling in Aberdeen.

He is survived by his widow, one son, George E., San Diego, Calif., two daughters, Mrs. George Lovell and Mrs. Fred A. Bull, both of Aberdeen, two sisters, Mrs. Polly Avery, Aberdeen, and Mrs. Rebecca Mackness, Ellingson, and two brothers, Charles Mould, Rushden, Northants, England and George Mould, New England, Northants, England.

Aberdeen, South Dakota newspaper
July 15, 1936   page 5

Charles Mould

Mr. C. Mould, Higham Ferrers

The death occurred on Saturday of Mr. Charles Mould, of 2, Grove-street, Higham Ferrers. He had been in Northampton General Hospital for 14 weeks and had been home for a fortnight before his death.

Aged 73 years, Mr. Mould was born at Peterborough, came to Higham Ferrers as a boy, and spent his working life in the boot trade, retiring three years ago. For some years he was a Sunday School teacher and superintendent of the Band of Hope at the Methodist Church, but in recent years had attended the Milton Hall Chapel.

A daughter, Mrs. I. Lovell, had been living with him. His wife died three years ago, and two sons, six daughters and 12 grandchildren are left.

The funeral took place on Tuesday, and the service was conducted at the home by the Rev. T.S. Kee, of the Rushden Independent Wesleyan Church, before interment at the Higham Ferrers cemetery. Mourners were : Mr. and Mrs. C. Headland, Rushden, Mr. and Mrs. J.W. Barrett, Northampton, Mr. and Mrs. R.E. Roberts, Higham Ferrers, Mr. and Mrs. J. Sharp, Rushden, Gnr. H. Eaton and Mrs. Eaton, Souldrop, (sons-in-law and daughters), Mr. and Mrs. B. Mould (son and daughter-in-law), Mr. and Mrs. A.T. Lovell (son-in-law and daughter), Mr. and Mrs. P. Mould (son and daughter-in-law), Mr. G. Mould (brother), Mrs. E. Mould (niece), Mrs. H. Durham, Mrs. W. Hensman (sisters-in-law), Mrs. E. Wrighton (cousin), and Mrs. Firkins (friend). Several friends of the Milton Chapel attended, these including Mr. L. Bradshaw, Mr. J. Lynn and Mr. W. Marriott.

Messrs. T. Swindall and Sons were the undertakers.

Rushden Echo & Argus
Friday, March 9, 1945   Page 2

Emily Jane Mould

Mrs. E. J. Mould, Higham Ferrers

Mrs. Emily Jane Mould (69) of 2, Grove-street, Higham Ferrers, who had been in failing health for about a year although she had only been seriously ill for about 17 weeks, passed away on Tuesday. Mrs. Mould was born at Rushden and went to live at Higham at the time of her marriage. She had been associated with the Rushden Salvation Army Corps and more recently with the Higham Ferrers Baptist Mission. Her husband, who, until he retired, was employed as a finisher by Messrs. B. Ladds, of Rushden, six daughters and two sons survive.

Rushden Echo and Argus
Friday, April 24, 1942   Page 9

George Mould

Death Fall Day After Marriage

Married on Easter Monday, Mr. George Mould, 79, of 3 Rose Cottages, Broughton, Hunts - a retired dairyman who formerly lived in Gilpin-street, Peterborough - fell from his cycle the following day and died in Huntington County Hospital on Thursday from injuries received in the fall.

At an inquest held on Saturday, the coroner, Mr. Philip Davies, the jury, and Inspector H. F. C. Busby all expressed their sympathy to the relatives and the widow.

Mrs. Dorothy Mould, said that on the Tuesday afternoon she went for a cycle ride with her husband.

RATHER FAST

"We were going down Fenton Hill," she said, "and as he was going rather fast. I called out to him to be careful.

"I released my brakes to catch him up."

"He wobbled three times and then fell off on his head and was immediately unconscious."

"There was no obstacle of any kind in the road and I could not see what caused him to wobble."

P.c. D. D. Walker, Ramsey, said that when he arrived on the scene he found Mould lying on the side of the road. His wife was holding him in a sitting position.

The head of the handlebars was bent. The bicycle, including the brakes was in a fairly good state of repair.

Dr. R. P. Walker, house surgeon at the County Hospital, said that Mould was unconscious when admitted to the hospital, the injuries suggested he had a fractured skull and had laceration of the brain.

A verdict of Accidental Death was recorded.

Unknown newspaper

Fannie Mould

Death of Mrs. F. Mould

Mrs. Fannie Mould, wife of Mr. Geo Mould, 59, Gilpin-st., died at Bracebridge Hospital, Lincoln, on Saturday, aged 76. Formerly Miss Mills, she was born in one of the G.N.R. Cottages, and for 13 years, in Canon Ball's time, was a teacher at New England Church schools. Mr. And Mrs. Mould were married at St. Paul's 48 years ago, and Mr. Mould has been a dairyman nearly 60 years, carrying on the business started by his father, Mr. Thomas Mould at Gunthorpe. Five sons and three daughters survive. Mr. C. Mould, 48, Silverwood-rd; Mr. B. Mould, 19, Priory-rd; Mr. E. Mould, 65, Exeter-rd; Mr. G.T. Mould, 97,Fulbridge-rd; Sgt. H. Mould, with the 11th ?????in Germany; Mrs. D. Maile, Gilpin-st; Miss M. Mould and Miss I. Mould, Gilpin-st. The funeral yesterday at St. Paul's was conducted by the Vicar, and the mourners were Mr. G. Mould (husband); Mr. And Mrs. C. Mould, Mr. And Mrs. B. Mould, Mr. And Mrs. E. Mould, Mr. And Mrs. G.T. Mould (sons and daughters-in-law); Mr. And Mrs. E. Maile, Miss M. Mould, Miss I. Mould (son-in-law and daughters); Mr. W. Mills, Holme (brother); Miss O. Mould, Miss A. Mould (grand-daughters); Mr. A. May, Mr. C. Butler and Mrs. Patchett (friends).

Peterborough Standard
Friday, February 21, 1947

Herbert Baldwin

Kissed His Wife Farewell, Drowned

It's no good. I have come to the end of my tether. Since boyhood days I have been _____ with a frail body.

That letter was written to his wife by a man who despaired in the struggle with life. Mr. Herbert A. Baldwin of Epsom, Surrey a _____ business man, aged fifty-nine.

He is reported to have fallen overboard soon after the night boat PARIS left Newhaven for Dieppe on Good Friday.

Tears filled the eyes of his wife as she quoted part of the letter to the Daily Mirror _____ day at her daughter's home at Allen??? Dulwich.

"He has been telling me good-bye for weeks past", she said "and we could not understand the pathetic farewells. I thought he might be thinking he would die within a short time."

Mr. Baldwin's brother, Mr. ? J. Baldwin, told the Daily Mirror, "He had a severe break-down after receiving head injuries while riding a horse at

Epsom two years ago and after that he seemed to go to pieces.

The Daily Mirror
April 18, 1938

Ellen (Nellie) Prentice

On August 11th at Peakirk, Ellen (Nellie) Prentice, eldest daughter of the late John William and Rose Prentice. On Page 2.

The Rector of Newborough (Rev. C.J. Newman) conducted the funeral service at Peakirk on Wednesday (14th) of Miss Ellen Prentice, eldest daughter of Mr. And Mrs. Prentice. The mourners included relatives and many friends.

Peterborough Citizen and Advertiser
Friday August 16, 1946   Page 2

Dora Prentice

Dora Prentice - Suddenly on (Monday) Dec. 20th at Peterborough Memorial hospital, Dora aged 66 yrs. Funeral service at St. Pega's Peakirk, Thursday Dec. 23rd at 2pm followed by cremation at Marholm.

Peterborough Citizen and Advertiser
Friday December 24, 1965

Second Obituary of Dora Prentice

Miss D. Prentice

Miss Dora Prentice, of Rectory Lane, Peakirk, died in Peterborough Memorial Hospital, the day after she had been playing the organ at St. Pega's Church, Peakirk, for the service of nine lessons and carols.

She was 66.

The funeral service was at St' Pega's, Peakirk, yesterday, conducted by the Rev. K. Sear, assisted by Archdeacon C.J. Grimes. The organist was Mr. Stanley Vann, director of music at the Peterborough Cathedral.

Apart from playing the organ in the church, Miss Prentice was a churchwarden for many years and had held the posts of secretary and treasurer of the Church Council. She was also a school manager.

She was well known in Peterborough having been a secretary in the

Chapter office.

For many years she was a correspondent for the "Advertiser".

The Rev. K. Sear said of Miss Prentice: "It is with great sorrow that we have to report the death of Miss Prentice. For many years she had been people's warden, secretary and treasurer of the Church Council, organist and school manager as well as holding in the past many other positions and responsibilities in the Church and village, to which she gave much time and devotion. The Church at Peakirk and the Cathedral were her two great interests and she was for them an indefatigable worker."

Peterborough Citizen and Advertiser
December 24, 1965

Third Obituary of Dora Prentice

Dora Prentice

Miss D. Prentice

The funeral service for Miss D. Prentice, Peakirk, whose sudden death was reported last week, was conducted at St. Pega's Church on December 23 by the Rev. R.K. Sear, assisted by Dr. C.J. Grimes. Mourners were: Mr. And Mrs. G.H. Prentice, Mr. J.F. Prentice (brothers and sister-in-law), Mr. John Prentice (nephew), Mr. And Mrs. Blanchard (cousins), Mrs. S. Rose (niece), Miss L. Prentice (sister) was unable to attend.

In church were the Archdeacon of Oakham (the Ven E.N. Millard), the Precenter Peterborough Cathedral (the Rev P.C. Nicholson), Mr. G. Elliott (Diocesan secretary), Mr. Brook (verger, Peterborough Cathedral), Mr. C.P. Tutt (representing Friends of the Cathedral), Miss M. Shipley Ellis, Mrs. Wood Canon H.G. Herklots, Canon and Mrs. J.C. Cartwright, Miss C. Gutteridge, Mr. And Mrs. S.E. Shearing, Mr. J.H. Woolgar, Mr. J.W.L. Samworth, Mr. J.G. Harrison (representing staff, John Lucas), Mrs. G.W. Wisbey (also representing Wisbey), Mrs. R.K. Sear, Mrs. H. Pearson, Mrs. Sibley, Miss M. Purcival, Mrs. C. Perrin, Mrs. E. Wilkinson, Mrs. H. Dudley, Mrs. Ewart, Miss L. Strange, Mr. P. Walker, Mr. And Mrs. J. Harris, Miss D. Neaverson, Mrs. H. Stimson (also representing Mrs. J. Pulley), Mrs. H. Wathen, Mrs. A Williams, Mrs. Palmer (representing the Wild Fowl Trust), Mr. And Mrs. G. Dunn, Miss Wheeler, Sister Sheila and Sister Jean, Mrs. E. Pearson (also representing Glinton Church Council), Mrs. C. Percival, Mrs. P. Noble (also representing Mr. Noble and the Village Hall Committee).

Mr. T. Neaverson, Miss F. Neaverson, Mr. and Mrs. C. Neaverson, Mr. and Mrs. A. Neaverson, (Mrs. Neaverson also representing the Women's Institute), Mr. E. Neaverson (representing Mrs. Neaverson), Mrs. Patterson, Mr. J. Patterson, Mr. Lang (representing Mrs. Lang and the Misses Welbon, Glinton), Miss Robinson, Mr. Wade, Peterborough, Mrs. N. Green, Mr. and Mrs. Lenton, Miss M. Sprigge (also representing Miss V. Sprigge), Mrs. C.

Green, Mrs. O. Green.
  Mr. Stanley Vann of Peterborough Cathedral, was organist.
  There were many floral tributes from friends and organizations.

Peterborough Citizen and Advertiser
December 31, 1965

Rose Lovell

Mrs. Lovell

SERVICES for Mrs. George (Rose M.) Lovell, 88, former Aberdonian, were held in National City, Calif., with burial in Glen Abby Memorial Park in Chula Vista, Calif.
  She died Jan. 26 in Chula Vista
  Mrs. Lovell was born Jan. 1, 1885, in Rushden, England, and came to Aberdeen in 1911 where she was married to George H. Lovell. The couple owned and operated the Cottage Grocery on 7th Ave. S.E. until 1946, when they retired and moved to California.
  Survivors include one son, James, of Imperial Beach, Calif.; one daughter, Mrs. A.C. (Hazel) Ritter, Chula Vista; one sister, Mrs. Fred A. (Annie) Bull, Aberdeen; and three grandson.
  She was preceded in death by her husband and a brother, George E. Mould.

Aberdeen, South Dakota newspaper
January 30, 1973   page 3

Annie Beatrice Bull

Mrs. Bull

Mrs. Fred A. (Annie Beatrice) Bull, 82, of 207 4th Ave. N.E., died Saturday night at St. Luke's Hospital.
  Services will be at 2pm Tuesday at the Gates-Vik Funeral Home with the Rev. Robert Brown of the First United Methodist Church officiating. Burial will be in Riverside Memorial Park Cemetery.
  Visitation will begin Monday night and continue until the time of service.
  Annie Beatrice Mould was born on Oct. 6, 1891 at Rushden-Northamptonshire, England. She came with her family to Aberdeen, in 1912. She married Fred A. Bull on July 11, 1915 at Aberdeen. They moved to Denver, Colo. in 1941 and then returned to Aberdeen in 1961.
  She was baptised in the Wesleyan Methodist Church in England and was a member of the Friendly Neighbors Club and the Royal Neighbors of America.

Survivors include her husband; one son, Alfred, of Aberdeen; one daughter, Mrs. Richard (Helen) Klapper, Borger, Tex.; and four grandchildren.

Aberdeen, South Dakota newspaper
March 16, 1974

Second Obituary for Annie Bull

Mrs. Bull

SERVICES for Mrs. Fred A. (Annie Beatrice) Bull, 82, of 207 4th Ave. N.E., were Tuesday afternoon at the Gates-Vik Funeral Home.
She died Saturday, March 16 at St. Luke's Hospital.
The Rev. Robert Brown of the First United Methodist Church officiated and burial was in Riverside Memorial Park Cemetery.
Pallbearers were Gordon Goodspeed, Dr. W.J. Rivett, Ray H. Anderson, Robert Frieh, Leslie Zumm and Earl Coyne.
Robert Olson was soloist and Mrs. Karlon Kempf, organist.
Members of the Friendly Neibors Club attended in a group.

Aberdeen, South Dakota newspaper
March 19, 1974

Fred Bull

Fred Bull - Aberdeen

FRED Bull, 92, of 207 4th Ave. N.E., died of a heart attack Wednesday, Nov. 24, at his home.
Services will be 2p.m. Saturday, Nov. 27, at the Gates-Vik Funeral Home, 320 6th Ave. S.E., with the Rev. Allen Lang of the Plymouth Congregational United Church of Christ officiating.
Burial will be in Riverside Memorial Park.
Visitation will be Friday evening and until the service Saturday at the funeral home.
The family prefers memorials to the Senior Citizens Center.
Fred Albert Bull was born May 10, 1890, at Rushden, Northamptonshire, England. He attended school there and came to the U.S. where he joined in the operation of the Bull Brothers Dairy. He married Annie Mould July 11, 1915, at Aberdeen. In 1944 they moved to Denver, Colo., where he was a technician in the blood bank of the Fitzsimmons Army Hospital. They retired in 1960 and returned to Aberdeen where he has since resided. Mrs. Bull died in 1974.
Survivors include one son, Alfred, Aberdeen; one daughter, Mrs. William (Helen) Klapper, Borger, Texas; and four grandchildren.

Casketbearers will be Willard Ellis, Ray Stewart, Leslie Zulmm, R.N. Fossum, Howard Froiland and Joseph Leon. Larry Arndt will be the soloist and Mrs. John Evens will be the organist.

Aberdeen, South Dakota newspaper
November 24, 1982

Jessie Barrett

Barrett On July 2, peacefully at St. Edmund's Hospital after a long illness bravely borne, Jessie, aged 82, widow of John Barrett, of 118 St. James Park Road, Northampton. Sadly missed by relatives and many friends. Service at Kettering Crematorium on Friday 8th July at 3pm. No flowers by request.

Northampton Chronicle and Echo
Tuesday, July 5th,   page 2

John William James Barrett

Deaths

Barrett - On May 9, after a short illness, at Northampton General Hospital, John William James, aged 73, of 118, St. Jame's Park-road. Beloved husband of Jessie, and dear brother of Ivy. Resting in the Lord. Funeral service, Monday, May 13, at 1:45pm at Princes-street Baptist Church. No flowers please.

Northampton Chronicle and Echo
Friday May 10, 1957   Page 12

Robert Edward Roberts

Suddenly on Feb. 12th 1971 at the General Hospital, Kettering, Robert Edward aged 73 years, beloved husband of Violet of 50 Wellingborough Road, Rushden, formerly of Souldrop. Father to Jeff, Pauline and John. Interred at Higham Ferrers on Wednesday.

Wellingborough News
Friday, February 19, 1971   page 2

Alfred James Sharp

Funeral of Mr. A. J. Sharp

The funeral of Mr. Alfred James Sharp, of 19, Wentworth Road, Rushden, who died in the Northampton General Hospital, took place on November 18, the service being conducted by the Rev. John Renison at the Independent Wesleyan Church.

Mr. C. Headland (brother-in-law) at the organ accompanied the hymns "Jesu, Lover of my Soul" and "In Heavenly Love Abiding" and played "O Rest in the Lord" and Handel's "Largo".

The coffin was draped with the Union Jack and among those present were representatives of the Independent Wesleyan Women's Auxiliary, the C.W.S. Boot Works (clicking department), the British Legion and Messrs. W. Sargent (closing department).

Mourners were: Mrs. D. Sharp (widow), Mr. And Mrs. W. Sharp (father and mother), Mr. And Mrs. P. Sturgess (brother-in-law and sister), Mr. And Mrs. C. Headland, Mrs. J. Barrett, Northampton, Mr. And Mrs. J.E. Roberts, Mr. And Mrs. H. Eaton, Mr. And Mrs. B. Mould, Mr. And Mrs. A.T. Lovell, and Mr. And Mrs. P. Mould (brothers-in-law and sisters-in-law), Messrs. P. Sturgess, N. Mould, P. Mould and P. Eaton (nephews), and Miss P. Roberts and Miss D. Lovell (nieces). Mrs. Firkins, Souldrop, and Mr. T. Wright (friends).

The interment was at the Higham Ferrers Cemetery.

Rushden Echo and Argus and Northampton Advertiser Higham Ferrers, Irthlingborough and Raunds Free Press
Friday November 26, 1948   Page 9

Bob Lovell

On March 3rd, 1965 at 40 High Street South, Rushden, Archibald Thomas (Bob) Lovell, beloved husband of Ivy Doreen Lovell, dear Father of Doreen and dearest Pappy of Heather and Paul, aged 57 years. Cremation at Kettering today.

Northamptonshire Advertiser
Friday, 5th March 1965   page 6

This announcement was repeated in the same newspaper on Friday, March 12th with a spelling correction (Heather's name) and a statement that the cremation had happened.

Second Obituary of Bob Lovell

Mr. A.T. Lovell, Rushden

Rushden hairdresser Mr. Archibald Thomas 'Bob' Lovell, 40 High Street South, died at his home after a short illness. He was 57.

When Mr. Lovell was 21, he moved from Rushden to London and worked there in the hairdressing trade.

Mr. Lovell left London during the last war and set up his hairdressing business in Rushden in 1945. For a short time, he was chairman of the Rushden Hairdressers Association.

He leaves a widow, Ivy Doreen, a sister, Mrs. Lilian Whitehead, a daughter, Doreen and grandchildren Heather and Paul.

The funeral was at Kettering Crematorium.

Ernest Victor Maile

Mr. E. V. Maile - After a long illness Mr. Ernest Victor Maile, 59 Gilpin-street, died in St. John's Hospital on Sunday at the age of 56. Born in Peterborough Mr. Maile was the eldest son of the late Mr. And Mrs. J. T. Maile and for some years worked in the oven shop of Baker Perkins Ltd. Twenty-five years ago he married Miss Doris Irene Mould, of St. Leonard's-on-Sea, and, for some years he and his wife kept a newsagent's and tobacconist's shop in the town returning to Peterborough about 16 years ago. The funeral took place at All Soul's yesterday.

Peterborough Standard
Friday February 8, 1957   Page 10

Joan Brushett

BRUSHETT - On November 4, 1996 HELENA JOAN. Service at Cheam Road Hall, 14 Cheam Road, Sutton, Surrey on Wednesday November 13, 1996 at 12.30 p.m. followed by interment at Sutton Cemetery at 1.30 p.m. Donations, if desired, to The Trinitarian Bible Society, Tyndale House, Dorset Road, London 3NN or flowers to W.A. Truelove & Son, 118 Carshalton Road, Sutton, Surrey.
"With Christ" Philippians 1-23.

Unknown newspaper - probably local Sutton newspaper

Annie Mould

Mould - Peacefully at Fenland Wing (Peterborough Hospital per Joan Bolton) on 10th October, Annie Louisa of Priory Road, Peterborough aged 88 years. Beloved wife of Bernard, Mother of Enid and Derek, mother-in-law of Joan and dear grandma of Simon and Christopher. Funeral service at St. John's Church Peterborough on Friday 15th October at 2:15pm followed by cremation. Family flowers only. Donations for Friends of Peterborough Hospital in lieu of flowers may be sent to John Lucas Funeral Directors, 31 Dogsthorpe Rd. Peterborough.

Peterborough Evening Telegraph
October 13, 1993

Eric Mould

On 24th April, Eric aged 90 years, beloved husband of the late Mary Ethel (Polly), much loved father of Ann and father-in-law of Ken, and a loving granddad of Keith and John. Funeral service at St. Paul's Church on Monday 1st May, followed by cremation. Family flowers only. Donations for Hospital at home to John Lucas Funeral Directors.

Peterborough Evening Telegraph
April 27, 1995

Alfred Bull

Aberdeen: The funeral service for Alfred Bull, 92, formerly of Aberdeen, will be 10:30 a.m. Saturday, Aug. 6, 2009, at Spitzer-Miller Funeral Home with Pastor Tom Haggar officiating.

Burial will take place at the Faulkton Cemetery, Faulkton, S.D.

Alfred Bull died Tuesday, Aug. 4, 2009 in Blaine, Minn.

Visitation is 1-7 p.m. Friday with family present from 5-7 p.m. at Spitzer-Miller Funeral Home, 1111 S. Main St., Aberdeen

Alfred M. Bull, a well-known and longtime resident of Aberdeen, died of advanced Parkinson's disease and pneumonia at the age of 92 on Aug. 4, 2009, in Blaine, Minn.

He taught high school physics, chemistry and advanced mathematics at Aberdeen Central High School between 1955 and 1982.

Alfred had a lifelong love of learning and kept up with new developments in science to the very end of his life. He also enjoyed music and theater. He was active in many community organizations. He was a devoted husband, father and public servant. He took great pride in the accomplishments of his many students over the years.

He was preceded in death by his wife, Lois, in 2004.

He is survived by one son, Richard (Linda) Bull of Palo Alto, Calif., and one daughter, Marilyn (Peter) Pash of Blaine, Minn.; sister Helen Klapper of Estes Park, Colo., and her two sons, Richard and Fred and grandnephew, Andrew.

Memorials preferred to the National Science Foundation.

Aberdeen, S.D. newspaper
August 6, 2009

Lois Eliza Frad

Lois Eliza Frad was born October 17, 1914 in Faulk County, SD, to William J. and Lulu (Pickler) Frad. The family moved to Redfield, SD, where she attended school and graduated from Redfield High School in 1933. She then attended Yankton College where she earned a Baccalaureate Degree. She served for three years on the high school faculty in Bonilla, SD. There she met and married Alfred Bull on May 26, 1940, at Faulkton, SD. They moved to Paxton, NE where they taught. Alfred entered the Navy during WWII and she moved with him to Sioux Falls, SD and Corpus Christi, TX. After his discharge from the service, they moved to Highmore, SD and then to Faulkton, SD, where she raised her family and assisted her husband in those school systems. They then moved to Aberdeen in 1955 where she was instrumental in developing the Special Education program in Aberdeen. She completed an investigative thesis on the retarded child in Eastern South Dakota for her Masters Degree earned in 1963. She retired in 1971 due to health reasons and became extremely active in a variety of community activities. As the last surviving heir to the historic Pickler home in Faulkton, SD, she deeded the home to the Faulk County Historical Society in September of 1987.

She was a member of the First United Methodist Church and also, at one time, directed the church choir. She loved reading, music, history and theater.

Her memory lives on with her husband, Alfred Bull of Aberdeen, SD, one son Richard (Linda) Bull of Santa Maria, CA, and one daughter, Marilyn (Peter) Pash of Blaine, MN.

She was preceded in death by her parents, one brother, William, and one sister, Alice.

Taken from the funeral bulletin of Lois Bull

William Richard Klapper

Funeral services for William Richard Klapper, 55, of 401 Dolomita, will be at 10 a.m. Friday in the First Christian Church with Dr. Kenneth E. Jones, pastor, officiating.

The casket will remain closed during the service.

Burial will be at 9 a.m. Saturday in Coleman City Cemetery in Coleman under the direction of Simpson Funeral Home of Borger.

Klapper died at 5:15p.m. Tuesday in North Plains Hospital.

He was born August 13, 1920 in Coleman and came to Borger in 1945. He has been an employee of Phillips Petroleum Company since that time and was currently a chemical engineer and supervisor at the Copolymer Plant.

He was a member of Adobe Walls Masonic Lodge 1355 and the First Christian Church where he served as deacon, elder and a member of the church board. He was also active in the Boy Scout program for several years.

Survivors include his wife, two sons, his mother and a sister.

Pall bearers will be W.G. Chapman, Wayne Hopkins, J.R. Edwards, G.G. Nicholas, Leo Robinson, J.B. McCombs, Don Rumold and Clarence McDaniel.

The family requests memorials be made to the Cancer Fund in care of Panhandle Bank & Trust of Borger.

Borger News Herald
January 1, 1976

Second Obituary of William Richard Klapper

County Native Dies In Borger Burial Here

William Richard Klapper, 55, who was born in Coleman August 13, 1920, died in Borger at 5:15 p.m. Tuesday, December 30, 1975. Funeral services will be held there Friday at 2:00 p.m. and burial will be in Coleman City Cemetery at 9:00 a.m. Saturday.

Mr. Klapper, a member, past deacon and past elder of First Christian Church of Borger, was married to Miss Helen Bull in 1944. A chemical engineer for Phillips Petroleum Company for 30 years, he was a Mason, and an active worker in the Boy Scout program.

Surviving him are his wife of Borger; two sons, Fred Klapper of Borger and Rick Klapper of Houston; his mother, Mrs. Mae Klapper of Abilene; and a sister, Mrs. Mary Ellen Lessing of Abilene.

Stevens Funeral is in charge of local arrangements.

Coleman County Chronicle
January 2, 1976

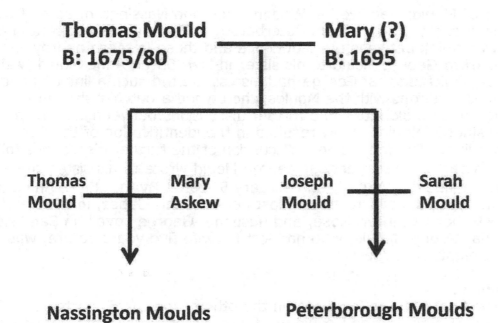

Thomas Mould
B: 1675/80

Mary (?)
B: 1695

Thomas
Mould

Mary
Askew

Joseph
Mould

Sarah
Mould

Nassington Moulds

Peterborough Moulds

Appendix XXV

Link With
Nassington Moulds

As we researched this book it became apparent that a large number of Moulds had lived in Woodnewton and Nassington, both of which are only a short distance from Peterborough. The authors felt certain that there was a link between our Mould line and those in these nearby villages. A letter from George Mould to his sister-in-law, Sarah Anne Mould (widow of Jabez) indicated that George had also suspected such a link and had pursued discussions with the Moulds who owned a butcher shop in Nassington. This old letter and further discussions between Joan Bolton and the Nassington Moulds finally resulted in the identification of the link between lines. The letter and a discussion of the further discussions follows.

This is part of the letter that George Mould wrote to his sister-in-law, Sarah Ann Mould, ("Annie") on February 5, 1952. By that time, Annie was an eighty-year-old widow, having lost her husband, Jabez, in 1936 and was living with her daughter, Rose, and husband, George Lovell, in San Ysidro, California. George Mould, who had lost his wife five years before, was seventy-eight. He wrote:

Dear Annie,

You will note by the few lines on the other page that I started to write to you a month ago, but as I could not finish it that night, it got put on one side ...and put off night after night, until now we are well into February. I'll tell you how it is: the last few weeks the weather has been cold and in the evening the table has been pushed back and the chairs drawn round the fire...and when all are gathered round, each with a book, it seems so much easier to sit and enjoy the fireside than to set about writing a letter.

Well, as I have said, you may be interested to know how we have fared during the past year. On the whole, we had a very good year. Personally, I have had good health all through the year. Except for an accident I had last March. I don't know if you heard of it through Annie and Fred (Bull - Annie Mould's daughter and son-in-law). Anyway, if not, I will just say that I fell over with my bike and got a nasty cut on my forehead and a cracked bone in the pelvis. But thank God I got over it and made a good recovery. I was out of action for three weeks but have been able to carry on alright ever since.

I bought myself a new bike and, during the summer, had several very nice runs into the country. One afternoon after dinner, I rode to Stamford and back via Wansford and Castor - in all, about 32 miles. It was a lovely afternoon and just at the time when the corn was white unto harvest ...and what a glorious view I had from the hill tops! From some points, you could see across country for miles. I couldn't help saying to myself - "This England! No wonder her sons went out to fight for her, and for all those they held dear." I don't think any country in the world can compare with our countryside, with its winding lanes, the green fields enclosed with their hedges and noble trees. With the picturesque old villages and the church spires peeping among the trees.

As I rode through Castor, I noted an old-fashioned Inn, with its thatched roof showing one of the finest examples of the thatcher's art and skill.

My last trip out was to Nassington. Some thirty years ago I rode through it with the boys and saw my name over a butcher's shop. Knowing that our family came from that part, and Kingscliffe, I thought to myself then: 'Some day I will come and see if I can find out anything about our family history.' So now that I have a little more time, I thought I would have a ride out. When I got there, I found that my name was still over the shop. I knocked at the door and it was answered by a young woman. When I told her my name and why I had called, she said, 'Oh, it will be Uncle you want to see.' She sent her little boy to show me where he lived and we found him in his garden.

I told my 'namesake' that I had come on a voyage of discovery. When I explained who I was, he shook hands and said he was very pleased to see me. We had quite a nice long talk. He called his wife and introduced me to her. It appeared that he had given up his business to his nephew a few years ago. Owing to the rationing, it had become very difficult to get supplies to satisfy customers. **He thought - like myself - that our families were very closely related a few generations back. He said there were a lot of our name at Woodnewton and Kingscliffe.**

He was interested in music and knew the Rushden Temperance Band years ago. He knew Joe Abbott and **Joe Mackness***, also Berkinshore, their conductor. So, you will understand we had quite an interesting talk. They hoped I would return to see them again.

One other little trip I must tell you about was my visit to the Rector of Etton. There had been an appeal for funds for the restoration of the Church. I had sent a small donation and a letter saying that I was very interested because my Father and Mother were married there in 1852. The result was that I had an invitation to call on him. I found both him and his wife very nice people indeed. The Rector accompanied me to the Church, pointing out all items of interest. After which we went up the tower to the belfry. He explained that it had been rebuilt from the inside and the bells re-hung on steel girders. Then we went into the Vestry where he took out the Register I had asked to see. We turned back the pages until we found, in faded writing, the marriage entry for Thomas Mould and Rose Ann Mackness on April 5th 1852. And there was the Altar where my dear parents, in the presence of the family, were married. You will understand how thrilled I was, and how I visualised the scene on that bright Easter morning, nearly a century ago!

George then returns to the present before drawing his letter to a close: 'I myself am keeping real well; I go out each morning and give Eric a hand on his round. I think the exercise and fresh air help me to keep fit. All the boys are well '......etc..

When George Ewart Mould gave Joan Mould her Grandfather's original letter in the summer of 1963, she was delighted! She was visiting George and his sister, Rose Lovell, in San Ysidro, California where she met several members of their family. (Joan had already met Annie Mould Bull and family earlier in South Dakota.) After being given the letter from her grandfather while visiting America in 1963, Joan Bolton took a keen interest in possible links between her own branch and the Nassington Moulds. Once her 'distant' cousin, Richard Klapper, enlisted her help in writing this book early in 2001, there was no holding her, of course!

First she telephoned Margaret Mould in Nassington. This was the widow of Jack who had taken over the butcher's shop when his Uncle George retired. She suggested Joan contact Rachelle Mould, her son, Richard's wife. Joan learned from Rachelle that it was her husband who was running the shop with his brother, Simon. Also, armed with more information, Joan worked out that her Grandfather not only met his 'namesake', George the butcher, but also the lady he spoke to must have been Margaret, and her little boy none other than Richard, whom we later met. Born in June, 1947, he would have been four years old in the summer of 1951: how smoothly it all connects! **

When Richard and Linda Klapper came over to England in the spring of 2003 to meet up with Joan in Peterborough, they were able to call on Richard and Rachelle at the butcher's shop. 'But,' they were told, 'the person you need to talk to is Richard's brother, Howard. He's the one interested in the family history. And they were right! In the summer of 2008, Howard was kind enough to send Joan a copy of the Nassington Moulds' Family Tree.

From this chart, the connection is clear to see: Whereas the Moulds of Peterborough descend from Joseph Mould (and Sarah Askew), the Nassington line comes down through his brother, Thomas Mould (and Mary Askew).

Presumably the wives must also be related, (sisters, even), in which case the blood line is even closer!

*Footnote: Joe Mackness was his brother-in-law, Joseph, married to Rebecca. See Chapter 8.

** Footnote: When we all met up with Richard Mould in the spring of 2003, how little we thought that he would die so soon. Very sadly, he passed away on September 11, 2007, aged 60.

Jabez and Mary Mackness - parents of Rose Ann
Mould; Brigstock, England

Appendix XXVI

Family Grave Headstone Inscriptions

In March 2003 Joan Bolton and Richard and Linda Klapper visited the churchyards in the villages around Peterborough where many of the Mould ancestors are buried. Many of the headstones are badly worn and/or corroded. It was apparent that many of the inscriptions will be lost forever in another twenty or thirty years so a decision was made to transcribe them and include them in this book for future researchers. A '/ ' is used to denote separate lines on the headstone.

Brigstock
Jabez & Mary Mackness: In / Affectionate Remembrance of / Jabez Mackness, / Who died Decr 28th 1865 / Aged 72 Years / Also of / Mary Wife of the Above / Who died August 2 1867 / Aged 68 Years /

Etton
Susannah Mould: In / Affectionate Remembrance Of (Susannah)(?) / Mould Who Died / July 12, 1868 / Aged 28 Years / Thou Shouldst .... /

William Mould: ..../ William Mould / .... / .... / .... /

Glinton
Joseph and Martha Mould: In Loving Memory Of / Martha / The Beloved Wife Of / Joseph Mould Who Died May 23, 1891 / Aged 63 Years / Also / Joseph Mould who died Jan 5, 1894 / Aged 68 Years / Thy Will Be Done

Joseph and Betsy Day: Beloved Companion / Betsy the Beloved Wife of / Joseph Day / Who Died October 13, 1914 / Aged 58 Years / Also of / Joseph Day / Who Died March 4, 1917 / Aged 67 Years

Jesse Day: In ..../ Jessie / The Daughter of / Joseph & Betsy Day / Died (July)(?) 30, 1911 / .... /

Helpston
John Moulds: Sacred To The Memory Of / John Moulds / Who Died / On the 8th Day of May 1857 Aged 56 Years / ..../ More writing illegible but smaller writing so probably just an inscription /

Sarah Moulds: In / Affectionate Memory Of / Sarah Wife Of / John Moulds / Who Died June 6, 1846 / Aged 38 Years / .... / Also of Edith Mary Daughter of / John & Sarah Moulds / Who Died ??? 18??

Edith Mary Moulds: In / Affectionate Memory Of / Sarah Wife Of / John Moulds / Who Died June 6, 1846 / Aged 38 Years / .... / Also of Edith Mary Daughter of / John & Sarah Moulds / Who Died ??? 18??

John & Mary Fisher: John Fisher / Who Departed This Life / April 17, 1887 / Aged 66 Years/ Also Of Mary Fisher / Beloved Wife Of Above / REMAINDER UNREADABLE
NOTE: This grave is not in the churchyard but in the cemetery 2 blocks away.

Higham Ferrers
Charles and Emily Mould: In Loving Memory of / Emily Jane / the Beloved Wife of / Charles Mould / Who Passed Away / 21st April 1942 / Aged 69 Years / Only A Step Removed / We Soon Again Shall Meet / Our Own Our Dearly Loved / Around The Savior's Feet / Also of / Charles / Beloved Husband of the Above / Who Died March 3rd 1945 / Age 75 Years / Reunited

Maxey
John and Susannah Mould: In / Loving Memory Of / John Mould / Who Departed This Life January 1, 1893 / Aged 72 Years / Thou Hast come To The Grave In A Full Age / Like As A Shock Of Corn Cometh In In His Season / .... / In / Affectionate Remembrance Of / Susannah Moulds / Who Departed This Life Sep 23, 1880 / Aged 35 Years / Prepare To Meet Thy God Amen(?)

Paston
Thomas & Rose Ann Mould: In Loving Memory / of / Thomas Mould, / (of Gunthorpe). / Who Fell Asleep Jan: 26: 1906 / Aged 78 Years / ----- / Also Rose Ann, / His Beloved Wife / Who Fell Asleep July 25: 1908 / Aged 79 Years. / ---- / "Thanks Be To God which Giveth Us / The Victory. Through Our Lord / Jesus Christ."

Joseph Mould: In memory of Joseph. The beloved son of Thomas and Roseann Mould. Who died March 31st 1900 aged 35 years. Gone but not forgotten.
NOTE: This inscription recorded by Alan Marks of Paston who recorded this cemetery. At the time of a visit in March 2003 the stone was broken and most of it was missing.

Peakirk
John Day and John Joseph Day: In Loving Memory / of / John / youngest son of John & Elizabeth Day / Born DecR 31st 1853, / Died May 14th, 1882 / Also of / John Joseph Day, / Born June 19th 1876, / Died May 1st 1882. / Nephew Of The Above

Robert Day: Sacred / To The / Beloved Memory of / Robert / The Eldest

Son of / John & Elizabeth Day / Born August 20, 1845 / Died May 9, 1866

Ellen, Dora and Lilian Prentice: In Loving Memory Of / Ellen Prentice / Born March 18th 1888 / Died August 11th 1946 / Underneath Are The Everlasting Arms / Also Dora Evelyn / Prentice, / Born Jan. 2nd 1899. / Died Dec. 20th 1965. / Rest In Peace / Also / Lilian Prentice / Born March 9th 1889 / Died Nov 16th 1967 / Re-United /

John Edward Dale Avery: In Loving Memory / Of / James Edward Dale Avery, / Who Died Feby 15th 1919, / Aged 56 Years. / "In The Midst Of Life We Are In Death."

John William & Rose Prentice: In / Loving Memory Of / John William Prentice / Born Nov: 4 1858 / Died Aug 26: 1919 / "Rock Of Ages: Cleft For Me, / Let Me Hide Myself In Thee." / Also Of Rose / Dearly Beloved Wife Of The Above / Born Nov: 2: 1858, / Died June 25: 1925. / Let Not Your Heart Be Troubled, Neither / Let It Be Afraid. / He That Endureth To The End Shall Be Saved.

John & Elizabeth Day: They are buried in Peakirk but their graves are unmarked. According to church records they have plots 14, 15 and 16 which are next to the headstone of Elizabeth Blake.

Peterborough
Ernest Maile: Memories / In the most holy name of / Jesus pray for the repose of the soul / of Ernest Victor Maile / who departed this life February 3rd 1957 / aged 54 years / RIP

Doris Maile: Plot next to her husband, Ernest, but no headstone.

George & Fanny Mould: In / Loving Remembrance Of / Fanny Mould / Who Departed This Life Feby 15 th 1947 / Aged 76 Years. / RIP / Also Of George Mould / Who Enterred Into Rest April 9th 1953 / Aged 79 years / Re-United

Marjorie Mould: In / Loving Memory Of / Marjorie Edna / Mould / Called To Rest / August 16th 1953 / Aged 43 Years
NOTE: Common headstone with Iris Mould.

Iris Mould: Also Of / Iris Teresa / Mould / Called To Rest / Nov 8th 1964 / Aged 51 years / R.I.P.
NOTE: Common headstone with Marjorie Mould.

Index of Individuals